Legal Actions for Future Generations

PETER LANG

Normandy Chair For Peace Collection

The purpose of this collection is to promote the work carried out by the Normandy Chair for Peace, which investigates the rights of future generations and Peace with the Earth. Resolutely open to the international scene and committed to multidisciplinarity, the Normandy Chair for Peace will publish here the proceedings and scholarship it has coordinated in fields as varied as: the legal protection of the planet, the rights of indigenous peoples, the rights of nature, animals, success stories, and environmental peace-building. This collection strives for coherence among the various transformations currently under way in international, regional, and national legal systems with a view toward establishing sustainable protection of the environment, environmental rights, and the future. The collection also explores the protection of the future human condition along with bioethical issues that are constantly renewing the legitimate fields of law.

Drawing on the immemorial wisdom of Humankind, this collection intends to promote all types of work illustrating the imperative of civilization according to which: "We shall have peace on Earth when we live in Peace with Earth."

Heads of the Normandy Chair For Peace Collection

Tony Oposa, Leader of the Normandy Chair for Peace (2019–2023), Public Interest Environmental Lawyer (Philippines)

Nicholas Robinson, Chair Emeritus of the Normandy Chair for Peace, University Professor for the Environment at Pace University, Co-Director, Global Center for Environmental Legal Studies (United States)

Emilie Gaillard, General Coordinator of the Normandy Chair for Peace, Professor of International Environmental & Human Rights Law at Sciences Po Rennes (France)

David Forman, Director, Environmental Law Program, University of Hawai'i at Mānoa (United States)

Emilie Gaillard & David M. Forman (eds.)

Legal Actions for Future Generations

Normandy Chair for Peace Collection
Vol. 1

With the support of
The "Mission Droit et Justice" (French Ministry of Justice);
The Normandy MRSH (CNRS)
The International Center for Comparative Environmental Law (CIDCE- Limoges);
The French Association for Environmental Law (SFDE);
The Demolombe Institute (Caen, Faculty of Law);
The Environmental Law Program, William S. Richardson School of Law, University of Hawai'i at Mānoa; The Global Center for Environmental Legal Studies, Elisabeth Haub School of Law at Pace University (USA).

"We will have Peace on Earth when we have Peace *with* the Earth."

Cover illustration: NASA/NOAA/GSFC/Suomi NPP/VIIRS/Norman Kuring
Cover design: Anne Lacherez

This publication has been peer reviewed.

ISSN 2736–3279
hardback ISBN 9782-8076-1528-1
paperback ISBN 978-2-8076-1534-2
ePDF 978-2-8076-0905-1 ePUB
978-2-8076-0906-8 MOBI
978-2-8076-0907-5 DOI 10.3726/
b16625 D/2020/5678/06

Bibliographic information published by "Die Deutsche Nationalbibliothek".

"Die Deutsche National Bibliothek" lists this publication in the "Deutsche Nationalbibliografie"; detailed bibliographic data is available on the Internet at <http://dnb.de>.

Richard L. OTTINGER

Foreword

Don't these people have (or at least know some) children? Don't they care?

- Climate deniers willing to sacrifice their children along with the lives of children throughout the world for the sake of short-term profits for their sponsors?
- Fossil fuel executives themselves, using their profits to persuade their governments to eliminate regulations that provide for the health and safety of future generations?
- Nuclear weapons industrialists promoting "mutually assured destruction," with ever more useable "small" weapons and elimination of agreements to reduce and control nuclear weaponry, engaging in weapon tests that cause…?
- Weapons manufacturers and sellers who resist legislation that would keep their guns out of the hands of unstable people, and permit the sale of even military weapons produced for the sole purposes of maximizing mass killing of humans.
- Lobbyists willing to make a living by threatening the lives of others?
- Governmental leaders and legislators who undermine regulations protecting the public against death-dealing climate change consequences of floods, droughts, hurricanes, diseases, air and water pollution, as well as agricultural disruptions that jeopardize food supplies?
- Members of the public who enable these miscreant leaders?

So, what is a child to do? Sue.

A new legal day is dawning all over the world, in which courts are finding a basis in their respective constitutions and laws to bring legal actions on behalf of future generations, ordering their governments to take action to protect against threats to the lives, health, safety and well-being of their citizens. Many of these lawsuits are being brought by, or in the name of, affected children themselves.

This monumental study systematically explores the worldwide movement to empower legal action to protect future generations. It attracts many of the world's leading experts, who examine this legal revolution across a wide variety of applications. The driving goal of this book, as so well stated therein, is "to promote ideas relating to the rights of future generations offered by lawyers, sociologists, philosophers and scientists (both academics and practitioners), with the sincere hope that doing so will help humankind as a whole 'become good ancestors' as urged Professor Nicholas Robinson in his essay #3 on 'Evolutionary Roots Nurturing Equity Across Generations' in the first Part of this book".

The history of our human race has been plagued by death-dealing events that legal actions have, so far, proved inadequate to prevent. World history is replete with wars, perfection of the weapons of death and destruction, as well as hideous dictatorships including the Hitler regime that engaged in the mass systematic murder known as the Holocaust. The United States was the first nation to use nuclear weapons to cause the death of entire municipal populations during the World War II attacks on Hiroshima and Nagasaki. Today, the killing spree continues with the use of chemical weapons and drone bombings to achieve mass killings and starvation of populations in Syria. Organized killings and destruction also continue in the Middle East, China, and many other parts of the world.

Much of the effort to civilize the world has been devoted to creating laws and institutions to settle the world's disputes by creating legal organizations designed to resolve disputes by peaceful means, such as the establishment of the United Nations and the World Court. The World Bank and regional banks have also been created to help nations alleviate situations of poverty that can lead to war. And treaties have been negotiated that limit the use of nuclear and chemical weapons. These efforts have brought some significant successes, namely the absence of a third world war, and prevention of the use of nuclear weapons.

However, the world is now faced with a threat of far greater proportion than any previously experienced. The advent of global warming threatens the universal extinction of all living things including people, if extraordinary action is not taken to mitigate and adapt to its consequences. This threat calls for global legal action far beyond anything that has been undertaken ever before. Since these dire consequences will face future generations with the possibility of extinction if not rapidly curbed, this study explores in depth the legal actions that can be taken for their protection.

The study describes in depth lawsuits that have been brought on behalf of future generations in many countries and international forums, in addition to the treaties, laws national and international, and agreements that have been relied upon (and are currently being drafted), as well as the philosophical and scientific bases for such initiatives.

The remarkable progress towards achieving near universal commitments to address climate change under the UNFCCC Paris Agreement of 2015 have proved to be far too short of meeting its goals. Taking legal action in the name of our children and grandchildren to protect their interests has universal appeal, which can help spur acceptance of the challenging next steps that must now be taken.

Is there still hope that this can happen? The inspiring environmental lawyer/advocate, Anthony A. Oposa, Jr., succeeded without funding and against all odds to persuade the Supreme Court of the Philippines, in a law suit that he brought in the name of his children and other minors in the Philippines, to require the government to preserve the last 800 hectares of virgin forests. He also took action to clean up the pollution in Manila Bay, and risked his own life by undertaking citizen enforcement actions to prevent the dynamiting of fish. The study concludes with a poem written by Oposa, in which he encourages us all to "make a little difference".

Professors Emilie Gaillard of Sciences Po Rennes and MRSH (Maison de la Recherche en Sciences Humaines), CNRS (Centre National de la Recherche Scientifique)/University of Caen, France and David Forman of the University of Hawai'i, along with their remarkable authors, have made an important contribution toward exploring new paths for resolving this most critical threat to our planet. We can only hope that this book will make at least a little difference, but I believe it will do much more.

Acknowledgments

This book constitutes the publication of the proceedings of the international conference organized on 17 and 18 November 2017 by the MRSH, CNRS/University of Caen Normandy. This conference benefited from the label and financing mechanism "Normandy for Peace", set up by the Normandy Region. It was organized with the support of the:

- Groupement d'Intérêt Public (GIP) Research Mission Law and Justice, French Ministry of Justice;
- Institute Demolombe at the Law School of Caen;
- Sciences Po Rennes;
- Institute of West Law and Europe (I.O.D.E., Faculty of Law of Rennes);
- Chair of Excellence Jean Monnet of Rennes;
- French Society for Environmental Law (SFDE Strasbourg);
- International Center for Comparative Environmental Law (CIDCE-Limoges); and
- Générations Futures Association.

The conference was also sponsored by the:

- World Commission on Environmental Law, International Union for the Conservation of Nature;
- Environmental Law Program at the William S. Richardson School of Law, University of Hawai'i at Mānoa (Honolulu, United States); and
- Global Center for Environmental Legal Studies, Elisabeth Haub School of Law at Pace University (New York, United States).

I have had the immense honor and pleasure of organizing this conference including stakeholders with whom I work regularly, and I wish to thank them warmly for their commitment to the rights of future generations.

I would like to thank in particular my colleague David Forman who agreed to assist me as co-editor in the elaborate preparation of this book. I have no doubt the book would not have come to life without his invaluable help.

Finally, we warmly thank our publisher for his support and express our wish that this book be widely shared and disseminated.

Emilie GAILLARD

Notes from the Editors

On Building Interdisciplinary and Cultural Bridges

Between sessions at the 15th Annual Colloquium of the International Union for the Conservation of Nature (IUCN) Academy of Environmental Law (IUCNAEL) in Cebu, Philippines, Professor Emilie Gaillard asked me to join the comité scientifique, or Scientific Committee, for a funding proposal in response to a call from Région Normandie relating to Normandie Pour La Paix (Normandy for Peace) – an annual world event inspired by the Davos Forum, bringing people from around the world together to address issues related to global peace and security. In addition to the November 2017 symposium that brought together the authors featured in this book, this successful proposal also included the fourth Antonio A. Oposa, Jr. Intergenerational Moot Court held June 2018 in Caen, France.

Professor Gaillard and I met for the first time in connection with the inaugural Oposa Moot Court held at the 2016 World Conservation Congress in Honolulu, Hawai'i. We reunited eight months later as mock judges of the International Court of Justice (ICJ) for the second Oposa Moot Court at the IUCNAEL colloquium in Cebu, co-hosted by none other than Attorney Oposa. This unique, collaborative moot court is unlike typical interscholastic moot court competitions. Law students from around the world were invited to draft written submissions involving a hypothetical issue of international environmental law and future generations. We then provided constructive feedback from expert commentators designed to make the students' final submissions useful (as a practical matter) for future advocates who might be dealing with analogous real-life issues. The written memorials and video recordings of the students' oral submissions are available on the University of Hawai'i Environmental Law Program website. *See* http://blog.hawaii.edu/elp/international (scroll down at the column on the right side). To make the experience even more meaningful, the students register for and participate in international proceedings that each of the moots are organized around.

Professor Gaillard and I are grateful to Richard L. "Dick" Ottinger, Dean Emeritus of the Elisabeth Haub School of Law at Pace University in White Plains, New York, for facilitating our initial connection after discovering that Professor Gaillard wrote her doctoral dissertation on the Rights of Future Generations. Aware of my collaboration on this topic with his colleague, University Professor Nicholas Robinson (who happens also to be one of the

IUCNAEL co-founders), Ottinger suggested that we consider Professor Gaillard as a member of our pool of international experts. Thankfully, Professor Gaillard (1) agreed to serve on the expert panel, (2) recruited one of her students to participate in the inaugural moot alongside students from the Philippines, the Republic of Korea, Brazil, Hawai'i and New York, and (3) joined the distinguished panel of judges for our mock International Court of Justice. Less than a year later, Professor Gaillard recruited two more French students to participate in the second Oposa Moot Court alongside a team of students from the Philippines. In addition to myself, Professor Robinson, another professor from Japan, and a member of the Philippine judiciary joined Professor Gaillard on the panel of mock ICJ judges.

The innovative moot continued in March 2018 as a special event during the 8th World Water Forum in Brasilia, Brazil, thanks to my Law School colleague Associate Dean and Professor Denise Antolini (who serves as Deputy Chair of the World Commission on Environmental Law, and also served as an elected member of the IUCN U.S. National Committee). The third Oposa Moot Court featured students from the Netherlands, Kenya, Hawai'i, New Zealand, Pakistan, and Brazil. Less than three months later in June 2018, the fourth Oposa Moot Court brought together students from New York, France, the Philippines, Kenya, and Hawai'i. These students also attended the 1st World Peace Forum, representing future generations at this prestigious event by speaking about their experiences with the Oposa Moot Court.

It is worth noting that Tony Oposa's personality and approach syncs perfectly with sentiments expressed by the great Quebec storyteller Fred Perellin – as quoted by Professor Louise Vandelac at the close of her essay #18 on "The Posthumous Post-human, or Abolishing The Future of Generations: By What Right?". The punchline of Perellin's joke explains that "a lot of people standing up together" in "a world that dances and sings" will be "pretty hard to tear down". Attorney Oposa lives Perellin's message by insisting that his audiences stand together and sing – better yet, to dance as well; in addition to engaging in other artistic pursuits like poetry, painting, or theater, as encouragement for creative thinking about how best to make a difference for future generations. *See* essay #21 on "Making a Difference for Future Generations".

The driving goal behind this book is to promote ideas relating to the rights of future generations by lawyers, sociologists, philosophers, and scientists (including academics as well as practitioners), with the sincere hope that this approach will help all humankind "become good ancestors", as urged by Nicholas Robinson in his essay #3 on "Evolutionary Roots Nurturing Equity Across Generations", if not "the best ancestors possible" as implored by Juan Ignacio

Pereyra in his essay #13 on “The Recognition of Rights for Future Generations in Argentinian Lawsuits: Review and Prospects”. During the editing process, the challenges of making this book accessible for readers from multiple disciplines were manifested in new and unexpected ways – some seemingly mundane, others more substantive in nature. In addition to conforming our colleagues’ wonderful submissions to the Author’s Guidelines provided by Peter Lang Publishing, we adopted a hybrid citation style that is based in part on the assumption that many of our readers may lack French language competence – as I do. I admit there were times when I was tempted to give in to a desire for mental enhancement along the lines discussed by Professor Vandelac in her essay #18 (referenced above) – at least to address my linguistic deficiencies. Rather than transforming myself into a transhumanist in search of perfection, I chose instead to accept the limitations and imperfections of my existence and apply a version of the precautionary principle. Thus, we have included within brackets our attempts to translate non-English source titles for the benefit of our non-Francophone readers. Except for titles of sources or quotations that follow British spelling, we opted to follow American spelling instead.

To the extent that the poetry inherent in the French language got lost in translation, those errors are ours alone as editors. Likewise, we are responsible for what may seem repetitive to some readers as a result of our efforts to clarify what is otherwise implicit in French. We believe this choice better serves readers who are less familiar with the subject matter or are accustomed to more direct writing styles. Rather than assuming shared knowledge about the niceties of citation forms in various disciplines, we also decided to depart from the traditional “rules” and present identifying information about our authors’ sources in a format accessible to a broad range of readers. I freely admit my inability to make the adjustment to « European quotes », so I welcomed Professor Gaillard’s willingness to accommodate some of my peccadilloes like using “smart quotes” in place of "straight quotes" – among many of my other quirks concerning punctuation and writing style. In turn, I conceded more than a few stylistic decisions that might cause American lawyers (particularly my academic colleagues, if not also those in other professions) to raise an eyebrow or two.

To the extent that Professor Gaillard and I may have succeeded in our attempts to harmonize this book across a variety of disciplines and cultures, I suspect this is the result of a shared appreciation for cross-cultural exchange and interdisciplinary or multidisciplinary initiatives based on our respective personal histories. My own contributions toward this goal were aided by knowledge passed down from my parents: Dr. Sheila M. Forman (one of many highly educated Filipinas who constantly demonstrated the truth behind falsehoods often associated with denigrating stereotypes in Hawai'i, which are rooted in the former plantation economy that ruled these islands in the middle of the Pacific Ocean where my family now lives – not to mention the shared experiences associated with centuries of colonization in my mother's native country); and Dr. Michael L. Forman, one of the first Peace Corps volunteers in the Philippines, Emeritus Professor of Linguistics with the University of Hawai'i at Mānoa, who published a dictionary for one of the twenty-seven major Philippine languages, and taught himself 'Ōlelo Hawai'i (the native Hawaiian language) in order to supervise the first doctoral dissertation written in 'Ōlelo Hawai'i. In addition to training subsequent Peace Corps volunteers, my parents were often hired by the State of Hawai'i Judiciary and other government agencies to provide cultural awareness training to federal, state, and county employees. My own multidisciplinary experiences include an undergraduate degree in Physical Sciences prior to my law degree, and courses in physical oceanography and ocean engineering on my way to a Graduate Ocean Policy Certificate from the School of Ocean and Earth Science and Technology, University of Hawai'i at Mānoa.

Ultimately, Professor Gaillard and I endeavored to achieve compromises that reflect a level of cross-cultural understanding rooted in the belief that neither of our respective approaches is necessarily right, or wrong; instead, our differences merely provide examples of the many diverse ways there are to look at the world and express ourselves.

David FORMAN

On the Technical Structure of the Book

This book is possible only because of the legal case on behalf of future generations won by attorney Antonio A. Oposa, Jr., in 1993 (authored by the Honorable Hilario G. Davide, Jr., Justice of the Supreme Court of the Philippines),[1] which

1 *Minors Oposa v. Factoran*, General Register No. 101083, Supreme Court of the Philippines, *International Law Materials*, 30 July 1993, Vol. 33, p. 173, *available online at* http://www.lawphil.net/judjuris/juri1993/jul1993/gr_101083_1993.html (accessed 15 June2019). Named Chief Justice for the Supreme Court of the Philippines in 1998, Davide served in that capacity until he reached the age of mandatory retirement. Chief Justice Davide later served as Ambassador/Permanent Representative of the Permanent Mission of the Philippines to the United Nations in New York City where, among other things, he was instrumental in breaking years of deadlock and successfully facilitated adoption of the UN Declaration on the Rights of Indigenous Peoples. *See, e.g.*, V. Tauli-Corpuz, "How the UN Declaration on the Rights of Indigenous Peoples Got Adopted", *available online at* http://www.tebtebba.

paved the way to a new legal and judicial era. Several themes explored in this book illustrate the ongoing impact of Oposa's pathbreaking work (and Justice Davide's eloquent opinion) across multiple disciplines.

In the first Part, three mentors of the law of future generations – namely, Professors Delmas-Marty, Brown Weiss and Robinson (key figures in international human rights and environmental law) – demonstrate the theoretical necessity of rights for future generations in the era of the Anthropocene (*Part 1*).

In the second Part, the nuclear industry and nuclear weapons in particular raise various lines of inquiry concerning justice for future generations. Mr. Alyn Ware (winner of the Livelihood Award in 2009) and Mr. Jean Marie Collin of ICAN (2017 Nobel Peace Prize) both provide insights into the topic of nuclear disarmament and the treaty to ban nuclear weapons. Professor Frédérick Lemarchand, a sociologist and anthropologist who specializes in the thought of catastrophism, offers a dive into the thought of Günther Anders. Anders and his fellow philosopher Jean-Pierre Dupuy help identify the conceptual paradoxes at the heart of the disaster. It is impossible to discuss the nuclear industry without giving the floor to two distinguished members of International Physicians for the Prevention of Nuclear War (which received the 1985 Nobel Peace Prize). Dr. Martin Walter and Professor Andreas Nidecker vividly demonstrate the reality of transgenerational genetic damage resulting from exposure to ionizing radiation. Sophisticated new research methods demonstrate that barn swallows, cattle and butterflies are already victims of genetic mutation near the sites of nuclear disasters; descendants of nuclear power plant operators and firefighters also suffer from increased mutations including leukemia and non-Hodgkin's lymphoma (*Part 2*).

The third Part studies a global diffusion of climate justice actions brought by civil society, youth, and sub-national governments. Attorney Christian Huglo argues that we are on our way toward a global judicial revolution. Our Children's Trust lawyers Elizabeth Brown and Danny Noonan, along with Professor John Davidson, shed light on the status of litigation under the North American Public Trust Doctrine as applied to climate change. Ms. Agnès Michelot takes us on a stroll through the international and French legal systems, including a report on the theme of climate justice for the French Economic and Social Council that she worked on as rapporteur alongside the famous Dr. Jean Jouzel, Director of Research at CNRS. Michelot and Jouzel also made proposals to the European Economic and Social Council regarding the rights of future generations (*Part 3*).

---

org/index.php/all-resources/category/20-un-declaration-on-the-rights-of-indigenous-peoples?download=333:how-the-un-declaration-on-the-rights-of-indigenous-peoples-got-adopted (accessed 15 June 2019).

In the fourth Part, it seemed necessary to study possible ways that new legal actions on behalf of future generations could be pursued in the future. Dr. Marie-Angèle Hermitte, Emeritus Director of Research at CNRS, has influenced French thought on countless major issues of our time. At the symposium, she made a presentation specifically focusing on the rights of nature by going beyond the distinction between subjects and objects of rights inherited from Roman law. According to Hermitte, we are instead entering a new era described by new forms of legal animism. There is no doubt that the justiciability of the rights of nature is part of a judicial evolution that converges with recognition of the rights of future generations. Ph.D. candidate Mathias Petel next provides an overview of the rights of nature, identifying the philosophical, economic and legal contours of this paradigm shift that converges nicely with litigation on behalf of future generations.

Attorney Juan Ignacio Pereyra, who testified about the harmful effects of pesticides in Argentina at the International Monsanto Tribunal and before the UN Human Rights Council, provides an encouraging inventory of the progress of these new rights in his country. Mr. David M. Forman brings some very interesting insights from Hawai'i, which has been a place of experimentation for the biggest multinational producers of pesticides before placing their genetically engineered organisms on the market. After fifty years of open-air field tests, local efforts to regulate these practices failed after the companies successfully removed the litigation from state to federal courts.

Part four concludes by presenting proposals for changes in the law that are currently being drafted to meet these new challenges. Among these proposals is the draft Third International Covenant on the Human Right to a Healthy Environment. Professor Michel Prieur describes this project marking a new evolutionary stage where human rights converge with environmental law on both international and national scales. The International Center for Comparative Environmental Law has deposited this draft covenant with the Human Rights Council in Geneva. Corinne Lepage's draft Universal Declaration of the Rights and Duties of Humankind is part of the same dynamic renewal of contemporary legal humanism. This initiative is perhaps even more daring, in that it intends to further elevate the level of evolution in human rights. Seventy plus years after the 1948 Universal Declaration of Human Rights, is it not time for the rights of humanity to be extended to future generations? (*Part 4*).

In the fifth Part, the book raises new and particularly difficult questions from a philosophical and legal point of view. Transhumanism marks the advent of a new ideology, with multiple faces that aim to "improve" the human being and create a new form of humanity. Judge Christian Byk, Court of Appeal of Paris, and

President of the UNESCO Intergovernmental Bioethics Committee, examines this new search for perfectibility of the human being. Professor Louise Vandelac questions the right to make a new human species, and asks what this means in terms of anthropological categories? As a true pioneer who has addressed many other bioethics themes, Dr. Amandine Cayol joins me in highlighting the many risks that arise for future generations. Cayol and I propose some milestones to consider when facing the numerous and thorny legal issues raised by transhumanism. This theme will undoubtedly require further study in coming years (*Part 5*).

In conclusion, the sixth Part provides an overview of the foundations that can be mobilized to provide legal protection for future generations. From the theoretical and practical point of view, directly or indirectly, many legal channels are possible. Above all, this book is a tribute to the pioneering judicial work opened by Tony Oposa; accordingly, the book concludes with his kind encouragement that we, lawyers and scientists from all over the world, can participate in protecting our future by making a difference for future generations (*Part 6*).

Emilie GAILLARD

Contents

List of Acronyms 23

PART 1. EXPLORING THEORETICAL FRAMEWORKS FOR APPLYING INTERGENERATIONAL EQUITY

Mireille DELMAS-MARTY
1. Adapting Juridical Order in the Age of the Anthropocene 29

Edith BROWN WEISS
2. Intergenerational Equity as a Change of Paradigm 43

Nicholas A. ROBINSON
3. Evolutionary Roots Nurturing Equity Across Generations 51

PART 2. THE NUCLEAR INDUSTRY AND THE RIGHTS OF FUTURE GENERATIONS

Alyn WARE
4. Nuclear Weapons and Law for the Future: The Application of Principles Protecting Future Generations in International Tribunals 63

Jean–Marie COLLIN
5. Treaty on the Prohibition of Nuclear Weapons: A Move Towards New Legal Action to Protect Future Generations? 83

Frédérick LEMARCHAND
6. The Bomb as a New Definition of Present and Future Humanity: What We Owe to Günther Anders' Thoughts 103

Martin WALTER & Andreas NIDECKER
7. Effects of Ionizing Radiation – Evidence of Genetic Effects: Greater Risks for Transgenerational Damage 113

PART 3. PROTECTING FUTURE GENERATIONS THROUGH CLIMATE JUSTICE LITIGATION

Christian HUGLO
8. Global Warming and the National Courts: A Global Legal Revolution? 133

Elizabeth BROWN, John DAVIDSON & Danny NOONAN
9. Securing the Legal Right to a Healthy Atmosphere and Stable Climate for the Benefit of All Present and Future Generations 153

Agnès MICHELOT
10. Climate Justice for Future Generations: From International to French Perspectives 171

PART 4. PROSPECTIVE LEGAL ACTIONS ON BEHALF OF FUTURE GENERATIONS?

Marie-Angèle HERMITTE
11. Each Object Has Its Own Subject! The Legal Revolutions of the Human-Nature Relationship 185

Matthias PETEL
12. The Rights of Nature: A Legal Revolution for Ecological Justice 211

Juan Ignacio PEREYRA
13. The Recognition of Rights for Future Generations in Argentinian Lawsuits: Review and Prospects 243

David M. FORMAN
14. Marooned in the Doldrums While Ignoring Indigenous Ecological Knowledge: Attempting to Regulate Pesticide Use in Hawai'i 261

Michel PRIEUR
15. Draft International Covenant on the Human Right to the Environment 285

Corinne LEPAGE & Emilie GAILLARD
16. For the Recognition of the Rights & Duties of Humankind 315

PART 5. PROTECTING THE HUMAN CONDITION OF FUTURE GENERATIONS, A NEW LEGAL QUESTION?

Christian BYK
17. Law and the Idea of Human Perfectibility 333

Louise VANDELAC
18. The Posthumous Post-Human, or Abolishing the Future of Generations: By What Right? 353

Amandine CAYOL & Emilie GAILLARD
19. Transhumanism(s) & Law(s): First Tracks and Thoughts 379

PART 6. THE IMPERATIVE TO LOOK FORWARD

Emilie GAILLARD
20. Legal Bases for Protecting Future Generations 397

David M. FORMAN & Antonio A. OPOSA, Jr.
21. Making a Difference for Future Generations 421

List of Figures 433

List of Tables 435

Select Bibliography 437

Select Case Law 465

Notes on Editors 473

Notes on Contributors 475

Index 485

Board of Advisers – Normandy Chair For Peace Collection 493

List of Acronyms

AAP	American Academy of Pediatrics
AI	Artificial Intelligence
AMAC	ʻAha Moku Advisory Committee
APHIS	Animal and Plant Health Inspection Service (United States Department of Agriculture)
Bt	Bacillus thuringiensis
CARICOM	Caribbean Community
CD	Conference on Disarmament
CEO	Chief Executive Officer
CERREV	Centre de Recherche – Risques & Vulnérabilités [Center for Research on Risks and Vulnerabilities]
CESE	Conseil Économique, Social et Environnemental [French Economic, Social and Environmental Council]
CIDCE	Centre International de Droit Comparé de l'Environnnement [International Center for Comparative Environmental Law]
CNRS	Centre National de la Recherche Scientifique [National Center for Scientific Research]
COMEST	World Commission on the Ethics of Scientific Knowledge and Technology
COP	Conference of the Parties
CRIDEAU	Centre de Recherches Interdisciplinaires en Droit de l'Environnement de l'Aménagement et de l'Urbanisme [Center for Interdisciplinary Research in Environmental Law and Urban Planning]
CRISPR	Clustered Regularly Interspaced Short Palindromic Repeats
CTBT	Comprehensive Nuclear-Test-Ban Treaty
CTBTO	Comprehensive Test Ban Treaty Organization
DDHu	Déclaration Universelle des Droits de L'Humanité [Universal Declaration of the Rights and Duties of Humankind]

DNA	Deoxyribonucleic acid
EA	Environmental Assessment
EC	European Commission
EESC	European Economic and Social Committee
EIA	Environmental Impact Assessment
ELP	Environmental Law Program, William S. Richardson School of Law, University of Hawai'i at Mānoa
ENMOD	Environmental Modification [Convention]
EPA	United States Environmental Protection Agency
FDA	United States Food and Drug Administration
GAFAM	Google, Amazon, Facebook, Apple and Microsoft (sometimes also including Twitter, Yahoo, and PayPal)
GE	Genetically Engineered
GHG	Greenhouse Gas
GIP	Groupement d'intérêt public [Public Interest Group]
GMO	Genetically Modified Organism
GRIP	Group for Research and Information on Peace and Security
HAARP	High-frequency Active Auroral Research Program
HDOA	State of Hawai'i Department of Agriculture
IALANA	International Association of Lawyers Against Nuclear Arms
ICAN	International Campaign to Abolish Nuclear Weapons
ICC	International Criminal Court
ICJ	International Court of Justice
ICRP	International Commission on Radiological Protection
IEL	International Environmental Law
IHL	International Humanitarian Law
IPCC	Intergovernmental Panel on Climate Change
IPPNW	International Physicians for the Prevention of Nuclear War
IUCN	International Union for the Conservation of Nature
IUCNAEL	IUCN Academy of Environmental Law

LCNP	Lawyers' Committee on Nuclear Policy
LDGJ	Librairie Générale de Droit et de Jurisprudence [General Library of Law and Jurisprudence]
LLM	Master of Laws
MDG	Millenium Development Goals
MRSH	Maison de la Recherche en Sciences Humaines [House of Research in Human Sciences]
mSV	millisievert
NAS	National Academies of Sciences, Engineering and Medicine
NATU	Netflix, Airbnb, Tesla and Uber
NBIC	Nanotechnology, Biotechnology, Information Science and Cognitive Sciences
NEPA	National Environmental Policy Act
NGO	Non-Governmental Organization
NHL	Non-Hodgkins Lymphoma
NPT	Nuclear Non-Proliferation Treaty
NSWLEC	Land and Environment Court of New South Wales
OAR	Overall Abnormality Rate
OCT	Our Children's Trust
OEWG	Open-ended Working Group
PCB	Polychlorinated biphenyl
PIP	Plant-Incorporated Protectant
POP	Persistent Organic Pollutant
PNND	Parliamentarians for Nuclear Non-proliferation and Disarmament
PSR	Physicians for Social Responsibility
R&D	Research & Development
RERF	Radiation Effects Research Foundation
RNA	Ribonucleic acid
RR	Relative Risk
RWE	Rheinisch-Westfälisches Elektrizitätswerk

SDG	Sustainable Development Goals
SFDE	Société Française pour le Droit l'Environnement [French Society for Environmental Law]
SSBN	Nuclear-powered ballistic missile submarine
TNC	Transnational Corporation
TPNW	Treaty on the Prohibition of Nuclear Weapons
UDHR	Universal Declaration of Human Rights (1948)
UK or **U.K.**	United Kingdom
UN or **U.N.**	United Nations
UNEP	United Nations Environment Programme
UNESCO	United Nations Educational, Scientific and Cultural Organization
UNFCCC	United Nations Framework Convention on Climate Change
UNGA	United Nations General Assembly
UNICEF	United Nations International Children's Emergency Fund
US or **U.S.**	United States
USA or **U.S.A.**	United States of America
USDA	United States Department of Agriculture
VNTR	variable number of tandem repeats
WCEL	World Commission on Environmental Law
WMO	World Meteorological Organization

PART 1. EXPLORING THEORETICAL FRAMEWORKS FOR APPLYING INTERGENERATIONAL EQUITY

In the first Part of this book, we explore the concept of Future Generations in a general legal context. Our entry into the Anthropocene Era calls for an urgent Copernican Revolution, a new legal matrix that is not only thought of (and used) for humans today, but also for future generations, including all living species and Nature itself.

Professor Mireille Delmas-Marty sets the stage by criticizing static depictions of the juridical order and proposing, instead, a globalized approach that relies upon mobilized stakeholders to ensure a dynamic equilibrium that recognizes our interdependent responsibilities. Rejecting uniformity in favor of an "ordering pluralism" that is sustained by its differences, Professor Delmas-Marty contends that planetary solidarity can be achieved by relying on two international law mechanisms: the universal principle of equal dignity, and cultural diversity as a Common Heritage of Mankind. By regulating the dialectic winds advocated by globalized economic, scientific and civil stakeholders, we can avoid the doldrums that could otherwise be experienced across a spectrum from totalitarianism to cut-throat competition (essay #1 on "Adapting Juridical Order in the Age of the Anthropocene").

Professor Edith Brown Weiss is one of the leading authors in international law on the topic of Justice for Future Generations. She puts into perspective the strengths associated with a changing legal paradigm that integrates Intergenerational Justice (procedurally and substantively) as a normative framework involving both rights as well as obligations. Deeply rooted in diverse cultural and religious traditions, intergenerational equity has already been applied by judicial bodies in a growing number of countries and is receiving increasing recognition in international law. The intergenerational equity framework provides that all generations share in a planetary trust and are partners in caring for as well as using the Earth (essay #2 on "Intergenerational Equity as a Change of Paradigm").

Professor Nicholas Robinson is an internationally-recognized architect of international environmental law, and one of the world's most distinguished public intellectuals. He poses an important question: whether jurisprudence and the legal profession can craft rules and procedures to ensure a more holistic, intergenerational application of equitable principles? Recognizing that human society is out of balance with the Earth, Professor Robinson draws upon norms evolved by indigenous peoples that can be applied to help rebalance our "intergenerational" accounts. We must become good ancestors who act as stewards of our cultural and natural heritage, and who are committed to justice and fairness across generations. In this sense, the evolution of environmental norms provides a framework for applying equity in a manner that promotes the resilience necessary to sustain life (essay #3 on "Evolutionary Roots Nurturing Equity Across Generations").

Mireille DELMAS-MARTY

1. Adapting Juridical Order in the Age of the Anthropocene

Taking Legal Action on Behalf of Future Generations: it was an ambitious objective for just two days! However, Emilie Gaillard is not easily daunted, so we have agreed to begin with an even more ambitious challenge: "Adapting Juridical Order in the Age of the Anthropocene".

Many scientists believe that the Anthropocene is a new stage in the history of Mankind; one in which the human species could become its own telluric force, capable of interacting with other geophysical forces and bringing about sustainable consequences for the ecosystem. This type of interaction has been brought to light in a variety of domains, including geology, earth science, geography and climatology. However, professionals in the domain of human and social sciences are taking longer to catch on, perhaps because the temporalities are usually much shorter.

Yet the need to anticipate has begun to affect law and philosophy, reflected in the concept of "future generations", as well as terms such as "sustainable development" and "sustainable peace". Currently, this need to anticipate is largely, if not exclusively, focused on nuclear or climate change issues, which will be addressed herein.

In order to fight against climate disruption, the temporal anticipation process cannot be disassociated from a spatial extension process – a phenomenon we refer to as globalization. This globalization dramatically changes the juridical order traditionally identified with States. It is true that globalization in itself is not something new. Going back to the end of the eighteenth century, the philosopher Immanuel Kant based what he referred to as "the principle of universal hospitality" on the spherical form of the Earth. He was well ahead of his times. We know that this principle has not yet been applied *per se*, but the recent constitutionalizing of "fraternity" could mean that hospitality becomes part of our legal world, thus limiting the definition of the so-called "délit de solidarité", i.e., crime of hospitality.[1]

---

1 French Constitutional Council, Decision No. 2018-717/718 QPC, 6 July 2018, *available online at* https://www.conseil-constitutionnel.fr/decision/2018/2018717_718QPC.htm (accessed 15 June 2019).

The surprising thing is that, according to Kant, this principle of "universal hospitality" – from the first article of his Cosmo political law – was imposed because, as the Earth is round, "infinite dispersion is impossible". He announced that henceforth, ties between nations would be "increasingly close" to the point that, "a violation of rights in one place will be felt everywhere". The truth of this statement became evident as the two processes that characterize globalization developed: the extension of relations between nations, or globalization *stricto sensu* (globalization of flows, risks and even crimes); and, the universalization of values (the establishment of "human" rights and crimes against "humanity"). So, what is different about today's world?

First, demography: during the time of Kant, there were roughly 1 billion humans on the Earth. Now there are nearly 8 billion of us, and this is growing at a staggering rate: between 1950 (3 billion) and 2010 (7 billion), the population increased by 1 billion every 15 years. This will soon increase every 10 years. Second, interdependencies: another increase between what can be referred to as "les collectifs humains" or "the different collectives".[2] This has been noted between different human collectives (tribes, States, groups of States, transnational companies, NGOs, etc.), but also between human and non-human collectives (non-humans including animals and nature, and perhaps "smart objects" created by Artificial Intelligence).

All this reorganization of human societies includes the sphere of justice and the juridical field. It is definitely not by chance that during this period of transition, drafts have abounded, not unlike those of the 1780-89 period: the age of the French Declaration of the Rights of the Man and of the Citizen. Presently, new declarations are being drafted. These include the Declaration of the Rights of Mother Earth, the Universal Declaration of the Rights and Duties of Humankind (Déclaration Universelle des Droits de l'Humanité, or DDHu) or even the Third International Covenant on the Human Right to the Environment, formulated by jurists such as Professor Michel Prieur and Yann Aguila (following two other international covenants signed in 1966: the International Covenant on Civil and Political Rights, along with the International Covenant on Economic, Social and Cultural Rights).

These different texts share many common points, but one in particular stands out: times have changed since the eighteenth-century declarations, and even since the 1966 Covenants – we have gone from gaining independences to recognizing interdependencies. The word "interdependencies" is central as it obliges

2 P. Descola, *Par-delà nature et culture* [*Beyond Nature and Culture*], Gallimard, 2015.

us to acknowledge what I would call the duty of solidarity. We can already note the increase in power of new legal categories that modify relationships in space and time.

For space, these categories include: the "Common Heritage of Mankind", "Global Public Goods" (this term was borrowed from economists and could lead to the recognition of common goods) or "ecological prejudice". As for time, the new categories introduce precisely this concept of anticipation that was not customary in the legal domain. I mentioned earlier the terms "future generations", "sustainable development" and "sustainable peace". To these we can add "transgenerational damages", and also the principle of "non-regression" that was recently introduced to international law. Although this last is perhaps less ambitious than the others, it is more realistic.

Unfortunately, the way juridical order has been depicted does not facilitate such a metamorphosis. The legal vocabulary is still static: *foundations, grounds, fundamental rights, etc.* Furthermore, the metaphors – which have an even greater influence – are immobile: *pyramids, bases, pillars*, etc. Even when referring to "sources", we add the adjective, "fundamental", which renders them immovable. All this vocabulary spurs – even obliges – us to identify law with a given State, and juridical order to a fixed construction.

To depict these new assemblages, we would need a more radical epistemological break-up, one that moves from concepts to process, from static to dynamic, and from models to movement. To this end, I proposed the metaphor of winds[3] – which I would like to take as a starting point for this presentation, divided into three parts. First, an observation: globalization is caught up in a storm of opposing winds. Then, I will study the narrative of "mondialité" by writers from the Caribbean zone – such as Edouard Glissant or Patrick Chamoiseau – who thought extensively about humanizing globalization, proposing to refer to this people-centered globalization as "mondialité". Finally, we shall consider the new responsibilities as belonging to the world, which we are starting to refer to as "world citizenship".

I. Globalization in a Storm of Opposing Winds

To sustain what he referred to as *the new scientific spirit,* Bachelard appealed to the "imaginative forces of the spirit" and opposed false scientific objectivity with

3 M. Delmas-Marty, *Aux quatre vents du monde. Petit guide de navigation sur l'océan de la mondialisation* [*Four Winds of the World: A Short Guide to Navigating the Ocean of Globalization*], Seuil, 2016.

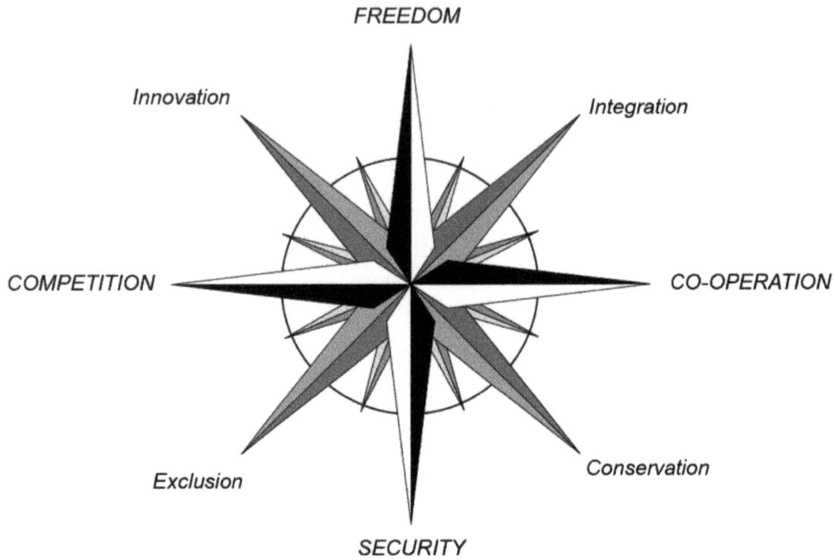

Fig. 1: *Wind Rose, Identifying Opposing Winds.*

a non-Cartesian epistemology. In the age of the Anthropocene, the renewal of political thought needs a *new legal spirit* that awakens the "imaginative forces of law" and opposes the widespread fallacy of a law that represents States with a "non-Kelsenian" epistemology. But how do we escape the "rigidity of blindly accepted convictions"? The philosopher wrote, "If we are unable immediately to attain to an ordered multiplicity, we can always resort to dialectics as to a clang that will awaken our dormant resonances".[4]

And Mr. Trump has helped us to discover the consequences of denying reality in a world becoming more and more interdependent. This reveals the emergency of introducing dialectics into the legal field. Two figures illustrate this theory: the wind rose to identify opposing winds (Fig. 1); and dancing with the winds (below, Fig. 2), to attempt to regulate them.

This is precisely the main objective of my imaginary wind rose: identifying contradictions. First, there are the dominant winds: freedom *versus* security; competition *versus* co-operation.

4 G. Bachelard, *The Psychoanalysis of Fire*, Routledge & K. Paul, 1964, pp. 6 and 110, translated by A.C.M. Ross.

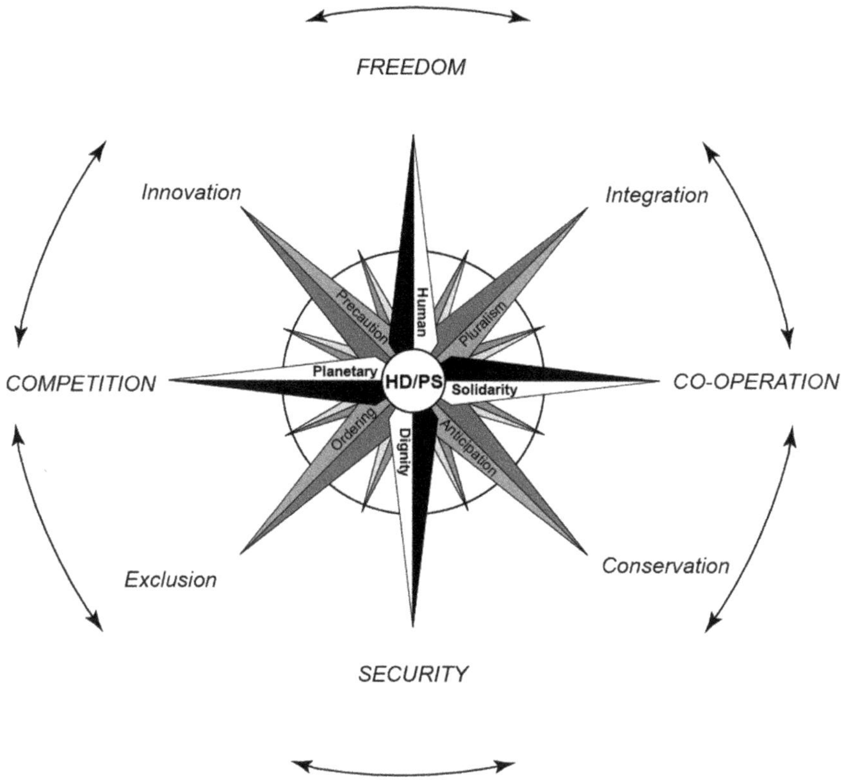

Fig. 2: *Wind Cycle, Dancing with the Winds.*

Then there are the intermediate winds, or the winds between winds: innovation *versus* conservation; exclusion *versus* integration.

The wind rose helps us to understand the issues – to know where we stand; but it does not indicate the direction to be taken. It doesn't show the direction for future global governance. It is true that for a long time each "human collective" has chosen its own direction, based on its own logic (or its ideologic). However, they remained within their own territories.

In the age of the Anthropocene, globalization is accompanied by deterritorialization, whether it be immaterial flows (financial flows or flows of information), global risks (climate or health risks), or global crimes (trafficking, corruption, terrorism or even ecocide). The borders that separated territories are becoming porous, and global governance, caught up in the storm of opposing winds, is drawing closer to the "doldrums": the place in the middle of the oceans where the meeting of north and south is so violent that their encounter produces, at best, calms (i.e., neutralizes one another and paralyzes vessels, that remain "becalmed") and, at worst, causes storms and shipwrecks.

It is true that every social (including legal) organization presupposes a minimum level of stability, at least temporarily. Even so, it must not prevent all movement during this period of major acceleration, when societies are continuously having to adapt themselves. To stabilize our societies without immobilizing them, we need to choose a direction.

Yet it appears impossible to favor one of the winds over the others without destroying the equilibrium. Security without freedom leads to totalitarianism, but freedom without security brings chaos; competition without co-operation leads to rule by force (military or economic), but cooperation without competition brings about collectivism; innovation without conservation could mean the collapse of the planet, but conservation without innovation leads to paralysis; exclusion without integration means imprisonment or war, but integration without exclusion could result in a deadly fusion.

In other words, the triumph of one single wind, whichever one it may be, will lead global governance into the doldrums: either the paralysis of a totalitarian system or a shipwreck in the great disorder of a world where cut-throat competition reigns; or a strange combination of them both.

On the other hand, the energy produced by these tensions could contribute – and here lies the gamble – to revitalizing action. Through a circular movement that resembles a sort of "wind cycle", this energy could generate legal principles that enable the regulation of opposing winds rather than the elimination of contradictions, thus producing a dynamic equilibrium.

This dynamic equilibrium is rather like the alternation of a world that breathes. Globalization would quickly be suffocated if alternation comes to a halt – for example, if security were to overrule rights or if competition were to extinguish the spirit of co-operation. To avoid this suffocation, each couple of opposing winds must be ordered around regulatory principles that allow "or" (that which opposes) to be replaced by "and" (that which composes).

For the intercardinal winds, regulation can be accomplished through a sort of balancing of interests that presupposes a logic of gradation, sometimes referred to as *fuzzy logic*. The principle of "precaution/anticipation" should, thus, reconcile the innovation/conservation couple – according to the degree of probability, seriousness and risk acceptability – stabilizing it without setting it in stone. The same applies to "ordering pluralism" (universal pluralism, harmonized plurality) that restores equilibrium to the "exclusion/integration" couple. It does not exclude all the differences, but instead permits integration with varied content and at several speeds. This is how the concept of the "domestic margin of appreciation" works at a European level and how "common but differentiated responsibilities" works at a global level, which we will return to later because it is included in the Paris Climate Agreement.

However, balancing is not yet possible: how do we balance freedoms with security? We need to choose a direction for stabilizing the route without setting the trajectory in stone, using both the attraction of common "inalienable" values and the repulsion of common "unsurmountable" prohibitions. Then, an agreement on the processes for determining relations between humans and non-humans would need to be settled.[5] It is difficult to decide between a separatist ideal (so-called "humanism") that separates Mankind from nature, and another so-called "naturalist" idea, that considers Mankind to be an element of nature (or of the ecosystem).[6]

Humanism seems to have prevailed on the international scene, from the philosophy of the Enlightenment through the UDHR. Beyond human rights, humanism further emphasizes the independence of humans according to a process of anthropocentric separation that favors Mankind and permits it to dominate nature. Its direction is the principle of equal dignity and its corollary, crimes against humanity and genocide, is otherwise called the prohibition of dehumanization.

Since the "Earth Summit" (Rio de Janeiro, 3-14 June 1992), Naturalism has been strongly expressed in many forms, culminating with the 17 Sustainable Development Goals (SDG, 25 September 2015), and then the Paris Climate Agreement (15 December 2015). It brings interdependencies between humans and other elements of the ecosystem into international law: "Recognizing the integral and interdependent nature of the Earth, our home" (Rio Declaration, 14 June 1992). It considers human collectivities as parts of the ecosystem, which should result in replacing the concept of an environment that puts Mankind at the center of the Earth (as in the days of old, when the Earth had been placed at the center of the solar system), with the concept of an ecosystem.

By prolonging a sort of universal fraternity, widened by the concept of "Mother Earth" to non-human living entities, the direction would be indicated by the

---

5 P. Descola, *Beyond Nature and Culture*, The University of Chicago Press, 2013, translated by J. Loyd.

6 D. Ander, *La silhouette de l'humain. Quelle place pour le naturalisme dans le monde d'aujourd'hui ? [The Silhouette of the Human: What Place for Naturalism in Today's World?]*, Gallimard, 2016.

concept of common goods in the purest sense of inappropriable and inalienable goods – of which the corollary could be the crime of ecocide (still a draft), as a companion to genocide, prohibiting denaturalization of the planetary ecosystem in order to achieve planet security.

Must we really make a choice? The very fact that we ask the question shows that although humans really are part of nature, they cannot be confused with other living entities – precisely because we are the only ones that are conscious and responsible. We must therefore find a path that would permit us to safeguard the equal dignity of humans and planetary common goods, while prohibiting genocide and ecocide. This would be a way of somehow avoiding both security excesses and abuses of freedoms, the excess of wars and markets, the abuse of fusional ecologism, in addition to a dehumanizing scientism.

Only a mobilization of all our energies that involves the complete responsibility of all stakeholders, will allow us to entertain the possibility of such a route.

In other words, we need a narrative that is centered on the wind cycle: where the letters HD stand for the equal dignity of human beings, and PS (or planetary solidarity) protects present and future generations, including both human and non-human living entities. This could be the deepest meaning of the narrative of globality.

II. The Narrative of "Mondialité": Towards a People Centered Globality

This word is difficult to translate into other languages, especially English. The concept "*Mondialité*" [globality] – coined in French by Edouard Glissant, who invented this concept and developed it in several of his works – is not utopia. It is a way of representing a reality that can already be seen: "Globality is this unprecedented adventure given to all of us to experience in a time-space; for the first time, truly and strikingly, it is at once unique and multiple and inextricable". He is not defining globality as a concept, nor describing it as a process, but perhaps rather explaining globality as a new narrative that I tried to summarize in a sort of manifesto ("Pour une mondialité apaisée" [For a pacified globality]), in three adjectives: all different (*see* Section II.A.), all interdependent (*see* Section II.B.), all acting together in solidarity (*see* Section II.C.).

A. All Different

Globality is not uniformity. What people fear most about globalization is the single model or, even worse, the hegemonic single model. Kant was already wary of a Universal Republic that he believed would lead to the most dreadful despotism. A century later, Tocqueville imagined that despotism in democracy would render humans so infantile that it would transform them into troops of docile animals. However, he had not envisaged the numerical revolution that aids his "soft" despotism – which everybody spontaneously takes part in – with mass surveillance tools. These are fed by big data that we contribute to, more or less consciously. The mass data is handled by algorithms that outrun us as artificial intelligence progresses and becomes more independent.

Globality on the other hand, recognizes these differences and is sustained by it. It is both unique and multiple: "multiple" to the extent that a degree of pluralism is involved, and "unique" in the sense that it does not stop at juxtaposing differences, but instead calls for common organization. In this respect, globality is close to what I referred to as "ordering pluralism" or pluralism that brings differences together without eliminating them, harmonizes diversity without destroying it, and pluralizes what is universal without replacing it with what is relative. So that there is common ground, differences must remain – but they must be compatible.

In order to make differences compatible, globality could rely on two mechanisms of international law: article 1 of the UDHR, already referred to, which establishes the equal dignity of human beings in the universal principle; and, article 1 of the United Nations Educational, Scientific and Cultural Organization (UNESCO) Universal Declaration on Cultural Diversity adopted in November 2001 in the tragic aftermath of 9/11 (then taken up again in the 2005 Convention), which proclaims cultural diversity to be the "Common Heritage of Mankind". Beyond the indication that, "No one may invoke cultural diversity to infringe upon human rights guaranteed by international law, nor to limit their scope" (art. 4, UNESCO Declaration), we still need to find a method for determining the threshold of compatibility that would enable us to reconcile the "irreconcilable".[7] Perhaps we must look for this method in the practices born of the second proposal.

B. All Interdependent

Interdependencies are an increasingly evident reality, to the extent that they have multiplied between human collectives, current and future generations, humans and non-human living entities, as well as between human subjects and intelligent objects. They received legal recognition at the Earth Summit (Rio 1992): "The

7 A. Meddeb, *Le temps des inconciliables* [*The Time of the Irreconcilable*], Contre-prêches 2, 2017.

planet Earth is a vast set of interdependencies". At first, this was a discreet entry, but we now find it in numerous drafts. Already in 2005, a "Declaration of Interdependency" was presented to the UN institutions; I know because I took part in its drafting along with the members of the *International Ethical, Scientific and Political Collegium* (including Michel Rocard, Milan Kucan, Stéphane Hessel, Fernando Henrique Cardoso, Edgard Morin and Peter Sloterdijk). During the ten years that followed, drafts have multiplied. These include the following: a "Universal Declaration of Human Obligations" (2011); in the light of the COP 21, a "Universal Declaration of the Rights and Duties of Humankind" and a proposal for a third UN Convention on the environment (2015); and, the Declaration of Poets published by Patrick Chamoiseau in 2017.[8]

Such effervescence is not surprising considering this is a true Copernican revolution: Copernicus discovered that the Earth is not the center of the solar system, and we have discovered that humans are not at the center of the Earth. Mankind is not the owner of nature but an element of the ecosystem. This calls for preference to be given to this term over the term "environment", which puts humans at the center. Incidentally, some languages do not include either the word or the concept of the environment.

But when we try to organize solutions to interdependencies, we must recognize that only humans ("endowed with reason and conscience", according to article 1 of the UDHR) are responsible. Their relationship with non-human entities is therefore asymmetric and without reciprocity, because the responsibility to promote solidarity lies with them.

C. All Acting in Solidarity

Moving from interdependency to solidarity requires us to explicate common targets. This method slowly expanded over the years: it began with the eight Millennium Development Goals – which were mainly focused on the fight against poverty, but still very vague (MDGs, UN Secretary General, 2000) – and has led to the 17 Sustainable Development Goals (SDGs 2015). The method was then clarified with more specific qualitative and quantitative goals: for the climate (Paris Agreement 2015) and perhaps for 2018, a draft World Charter of Migrants.

Planetary solidarity is possible when the legal spirit opens up to the world, if we consider common law as a common grammar even if the technical rules are different. This is also the basis for the idea of opening legal systems up to the

8 P. Chamoiseau, *Frères migrants* [*Migrant Brothers*], Seuil, 2017.

world, using processes that we employ for languages: dialog, or rather exchange; co-ordination between legal systems; and harmonization, which is a kind of translation because it involves looking for equivalents. We do not look for absolute identity but rather functional or symbolic equivalences – as with the concept of "domestic margin of appreciation". Finally, if we want to achieve a fusion that is acceptable to everyone, we must avoid unilateral transplantation and favor reciprocity, through a sort of reciprocal hybridization that evokes creolization, and creates the unexpected. For example, to define a crime against humanity truly acceptable by all nations, we must combine the different ideas of humanity from different cultures throughout the world.

Furthermore, we must be aware of the resistance we will face. Were planetary solidarity to be politically accepted by everyone, it would call for new responsibilities, perhaps paving the way for the birth of world citizenship.

III. New Responsibilities and World Citizenship

In international law, the States are still the main responsible stakeholders. What is new is the concept of "common but differentiated responsibilities": the responsibilities of the States are common (inasmuch that the common objectives are accepted by all) as with climate issues; however, their application or implementation is differentiated, or contextualized. The national context could be historical, economic, political, cultural, geographical, etc. However, contextualizing does not mean re-nationalizing: differentiation criteria are necessary to avoid arbitrariness.

This leads to the delicate issue of control. The Paris Agreement, for example, is mandatory – but what happens in cases of transgression? The ideal response would be that each transgression is directly sanctioned by a Court; thus, transitioning the agreement from soft law to hard law. The Paris Agreement currently allows for a transparency framework, in which the information provided by States may be published by a committee of experts and triggers a sort of symbolic sanction of public opinion as a result. Everything will depend on the way the globalization stakeholders use the text.

If they are not pushed into a corner, the States will not do anything. This demonstrates the importance of other stakeholders. For example, a national judge could pronounce sanctions. We are beginning to observe throughout the global space the role of national judges using international mechanisms to interpret domestic law. For example, the *Urgenda* ruling by a Dutch court sanctioned the Netherlands in 2015, because the State failed to respect its greenhouse gas

(GHG) emissions commitments. Subsequent essays in this book include similar examples and further develop the subject.

This first approach based on renewing responsibilities could contribute to transforming *solitary* sovereignty to sovereignty based on *solidarity*, marking the move from independence to interdependence. Given the strong resistance, however, we cannot limit responsibility to the States. This leads us to the role economic stakeholders play and a concept that entered into the legal vocabulary a few years ago: social and environmental responsibility (SER) for companies, including transnational corporations (TNCs). The TNCs have been making voluntary commitments since the year 2000: first, in adherence to the Global Compact principles; then, taking an increasingly active part in negotiations, including even the implementation of some international agreements. In the Climate Agreement negotiations, for example, the large corporations played a key role.

The ideal scenario would be to create an international environmental court that would have the power to judge both States and transnational corporations. We have already had the Rights of Nature Tribunals and the International Monsanto Tribunal (opinion tribunal for the Monsanto case). Furthermore, several texts, including the French Law of 2017, impose a duty of vigilance on parent companies – providing instruction for companies at a European and even global level. This could be extended by other legislations. Likewise, the famous crime of ecocide, if we manage to create it, must be imputable when necessary – not only to State leaders, but also to managers of large companies.

And of course, we could do nothing without the civil stakeholders, and that includes all of us! The group includes all those who already consider themselves as such, even if they do not yet have the corresponding legal status, as world citizens. We must likewise acknowledge the special role that scientists play; they are often those who give warnings and trigger legal responses, as the climatologists did for the climate.

Of course, we oppose them at times because of the risk of conflict of interests. However, there are solutions: we could define a status of global researcher and expert, both to protect their independence and to guarantee their competence. It is true that there are very few specialists in some domains, and they are all hired – a reality such specialists claim makes conflicts of interest inevitable: if you work with somebody competent, they will not be impartial; and, if you work with somebody impartial, they will not be competent. But there are solutions to this problem as well: including separation of the expert's role and the researcher's role, perhaps through registration of global expert status. Furthermore, scientists could contribute to clarifying the duties of humans towards other living entities. In this respect, I am interested in the parallel drawn by Marie-Angèle Hermitte between the animism of indigenous populations and scientific animism.

The last stakeholders are the civil stakeholders (last, but perhaps the first), especially NGOs, who are already formulating numerous texts and taking part in their implementation. Their status still needs to be defined and the civic initiative must be further developed. This procedure has not yet proved to be very fruitful in Europe, but it is starting to be included in the practices, and jurists could contribute to the creation of an analogy to the European Citizens' Initiative at a global level, including the protection of future generations. This would create technical problems that will be addressed later in this book. For example, how do we represent the rights of future generations? What about the rights of non-human living entities? Must we stop speaking of duties with respect to these categories? The debate about representation of collective interests stretches even further to address representation of the elements of the cosmos such as mountains and rivers. Jurists and anthropologists have begun to have useful discussions on all these issues.

To conclude, I hope that I have shown the extent to which the topics discussed in this book "Legal Actions for Future Generations" lay at the heart of efforts to recompose the global legal system in this age of the Anthropocene. Future generations still need to be included in the cycle. To this end, we must consolidate the legal mechanisms – but, also, adapt and renew them.

The book begins by addressing nuclear issues and the discovery of common goods. It then addresses the issue of climate justice and concludes with looking at transhumanism, which could lead to the explosion of a new post-human species. This goes to show the anthropological background that underpins all of this work. There are different aspects of Mankind we are invited to reflect upon: the separatist and dominant Mankind of the enlightenment philosophy; the interdependent Mankind of the ecologists; or, the enhanced Mankind that is looming on the horizon of transhumanism. Let's hope that they all learn to live together in peace, and learn to protect both human dignity and planetary solidarity within the ecosystem.

I would like to end by referring to Boutros Boutros Ghali's 1993 formula at the Vienna Summit, where he evoked the irreducible human. Irreducible Mankind is not the solitary man of the Enlightenment, nor the enhanced Mankind of the transhumanists. This definition refers instead to Mankind in a relationship, a sort of go-between: in solidarity with future generations, but with equal duties owed to non-human living entities. Irreducible Mankind must not only develop its memory and cognitive performance (the dream of enhanced Mankind), but also its imagination, creativity and – why not? – spirituality. Aware of its limits, irreducible Mankind does not expect to predict the unpredictable. If it does anticipate, it is within the limits of its finite humanity. This reminds me of a poem by René Char (*Feuillets d'Hypnos* [Leaves of Hypnos]) published during the war. While he was fighting with the Maquis, the poet dreamed of a humanism that was "aware of its duties, discreet about its virtues, wishing to reserve the inaccessible to be freely roamed by the imagination of its suns, and decided to pay the price for it". With a bit of luck, this new humanism will discover how to steer clear of the doldrums.

Edith BROWN WEISS

2. Intergenerational Equity as a Change of Paradigm

We live in an emerging Anthropocene Epoch, in which humans for the first time are the major force shaping our environment. All of us share the global environment; we are for the foreseeable future locked into the same atmosphere and biosphere. What we do in one place can severely affect the resilience and integrity of our planet. At the same time, we live in a kaleidoscopic world, in which people communicate instantaneously within and across borders and in which change is inherent and rapid. The kaleidoscopic world is more integrated, more fragmented, and more chaotic. We now have ever-shifting *ad hoc* coalitions as well as more formal groups, myriad individual initiatives, and do-it-yourself technologies emerging in synthetic biology and climate interventions, with long term implications for future generations.

Climate change has focused our attention, as perhaps nothing else, on the long-term implications of our actions and the risks that our actions pose for future generations, both for immediate future generations and those in the more distant future. We are accustomed to addressing problems in a near term perspective. But this paradigm no longer suffices because it does not adequately address the future. Youth are at the forefront today of appreciating the need to consider the future in the decisions we take today.

I. Framework of Intergenerational Equity

Intergenerational equity provides a framework for addressing the kaleidoscopic world of the Anthropocene Epoch. As a principle, it has deep roots in diverse cultural and religious traditions: common law, civil law, Islamic law, African customary law, Judeo-Christian tradition, and monotheistic and theistic traditions of Asia and South Asia. The report of the United Nations Secretary General on Intergenerational Solidarity and the Needs of Future Generations confirmed the principle of intergenerational equity.[1] The basic theoretical framework is that all generations share in a planetary trust and are partners in caring for and using the

---

1 UN Secretary General, *Intergenerational Solidarity and the Needs of Future Generations: Report of the Secretary-General,* UN Doc. A/68/322, 15 Aug. 2013.

Earth.[2] The present generation, those of us living today, must pass the Earth and our natural and cultural resources to future generations in at least as good condition as we received them, so that future generations can meet their own needs. Intergenerational equity is the foundation for sustainable development.

We can identify three components of the principle of intergenerational equity: options or comparable options; quality or comparable quality; and access or comparable non-discriminatory access among generations. These components satisfy four criteria: to encourage equality among generations, by not authorizing the present generation to exploit resources to the exclusion of future generations, and not imposing unreasonable burdens on the present generation to meet indeterminate future needs; to avoid making the present generation predict the values of future generations but, rather, giving them flexibility to meet their own goals according to their own values; to be reasonably clear in application to foreseeable situations; and, to be generally shared by diverse cultural traditions and acceptable to different economic and political systems.

The principle's three components – options, quality and access – are briefly considered below.

Comparable options is a component that calls for conserving the diversity of natural (and cultural) resources, so that future generations have a more robust and flexible heritage from which they can achieve their own well-being. This means, for example, conserving biological diversity, respecting ground water recharge rates, and in the case of resources for which there are no known substitutes for certain uses, by not releasing all of the resource as a byproduct of other resource exploitation.

Comparable quality calls for ensuring that the quality of the environment is on balance no worse than when we received it. Some actions generate long lasting and potentially irreversible harm. Reversing the contamination of a ground water aquifer may be too difficult and too costly, especially for larger aquifers. Inappropriate disposal of nuclear wastes may result in long term harm and disposal of such wastes, and other pollutants in the oceans may cause widespread essentially irreversible damage. The erosion and desecration of soils may render them unproductive.

Comparable access provides members of our generation with a reasonable, non-discriminatory right of access to the environment and its resources to use

---

2 E. Brown Weiss, *In Fairness to Future Generations*, Tokyo/New York, United Nations University/Transnational Publishers, 1989. The analysis that follows is based on this reference.

for our own benefit, and provides for equitable non-discriminatory access for future generations. An indication of comparable access would be, for example, whether the real prices of resources to future generations (or at least to immediate successor generations), were comparable to those today. One could also apply this component to climate change, if it were more costly for future generations to maintain a stable climate because the present generation had not taken needed measures, or if the impacts from climate change made access to resources more difficult or costly.

From the perspective of the intergenerational lens, a number of strategies follow. The most fundamental is to give future generations a voice in the decisions that we take today. Their interests are generally not included. Decisions are often taken for short-term political or other gains at the expense of their well-being. It is not easy to give future generations a voice, because we have to identify what their interests are and ensure that those claiming to represent their interests are not, instead, pursuing their own at the expense of the well-being of future generations. Nonetheless, a variety of proposals have emerged for altering the dialogue to include consideration of the interests of future generations. These include the proposal of the Mary Robinson Foundation for Global Guardians for Future Generations,[3] intergenerational pacts, and ombudspersons for future generations operating in various fora and at various levels.

The intergenerational lens also highlights the need for scientific research and technological development to understand the global and local environmental systems better, to identify and assess the impacts of our actions, to develop more efficient ways to extract and use resources, and to develop alternatives for meeting our needs that are less harmful to both present and future generations. Such research and development is critical to addressing climate change.

Another central strategy is to address the inequities among people who are living today. All people need to be able to live sustainably and to have reasonable non-discriminatory access to the environment and its resources. The United Nations Sustainable Development Goals address this issue. From an intergenerational perspective, though, still more needs to be done to ensure that the basic human needs of all people today are being met and that all people are willing and able to meet their obligations to future generations.

---

3 *See, e.g.*, Mary Robinson Foundation – Climate Justice, Global Guardians: A voice for future generations (Jan. 2018), *available online at* https://www.mrfcj.org/wp-content/uploads/2018/02/Global-Guardians-A-Voice-for-Future-Generations-Position-Paper-2018.pdf (accessed 15 June 2019).

In a kaleidoscopic world with a plethora of actors and coalitions along with individuals having increasing voice, the most basic strategy is to ensure that we share fundamental norms that are rooted in the diverse societies. These norms can be a unifying element in addressing problems to both present and future generations. The principle of intergenerational equity reflects one such norm.

II. Intergenerational Rights and Obligations

In considering a principle of intergenerational equity, a key question is whether this implies only obligations by the present generation to future generations or whether future generations also have rights. If the latter, then we can speak of intergenerational rights and obligations. While rights are always linked with obligations, obligations do not require rights. If rights exist, they provide stronger protection than obligations alone, since they represent specific interests that must be respected and are enforceable by the holders of the rights or their representatives. The principle of intergenerational equity provides the basis for a set of intergenerational rights and obligations, which derive from each generations' position as part of the intertemporal entity of human society.

Intergenerational rights are the rights of each generation to receive the Earth in no worse condition than did the previous generation, to inherit comparable diversity in natural and cultural resources and to have non-discriminatory access to use and benefit from the legacy. In the first instance, they represent moral protection of interests, which must be transformed into legal rights and obligations. The rights and obligations coexist in each generation. The rights of future generations are linked to the obligations of the present generation. The rights inherently adhere in all generations, whether immediately successive generations or ones more distant. Disposal of nuclear wastes, ozone depletion, climate change, loss of biological diversity and loss of the productivity of soils significantly affect the natural heritage of even the more distant generations.

Intergenerational rights may be regarded as group rights as distinct from individual rights in the sense that generations hold these rights as a group in relation to other generations past, present, and future. They exist regardless of the number and the identity and number of individuals making up each generation. When these rights are held by members of the present generation, they may acquire attributes of individual rights in the sense that there are identifiable interests of individuals that the rights protect. Remedies for violating these rights will benefit other members of the generation, not only the individual claiming the right. Intergenerational rights must be conceived in the context of generations, in which the present and future generations have rights in relation to other generations to use and benefit from the Earth. This is consistent with other views of rights, including the Islamic view, which treats human rights not only as individual rights but as rights of the community of believers as a whole.

We should also consider whether we may speak only of obligations toward future generations, without corresponding rights. The 1997 UNESCO Declaration on the Responsibilities of the Present Generation toward Future Generations speaks only of obligations. Theoretically, an obligation is not always engaged with a right. A moral charitable obligation, for example, does not give those who benefit a right to charity. The English philosopher John Austin describes some obligations as absolute duties, which exist independently of any correlative right.

In the intergenerational context, we can speak either of obligations or of rights and obligations. If we consider the fundamental temporal relationship that each generation has to all other generations, we can discern rights and obligations. If the obligations of the present generation are not linked with rights, the present generation has an incentive to bias the articulation of these obligations in favor of itself at the expense of future generations. If future generations have rights, we do not have to rely only on a sense of *noblesse oblige* by the present generation. Intergenerational rights have greater moral force than do obligations.

The principle of intergenerational equity frames the content of intergenerational rights and obligations. Within this context, every generation has the responsibility to set criteria for defining the actions that infringe upon these rights. Appropriate criteria would be whether activities have a significant harmful impact either spatially or over time; whether the effects are irreversible or reversible only with unacceptable costs; and whether the effects will be viewed as significant by a substantial number of people. Intergenerational rights may also be linked to certain procedural norms, such as generation of and access to information, participation in decision-making, monitoring and impact assessments that reflect the perspective of future generations.

The enforcement of intergenerational rights and obligations raises critical and difficult issues. Future generations are neither present in the decisions we take affecting them nor physically present in judicial procedures. Theoretically, States have the primary responsibility to enforce rights of future generations, and in this sense serve as guardian *ad litem* for future generations. More broadly, communities, non-governmental organizations, and even individuals have a duty to enforce rights of future generations. An ombudsperson for future generations, guardian *ad litem*, or other designated representative of future generations could be considered. One challenge is to ensure that any party seeking to enforce rights of future generations is not using future generations as a subterfuge for pursuing the party's own agenda at the expense of future generations.

III. Judicial Application of Intergenerational Equity

In the last two decades, judiciaries have had an increasingly important role in recognizing and ensuring respect for intergenerational equity. The decisions relate both to procedural issues in bringing cases and to the application of the substance of the principle. One of the most significant procedural issues relates to who has standing to represent future generations before judicial bodies. In the *Oposa* case, discussed later in the symposium, the Philippines Supreme Court gave standing to children as representative of future generations. Children also have requested standing in the atmospheric trust cases related to climate change in the United States and elsewhere across the world. In at least one country, an ombudsperson for future generations has been able to bring claims before a court.

National Supreme Court and lower court decisions in a growing number of countries have applied a principle of intergenerational equity.[4] Developments have been especially noteworthy in three countries: India, Colombia and Brazil. At least four decisions of the Supreme Court of India incorporate the principle of intergenerational equity. On 2 August 2017, the Supreme Court of India issued an historic decision in a large-scale mining case in which the Court specifically discussed the principle of intergenerational equity in its judgment. Although declining to impose a quantitative limit on the mining, the Court required the Government to develop an updated mineral policy by the end of 2017, which would include intergenerational equity.[5] The Government of India issued a new National Mineral Policy at the end of February 2019, which contains for the first time a section entitled "Intergenerational Equity" and establishes an Inter-Ministerial body to institutionalize a mechanism to ensure sustainable mining "keeping in mind the principles of sustainable development and intergenerational equity[…]".[6] In another case involving the state of Goa, the Indian Supreme Court said that the interests of future generations had to be taken into account in coal mining operations. Citing intergenerational equity, the Court: called for a committee to determine an appropriate limit to the amount that could be

4 E. Brown Weiss, *Establishing Norms in a Kaleidoscopic World*, The Hague Academy of International Law, 2018. The analysis that follows draws upon this reference.

5 Judgment, *Common Cause v. Union of India & others*, Case No. SC WP 2014, Supreme Court of India, 2 Aug. 2017.

6 Government of India, National Mineral Policy 2019, articles 10 & 11.

extracted; and required, as a condition for a permit to mine, that a trust fund be established for the benefit of future generations.[7]

In Latin America, the Supreme Court of Justice of Colombia in 2018 ordered the Presidency of the Republic and the Ministries of Environment and Agriculture to create an "intergenerational pact for the life of the Colombian Amazon" to eliminate deforestation and to take other measures to protect the area into the future.[8] The judgment responded to a lawsuit brought by a group of youth with the support of the non-governmental organization Dejusticia. In Brazil, the High Court has handed down at least five decisions between 2007 and 2011 that emphasized the constitutional duty to protect the environment for future generations. These cases involved threats to ecosystems from logging and other activities.[9] Other judicial decisions incorporating intergenerational equity can be found, for example, in the High Court of Kenya and in courts in Australia and New Zealand.[10]

At the level of international judiciaries, several Judges on the International Court of Justice have issued concurring or dissenting opinions that reference intergenerational equity. In his dissenting opinion for the Advisory Opinion on the *Legality of the Threat or Use of Nuclear Weapons*, the late Judge Weeramantry

---

7 *Goa Foundation v. Union of India & others*, Case No. 435 OF 2012, National Green Tribunal (India), 21 Apr. 2014.

8 "Climate Change and Future Generations Lawsuit in Colombia: Key Excerpts from the Supreme Court's Decision", *Dejusticia*, 13 Apr. 2018 (translating *José Daniel Rodríguez Peña & others v. Presidencia de la República de Colombia*, Supreme Court of Justice of Colombia, No. STC4360-2018, 4 Apr. 2018), *available online at* https://www.dejusticia.org/en/climate-change-and-future-generations-lawsuit-in-colombia-key-excerpts-from-the-supreme-courts-decision/ (accessed 15 June 2019).

9 *See, e.g., Ministerio Publico do Estado de Sao Paulo v. Companhia Acucareira Sao Geraldo* [*Sao Paulo State v. Sao Geraldo Sugar Co.*], Superior Tribunal de Justiça – RECURSO ESPECIAL, No. 948.921/SP (2d Panel), Relator: Ministro [Justice] António Herman Benjamin, 23 Oct. 2007; *Ministerio Publico Federal v. H Carlos Schneider S/A Comercio e Industria e Outro* [*Brazil v. H Carlos Schneider Inc.*], Superior Tribunal de Justiça – RECURSO ESPECIAL No. 650.728- SC (2d Panel), Relator: Ministro [Justice] António Herman Benjamin, 2 Dec. 2009.

10 *J. Waweru Karuma v. Republic of Kenya*, Case No. 166 OF 2016, High Court of Kenya (Kiambu), Criminal Appeal, 15 June 2017; *Northcompass Inc. v. Hornsby Shire Council*, Case No. NSWLEC 213, Land and Environment Court of New South Wales, 26 Aug. 1996; *BGP Properties Pty Limited v. Lake Macquarie City Council*, Case No. NSWLEC 399, Land and Environment Court of New South Wales, 12 Aug. 2004; *New Zealand Recreational Fishing Council v. Sanford Limited & others*, Case No. SC40/2008 NZSC 54, New Zealand Supreme Court, 28 May 2009.

discussed damage to future generations and wrote, "it is to be noted in this context that the rights of future generations have passed the stage where they are merely an embryonic right struggling for recognition. They have woven themselves into international law".[11] In his separate opinion in the 2014 *Whaling in the Antarctic* case, Judge Cançado Trindade wrote that intergenerational equity "marks presence nowadays in a wide range of instruments in international environmental law and indeed of contemporary public international law".[12] These are important indicators of the increasing recognition of intergenerational equity in international law.

Conclusion: A Moral Obligation

Underlying all of our most recent concerns about our impacts on Planet Earth and about the inheritance that we pass to future generations, is recognition of a profound moral obligation to those who succeed us. Pope Francis captured this in his Encyclical Letter *On Care for Our Common Home*.[13] The moral obligation is deeply rooted in all civilizations. Youth today are at the forefront of pressing for actions that consider the future and the integrity and robustness of our Planet. Through information technology, they can connect with other youth across the world. They recognize the moral obligation that all of us share. This moral obligation also underlies the principle of intergenerational equity.

The challenges we now face in ensuring the well-being of future generations mean that we can no longer ignore the future in our decisions today. Intergenerational equity provides a normative framework for the new Anthropocene Epoch in a kaleidoscopic world. Future generations have a fundamental entitlement, which we must respect. It is an entitlement that we hold as members of the present generation in relation to our ancestors and that we must now protect and ensure for our descendants.

---

11 Dissenting Opinion of Judge Weeramantry, Advisory Opinion, *Legality of the Threat or Use of Nuclear Weapons*, International Court of Justice Reports, 1996, p. 455.

12 Judgment, *Whaling in the Antarctic* (*Australia v. Japan; New Zealand intervening*), International Court of Justice, International Court of Justice Reports, 31 Mar. 2014, p. 226; *ibid.*, p. 366, paragraph 47 (Separate Opinion of Judge Cançado Trindade).

13 Laudato Si' *On Care for Our Common Home*, 24 May 2015.

Nicholas A. ROBINSON

3. Evolutionary Roots Nurturing Equity Across Generations

Equity is a fundamental component of justice. Without fairness, humans feel aggrieved. The psychology and sociology of equity are explored elsewhere. Here we focus on the legal dimensions of equity, not in the abstract, but amidst an epoch new in world history: The Anthropocene. Scientific assessments confirm that as the human species has multiplied in numbers – now at 7.6 billion and soon to be at 9 billion individuals – humans have stressed the climate with rapid rises in ambient atmospheric and marine temperatures, melted the cryosphere, gradually increased sea levels and coastal erosion, altered the carbon and hydrologic cycles, triggered a vast extinction of other species, and caused indigenous languages and whole ethnic communities to become extinct.[1]

What can equity mean in the Anthropocene? When extreme weather conditions disrupt traditional socio-economic life, people are displaced from homes and livelihoods. When contemporary governments boost their economies by borrowing to finance escalating patterns of consumption, they mortgage their children to cover today's debts, or trigger the collapse of the debt-ridden economy when funds are lacking to repay for past profligacy. Patterns of pollution mirror the unsustainable economy. The oceans are awash with plastic waste that nations refuse to prevent from entering their rivers and discharging into the seas. Massive dissemination of synthetic chemicals is evident in humans and all of nature, as industrial and commercial use of chemicals outstrip efforts for their environmental management. Widespread corruption in governments and commercial systems corrodes efforts to contain their pernicious trends.

The response of the jurisprudence to these trends is to insist upon the right to the environment.[2] However, recognition of this right, along with environmental

---

1 *See* the UN Environment GEO-5 Report, the Assessment Reports of the Intergovernmental Panel on Climate Change (IPCC), the Red Data Books of the Species Survival Commission of the International Union for the Conservation of Nature (IUCN), and the reports of Survival International on the fate of indigenous peoples.

2 *See* the Advisory Opinion of the Inter-American Court of Human Rights (2017), finding that there is an autonomous right to the environment, enforceable through agreed human rights procedures. *See also* the constitutions of 178 nations, which

due process of law,[3] comes so late in the onset of the Anthropocene that invoking the right alone cannot arrest the juggernaut of radical environmental change all over the Earth for the next two to three centuries. Adherence to the right may help stabilize global environmental change, such as driving back the current rise to four degrees Celsius (4°C) ambient atmospheric temperature rise back to closer to 3 degrees Celsius (3°C), if the carbon dioxide emissions are arrested and humans scrub the air of greenhouse gases. Humans can save the knowledge and DNA of species becoming extinct, but the diversity of biological life on Earth is being altered. Humans will have to retreat from the rising seas, as they did in past epochs after Ice Ages ended.

So, equity in the Anthropocene has two dimensions: first, equity with contemporaries. As societies plan for relocating coastal communities to inland human settlements, they can design the process and the new homes to eradicate poverty and ensure education, along with mutual respect for genders, as well as stewardship for flora and fauna. That would be equitable. Or, they can wait for disasters after hurricane storm surges, and let fate determine who wins and loses. Given human nature and past performance, that is likely, but inequitable. The United Nations proposes a set of Sustainable Development Goals (SDGs) to define the equitable "future we want".[4] What is needed to build the equitable path into this future? It is the contemporary generation that must design the plans and programs to ensure that all are treated fairly "today".

But then there is tomorrow. The second dimension of equity in the Anthropocene involves equity with future generations. Only this dimension of equity cannot be deemed a "second" class of concern. The bifurcation in jurisprudence between intra-generational and inter-generational equity is a synthetic artifice. It suggests that humans and their governments only live for today, and

---

now recognize the right to the environment. D.R. Boyd, *The Environmental Rights Revolution*, University of British Columbia Press, 2011.

3 The IUCN World Commission on Environmental Law, and the UN Environment, have recognized the binding character of environmental due process of law. United Nations and the Rule of Law, "Environmental Law", *available online at* https://www.un.org/ruleoflaw/thematic-areas/land-property-environment/environmental-law/ (accessed 28 June 2019); World Commission on Environmental Law, "Environmental Rule of Law", *available online at* https://www.iucn.org/commissions/world-commission-environmental-law/our-work/environmental-rule-law-1 (accessed 28 June 2019).

4 Adopted by the UN General Assembly in 2015, the SDGs are provided as a guide to integrate socio-economic and environmental cooperation to the year 2030. Sustainable Development Goals Knowledge Platform, "Sustainable Development Goals", *available online at* https://sustainabledevelopment.un.org/sdgs (accessed 28 June 2019).

so are free to divide up human interests into present or future interests. On a limited scale, by agreement, sharing among generations closely linked in time, may function – as when a trust is established[5] or a government offers a bond to borrow funds, to be paid off over a period of 40 years with interest. To more broadly assert one generation has a broad duty to a future generation, as the Brundtland Commission did in defining sustainable development,[6] is well intended but lacks the bond that ties now to then. Economists, political theorists and lawyers seek, with acknowledged difficulty, to define some methodology to bind the duties between present and future generations. They are not likely to succeed. The natural history of all life on Earth shows how this dichotomy is false. To continue to debate whether humans in the future have a seat at the table today is to ignore evolution.

Life on earth has evolved for eons, in integrated ways that humans are still coming to understand. Charles Darwin and Alfred Russel Wallace explained natural selection for species[7] in the nineteeth century, then Carl Woese and Nigel Goldenfeld did so again in the twentieth century – with horizontal and vertical transfers of genetic materials among species.[8] To these biological discoveries must be added the studies of cultural evolution.[9] Basic principles such as equity and derivative legal rules are evolved norms, which reflect a mix of cultural and biological evolution.[10] For example, the first "modern" environmental statute, the

---

5 At Common Law, trusts were limited by the Rule against Perpetuities, to last only so long as measured by a youngest life in being plus one generation more, 30 years and a 9-month gestation period of time.

6 United Nations World Commission on Environment and Development, *Our Common Future*, Oxford University Press, 1987 (defining sustainable development as "development that meets the needs of the present without compromising the need of future generations to meet their own needs").

7 C. Darwin, *On The Origin of Species*, J. Murray, 1859; A.R. Wallace, *Darwinism: An Exposition of the Theory of Natural Selection, With Some of its Applications*, Macmillan, 1889.

8 *See* the works of C. Woese, *available online at* https://academictree.org/chemistry/publications.php?pid=56761 (accessed 28 June 2019); D. Quammen, "The Scientist who Scrambled Darwin's Tree of Life", *New York Times Magazine*, 13 Aug. 2018, *available online at* https://www.nytimes.com/2018/08/13/magazine/evolution-gene-microbiology.html (accessed 28 June 2019).

9 L. Arnhart, *Darwinian Natural Right. The Biological Ethics of Human Nature*, State University of New York Press, 1998.

10 N.A. Robinson, "Evolved Norms: A Canon for the Anthropocene", *in Rule of Law for Nature*, C. Voigt (ed.), Cambridge University Press, 2013, p. 46.

Forest Charter of 1217, was born out of struggles to establish equitable access to nature in the thirteenth century England.[11]

To navigate through the disruptions to human life that will come to typify the Anthropocene, it will be essential to embrace a holistic understanding of life. It is not amenable to being disaggregated into here and now, *versus* then and far. Life evolves in a dynamic on-going fashion. Universal legal principles need to adapt to the coming physical conditions of the Anthropocene and evolve norms and the practical application for making the quest to provide environmental equity, both among generations of humans as well as between humans and other species. Seeking to be equitable then will be a reality, not just a slogan or a principle that we refer to without the burdens of putting it into practice.

Equity is not only what we owe to our descendants, we must become good ancestors in our generation for those who follow us. We carry the contributions to our present existence from those who came before us. All of us are struggling to seek justice and be just, as circumstances arise to test us. But we must also conserve our natural and cultural heritage and think: what has worked well in the past, that the past has given us, which we can nurture, enhance, and pass forward?

The Onondaga Nation of the Haudenosaunnee (in what is now called North America), in New York, is a nation that precedes both New York and the United States. The Onondaga understand that all relationships studied in ecology are interrelated, now and across time. Chief Oren Lyons described the ancestral mandate of the Peacemaker, who united seven nations into a confederacy more than 1,000 years ago, long before the United Nations attempts this task today. He said, "when you sit and you council for the welfare of the people, think not of yourself, or of your family, or even of your generation. He said, make your decisions on behalf of the seven-generation coming, those faces looking up from the earth, each generation waiting for them. Defend them; protect them, so that they may enjoy what you enjoy today".[12] The mission is not to set aside assets for

11 N.A. Robinson, "The Charter of the Forest: Evolving Human Rights in Nature", *in Magna Carta and the Rule of Law,* D.B. Magraw & others (eds.), American Bar Association, 2014, p. 311.

12 O. Lyons, "Scanno" [Skä-Noñh], *in* "Symposium the Prospects for the UN Declaration on the Rights of Indigenous Peoples", *Pace Environmental Law Review,* 2010, Vol. 28, Issue No. 1, sec. 334, *available online at* https://digitalcommons.pace.edu/pelr/vol28/ (click on "Issue 1" then scroll down to the second entry under "Confernence Proceedings") (accessed 28 June 2019). *See also Akwesasne Notes*, Native Voices eds., 1978, and the Great Law of Peace Center, *available online at* http://www.skanonhcenter.org/ (accessed 28 June 2019).

future persons, but to sustain all of life so that the continuous being is healthy and mingles together. When all is healthy, all is at peace. The evolved norms of the Onondaga have been sustained for a millenium.

If people today wish to be resilient enough to thrive amidst the Anthropocene, there is much to learn from the norms evolved by indigenous people. Their applications of Equity consider all their relationships, with all flora and fauna and their habitats, with the waters and soils, with the air. When laws commodify and disaggregate life in natural resources, they breach the whole. Some laws, such as requiring environmental impact assessment (EIA),[13] require taking the holistic approach; however, EIA laws are weakly enforced in all nations. The narrative of disaggregated nature, and the legal rights attached to commodified natural resources, eclipse a robust embrace of EIAs. Learned culturally evolved norms can suppress the application of deeper evolved norms associated with concepts of equity.

Perhaps the principle of resilience can be allied to equity, to enable human society to see its deeper values and act accordingly.[14] Resilience is a focus on the here and now at the same time frame as the future. It does not differentiate time. It focuses on systems analysis and capacity, and health. Acting on a duty to promote resilience advances a sense of time, which is very different than what we have today in our current politics and commerce. It can require patience and

---

13 Environmental Impact Assessment is required under Principle 17 of the UN Rio Declaration on Environment and Development, under Article 206 of the UN Convention on the Law of the Sea to protect the marine environment, and as a customary norm of international law. *Pulp Mills on the River Uruguay* (*Argentina v. Uruguay*), International Court of Justice, 20 Apr. 2010, *available online at* https://www.icj-cij.org/files/case-related/135/135-20100420-JUD-01-00-EN.pdf (accessed 28 June 2019).

14 On Resilience, *see* the Stockholm Resilience Center's studies, at the Stockholm University, *available online at* http://www.stockholmresilience.org/ (accessed 28 June 2019), and the proposed Article 16 on resilience in the Global Pact for the Environment, which reads "The Parties shall take necessary measures to maintain and restore the diversity and capacity of ecosystems and human communities to withstand environmental disruptions and degradation and to recover and adapt". Legal background for Article 16 is found in the essay by N.A. Robinson, "The Resilience Principle", *in IUCN Academy of Environmental Law eJournal,* 2014, Vol. 5, p. 19, *available online at* https://papers.ssrn.com/sol3/papers.cfm?abstract_id=2497244 (accessed 28 June 2019). *See also* the draft discussion paper prepared for study by the UN Development Programme, *available online at* http://earlyrecovery.global/sites/default/files/ttpr_discussion_paper_-putting_resilience_principles_into_practice_9042015_0.pdf (accessed 28 June 2019).

preparation for a range of future scenarios. Striving to be resilient is a self-discipline that cultivates a sense of deep perspective and respect for how long it takes to achieve things. Governments and communities would do well to learn from the Onondaga Nation and others who have that wisdom.

Humans have similarities because it is inbred in our human nature. Concepts of justice and fairness are things we learn from when we were very small children. Evolutionary psychologists along with other disciplines have demonstrated that the concept of cooperation is very much a hardwired instinct in the human species.[15] We know how to cooperate with each other whether we think we do or not. Methods for effective cooperation are very important tools for humans to develop and nurture. Humans cooperate from the time they are small children. Parents teach how to cooperate. Cooperation is a human instinct, but what are we cooperating for? This is where the evolved norms of equity and resilience become essential.

In the Anthropocene, survival will require humans to cooperate toward resilience in the face of new conditions. Humans will be cooperating not only for today, or for the immediate generation or family or clan, but also for us – or for the wider community of life, and with our ancestors, for our descendants. Nature is an essential part of this community. Humans grew out of nature, live within nature. Environmental laws, such as EIA, strive to make humans perform as stewards of nature. This is what Edward O. Wilson meant when he described "biophilia" as an integral component of human nature in 1978.[16] Humans are social animals in the context of Earth's environment, from within which Homo sapiens evolved. Their evolved norms reflect this heritage.

Can jurisprudence and the legal profession craft rules and procedures to make a holistic application of equity a reality? This challenge will define legal education and environmental public policy for the coming decades. The instinct for cooperation in the protection and stewardship of nature is inherited from what prior generations did to protect nature. How shall this generation bond with its past and future as one? The answers may appear opaque, or in doubt, because of fears of climate change in the most fundamental way. The heritage of Equity, and profound human instinct, suggest the human species has the capacity to evolve to be more just than is apparent today. Although humans, as a species, have inbred this concept of fairness, it is complex and difficult to apply. Human

---

15 *See* M.A. Nowak & R. Highfield, *Super Cooperators: Altruism, Evolution, and Why We Need Each Other to Succeed*, Free Press, 2011.

16 E.O. Wilson, *Biophilia: The Human Bond with Other Species*, Harvard University Press, 1976.

society will need to develop a set of guiding norms and practical rules that enable evaluation of how to apply fairness in different situations, and how to apply fairness amongst people but, importantly also, amongst species and with the natural environmental systems of the planet.

Unquestioned acceptance of, and dependence on, "business as usual" constrains such new thinking. Consider, for example, how governments foster development of society. When investing in infrastructure – the building of a school, or a hospital, or a road, or housing – often governments will finance that with borrowing. They will raise funds from a bond, essentially sale of a debt, and then they will pay back the loan, with interest, from their tax receipts or other income, over long periods of time. In this way governments spend money now that it does not have, knowing that it will amortize the debt over the lifetime of the bridge or the highway. In this way, everyone will get the benefit of it: our generation, and our children's generation, and even subsequent generations. But, this kind of financing is too easy sometimes, because governments borrow too much and it is too easy to have and spend the money now and then not work conscientiously on systematic ways to pay the funds back. Governments in the twenty-first century have developed a dependency on debt, which is destabilizing the economy – the human economy – around the world.

When one applies this concept through the "natural economy" of nature, the ecological systems and hydrologic cycles of Earth, it is evident that this "business as usual" approach is borrowing from and over-taxing the capacity of nature to serve present and future needs. This is most clearly evident with global warming and climate. Humans avoid the cost of controlling their pollution and tolerate the fiction that "externalities" to the classic economic model can go on forever. The same disruptions are evident in the nitrogen cycle and the other great geophysical cycles of the planet. Human society is out of balance with the Earth, the habitat of Homo sapiens.

When humans over-extend their economic cycle, they periodically experience a recession or economic depression. Such a human dislocation – with vast inequities in its wake – is as likely in the future as it has been in the past, and humans can recover their preferred model of economic relations. However, in the economy of nature, there is no recovery to a prior state of being. Evolution moves on as Earth's natural systems change. It is not so clear humans know how to restore a non-human thing like the planet Earth.

The economy of humans and its infrastructure produces acid rain, sea level rise, and an irreparably altered planet. These are among the host of challenges that are being passed on to this generation's children and grandchildren. Today's legacy can also be new ways of being, renouncing "business as usual," and embracing obligations to advance resilience in all dimensions of life.

Today's human legacy has both assets, and liabilities. We value for instance historic landmarks, great cultural buildings from the past; even archeological sites from pre-history are valued as contributions of what past generations have given to us, and we struggle to try and preserve them. But, at the same time we cut down the last tropical forest. We're not managing the great river ecosystems of the planet. We are dumping plastics into our rivers and gutters, and streams blindly and with abandon; there is estimated to be more plastic particles in the oceans then there are fish. Humans are fast depleting the oceans of fish by not sustainably caring for them and harvesting them. In short, our parents and we are creating enormous liabilities in our current system of governing how humans use the planet.

To rebalance our accounts, and come back into some kind of equity – for self-discipline, for not taking too much, not borrowing too much, not creating the debts in nature – human society will need a new paradigm. The mindset of the Onondaga is worth emulating. The search for such a more sustainable and wholesome, healthy and peaceful paradigm is what this conference, and all such conferences, must be about today. By probing the inequities of our age, we can strive to make environmental law relevant in the epoch of climate change. Evolved norms can guide humans as we learn to become good ancestors. With resilience and a drive to be equitable, we can renew environmental law to guide us away from of our worst instincts.

Let's take biodiversity. We are in the sixth great extinction of the loss of species. Species are thinning all around us and we are losing many species. In order to keep balance with nature, Edward O. Wilson has written a little book called *Half Earth*.[17] He proposes that we take the one half of the earth that is not now heavily developed and keep it primarily for nature. Humans can be there, and they will be there, but it should not be exploited and destroyed. It should in fact be extended. Now we are close to doing that with the oceans. We have marine protected areas that are developing throughout the oceans of the earth, and I think we can easily say most of the oceans if we try. We will have to come up with a way to temper our appetite for exploiting the oceans, but they are vast.

---

17 E.O. Wilson, *Half Earth: Our Planet's Fight for Life*, 2017, *available online at* https://www.half-earthproject.org/discover-half-earth/#half-earth-the-book (click on "Learn More") (accessed 28 June 2019).

Now on land, we still have half earth in much of the world. We have the great Amazon basin, we have the great Congo basin. We have seen the restoration of the northern forests in Canada and the United States come back after a period of deforestation. We have other regions that have rich natural resources that are untrammeled by men. The Zapovetniki of the former Soviet Union, now the Russian federation once again, is a vast area of wilderness and nature preserved for nature as a sacred beauty. So half of Siberia is saved already, if you will, and many other places in Russia. The same is the case in New York State, where one half of the State is protected in the State's constitutionally mandated Forest Preserve along with extensive other parks and protected areas. Protecting half of Earth for nature is essential to preserving the resilience of Earth's ecosystems and natural cycles. "Half" also manifests a commitment to equity, as well as testimony to equity.

We have taken these lessons and extended them through the United Nations Sustainable Development Goals (SDGs). In 2015, when the U.N. General Assembly adopted the Sustainable Development Goals for the first time, goals 14 and 15 were included as core values for all socioeconomic development. This means both the marine environment and the terrestrial environment must be protected. There is urgency in this and, by 2030, if we adhere to the SDGs, we should make great advances in attaining all of the sustainable development goals. If we do that, we can basically keep half the earth in balance with the half of the earth that we are heavily pressing down with our footprints. We can also maintain the great geophysical systems of the oceans and the atmosphere; but we will have to temper our appetite for exploiting nature.

The SDGs are an attempt to create justice and fairness amongst generations. They are consciously intergenerational, reflecting thinking across generations. When the United Nations was set up in 1945, it was to provide for succeeding generations. The U.N. was not a project just for the era after the second world war. The Universal Declaration of Human Rights is meant to serve for all time. We have had a hard time adapting and changing the U.N.'s deliberative systems, but the U.N. is evolving nonetheless. Member States are creating innovations, such as U.N. Environment, the next extension of the U.N. Environment Programme (UNEP). The U.N. Environment Assembly now meets in Nairobi, Kenya, and is refocusing nations on their obligations to end pollution. Humans have the technological knowledge to end pollution now, they just have to develop the political systems and the legal framework to ensure that it happens.

So, the U.N. can evolve and human society in turn can evolve with it. If concepts of justice and equity remain in the forefront, along with the UN Charter's vision of peace for succeeding generations, nations can find ways to navigate through the disruptions of the Anthropocene. This passage will be difficult. There will be mistakes and false starts, but nations can move toward accepting more holistic vision. China is doing so internally, with its concepts and policies for Ecological Civilization. States can rebalance today's "intergenerational" accounts onto one balance sheet. Socio-economic relations among nations are badly out of balance now, which is one motivation for negotiating the shared vision of the SDGs. This is a step toward enhancing equitable relations and fairness among peoples.

If there is another fundamental principle that leads to equity, it is the emergence of the right to the environment. This is an autonomous right, beyond human rights. The environmental right is expansive and includes the rights of all living systems, all living entities. All species – and their habits in air and water and land – have evolved together on this planet. The planet itself is a changing and dynamic physical and natural phenomenon. In the Anthropocene, the disruptions to natural conditions teach that humans need to relearn how to live with nature, design with nature, acknowledge our dependence on nature, and maintain the integrity and resilience of the natural systems around the world. This holistic recognition is at the heart of both the science of ecology and humanity's relationships with Earth's ecological systems. The environmental norms of environmental law have evolved out of this context, as a framework for seeking equity. Studying these dynamics is at the heart of defining the right to the environment.

The right to the environment now exists in more than 170 constitutions of the world.[18] It is a right that, by necessity, is more expansive than a human right. The right to the environment is fundamental to all life on this planet. Recognition of the right to the environment offers a foundation for those struggling to attain equity. Environmental justice based on a right to the environment provides a juridical basis for encouraging governments to promote resilience that sustains life through eight generations, in order to sustain Earth as a viable and healthful place for all of life through the changes of the Anthropocene. The right to the environment can engender appreciation also for ancestral times, when Homo sapiens has been the recipient of the bounty, the cornucopia of that past Earth.

18 D.R. Boyd, *The Environmental Rights Revolution. A Global Study of Constitutions, Human Rights, and the environment*, University of British Columbia Press, 2012.

PART 2. THE NUCLEAR INDUSTRY AND THE RIGHTS OF FUTURE GENERATIONS

In the second Part of the book, we explore the dangers and the specific concept of disasters at the nuclear age. The nuclear industry and, more particularly nuclear weapons, are generating absolute transgenerational threats to Humankind. This highlights the necessity of recognizing human rights for future generations.

Alyn Ware is a leading expert in the field of nuclear disarmament. His presentation shows that law relating to future generations, particularly the rights of future generations, is an emerging field with a range of aspects still being developed and defined. These include the scope of law applicable to the future, the collective rights of persons not yet existing, and in what ways future generations can have standing in current legal bodies. Ware's essay discusses ways these issues are being tested in international tribunals – both formal and informal – in relation to current activities that have considerable impact on future generations, specifically, the testing and use of nuclear weapons. Three cases at the International Court of Justice and an informal people's tribunal on nuclear weapons are considered. In addition, the essay also discusses the transtemporal nature of International Humanitarian Law (IHL) and issues surrounding the inclusion of nuclear-weapons-use as a crime under the jurisdiction of the International Criminal Court (essay #4 on "Nuclear Weapons and Law for the Future: The Application of Principles Protecting Future Generations in International Tribunals").

Jean-Marie Collin focuses on a new treaty that has been added to the constellation of treaties designed to control nuclear weapons and therefore the disarmament and non-proliferation processes. The "Treaty on the Prohibition of Nuclear Weapons" (TPNW) was signed on 7 July 2017. The TPNW came at a time when a large majority of States around the world had become aware of its ability to act in the face of the potential consequences of a nuclear weapons detonation. More than ever before, this is a treaty that has its roots in the rules of law related to humanitarian disarmament and supplied new elements, such as the notion of gender, but at the same time has seized upon already-existing concepts in treaties and agreements related to the environment (such as the polluter-pays principle) and innovative legal concepts, such as the rights of future generations, which are still in the process of gaining recognition (essay #5 entitled, "Treaty on the Prohibition of Nuclear Weapons: A Move Towards New Legal Action to Protect Future Generations?").

Professor Frédérick Lemarchand clearly presents Günther Anders' thoughts on the question of the Apocalypse and the possibility of humankind vanishing forever following our entry into the Nuclear Age. He exposes ten commandments, which focus on the need for a renewed philosophy because of the entry into a new era which is not prepared to think about the danger of nuclear arms. Anders emphasized the fact that humans are unable to think about the ethical problems of new technology, such as nuclear threats. We are incapable of being afraid and there is now a Promethean gap between the human moral rules and its new condition at the nuclear age. Many authors from the Frankfurt School are quoted, such as Hannah Arendt and Hans Jonas, both authors who also paved the way to think about our moral responsibilities towards Future Generations (essay #6 on "The Bomb as a New Definition of Presents and Future Humanity: What We Owe to Günther Anders' Thoughts").

Doctor Martin Walker and Professor Andreas Nidecker provide an essay on the effects of ionizing radiation, which includes evidence of transgenerational damage. In the past, genetic mutations occurring in children of irradiated parents have been the subject of considerable controversy. Recent research has produced persuasive evidence of genetic changes resulting from low-level ionizing radiation. Even more striking are studies of trans-generational genetic changes in animals as documented in publications of studies in the contaminated regions of Chernobyl and Fukushima. Studies on humans reveal increased mutation rates in the so-called minisatellite genome. Scientists from England hypothesize that workers employed at the Sellafield reprocessing plant have fathered increased numbers of children suffering from leukemia and non-Hodgkin's lymphoma. There now exists in the literature a mosaic of findings, which point to genetic damage in offspring caused by low-level ionizing radiation. This paper begins with a short introduction to the different forms of ionizing radiation, the known effects of radiation, and our current knowledge of its link to common diseases. It then looks in further detail at some of the existing scientific literature regarding the genetic effects of ionizing radiation on animals and humans (essay #7 on "Effects of Ionizing Radiation – Evidence of Genetic Effects: Greater Risks for Transgenerational Damage").

Alyn WARE

4. Nuclear Weapons and Law for the Future: The Application of Principles Protecting Future Generations in International Tribunals

Law relating to future generations, and in particular the rights of future generations, is an emerging field with a range of aspects still being developed and defined. These include the scope of law applicable to the future, the collective rights of persons not yet existing, and in what ways future generations can have standing in current legal bodies.

Some of these aspects are being tested in international tribunals – both formal and informal – in relation to current activities that have considerable impact on future generations, such as climate change and nuclear weapons.

With regard to nuclear weapons, legal responsibility to future generations has been considered in three cases at the International Court of Justice and in an informal People's International Tribunal on Nuclear Weapons and the Destruction of Human Civilisation.[1] Legal responsibility to future generations also features in efforts to include the deployment of nuclear weapons as a crime under the jurisdiction of the International Criminal Court.

I. 1974 International Court of Justice *Nuclear Tests* Cases

On 9 May 1973, Australia and New Zealand instituted proceedings against France concerning tests of nuclear weapons that France proposed to carry out in the atmosphere in the South Pacific region.[2] Already France had conducted

---

1 This People's tribunal was held in Australia; documents are available online. Unfold Zero, "People's tribunal on nuclear weapons convicts leaders – tribute to tribunal visionary", 17 Aug. 2016, *available online at* http://www.unfoldzero.org/peoples-tribunal-on-nuclear-weapons-convicts-leaders-tribute-to-tribunal-visionary/ (scroll to the bottom of the page under the heading "Key tribunal documents" for links to select documents) (accessed 28 June 2019).

2 *Nuclear Tests* (*Australia v. France*), International Court of Justice Reports, 9 May 1973, *available online at* https://www.icj-cij.org/files/case-related/58/13187.pdf (accessed 28 June 2019); *Nuclear Tests* (*New Zealand v. France*), International Court of

46 atmospheric nuclear explosions from their testing facilities on Moruroa and Fangataufa Atolls.

In their application to the Court, New Zealand alleged: that the nuclear tests conducted by France from 1966 to 1973 caused radioactive fallout to New Zealand and to territories under New Zealand's protection (Cook Islands, Niue and the Tokelau Islands); that this radioactive fallout constituted a hazard to human health and to the environment of these territories; and, as a consequence, the nuclear tests violated the sovereignty of New Zealand.[3]

New Zealand also alleged that the actions by France to cordon off areas of the high seas during nuclear tests were a violation of the right of New Zealand and others to freedom of navigation on the high seas.[4] New Zealand further argued that the tests were linked to the planning and preparation for nuclear war, which was inconsistent with the rights of the global community to peace and security, and the common aspirations for the elimination of nuclear weapons. As such, the harm to the populations of New Zealand and territories under its protection was not confined to damage or potential damage to physical health, but also to increased risks, anxieties and fears of global nuclear war.[5]

Indeed, the New Zealand application added a futures framework to the threat of nuclear war arising from the tests, stating that the tests "hinder the attainment of further disarmament measures which are universally considered essential for the attainment of future international Security".[6]

Reference to the future in the application also extended to the rights of future generations to be protected. New Zealand argued that the nuclear tests generated "hazards to the health of current and future generations" not only in New Zealand but globally due to "the dispersal over wide areas of the globe of radioactive fallout", as well as due to the long lives of radioactive isotopes from nuclear tests and the trans-generational impact of these isotopes through their damage to human genes and reproduction.[7]

Australia's application included many of the same arguments as New Zealand, including references to the rights of future generations. With regard to the

---

Justice Reports, 9 May 1973, *available online at* https://www.icj-cij.org/files/case-related/59/9447.pdf (accessed 28 June 2019).

3 *Nuclear Tests* (*New Zealand v. France*), paragraphs 12–14.

4 *Ibid.*, paragraph 28.

5 *Ibid.*, paragraph 24.

6 Note from New Zealand Embassy to French Ministry of Foreign Affairs, 5 June 1968. Appendix, *Nuclear Tests* (*New Zealand v. France*), 9 May 1973, p. 27.

7 *Nuclear Tests* (*New Zealand v. France*), paragraph 24.

harm to human health, Australia submitted that "Radiation exposure of human populations can be expected to bring about some increase in deleterious genetic mutations which can be transmitted to the offspring of exposed persons and to future generations".[8] Australia also highlighted the threats to peace and security of current and future generations, and the harm to mental health resulting from these threats:

> "In addition, peoples have been subjected to increasing mental stress resulting from fear and anxiety about the direct and indirect biological effects of nuclear explosions on present and future generations and by concern for the consequences of a possible proliferation in the number of States developing and testing nuclear weapons". And that "People feel a real concern that the testing of nuclear weapons in the atmosphere places their lives, health and well-being and that of their children and future generations in jeopardy".[9]

Decisions of the Court and Dissenting Opinions

Early in the proceedings (22 June 1973) the Court granted an injunction against further tests by France while the cases proceeded.[10] However, the merits (legal status) of the arguments presented by New Zealand and Australia were not tested by the Court because of the announcement by France on 11 October 1974 that they would no longer conduct atmospheric nuclear tests. As the object of the legal action by New Zealand and Australia had been met, i.e. the prevention of further atmospheric nuclear tests, the Court announced in judgments delivered on 20 December 1974 that they no longer were required to give a decision on the legality of the French nuclear tests.[11]

Not all the judges agreed with this decision. In a joint dissenting opinion, Judges Charles D. Onyeama, Hardy C. Dillard, Eduardo Jiménez de Aréchaga

---

8 *Ibid.*, paragraph 33.

9 *Ibid.*, paragraph 40.

10 Request for the indication of interim measures of protection, *Nuclear Tests* (*New Zealand v. France*), Order of 22 June 1973, *available online at* https://www.icj-cij.org/files/case-related/59/059-19730622-ORD-01-00-EN.pdf (accessed 15 June 2019); *Nuclear Tests* (*Australia v. France*), Request for the indication of interim measures of protection, Order of 22 June 1973, *available online at* https://www.icj-cij.org/files/case-related/58/058-19730622-ORD-01-00-EN.pdf (accessed 15 June 2019).

11 *Nuclear Tests* (*New Zealand v. France*), 20 Dec. 1974, *available online at* https://www.icj-cij.org/files/case-related/59/059-19741220-JUD-01-00-EN.pdf (accessed 15 June 2019); *Nuclear Tests* (*Australia v. France*), 20 Dec. 1974, *available online at* https://www.icj-cij.org/files/case-related/58/058-19741220-JUD-01-00-EN.pdf (accessed 15 June 2019).

and Sir Humphrey Waldock noted that there were a number of reasons that the case should have continued to be considered, most notable because there could be legal obligations arising from the "future damage" caused by the nuclear tests already conducted by France.

> Whatever impressions may be gained from *a prima facie* reading of the evidence so far presented to the Court, the questions of the materiality of the damage resulting from, and of the risk of future damage from, atmospheric nuclear tests, appear to us manifestly questions which cannot be resolved in preliminary proceedings without the parties having had the opportunity to submit their full case to the Court.[12]

II. 1996 ICJ Advisory Opinion on the *Legality of the Threat or Use of Nuclear Weapons*

On 8 July 1996, the International Court of Justice delivered a decision on a legal question asked of it by the United Nations General Assembly: "Is the threat or use of nuclear weapons in any circumstance permitted under international law?"[13]

The Court held that "the threat or use of nuclear weapons would generally be contrary to the rules of international law applicable in armed conflict, and in particular the principles and rules of humanitarian law"; but that there might be a possible exception to this prohibition, in that it "cannot conclude definitively whether the threat or use of nuclear weapons would be lawful or unlawful in an extreme circumstance of self-defence, in which the very survival of a State would be at stake".

Finally, the Court concluded unanimously that "there exists an obligation to pursue in good faith and bring to a conclusion[,] negotiations leading to nuclear disarmament in all its aspects under strict and effective international control".

It recognized that there is no specific treaty which provides a general or universal prohibition on the threat or use of nuclear weapons. However, the Court based its conclusion of general illegality on the application of customary law to nuclear weapons, in particular "principles and rules of international humanitarian law".[14]

---

12 Joint Dissenting Opinion of Judges Onyeama, Dillard, Jiménez de Aréchaga and Sir Humphrey Waldock, *Nuclear Tests* (*New Zealand v. France*), 20 Dec. 1974, paragraph 50.

13 Advisory Opinion, *Legality of the Threat or Use of Nuclear Weapons*, International Court of Justice, 8 July 1996, *available online at* https://www.icj-cij.org/files/case-related/95/095-19960708-ADV-01-00-EN.pdf (accessed 15 June 2019).

14 Dispositif, *Legality of the Threat or Use of Nuclear Weapons*.

In its decision, the Court referred a number of times to future generations or the transgenerational impact of nuclear weapons. The Court noted, for example, that:

> "the use of nuclear weapons would be a serious danger to future generations. Ionizing radiation has the potential to damage the future environment, food and marine ecosystem, and to cause genetic defects and illness in future generations". Earlier in the same paragraph, the Court observed "[b]y its very nature, that process, in nuclear weapons as they exist today, releases not only immense quantities of heat and energy, but also powerful and prolonged radiation. These characteristics render the nuclear weapon potentially catastrophic. The destructive power of nuclear weapons cannot be contained in either space or time".[15]

The Court noted that the destructive impact of nuclear weapons transcends not only multiple generations, but could cause the end to the future of humanity and the planet itself. "They have the potential to destroy all civilization and the entire ecosystem of the planet". The testimony by Lijon Eknilang describing some of the transgenerational impacts of nuclear tests (excerpt below) was very influential in the Court reaching this conclusion.

With regard to the law on transgenerational impact, the Court cited: Additional Protocol 1 of 1977 to the Geneva Conventions of 1949, Article 35, paragraph 3, which prohibits the employment of "methods or means of warfare which are intended, or may be expected, to cause widespread, long-term and severe damage to the natural environment"; and, the Convention of 18 May 1977 on the Prohibition of Military or Any Other Hostile Use of Environmental Modification Techniques, which prohibits the use of weapons which have "widespread, long-lasting or severe effects".[16]

Transgenerational Impact of Nuclear Tests in the Marshall Islands:

> My own health has suffered very much, as a result of radiation poisoning. I cannot have children. I have had miscarriages on seven occasions. On one of those occasions, I miscarried after four months. The child I miscarried was severely deformed; it had only one eye […]. Some of us had brain tumours and other cancers removed. In more recent years, we have come to learn that some of us had our entire thyroids removed […]. Women have experienced many reproductive cancers and abnormal births. Marshallese women suffer silently and differently from the men who were exposed to radiation. Our culture and religion teaches us that reproductive abnormalities are a sign that women have been unfaithful to their husbands. For this reason, many of my friends keep quiet about the strange births they had. In privacy, they give birth, not to children as we like

15 *Legality of the Threat or Use of Nuclear Weapons*, paragraph 35.
16 *Ibid.*, paragraph 27.

> to think of them, but to things we could only describe as "octopuses", "apples", "turtles", and other things in our experience [...]. One woman on Likiep gave birth to a child with two heads. Her cat also gave birth to a kitten with two heads.
>
> The most common birth defects on Rongelap and nearby islands have been "jelly-fish" babies. These babies are born with no bones in their bodies and with transparent skin. We can see their brains and hearts beating. The babies usually live for a day or two before they stop breathing. Many women die from abnormal pregnancies and those who survive give birth to what looks like purple grapes which we quickly hide away and bury.

Testimony of Lijon Eknilang, *Oral Presentation of the Marshall Islands to the International Court of Justice*, Tuesday 14 November 1995.

Transtemporal Application of Humanitarian Law

There is another aspect of the Court's deliberations, which relates to future generations: the Court's acceptance of the transtemporal nature of the application of international humanitarian law to specific weapons systems. This concept is expressed most clearly in the Martens Clause adopted in the Hague Conventions of 1899 and 1907, along with the Geneva Convention Protocols of 1977.

The Hague and Geneva Conventions prohibited methods of warfare that caused superfluous injury or unnecessary suffering, or that targeted civilians and other protected groups (such as prisoners of war), and also prohibited specific weapons systems which would violate these laws of warfare. The Martens Clause, named after Friedrich Martens, the Russian delegate to the Hague Peace Conferences of 1899, held that the laws of warfare also applied in circumstances and to weapons systems not specifically identified in the conventions.

> Until a more complete code of the laws of war is issued, the High Contracting Parties think it right to declare that in cases not included in the Regulations adopted by them, populations and belligerents remain under the protection and empire of the principles of international law, as they result from the usages established between civilized nations, from the laws of humanity and the requirements of the public conscience.[17]

In essence, the Martens clause indicates that the laws of warfare affirmed by the Hague and Geneva Conventions reach into the future to apply to weapons systems not yet invented, developed or deployed at the time of the adoption of the

---

17 Convention (II) with Respect to the Laws and Customs of War on Land and its annex: Regulations concerning the Laws and Customs of War on Land (The Hague Convention), The Hague, 29 July 1899, Preamble, paragraph 7, *available online at* https://ihl-databases.icrc.org/applic/ihl/ihl.nsf/Article.xsp?action=openDocument&documentId=9FE084CDAC63D10FC12563CD00515C4D (accessed 15 June 2019).

conventions. The International Committee of the Red Cross highlighted this transtemporal nature of international humanitarian law (IHL) when it noted in its commentary of 1987 that:

> First, despite the considerable increase in the number of subjects covered by the law of armed conflicts, and despite the detail of its codification, it is not possible for any codification to be complete at any given moment; thus the Martens clause prevents the assumption that anything which is not explicitly prohibited by the relevant treaties is therefore permitted. Secondly, it should be seen as a dynamic factor proclaiming the applicability of the principles mentioned regardless of subsequent developments of types of situation or technology.[18]

The Court upheld this interpretation of the transtemporal nature of IHL when it considered the application to nuclear weapons of law in the Hague Conventions of 1899 and 1907, along with the Geneva Protocol of 1925, even though these were adopted prior to the existence of nuclear weapons. In making this determination the Court specifically pointed to "the Martens Clause, whose continuing existence and applicability is not to be doubted, as an affirmation that the principles and rules of humanitarian law apply to nuclear weapons".[19] The Court re-affirmed the universal and transtemporal application of IHL when responding to the arguments of the nuclear armed States that the Geneva protocols of 1977 did not apply to nuclear weapons because nuclear weapons were not mentioned:

> It cannot be concluded from this that the established principles and rules of humanitarian law applicable in armed conflict did not apply to nuclear weapons. Such a conclusion would be incompatible with the intrinsically humanitarian character of the legal principles in question which permeates the entire law of armed conflict and applies to all forms of warfare and to all kinds of weapons, those of the past, those of the present and those of the future.[20]

The International Court of Justice's Conclusion

Consideration of the transgenerational impact of nuclear weapons was a strong contributing factor moving the Court to affirm the general illegality of the threat or use of nuclear weapons despite the fact, which the Court also recognised, that

---

18 International Committee of the Red Cross, *Commentary on the Additional Protocols of 8 June 1977 to the Geneva Conventions of 12 August 1949*, Martinus Nijhoff Publishers, Geneva, 1987, paragraph 55, *available online at* http://www.loc.gov/rr/frd/Military_Law/pdf/Commentary_GC_Protocols.pdf (accessed 15 June 2019).

19 *Legality of the Threat or Use of Nuclear Weapons*, paragraph 87.

20 *Ibid.*, paragraph 86.

nuclear deterrence was still accepted and relied upon by a considerable sector of the international community.

> The emergence, as *lex lata*, of a customary rule specifically prohibiting the use of nuclear weapons as such is hampered by the continuing tensions between the nascent opinio juris on the one hand, and the still strong adherence to the practice of deterrence on the other.[21]

As such, the Court did not legitimize the nuclear deterrent policies of the nuclear armed states; nor did the Court condemn them outright in its determination of general illegality. Some judges felt that the Court should have gone further and ruled 100% against the doctrine of nuclear deterrence based upon the principles of international humanitarian law and protection of future generations.

In a dissenting opinion, Judge Weeramantry for example, argued that any threat or use of nuclear weapons, without exception, would be illegal based on application of a wide body of law including the afore-mentioned principles.[22]

With regard to the rights of future generations, Weeramantry cited the responsibility under the UN Charter to "protect future generations from the scourge of war", observed that the atom bomb "is unique as a source of peril to the human future", and argued that "This Court [the ICJ], as the principal judicial organ of the United Nations, empowered to state and apply international law with an authority matched by no other tribunal must, in its jurisprudence, pay due recognition to the rights of future generations".

Furthermore, Judge Weeramantry argued that "It is to be noted in this context that the rights of future generations have passed the stage when they were merely an embryonic right struggling for recognition. They have woven themselves into international law through major treaties, through juristic opinion and through general principles of law recognized by civilized nations".

In supporting this position, Weeramantry cited a number of treaties that uphold the rights of future generations and the responsibility to protect these rights. He also noted that "a multiplicity of traditional legal systems across the globe protect the environment for future generations". He added that: "When incontrovertible scientific evidence speaks of pollution of the environment on a scale that spans hundreds of generations, this Court would fail in its trust if it

---

21 *Ibid.*, paragraph 73.

22 Dissenting opinion of Judge Weeramantry, *Legality of the Threat or Use of Nuclear Weapons*, *available online at* https://www.icj-cij.org/files/case-related/95/095-19960708-ADV-01-12-EN.pdf (accessed 15 June 2019).

did not take serious note of the ways in which the distant future is protected by present law".[23]

Judge Shahabudeen also cited protection of future generations in his dissenting opinion where he agreed with Weeramantry that international law rules out any use of nuclear weapons.[24]

Shahabudeen argued that the use of nuclear weapons not only impacts on future generations, but it would be an act of "war" on future generations. "The weapon continues to strike for years after the initial blow, thus presenting the disturbing and unique portrait of war being waged by a present generation on future ones – on future ones with which its successors could well be at peace".[25] Indeed, Shahabudeen indicates that the unique capacity of nuclear weapons to inflict indiscriminate damage across space and time require the application to nuclear weapons of legal principles protecting future generations in addition to the application of international humanitarian law.

> International law includes the principles of the law of armed conflict. These principles, with roots reaching into the past of different civilizations, were constructed on the unspoken premise that weapons, however destructive, would be limited in impact, both in space and in time. That assumption held good throughout the ages. New and deadlier weapons continued to appear, but none had the power to wage war on future generations or to threaten the survival of the human species. Until now.[26]

Judges Weeramantry and Shahabudeen presented dissenting opinions, and so it is not possible to claim that their opinions and conclusions reflect the corpus of the 1996 Advisory Opinion. On the other hand, the Declaration of Judge Bedjaoui, who presided over the case, is reflective of the Court's decision and can be seen as an explanation of the decision.[27] With regard to protection of future generations, Bedjaoui refers to the UN Charter obligation to save succeeding generations from the scourge of war. He then comments more directly on the threat of nuclear weapons to the "survival of mankind". He explains that in order

---

23 *Ibid.*, pp. 233–234.
24 Dissenting opinion of Judge Shahabudeen, *Legality of the Threat or Use of Nuclear Weapons*, *available online at* https://www.icj-cij.org/files/case-related/95/095-19960708-ADV-01-11-EN.pdf (accessed 15 June 2019).
25 *Ibid.*, pp. 160–161.
26 *Ibid.*, p. 158.
27 Declaration of President Bedjaoui, *Legality of the Threat or Use of Nuclear Weapons*, *available online at* https://www.icj-cij.org/files/case-related/95/095-19960708-ADV-01-01-EN.pdf (accessed 15 June 2019).

to exercise its responsibility to protect "mankind", the court turned the *Lotus* principle on its head with respect to nuclear weapons.

In the *Lotus* case of 1927, the Permanent Court of Arbitration held that actions, which are not specifically prohibited under international law are permissible.[28] Judge Bedjaoui explained that the Court's current decision indicates a presumption of illegality with regards to the threat or use of nuclear weapons, with any exception to that presumption needing to be established, rather than the reverse.

"I cannot sufficiently emphasize that the Court's inability to go beyond this statement of the situation can in no way be interpreted to mean that it is leaving the door ajar to recognition of the legality of the threat or use of nuclear weapons [...] the Court, in this Opinion, is far more circumspect than its predecessor in the 'Lotus' case in asserting today that what is not expressly prohibited by international law is not therefore authorized".[29]

The approach of the Court in the nuclear weapons case, as explained by its President, Judge Bedjaoui, has some similarities to the precautionary principle in international environmental law,[30] which provides some level of constraint regarding actions that could cause serious and irrevocable harm when there does not yet exist a clear and comprehensive legally binding prohibition on such actions.

In conclusion, one can argue that an emerging recognition of the rights of future generations was influential in the 1996 ICJ advisory opinion, but was not sufficiently strong to swing the decision from a precautionary approach regarding the legality of threat and use of nuclear weapons, to a comprehensive legal proscription with no possible exceptions.

---

28 *The Case of the S.S. Lotus* (*France v Turkey*), Permanent Court of Arbitration, 7 Sep. 1927, *available online at* http://www.worldcourts.com/pcij/eng/decisions/1927.09.07_lotus.htm (accessed 15 June 2019).

29 Declaration of President Bedjaoui, *Legality of the Threat or Use of Nuclear Weapons*, paragraphs 11 & 15.

30 The precautionary principle holds that parties should refrain from specific actions if there is reasonable cause to believe that such actions could result in serious, detrimental impact to the environment or to human society. The principle finds expression in various environment declarations and agreements including the World Charter for Nature adopted by the United Nations General Assembly in 1982, the 1987 Montreal Protocol on Substances that Deplete the Ozone Layer, the 1992 Rio Declaration on Environment and Development and the 1997 Kyoto Protocol on Climate Change.

III. 2016 International Court of Justice Nuclear Disarmament Cases

On 24 April 2014, the Marshall Islands filed applications in the International Court of Justice against the three nuclear-armed states, which accept compulsory jurisdiction of the International Court of Justice for contentious cases (India, Pakistan and the United Kingdom). The Marshall Islands charged these countries[31] with not fulfilling their treaty and customary obligations to negotiate for the comprehensive prohibition and elimination of nuclear weapons.[32]

In their applications, the Marshall Islands cited the conclusion of the ICJ 1996 case that:

> "[t]he destructive power of nuclear weapons cannot be contained in either space or time" and that such weapons "have the potential to destroy all civilization and the entire ecosystem of the planet" and make it imperative for the court to take account of "the unique characteristics of nuclear weapons, and in particular their destructive capacity, their capacity to cause untold human suffering, and their ability to cause damage to generations to come".[33]

---

31 Marshall Islands filed memorials brief charging the other six nuclear-armed states, and requesting those states to accept legal proceedings in the ICJ on the question of their compliance with nuclear disarmament obligations; none of these six acquiesced to the request. Nuclear Age Peace Foundation, "#nuclear ZERO", *available online at* www.wagingpeace.org/nuclearzero.org/ (scroll down under "International Court of Justice Documents" for links to.pdf copies of the initial documents filed in each case) (accessed 28 June 2019).

32 *See generally*, Judgment, *Obligations Concerning Negotiations Relating to Cessation of the Nuclear Arms Race and to Nuclear Disarmament* (*Marshall Islands v. India*), International Court of Justice, 5 Oct. 2016, *available online at* https://www.icj-cij.org/files/case-related/158/158-20161005-JUD-01-00-BI.pdf (accessed 15 June 2019); Judgment, *Obligations Concerning Negotiations Relating to Cessation of the Nuclear Arms Race and to Nuclear Disarmament* (*Marshall Islands v. Pakistan*), International Court of Justice, 5 Oct. 2016, *available* online *at* https://www.icj-cij.org/files/case-related/159/159-20161005-JUD-01-00-EN.pdf (accessed 15 June 2019); Judgment, *Obligations Concerning Negotiations Relating to Cessation of the Nuclear Arms Race and to Nuclear Disarmament* (*Marshall Islands v. United Kingdom*), International Court of Justice, 5 Oct. 2016, *available online at* https://www.icj-cij.org/files/case-related/160/160-20161005-JUD-01-00-EN.pdf (accessed 15 June 2019).

33 Application Instituting Proceedings, *Obligations Concerning Negotiations Relating to Cessation of the Nuclear Arms Race and to Nuclear Disarmament* (*Marshall Islands v. United Kingdom*), International Court of Justice, 24 Apr. 2014, p. 6, paragraph 3 & footnotes 5–6 (citing *Legality of the Threat or Use of Nuclear Weapons*, paragraphs 35 and 36), *available online at* https://www.icj-cij.org/files/

The Marshall Islands cited evidence from its testimony to the Court in 1995 on the devastating transgenerational impacts of nuclear weapons tests to the population and environment of the Marshall Islands. In addition, they submitted evidence that was not available in 1995 on the catastrophic and transgenerational impact of the use of nuclear weapons on the global economy and on the climate. They cited the conclusion of the Vienna Conference on the Humanitarian Impacts of Nuclear Weapons that:

> The impact of a nuclear weapon detonation, irrespective of the cause, would not be constrained by national borders and could have regional and even global consequences, causing destruction, death and displacement as well as profound and long-term damage to the environment, climate, human health and well-being socioeconomic development, social order and could even threaten the survival of humankind.[34]

The Court did not consider the merits of the cases, dismissing them on admissibility and jurisdictional grounds.[35]

IV. 2017 People's International Tribunal on Nuclear Weapons and the Destruction of Human Civilisation

In August 2017, a People's International Tribunal on Nuclear Weapons and the Destruction of Human Civilisation was held in Sydney to consider the application of international law to nuclear weapons and the responsibility of those

---

case-related/160/160-20140424-APP-01-00-EN.pdf (accessed 28 June 2019); Application Instituting Proceedings, *Obligations Concerning Negotiations Relating to Cessation of the Nuclear Arms Race and to Nuclear Disarmament (Marshall Islands v. Pakistan)*, International Court of Justice, 24 Apr. 2014, p. 6, paragraph 1 & footnotes 2–3 (same), *available online at* https://www.icj-cij.org/files/case-related/159/159-20140424-APP-01-00-EN.pdf (accessed 28 June 2019); Application Instituting Proceedings, *Obligations Concerning Negotiations Relating to Cessation of the Nuclear Arms Race and to Nuclear Disarmament (Marshall Islands v. India)*, International Court of Justice, 24 Apr. 2014, p. 6, paragraph 1 & footnotes 2-3 (same), *available online at* https://www.icj-cij.org/files/case-related/158/158-20140424-APP-01-00-EN.pdf (accessed 28 June 2019).

34 Memorial of the Marshall Islands, *Marshall Islands v. United Kingdom*, 16 Mar. 2015, pp. 19–20, paragraph 26, *available online at* https://www.icj-cij.org/files/case-related/160/160-20150316-WRI-01-00-EN.pdf (accessed 28 June 2019); Memorial of the Marshall Islands, *Marshall Islands v. Pakistan*, 12 Jan. 2015, p. 5, footnote 1, *available online at* https://www.icj-cij.org/files/case-related/159/159-20150112-WRI-01-00-EN.pdf (accessed 28 June 2019).

35 Judgment, *Marshall Islands v. United Kingdom*, p. 856, paragraph 58.

most responsible for nuclear weapons policies. Civil society tribunals do not have formal legal standing and their findings do not have compulsory legal force. However, they provide a court-like environment with the prosecution and defense putting forward legal arguments and evidence, as well as opportunities for testimony from witnesses, and judges or a jury who are required to make a judgment based on the evidence and law presented to them. In this way, they can provide a test of legal arguments applicable to the situation at hand.[36]

As such, they not only contribute to *opinio juris* (as a reflection or interpretation of international custom, general principles of law and the teachings of highly qualified publicists), but they can also pave the way for applications to formal courts. The London Nuclear Warfare Tribunal of 1985, for example, paved the way for an international network of lawyers, medical professionals and peace activists to launch the successful effort to get the case on legality of the threat or use of nuclear weapons into the International Court of Justice.

The People's International Tribunal on Nuclear Weapons and the Destruction of Human Civilisation laid "charges" against the leaders of the nine nuclear armed States (China, France, India, Israel, North Korea, Pakistan, Russia, United Kingdom and the United States) and the leader of Australia – a state relying on extended nuclear deterrence from the United States.[37]

On August 16, the Tribunal delivered its verdict. The leaders of the nuclear armed States were "convicted" of war crimes, crimes against humanity, crimes against peace and crimes of threatening, planning and preparing acts which would constitute genocide, ecocide and omnicide. In addition, the tribunal "convicted" the leader of Australia for complicity (i.e., aiding and abetting the planning and preparation for the use of nuclear weapons), which would constitute a crime, and for making illegal threats to facilitate and support the use

36 *See* Dr. T. Kerns, "Environment and Human Rights: Citizens Tribunals", *available online at* https://environmentandhumanrightscourse.info/lecsite/CitsTribunal.html (mini-lecture from Philosophy course) (accessed 28 June 2019); *cf.* B. Barrillot, "Essais nucléaires français. L'héritage empoisonné" [French Nuclear Tests: The Poisoned Inheritance], Observatoire des Armements/Centre de Documentation et de Recherche sur la Paix et les Conflits Editions, 2012; B. Barrillot, *L'Héritage de la bombe : Polynésie – Sahara 1960-2002* [*The Legacy of the Bomb: Polynesia – Sahara 1960–2002*], Centre de Documentation et de Recherche sur la Paix et les Conflits Edition, 2002.

37 Prosecution Memorial, People's International Tribunal on Nuclear Weapons and the Destruction of Human Civilisation, Centre for Peace and Conflict Studies, University of Sydney, 7–8 July 2016, *available online at* http://sydney.edu.au/arts/peace_conflict/practice/Alyn%20Ware%20TMay%20version%20Peoples%20Tribunal%20Prosecution%20Memoriall%20FINAL%203%20July%202016.pdf (accessed 15 June 2019).

nuclear weapons.[38] In reaching its decision the tribunal considered the application of international humanitarian law and the law on peace and security, as well as human rights, environmental, and criminal law. Most significantly, the tribunal included a specific focus on protecting the rights of future generations.

In testimony to the court, Professor Emilie Gaillard provided considerable theoretical and legal background on the status of inter-generational justice, the rights of future generations under international law, and the responsibility to protect future generations. She gave evidence of the increasing recognition at international and national levels of these legal principles, through treaties, national laws, judicial decisions and academic writings. In applying this growing body of law on inter-generational justice to nuclear weapons, Professor Gaillard argued that policies to threaten or use nuclear weapons would violate the rights of future generations, and those responsible for such acts would be criminally responsible.[39]

The Prosecution Memorial also included a focus on inter-generational justice and the rights of future generations. It argued that the development of international human rights, environmental and intergenerational law since the 1996 ICJ advisory opinion closed the uncertainty gap left by the Court in 1996 on the legality of the threat or use of nuclear weapons in the extreme circumstance of self-defense when the very survival of a state is at stake.

> Finally, if there is any remaining doubt that every use of nuclear weapons is now clearly illegal, the inter-generational application of international humanitarian law closes and locks the door completely. Even if there was some remaining possibility that a nuclear weapon could be used on military installations and personnel in a way that did not spread radiation to civilians, the offspring of surviving military personnel, and their subsequent generations, would be impacted by the radiation – both through long-lasting radionuclides and through inter-generational damage to genes. It is clearly illegal for the weapons to cause this damage to future generations. They may be offspring of military personnel, but they have their own human rights and are protected under international humanitarian law.[40]

---

38 Indictment, People's International Tribunal on Nuclear Weapons and the Destruction of Human Civilisation, Centre for Peace and Conflict Studies, University of Sydney, 16 Aug. 2016, *available online at* http://www.global-directions.com/ipt.pdf (accessed 15 June 2019).

39 *Amicus brief on Emerging law: Ecocide and the Rights of Future Generations*, Professor Emilie Gaillard, People's International Tribunal on Nuclear Weapons and the Destruction of Human Civilisation, Centre for Peace and Conflict Studies, University of Sydney, *available online at* http://www.unfoldzero.org/wp-content/uploads/Emerging-law-.EGAILLARD.pdf (accessed 15 June 2019).

40 Prosecution rebuttal and closing statement, People's International Tribunal on Nuclear Weapons and the Destruction of Human Civilisation, Centre for Peace and Conflict

The tribunal judges placed a high importance on the issue of inter-generational justice and rights of future generations in their judgment, dedicating a whole chapter on the issue. The Tribunal concluded, with specific reference to inter-generational justice, that:

> The evidence before the Tribunal showed the impossibility of the use of nuclear weapons, not stopping at neutral borders, wreaking destruction on present and future generations, thus breaching all of the above and therefore being unlawful.[41]

The Tribunal also held that, in light of developments in international law over the past two decades, the principle arguments and conclusion by Judge Weeramantry in his dissenting opinion in the 1996 ICJ case, in particular the "proposition of his finding that use or threat of nuclear weapons is illegal, has moved from 'dissent' to the interpretation of the majority of the international community".[42]

The Tribunal then reaffirmed that the threat or use of nuclear weapons would violate a number of principles and expressions of international law including "Protection of future generations – the widespread damage by nuclear weapons [...] environmental, ecological and genetic would be on such a scale that the fundamental human rights of those future generations and the legal protections afforded to them would be totally breached".[43]

V. Nuclear Weapons in the International Criminal Court

During the negotiations in 1997 and 1998 for the establishment of an International Criminal Court, the Philippines proposed that the employment of nuclear weapons be included as a crime under the jurisdiction of the court.[44] The proposal found support from the majority of countries participating in the negotiations, but was not included in the adopted Rome Statute due to the realization that if such a provision was included it would likely prevent any nuclear armed or allied state from signing or ratifying the statute. As one commentator noted after the adoption of the Rome Statute:

Studies, University of Sydney, available online *at* http://sydney.edu.au/arts/peace_conflict/practice/Prosecution%20rebuttal%20and%20closing%20statement%20Alyn%20Ware.pdf (accessed 15 June 2019).

41 Indictment, People's Tribunal on Nuclear Weapons and the Destruction of Human Civilisation, paragraph 220.

42 *Ibid.*, paragraph 230.

43 *Ibid.*, paragraph 263.

44 *See* M. Glasius, *The International Criminal Court: A Global Civil Society Achievement*, Routledge, London, 2006, p. 100.

> A majority of states addressing the issue supported options in the draft Statute, in the prohibited weapons section, that either expressly identified nuclear weapons or contained a general provision regarding weapons that cause unnecessary suffering or indiscriminate damage that would implicitly cover nuclear weapons. The Non-Aligned Movement of more than 100 states, in its Cartagena meeting a month before, had made inclusion of use of nuclear weapons and of aggression as crimes key objectives. Of course, the nuclear weapon states absolutely refused a Statute that would clearly criminalize use of nuclear weapons.[45]

What these states were able to achieve was the inclusion in the Rome statute of language that, while not specifically mentioning nuclear weapons, would most likely provide jurisdiction of the court for the use of nuclear weapons either by nationals of States Parties or on the territories of States Parties. Such use would fall under Article 8 of the Statute, which holds inter alia that "War Crimes" under the court's jurisdiction include:

> Intentionally launching an attack in the knowledge that such attack will cause incidental loss of life or injury to civilians or damage to civilian objects or widespread, long-term and severe damage to the natural environment which would be clearly excessive in relation to the concrete and direct overall military advantage anticipated.[46]

In an attempt to preclude the application of Article 8 to nuclear weapons use, and in particular to the freedom of themselves to use nuclear weapons, the government of France attached an interpretive declaration to their ratification of the Rome Statute stating:

> The provisions of Article 8 [war crimes] of the Statute, and in particular those of paragraph 2(b) [war crimes in international armed conflict], exclusively concern conventional weapons and could not regulate or prohibit the possible use of nuclear weapons or prejudice other rules of international law that apply to other weapons which are necessary in the exercise of France's inherent right of self-defense [...].[47]

The Lawyers' Committee on Nuclear Policy responded with a critique of the French declaration stating that their interpretation of Article 8 was legally

---

45 J. Burroughs, "The International Criminal Court, Weapons of Mass Destruction, NGOs and Other Issues: A Report on the Negotiations and the Statute, *Lawyers Committee on Nuclear Policy*, New York, Apr. 1999, *available online at* http://lcnp.org/global/icc.htm (accessed 15 June 2019).

46 Rome Statute of the International Criminal Court, Rome, 17 July 1998, Article 8.2(b)(4), *available online at* https://www.icc-cpi.int/NR/rdonlyres/ADD16852-AEE9-4757-ABE7-9CDC7CF02886/283503/RomeStatutEng1.pdf (accessed 15 June 2019).

47 *Interpretative Declaration by France Upon Ratifying Rome Statute of the International Criminal Court*, 9 June 2000, Unofficial translation from the French by Lawyers' Committee on Nuclear Policy.

incorrect. "It should go without saying that humanitarian law applies to nuclear weapons just as it does to all other weapons". In addition, LCNP argued that the attempt by France to exclude any French use of nuclear weapons from the Court's jurisdiction "purports to exclude or modify the legal effect of certain provisions of the treaty in their application to that State" and as such the declaration "amounts to a reservation, and reservations are barred by the Statute, Article 120".[48]

New Zealand subsequently added an interpretative declaration to their ratification of the Rome Statute, picking up the arguments provided by LCNP and also challenging the validity of the French declaration.

> The Government of New Zealand notes that the majority of the war crimes specified in article 8 of the Rome Statute, in particular those in article 8(2)(b)(i)-(v) and 8(2)(e)(i)-(iv) (which relate to various kinds of attacks on civilian targets), make no reference to the type of the weapons employed to commit the particular crime. The Government of New Zealand recalls that the fundamental principle that underpins international humanitarian law is to mitigate and circumscribe the cruelty of war for humanitarian reasons and that, rather than being limited to weaponry of an earlier time, this branch of law has evolved, and continues to evolve, to meet contemporary circumstances. Accordingly, it is the view of the Government of New Zealand that it would be inconsistent with principles of international humanitarian law to purport to limit the scope of article 8, in particular article 8(2)(b), to events that involve conventional weapons only.

In addition, New Zealand referred in their interpretive declaration to the 1996 ICJ Advisory Opinion with regard to the universal and transtemporal nature of international humanitarian law:

> the Court stated that the conclusion that humanitarian law did not apply to such weapons would be incompatible with the intrinsically humanitarian character of the legal principles in question which permeates the entire law of armed conflict and applies to all forms of warfare and to all kinds of weapons, those of the past, those of the present and those of the future.[49]

Specific Reference to Nuclear Weapons Through Amendment

In 2010, the government of Mexico proposed an amendment to the Rome Statute to include the crime of nuclear weapons threat and use under the Court's

48 J. Burroughs, "The French Interpretative Declaration Regarding Nuclear Weapons", Lawyers Committee on Nuclear Policy, New York, 3 July 2000.

49 "Interpretative declaration made by the Government of New Zealand on ratification of the Rome Statute of the International Criminal Court", New Zealand instrument of ratification of the Rome Statute, 23 Sep. 2000.

jurisdiction.[50] In its proposal, Mexico cited the destructive impact on human civilization, and the long-term and severe damage to the environment from the use of nuclear weapons.

Mexico was one of the countries which, during the negotiations for the Rome Statute, supported including the use of nuclear weapons as a War Crime, but dropped their insistence that it be included to ensure that nuclear armed and allied States could join the Rome Statute.

Mexico tried the amendment approach in 2010 because the adoption of such an amendment to the Statute would not necessarily result in nuclear armed and allied States withdrawing from the International Criminal Court. Article 121 of the Statute provides that amendments to the Statute are only binding on those states which ratify them.

Until now there has been insufficient political *momentum* to get the amendment considered and adopted by States Parties. However, the recent adoption of a Treaty on the Prohibition of Nuclear Weapons,[51] which was negotiated and adopted under the auspices of the United Nations, and which refers to criminal responsibility[52] and to the rights of future generations,[53] might generate additional political will and legal incentive for taking forward the Mexican proposal.

Conclusion

The rights of future generations, and the responsibilities to protect future generations from the harm of the inter-generational impact of nuclear weapons, have been considered in international tribunals seized of the issue of nuclear

50 *Amendment to article 8 of the Rome Statute of the International Criminal Court regarding the use of Nuclear Weapons*, submitted by Mexico to the Review Conference of the Rome Statute of the International Criminal Court, Kampala, 31 May to 11 June 2010, Document ICC-ASP/8/43/Add.1.

51 Treaty on the Prohibition of Nuclear Weapons (TPNW), adopted in New York 7 July 2017, and opened for signature in New York on 20 Sep. 2017.

52 "Each State Party shall take all appropriate legal, administrative and other measures, including the imposition of penal sanctions, to prevent and suppress any activity prohibited to a State Party under this Treaty undertaken by persons or on territory under its jurisdiction or control", TPNW, New York, 7 July 2017.

53 The TPNW refers to protection of future generations in its preamble which states that "the catastrophic consequences of nuclear weapons cannot be adequately addressed, transcend national borders, pose grave implications for human survival, the environment, socioeconomic development, the global economy, food security and the health of current and future generations".

weapons. These considerations were not influential in the 1975 Nuclear Tests Case, which was concluded without any legal determination; nor were these considerations influential in the 2016 Nuclear Disarmament Obligations cases (Marshall Islands versus the nuclear-armed States), which were dismissed on admissibility and jurisdictional grounds. Considerations of the rights of future generations also have not been effective so far in attempts to include the threat or use of nuclear weapons as a War Crime through amendment of the Rome Statute for the International Criminal Court. However, considerations of protecting future generations appeared to be very influential, even if not 100% decisive, in contributing to the International Court of Justice decision in 1996 to affirm the general illegality of the threat or use of nuclear weapons. Finally, considerations of the rights of future generations were fundamental to the conclusions of the People's International Tribunal on Nuclear Weapons and the Destruction of Human Civilisation that any threat or use would be illegal and criminal.

What this indicates is that consideration of principles of inter-generational justice provides possibilities to strengthen legal norms and influence judicial decisions, especially in relation to nuclear weapons. Such principles are not yet strong enough to be decisive in most circumstances, but the evolution and strengthening of these principles could indeed make them much more influential in the future.

Jean-Marie COLLIN

5. Treaty on the Prohibition of Nuclear Weapons: A Move Towards New Legal Action to Protect Future Generations?

Law is like a living thing. It evolves, it breathes; sometimes, it can even hiccup. But the law is always improving, so that anyone can make it her or his own; it can also become common property – in this way, law is truly a "transformative process".[1] But law also upsets; obviously so. Law's aim is to create rules; in other words, constraints and obligations that can be difficult to accept or, worse, may even be rejected. This was as much the case, for example, with laws abolishing slavery and apartheid, as for the creation of treaties for nuclear weapon control and non-proliferation.[2] Despite this, law is accepted, respected and – more than this – sought after. Indeed, law has no other purpose than to protect (us) here and now, including protection of our families, our environment, and our future.

In 2018, nine States[3] – that is simultaneously few and many – possess nuclear weapons. A global nuclear arsenal consisting of almost 14,465 weapons,[4] of which nearly 4,000 are operational and some 1800 are in a state of alert, ready to be used. In other words, 24 hours a day, 7 days a week, a French nuclear-powered ballistic missile submarine (SSBN)[5] – but not just French, also a British,

1 M. Delmas-Marty, "*Etudes juridiques comparatives et internationalisation du droit 'Cours : vers une communauté de valeurs ? – Les droits fondamentaux'*" [Comparative legal studies and the internationalization of law, "Lecture: Moving Towards a Community of Values? – Fundamental Rights"], *available online at* goo.gl/obJZhc (accessed 15 June 2019).

2 Thus, the Nuclear Non-Proliferation Treaty signed on 1 July 1968, entered into force in 1970 despite being rejected by France and China. These two States later decided to sign and ratify the treaty in 1992.

3 According to the Stockholm International Peace Research Institute in 2018, the States possessing nuclear weapons are: the United States, Russia, the United Kingdom, France, China, Israel, India, Pakistan, North Korea.

4 SIPRI [Stockholm International Peace Research Institute] Yearbook 2018, *Armaments, Disarmament and International Security*, 2018.

5 A French SSBN can carry a total of 16 missiles (type M51, with a range of 6000 to 9000 Km). Each missile can carry a total of 6 nuclear warheads, with a unitary power of 150 kilotons.

American and Russian SSBN[6] – is operationally on standby, ready to launch its nuclear missiles if its commander in chief (President or Head of Government) gives the order. Today, the world's nuclear arsenal is much smaller than it was in the middle of the 1980's, when the number of nuclear weapons reached 64,449.[7] It is impossible to deny, therefore, the existence of a process of reduction of this type of armament. A quantitative reduction of this scale (reduction from 64,449 to 14,465) needs to be seen in the context of a qualitative improvement of the current arsenals. Indeed, the current arsenals are undergoing a global wave of modernization and renewal. We could even call it a new nuclear arsenal race. A fact that was openly stated in 2014 by the French Prime Minister, Emmanuel Valls: "Throughout the cold war, France made a considerable effort to avoid being out-distanced by the two great powers of the period. But now France is in the lead when it comes to deterrent technologies"[8] their launch of nuclear arsenal modernization and renewal processes, the phenomenon of the nuclear arms race is manifested in the different States. In France, during a speech to the armed forces (Toulon, 23 January 2018), President Macron indicated that he was in favor of the renewal of the air and submarine nuclear components. The voting-in by the French Parliament of the Military Programming Law[9] over the 2019/2025 period is the enactment of this intention, with an increase in the deterrence budget of 60%[10] and a commitment to retain nuclear systems until at least 2080.[11]

It is clear to many that nuclear weapons, arms of mass destruction, constitute a very serious international security problem. It is for this reason that,

6 Only these four States have this capacity permanently.

7 H.M. Kristensen & R.S. Norris, "Global nuclear weapons stockpiles, 1945–2013", *Bulletin of the Atomic Scientists*, Sep. 2013, p. 75.

8 Speech given by Manuel Valls, Prime Minister, 23 Oct. 2014.

9 Ministry of Defence, Military Programming Law 2019–2025, legislative texts, *available online at* https://www.defense.gouv.fr/english/actualites/articles/le-president-de-la-republique-promulgue-la-loi-de-programmation-militaire-2019-2025 (scroll down and click on the link: Téléchargez la Loi no 2018-607 du 13 juillet 2018 relative à la programmation militaire pour les années 2019 à 2025 (Légifrance, PDF, 610Ko)) (accessed 15 June 2019).

10 J.-M. Collin, "*Loi de programmation militaire : le Parlement atomisé ?*" [Military Planning Act: The Atomic Parliament?], *La Tribune*, 8 Feb. 2018.

11 J.-M. Collin, P. Quilès & M. Drain, *L'Illusion nucléaire : La face cachée de la bombe atomique* [*Nuclear Illusion: The Hidden Side of the Atomic Bomb*], éditions Charles Léopold Meyer, 2018.

since mankind entered the military nuclear era,[12] a "constellation" of treaties[13] has come into existence, and bilateral agreements (the latter involving just the United States and Russia), designed to control nuclear weapons and therefore the disarmament and non-proliferation processes. The Nuclear Non-Proliferation Treaty (NPT) is the cornerstone of this regime. To these treaties we can add a whole set of texts that, according to where they come from, do or do not create obligations for States. We might list the resolutions issued by the United Nations Security Council, the resolutions taken by the Red Cross Red Crescent Council of Delegates, by the Inter-Parliamentary Union,[14] and by the OSCE Parliamentary Assembly. We could also mention the rules proper to each State, some of which – e.g., Mongolia (1992), Austria (1999) – decided to inscribe the principles governing nuclear weapons into their constitutions. Finally, on 7 July 2017 a new star was added to this constellation, known as TPNW, short for the "Treaty on the Prohibition of Nuclear Weapons".[15] Two days before the TPNW was opened for signature, the French Minister for Foreign Affairs uttered harsh words about this treaty and the 122 States that voted its adoption at the United Nations General Assembly: "A policy of incantation confines us to irresponsibility".[16] This sentence demonstrates the tension born of the so-called "humanitarian initiative" that took place between 2010 and 2017, and of the creation of this new legal instrument whose role is to ban a type of weapon of mass destruction. The scope of this treaty will also impact upon future generations.

From Military Theory to Humanitarian Reality

During the months following the use of the *Little Boy* and *Fat Man* nuclear bombs at Hiroshima and Nagasaki, organizations such as the International Committee

---

12 On 16 July 1945, the date of the first atmospheric nuclear test conducted at the U.S. test site of Alamogordo.

13 *See* the list of treaties on the Arms control Association internet site, "Treaties & Agreements", https://www.armscontrol.org/treaties (accessed 15 June 2019).

14 The Inter-Parliamentary Union and the Parliamentarians for Nuclear Non-proliferation and disarmament: Supporting Nuclear Non-Proliferation and disarmament – Handbook for Parliamentarians, No. 19, 2012.

15 The treaty has been open for signature since 20 September 2017. It will come into force once fiftieth instrument of ratification has been deposited. In February 2019, the number of States having signed the treaty was 70, with 21 ratification deposits.

16 Press conference of M. Jean-Yves Le Drian, General Assembly of the United Nations, 18 Sep. 2017.

of the Red Cross[17] and pacifist movements (for example the Stockholm Appeal launched on 19 March 1950) were ringing alarm bells about the humanitarian and environmental risks of the use and consequences of this type of weapon. U.S. scientific and military authorities were aware of the dangers for mankind, and studied the survivors of the atomic bombings – nicknamed "Hibakushas" – as well as inhabitants born after these bombings.[18] Volunteer experiments carried out during atmospheric nuclear tests[19] affected thousands of people (both military and civilian), sometimes transmitting radiation-induced diseases to subsequent generations. Women were unfortunately more affected than men from a social perspective (some, for example, being openly rejected after having survived the nuclear bombing of Japan),[20] others giving birth to what were termed "jellyfish babies". Darlène Keju-Johnson, Family Planning Director on the Marshall Islands (1987-1992), tells of these strange births: "We currently have a problem that we refer to as the "jellyfish babies". At birth these babies look like jellyfish. They have no eyes. They have no heads. They have no arms. They have no legs. They don't look human. When they die, they are immediately buried. Often the mother is not allowed to see her baby, because she would go mad if she did. It's inhuman".[21] The environmental impact of this nuclear experimentation is visible at test sites across the entire globe: in the Steppes of Kazakhstan (456 tests carried out between 1949 and 1989 by the Soviet Union), at the British Maralinga site

---

17 International Committee of the Red Cross, "Atomic weapons and non-directed weapons", *International Review of the Red Cross*, Vol. III, No. 4, Apr. 1950, p. 70.

18 Kyodo, "Huge scale of A-bomb gene study revealed. Medical records of 1,200 babies of hibakusha shipped to U.S.", *Japan Times*, 23 Apr. 2012.

19 As part of the *Desert Rock* operation in the United States, the military conducted a series of nuclear tests in Nevada between 1951 and 1957, exposing thousands of participants – both military and civilian – to high levels of radiation. As for France, French troops were sent to the so-called "Green Jerboa" (Gerboise Verte) nuclear test conducted on 25 April 1961. On 14 September 1954, Soviet troops conducted a similar exercise during their "Totskoye" operation near the city of Orenburg.

20 A.G. Dimmen, "Gendered Impacts: The Humanitarian Impacts of Nuclear Weapons from a Gender Perspective", *International Law and Policy Institute – United Nations Institute for Disarmament Research Vienna Conference Series*, Paper No. 5 of 6, Dec. 2014.

21 Bikini Atoll is an atoll of the Marshall Islands. It was the scene of atomic weapon tests undertaken by the United States from 1 July 1946. Sixty-seven nuclear experiments were conducted between 1946 and 1958, including the most powerful U.S. H-bomb "Castle Bravo". Quotation from the *Nuclear Disarmament Resource Guide* of Religions for Peace, 2013.

(7 tests in 1957), up to the French Atolls of Fangataufa and Mururoa (193 tests carried out between 1966 and 1996). At some sites the pollution is "invisible" confined within the depths of underground wells hollowed out in deep galleries. But for how long? The only thing that is certain is that future generations will have to deal with these sites and it is their task to continue to remember that these sites are forever polluted.

In 2010, during the 8th Nuclear Non-Proliferation Treaty Review Conference, the following consensus statement was made: "The Conference expresses its deep concern at the catastrophic humanitarian consequences of any use of nuclear weapons". These words opened the door to the so-called "Humanitarian Initiative" movement. Over the course of the years, more and more States joined it and it was (and still is) at the heart of the International Campaign to Abolish Nuclear Weapons – ICAN. This awareness demonstrates a dual goal on the part of these States. On one hand, consciousness of the real and permanent danger of nuclear weapons and, on the other hand, consciousness that all [States] need to play their part to increase international security. Until this period, the conferences of United Nations bodies[22] always concentrated on political concepts (such as deterrence) and nuclear non-proliferation. If these discussions have pushed the "nuclear weapons" issue to the forefront, they largely ignore the real threat posed by these weapons to all life on earth. The avoidance of this reality might be explained by the fact that the negotiations and the schedule for disarmament and non-proliferation have principally been led by the States that possess this type of weapon. Therefore, over the last 20 years, an almost total absence of real progress can be observed, if not a regression in the application of some treaties.[23]

In order to understand more clearly the incentives that inspired these States to act, we can take the analogy of smokers. Clearly, people who are dependent on cigarettes are not the ones who will impose rules and behaviors that limit their consumption or force them to stop smoking. No, it is other people who

22 Such as the General Assembly of the United Nations, the UN Disarmament and International Security First Committee, the Conference on Disarmament, the NPT Review Conferences and Preparatory Committees.

23 Since 1996, the Conference on Disarmament has failed to produce any real results, the Fissile Material Cut-off Treaty is still in the discussion stage, and the Comprehensive Nuclear-Test-Ban Treaty is not yet in force. The Intermediate Range Nuclear Forces Treaty seems under to be threat from both Russia and the United States; the latter having also decided in 2003 to withdraw unilaterally from the Anti-Balistic Missile (ABM) Treaty created in 1972 to restrict the arsenal race between Moscow and Washington.

make the rules – specifically, the non-smokers who make up the majority of the population. In the first place for their own sakes (the wish to put an end to passive smoking through the French Évin Law, for example[24]), restricting the extent of the nuisance generated by smokers. Then, in time the rule is imposed on everyone through stronger prohibitions, increased prices, and neutral packaging that dissuade people from smoking for good! In our situation the same principle is at work, where the majority seize (upon) the problem in order to ensure their own safety. Nuclear disarmament is a global task and carries collective responsibility. The Humanitarian Initiative therefore brought to the forefront the "catastrophic humanitarian consequences"[25] that the use of nuclear weapons would have, as well as the issues that this utilization or threat of utilization raises in terms of respect for international humanitarian law, and made sure that these considerations were at the heart of the debate on nuclear disarmament.

Three intergovernmental conferences[26] on the humanitarian consequences of nuclear weapons were held (in Oslo in 2013, in Nayarit and Vienne in 2014). The aim was to inform the States on the hazards and risks of detonation of a military nuclear device whether accidentally[27] or deliberate. Each time, the number of States present increased, from 128 to 146, and finally up to 156 States.[28] The conclusions heard, repeated and emphasized during these three conferences confirmed that:

---

24 The Loi Évin (10 Jan. 1991), bans smoking in public communal areas, as well as in public transport premises and vehicles.

25 Final document of the Review Conference of the Parties to the Treaty on the Non-Proliferation of Nuclear Weapons in 2010, NPT/CONF.2010/50, New York, 2010.

26 J.-M. Collin, "L'impact humanitaire des armes nucléaires: un nouveau forum du désarmement ?" [The Humanitarian Impact of Nuclear Weapons: A New Forum for Disarmament], Group for Research and Information on Peace and Security Analysis Note, 2013; J.-M. Collin, "Nayarit conference on the humanitarian impact of nuclear weapons: A point of no-return!", Group for Research and Information on Peace and Security Analysis Note, 2014; J.-M. Collin, "3rd conference on the humanitarian impact of nuclear weapons, a new cycle of action", Group for Research and Information on Peace and Security Analysis Note, 2015.

27 J.-M. Collin, "Dimension humanitaire du désarmement nucléaire et danger du nucléaire militaire en France" [The Humanitarian Dimension of Nuclear Disarmament and the Danger of Nuclear Energy in France], Group for Research and Information on Peace and Security Analysis Note, 16 Sep. 2015.

28 It is worth noting that at this last conference in Vienna, of the 28 Members States of the European Union only France was absent. Moreover, the United States and the United Kingdom, two of the official Nuclear Powers as regards the NPT attended a humanitarian conference for the first time.

- Nuclear weapons are unique by reason of their destructive power and the terrible suffering they induce. Their use, even on a small scale, would have catastrophic and enduring consequences for human health, environment, climate, food production and socio-economic development.
- The impact of these weapons on health can last for decades and affect the children of survivors through the genetic damage passed on by their parents. This evidence was confirmed when nuclear weapons were set off in tests.
- No solution can be found to help large numbers of survivors of a nuclear explosion while suitably protecting those providing assistance.
- The humanitarian consequences of the explosion of nuclear weapons would not be limited to the State(s) where it occurred; other States and their populations would also be affected.

After the 3rd conference on the humanitarian consequences of nuclear weapons (2014), Austria decided to make a commitment to the civil society organizations and the international community[29] in a political declaration, called the "Humanitarian Pledge". This declaration[30] consisted in "identifying and applying effective measures to fill the legal gap for the prohibition and elimination of nuclear weapons". By "legal gap", "it should be understood that there is no allusion to the absence of a general ban on the development, possession, or use of nuclear weapons as established in the case of regimes prohibiting comparable weapons"; in other words, as we can find in the chemical and biological weapons conventions.

The NPT, which is the cornerstone of the non-proliferation regime, is not, in fact, a global treaty. The authors did not include all the obligatory constraints in terms of nuclear disarmament and non-proliferation. For example, the regime did not explore:

---

29 J.-M. Collin, "Les postures d'Etats européens face au processus de désarmement nucléaire dans le cadre de l'initiative humanitaire sur les armes nucléaires" [The Postures of European States in the Process of Nuclear Disarmament Under the Humanitarian Initiative on Nuclear Weapons], Repenser les stratégies nucléaires entre ruptures et continuités, Journées d'étude en hommage à Lucien Poirier, Lyon III University, 11 Dec. 2015. In less than 6 months this Commitment was made by 107 States, so rapidly that it was renamed during the course of the NPT Review Conference of May 2015 the "Humanitarian Pledge" to give it broader international scope.

30 ICAN France, "L'engagement Humanitaire" [The Humanitarian Commitment], *available online at* http://icanfrance.org/lengagement-autrichien/ (accessed 15 June 2019).

- The total prohibition of nuclear testing. It authorized (in Article V) "the potential benefits from any peaceful applications of nuclear explosions". The creation of the Comprehensive Nuclear-Test-Ban Treaty (CTBT) was thus brought in to fill in the prohibition "gap". Even if this treaty has not yet come into force, it reinforced the NPT by becoming "the universally accepted norm against nuclear testing".[31]
- The wish of the overwhelming majority of States to implement a Treaty banning the production of fissile material for the manufacture of weapons and other nuclear explosive devices comes from the same logic. The aim of these measures is to reinforce the NPT, which is the "global nuclear 'breakwater' ".[32] Finally, and this is the ultimate goal, this prohibition treaty should be the point of departure of a global nuclear disarmament process, in other words the elimination of all nuclear weapons.
- Articles I and II of the NPT prohibit the manufacture and acquisition of nuclear weapons for non-nuclear-weapon States but authorize the transfer of technologies between nuclear-possessing States. This is the situation between the Americans and the British (since the mid-1950's), but also between the French and the British (Treaty between France and the United Kingdom for joint radiographic and hydrodynamic facilities, signed in London on 2 November 2010).

Progressing Towards a Treaty on the Prohibition of Nuclear Weapons

In parallel with these non-United Nations conferences, this approach to humanitarian disarmament was largely relayed to the Conference on Disarmament (CD), the Preparatory Committees (2012, 2013, 2014 & 2017) and review of the NPT (2015), and annual meetings of the UN Disarmament and International Security First Committee. The debates and deliberations during the various works carried out by these fora were finally expressed in declarations entitled in turn "Humanitarian Consequences of Nuclear Weapons", "Humanitarian Dimension of Nuclear Weapons", and "Humanitarian Consequences of

31 Comprehensive Test Ban Treaty Organization (CTBTO) Executive Secretary Lassina Zerbo spoke of the "unusual seismic event detected in the Democratic People's Republic of Korea". CTBTO, Press Release, 3 Sep. 2017.

32 J.-M. Collin, "L'Assemblée générale de l'ONU ouvre la porte à un traité d'interdiction des armes nucléaires" [UN General Assembly Opens the Door to a Nuclear Weapons Ban Treaty], Group for Research and Information on Peace and Security (GRIP) – *Annuaire français de relations internationales* (AFRI), Vol. XVIII, Dec. 2016.

Nuclear Weapons", delivered respectively by Switzerland,[33] South Africa,[34] New Zealand[35] and Austria.[36]

---

33 "Joint Statement on the humanitarian dimension of nuclear disarmament by Austria, Chile, Costa Rica, Denmark, Holy See, Egypt, Indonesia, Ireland, Malaysia, Mexico, New Zealand, Nigeria, Norway, Philippines, South Africa, Switzerland", First Session of the Preparatory Committee for the 2015 Review Conference of the Parties to the Treaty on the Non-Proliferation of Nuclear Weapons, *available online at* http://bit.ly/1rwuvvw (accessed 15 June 2019).

34 "Joint Statement on the humanitarian impacts of nuclear weapons", Second Session of the Preparatory Committee for the 2015 Review Conference of the Parties to the Treaty on the Non-Proliferation of Nuclear Weapons, Geneva, 24 Apr. 2013, Delivered by Ambassador Abdul Samad Minty, Permanent Representative of South Africa to the United Nations, *available online at* http://bit.ly/1kdjP4z (speaking on behalf of Algeria, Argentina, Austria, Belarus, Bangladesh, Bosnia and Herzegovina, Botswana, Brazil, Burkina Faso, Cambodia, Chile, Colombia, Costa Rica, Ivory Coast, Cyprus, Cuba, Denmark, Djibouti, Ecuador, Egypt, El Salvador, Ethiopia, Ghana, Georgia, Grenada, Guatemala, Holy See, Honduras, Iceland, Indonesia, Iran, Ireland, Jamaica, Jordan, Kazakhstan, Kenya, Kuwait, Lebanon, Lesotho, Liechtenstein, Luxembourg, Malaysia, Maldives, Malta, Mauritius, Mexico, Morocco, Mozambique, Namibia, Nepal, New Zealand, Nicaragua, Niger, Nigeria, Norway, Palau, Panama, Papua New Guinea, Paraguay, Peru, Philippines, Qatar, Serbia, Samoa, Singapore, Solomon Islands, Swaziland, Switzerland, Tanzania, Thailand, Togo, Tonga, Trinidad and Tobago, Tunisia, Uganda, Ukraine, Uruguay, Yemen, Zambia, and South Africa) (accessed 27 June 2019).

35 "Joint Statement on the Humanitarian Consequences of Nuclear Weapons", UNGA 69: First Committee, 20 Oct. 2014, Delivered by Ambassador Dell Higgie (New Zealand), *available online at* http://bit.ly/1wjO8HM (speaking on behalf of Afghanistan, Algeria, Andorra, Angola, Antigua and Barbuda, Argentina, Armenia, Austria, Azerbaijan, Bahamas, Bahrain, Bangladesh, Barbados, Belarus, Belize, Benin, Bolivia, Bosnia and Herzegovina, Botswana, Brazil, Brunei Darussalam, Burkina Faso, Burundi, Cabo Verde, Cambodia, Cameroon, Central African Republic, Chad, Chile, Colombia, Comoros, Congo, Costa Rica, Ivory Coast, Cuba, Cyprus, DR Congo, Denmark, Djibouti, Dominica, Dominican Republic, Ecuador, Egypt, El Salvador, Equatorial Guinea, Eritrea, Ethiopia, Fiji, Finland, Gabon, Gambia, Georgia, Ghana, Grenada, Guatemala, Guinea, Guinea Bissau, Guyana, Haiti, Honduras, Iceland, Indonesia, Iraq, Ireland, Jamaica, Japan, Jordan, Kazakhstan, Kenya, Kiribati, Kuwait, Kyrgyzstan, Lao PDR, Lebanon, Lesotho, Liberia, Libya, Liechtenstein, Macedonia, Madagascar, Malawi, Malaysia, Maldives, Mali, Malta, Marshall Islands, Mauritania, Mauritius, Mexico, Federated States of Micronesia, Republic of Moldova, Mongolia, Montenegro, Morocco, Mozambique, Myanmar, Namibia, Nauru, Nepal, Nicaragua, Niger, Nigeria, Norway, Oman, Palau, Panama, Papua New Guinea, Paraguay, Peru, Philippines, Qatar, Rwanda, Saint Kitts and Nevis, Saint Lucia, Saint Vincent and the Grenadines, Samoa, San Marino, Sao Tome and Principe, Saudi Arabia, Senegal, Serbia, Seychelles, Sierra Leone, Singapore, Solomon Islands, Somalia, South Africa, South Sudan, Sudan, Suriname, Swaziland, Sweden, Switzerland, Tanzania, Thailand, Timor-Leste, Togo, Tonga, Trinidad and Tobago, Tunisia, Tuvalu, Uganda, Ukraine, United Arab Emirates, Uruguay, Vanuatu, Venezuela, Viet Nam, Yemen, Zambia, and New Zealand) (accessed 27 June 2019).

36 "Joint Statement on the Humanitarian Consequences of Nuclear Weapons", 2015 Review Conference of the Parties on the Non-Proliferation of Nuclear Weapons, 28

The number of States endorsing these declarations continues to rise.[37]

Also, in 2013, and in 2016,[38] an Open-ended Working Group (OEWG) was created with the task of taking forward multilateral negotiations on nuclear disarmament.[39] In this context, it is worth noting that various working documents filed by the States during the course of the second OEWG mentioned the term "future generations", demonstrating the growing interest in this concept. Thus, Iran reminded us of the effects of nuclear weapons, which are "unique in their destructive power, in the unspeakable human suffering they cause, [...] and in the threat they pose to

---

Apr. 2015, Delivered by H.E. Sebastian Kurz, Federal Minister for Europe, Integration and Foreign Affairs of Austria, *available online at* http://bit.ly/1KY2d5m (speaking on behalf of Afghanistan, Algeria, Andorra, Angola, Antigua and Barbuda, Argentina, Armenia, Azerbaijan, Bahamas, Bahrain, Bangladesh, Barbados, Belarus, Belize, Benin, Bolivia, Bosnia and Herzegovina, Botswana, Brazil, Brunei Darussalam, Burkina Faso, Burundi, Cabo Verde, Cambodia, Cameroon, Central African Republic, Chad, Chile, Colombia, Comoros, Congo, Cook Islands, Costa Rica, Ivory Coast, Cuba, Cyprus, DR Congo, Denmark, Djibouti, Dominica, Dominican Republic, Ecuador, Egypt, El Salvador, Equatorial Guinea, Eritrea, Ethiopia, Fiji, Finland, Former Yugoslav Republic of Macedonia, Gabon, Gambia, Georgia, Ghana, Grenada, Guatemala, Guinea, Guinea Bissau, Guyana, Haiti, Holy See, Honduras, Iceland, Indonesia, Iran, Iraq, Ireland, Jamaica, Japan, Jordan, Kazakhstan, Kenya, Kiribati, Kuwait, Kyrgyzstan, Lao PDR, Lebanon, Lesotho, Liberia, Libya, Liechtenstein, Madagascar, Malawi, Malaysia, Maldives, Mali, Malta, Marshall Islands, Mauritania, Mauritius, Mexico, Federated States of Micronesia, Republic of Moldova, Mongolia, Montenegro, Morocco, Mozambique, Myanmar, Namibia, Nauru, Nepal, New Zealand, Nicaragua, Niger, Nigeria, Norway, Oman, Palau, State of Palestine, Panama, Papua New Guinea, Paraguay, Peru, Philippines, Qatar, Rwanda, Saint Kitts and Nevis, Saint Lucia, Saint Vincent and the Grenadines, Samoa, San Marino, Sao Tome and Principe, Saudi Arabia, Senegal, Serbia, Seychelles, Sierra Leone, Singapore, Solomon Islands, Somalia, South Africa, South Sudan, Sri Lanka, Sudan, Suriname, Swaziland, Sweden, Switzerland, Tajikistan, Tanzania, Thailand, Timor-Leste, Togo, Tonga, Trinidad and Tobago, Tunisia, Tuvalu, Uganda, Ukraine, United Arab Emirates, Uruguay, Vanuatu, Venezuela, Viet Nam, Yemen, Zambia, Zimbabwe and Austria) (accessed 27 June 2019).

37 Only 16 States supported the Swiss declaration in 2011, while 159 States co-signed the Austrian declaration of 28 Apr. 2015.

38 J.-M. Collin, "Groupe de travail de l'ONU sur le désarmement nucléaire : bilan de ses sessions de travail de janvier à mai 2016" [UN Working Group on Nuclear Disarmament: Review of its Working Sessions from January to May 2016], *Note: Multipol*, 21 July 2016.

39 Reaching Critical Will, "Open-ended working group on nuclear disarmament", *available online at* http://bit.ly/2KToZl4 (accessed 15 June 2019).

the environment, to future generations".[40] The Group of African States, by using the expression "succeeding generations", called upon the "nuclear weapon-possessing States to respect their commitment to a joint undertaking to protect [from all catastrophic nuclear consequences] and preserve our planet for future generations".[41] Ireland, for whom the matter of gender has become a priority, pointed out that: "The disproportionate effect [of nuclear weapons] on women and girls has repercussions for subsequent generations".[42]

The final report of the 2016 OEWG also included in the section entitled "Concrete effective legal measures, legal provisions and norms that will be needed to attain and maintain a world without nuclear weapons" Point 61, informing us that the "Working Group also stressed the importance of engaging young people, including through the promotion of special youth communicators and student peace ambassadors, in order to pass on knowledge to future generations".[43] The concept of future generations is therefore consistently present in these working documents and has become intrinsic to the thinking and the work of nuclear disarmament.

On the strength of all these works, a group of States submitted during the UNGA of 2016 a resolution (L41) entitled "Taking Forward Multilateral Nuclear Disarmament Negotiations",[44] which requested the start of negotiations in 2017 on a legally binding instrument on nuclear weapons. For the first time in two decades, the States could adopt or reject a concrete proposal for a resolution intended to take forwards multilateral negotiations on nuclear disarmament. This resolution was approved (113 for, 35 against, 13 abstentions) on 23 December 2016.[45] The negotiations for this future legal instrument were carried out over the course of two sessions (March and June/July 2017).[46] On 7 July 2017, the Ambassador of Costa Rica, Elayne Whyte Gómez, president of this conference, announced the adoption of the Treaty on the Prohibition of Nuclear Weapons (TPNW) following

40 Working paper of the Islamic Republic of Iran, A/AC/286/WP.7, 2016.
41 Declaration of the Group of African States, OEWG, 2 May 2016.
42 Working paper of Ireland, A/AC.286/WP.35.
43 Final report of OEWG, A/71/371, 1 Sep. 2016.
44 J.-M. Collin, "L'Assemblée générale de l'ONU ouvre la porte à un traité d'interdiction des armes nucléaires" [UN General Assembly Opens the Door to a Nuclear Weapons Ban Treaty], Group for Research and Information on Peace and Security Analysis Note, 9 Dec. 2016.
45 For information, on 27 October 2016, the UN First Committee had adopted this resolution by 123 votes for, 38 against and 16 abstentions.
46 J.-M. Collin, "La convention d'interdiction des armes nucléaires : de la négociation au premier draft " [Nuclear Weapons Convention: From Negotiation to First Draft], Group for Research and Information on Peace and Security Note, 12 June 2017.

a vote with a resounding majority (122 States for; one against, the Netherlands; one abstention, Singapore). In concluding the conference, the President declared that: "The delegates will leave today with the satisfaction of having accomplished their duty [and that it] is indeed possible for future generations to inherit a world without nuclear weapons".[47] These future generations were also at the heart of the declarations of the representative of Trinidad-and-Tobago who, speaking on behalf of the Caribbean Community (CARICOM), declared that future generations would remember that the Treaty had advanced the process of multilateral disarmament. Thailand also concluded that adoption was "a triumph for humanity and the heritage of future generations".[48] This prohibition treaty, once in force, will make nuclear weapons illegal before international law and will be the start of the process of global nuclear disarmament: that is to say, the process for the reduction and elimination of nuclear weapons.

Future Generations at the Heart of the Treaty on the Prohibition of Nuclear Weapons

The general architecture of the Treaty on the Prohibition of Nuclear Weapons (TPNW) – comprising a preamble of 24 paragraphs and 20 Articles – is based on the conclusions issued at the different conferences on the catastrophic humanitarian consequences that would result from the detonation of nuclear weapons and on international humanitarian law and human rights. This legal text is therefore one more in a series of humanitarian instruments[49] of arms control aimed at banning entire categories of weapons.

The preamble of the treaty presents the objectives of the TPNW in a humanitarian framework. The ultimate goal being: "[the necessity] to completely eliminate such weapons [nuclear]" (paragraph 2), further stating that "a legally binding ban of nuclear weapons constitutes an important contribution towards the achievement and maintenance of a world free of nuclear weapons, including the irreversible, verifiable and transparent elimination of nuclear weapons, and determined to act towards that end" (paragraph 15). This preamble reveals that this treaty is the result of a lengthy process[50] and accordingly makes a number of direct references to the

47 Conference on Nuclear Weapons, 28th & 29th meeting, DC/3723, 7 July 2017.

48 *Ibid.*

49 Convention on the Prohibition of anti-personnel Mines (1997), and Convention Banning Cluster Munitions (2008).

50 Contrary to the claims of, for example, Alice Guitton, French Ambassador, at the Conference on Disarmament: "France is opposed to the Treaty for the Prohibition of

UN machinery for disarmament. First, by citing the first resolution of the General Assembly of the United Nations of 24 January 1946 ("and subsequent resolutions which call for the elimination of nuclear weapons"), then by describing the application of the Treaty on the Non-Proliferation of Nuclear Weapons as a "cornerstone element of the nuclear disarmament and non-proliferation regime". Finally, by recognizing "the vital importance of the Comprehensive Nuclear-Test-Ban Treaty and its verification regime as a core aspect of the nuclear disarmament and non-proliferation regime".

For the first time the English term "future generations" (directly transposed into French as générations futures) was used in a treaty prohibiting a weapon of mass destruction.[51] In treaties prohibiting indiscriminate weapons, the will is emerging to take into account the impact of the weapons on future generations. Thus, in the Convention on the Prohibition of Anti-personnel land mines (1997), the first paragraph includes the following: "Determined to put an end to the suffering and casualties caused by anti-personnel mines that [...] have other severe consequences for years after emplacement". Similar phraseology was used in 2008 when drawing up the Convention on Cluster Munitions. Indeed, there is an arms control treaty that explicitly uses this term "future generations". It is the ENMOD convention (1976),[52] which is largely unknown[53] despite being officially in force. The term is present in the preamble (paragraph 5), although the English is rendered slightly differently in the French translation as "generations to come" (générations à venir).

This concept of future generations has been used at various times during negotiations of the TPNW; initially, by the International Committee of the Red Cross during the first day of negotiations (27 March 2017). The president, Mr. Peter Maurer, emphasized in his statement that: "Nuclear weapons are the most terrifying weapon ever invented. They threaten irreversible harm to the environment and to future generations". The Republic of the Marshall Islands, whose fight against nuclear weapons is perhaps more legitimate than

---

Nuclear Weapons, hastily negotiated last year", opening speech of the 2018 session of the Conference on Disarmament, 23 Jan. 2018.

51 The Conventions on the prohibition of biological and chemical weapons make no reference to this notion.

52 Convention on the Prohibition of Military or Any Other Hostile Use of Environmental Modification Techniques.

53 L. Mampaey, "The ENMOD convention and the Programme HAARP: challenges and scope", *Analysis Note, GRIP*, June 2008.

any,[54] also emphasized the term during its contribution to discussions about the preamble (15 June): "We have a moral obligation towards our youngest generations and future generations".[55] At paragraph 4 of the TPNW, the first direct reference is made to the concept of "future generations":

> Cognizant that the catastrophic effects of nuclear weapons cannot be adequately addressed, transcend national borders, pose grave implications for human survival, the environment, socioeconomic development, the global economy, food security and the health of current[56] and future generations, and have a disproportionate impact on women and girls, including as a result of ionizing radiation.

It should also be noted that by introducing in this paragraph the notion of gender (which is also a first in a treaty on weapons of mass destruction) and the more significant effects of nuclear weapons on "women and girls", the wish to preserve their health and their capacity to give life to new generations is obviously implied.

The second reference is made at the end of the preamble (paragraph 23): "Recognising also the importance of peace and disarmament education in all its aspects and of raising awareness of the risks and consequences of nuclear weapons for current and future generations, and committed to the dissemination of the principles and norms of this Treaty". Moreover, a third reference can be found in this preamble, albeit an indirect one. To make it clear that this treaty follows in the wake of the Charter of the United Nations, the first paragraph of the preamble describes the will of the States Parties to "contribute to the realization of the purposes and principles of the Charter of the United Nations". A Charter of which, indeed, the first sentence of the preamble explicitly cites the wish to ensure peace for future generations: "We peoples of the United Nations, determined to save succeeding generations from the scourge of war, which twice in our lifetime has brought untold sorrow to mankind".[57]

---

54 J.-M. Collin, "La bombe juridique des îles Marshall contre les puissances nucléaires" [The Marshall Islands' Legal Bomb Against the Nuclear Powers], *Le Monde Diplomatique*, June 2016.

55 Discussion on Preambular Elements, Delivered by Her Excellency Ms. Amatlain Elizabeth Kabua, Permanent Representative, Mission of the Republic of the Marshall Islands to the United Nations, 15 June 2018.

56 The word "current", was added at the request of Egypt during the discussions on the preamble. The delegate wished thus to make it clear that these health issues already affect populations.

57 The Charter is posted on the United Nations site, *available online at* https://www.un.org/fr/charter-united-nations/ (accessed 15 June 2019).

The Treaty comprises 20 Articles, seven of which set out the principles of the treaty, the other thirteen being dedicated to the functioning of the treaty. The list of the various prohibitions is given in the first article. The treaty expressly prohibits the use of nuclear weapons, as well as any activities that make their use possible, on the basis of their catastrophic consequences from a humanitarian perspective: "Each State undertakes never under any circumstances to: develop, test, produce, manufacture, otherwise acquire, possess or stockpile, transfer, receive, allow any stationing, installation or deployment of any nuclear weapons or other nuclear explosive devices". In addition to the usual prohibitions, what is striking is the move to prohibit all possibility of a policy of deterrence by prohibiting the "threat to use nuclear weapons", since the nuclear deterrent consists in a permanent threat of the use of nuclear weapons hanging over towns and centres of power where civilian communities live, and creating in this way a global sentiment of insecurity and an arsenal race.

In Articles 6 and 7, which are about positive obligations, we can see the intention to take into account future generations. In fact, this treaty demands not only the implementation of a nuclear disarmament process (Article 4), together with verification, but also rehabilitation following past actions. There is a need expressed by the authors to track the past so that communities today and in the future will be able once again to live in a healthy environment without suffering the radioactive pollution that is still around in the parts of the world where nuclear tests have been conducted. Article 6 (Victim assistance and environmental remediation) states that the States Parties that have conducted nuclear tests must "provide adequate assistance to affected States Parties, for the purposes of victim and environmental remediation". These provisions – which are no more than an unusual application of the polluter-pays principle – are the result of the very firm intention of States such as Algeria, Ecuador and Vietnam, to compel the States responsible for this type of health and environmental damage to shoulder their responsibility. It should be noted that the inclusion of this concept of reparation in this type of treaty is highly innovative. It has never been included before. For example, the inclusion of the idea of rehabilitation of environments affected by nuclear tests would have been logical in the CTBT treaty. Only the treaty that created the nuclear weapon-free zone in Central Asia, the Treaty of Semipalatinsk, states in Article 6 (environmental security) that environmental damage environmental damage caused by a nuclear test program must be repaired: "Each Party undertakes to assist any efforts toward the environmental rehabilitation of localities contaminated as a result of past activities related to the development, production or storage of nuclear weapons or other nuclear explosive devices, in particular uranium tailings storage sites and nuclear test sites".

The Treaty on the Prohibition of Nuclear Weapons that Links Current and Future Generations

Nuclear weapons are weapons with enduring effects at every stage of their life. Prior to their use, the production and testing of these weapons create radioactive waste and zones where healthy life is impossible. Following their use, any survivors are confronted with major health problems from radiation,[58] and the contamination of bombed areas remains high.[59] Finally, the generations born after the production, testing and use of these weapons may also have radiation-induced diseases transmitted to them and suffer their effects if affected areas are not decontaminated. It was therefore illogical to continue to exclude future generations from all legal considerations relating to nuclear weapons. It can be observed that since the TPNW was opened for signature this link between "future generations and nuclear weapons" has been highlighted on three significant occasions. The Holy See is the first State (on 20 September 2017) to have ratified the TPNW. In accordance with the obligation set out in Article 12,[60] "Universality": this State organized the first major conference (10/11 November 2017) to promote the TPNW. In his opening message, the Holy Father took care to remind us that the international community is aware of the effects of nuclear weapons and that it cannot accept them for its descendants: "Essential in this regard is the witness given by the Hibakushas, the survivors of the bombings of Hiroshima and Nagasaki, together with other victims of nuclear weapons testing. May their prophetic voice serve as a warning, above all for coming generations!".[61] On 10 December 2017, the Nobel Committee awarded a Nobel Peace Prize to the International Campaign to Abolish Nuclear Weapons (ICAN). Setsuko Thurlow, a survivor of the nuclear bombing of Hiroshima, on receiving this prize, said: "Nine nations still threaten to incinerate entire cities, to destroy life on earth, to make our beautiful world

---

58 Evidence from the experience of the hibakushas and populations that have taken part in nuclear tests demonstrates this.

59 Unless decontaminated. Typhoon Makurazaki hit the city of Hiroshima on 17 and 18 September 1945; although the typhoon did tremendous damage, it also "cleaned" the city of radioactive contamination from the explosion of 6 August 1945.

60 Article 12, Universality: "Each State Party shall encourage States not party to this Treaty to sign, ratify, accept, approve or accede to the Treaty, with the goal of universal adherence of all States to the Treaty".

61 Address of His Holiness Pope Francis to participants in the international symposium: "Prospects for a World Free of Nuclear Weapons and for Integral Disarmament", Vatican State, 10 Nov. 2017.

uninhabitable for future generations".[62] Finally, the Secretary-General of the United Nations, António Guterres, presented an agenda with the purpose of "Securing Our Common Future", in which he listed three priorities: "My agenda has three priorities: disarmament to save humanity, disarmament to save lives, and disarmament for future generations".[63] Obviously, none of these three pronouncements has any legal weight. Nevertheless, such affirmations clearly demonstrate that the subject of "nuclear weapons", traditionally solely a military issue, has become inseparably intertwined with the concept of "future generations". The concept is henceforth loaded with new legal implications related to the protection of the environment and health.

Acting with Justice in the Name of Future Generations: A Return to the ICJ?

In 1996, two requests for advisory opinion were referred to the International Court of Justice.[64] The first came from the World Health Organization[65] and the second from the General Assembly of the United Nations, which asked: "Is the threat or use of nuclear weapons in any circumstance permitted under international law?" The ICJ failed to make an unequivocal ruling, remaining somewhat ambiguous. It is interesting, however, that in the grounds for its decision[66] the Court states that: "The question put to the Court by the General Assembly is indeed a legal one, since the Court is asked to rule on the compatibility of the threat or use of nuclear weapons with the principles and rules of international law".

The court duly: "recognizes that the environment is under daily threat and that the use of nuclear weapons could constitute a catastrophe for the environment. It also recognizes that the environment is not an abstraction but represents the living space, the quality of life and the very health of human beings, including generations unborn". And continues: "Further, the use of nuclear weapons would be a serious danger to future generations", adding that: "In consequence, in order

62 Nobel Lecture given by the Nobel Peace Prize Laureate 2017, ICAN, delivered by Beatrice Fihn and Setsuko Thurlow, Oslo, 10 Dec. 2017.

63 Secretary-General's remarks at the University of Geneva on the launch of the Disarmament Agenda, 24 May 2018.

64 Advisory Opinion, *Legality of the threat or use of nuclear weapons*, International Court of Justice Reports, 8 July 1996.

65 The Court considered that it was not in a position to give the advisory opinion sought by the World Health Organization. *Ibid.*

66 *Ibid.*, paragraphs 29, 35 & 36.

correctly to apply to the present case the Charter law on the use of force and the law applicable in armed conflict, and in particular humanitarian law, it is imperative for the Court to take account of the unique characteristics of nuclear weapons, […] their capacity to cause untold human suffering, and their ability to cause damage to generations to come". The possible entry into force of the TPNW (end 2019/start 2020) necessarily entails the development of the legal perspective. The TPNW, which is a humanitarian disarmament treaty, backed up by IHL and expressly prohibitive in Article 1 (of the threat or use of nuclear weapons), should constitute a new basis for legal action and lead to a procedure in the ICJ. Frankly, if the ICJ were again referred to by the General Assembly of the United Nations (which, objectively, ought to be the case), how could the Court fail to recognize – with the existence of the TPNW – the illegality of using or threatening to use nuclear weapons? From a legal point of view the result would be tremendous.

Such a decision would also highlight and reinforce the conclusions of the UN[67] and intergovernmental[68] conferences on "the humanitarian consequences of nuclear weapons", and thus accentuate the notion of the protection of "future generations" in this context. States that possess nuclear weapons, like those that pursue a policy of nuclear deterrence because of their military alliances, will be faced with a choice: renege on an international court ruling or pursue a path of "exclusion" from the nations that comply with international law. There is no doubt that a legal battle would ensue (and hence deepen the rise in public awareness of the danger of nuclear weapons) on the part of the States in favor of keeping nuclear weapons; they would no doubt refer to declarations made just minutes after the adoption of the TPNW on 7 July 2017: "We do not intend to sign, ratify or ever become party to this treaty. Therefore, there will be no change in the legal obligations of our countries with respect to nuclear weapons. For example, we would not accept any claim that this treaty reflects or in any way contributes to the development of customary international law (or customary norm)".[69] There is no doubt that the legal weight of the TPNW and of such a

67 *See* work of the Open-ended Working Group (of 2013, then of 2016) given the task of taking forward multilateral negotiations on nuclear disarmament.

68 Intergovernmental Conferences in Oslo (Mar. 2013), Nayarit (Feb. 2014) and Vienna (Dec. 2014) on the humanitarian impact of nuclear weapons.

69 Press statement of the permanent representatives to the United Nations of the United States, the United Kingdom and France following the adoption of the Treaty on the Prohibition of Nuclear Weapons – New York, on 7 July 2017.

decision in the future would weaken the legal standing of these declarations, and equally demonstrate the absence of "good faith" (Article 6) of the Nuclear Weapons States[70] with regard to nuclear disarmament. Furthermore, parliaments and civil society[71] would obviously also seize upon this legal aspect, adding impetus to the construction of new national and international law.

Conclusion

The treaty prohibiting nuclear weapons has come at a time when a large majority around the world has become aware of its ability to act in the face of the potential consequences of a nuclear weapons detonation. The TPNW will come into force once 50 States have ratified it (Article 15). There is no doubt that this treaty will, at the end of 2019 (or start of 2020), be a rule of law. On 25 February 2019, 21 States had already ratified and 70 States had signed the text. Once in force, this treaty will reinforce the international rule of law against nuclear weapons. It will give new impetus to nuclear disarmament and give civil society a new tool in the fight for a world free of nuclear weapons. It will put increased pressure on the nuclear-weapon-possessing States or those that have adopted a policy of nuclear deterrence. More than ever before, this is a treaty that has its roots in the rules of law related to humanitarian disarmament; in other words, the will to take into account the consequences of a weapons system for civilian communities. This treaty has supplied new elements, such as the notion of gender, but at the same time has seized upon already-existing concepts in treaties and agreements related to the environment (such as the polluter-pays principle) and legal concepts – such as the rights of future generations – that are still in the process of gaining recognition. Clearly, the nuclear disarmament community has taken a huge stride forwards, by showing that not only do nuclear weapons create a problem of international insecurity but that, more than that, they represent an environmental, humanitarian and health hazard. Henceforth, it is to be expected that new legal ground rules should be integrated into nuclear disarmament law.

70 It is worth noting that the Republic of the Marshall Islands in its case against the nuclear powers also confronted the States that were not members of the NPT with this notion of "good faith". *See* "Obligations concerning Negotiations relating to Cessation of the Nuclear Arms Race and to Nuclear Disarmament", International Court of Justice Reports, 2014.

71 For example, through a similar approach to the "Monsanto tribunal" – a citizens' proceeding (without official recognition) that aimed to arouse public opinion and move the law forward. *See* International Monsanto Tribunal, *available online at* http://fr.monsantotribunal.org (accessed 27 June 2019).

Frédérick LEMARCHAND

6. The Bomb as a New Definition of Present and Future Humanity: What We Owe to Günther Anders' Thoughts

"I have seen the world spirit, not on horseback, but on wings and without a head, and that refutes, at the same stroke, Hegel's philosophy of History"

T. Adorno, Minima Moralia: Réflexions sur la vie mutilée [Minima Moralia: Reflections on a Damaged Life], Payot, 2016, p. 53

On the day after the explosion of the first atomic bomb on 7 August 1945, Albert Camus authored an editorial in the newspaper *Combat* that closed with the following words:

> The world is what it is, that it is to say not much. We all know this as of yesterday, thanks to the formidable chorus broadcast by radio, newspapers and news agencies on the subject of the atomic bomb. They effectively told us, in the midst of a host of enthusiastic commentaries, that any average sized town can be completely levelled by a bomb the size of a football [...]. We can sum it up in one sentence: mechanical civilization is about to set upon its ultimate phase of barbarism. A choice must be made, in the near or not too distant future, between collective suicide or the intelligent use of scientific conquests.[1]

A single voice pierced the clapping crowd of western citizens blindly cheering for the anonymous forces that had just triumphed over evil without caring about the apocalyptic destruction of the City of Hiroshima – whose immediate death toll rose to some 70,000. Like the concentration camps, the horrific impacts of this disaster were impossible to imagine and comprehend.[2] Two days later,

---

1 A. Camus, "Albert Camus on Hiroshima", *Combat*, 8 Aug. 1945, *available online at* https://www.humanite.fr/albert-camus-sur-hiroshima-leditorial-de-combat-du-8-aout-1945-580990 (accessed 27 June 2019).

2 K. Oe, *Hiroshima Notes*, M. Boyars Publishers, 2000, translated by T. Yonezawa & D.L. Swain (citing testimony obtained from direct witnesses who survived the bombing, originally published in 1965); *cf.* B. Barrillot, "Essais nucléaires français. L'héritage empoisonné" [French Nuclear Tests: The Poisoned Inheritance], Observatoire des Armements/Centre de Documentation et de Recherche sur la Paix et les Conflits

the experiment was repeated without justification; this time using a plutonium bomb that destroyed the whole city of Nagasaki. The two bombs killed a total of 250,000 people. Although, this number of deaths was appalling, the second World War had already killed 70 million people. What led us into a new era instead was the apocalyptic potential of such a new weapon.

Another discordant voice rose, that of philosopher Günther Anders. Over the decades and preceding his death in 1992, Anders kept striving to establish the foundations for reflecting on both what happened in Japan and the worldwide consequences of entering into the nuclear age.[3] The inaugural text of "Reflections on the H Bomb" was written in the decade that followed the Hiroshima bombing, later published in 1956 under the title "On the Bomb and the Roots of our Blindness toward the Apocalypse". An essay included in *The Obsolescence of Man*, contains a philosophical program that redefined the human condition in the nuclear era.[4] Anders later recalled that "this concern for the possible end [of the world], appeared immediately on the day of Hiroshima (6 August 1945). [But he was not] able to transform this concern into 'texts' ".[5] We will not be able to develop here the entirety of this ontological project, which proposes a negative redefinition of our anthropology[6] after the atomic bombings. Instead, we will simply say that the work of Anders – whose text on the bomb constitutes one of the inaugural moments – is probably the most relevant and contemporary attempt at thinking about the issues of modern technology, distinguishing Anders from the legacy of his teachers Heidegger and Husserl.

Editions, 2012; B. Barrillot, *L'Héritage de la bombe : Polynésie – Sahara 1960–2002* [*The Legacy of the Bomb: Polynesia – Sahara 1960–2002*], Centre de Documentation et de Recherche sur la Paix et les Conflits Edition, 202.

3 Anders published three essays (1958–1964) *in* G. Anders, *Hiroshima ist überall* [*Hiroshima is Everywhere*], Munich, C.H. Beck, 1963, including "Der Mann auf der Brücke: Tagebuch aus Hiroshima und Nagasaki" [The Man on the Bridge: A Diary from Hiroshima and Nagasaki], written by Anders during an August 1958 visit to Japan.

4 G. Anders, "Les bombes et les racines de notre aveuglement face à l'apocalypse" [The Bombs and the Roots of Our Blindness to the Apocalypse], *in* G. Anders, *L'Obsolescence de l'homme : Sur l'âme à l'époque de la deuxième révolution industrielle* [*The Obsolescence of Man: On the Soul at the Time of the Second Industrial Revolution*], Éditions de l'Encyclopédie des Nuisances-Ivréa, 2002, Translated from the original 1956 version published by Beck'sche Reihe, pp.261–361.

5 G. Anders, *L'homme sans monde. Écrits sur l'art de la littérature* [*Man without World: Writings on the Art of Literature*], Fario, 2015.

6 Meaning the way that each society defines for itself mankind's humanity.

Before going into the details, it should be noted further that Anders uses neither the words "atomic bomb" nor "the bombs" (as objects) but "THE bomb". Creating an interpretative paradigm for the unprecedented nature of this new era – namely, that of "the apocalypse". As Professor Delmas-Marty quite rightly reminded us in the opening address of this colloquium, the one thing that distinguishes us from our ancestors is the ability to act on the world – and on ourselves – with greater responsibility. Remaining faithful to the Frankfurt School's methods, Anders pushed this assumption to the extreme: what is new is the capacity of mankind to destroy itself through the destructive power of nuclear weapons. Thus, "the bomb" may be translated as both "technical power" and "apocalypse" – whose non-religious meaning (naked apocalypse) evokes the Greek sense of "reversal" and "collapse". We propose a ten-point exegesis of the original 1956 text, which could be called the Ten Commandments of the atomic age; this has since been followed by many other publications on nuclear issues.

As we reflect on how the bomb leads us to consider a tragic redefinition of mankind's humanity what appears fundamental to us is the universal dimension and its wholly anthropological dimension: we are made by our own inventions as much as we produce them – they structure us, limit us (or, rather, constrain us) in our capacities for action; as opposed to the *doxa* that makes us believe that we *master* technique just as we *master* nature. Both are now returning to humanity, in the double sense of the term referring to both living biological species as well as the way we think of ourselves as human beings rather than barbarians, animals, or machines.

Commandment 1: *Moral philosophy has always believed that there would always be human beings.* Anders is the first philosopher to start his line of thinking with the idea that humans now have the means of self-destruction. This is of course a fresh reconsideration of the Kantian heritage, "in the shadow of the threat", from the experience of Hiroshima. In this way, Anders introduces to moral philosophy the question of *future generations*, which will be taken up by Jonas[7] in the 1980s and by "catastrophists" like the French philosopher Jean-Pierre Dupuy.[8]

Commandment 2: *The bomb could only be produced in the absence of moral conscience.* If the bomb is the natural outcome of a project, like any technical object, it is also the result of a process. The number of workers who worked to achieve

7 H. Jonas, *The Imperative of Responsibility: In Search of an Ethic for the Techonological Age*, University of Chicago Press, 1985.

8 J.-P. Dupuy, *Pour un catastrophisme éclairé. Quand l'impossible devient certain* [*For an Enlightened Catastrophism: When the Impossible Becomes Certain*], Points Essais, éditions Seuil, 2004.

that outcome can be estimated at several hundred thousand, but most of them were not aware of its consequences. The fact remains that many of the artisans who were confined to the site at Los Alamos in New Mexico – that is to say, the manufacturers and designers (including scientists and engineering technicians) – could no longer ignore what they had contributed to especially after the first test at Alamogordo (16 July 1945). Under what conditions could men of science and technicians who most certainly were "good father figures" have knowingly contributed to the making of such a ignominy? If psycho-sociologist Stanley Milgram's research on the conditions of transferring responsibility to a higher authority[9] can provide partial answers to such questions, the Andersian analysis of work gives us a more general understanding of the problem: rationalized work doubly exceeds our imagination. Ultimately, we have no valid perception of what we are doing in our everyday life; we are trapped by a segmented division of labor, and by the same disaster that irritates our senses. The consequence is that our once unitary conception of the subject breaks into fragments of "faculties" – i.e., human fragments specializing in "productive being", "sensitive being", "ability to enjoy", "ability to imagine", etc. This explains how the torturer and the atomic bomb maker can, at the same time, be good father figures. Anders concludes that schizophrenia is no longer an isolated psychic illness; instead, it becomes the unsurpassable condition of the modern man.

Commandment 3: *The bomb is not a means, because it exceeds all ends.* If it made sense to destroy the Earth even once, why give yourself the means to destroy it several times over? This brings us back to a metaphysical question. Through its power, the bomb exceeds all the means ever invented by humans to influence the world. It is from this theoretical – but, at the same time, very tangible hypothesis, that Anders questions the transformational movement from means to ends. Critical theory certainly understood the way unforeseen ends can be ignored while focusing instead on the ever-growing empire of means – ask a researcher to provide an early justification for plant transgenesis or animal cloning, for example! However, Anders goes further: It is now a question of considering former aspirations and, ultimately, humans (but also freedom and happiness) as means without ends. The bomb inaugurates this era by turning modern technology into a new transcendence. Thus, Vietnam did not contribute to the production of weapons for the war, but rather, to the production of a war for weapons.

9 S. Milgram, *Obedience to Authority: An Experimental View*, Harper Collins, 2004.

Commandment 4: *The bomb is used every day … as a means of blackmail.* Far from constituting a "weapon of peace" or some other stabilizing actor (as nuclear doxa has taught since the beginning of the cold war), the bomb is far from a harmless object forgotten at the bottom of a silo but nevertheless available for use "just in case". Rather, the bomb's mere existence precludes its use in the real world. Anders contends that the bomb places humanity in an unprecedented posture of vulnerability, making humans – rich or poor, whether or not they own a fallout shelter – a disillusioned and, potentially, vulnerable being. To live in the atomic age is to become a "being-in-suspension", a human who has not yet been killed. We have entered the Damoclean era, as permanent victims of blackmail for peace while we face the prospect of total destruction on the horizon. Anders states that, after Auschwitz, humanity became killable (murderable); after Hiroshima, humanity faces extinction.

Commandment 5: *Nuclear "tests" are not tests.* As opposed to abstract philosophers, Anders' substantialist approach to the inherent danger interprets the term "tests" as concrete elements of reality. In other words, these tests are now part of our world: think about 2,000 nuclear tests – half of which were conducted in open air; most of them ten times more powerful than the bomb dropped on Hiroshima. The environmental consequences of those tests were carefully studied in Hiroshima for the sole purpose of seeing if the damage met expectations; we know today the dramatic ecological impact of all the nuclear tests carried out in the Pacific,[10] and in the Sahara.[11] Plutonium is one of the world's most toxic substances, it is now known that very small amounts of contaminants can have lethal effects on health because, in real life, substances often act in combination. Thus, the new paradigm of environmental health highlights the combined, potential, delayed, and transgenerational effects of pollution – challenging the old belief that "the dosage makes the poison".[12]

Accordingly, radioactive substances are often referred to as "low doses" (implying harmlessness) when they actually display effects that are fully comparable

---

10 W. Sage, "The Transformation of Polynesian Society with Nuclear Tests", Symposium Taking Legal Action on Behalf of Future Generations, 17–18 Nov. 2017, Caen, France (demonstrating how "testing" creates a destructive nuclear economy in local societies).

11 The Béryl nuclear accident (code name of the test) occurred on 1 May 1962, when France carried out its second underground nuclear test at In Ecker, north of Tamanrasset, in the Algerian Sahara. It contaminated an area of 150 km radius whose effects on the health of local populations are proven but not recognized. *Cf.* Gerboise bleue, documentaire de Djamel Ouahab, Kalame films, 2009.

12 Paracelse (1493–1541).

to those of endocrine disruptors. The nuclearized world, therefore, embodies Philippe Roquelo's conception of technique: "every technical object is the petrification of social relations that it contributes to both establishing, perpetuating and modifying and that's precisely why it is possible to perceive the essential social characteristic of the technique".[13]

Commandment 6: *We have become bigger than ourselves.* Like his first wife Hannah Arendt, Anders places at the heart of his thoughts the question of knowing what we are doing. At the same time, he questions our ability to understand what we are doing – especially with respect to hyper technology (bombs, media, biotechnology, etc.) – through his central hypothesis about man's obsolescence: we are not, in imagination or feeling, at the height of what we produce. The demiurge man seeking to produce hyperpower and complex machines, some even autonomous, instead begets Golem or Frankenstein-like creatures. Technology transcends and leaves us behind: we have become bigger than ourselves, our creations are no longer human … instead, they have become foreign to us and incomprehensible.

Hence the second assertion: *We have become smaller than ourselves.* Our inability to apprehend what we are doing turns us into imperfect beings, as opposed to the perfection of machines. Jean-Michel Besnier summed up the situation very well with regard to transhumanism: the optimised man is first and foremost a diminished man, cut off from his faculties of comprehension.[14] In other words, Anders uses the concept of supra-linearity to refer to the phenomena that goes beyond human understanding (initially, the bomb), such as the consequences of a 4°C global warming, and infra-linearity to designate what escapes our immediate perception (like the bomb that lurks at the bottom of the ocean in the form of a strategic submarine; in addition to environmental pollution, or climate change).[15]

Commandment 7: *We are incapable of being afraid.* Catastrophists have always taken great interest in the notion of fear, beginning with Hans Jonas who used it as a heuristic foundation in his new ethic for techno-scientific societies: listen to your fears and you will truly know what matters to you.[16] Paradoxically, Anders

---

13 P. Roqueplo, *Penser la technique : pour une démocratie concrète* [*Thinking Technique: For a Concrete Democracy*], Seuil, 1983.

14 J.-M. Besnier, *L'Homme simplifié* [*Simplified Man*], Paris, Fayard, 2012.

15 G. Anders, 2002, p. 291.

16 H. Jonas, *Le principe responsabilité : une éthique pour la civilisation technologique* [*The Principle of Responsibility: An Ethic for Technological Civilization*], Champs essais, 1995, translated by J. Greisch, p. 66.

neither refutes nor criticizes fear which is a traditional obstacle to self-realization or great ideals in modern thought. But he wonders why we are not afraid of future disasters, despite the presence of signs that have gathered and are readable around us like in the oracles.[17] Simply waking up in a condemned world – not only under the threat of the bomb – should produce a sense of fear, which could drive us to collective action: demand nuclear disarmament wherever atomic weapons exist. The catastrophism of Jean-Pierre Dupuy[18] is based on the idea that catastrophe must be ontologically conceived and sufficiently credible, so as to give the future an image repulsive enough for us to fight against its occurrence. To the contrary, the occurrence of catastrophes in the real world – and, more precisely, the various ends of the world made possible by the bomb – somehow overturned the perspective between real and imaginary catastrophes; thus, annihilating the fear that animated ancient imaginations of the catastrophe.[19] So, at the very moment when we should apprehend – in its dual sense of grasping and being afraid – what we are doing, the makers of end-of-the-world instruments seem devoid of any moral conscience and, therefore, of any *sense* of concern for the world. The responsible human is a worried, concerned person; so, we should be more scared than ever. Our lack of fear, says Anders, is part of our pathology.[20]

Commandment 8: *There are Promethean disparities: fear is not equal to the task, with respect to what the other faculties are able to generate.* The anthropological-psychological analysis of the subject (or, rather, the fragmentation of the subject) opens a fundamental perspective on man within scientific societies. It would be difficult to summarize in just a few words the question of man's destiny: are we part of history – created by men caught up in the balance of power – or, are we part of a socio-technological evolution where technique plays a role by giving competitive advantage to some rather than others, like the role played by genes in the evolution of life? I know that such a question will be swept aside by many philosophers and academic sociologists; however, it deserves to be examined – at least as a hypothesis – if we want to understand why what is happening seems to be beyond our reach. Not that we lack knowledge, because *we know*; science enlightens us through the power of logos, and information is accessible to most through the World Wide Web. However, as Anders boldly announces: indeed, we know but *don't dare believe* what we know. Here, he introduces a distinction

17 G. Anders, 2002, p. 49.
18 J.-P. Dupuy, *Petite métaphysique des tsunamis* [A Short Treatise on the *Metaphysics of Tsunamis*], Seuil, 2005, translated by M.B. DeBevoise.
19 A. Le Brun, *La perspective dépravée* [*The depraved perspective*], Éditions du Sandre, 2011.
20 G. Anders, 2002, p. 49.

between abstract and disconnected information from experience, on the one hand, and the social imaginary of the catastrophe, on the other hand. We lack an anthropological base within which to inscribe the catastrophe (here, the nuclear apocalypse), rather than taking refuge behind absurd theories such as "the balance of terror"[21] or, more broadly, the "management" of calculable risk. Our task from now on per Anders, is to develop our "moral imagination" – including the possibility of imagining the very worst (in other words, the end of the human species).

Commandment 9: *The problem: our belief in Progress.* As an anthropologist, Anders tirelessly probes our social imagination – in other words, this collective and immaterial instance that forms an image of what we want to be, of what we are, and of the world. The concepts of Progress and its corollary, Historical Time, give structure to progressive and developmentalist ideals; the history of the lived world shows us that these concepts and ideals are the source of catastrophes. As previously stated, Anders is one of, if not the, first to consider that we must equip ourselves with a new temporality. The future is no longer that horizon of possibilities – of which only one can come to be – that connects us through an arborescence of causality, where each bifurcation provides an opportunity to assert our freedom of choice. Instead, our new destiny is a fixed point: catastrophe. The effects of human activity in the Anthropocene[22] are such that the future is literally colonized by what we do: a process of climatic turmoil for the next 10,000 years (even if we immediately stop emitting CO_2); long lived nuclear waste[23]; biodiversity erosion, placing us in the sixth phase of species extinction; and, environmental xenobiotic pollution that has profoundly altered the logic of the living, as well as the reproduction of species.[24]

---

21 The doctrine known as Mutually Assured Destruction (or MAD – i.e., "crazy") anticipates that the large-scale use of nuclear weaponry by one of two belligerents would certainly cause the destruction of both camps, and thus precludes implementation of the weapons.

22 Name given by atmospheric chemist Paul Crutzen to the new geological era marked by the significant global impact of human activities on the terrestrial ecosystem.

23 France has produced 2700 m^3 of high-level waste, representing 0.2% of the volume of waste, and accounting for 96% of the activity. The lifespan of some isotopes is millions of years.

24 *See* G.-E. Seralini, "The transgenerational effects of pesticides and pollutants: how and why?", Taking Legal Action on Behalf of Future Generations, 17–18 Nov. 2017, Caen, France; G.E. Seralini, *Le sursis de l'espèce humaine* [*The reprieve of the human species*], Belfond, 1998.

Commandment 10: *Only own things whose precepts could also become the maxims of your action.*[25] Before Jonas, Anders formulated the precepts of a new ethic adapted to the *new* New World created by westerners. But, would those precepts in turn adapt to the new type of human, the fragmented and short-sighted man generated by the technoscientific economy? This is the whole source of Ander's methodological despair, as expressed in the provocative title of his published biography: *And if I'm desperate, what can I do?*[26] We need to base our ethics on a methodological rather than psychological despair; we must "start from the worst hypothesis" as the basis of elementary prudence. The invitation is clear. We must refrain from acquiring new technologies that threaten humanity anthropologically and ontologically. This is indeed what guides the whole movement for global nuclear disarmament (such as the Nuclear Disarmament Initiatives Movement).[27] It comes fifty years before the "neo-luddite" thinkers – e.g., American computer scientist Bill Joy, who published an article in *Wired magazine* in 2000 entitled "Why the future does not need us".[28] At the end of this article, Joy concludes that all progress in technical knowledge – particularly posthumanism research (e.g., artificial intelligence, biotechnologies) – brings us closer to the end of humanity. So, to save ourselves, we must *forego knowing.*

To conclude, Anders installs new hope in a possible transformation of the idea of humanity. The enlightenment shaped an abstract idea whose morals were unable to prevent the catastrophes of the twentieth century (wars and genocides). Instead, we need a *coherent and united humanity* that shares an interest in survival. Thus, the major ecological crisis is perhaps a chance to be seized – in order to expand the space of imaginations envisaged by the author. As Anders wrote, "the bomb has succeeded [...] where all philosophies, religions and empires had failed: it turned us into a humanity". Will he be proved right by the famous, very Hegelian, quote from the poet Hölderlin: "where the danger is, also grows the saving power"?

---

25 G. Anders, *De la Bombe et notre aveuglement face à l'apocalypse* [*The Bomb and our Blindness to the Apocalypse*], Titanic, 1995, p. 95 ("Ne possède que les choses dont les préceptes pourraient également devenir les propres maximes de ton action").

26 G. Anders, Interview with M. Greffath, Editions Allia, 6th edition, 2016.

27 *See* J.-M. Collin's essay #5 (this book) on "Treaty on the Prohibition of Nuclear Weapons: A Move Towards New Legal Action to Protect Future Generations"; A. Ware's essay #4 (this book) on "Nuclear Weapons and the Law for the Future: The Application of Principles Protecting Future Generations in International Tribunals".

28 B. Joy, "Why the Future doesn't need us", *Wired Magazine*, 4 Jan. 2000, *available online at* https://www.wired.com/2000/04/joy-2/.

Martin WALTER & Andreas NIDECKER

7. Effects of Ionizing Radiation – Evidence of Genetic Effects: Greater Risks for Transgenerational Damage

Introduction

Ionizing radiation can enter the nucleus and the body of any cell and can lead to cell death or cell damage. A damaged cell may repair itself or the cell damage may be passed on to subsequent generations if a genetic alteration has been brought about (Figs. 1 and 2).

Earlier Paradigm

There are various forms of ionizing radiation and all have the potential to cause damage. These forms differ in their impact on organic tissue. The most potent of the three types is gamma radiation. It can penetrate walls and human bodies and travels the longest distance (several meters). X-rays (which have essentially the same characteristics as gamma-rays) are used in a controlled manner by radiologists. The X-ray tube produces X-rays in order to create radiographs or do fluoroscopy. When the tube is switched off, radiation ceases to emanate from the X-ray machine. Lead-lined walls or lead aprons protect people from direct exposure to X-ray radiation during the procedure.

Among the radioactive so-called isotopes, Iodine-131 or Cesium-137 emit gamma rays which can be detected in a patient with a whole body counter. Alpha and beta particles emit radiation over a much shorter range and alpha particles may even be blocked by a sheet of paper. However, locally they have an equally strong effect on surrounding cells. This may be the case when these radionuclides enter the body of a living human, animal or plant. This can happen indirectly by eating, for example, contaminated fish or meat from animals which have grazed on contaminated pastures – such as the reindeer in Sweden following the Chernobyl accident. Strontium-90 is a beta emitter and behaves in the body like calcium. It "seeks out" bone where it settles and continues to radiate locally. This radiation has the potential to create bone tumors (Fig. 3) or leukemia.

One of the most dangerous substances is Plutonium-239. It has a very long half-life (the time in which it loses half of its radioactivity) of 24,000 years. A quantity as little as a few micrograms can cause lung cancer or cancer of

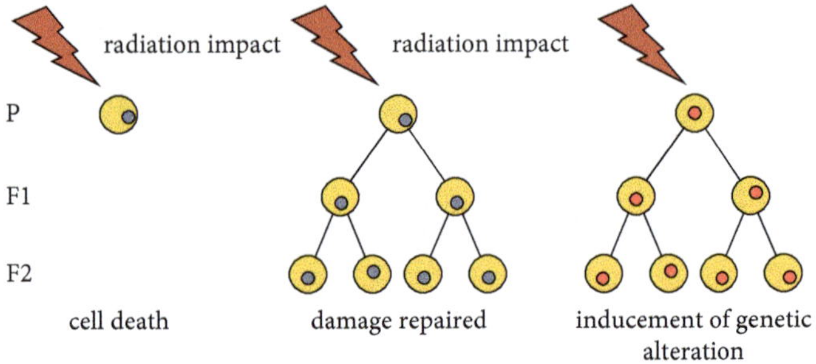

Fig. 1: *The clonal theory.* Source: Adapted from E.G. Wright, "Radiation-induced Genomic Instability and Bystander Effects: implications for radiation leukaemogenesis", International Scientific Conference on Childhood Leukaemia, Sep. 2004, London (powerpoint presentation), *available online at* http://cwl2004.powerwatch.org.uk/programme/speakers/day2-wright-pres.pdf.

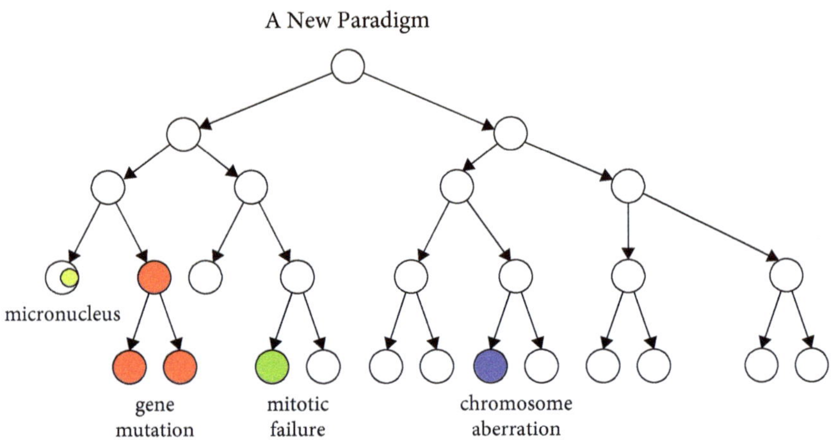

Fig. 2: *Genomic Instability*. Source: Adapted from E.G. Wright, 2004

F1 and F2 of the irradiated cell do not show visible damage, but subsequent generations begin to show signs of damage. White colored cells are normal cells. The damage is the consequence of so-called "bystander" effects on neighboring and distant cells and indicate genomic instability which is transferred to the germline and may be passed on to following generations.

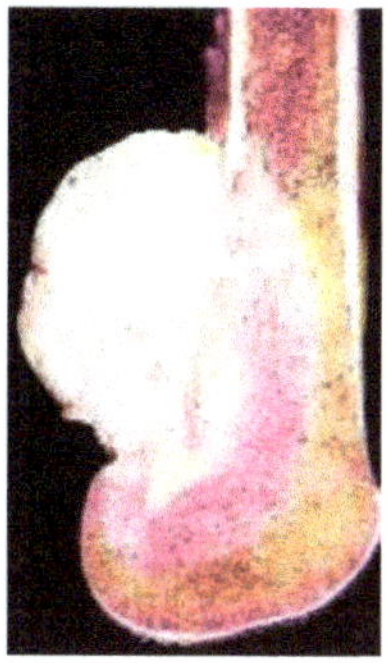

Fig. 3: *Histological slide of bone tumor (white mass) in the lower part of a femur.*
Source: Institute of Pathology, University of Basel.

the stomach. The risks and dangers of ionizing radiation were recently studied at a meeting in Ulm in October 2013.[1] Physicians, epidemiologists and other scientists reviewed the current data on the health effects of ionizing radiation but did not focus on the genetic effects. The data showed that all forms of ionizing radiation (background radiation, radiation used in medicine and radioactivity released in the civil and military nuclear industry) can cause epidemiologically measurable health effects. The findings of these studies make more realistic risk assessments possible. Additionally, the data indicate that there is no threshold below which radiation can be considered harmless. Even doses under 1 millisievert (mSv) can cause epidemiologically measurable health effects.[2] Other studies indicate, that even nuclear power plants in normal operation can cause quantifiable, adverse health effects.[3] If the concept of collective dose is used

1 International Physicians for the Prevention of Nuclear War, "Health effects of ionising radiation: Summary of expert meeting in Ulm, Germany, October 19th, 2013", *available online at* http://www.fukushima-disaster.de/information-in-english/information-on-radioactivity.html.

2 J.D. Mathews, A.V. Forsythe, Z. Brady, M.W. Butler & others, "Cancer risk in 680,000 people exposed to computed tomography scans in childhood or adolescence: data linkage study of 11 million Australians", *British Medical Journal*, 21 May 2013, Vol. 346, doi: 10.1136/bmj.f2360, *available online at* https://www.ncbi.nlm.nih.gov/pmc/articles/PMC3660619/.

3 P. Kaatsch, C. Spix, S. Schmiedel, R. Schulze-Rath & others, "Epidemiologische Studie zu Kinderkrebs in der Umgebung von Kernkraftwerken (KiKK-Studie)" [Epidemiological Study on Childhood Cancer in the Vicinity of Nuclear Power Plants (KiKK Study)],

in epidemiological studies, health risks of low-level radiation exposure can be reliably predicted and quantified.[4] One of the conclusions of the Ulm meeting was that the International Commission on Radiological Protection (ICRP) practice of using studies on Hiroshima and Nagasaki survivors as a basis for determining risk factors for low-level radiation has led to an under-estimation of the risk. Therefore, previous ICRP guidelines should be regarded as outdated and need to be revised.[5]

Known Effects of Chronic Internal Low-Level Ionizing Radiation

Leukemia is one of the most common types of cancer following exposure to radiation. It is usually diagnosed within 2 to 5 years following exposure and has been observed in the victims of the Hiroshima and Nagasaki atomic bombings[6] and in small children living in the vicinity of nuclear reactors.[7] Also extensively

---

Vorhaben 3602S04334, Deutsches Kinderkrebsregister, Mainz, Herausgegeben vom Bundesamt für Strahlenschutz (BfS), Salzgitter, 2007.

4 M.S. Pearce, J.A. Salotti, M.P. Little, K. McHugh & others, "Radiation exposure from CT scans in childhood and subsequent risk of leukaemia and brain tumours: a retrospective cohort study", *The Lancet*, 2012, Vol. 380, Issue 9840, pp. 499–505, *available online at* https://europepmc.org/articles/pmc3418594; D.L. Miglioretti, E. Johnson, A. Williams, R.T. Greenlee & others, "The Use of Computed Tomography in Pediatrics and the Associated Radiation Exposure and Estimated Cancer Risk", *JAMA Pediatrics*, 10 June 2013, Vol. 167, No. 8, pp. 700–707, doi:10.1001/jamapediatrics.2013.311, *available online at* https://jamanetwork.com/journals/jamapediatrics/articlepdf/1696279/poi130056.pdf; D.A. Pierce & D.L. Preston, "Radiation-Related Cancer Risks at Low Doses among Atomic Bomb Survivors", *Radiation Research*, 2000, Vol. 154, No. 2, pp. 178–186.

5 International Commission on Radiological Protection, Publication 103, "The 2007 Recommendations of the International Commission on Radiological Protection", 2007, Vol. 37, pp. 2–4.

6 Committee for the Compilation of Materials on Damage Caused by the Atomic Bombs in Hiroshima and Nagasaki, *Hiroshima and Nagasaki: The Physical, Medical, and Social Effects of the Atomic Bombings*, translated by E. Ishikaa & D.L. Swain, New York Basic Books, 1981.

7 A. Köerblein, "Kinderleukämie um Kernkraft-werke: Neue episdemiologische Studie aus Frankreich" [Childhood Leukemia around Nuclear Power Plants: New Epidemiological Study from France], *Strahlentelex mit ElektrosmogReport*, 2 Feb. 2012, Vol. 26, No. 602–603, ISSN 0931-4288, *available online at* http://www.strahlentelex.de/Stx_12_602_S01-03.pdf.

documented are carcinomas of the thyroid gland in children and thyroiditis following exposure to radiation[8] in populations where no attempts were made by the authorities to protect the thyroid gland with iodine tablets following a nuclear accident.[9] As documented above, solid cancers may develop years after irradiation occurs. All parts of the body may be affected, the most common being stomach, bone, kidneys, lungs and pancreas.

Less well-known effects of ionizing radiation in contaminated regions may also be observed. These include non-cancerous diseases such as cesium cardiomyopathy[10] and vascular diseases involving large and small vessels such as the coronary arteries and the small arteries of the retina.[11] There are also many reports on harmful effects of ionizing radiation on the brain, and some authors see a relation to certain mental disorders.[12]

---

8 E. Cardis & others, "Cancer consequences of the Chernobyl accident: 20 years on", *Journal of Radiological protection*, June 2006, Vol. 26, No. 2, pp. 127–140; F. Pacini & others, "Thyroid consequences of the Chernobyl nuclear accident", *Acta Paediatra Supplementum*, Dec. 1999, Vol. 88, Issue s433, pp. 23–27.

9 World Health Organization, Technical brief, "Use of potassium iodide for thyroid protection during nuclear or radiological emergencies", 31 Mar. 2011, *available online at* http://www.who.int/ionizing_radiation/pub_meet/tech_briefings/potassium_iodide/en/.

10 G.S. Bandazhevskaya & others, "Relationship between Caesium (^{137}Cs) load, cardiovascular symptoms, and source of food in 'Chernobyl' children – preliminary observations after intake of oral apple pectin", *Swiss Medical Weekly*, 18 Dec. 2004, No. 134(49–50), pp. 725–729.

11 P. Fedirko, V. Sakovich & N. Garkava, "Vascular Pathology of an eye and the threat of developing age-related macular degeneration after radiation exposed", *Eureka: Health Science*, Nov. 2017, No. 6, pp. 3–9; L. Spielberg, P. Potter & A. Leys, "Chapter 58. Radiation Retinopathy", *in RETINA*, S.J. Ryan, R.S. Srini, D.R. Hinton, A.P. Schachat, C.P. Wilkinson & P. Wiedemann (eds.), 2013, pp. 1083 -1090.

12 European Committee on Radiation Risks, *2010 Recommendations of the European Committee on Radiation Risk. The Health Effects of Exposure to Low Doses of Ionizing Radiation*, C. Busby, R. Bertell, I. Schmitz-Feuerhake, M. Scott Cato & A. Yablokov (eds.), Green Audit, 2010, p. 141 & pp. 163–172; D. Green-Schloesser, M.E. Robbin, A.M. Pfeiffer & others, "Radiation-induced brain injury: a review", *Frontiers in Oncology*, 19 July 2012, *available online at* https://doi.org/10.3389/fonc.2012.00073/full; K.N. Loganovsky, S.V. Volovik, K.G. Manton & others, "Whether ionising radiation is a risk factor for schizophrenia spectrum disorders?", *The World Journal of Biological Psychiatry*, 2005, Vol. 6, Issue 4, pp. 212–230.

Genetic Effects

Genetic effects in children of irradiated parents are a matter of some dispute in the radiation literature.[13] In the Live Span Study of the Radiation Effects Research Foundation (RERF), only minimal effects could be identified in the children of the surviving nuclear bomb victims.[14] More recent papers, however, do indicate that genetic effects may be found following exposure to low-level radiation.[15] There is also a body of papers available which show effects of low-level radiation in animals, and some of them will be referenced below.

Early Studies of Genetic Damage Resulting from Ionizing Radiation

In 1927, Hermann J. Muller was the first to produce genetic effects in fruit flies by using ionizing radiation. His experiments earned him the Nobel Prize for Physiology and Medicine in 1947.[16] Muller was an outspoken scientist and even in those early years warned that ionizing radiation could have effects on the most important "asset" of human beings, namely our genetic material. After the atomic bombing of Hiroshima and Nagasaki in 1945 initial studies did not reveal any significant radiation effects on the genome of the children of the survivors.[17] For this reason, discussions of any such effects were considered controversial and rather played down at the time by science.[18]

Mutation studies are difficult to perform because phenotypical events and spontaneous mutations in fruit flies are rare in nature. By using X-rays, however,

---

13 O. Handt, M. Krings, R.H. Ward & S. Pääbo, "The retrieval of ancient human DNA sequences", *The American Journal of Human Genetics*, 1996, Vol. 59, Issue 2, pp. 368–376; V.N. James & W.J. Schull (eds.), *The Children of Atomic Bomb Survivors: A Genetic Study*, National Academies Press, 1991.

14 V.N. James & W.J. Schull, 1991.

15 J.D. Matthews & others, 2013; M.S. Pearce & others, 2012; D.L. Miglioretti & others, 2013.

16 J.M. Hermann, "Artificial transmutation of the gene", *Science*, 1927, Vol. 66, pp. 84–87.

17 *European Committee on Radiation Risk*, 2010.

18 D. Sumner, T.E. Wheldon & W. Watson (eds.), *Radiation risks: an evaluation*, Tarragon Press, 1990; ICRP [International Commission on Radiological Protection] Publication 103, "The 2007 Recommendations of the International Commission on Radiological Protection", 2007, Vol. 37, pp. 2–4; Publications of the Radiation Research Foundation, *available online at* http://www.rerf.jp/library/archives_e/lsstitle.html.

Fig. 4: *Normal fruit fly on the left. Phenotypical aberration on the right (lack of wings).* Source: https://bugscope.beckman.illinois.edu/pdfs/insects/mutant.pdf.

Fig. 5: *Genetic effects in barn swallows.* Sources: T.A. Mousseau (c) 2006 (left and middle pictures); T.A. Mousseau (c) 2005 (right picture).

Picture on the left shows a normal bird, with proper plumage. Middle picture shows a bird with genetic mutations, displaying albinism and thinner plumage.

Picture on the right shows animal with asymmetrical wings and tail.

Muller was able to produce large numbers of phenotypically visible mutations that showed for the first time that X-rays could have such an effect (Fig. 4).

Some Studies from the Chernobyl Region

Due to the faster reproduction cycles of many animals, genetic effects are more easily seen in animals such as barn swallows (hirundo rustica). Studies in the Chernobyl region have demonstrated a loss of physical fitness in these birds. They have also been found to exhibit partial albinism, microcephaly, morphological abnormalities in feathers and wings (Fig. 5), a reduction in reproductive

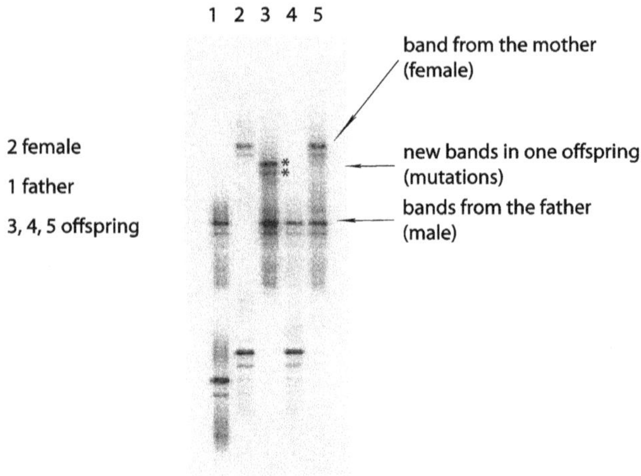

Fig. 6: *Examples of microsatellite germline mutations in three offspring (columns 3, 4 and 5) from barn swallows (father and mother, columns 1 and 2).* Source: Adapted from H. Ellegren & others, 1997.

The new bands (marked red) indicate a mutation in one offspring.

capacity and premature death.[19] Partial albinism has additionally been observed even in mammals in the Fukushima region.

It is possible that the partial albinism of cattle has the same origin as that of the swallows. Besides those phenotypical aberrations, Ellegren & others[20] have found increased mutation rates in the so-called microsatellite genome in the offspring of breeding barn swallows, by carrying out genetic studies in whole blood samples taken from the birds (Fig. 6). Swallows in Northern and Central Italy, and from uncontaminated areas in the former Soviet Union, did not show such pathologies.[21] Since 2012

19 A.P. Møller, A. Bonisoli-Alquati & T.A. Mousseau, "High frequency of albinism and tumours in free-living birds around Chernobyl", *Mutation Research,* 18 Sep. 2013, Vol. 757, Issue 1, pp. 52–59, doi: 10.1093/jhered/esu040; T.A. Mousseau & A.P. Møller, "Genetic and Ecological Studies of Animals in Chernobyl and Fukushima", *The Journal of Heredity,* 1 Sep. 2014, Vol. 105, Issue 5, pp. 704–709, *available online at* https://academic.oup.com/jhered/article/105/5/704/2961808.

20 H. Ellegren, G. Lindgren, C.R. Primmer & A.P. Møller, "Fitness loss and germline mutations in barn swallows breeding in Chernobyl", *Nature,* 9 Oct. 1997, Vol. 389, No. 6651, pp. 593–596, doi: 10.1038/39303.

21 *Ibid.*

Fig. 7: *Zizeeria maha, pale grass butterfly.* Source: https://en.wikipedia.org/wiki/Pseudozizeeria_maha.

this partial albinism has also been seen in the vicinity of Fukushima among swallows and cattle.

Studies from the Fukushima Region

Following the nuclear catastrophe on 11 March 2011 (due to an earthquake followed by a tsunami), large amounts of radioactive isotopes were released into the environment, leading to widespread contamination of the biosphere. An environment was thus created which allowed research into the effects of low-level radiation on the fauna and flora. Yamato Shijimi (Zizeeria maha, pale blue grass butterfly) (Fig. 7) is widely distributed in Japan, and was therefore selected as an environmental indicator and model by a scientific group at the Ryukyus University in Okinawa, in the uncontaminated far south of Japan.[22] By May 2011 these researchers had collected 144 hatched butterflies. Their larvae had managed to survive the winter close to the ground and received nourishment from leaves of contaminated oxalis corniculata (sorrel), a plant which grows widely in

22 A. Hiyama, C. Nohara, S. Kinjo, W. Taira, S. Gima, A. Tanahara & J.M. Otaki, "The biological impacts of the Fukushima nuclear accident on the pale grass blue butterfly", *Scientific Reports,* 2012, Vol. 2, Article no. 570, doi: 10.1038/srep00570, *available online at* https://www.nature.com/articles/srep00570; A. Hiyama, C. Nohara, W. Taira, S. Kinjo, M. Iwata & J.M. Otaki, "The Fukushima nuclear accident and the pale grass blue butterfly: evaluating biological effects of long-term low-dose exposures", *BMC Evolutionary Biology*, 2013, Vol. 13, pp. 13–25, *available online at* http://www.biomedcentral.com/1471-2148/13/168.

Fig. 8: *Study concept relating to the blue grass pale butterfly after the Fukushima disaster.* Source: A. Hiyama & others, 2012.

Japan and which does not grow higher than 10 cm. Z. maha is monophagous and this plant is the sole source of nourishment for these butterflies.

The living butterflies were immediately transported to Okinawa, which had not been affected by radioactive contamination (Fig. 8). Measurements of radioactivity at the individual catchment sites were made and gamma doses between 0.09 to 3.09 μSv/h were found. In this manner, in a clean environment, eggs were harvested from the females and reared to generation F1. The butterflies were reared separately according to the location from which they had originally been

Fig. 9: *Morphological damage in F1 and F2 butterfly generations.* Source: A. Hiyama & others, 2012.

collected. Later, they were mated according to different criteria,[23] and the generation F2 was reared. F1 and F2 follow-up generations were all subsequently examined in Okinawa.

Although there were already minor dysplastic changes in the original butterflies taken from Fukushima, morphological damage was much more evident in generations F1 and F2. There were changes in the wing length, in the pattern of the spots, the appendages, eyes and there were tumours on the chest. Furthermore, delayed hatching and reduced life expectancy were observed. A very important point was that the pathologies in the wing spot pattern were again seen in the F2 generation (Fig. 9).

In order to test their hypothesis that ionizing radiation and not other environmental influences were the cause of the increased trans-generational damage in F1 and F2, the researchers collected healthy butterflies from non-contaminated areas in Japan and exposed these to external radiation and to oxalis leaves from contaminated and non-contaminated regions. It was then possible to demonstrate the identical changes as compared to the butterflies collected in the originally contaminated environment of Fukushima. For the purpose of analysis, an overall abnormality rate (OAR) was calculated and statistically defined. In generation P (parents), butterflies originally collected in Fukushima, (which had been exposed through external or internal radiation due to eating contaminated leaves in their larval stage), there were 12.4% to 13.2% abnormality rates. The

23 A. Hiyama & others, 2012.

Tab. 1: *Abnormality rate of Zizeeria maha.* Source: A. Hiyama & others, 2012.

Overall abnormality rate (OAR) of adults	
Adult samples	OAR (%)
Field-caut P generation in May (7 localities)*	12.4
Field-caut P generation in May (10 localities)	13.2
F1 from the May samples (8 localities)	18.3
F2 from the May samples (6 localities, 9 strains	33.5
Field-caut P generation in September (7 localities)*	28.1
F1 from the September samples (6 localities including Kobe)	51.9
F1 from the September samples (5 localities excluding Kobe)	60.2
External radiation exposure	31.7
Control (no exposure)	16.7
Internal radiation (excluding the Ube samples)	39.6
Internal radiation (excluding the Ube samples)	24.5
*can be compared directly	

original collection in 2011 was done during May and September. In generations F1 and F2, the rate of abnormality increased significantly, even though the animals were fed and raised in a clean environment, indicating trans-generational damage had taken place. The results are shown in Tab. 1. As the genome of Zizeeria maha has not been sequenced yet, no mutation analyses in the DNA of the damaged butterflies can be made, as was possible for the swallow study by Ellegren & others.

Whether or not albinism even in livestock (Fig. 10) is related to environmental nuclear contamination has not been conclusively proven, even though farmers in the Fukushima region report never having seen such white spots in their own animals.[24]

24 T.A. Mousseau & A.P. Møller, "Biological Consequences of Chernobyl and Fukushima" (powerpoint presentation), *available online at* http://www.chernobylcongress.org/fileadmin/user_upload/Arnoldshain_Doku/Mousseau_March2014-small.pdf.

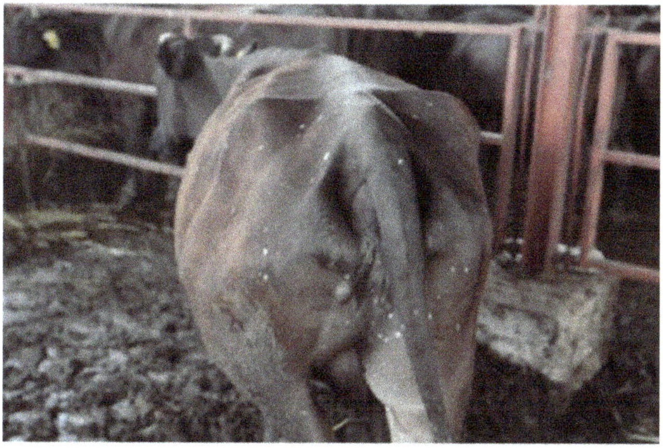

Fig. 10: *Cow from a farm in the Fukushima prefecture with white spots on fur, indicating the possibility of radiation induced albinism.* Source: T.A. Mousseau & A.P. Møller, 2014.

Is Genetic Damage in Humans Possible and Can It Be Passed on to Following Generations?

The Sellafield Story

In Cumbria, England at the Windscale nuclear reprocessing site (later renamed Sellafield), Yorkshire Television in 1983 broadcast the film "Windscale: the Nuclear Laundry". This documentary highlighted, for the first time, a disturbingly high rate of childhood leukaemia among people living in Seascale, a village next to the plant.[25] The official report by Sir Black and his advisory committee confirmed that the incidences of leukemia and Non-Hodgkin-Lymphoma (NHL) were abnormally high in that region. Black suggested further studies be done and Gardner and colleagues found, in a case control study in 1990, that, with regard to leukemia and NHL, the relative risk (RR) for children of fathers working at the Sellafield nuclear plant and receiving a total pre-conception ionizing radiation dose of 100 mSv or more, was 6.24 (Tab. 2). As one would normally expect a non-radiation value of 1.0, this may be regarded as significantly

25 Sir Douglas Black (ed.), *Investigation of the possible increased incidence of cancer in West Cumbria. Report of the Independent Advisory Group,* Stationery Office Books, 1984.

Tab. 2: *Increased relative risk (RR) for children of fathers working at the Sellafield nuclear plant and receiving a total pre-conceptional ionizing radiation dose of 100 mSv or more.* Source: Adapted from M.J. Gardner & others, 1990.

LNHL (leukemia and non-Hodgkin Lymphoma) 66 cases (<25 yrs old people) and preconception dose of Sellafield workers in West Cumbria, U.K.	
Dosis (mSv)	Relative risk (area controls)
1-49	1.06
50-99	1.16
≧100	6.24

elevated.[26] Gardner's hypothesis could not be confirmed in recent studies, but there is no other immediately apparent explanation for the elevated rates of leukemia and NHL in children and young adults.

In another separate epidemiological study at Sellafield, Dr. Louise Parker & others found a significant risk correlation of babies being stillborn and the fathers' total exposure to external ionizing radiation prior to conception, which once again, would indicate a trans-generational pathway.[27]

26 M.J. Gardner, M.P. Snee, A.J. Hall, C.A. Powell, S. Downes & J.D. Terrell, "Results of case-control study of leukaemia and lymphoma among young people near Sellafield nuclear plant in West Cumbria", *British Medical Journal,* 17 Feb. 1990, Vol. 300, pp. 423–429, *available online at* https://pdfs.semanticscholar.org/d70b/e3ce2fc5b1491787ffb7b2b8788c3f4cf8dc.pdf; M.J. Gardner, A.J. Hall, M.P. Snee, S. Downes, C.A. Powell & J.D. Terrell, "Methods and basic data of case-control study of leukaemia and lymphoma among young people near Sellafield nuclear plant in West Cumbria", *British Medical Journal,* 17 Feb. 1990, Vol. 300, pp. 429–34, *available online at* https://pdfs.semanticscholar.org/6f1d/60df800beed2d471831a142afef3330c1ce7.pdf.

27 L. Parker, M.S. Pearce, H.O. Dickinson, M. Aitkin & A.W. Craft, "Stillbirths among offspring of male radiation workers at Sellafield nuclear reprocessing plant", *The Lancet,* 23 Oct. 1999, Vol. 354, Issue 9188, pp. 1407–1414, doi: https://doi.org/10.1016/S0140-6736(99)04138-0.

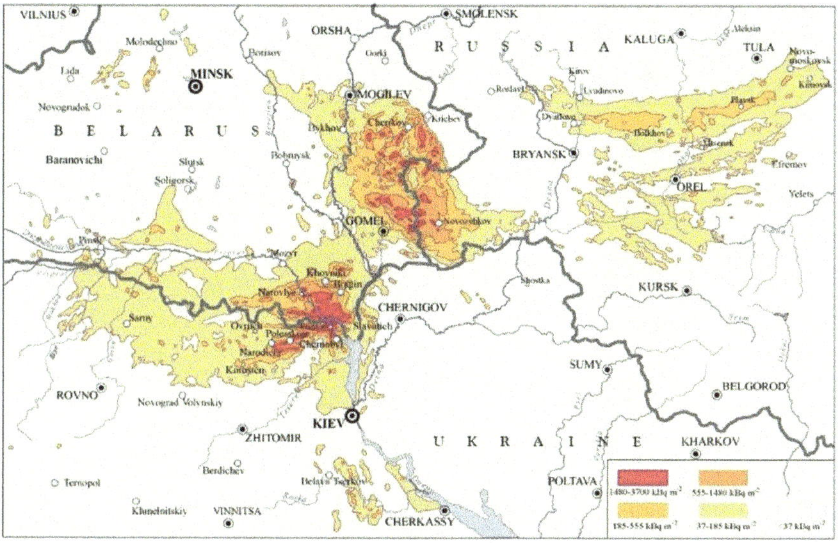

Fig. 11: *Contamination of the Mogilev Region.* Source: United Nations Scientific Committee on the Effects of Atomic Radiation (UNSCEAR), Maps of radionuclide deposition, Fig. VI, *available online at* http://www.unscear.org/unscear/en/chernobylmaps.html

Mutations in the Minisatellite Genome

In 1996, Dubrova & others published a paper which showed an increased rate of mutations in the minisatellite[28] genome.[29] Children, who had been born between February and September 1994 in the Mogilev region (Fig. 11), whose fathers and

28 A minisatellite is a tract of repetitive DNA in which certain DNA motifs (ranging in length from 10–60 base pairs) are typically repeated 5–50 times. Minisatellites occur at more than 1,000 locations in the human genome and they are notable for their high mutation rate and high diversity in the population. Minisatellites are prominent in the centromeres and telomeres of chromosomes, the latter protecting the chromosomes from damage. The name "satellite" refers to the early observation that centrifugation of genomic DNA in a test tube separates a prominent layer of bulk DNA from accompanying "satellite" layers of repetitive DNA. Minisatellites and their shorter cousins, the microsatellites, together are classified as VNTR (variable number of tandem repeats) DNA. Confusingly, minisatellites are often referred to as VNTRs, and microsatellites are often referred to as short tandem repeats (STRs) or simple sequence repeats (SSRs).

29 Y.E. Dubrova, V.N. Nesterov, N.G. Krouchinsky, V.A. Ostapenko, R. Neumann, D.L. Neil & A.J. Jeffreys, "Human minisatellite mutation rate after the Chernobyl accident", *Nature*, 25 Apr. 1996, Vol. 380, Issue 6576, pp. 683–686.

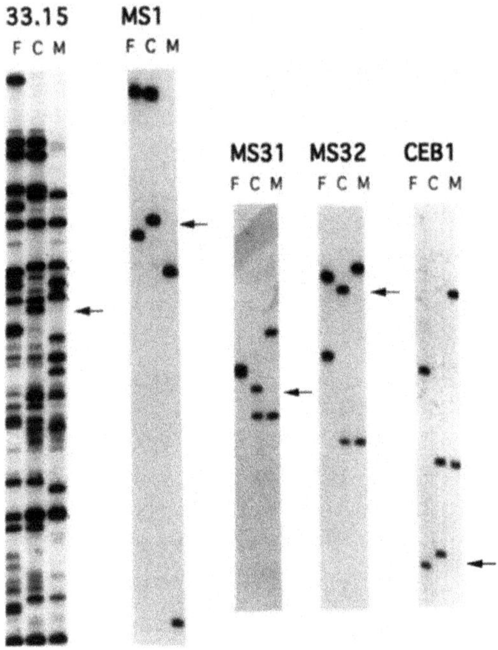

Fig. 12: *Examples of human minisatellite germline mutation.* Source: Y.E. Dubrova & others, 1996.

DNA profiles were produced for each father (F), child (C) and mother (M) using probes 33.15, MS1, MS31, MS32 and CEB1. New mutant bands are arrowed.

mothers had always lived in the villages of Bykhov, Krasnopolye and Cherikov, were examined by means of DNA fingerprinting (Fig. 12). They were compared with a control of group of sex- and age-matched children from non-contaminated regions in England. By correlating the level of ground contamination with the mutation rates in the two groups the researchers discovered, on average, a twofold increase in the mutation rate of the minisatellite genome (Tab. 3). Using the same method, children from survivors in Hiroshima and Nagasaki were tested. However, in those children, no increased mutation rates were found. This nevertheless raises an important question.

Could a low dosage rate through long term internal contamination by consumption of contaminated food be more dangerous than the genetic effects following an acute evet involving external ionizing radiation caused by a nuclear bomb or catastrophe?

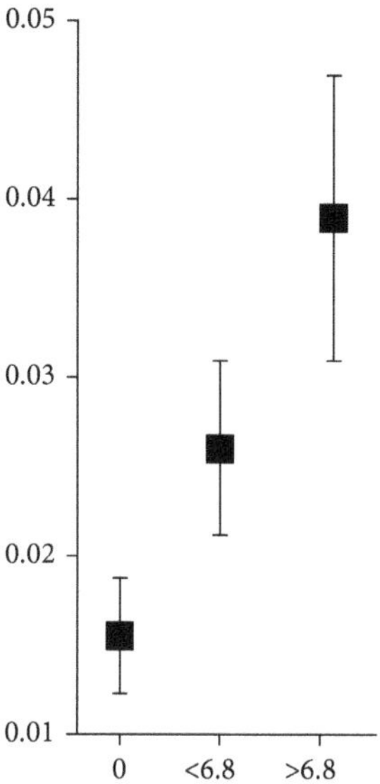

mutation rate per band (controls)	0.0154	twofold increase of the mutation rate in Mogilev children versus UK controls
mutation rate per band (exposed)	0.0303	

Curie (Ci) / km^{-2}

^{137}Cs surface contamination (6.8 Ci km^{-2} = 251.6 Bq m^{-2}) correlates with mutation rate

Tab. 3: ^{137}*Cs surface contamination correlates with mutation rate.* Source: Adapted from Y.E. Dubrova & others, 1996.

It should be acknowledged that Dubrova's work has been criticized for the fact that the control group was from England. However, due to the widespread contamination of Belarus no other control group was available. It would have been difficult to find families living in an uncontaminated part of Belarus. According to the authors, in all examples the trans-generational effects of ionizing radiation were clearly identified.

Children of Nuclear "Liquidators"

Weinberg & others examined the children of fathers who, following the nuclear catastrophe of Chernobyl, had worked on cleaning up the contaminated site and had experienced frequent exposure to high levels of ionizing radiation. The children of those men, born before the accident, were compared with children conceived and born after the accident. These authors examined the minisatellite genome using a similar method to that of Dubrova. These authors found a significant increase in the mutation rate, namely a seven-fold increase in new bands in the children born after the accident as compared to their siblings born before.

Weinberg & others also regard a germline mutation in the fathers as the origin of these subsequent mutations. They saw that the ionizing radiation has had transgenerational consequences.[30]

Conclusion

There is now ample evidence produced by sophisticated newly available research methods into genetic effects of ionizing radiation. Insects were once thought to be resistant to radiation. New scientific studies on butterflies in Japan have demonstrated the contrary as has been documented in several papers.[31] Furthermore, studies in the regions of Chernobyl and Fukushima have provided evidence of genetic mutations in birds and observed partial albinism both in birds and cattle in those regions where the worst nuclear power plant catastrophes have taken place.

Studies of human populations in the Mogilev region close to Chernobyl, involving descendants of nuclear power plant operators in England and liquidators of the Chernobyl fire, conclusively document a clear increase in mutations in children conceived and born after the return home of those brave people, compared with children born prior to the catastrophe.

We conclude that available epidemiological studies prove, without doubt, that ionizing radiation has the potential to cause significant damage to the human germline and needs to be addressed. Compared with short term external radiation, this seems particularly to be the case in situations of long-term exposure to internal radiation in humans and animals living in or near contaminated regions.

In our opinion, with regard to these risks, the precautionary principle[32] should be strictly adhered to. New legal bases need to be established globally for the protection of future generations. A new standard in human rights legislation is called for.

---

30 H.S. Weinberg, A.B. Korol, V.M. Kirzhner, A. Avivi, T. Fahima, E. Nevo, S. Shapiro, G. Rennert, O. Piatak, E.I. Stepanova & E. Skvarskaja, "Very high mutation rate in offspring of Chernobyl accident liquidators", *Proceedings of the Royal Society of London, Series B: Biological Sciences,* 22 May 2001, Vol. 268, Issue 1471, pp. 1001–1005, *available online at* https://rampages.us/vcugenetics/wp-content/uploads/sites/4855/2015/01/WeinbergEtAl2001.pdf.

31 A.P. Møller & others, 2013; T.A. Mousseau & A.P. Møller, 2014; H. Ellegren & others, 1997.

32 World Commission on the Ethics of Scientific Knowledge and Technology, Report, *The Precautionary Principle,* United Nations Educational, Scientific and Cultural Organization, 2005.

PART 3. PROTECTING FUTURE GENERATIONS THROUGH CLIMATE JUSTICE LITIGATION

In the third Part of the book, we explore the protection of future generations through Climate Justice Litigation. Undoubtedly, we are observing a historical call for Climate justice all around the world.

Attorney Christian Huglo is famous for having paved the way in environmental justice litigation. He has been devoted to the defense of important litigation such as Amoco Cadiz. We are living a Global Legal Revolution that Attorney Huglo describes through several examples of global warming cases brought into National Courts. Something very particular and special is at stake: We have entered the era of Climate Justice. This asks us to think out of the box. Two main types of Climate Litigation can be identified: Legal action against States and others against companies. He emphasized the specificity of the Our Children's Trust Climate Change litigation in the U.S. It necessarily generates a Legal Revolution on the application of procedural and substantive rules (essay #8 on "Global Warming and the National Courts: A Global Legal Revolution?").

Attorney Elizabeth Brown, Professor John Davidson and former Global Program Coordinator Danny Noonan provide a clear explanation of the roots concerning the Public Trust Doctrine at the core of the Our Children's Trust Climate litigation. They first provide an overview of Climate litigation, then explain the Public Trust Doctrine as applied in and outside the United States. The Juliana v. United States case *is then described. It is a privilege to share their analysis from the inside. The goal is no more or less than Securing the Legal Right to a Healthy Atmosphere and Stable Climate for the Benefit of All Present and Future Generations (essay #9 on "Securing the Legal Right to a Healthy Atmosphere and Stable Climate for the Benefit of All Present and Future Generations").*

Professor Agnès Michelot is at the Head of the French Association for Environmental Law and as such is rapporteur of two reports on Climate Justice. The first was delivered to the French Environmental, Social and Economic Counsil (CESE) and the second to the European Economic and Social Committee. Professor Michelot provides an analysis of Climate Justice from International Law to French Perspectives. She explains how the Right of Future Generations to a preserved environment is enriching the very concept of dignity and also provides the basis for the concept of Ecological Integrity. Undoubtedly, Climate Justice seeks Justice for Future Generations. New legal principles can lead to this goal, such as the principle of non-regression and the principle of ecological solidarity (essay #10 on "Climate Justice for the Future Generations: from International to French Perspectives").

Christian HUGLO[1]

8. Global Warming and the National Courts: A Global Legal Revolution?

Climate litigation has come to fill the legal *vacuum* left by the traditional approach of international law – which, officially, only takes into account essential treaty law and decisions of the International Court of Justice in The Hague. As it stands, this court cannot institute effective legal protection of the global climate. However, we have entered a new epoch called the Anthropocene.

In this new era, the office of judge has changed; judges must now consider and provide justice on global and transgenerational issues. The role of the national court is traditionally subordinate to the rule of the three unities: time, place and action. Today, these courts are confronted with the question of preventing and anticipating damage caused by all to all – with approximately 900 climate litigation cases to date and counting (in the United States, Australia, India, Belgium, Norway, Austria, South Africa, etc.). The first type of litigation includes the non-contentious cases involving environmental impact studies. The second type aims to put in issue the responsibility of States, with two variants: annulment of decisions and the possibility for the court to replace the State by means of proceedings for failure to act. The third and final type of litigation concerns the liability of companies for their share of responsibility for global warming. For example, the action brought by a Peruvian farmer against a German company provides an interesting illustration in addition to cases involving climate refugees.

We shall therefore examine the following in order: first, the field and forms of climate litigation (*see* Part I below); and second, how national courts are addressing the subject in a revolutionary way, with respect as much to the traditional application as to the traditional substance of the rules of procedure (*see* Part II below).

---

1 In conjunction with Chancia Plaine, jurist at the Huglo Lepage Avocats lawyers' office. Attorney Huglo recently published a book that provides an in-depth study of climate justice litigation. See C. Huglo, *Le contentieux climatique : une révolution judiciaire mondiale* [Climate Litigation: A Global Judicial Revolution], éditions Bruylant, 2018.

I. The Field and Forms of Climate Litigation.

In the absence of global solutions due to the current impossibility of creating an effective international jurisdiction, it is to the national jurisdictions that one must turn (*see* Section I.A. below). The national litigation in the United States of America is a particularly complex situation (*see* Section I.B. below).

A. The Two Main Types of Climate Litigation

In 2015, Professor Meredith Wilensky (former Associate Director of the *Sabin Center for Climate Change Law*),[2] followed up the work of professors David Markell (*Florida State University College of Law*) and J. B. Ruhl (*Vanderbilt University Law School*) on the classification of legal actions arising from climate litigation,[3] with legal actions against the States on the one hand (*see* subsection I.A.1. below) and, on the other hand, legal actions against companies (*see* subsection I.A.2. below). It is in the light of this classification that national climate litigation will be analyzed.

1. Legal Action Against States

According to the conclusions of a search of the "Non U.S. Climate Change Litigation Chart",[4] which covers all disputes tried to date outside the United States, four types of legal action taken against the State have been identified. Firstly, there are those relating to adaptation and/or mitigation measures; secondly, those relating to the obligation to estimate environmental impact taking into account the foreseeable climatic upheaval dimension; thirdly, actions that center around fundamental rights such as human rights; and, finally, actions that involve climate science itself.

Between the years 2012-2015, no legal action relating to adaptation or mitigation measures had been brought before the federal courts in the United States. Linked to the proximity of the United Nations Framework Convention on Climate Change conference of the parties (COP) held 21 November 2015

2 M. Wilensky, "Climate Change In The Courts: An Assessment Of Non-U.S. Climate Litigation", *Duke Environmental Law & Policy Forum*, Fall 2015, Vol. 26, p. 131, note.

3 *Ibid.*, pp. 135–137 (discussing D. Markell & J.B. Ruhl, "An Empirical Assessment of Climate Change in the Courts: A New Jurisprudence or Business as Usual?", *Florida Law Review*, 2012, Vol. 64, pp. 15–86).

4 Sabin Center for Climate Change Law, "Non U.S. Climate Change Litigation Chart", *available online at* http://climatecasechart.com/non-us-climate-change-litigation/ (accessed 14 June 2019).

in Paris, the successes of the climate cases against *Urgenda* in the Netherlands and *Leghari* in Pakistan inspired citizens of other nations. In turn, these citizens instituted legal proceedings for the first time arguing that the mitigation and adaptation measures prescribed by regulations governing greenhouse gas emissions were inadequate in the face of climate change.

A perfect illustration of litigation relating to mitigation and adaptation is the *Urgenda* case, in which the Dutch judge specifically pronounced with regard to adaptation that "[t]he dispute between the Parties [...] does not concern the need for mitigation but rather the pace, or the level, at which the State needs to start reducing greenhouse gas emissions".[5] The court concluded that the Dutch State had a duty to take climate change mitigation measures, explaining that in view of the "severity of the problem of hazardous climate change, climate scientists have investigated with which degree of probability current human actions have negative or positive effects on future climate change".[6] According to the Swiss plaintiffs, the government did not heed the emission reductions required to comply with the objective of keeping the global temperature increase below 2°C. Another illustrative case is *In re Court on its own Motion v. State of Himachal Pradesh & others* delivered on 9 May 2016 in India,[7] based on Article 21 under the Constitution of India. The National Green Tribunal ordered the government of Himachal Pradesh to impose a series of traffic restrictions and to undertake a reforestation program, with the aim of reducing greenhouse gas emissions and remedying diverse environmental damage; the Indian judge did not issue an injunction against the Himachal Pradesh province requiring mitigation of global warming.

An examination of legal actions arising from compulsory environmental impact studies that take global warming into account is also of some interest. The mechanism of the environmental impact study came from the United States[8]

---

5 *Urgenda Foundation v. Kingdom of the Netherlands*, Case No. C/09/456689/HA ZA 131396, The Hague District Court, 24 June 2015, paragraph 4.32, *available online at* http://blogs2.law.columbia.edu/climate-change-litigation/wp-content/uploads/sites/16/non-us-case-documents/2015/20150624_2015-HAZA-C0900456689_decision.pdf (accessed 7 January 2020).

6 *Ibid.*, paragraph 4.19.

7 *In re Court on its own Motion v. State of Himachal Pradesh & others*, Application No. 237 (T_{HC}) of 2013, National Green Tribunal (India), 9 May 2016, *available online at* http://climatecasechart.com/non-us-case/in-re-court-on-its-own-motion-v-state-of-himachal-pradesh-and-others/?cn-reloaded=1 (accessed 14 June 2019).

8 C. Huglo & C. Constantin, "Comment apprécier la portée de la réforme du droit des études d'impact issue du décret du 29 décembre 2011 au regard du droit de l'Union

following the adoption of the National Environmental Policy Act (NEPA).[9] NEPA obligates environmental studies on the effects of a project, followed by a public discussion in the presence of those responsible for the project with a view to mitigating or correcting the project's foreseeable effects. A case that came up on the African continent was one of the first successes[10] of climate litigation: *Earthlife Africa Johannesburg v. Minister of Environmental Affairs*,[11] before the Supreme Court of South Africa, where EarthLife Africa Association contested approval by the Ministry of Environmental Affairs for a 1200 MW Thabametsi coal-fired power plant project to operate in the province of Limpopo until 2060.[12] The High Court of Pretoria ordered that the validation of the Thabametsi project be subject to the condition that an assessment of the consequences of climate change impact be carried out within a six-month deadline.

Legal action constituting an invocation of human rights based on the fundamental right to a healthy and ecologically balanced environment is classified as a third generation right.[13] This category of rights was notably enshrined in Article 24 of the African Charter on Human and Peoples' Rights,[14] which states that "All peoples shall have the right to a general satisfactory environment favourable to their development".[15] Three other climate litigation cases that involved human rights claims also merit mention. In chronological order, two disputes went to

---

européenne ?" [How to Assess the Scope of the Reform of the Law of Impact Studies Resulting from the Decree of 29 December 2011 with regard to European Law], *in Environnement et Développement*, Apr. 2012, p. 9.

9 National Environmental Policy Act of 1969, United States Code, Vol. 42, sections 4321 to 4370m-12.

10 T. Khan, "How climate change battles are increasingly being fought and won in court", *The Guardian*, 8 Mar. 2017, *available online at* www.theguardian.com/environment/2017/mar/08/how-climate-change-battles-are-increasingly-being-fought-and-won-in-court (accessed 14 June 2019).

11 *Earthlife Africa Johannesburg v. Minister of Environmental Affairs & others*, Case. No 65662/16, High Court of South Africa (Pretoria), 8 Mar. 2017, *available online at* http://blogs2.law.columbia.edu/climate-change-litigation/wp-content/uploads/sites/16/non-us-case-documents/2017/20170306_Case-no.-6566216_judgment.pdf (accessed 14 June 2019).

12 *Ibid.*, paragraph 1, p. 1.

13 M. Dutu, "Climate change and human rights: emergence of a new fundamental right to proper climate", *in* A. Michelot (ed.), *Justice climatique: enjeux et perspectives* [Climate Justice: Issues and Perspectives], Bruylant, 2016, p. 311.

14 African Union Organization, *African Charter on Human and Peoples' Rights*, 27 June 1981.

15 *Ibid.*

court in 2005: *Shell v. Nigeria*[16] in Africa, the other a non-contentious case illustrated by the petition of the *Inuits*[17] of Canada; and, third, the 2014 *Tuvalu*[18] case tried before a judge in New Zealand. In the former case involving the Ogoni people,[19] the African Charter on Human and Peoples Rights concluded that the Nigerian government had not taken the necessary protective measures and had not informed the community of the dangers created by the activities envisaged nor given the community the opportunity to take part in procedures and decisions relating to these activities.[20] In other words, Nigeria violated the right of the people to a healthy environment. Thus, a new fundamental human right designated as the "right to a proper climate"[21] emerged – i.e., the right to a healthy climate.

2. *Legal Action Against Companies*

Here we distinguish between legal action taken against companies for *Greenwashing* on the one hand, and legal action undertaken by companies

16 *Gbemre v. Shell Petroleum Development Company of Nigeria Ltd. & others*, Suit No. FHC/B/CS/53/05, Federal High Court of Nigeria (Benin), 14 Nov. 2005, *available online at* http://blogs2.law.columbia.edu/climate-change-litigation/wp-content/uploads/sites/16/non-us-case-documents/2005/20051130_FHCBCS5305_judgment-1.pdf (accessed 14 June 2019) (certified copy 30 Nov. 2015).

17 Inter-American Commission on Human Rights (petition), "Seeking Relief from Violations Resulting from Global Warming Caused by Acts and Omissions of the United States", 7 Dec. 2005.

18 *AD (Tuvalu)*, [2014] NZIPT 501370-371, New Zealand: Immigration and Protection Tribunal, 4 June 2014, *available online at* https://www.refworld.org/cases,NZ_IPT,585152d14.html (accessed 3 Mar. 2019).

19 *Social and Economic Rights Action Center (SERAC) and Center for Economic and Social Rights (CESR)/Nigeria*, Decision 155/96, African Commission on Human and People's Rights, 13–27 Oct. 2001, *available online at* http://www.achpr.org/communications/decision/155.96/ (accessed 14 June 2019).

20 *Ibid.*, paragraph 53 ("Government compliance with the spirit of Article 16 and Article 24 of the African Charter must also include ordering or at least permitting independent scientific monitoring of threatened environments, requiring and publicising environmental and social impact studies prior to any major industrial development, undertaking appropriate monitoring and providing information to those communities exposed to hazardous materials and activities and providing meaningful opportunities for individuals to be heard and to participate in the development decisions affecting their communities").

21 *Earthlife Africa*, p. 312.

related either directly or indirectly to regulations established in favour of the fight against global warming, on the other hand.

Firstly, legal action taken on the grounds of Greenwashing is interesting as the court sets boundaries that must not be crossed and does not hesitate to condemn false posturing. Litigation related to climate greenwashing[22] has taken place in Australia, for example. In all of these cases, the defendant companies were condemned and constrained to change their practices.[23] The best-known case concerned the falsification of diesel vehicle tests by the German automobile manufacturer Volkswagen. Following an investigation by the United States Environmental Protection Agency (EPA),[24] the U.S. Department of Justice filed a civil lawsuit against the Volkswagen (VW)[25] demanding an injunction against the company as well as financial penalties. Several U.S. states filed suits against VW.[26] A former VW executive who headed the company's environment office in Detroit, Oliver Schmidt, was accused of covering up cheating by VW on diesel emission tests; on 6 December 2017, he was sentenced to a maximum seven years in federal prison and fined $400,000.[27] Engineer James Liang cooperated with the inquiry and received a 40-month prison sentence.[28]

---

22 M. Wilensky, 2015, pp. 153–54 & 158.

23 *Ibid.*

24 *See* United States Environmental Protection Agency, "Learn About Volkswagen Violations", https://www.epa.gov/vw/learn-about-volkswagen-violations (accessed 3 Mar. 2019).

25 *United States of America v. Volkswagen AG*, Case No 2:16-cv-10006-LJM-MJH, United States District Court for the Northern District of California, 4 Jan. 2017; *see also* United States Department of Justice, "U.S. v. Volkswagen, 16-CR-20394: Volkswagen Diesel Engine Matters, Case No. 2:16-cv-120394-SFC-APP (E.D. Mich.)", 18 Dec. 2018, *available online at* https://www.justice.gov/usao-edmi/us-v-volkswagen-16-cr-20394 (accessed 14 June 2019).

26 *See* D. Shepardson, "Three U.S. states sue Volkswagen, say executives covered up diesel cheating", *Reuters*, 19 July 2016, *available online at* https://www.reuters.com/article/us-volkwsagen-emissions-idUSKCN0ZZ1X3 (accessed 14 June 2019) (discussing nearly identical lawsuits separately filed by New York, Massachusetts, and Maryland).

27 *See* D. Rushe & agencies, "Oliver Schmidt jailed for seven years for Volkswagen emissions scam", *The Guardian*, 6 Dec. 2017, *available online at* https://www.theguardian.com/business/2017/dec/06/oliver-schmidt-jailed-volkswagen-emissions-scam-seven-years (accessed 14 June 2019).

28 *See* D. Shepardson, "VW engineer sentenced to 40-month prison term in diesel case", *Reuters*, 25 Aug. 2017, *available online at* https://www.reuters.com/article/us-volkswagen-emissions-sentencing/vw-engineer-sentenced-to-40-month-prison-term-in-diesel-case-idUSKCN1B51YP (accessed 14 June 2019).

Litigation relating to or motivated by environmental regulations supporting the fight against global warming was brought before the Court of Justice of the European Union, referenced for a preliminary ruling by national jurisdictions. These cases are concerned as much with quotas as questions of environmental taxation. Several examples exist of relevant litigation in France,[29] Spain,[30] Sweden,[31] and Germany.[32] The European court therefore concluded that the Member States should apply a more restrictive definition of dual use and choose to impose dual use energy products, on condition that the Member States exercise their power in accordance with European law.

Litigation relating to responsibility of the State for default remains rather difficult to implement, as much for procedural reasons as the question of separation of powers. Direct litigation against companies principally encounters the problem of proof.

B. The Specifics of U.S. Litigation

The public trust doctrine predominates legal actions taken by young Americans (*see* subsection I.B.1. below) seeking regulation of greenhouse gas emissions at the federal level. After the U.S. EPA issued its Clean Power Plan in the summer of 2015, several states and industries instituted proceedings demanding the suspension of the new regulations (*see* subsection I.B.2. below).

---

29 *Agrargenossenschaft Neuzelle eG v. Landrat des Landkreises Oder-Spree*, Case No. C-545/11, Court of Justice of the European Communities (Fourth Chamber), 14 Mar. 2013, *available online at* http://www.bailii.org/eu/cases/EUECJ/2013/C54511.html (accessed 14 June 2019).

30 *Iberdrola S.A. & others*, Case No. C-566/11, European Court of Justice (Fifth Chamber), 17 Oct. 2013, *available online at* http://blogs2.law.columbia.edu/climate-change-litigation/wp-content/uploads/sites/16/non-us-case-documents/2013/20131017_2013-Case-C-56611_judgment-1.pdf (accessed 14 June 2019).

31 *Billerud Karlsborg AB and Billerud Skärblacka AB v. Naturvardsverket*, Case No. C-203/12, European Court of Justice (Second Chamber), 17 Oct. 2013, *available online at* http://blogs2.law.columbia.edu/climate-change-litigation/wp-content/uploads/sites/16/non-us-case-documents/2013/20131017_2013-Case-C-20312_judgment.pdf (accessed 14 June 2019).

32 E. Sharpston, Advocate General, Request for preliminary ruling from Gerechtshof's-Hertogenbosch Regional Court of Appeal (*Demande de décision préjudicielle formée par le Gerechtshof's-Hertogenbosch c. Netherlands*), Case No. C 426/12, 22 May 2014.

1. The Actions of Our Children's Trust

Among fundamental rights often disputed in the broad context of environmental protection is the right of legal recourse guaranteed by the fifth amendment to the United States Constitution.[33] Very importantly, the public trust doctrine is intended to protect vital resources of the State. The doctrine provides the legal foundation for proceedings brought by non-governmental organizations (NGOs) such as Our Children's Trust. The federal courts have great independence and their preoccupation with climate future is very real. The public trust doctrine is the core principle of climate litigation that young Americans have used to establish the legal basis of their recourse to the U.S. courts.

The climate dispute decided by the Superior Court of the State of Washington for King County District on 19 November 2015,[34] was also based on the public trust doctrine: the plaintiffs sought an injunction against the federal State of Washington obliging it to establish a regulation that would reduce greenhouse gas emissions. Judge Hollis R. Hill issued a ruling accepting the claimants' fundamental arguments, but rejecting their demand for an injunction based on asserted public trust obligations under Article XVII, section 1, of the state's Constitution.[35] In other words, Judge Hollis concluded that he could not force the agency to make a new regulation where the Governor was already committed to this type of action.

In parallel, the NGO Our Children's Trust filed a series of climate lawsuits in the State of Oregon since 2011. The claimants alleged that the federal government is violating the current generation of youths' fundamental constitutional rights under the fifth amendment to the United States Constitution, which

---

33 The Fifth Amendment states that: "the victims of a constitutional violation by a federal agent have the right to recover damages against the official in a federal court despite the absence of any statute conferring such a right".

34 *Zoe and Stella Foster v. Washington Department of Ecology*, No. 14-2-252951 SEA, Superior Court, State of Washington (King County), 19 Nov. 2015 (accessed 14 June 2019).

35 *Ibid.*, p. 8; *but see Foster v. Washington Department of Ecology*, No. 75374-6-I, Court of Appeals, State of Washington, 5 Sep. 2017 (unpublished opinion) (reversing trial court judgment as an abuse of discretion, where the petitioners failed to demonstrate "extraordinary circumstances" warranting relief), *available online at* http://blogs2.law.columbia.edu/climate-change-litigation/wp-content/uploads/sites/16/case-documents/2017/20170905_docket-75374-6-1_opinion.pdf (accessed 14 June 2019).

purportedly protects present and future generations from inaction by the federal government.[36]

On 11 December 2017, during a hearing at the United States Court of Appeal for the Ninth Circuit, the arguments of young people in the case of *Juliana v. United States* came before the judges. On 7 March 2018, the Court of Appeal for the Ninth Circuit rejected attempts by the Trump administration to paralyze the proceedings by rejecting the petition for a *writ of mandamus* and allowing the young claimants to go ahead with this eagerly awaited, historic climate trial.[37]

2. *Litigation Based on the Clean Power Plan*

The Clean Power Plan regulations[38] are part of a series of U.S. administrative rules aimed at ensuring environmental protection in the fight against greenhouse gas emissions. The rules were established under the Obama administration with a view to fulfilling the objectives of the United States with regard to their national contribution to COP 21.[39] Adopted in August 2015, the Clean Power Plan imposed a 32% reduction of power stations' CO_2 emissions by 2030 compared with historic 2005 emissions. Under the Clean Power Plan, every state

---

36 D. Estrin, "Limiting Dangerous Climate Change: The Critical Role of Citizen Suits and Domestic Courts, Despite the Paris Agreement", *Centre for International Governance Innovation*, 10 May 2016, No. 101, p. 19, *available online at* https://issuu.com/cigi/docs/paper_no.101.

37 *United States v. District Court of Oregon*, No. 17-71692, United States Court of Appeals for the Ninth Circuit, *Federal Reporter, Third Series*, West Publishing, 2018, Vol. 884, p. 830 (Opinion by Chief Judge Thomas). The order on appeal was previously issued by Judge Ann Aiken, denying the Trump Administration's motion to dismiss the case. *Juliana v. United States*, No. 6:15-cv-01517-AA, United States District Court for the District of Oregon, *Federal Supplement, Third Series*, West Publishing, 2016, Vol. 217, p. 1224. As a result of further legal maneuvering, the trial has yet to take place. *See* E. Brown, J. Davidson & D. Noonan, essay #9 (this book) on "Securing the Legal Right to a Healthy Atmosphere and Stable Climate for the Benefit of All Present and Future Generations".

38 Environmental Protection Agency, Final Rule, "Carbon pollution emission guidelines for existing stationary sources: electric utility generating units", *Federal Register*, 23 Oct. 2015, Vol. 80, pp. 64,661 & 64,663.

39 D. Vine, "Achieving the United States' Intended Nationally Determined Contribution", *Center for Climate and Energy Solutions*, Sep. 2016, *available online at* https://www.c2es.org/site/assets/uploads/2016/09/achieving-us-indc-nov-2016.pdf (accessed 14 June 2019).

in the Union was required to submit a strategy for meeting this target before 6 September 2016 (or 6 September 2018 at the latest).

In 2007, the United States Supreme Court in *Massachusetts v. Environmental Protection Agency* (EPA),[40] determined that the EPA was competent to regulate greenhouse gas emissions under article 202(a)(1) of the Clean Air Act. The litigation involved a full-flung battle against new regulations reforming the Clean Air Act even before the U.S. EPA formally adopted the Clean Power Plan. Two cases are at the very heart of the climate litigation based on the Clean Power Plan: *West Virginia v. Environmental Protection Agency*, and *North Dakota v. Environmental Protection Agency*.

In *West Virginia v. Environmental Protection Agency*, numerous arguments on substantive issues were put forward and debated – particularly examining the applicable standard under section 111(d) of the Clean Power Plan, in addition to the proper interpretation of section 112.[41] The parties alleged that the standards of assessment used by the U.S. EPA with regard to section 111(d) needed to be interpreted in accordance with *Chevron v. Natural Resources Defense Council, Inc.*[42] The *Chevron* case concluded that it is possible for an agency to effect a reasonable interpretation of its enabling act and, therefore, of the powers delegated to the agency by the U.S. Congress. The claimants maintained that, to their point of view, the EPA is a purely regulatory body. The agency and its defenders replied that *Chevron* authorized the EPA to adopt *best system* criteria. Following the election of President Donald Trump, the question now being asked is whether a trial based on substantive issues will ever see the light of day – which seems unlikely.

Secondly, the climate litigation in *North Dakota v. Environmental Protection Agency*,[43] was based on section 111(b) of the Clean Air Act. Twenty-five states

---

40 *Massachusetts v. Environmental Protection Agency*, United States Supreme Court, *United States Reports*, United States Government Publishing Office, 2 Apr. 2007, Vol. 549, p. 497; *see also* "Emission standards for new motor vehicles or new motor vehicles engines", *United States Code*, Vol. 42, section 7521(a)(1).

41 *See, e.g.*, Respondent EPA's Opposition to Motions to Stay Final Rule (Document #1586661), *West Virginia v. United States Environmental Protection Agency*, No. 15-1363, United States Court of Appeals for the District of Columbia Circuit, 3 Dec. 2015, p. 23, *available online at* https://ago.wv.gov/publicresources/epa/Documents/EPA%20opp%20-%20total%20file%20(M0111970xCECC6).pdf (accessed 14 June 2019).

42 *Chevron U.S.A., Inc. v. Natural Resources Defense Council, Inc.*, No. 82-1005, United States Supreme Court, *United States Reports*, United States Government Publishing Office, 25 June 1984, Vol. 467, p. 837.

43 Petition for Review, *North Dakota v. Environmental Protection Agency*, No. 15-1381, United States Court of Appeals for the District of Columbia Circuit, 23 Oct. 2015,

challenged the EPA's issuance of regulations governing "Greenhouse Gas Emissions from New, Modified, and Reconstructed Stationary Sources: Electric Utility Generating Units" in the United States Court of Appeals for the D.C. Circuit. The lawsuit contested the EPA's authority to base the agency's establishment of energy performance standards for carbon sequestration and storage on Clean Air Act section 111(b).[44] The adoption of New Source Performance Standards measures in keeping with this statutory provision is a prerequisite invoking the authority under section 111(d) to regulate existing sources pursuant to the Clean Power Plan. The plaintiff states in *North Dakota v. Environmental Protection Agency* obviously sought to impact the future existence of the Clean Power Plan regulations – which was later accomplished as a result of policy change.

One of the reasons that the study of federal litigation via these two cases is so interesting is the fact that the legal actions date from before and (even more importantly) after the radical change of perspective that accompanied President Donald Trump's rise to power.

II. Climate Litigation: Legal Revolution on the Horizon?

Climate litigation courts are generally confronted with various difficulties involving the application of procedural rules (*see* Section II.A. below) as well as substantive issues (*see* Section II.B. below).

---

available online at http://blogs2.law.columbia.edu/climate-change-litigation/wp-content/uploads/sites/16/case-documents/2015/20151023_docket-15-1381_petition-for-review-1.pdf (accessed 7 January 2020).

44 Subsequent history for this case is *available online at* http://climatecasechart.com/case/north-dakota-v-epa/. The D.C. Circuit issued an order holding the case in abeyance temporarily, following President Trump's issuance of Executive Order 13783 (28 Mar. 2017) ordering EPA to review the standards for possible suspension, revision, or rescission. Order, *North Dakota v. Environmental Protection Agency*, No. 15-1381, United States Court of Appeals for the District of Columbia Circuit, 28 Apr. 2017, *available online at* http://blogs2.law.columbia.edu/climate-change-litigation/wp-content/uploads/sites/16/case-documents/2017/20170428_docket-15-1381_order.pdf (accessed 14 June 2019). Eventually, the D.C. Circuit decided to hold the cases in abeyance until further order, with status reports filed every ninety days. Order, *North Dakota v. Environmental Protection Agency*, Case No. 15-1381, United States Court of Appeals for the District of Columbia Circuit, 10 Aug. 2017, *available online at* http://blogs2.law.columbia.edu/climate-change-litigation/wp-content/uploads/sites/16/case-documents/2017/20170810_docket-15-1381_order.pdf (accessed 14 June 2019).

A. On the Application of Procedural Rules

The demands of jurisdictional competence include the separation of powers issue as it arguably applies to questions of climate dispute. In addition, the question of interest to act (whether the plaintiff has standing to sue), since this conditions access to civil society courts. Moreover, the burden of proof in the field of climate change remains a central issue, as does the matter of executing the judicial decision.

The process of determining the court's jurisdictional competence consists of, generally, defining a connection between the forum, the claimants and the facts at issue in the dispute.[45] In fact, the judicial competence question determines whether or not the claimant has a case to bring. In classical civil law countries *forum non conveniens* (forum not agreeing) – recognized notably in Canada and the United States – may be applied by certain courts to conclude that they do not have jurisdictional competence over climate disputes.[46]

The Canadian court gave its opinion on this question in two cases involving the Kyoto Protocol: *Turp v. Minister of Justice and Attorney General of Canada*,[47] relating to the withdrawal of the Canadian government from the Kyoto Protocol; and *Friends of the Earth v. the Governor in Council & others*,[48] where the claimants

45 Environmental Law Center, University of Victoria, "Climate change litigation", 3 Dec. 2007, p. 2, *available online at* www.elc.uvic.ca/wordpress/wp-content/uploads/2015/02/C1_ClimateChangeLitigationBackgrounder-2007Dec3.pdf (accessed 14 June 2019).

46 D. Saxe & K. Mikadze, "The Dutch Climate Case: Beginning of a New Era of Climate Litigation?", *Slaw: Canada's online legal magazine*, 21 Aug. 2015, *available online at* http://www.slaw.ca/2015/08/21/the-dutch-climate-case-beginning-of-a-new-era-of-climate-litigation/ (accessed 14 June 2019).

47 *Turp v. Minister of Justice and Attorney General of Canada*, Docket No. T-110-12, Federal Court of Canada, *Federal Court Reports*, 17 July 2012, p. 893, *available online at* https://www.canlii.org/en/ca/fct/doc/2012/2012fc893/2012fc893.pdf (accessed 14 June 2019).

48 *Friends of the Earth v. Canada (Governor in Council)*, Docket Nos. T-2013-07, T-78-08 & T-1683-07, Federal Court of Canada (CanLII), *Federal Court Reports*, 18 June/20 Oct. 2008, p. 1183, *available online at* http://blogs2.law.columbia.edu/climate-change-litigation/wp-content/uploads/sites/16/non-us-case-documents/2008/20081020_2008-FC-1183-2009-FCA-297_decision.pdf (accessed 14 June 2019), *affirmed*, Docket No. A-572-08, Federal Court of Appeal, *Federal Court of Appeal Decisions*, 15 Oct. 2009, p. 297, *available online at* http://blogs2.law.columbia.edu/climate-change-litigation/wp-content/uploads/sites/16/non-us-case-documents/2009/20091015_2008-FC-1183-2009-FCA-297_decision.pdf (accessed 14 June 2019).

accused the government of a breach of its obligations with regard to climate change in virtue of the law implementing the Kyoto Protocol.

The climate problem is both global and local and this dual aspect cannot hinder the competence of a national judge.

In the *Klimaatzaak* case,[49] the claimants believed they could overcome the judicial competence hurdle by invoking Article 144 of the Belgian Constitution.[50] The Belgian Court of Cassation previously confirmed that judicial power is competent for preventative purposes as well as actions seeking indemnification based on the irregular infringement of a subjective right through the administration's exercise of purportedly unbound jurisdiction.[51]

In the United States, the separation of powers doctrine originated in the nineteenth century Supreme Court decision of *Marbury v. Madison*.[52] Separation of powers has been broadly interpreted by the majority of federal courts. According to Professor Neyret,[53] the obstacle to establishing State responsibility for climate change in U.S. litigation under the separation of powers doctrine, is that climate issues must be handled exclusively by the U.S. Congress rather than U.S. courts.

Although the separation of powers question remains a serious obstacle to judicial oversight of executive institutions (e.g., Parliament), the same does not appear to be true for questions involving public trust obligations. Application of the public trust doctrine[54] was preliminarily addressed in November 2016 by Judge Aiken in *Juliana v. United States* (to be tried in the State of Oregon). Judge Aiken determined that the government has an obligation to preserve natural resources held in trust,[55] and violated this duty by ignoring the climate change effects of governmentally authorized activities. Likewise, an April 2016

---

49 *See, e.g.*, Phillippe & Partners, "Citation", *available online at* https://affaire-climat.be/documents/affaire_climat_Citation_fr.pdf (accessed 14 June 2019) (listing "Asbl Klimaatzaak" as one of the Requerants [Applicants] and summarizing the Belgian court's decision).

50 *Ibid.*, p. 33.

51 *Ibid.*, p. 33, paragraph 19.

52 *Marbury v. Madison*, United States Supreme Court, *United States Reports* (Cranch, Vol. 1), 24 Feb. 1803, Vol. 5, p. 137.

53 L. Neyret, "La reconnaissance de la responsabilité climatique" [Recognition of Climate Responsibility], *Recueil Dalloz*, 2015, p. 2278.

54 J.L. Sax, "The Public Trust Doctrine in Natural Resources Law: Effective Juridical Intervention", *Michigan Law Review*, 1970, Vol. 68, p. 188.

55 *Ibid.*, p. 196.

constitutional petition filed in Pakistan[56] invoked echoes of the public trust doctrine. It is also worth noting that the *Urgenda* court made similar reference to the public trust doctrine.[57]

If a court does not reject an application for declaratory judgment, it may: order measures to reduce greenhouse gas emissions to be taken, order measures of adaptation, or impose an environmental impact study requirement. In other words, like *Urgenda,* a court could issue a declaratory judgment pronouncing the national government's obligation to limit carbon emissions and directing the State to take the appropriate measures; however, there is no power of coercion.

No U.S. court has yet ruled against the Trump administration's inaction and in favor of a climate change policy.[58] To do so would effect nothing less than a global legal revolution, by notably sidestepping applicable rules of procedure.

---

56 Constitutional Petition, *Rabab Ali v. Federation of Pakistan & Another*, Supreme Court of Pakistan, 1 Apr. 2016 (decision pending).

57 *Urgenda Foundation v. Kingdom of the Netherlands*, Case No. C/09/456689/HA ZA 131396, The Hague District Court, 24 June 2015, paragraph 4.54.

58 *But see American Electric Power Company v. Connecticut*, United States Supreme Court, *United States Reports*, United States Government Publishing Office, 20 June 2011, Vol. 564, p. 410 (relying on the political question doctrine to dismiss lawsuits filed by eight states, New York City, and three land trusts based on the conclusion that any federal common-law right to seek abatement of carbon-dioxide emissions from fossil-fuel fired power plants was displaced by the Clean Air Act, including actions the Environmental Protection Agency is authorized to take pursuant to the Clean Air Act); *Native Village of Kivalina v. ExxonMobil Corporation*, No. 09-17490, United States Court of Appeals for the Ninth Circuit, *Federal Supplement, Third Series*, West Publishing, 21 Sep. 2012, Vol. 696, p. 849 (holding that federal common-law nuisance claims against multiple oil, energy, and utility companies alleging that their massive greenhouse gas emissions resulted in global warming that severely eroded land upon which the city was situated, were displaced by adoption of the Clean Air Act), *certiorari denied*, United States Supreme Court, *United States Reports*, United States Government Publishing Office, 20 May 2013, Vol. 569, p. 1000; Order Granting Defendants' Motion to Dismiss, *Comer v. Murphy Oil USA, Inc.*, Civ. No. 1:05-CV-436-LG-RHW, United States District Court for the Southern District of Mississippi, Civ. No. 1:05-CV-436-LG-RHW, *Westlaw*, Westlaw Publishing, 30 Aug. 2007, p. 6942285 (holding that "Plaintiffs' claims are non-justiciable pursuant to the political question doctrine"), *appeal dismissed*, United States Court of Appeals for the Fifth Circuit, *Federal Reporter, Third Series*, West Publishing, 28 May 2010, Vol. 607, p. 1049; *People of the State of California v. General Motors Corporation*, No: C-06-05755 MJJ, United States District Court for the Northern District of California, *Westlaw*, Westlaw Publishing, 17 Sep. 2007, p. 2726871 (dismissing public nuisance claims seeking damages under

B. On the Application of Substantive Rules

In climate litigation, certain substantive rules closely linked to environmental law apply as much to States (*see* subsection II.B.1. below) as to companies (*see* subsection II.B.2. below). As we shall see, whether it be in litigation against the States or by or against private individuals, the substantive rules applied by the different judges consistently involve the notion of default by the higher duties. Often referred to as the duty of care, these substantive rules appear to derive from basic principles of liability enunciated in both public international law and national environmental law.

1. *The Substantive Rules Applied in Proceedings Against the State*

In proceedings against the State, plaintiffs often invoke constitutional rights. However, another type of obligation has been invoked several times by the parties in climate trials – namely, a duty of care owed by the State. This concept was at the forefront of the 1932 United Kingdom case of *Donoghue v. Stevenson*,[59] concerning tort liability in the field of consumer law. Aside from this important duty of care rule, States must also comply with other legal principles intrinsic to climate law.

In *Urgenda*, the Dutch judge asked about the legal foundations supporting the alleged duty of care owed by the Dutch State. The judge concluded that European Court of Human Rights jurisprudence should be considered to determine the court's capacity to interpret the duty of care,[60] and that the Dutch State's inherent obligation was founded on Article G 162 of the Civil Code of the Netherlands – under which responsibility is established for tortious acts. In defining the Dutch State's duty of care, the judge identified a number of criteria[61] as follows:

> Therefore, these objectives and principles constitute an important viewpoint in assessing whether or not the State acts wrongfully towards Urgenda [...]. In determining the scope of the duty of care of the State, the court will therefore take account of: (i) the nature and extent of the damage ensuing from climate change, (ii) the knowledge and foreseeability of this damage, (iii) the chance that hazardous climate change will occur, (iv) the nature of the acts (or omissions) of the State, (v) the onerousness of taking

---

federal common law and California law against various automakers for creating and contributing to global warming as non-justiciable political questions).

59 *Donoghue (or McAlister) v. Stevenson*, Case No. AC562, House of Lords, *The All England Law Reports*, 26 May 1932, p. 1.

60 *Urgenda*, paragraph 4.46.

61 *Ibid.*, paragraph 4.63.

precautionary measures, (vi) the discretion of the State to execute its public duties – with due regard for the public-law principles, all this in light of: the latest scientific knowledge, the available (technical) option to take security measures, and the cost-benefit ratio of the security measures to be taken.

The Court then considered that the increase in greenhouse gas emissions demonstrated in the Netherlands could properly be attributed to the government's inaction. Nevertheless, the judge did not specify how the Dutch government should meet the applicable reduction objectives.

Additional substantive rules originate from Principles of European law concerning failure to transpose directives. For example, the European Commission brought an action against the Italian Republic[62] for failure to adopt all legislative, regulatory and administrative provisions necessary to comply with Directive 2003/87/EC.[63] Thus, the Court of Justice of the European Union concluded that the Italian Republic failed to fulfil its obligations under Article 31, paragraph 1, of Directive 2003/87.

Finally, the notion of State responsibility seems to be spreading. National courts notably recognized State responsibility, for example, in Canada,[64] the United States,[65] Pakistan[66], Ukraine,[67] and Poland.[68] According to Roger

62 *Commission of the European Communities v. Italian Republic*, Case No. C-540/07, European Court of Justice, 19 Nov. 2009.

63 Directive 2003/87/EC of the European Parliament and the Council of 13 October 2003 establishing a scheme for greenhouse gas emission allowance trading within the Community and amending Council Directive 96/61/EC.

64 *Friends of the Earth v. Canada*, 2008.

65 *Kanuk v. Alaska Department of Natural Resources*, No. S-14776, Supreme Court of Alaska, *Pacific Reporter, Third Series*, 12 Sep. 2014, Vol. 335, p. 1088; *Juliana v. United States*, No. 6:15-cv-01517-TC, United States District Court for the District of Oregon, *Federal Supplement, Third Series,* 10 Nov. 2016, Vol. 217, p. 1224.

66 *Ashgar Leghari v. Federation of Pakistan*, Case W.P. No. 25501/2015, High Court of Lahore, 14 Sep. 2015, *available online at* http://blogs2.law.columbia.edu/climate-change-litigation/wp-content/uploads/sites/16/non-us-case-documents/2015/20150414_2015-W.P.-No.-25501201_decision.pdf (accessed 7 January 2020).

67 *Environment-People-Law v. Cabinet of Ministers of Ukraine and National Agency of Environmental Investments*, Llviv Circuit Administration Court, 2 Feb. 2010 (pending).

68 Sabin Center for Climate Change Law, "*ClientEarth v. Enea*", *available online at* http://climatecasechart.com/non-us-case/clientearth-v-enea/ (accessed 7 January 2020) (discussing a claim filed at the Regional Court in Poznań (Poland), on 24 October 2018, which is not yet publicly available). *See also, e.g.*, ClientEarth, "World-first climate risk case launched over major coal plant in Poland", 29 Oct.

Cox,[69] advocate for the plaintiff in *Urgenda*, any Member State of the European Union could be held liable for the climate.

2. *The Substantive Rules Applied in Proceedings Against Companies*

As regards proceedings against companies, the rules of duty of care and due diligence are, ultimately complementary – both rules revolve around the idea that a particular duty must be accomplished in the face of situations created by the company that are also likely to cause external damage. The duty of care has been illustrated in the *South-East Asia Greenpeace* petition[70] based on the Heede report, which calculated the share of liability for certain companies in global warming.[71] Another example is the case involving the Peruvian farmer[72] mentioned in the Introduction above.

2019, *available online at* https://www.clientearth.org/world-first-climate-risk-case-launched-over-major-coal-plant-in-poland/ (accessed 7 January 2020); ClientEarth, Briefing – Ostrołeka C: Energa's and Enea's Board Members' Fiduciary Duties to the Companies and Shareholders, 20 Sep. 2018, *available online at* http://blogs2.law.columbia.edu/climate-change-litigation/wp-content/uploads/sites/16/non-us-case-documents/2018/20180920_Not-Available_na-1.pdf (accessed 7 January 2020).

69 R.H.J. Cox, "The Liability of European States for Climate Change", *Utrecht Journal of International and European Law*, 2014, Vol. 30(78), pp. 125–235.

70 *In re Greenpeace Southeast Asia*, Case No. CHR-NI-2016-001, Philippine Commission on Human Rights, 12 May 2015, Petition, *available online at* http://blogs2.law.columbia.edu/climate-change-litigation/wp-content/uploads/sites/16/non-us-case-documents/2015/20150512_Case-No.-CHR-NI-2016-0001_petition-1.pdf (accessed 14 June 2019); *see also* http://climatecasechart.com/non-us-case/in-re-greenpeace-southeast-asia-et-al/ (accessed 14 June 2019) (providing links to responses filed by named parties, and two press releases issued by the Commission).

71 R. Heede, "Tracing anthropogenic carbon dioxide and methane emissions to fossil fuel and cement producers, 1854–2010", *Climatic Change*, 2014, Vol. 122, Issue 1–2, pp. 229–241, *available online at* https://link.springer.com/article/10.1007/s10584-013-0986-y (accessed 14 June 2019).

72 Decision, *Lliuya v. RWE AG*, File No. 2 O 285/15, Regional Court Essen, 15 Dec. 2016, *available online at* http://blogs2.law.columbia.edu/climate-change-litigation/wp-content/uploads/sites/16/non-us-case-documents/2016/20161215_Case-No.-2-O-28515-Essen-Regional-Court_decision.pdf (accessed 14 June 2019) (unofficial English translation); *see also ibid.*, 11 Dec. 2017, Order, *available online at* http://blogs2.law.columbia.edu/climate-change-litigation/wp-content/uploads/sites/16/non-us-case-documents/2017/20171211_Case-No.-2-O-28515-Essen-Regional-Court_order-1.pdf (accessed 14 June 2019) (unofficial English translation).

One could rely on all these concepts to imagine what an international court might do with all the climate causes. That would be a feasible exercise. One could also imagine instead of a right to the environment, the logical corollary based on duties owed by the State. In what form might we one day envisage an *ad hoc* tribunal? This was the experience illustrated by the International Monsanto Tribunal, a tribunal of opinion that could eventually broaden the possibilities of climate litigation.

Conclusion: The Future of Climate Litigation

In the wake of the International Monsanto Tribunal,[73] it seems possible to consolidate a climate trial that is founded on criminal law with inherent subtleties that must be addressed with precision. The advisory opinion of the International Monsanto Tribunal included documents on glyphosate assembled by associations. The judges referred to international law when giving their legal opinion. It was a consultation given by independent judges. Worth pointing out here, is a contrast with the Russell-Sartre Tribunal: the International Monsanto Tribunal was not, in essence, a popular tribunal. Instead, it proceeded according to rules defined by the International Court of Justice. The tribunal took place from 14 to 16 October 2016 at The Hague in the Netherlands – a deeply symbolic location given that the city is the seat of the International Court of Justice (ICJ), and of the International Criminal Court (ICC), which tries crimes against humanity.

One of the goals set by the tribunal was to assess Monsanto's compliance with regard to human rights, including the right to life, the right to a healthy environment, and the rights of future generations. The International Monsanto Tribunal constituted a new model for the expression of justice: firstly, through the composition of the judges at the tribunal, who were eminent practitioners of law from various different legal cultures; secondly, through the diversity of the legal standards at the heart of the issue; but, also, through the conclusions submitted to the judges by victims' advocates who plead before the ICJ in The Hague.

Transposing the International Monsanto Tribunal procedure to the global warming context would involve both procedural as well as substantive advantages. Regarding procedure, Catherine Le Bris pointed out the tribunal's emulation of existing international jurisdictions, along the diversity of law applied by the judges.[74] As long as the exercise of consultative jurisdiction complies

---

73 All documents and information *available online at* https://en.monsantotribunal.org (accessed 14 June 2019).

74 E. Gaillard, "*Le Tribunal international Monsanto, un tribunal d'opinion atypique et audacieux*" [The International Monsanto Tribunal, an Atypical and Audacious Tribunal

with rules governing trial proceedings – including basic procedural criteria like the right of defence and statement of reasons upon which decisions are based – it will be entitled to a certain recognition. Transposition of the International Monsanto Tribunal would possibly signal a move towards clearer determination of the responsibility of large companies in the matter of global warming.

The importance of opinion tribunal lies in the fact that they are "a type of practice that, while potentially contributing to training and the work of formal courts, exist to build solidarity and recognition of the experiences of those who have suffered violations of human rights". According to Magistrate Ghislain Poissonnier, the goal of the International Monsanto Tribunal was to give a voice to the victims, raise international public awareness and contribute to a change in international law.[75]

Finally, the conversion of a judge to the environment is fortunately no longer the privilege of only European judges, whether national or not. This possibility has been extended to international judges in their capacity as such, thanks to the ICJ ruling of 2 February 2018, which established the right to compensation for ecological damage in the case of *Costa Rica v. Nicaragua*.[76] This was an important and fundamental step for environmental law, since the law of ecological damage liability historically brought to life the law of environmental prevention and precaution upon which climate litigation is based.

---

of Opinion], *Energie-Environnement-Infrastructures*, June 2017, No. 6, pp. 62–63; C. Le Bris, "*Le Tribunal Monsanto ou l'écocide face à la justice des peuples*" [The Monsanto Tribunal or the Ecocide Against the Justice of Peoples], *Droit de l'environnement*, Jan. 2017, No. 252, pp. 2–4.

75 G. Poissonnier, "*Tribunal Monsanto: vers une définition de l'écocide?*" [Monsanto Tribunal: Toward a Definition of Ecocide?], *Recueil Dalloz*, 2016, p. 2512.

76 Order, *Maritime Delimitation in the Caribbean Sea and the Pacific Ocean (Costa Rica v. Nicaragua)*, International Court of Justice Reports, 2 Feb. 2018, *available online at* https://www.icj-cij.org/files/case-related/157/157-20180202-JUD-01-00-EN.pdf (accessed 14 June 2019).

Elizabeth BROWN, John DAVIDSON & Danny NOONAN

9. Securing the Legal Right to a Healthy Atmosphere and Stable Climate for the Benefit of All Present and Future Generations

Introduction

Global climate change is the most pressing ecological and human rights issue of our time. To protect our planet's climate system and ensure that the fundamental rights of young people and future generations are protected, climate policies of governments *must* be based on the best climate science. The best climate science requires states to completely decarbonize their energy systems by 2050, and to sequester atmospheric carbon dioxide (CO_2) through massive reforestation, improved land management and other natural sequestration methods.

The worldwide political class, as a whole, has been reluctant to adopt the measures necessary to remedy the climate crisis. Instead, the policies and actions of governments around the world – in continuing to promote and incentivize fossil fuels – have sacrificed critical, long-term social and environmental needs in favor of the short-term profit of a few. This tragic state-of-affairs is perpetuated by the fact that those most harmed by such policies have essentially no present political influence: children and future generations. Conventional politics, statutes, treaties, and litigation also contribute to this global tragedy of the commons by, on the one hand, promising solutions but, on the other hand, consistently failing to bring about the necessary changes.

One innovative strategy that is gaining increasing attention and success involves a direct appeal to independent judiciaries. These appeals are based on fundamental rights including, most notably, what is commonly-called the Public Trust Doctrine. The Public Trust Doctrine is an ancient rule of law that encompasses the most essential purpose of government: the protection of vital natural resources for the continuing survival and welfare of present and future generations. Every government possesses, therefore, both the authority *and the duty* to safeguard these crucial natural resources, such that citizens have inalienable and actionable rights to benefit from these resources in perpetuity.[1]

---

1 M.C. Wood & G. Levitt, "The Public Trust Doctrine in Environmental Decision Making", *in* L. Paddock & others (eds.), *Decision Making in Environmental Law*, Edward

A key group at the forefront of this emerging legal movement is Our Children's Trust (OCT). OCT is a nonprofit public interest law firm that provides strategic, campaign-based legal services to youth from diverse backgrounds to secure their legal rights to a safe climate.[2] In the most notable case, *Juliana v. United States*, OCT supports 21 youth plaintiffs who are suing the U.S. federal government for violating their rights under the U.S. Constitution.[3] In a historic ruling, the court rejected the government's motion to dismiss the youth's legal claims from moving forward to a trial. In doing so, a judge of the U.S. federal district court (District Court) formally recognized the existence of a constitutional right to a climate system capable of sustaining human life, as well as the right of the youth plaintiffs and future generations to bring a case to enforce that right through the court system.

The remainder of this paper will consider, first, the nature and dimensions of the problem of climate change and, second, the origins of the theories at the heart of this novel legal strategy and their implementation through the *Juliana* case in particular.

I. Climate Change – an Overview

In 2015 global average surface temperatures reached 1°C above pre-industrial levels for the first time on record.[4] Populations around the world are already experiencing significant impacts from this warming.[5] These include more

---

Elgar Publishing, 2016, chapter 6; *see also ibid.*, p. 2 (draft prior to publication), *available online at* https://law.uoregon.edu/sites/law1.uoregon.edu/files/mary-wood_0/mary-wood/FINAL_PDF_For_DISTRIBUTION_Encyclopedia_Public_Trust1.pdf (accessed 7 January 2020).

2 *See* Our Children's Trust, *Mission Statement*, *available online at* http://www.ourchildrenstrust.org/mission-statement/. *See also* O. Molodanof & J. Durney, "Hope is a Song in a Weary Throat: An Interview with Julia Olson", *Hastings Environmental Law Journal*, 2018, Vol. 24, p. 213.

3 Amended Complaint, *Juliana v. United States*, No. 6:15-cv-01517-AA, United States District Court for the District of Oregon, 10 Sep. 2015.

4 World Meteorological Organization (WMO), *WMO Statement on the Status of the Global Climate in 2015*, 2016, WMO-No. 1167, pp. 1, 5, *available online at* http://www.cma.gov.cn/en2014/news/News/201603/P020160322334697539255.pdf; *see also* J. Hansen & al, "Global Temperature in 2015", *Climate Science, Awareness and Solutions*, 2016, *available online at* http://csas.ei.columbia.edu/2016/01/19/global-temperature-in-2015/.

5 For a list of global impacts felt in 2015, *see, e.g.*, WMO, *Status Global Climate 2015*, 2016, pp. 11–20.

frequent and severe extreme weather events such as drought and flooding, ocean acidification, expansions of the range of vector-borne infectious disease, and accelerated mass extinction.[6] These impacts constitute harbingers of far more dangerous changes to come.

If unabated, continued greenhouse gas emissions "will initiate dynamic climate change and effects that spin out of human control, as the planet's energy imbalance triggers amplifying feedbacks and the climate and biological systems pass critical tipping points".[7] Such changes would be irreversible and create a different planet from the one on which human civilization developed.[8] Failure to repair Earth's energy imbalance risks economic collapse, social disintegration, and the loss of essential natural and human services. That future may be marked by rising seas, disruption of coastal cities, mass migrations, resource wars, food shortages, heat waves, mega-storms, soil depletion and desiccation, freshwater shortage, collapse of public health systems, and the extinction of increasing numbers of species. As numerous studies and international bodies have recognized,[9] young people have the most to lose as climate change worsens over time. That is, young people have no present voice in the democratic process, will shoulder a disproportionately-large burden of the harms of climate change,

---

6 Our Children's Trust, "Government Climate and Energy Actions, Plans, and Policies Must Be Based on a Maximum Target of 350 ppm Atmospheric CO2 and 1°C by 2100 to Protect Young People and Future Generations", 2018, *available online at* http://www.ourchildrenstrust.org/s/OCT_Why350ppm_2018.pdf; *see also* A.J. McMichael, "Globalization, Climate Change, and Human Health", *New England Journal of Medicine*, 2013, Vol. 368, pp. 1335, 1340; *see also* M.C. Urban, "Accelerating Extinction Risk from Climate Change", *Science*, 2015, Vol. 348, pp. 571, 572.

7 Declaration of Dr. James E. Hansen in Support of Our Children's Trust & others' Submission to the UN Committee on the Rights of Child Regarding State Obligations, Children's Rights and Climate Change, 19 Aug. 2016, 17, *available online at* http://www.ourchildrenstrust.org/s/HansenCRCDeclaration.pdf. *See also* Why 350, pp. 4–6.

8 *Ibid.*, pp. 3–4.

9 *See, e.g.*, F.P. Perera, "Children Are Likely to Suffer Most from Our Fossil Fuel Addiction", *Environmental Health Perspectives,* Aug. 2008, Issue No. 116(8), pp. 987–990; UNICEF United Kingdom, *Climate Change: Children's Challenge* (2013), *available online at* https://www.unicef.org.uk/publications/climate-change-report-jon-snow-2013/; Z. Xu & others, "The Impact of Heat Waves on Children's Health: A Systematic Review", *International Journal of Biometeorology,* 2014, p.239; American Academy of Pediatrics Council on Environmental Health (AAP), "Policy Statement on Global Climate Change and Children's Health", *Pediatrics,* 1 Nov. 2018, Vol. 136, pp. 992–997; J. Currie & L. Deschênes, "Children and Climate Change: Introducing the Issue", *The Future of Children,* Vol. 26, No1, Children and Climate Change, pp. 3–9.

and have reaped a disproportionately-small share of the benefits of accumulated anthropogenic greenhouse gas emissions. The myriad impacts of climate change on young people are set out below.

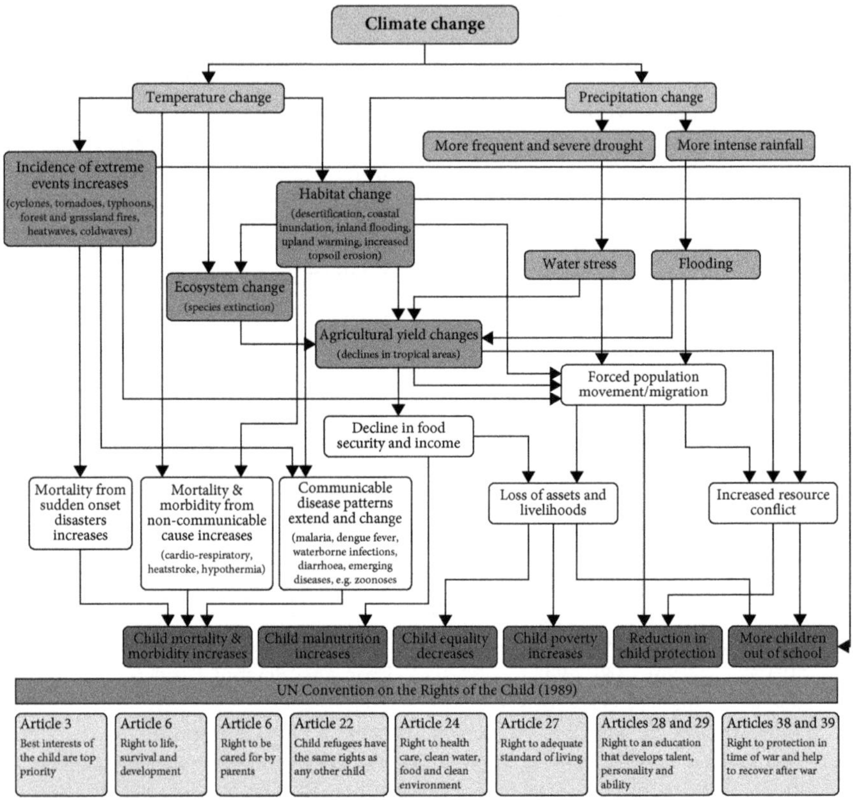

Figure: *Climate change impacts and harm to children's rights.*[10]

Neither the Paris Agreement nor its parent treaty, the United Nations Framework Convention on Climate Change (UNFCCC), respond adequately to the risks described above. Under the Paris Agreement itself, parties aspire

10 UNICEF, "A brighter tomorrow: Climate change, child rights and intergenerational justice", 2010, *available online at* https://downloads.unicef.org.uk/wp-content/uploads/2010/09/intergenerationaljustice.pdf.

to a non-binding target of temperature increases "well below" 2°C above pre-industrial levels and agree to "pursue efforts" to limit global temperature increase to 1.5°C.[11] Yet the Agreement only requires parties to submit non-binding emission reduction pledges. Even if these pledges are met, it is projected that they will result in an *increase* in emissions through 2030 and cause climate warming of between 2.6°C and 3.5°C.[12]

Even the lowest of the Paris Agreement's politically-determined targets, 1.5°C, is dangerously high from a scientific standpoint, especially as climate change-related harms are already occurring at present levels of warming. Instead, the best and most-current science indicates that, to redress these harms, *long-term* global average surface temperatures must return to less than 1°C above pre-industrial levels.[13]

This requires reducing atmospheric CO_2 from its current concentration of approximately 410 ppm to less than 350 ppm by the end of this century.[14]

---

11 Paris Agreement, FCCC/CP/2015/L.9, 12 Dec. 2015, p. 20, *available online at* http://unfccc.int/resource/docs/2015/cop21/eng/l09.pdf. While earlier models of climate change dynamics indicated that a 2°C increase might be sustainable, these models failed to incorporate the slow feedback, system inertia and other dynamics that influence the effect of current temperature change on future climate change. J. Hansen & others, "Assessing 'Dangerous Climate Change': Required Reduction of Carbon Emissions to Protect Young People, Future Generations and Nature", *Public Library of Science ONE,* 3 Dec. 2013, 8(12):e81648, p. 15.

12 L. Jeffrey & others, "2.7°C is Not Enough—We Can Get Lower", *Climate Action Tracker Update*, 8 Dec. 2015, *available online at* http://climateactiontracker.org/news/253/Climate-pledges-will-bring-2.7C-of-warming-potential-for-more-action.html; Climate Interactive, *Climate Scoreboard: UN Climate Pledge Analysis, available online at* https://www.climateinteractive.org/programs/scoreboard/; J. Rogelj & others, "Paris Agreement climate proposals need a boost to keep warming well below 2°C", *Nature,* 30 June 2016, Vol.534, pp. 631, 639.

13 Given the long-term effects of CO_2 in the atmosphere, past emissions may result in 1.5°C peak in global surface heating for a period of time; however, emissions must be reduced to ensure that long-term temperatures, after peaking, stabilize at no more than 1°C above preindustrial levels. To stabilize at 1°C requires a mean atmospheric concentration of CO_2 of no more than 350 ppm. *See* J. Hansen & others, 2013, "*Assessing "Dangerous Climate Change". See also* J. Hansen & others, "Ice Melt, Sea Level Rise and Superstorms; Evidence from Paleoclimate Data, Climate Modelling, and Modern Observations that 2°C Global Warming Could be Dangerous", *Atmospheric Chemistry and Physics*, 2016, Vol.16, pp. 3761–3812; J. Hansen, *Storms of My Grandchildren: The Truth About the Coming Climate Catastrophe and Our Last Chance to Save Humanity,* Paperback, 2009, p. 166.

14 *See* J. Hansen, Why 350, 2016.

Permitting global average surface temperatures to approach 2°C and atmospheric CO_2 to approach 450 ppm for any length of time would be highly dangerous.[15] In the face of this scientific evidence, and in light of ongoing political intransigence, one of the world's leading climate scientists has concluded that litigation and judicial intervention is needed to "unburden our children from the ravages of climate chaos that [governments'] choices to date have done so much to ensure".[16] The Public Trust Doctrine provides one such avenue for this kind of litigation.

II. The Public Trust Doctrine

The Public Trust Doctrine is an ancient legal principle that confirms a government's obligation to hold critical natural resources in trust for the benefit of present and future generations. An early codification of the doctrine can be found in the *Institutes* of the Roman Emperor Justinian, which declared "the following things are by natural law common to all – the air, running water, the sea, and consequently the seashore".[17] The doctrine "speaks to one of the most essential purposes of government: protecting crucial ecology for the continuing survival and welfare of citizens".[18] Under the doctrine, citizen beneficiaries of vital natural resources held in trust by governments have reserved and inalienable rights to "a sustained natural endowment".[19]

---

15 *See* J. Hansen, Why 350, 2016, pp. 3–4; *see also* J. Hansen & others, "*Assessing Dangerous Climate Change*", 2013, p. 15 (noting that a 2°C increase would result in an "unacceptably high risk of global catastrophe").

16 Supplemental Declaration of Dr. J.E. Hansen in Support of Plaintiffs' Opposition to Defendants' Motion to Dismiss, Docket No. 47, *Juliana v. United States*, No. 6:15-cv-01517-TC, United States District Court for the District of Oregon, 8 Jan. 2016, p. 37. *See also* J. Hansen, "Our Children's Right to a Viable Future", 2016, *available online at* http://csas.ei.columbia.edu/2016/03/09/our-childrens-right-to-a-viable-future/.

17 J.B. Moyle, *The Institutes of Justinian*, Oxford, 5th edition, 1913, Book 2, Title 1.1, *available online at* https://droitromain.univ-grenoble-alpes.fr/Anglica/just2_Moyle.htm#I.

18 Wood & Levitt, 2016; *see also ibid.*, p. 2 (draft prior to publication), *available online at* https://docplayer.net/57810584-Abstract-table-of-contents.html (accessed 14 June 2019).

19 M.C. Wood & D. Galpern, "Atmospheric Recovery Litigation: Making the Fossil Fuel Industry Pay to Restore a Viable Climate System", *Environmental Law*, Spring 2015, Vol. 45, Issue 2, pp. 259–335, *available online at* https://static1.squarespace.com/static/571d109b04426270152febe0/t/57ae174cb3db2b8d0ea58e22/1471027050464/2015_Wood_Atmospheric+Recovery+Litigation-Making

The essence of the doctrine is the fiduciary duty of governments to protect the public's crucial natural resources from irrevocable privatization or destruction. This duty is an aspect of its sovereignty and so cannot be abdicated. Additionally, governments owe this duty equally to present and future generations to protect these resources.[20] Governments are therefore prohibited from destroying or causing irreparable harm to these natural resources,[21] necessitating judicial enforcement when the political branches of government fail to uphold their fiduciary obligations.

In the United States, the Public Trust Doctrine has long been closely linked to a broader responsibility to protect the sovereign interests of later generations.[22] The foundational U.S. public trust cases[23] affirm that, as part of this responsibility, governments cannot substantially impair or alienate resources crucial to the public welfare. The public trust concept is also reflected in the writings of the founders of the United States, including in Thomas Jefferson's famous letter to

+Fossil+Fuel+Industry+Pay+to+Restore+Viable+Climate+System.pdf (accessed 14 June 2019).

20 Restatement (Second) of Trusts, 1959, section 183.

21 *Arizona Center for Law v. Hassell*, No. 1 CA-CV 89–134, Arizona Court of Appeals, *Pacific Reporter, Second Series*, West Publishing, 6 Oct. 1992, Vol. 837, pp. 158, 169.

22 This broader conception of the trust principle is commonly referred to as the "reserved powers doctrine", which stipulates that today's legislature cannot bind future legislatures. This means the current legislature cannot deprive future legislatures the capacity to manage commonly-owned natural resources. *See* J. Eule, "Temporal Limits on the Legislative Mandate: Entrenchment and Retroactivity", *American Bar Foundation Research Journal*, Spring-Summer 1987, Vol. 12, No. 2/3, pp. 379–459; M. J. Klarman, "Majoritarian Judicial Review: The Entrenchment Problem", *Georgetown Law Journal*, 1997, Vol. 85, pp. 491, 491–92; D. Dana & S. Koniak, "Bargaining in the Shadow of Democracy", *University of Pennsylvania Law Review*, 1999, Vol. 148, pp. 473–533.

23 *See, e.g., Stone v. Mississippi*, United States Supreme Court, *United States Reports*, United States Government Publishing Office, 1 Oct. 1879, Vol. 101, pp. 814, 819–20; *Newton v. Commissioners of Mahoning County*, United States Supreme Court, *United States Reports*, United States Government Publishing Office, 1 Oct. 1879, Vol. 100, p. 548; *Illinois Central Railroad Co. v. Illinois*, Nos. 419, 608 & 809, United States Supreme Court, *United States Reports*, United States Government Publishing Office, 5 Dec. 1892, Vol. 146, p. 387; *Geer v. Connecticut*, No. 87, United States Supreme Court, *United States Reports*, United States Government Publishing Office, 2 Mar. 1896, Vol. 161, pp. 519, 533–34; *Missouri v. Holland*, No. 609, United States Supreme Court, *United States Reports*, United States Government Publishing Office, 19 Apr. 1920, Vol. 252, pp. 416, 435.

James Madison of September 6, 1789: "I set out on this ground, which I suppose to be self-evident, '*that the earth belongs in usufruct to the living*' [...]".[24]

The relevance of both the Public Trust Doctrine and broader intergenerational principles to the climate crisis is inescapable. As Dr. James Hansen has warned, "sovereign governments around the world are on the verge of collectively imposing an overwhelming burden – intergenerational injustice in the extreme – upon young people and future generations who stand to inherit a climate system that is not at all conducive to their well-being or survival".[25] In the context of the climate crisis, the Public Trust Doctrine thus provides both a conceptual and legal framework to clarify the intergenerational obligations of governments and affirm the fundamental rights of future generations.

III. Public Trust Principles Outside the United States

These principles underpinning the Public Trust Doctrine are not unique to the United States, or to common law countries. Many nations around the world "embrace the doctrine as a central principle in their legal systems", and "the overarching position of the public trust in political and legal traditions around the world reflects the character of the doctrine as a fundamental attribute of sovereignty – a constitutive principle that government cannot shed".[26] Legal scholars Michael Blumm and Rachel Guthrie have concluded that the doctrine is evolving "towards becoming a general principle of international law".[27]

---

24 Letter from Thomas Jefferson to James Madison, 6 Sep. 1789, *in* J.P. Boyd & others (eds.), *The Papers of Thomas Jefferson,* 1958, Vol. 15, p. 392 (emphasis in original).

25 Declaration of Dr. James E. Hansen in Support of Our Children's Trust & others' Submission to the UN Committee on the Rights of Child Regarding State Obligations, Children's Rights and Climate Change, 19 Aug. 2016, paragraph 41, *available online at* http://www.ourchildrenstrust.org/s/HansenCRCDeclaration.pdf.

26 G. Levitt, N. Bellinger, J. Margolis & D. Quirke, *Public Trust Doctrine in Environmental Decision Making*, Mar. 2016, The Environmental & Natural Resources Law Center, p. 2 (internal citations omitted), *available online at* https://law.uoregon.edu/images/uploads/entries/environmental_decision_making_-_EK_edit.pdf.

27 M.C. Blumm & R.D. Guthrie, "Internationalization of the Public Trust Doctrine: Natural Law and Constitutional and Statutory Approaches to Fulfilling the Saxion Vision", *University of California Davis Law Review*, 2012, Vol. 45, p. 741. *See also* M. Turnipseed & others, "Reinvigorating the Public Trust Doctrine: Expert Opinion on the Potential of a Public Trust Mandate in U.S. and International Environmental Law", *Environment Magazine*, 2010, Vol. 52, No. 5, p. 12; D. Takacs, "The Public Trust Doctrine, Environmental Human Rights and the Future of Private Property", *New York University Environmental Law Journal*, 2008, Vol. 16, pp. 711, 746.

In the landmark case *Oposa v. Factoran*, the Supreme Court of the Philippines interpreted "the right to a balanced and healthful ecology" as "concern[ing] nothing less than self-preservation and self-perpetuation", and held that "these basic rights need not even be written in the Constitution, for they are assumed to exist from the inception of humankind".[28] The Court declared that without these basic rights, "the day would not be too far when all else would be lost not only for the present generation, but also for those to come – generations which stand to inherit nothing but parched earth incapable of sustaining life".[29] The Court also ruled that "every generation has a responsibility to the next to preserve that rhythm and harmony for the full enjoyment of a balanced and healthful ecology".[30]

In addition to the essentially-domestic law duties that the public trust doctrine imposes on governments for the protection of their own natural resources, governments have international responsibilities to safeguard resources shared in common with other nations. For example, the atmosphere, oceans, and climate system are all shared planetary resources that cannot be divided, and the harm of climate change occurs both *within* and *outside* the national borders of those responsible for these harms. These circumstances necessitate that governments act as co-tenants and co-trustees of these *global trust resources*.[31] Each government, therefore, has a shared obligation to manage the global trust resources so as to avoid waste and destruction of the resources, and in a manner analogous to any co-tenant of a shared piece of property.[32]

---

28 *Minors Oposa v. Factoran*, General Register No. 101083, Supreme Court of the Philippines, *Supreme Court Reports, Annotated*, 30 July 1993, Vol. 224, p. 792, General Register No. 101083.

29 *Ibid.*

30 *Ibid.*

31 M.C. Wood, *Nature's Trust: Environmental Law for a New Ecological Age*, 2013, p. 213; *see also* P.H. Sand, "Sovereignty Bounded: Public Trusteeship for Common Pool Resources", *Global Environmental Politics*, 2004, Vol. 4, pp. 47–57.

32 For an application of the property doctrines of waste and co-tenancy to a global atmospheric trust, *see* J.W. Singer, *Property Law: Rules, Policies, and Practices*, 2010, 5th edition, pp. 664–665; "Co-tenancy and Joint Ownership", *American Jurisprudence*, Second Edition, 2012, Vol. 20, section 1. For its application to the global trust, *see* M.C. Wood, *Nature's Trust*, 2013, pp. 212–213; E. Fox-Decent, "From Fiduciary States to Joint Trusteeship of the Atmosphere: The Right to a Healthy Environment Through a Fiduciary Prism", *in* K. Coghill & others (eds.), *Fiduciary Duty and the Atmospheric Trust*, 2012, p. 263 (discussing the global trust through the lens of a human rights analysis of climate obligations and indicating that "the idea that states are essentially joint trustees of the earth's atmosphere").

Public trust principles are also embedded in international agreements. The preamble of the UNFCCC embodies the public trust principle of intergenerational responsibility: "The Parties should protect the climate system for the benefit of present and future generations of humankind, on the basis of equity and in accordance with their common but differentiated responsibilities and respective capabilities". Similarly, UNESCO's 1997 *Declaration on the Responsibilities of the Present Generations towards Future Generations* offers one of the most comprehensive statements of intergenerational obligation in international law. Specifically, the declaration recognizes that *present generations* "have the responsibility of ensuring that the needs and interests of future generations are fully safeguarded" and "the responsibility to bequeath to future generations an Earth which will not one day be irreversibly damaged by human activity", and consequently "should preserve for future generations natural resources necessary for sustaining human life and for its development".[33]

Additionally, public trust principles reflect the shared reasoning underlying the moral values and religious teachings of many faiths.[34] In the papal encyclical, *Laudato Si'*, Pope Francis asked, "What kind of world do we want to leave to those who come after us, to children who are now growing up? The question not only concerns the environment in isolation; the issue cannot be approached piecemeal".[35] He asserts that, "Whether believers or not, we are agreed today that the earth is essentially a shared inheritance, whose fruits are meant to benefit everyone"[36] and that "[e]ach community can take from the bounty of the earth whatever it needs for

33 *See* Arts. 1, 4 and 5.

34 *See, e.g.*, "Islamic Declaration on Global Climate Change", International Islamic Climate Change Symposium, 18 Aug. 2015, *available online at* http://www.ifees.org.uk/wp-content/uploads/2016/10/climate_declarationmMWB.pdf; *Hindu Declaration on Climate Change* (23 Nov. 2015), *available online at* http://www.hinduclimatedeclaration2015.org/english; *see also*, M.C. Wood, *Nature's Trust*, 2013, pp. 279–280 (citing multiple faiths as recognizing public trust obligations to present and future generations); "To the Jewish People, to all Communities of Spirit, and to the World: A Rabbinic Letter on the Climate Crisis", signed by 425 Rabbis of all streams of Judaism, originally published May 2015, *available online at* https://theshalomcenter.org/RabbinicLetterClimate.

35 Francis, *Encyclical Letter Laudato Si' of the Holy Father Francis On Care for Our Common Home*, Vatican Press, 2015, pp. 118–19, originally published in Latin, English translation *available online at* http://w2.vatican.va/content/dam/francesco/pdf/encyclicals/documents/papa-francesco_20150524_enciclica-laudato-si_en.pdf"http://w2.vatican.va/content/dam/francesco/pdf/encyclicals/documents/papa-francesco_20150524_enciclica-laudato-si_en.pdf.

36 Francis, *Laudato Si'*, 2015, p. 68.

subsistence, but it also has the duty to protect the earth and to ensure its fruitfulness for coming generations".[37] In a similar vein, Islamic scholars and theologians came together in 2015 to put out the Islamic Declaration on Global Climate Change, which elaborates on the environmentalist and conservationist ethics inherent in Islamic teachings. The declaration both reminds humanity that our species is a caretaker and steward on this earth and poses the question: "What will future generations say of us, who leave them a degraded planet as our legacy"?[38] These questions embody a moral clarity and broader intergenerational justice principles that are increasingly being voiced through the courts.

IV. Youth Seeking Systemic Change in *Juliana v. United States*

In August 2015, Our Children's Trust supported 21 young people ("the Youth") in filing a lawsuit against the U.S. government, the President, and the major executive departments. "Future generations" are also named plaintiffs in the case. The Youth allege that the very survival of young people – their right to life – is being threatened by U.S. government actions that have created and aggravated a dangerous climate system.

As the judge presiding over the case has noted, "This is no ordinary lawsuit".[39] Rather, it is in many aspects an unprecedented case using recognized precedial claims, brought in response to an extraordinary and unprecedented crisis. Climate change is a problem of such systemic scope that no challenge to an individual project or policy, based on a particular regulation or piece of legislation, would be remotely adequate to address the challenge. Instead, comprehensive judicial action is required in order to bring about a paradigm shift in national, and indeed global, energy policy, based on precedent such as *Brown v. Board of Education*.[40]

To achieve this systemic paradigm shift, the Youth are challenging the entire U.S. fossil fuel energy system and all of the federal government's actions that have facilitated and subsidized the fossil fuel industry. In other words, the Youth are not suing merely on the basis of the government's *inaction* on climate change, but are foremost challenging the government's *intentional, affirmative activities* that

37 Francis, *Laudato Si'*, 2015, p. 49.

38 Islamic Declaration on Global Climate Change.

39 *Juliana v. United States,* No. 6:15-cv-01517-AA, District Court for the District of Oregon, *Federal Supplement, Third Series,* 2016, Vol. 217, p.1224, p. 1234 (order denying motion to dismiss).

40 *Brown v. Board of Education*, United States Supreme Court, *United States Reports*, United States Government Publishing Office, 31 May 1955, Vol. 349, p. 294; *Brown v. Board of Education*, United States Supreme Court, *United States Reports*, United States Government Publishing Office, 17 May 1954, Vol. 347, p. 483.

have exacerbated this ongoing crisis. As a result, the Youth are not using the traditional litigation approach of "whack-a-mole"; that is, they are not challenging individual projects and agencies on a piecemeal basis, in circumstances where no single successful individual challenge would alleviate the present and future climate harm to the Youth. The Youth have instead simultaneously targeted all of the major departments and agencies in the federal government that play a role in energy supply and production, and pollution control.

A. *Juliana*: Historical Knowledge and Deliberate Indifference

The Youth in *Juliana* argue that the U.S. federal government has known for decades that carbon dioxide pollution was causing catastrophic climate change and that massive emission reductions and a nationwide transition away from fossil fuels were needed to protect the Youth's constitutional rights.[41] As an example of this long-standing governmental knowledge, fifty-three years ago President Lyndon B. Johnson's White House released a report that confirmed that anthropogenic carbon dioxide threatens the health and livelihood of citizens.[42] This was followed by revelations during the Nixon Administration that described CO_2 pollution from the burning of fossil fuels in terms of "apocalyptic change"[43] and warned that "[i]n the longer term, the quality of the atmosphere may well determine whether man survives or perishes".[44]

Based on these and other pieces of evidence, the Youth argue that – despite this knowledge – the U.S. government has spent nearly 60 years implementing systemic energy programs, plans, and national policies, and issuing thousands of authorizations and permits that, in the aggregate, have facilitated and subsidized the extraction, production, consumption, transportation and exportation of fossil fuels.[45]

---

41 Amended Complaint, *Juliana v. United States*, pp. 51–56.

42 R. Revelle, W. Broecker, H. Craig, C.D. Keeling & J. Smagorinsky, The Environmental Pollution Panel on the President's Science Advisory Committee, *Restoring the Quality of Our Environment – Atmospheric Carbon Dioxide*, 1965, Appendix, pp. 1–2, 4, 193.

43 D.P. Moynihan, *White House memorandum to John Erlichman*, 17 Sep. 1969, p. 1, *available online at* https://www.nixonlibrary.gov/sites/default/files/virtuallibrary/documents/jul10/56.pdf.

44 U.S. Department of Commerce & others, *World Weather Plan for Fiscal Year 1971*, 1970, p. iv.

45 Amended Complaint, *Juliana v. United States*, pp. 56–64.

B. *Juliana*: Legal Claims

The Youth's first legal claim in *Juliana* involves an alleged violation of the "due process clause" of the Fifth Amendment to the U.S. Constitution.[46] Specifically, the Youth argue that the Defendants "knowingly endanger Plaintiffs' health and welfare by approving and promoting fossil fuel development, including exploration, extraction, production, transportation, importation, exportation, and combustion".[47] This claim highlights the federal government's historical responsibility for the climate crisis, their historical knowledge of the consequences of continued reliance on fossil fuels, and their deliberate indifference to that knowledge and responsibility.

The Youth's second claim argues that a life-sustaining climate system is a precondition for civilization, without which all other rights would be rendered moot, and as a result deserves judicial protection.[48] In building on recent U.S. Supreme Court precedent supporting the existence of unenumerated fundamental rights that are implicit in the Constitution's Fifth Amendment protections,[49] and in appealing to the historical and philosophical origins of the Public Trust Doctrine and the principle of intergenerational equity, Youth assert that the U.S. government's myriad actions unjustifiably violate their fundamental right to a stable climate system. The District Court's order agreed, and in doing so endorsed the intergenerational dimensions of this right by citing the Philippines Supreme Court's finding in *Oposa v. Factoran* that "without 'a balanced and healthful ecology', future generations 'stand to inherit nothing but parched earth incapable of sustaining life' ".[50]

---

46 Plaintiffs' First Amended Complaint, *Juliana v. United States*, No. 6:15-cv-01517-TC, United States District Court for the District of Oregon, 10 Sep. 2015, paragraphs 277–289, *available online at* https://static1.squarespace.com/static/571d109b04426270152febe0/t/57a35ac5ebbd1ac03847eece/1470323398409/YouthAmendedComplaintAgainstUS.pdf. The Fifth Amendment states "nor shall any person [...] be deprived of life, liberty, or property, without due process of law".

47 Plaintiffs' First Amended Complaint, *Juliana v. United States*, paragraph 280; *see also Juliana v. United States*, p. 1248.

48 *Juliana v. United States*, No. 6:15-cv-01517-AA, United States District Court for the District of Oregon, *Federal Supplement, Third Series,* 10 Nov. 2016, Vol. 217, p. 1224, p. 1250 (order denying motion to dismiss).

49 *Obergefell v. Hodges*, No. 14-556, United States Supreme Court, *Supreme Court Reporter*, West Publishing, 26 June 2015, Vol. 135, pp. 2584, 2598.

50 *Juliana v. United States*, 2016, p. 1250 (citing *Maynard v. Hill*, United States Supreme Court, *United States Reports*, United States Government Publishing Office, 1888, Vol. 125,

In their third legal claim, the Youth argue that the government's actions violate the equal protection principles embedded in the Fifth Amendment. This argument embodies the intergenerational equity principles discussed above. The Youth maintain that there is a long history and pattern of deliberate actions by the government promoting and benefiting the short-term economic interests of the fossil fuel industry to the extreme detriment of children and future generations. The Youth argue that these government actions discriminate against young people and future generations who, as a sector of society, are disproportionately impacted by climate change.

The Youth's final legal claim asserts a violation of the Public Trust Doctrine, the basis for which is described above. Judge Aiken recognized that the Youth's "public trust rights both predated the Constitution and are secured by it".[51] Judge Aiken emphasized the vast scope of the doctrine,[52] and that it implicates protection of the atmosphere.[53] In recognizing the inextricable connection between the Public Trust Doctrine and sovereignty, the District Court also found that, contrary to Defendants' contentions, the Public Trust Doctrine applied equally to the federal government as to the 50 U.S. States,[54] and could not be displaced by legislation.[55]

C. *Juliana*: Remedy

The Youth in *Juliana* want to hold the U.S. government, and its constellation of laws, regulations and policies, ultimately responsible for the country's historical cumulative emissions, among other equitable remedies which are

---

pp. 190, 211); *Minors Oposa v. Factoran*, General Register No. 101083, Supreme Court of the Philippines, *International Law Materials*, 30 Jul. 1993, Vol. 33, pp. 173, 187–188.

51 *Juliana v. United States*, 2016, p. 1260; *ibid.*, p. 1261 ("Although the public trust predates the Constitution, plaintiffs' right of action to enforce the government's obligations as trustee arises from the Constitution. […] plaintiffs' public trust claims are properly categorized as substantive due process claims. […] Plaintiffs' public trust rights, related as they are to inherent aspects of sovereignty and the consent of the governed from which the United States' authority derives, satisfy both tests. […] But it is the Fifth Amendment that provides the right of action".).

52 *Ibid.*, pp. 1252–53 ("In its broadest sense, the term 'public trust' refers to the fundamental understanding that no government can legitimately abdicate its core sovereign powers" and that the doctrine "rests on the fundamental principle that '[e]very succeeding legislature possesses the same jurisdiction and power with respect to [the public interest] as its predecessors'") (internal citations omitted).

53 *Ibid.*, p. 1255.

54 *Ibid.*, pp. 1253, 1256–59.

55 *Ibid.*, pp. 1259–1260.

25% of total, cumulative global emissions. The Youth are requesting not only a judicial declaration that the Defendants' actions have violated their fundamental rights under the Constitution and the Public Trust Doctrine, but also an order that the Defendants prepare and implement a national "climate recovery plan" to phase out fossil fuel emissions and draw down excess atmospheric carbon dioxide commensurate with safe levels (i.e. < 350 parts-per-million).[56]

In an unprecedented early success in the case, Judge Ann Aiken issued an emphatic order in November 2016 that denied the government's motion to dismiss and affirmed the judiciary's role as a "coequal branch of government" in addressing the climate crisis.[57] Importantly, the District Court's order found that the Youth's requested relief would not contravene the Constitutional separation of powers,[58] and – given the U.S.'s proportionately-large national emissions – would actually redress the Youth's injuries by at least slowing or mitigating the alleged harms.[59]

Going Forward

Following the District Court's order in *Juliana* denying the U.S. government's motion to dismiss, the Trump administration has pursued a series of dilatory tactics to try and stop the case from going to trial. Multiple attempts to resort to rarely-used and even more rarely-granted appeals have been denied by the District Court, by the Ninth Circuit Court of Appeals, and most recently by the U.S. Supreme Court.[60] The District Court set a trial date for October 29, 2018 and

---

56 *Ibid*, p. 1239. *See also* Plaintiffs' First Amended Complaint, *Juliana v. United States*, pp. 94–95.

57 *Juliana v. United States*, 2016, pp. 1262–63 ("Federal courts too often have been cautious and overly deferential in the arena of environmental law, and the world has suffered for it. […] 'A strong and independent judiciary is the cornerstone of our liberties'. These words, spoken by Oregon Senator Mark O. Hatfield, are etched into the walls of the Portland United States courthouse for the District of Oregon. The words appear on the first floor, a daily reminder that it is 'emphatically the province and duty of the judicial department to say what the law is'. *Marbury v. Madison*, [… p. 177]. Even when a case implicates hotly contested political issues, the judiciary must not shrink from its role as a coequal branch of government".).

58 *Juliana v. United States*, 2016, pp. 1239–1240.

59 *Ibid.*, pp. 1245–1247.

60 *See* L. Hurley, "Supreme Court rejects Trump bid to halt climate change case", *Reuters*, 31 July 2018, *available online at* https://www.reuters.com/article/us-usa-court-climate/supreme-court-rejects-trump-bid-to-halt-climate-change-case-idUSKBN1KK2FY.

ordered the parties to "get prepared".[61] However, the trial has not yet taken place due to additional legal maneuvering by the Trump Administration.[62]

Beyond the case itself, *Juliana* has helped inspire and is itself part of a growing global movement of young people demanding science-based climate action from their governments – actions which the Paris Agreement failed to achieve. Courts around the world are beginning to confirm that governments have a duty to safeguard the climate for present and future generations. Valuable legal precedents

61 Reporter's Transcript of Proceedings, *Juliana v. United States of America*, No. 6:15-CV-1517-TC, District Court for the District of Oregon, 10 May 2018, p. 28.

62 *See, e.g.*, Our Children's Trust, "Landmark U.S. Federal Climate Lawsuit: Major Court Orders and Filings", *available online at* https://www.ourchildrenstrust.org/court-orders-and-pleadings. United States Supreme Court Chief Justice John G. Roberts, Jr. issued an order staying the trial. *In re United States*, No. 18A410, United States Supreme Court, *Supreme Court Reporter*, United States Government Publishing Office, 19 Oct. 2018, Vol. 139, p. 16. Two weeks later, a majority of the Court (not including dissenting Justices Clarence Thomas and Neil A. Gorsuch) vacated the Chief Justice's order. *Ibid.*, 2 Nov. 2018, Vol. 139, p. 452 (memorandum opinion). The Ninth Circuit then granted a temporary stay of the district court proceedings pending resolution of another petition for *writ of mandamus* (later denied as moot). *In re United States*, No. 18-73014, United States Court of Appeals for the Ninth Circuit, 8 Nov. 2018 (slip opinion); *ibid.*, 26 Dec. 2018 (slip opinion). In the interim, District Judge Aiken certified the case for interlocutory appeal to the Ninth Circuit. *Juliana v. United States*, No. 6:15-cv-01517-AA, United States District Court for the District of Oregon, 21 Nov. 2018 (slip opinion). In a split decision (with Circuit Judge Michelle Taryn Friedland dissenting), the Ninth Circuit granted permission to appeal. *Juliana v. United States*, No. 18-80176, United States Court of Appeals for the Ninth Circuit, 26 Dec. 2018 (slip opinion). The court subsequently granted the youth plaintiffs' request for expedited briefing. *Juliana v. United States*, No. 18-36082, United States Court of Appeals for the Ninth Circuit, 7 Jan. 2019 (slip opinion). Oral argument took place on 04 June 2019. *See, e.g.*, United States v. United States District Court for the District of Oregon, No. 17-1692, United States Court of Appeals for the Ninth Circuit, 4 June 2019, *available online at* https://www.ourchildrenstrust.org/juliana-v-us (scroll down and click on YouTube link to view a video recording of oral arguments in the case). *Editors' note*: On 7 January 2020, the Ninth Circuit recognized the gravity of the evidence on the Youth's injuries from climate change and the government's role in causing them, but issued a split decision (with Judge Josephine Laura Staton dissenting) "reluctantly" concluding that the Youth's requested remedies should instead be addressed by the executive and legislative branches. *Juliana v. United States*, No. 18-3602, United States Court of Appeals for the Ninth Circuit, 17 Jan. 2020 (slip opinion). The Youth's attorneys filed a petition on 2 March 2020 seeking rehearing en banc before a new panel of 11 circuit court judges. Petition for Rehearing *En Banc* of Plaintiffs-Appellees, *Juliana v. United States*, No. 18-3602, United States Court of Appeals for the Ninth Circuit, 2 Mar. 2020.

are being set that will hopefully continue to instigate a wave of successful climate change court cases against governments worldwide.[63]

Perhaps the most significant of this recent wave of litigation was brought by 25 young people in Colombia. The youth plaintiffs in this case used a unique procedural mechanism under Colombia's Constitution called a "tutela". This mechanism permitted the plaintiffs to receive an expedited hearing of their claim that the Colombian government, in failing to prevent deforestation, has violated their constitutional rights. The Colombia Supreme Court found in favor of the plaintiffs in a judgment permeated by intergenerational principles. For instance, with regards to the importance of protecting the climate across generations, the Court stated:

> Without a healthy environment we subjects of rights and human beings in general cannot survive, much less safeguard those rights for our children nor for the generations to come. Neither could the existence of the family, of society, or the State itself be guaranteed. The growing deterioration of the environment is a grave attack against present life and life to come and all the fundamental rights; furthermore, it gradually depletes life and all of the rights connected to it.[64]

---

63 *See, e.g., Merriman & others v. Fingal County Council & others; Friends of the Irish Environment CLG v. Fingal County Council & others*, Case No. 344 JR, High Court of Ireland, *High Court of Ireland Decisions* 695, 21 Nov. 2017, pp. 9–17, 264 (recognizing an unenumerated right to "an environment that is consistent with the human dignity and well-being of citizens at large", but ultimately denying relief on the basis that plaintiffs' claims were non-justiciable and otherwise brought out-of-time), *available online at* https://www.elaw.org/system/files/attachments/publicresource/Airport_judgment_Barret_J_21.11.17.pdf; *Föreningen Greenpeace Norden & Natur og Ungdom v. The Government of Norway through the Ministry of Petroleum and Energy*, No. 16-166674TVI-OTIR/06, Oslo District Court, 4 Jan. 2018 (Unofficial English Translation) at 3.1, 5.2.1–5.2.2 (recognizing an individually-enforceable constitutional right to "an environment that is conducive to health", but finding that this right could not be used to invalidate oil leases on the basis of Norwegian oil and gas combustion emissions occurring outside of Norway), *available online at* http://blogs2.law.columbia.edu/climate-change-litigation/wp-content/uploads/sites/16/non-us-case-documents/2018/20180104_16-166674TVI-OTIR06_judgment-2.pdf.

64 *Future Generations v. Ministry of the Environment & others*, STC4360-2018, Radicación No. 11001-22-03-000-2018-00319-01, Corte Suprema de Justicia de Colombia, 5 Apr. 2018, pp. 13–14 (unofficial English translation). Original text: "Sin ambiente sano los sujetos de derecho y los seres sintientes en general no podremos sobrevivir, ni mucho menos resguardar esos derechos, para nuestros hijos ni para las generaciones venideras. Tampoco podrá garantizarse la existencia de la familia, de la sociedad o del propio Estado. El deterioro creciente del medio ambiente es atentado grave para la vida actual y venidera y de todos los otros derechos fundamentales; además, agota paulatinamente la vida y todos los derechos conexos con ella".

The Court went on to say that:

> In keeping with the criteria of intergenerational equity, the transgression is obvious, in keeping with the prognosis that an increase in temperature for the year 2041 will be 1.6 degrees and in 2071 up to 2.14 degrees, being that future generations, amongst them, the children who lodge this safeguard, will be directly affected, unless the present [generations], reduce to zero the level of deforestation.[65]

Conclusion

Throughout the history of liberal democratic thought, it has been recognized that one of the most fundamental sovereign duties of governments is to ensure that the means and necessities of self-government are preserved for the next generation and in perpetuity. The Public Trust Doctrine – and the broader principles of sovereignty, preservation of natural resources, intergenerational equity and equal protection that it embodies – provide an apt framework for grappling with the unprecedented challenges of the present climate crisis. That is to say, a litigation strategy predicated on the Public Trust Doctrine and other fundamental rights, and targeting the systemic actions of governments in causing the climate crisis, is uniquely-capable of placing the morality and fairness of present government actions to future generations squarely before the courts. Faced with the recalcitrance and short-sightedness of today's political leaders, young people are therefore increasingly appealing to the judiciary to safeguard their fundamental rights and those of future generations.

Through these legal actions, the jurisprudential and philosophical foundations of the Public Trust Doctrine are finding new meaning and relevance. As recognized by Judge Aiken in *Juliana v. United States*, denying legal recourse to young people to prevent the destruction of the climate and other essential natural resources safeguarded by the Public Trust Doctrine "would be to say that the [U.S.] Constitution affords no protection against a government's knowing decision to poison the air its citizens breathe or the water its citizens drink".[66] Courts throughout the world are thus increasingly recognizing the severity of the climate crisis and the necessity of intervening to ensure that future generations are not deprived of a habitable climate system.

---

65 *Ibid.*, p. 37 (unofficial English translation). Original text: "En cuanto al criterio de equidad intergeneracional, es obvia su transgresión, en tanto que el pronóstico de incremento de la temperatura para el año 2014, será de 1,6°, y en 2071 hasta de 2,14°, siendo las futuras generaciones, entre ellos, los infantes que interponen esta salvaguarda, las que serán directamente afectadas, a menos que las presentes, reduzcan a cero la tasa de deforestación".

66 *Juliana v. United States*, 2016, p. 1250.

Agnès MICHELOT

10. Climate Justice for Future Generations: From International to French Perspectives

The Paris Agreement makes a brief reference to the concept of "climate justice" in the preamble, perhaps thus opening new perspectives for the understanding of and fight against climate change. Perspectives that would be more in phase with the demands, significantly on the rise since the early years of the century, of the international networks of civil society groups for whom economic, social and ecological crisis are all intertwined. As an aggravating factor in inequality, climate change raises crucial questions about the responsibility of present generations towards future generations.

Confronted with these issues, civil society is trying to propose solutions as part of a collective and concerted approach. In its 27 September 2016 opinion on "Climate Justice: issues and perspectives for France", the French Economic, Social and Environmental Council (2016 French CESE opinion) reminded us that "even if limited to 2°C, global warming will have significant consequences to which our society will have to adapt, carrying, in the absence of suitable measures, the risk that inequalities will deepen between those who have and those who do not have the means to achieve this".[1]

A year later, on 19 October 2017, the European Economic and Social Committee (EESC) adopted an opinion[2] in the same spirit that defined global climate change as a political and ethical issue, rather than exclusively environmental. The EESC highlighted the "observation that the most vulnerable categories and the poorest members of society are often those most affected by the effects of climate change, and this despite the fact that these same categories are the least responsible for the emissions that have led to the climate crisis".

---

1 J. Jouzel & A. Michelot, *La Justice climatique : enjeux et perspectives pour la France* [*Climate Justice: Challenges and Prospects for France*], Les Éditions des Journaux Officiels, CESE, 27 Sep. 2016, p. 12, *available online at* http://www.lecese.fr/sites/default/files/pdf/Avis/2016/2016_10_justice_climatique.pdf.

2 European Economic and Social Committee, *Climate justice (own-initiative opinion)*, 19 Oct. 2017, C. Lohan (reporter), pp. 1–12.

In the categories that are least responsible for climate change, the group most in the foreground is that of future generations. They are also the ones who will be subject to the full force of the effects of the climate change – which is producing an increasingly inegalitarian society and is, therefore, full of menace and danger for the future. Global warming has become a matter of international security. The risks related to global warming that now hang over food and health safety are major issues for tomorrow's societies.

In this context, to what extent is the concept of climate justice embedded in the rights of future generations? And what are the prospects of climate justice reinforcing protection of the interests of future generations?

I. Climate Justice: A Concept Rooted in the Rights of Future Generations.

The origins of the movements demanding climate justice are to be found principally in the gathering of activists around the Conferences of the Parties to the United Nations Framework Convention on Climate Change. Little by little, the demands made during these gatherings have spread and diversified at an international level. These demands bring together environmental NGOs and specialists in the defense of human rights. Trade union and religious movements have also become interested in the subject. Despite the diversity of those involved, there is general agreement on: the fact that the world lacks equity, and about the risk to social cohesion caused by climate change. Climate justice is the project of a human community that is fighting a "climate divide" that goes against the essential values of equality and solidarity. Whether through respect for the right to a quality environment – which implies an individual approach to the rights of future generations – or the seeking of climate justice for all of humanity throughout time, the rights of future generations are at the very heart of the aims of climate justice.

A. The Right of Future Generations to a Preserved Environment: Human Dignity and Ecological Integrity as the Basis for Climate Justice

The international clamor for climate justice finds expression in demands that reside, in the first instance, under the right not to suffer the consequences of climate change or any form of ecological degradation. The Principles of Climate Justice Charter[3] drawn up by a NGO network and activists in 2002 are a relatively

3 Bali Principles of Climate Justice, 29 Aug. 2002, *available online at* http://www.ejnet.org/ej/bali.pdf.

symbolic representation of this demand; while in international law, the demand has found expression following the 1972 Stockholm Conference under Principle 1 of the Declaration on the Human Environment: "Man has the fundamental right to freedom, equality and adequate conditions of life, in an environment of a quality that permits a life of dignity and well-being. He bears a solemn responsibility to protect and improve the environment for present and future generations". This principle is specifically referenced in the 2016 French CESE opinion.

The observance of this fundamental right is owed to the humanity of today, as well as the future. At the root of this international environmental law is the fundamental link between the rights of future generations and the protection of the environment. Principle 2 of the Stockholm Declaration thus proclaims our responsibility to preserve the natural resources of the planet for the benefit of present generations and those to come.

Other international texts also establish this link between the environment and the rights of future generations, notably from the point of view of natural heritage. For its part, the United Nations Framework Convention on Climate Change states that it is up to the Parties to protect the climate system in the interest of future generations. Following this, the Declaration on the Responsibilities of the Present Generations Towards Future Generations of 12 November 1997 proclaims, in Article 5 dedicated to the protection of the environment, that "In order to ensure that future generations benefit from the richness of the Earth's ecosystems, the present generations should strive for sustainable development and preserve living conditions, particularly the aspect and integrity of the environment". The Declaration of Ethical Principles in Relation to Climate Change adopted during the thirty-ninth session of the General Conference of UNESCO in 2017, confirms the importance of taking measures to protect ecosystems for present and future generations (Article 4.2, equity and justice).

Indeed, a well-preserved environment is the essential condition for a life of dignity and well-being. In the context of climate justice, respect for the right of every person to a healthy environment and dignified living conditions is fundamental. Dignity signifies that every individual should benefit from the protection of law and that no-one should be crushed or see his or her rights annihilated by those in power (whether political, economic or other). In the same way, one's right to dignity cannot be questioned in the name of others' rights. This brings us back to the principle of equality, which is also fundamental to climate justice. A person who is weak should see his/her rights protected in the same way that others' rights are protected, particularly when it comes to the right to life and the right to health.

The right to a healthy environment, which is at the heart of climate justice, depends upon the protection of the quality and integrity of the environment. The destruction of the climate system is a violation of human dignity. The reference to dignity is particularly relevant from our point of view in facilitating the presentation of three considerations that are pillars of climate justice:

(1) Each person deserves to be respected as he/she is and for who he/she is regardless of his/her social status, economic power, gender, state of health … his/her weakness or vulnerability should not lead to a denial of the most essential rights. The right to life and the right to the environment are closely related. For this reason, the climate challenge must be considered from the perspective of respect for human dignity.
(2) Each person is unique and consequently we are moving away from the "rule of equivalence and compensation". Not everything has an equivalent. Thus, we also move away from the reign of the technology of compensation and utilitarianism.
(3) The interaction of humans and ecosystems is an essential aspect of climate justice. The conservation of human dignity depends on the conservation of ecological integrity. More fundamentally still, the counterpart of human dignity from the point of view of ecosystems is ecological integrity. Respect for ecological integrity allows a different approach to the protection of the environment from that delivered by ecosystem and/or environmental services, which induce us to think about our relationship with nature from the perspective of the "segmented" services that they offer. Human life is unique, in the same way that the climate system is unique. Human dignity cannot be "dissected": it concerns the human family in its entirety and in its continuity.

B. Climate Justice for the Humanity of the Future

The 2016 French CESE opinion clearly sets out the matter of "beneficiaries" of climate justice.[4] After stating what climate justice consists of, its aims and objectives, the next thing to consider is whom it addresses. The legal approach facilitates an approach from the perspective of the subjects of law, considering the necessity to defend in an articulate and dynamic way the rights of several beneficiaries.

---

4 J. Jouzel & A. Michelot, 2016, p. 16.

Therefore, climate justice breaks down into justice between individuals or certain groups of individuals, justice between States, justice between different generations (thus, for present and future humanity), and justice for nature. This last aspect led to a certain amount of debate within the CESE's environment section that was in charge of preparing the opinion; however, the problem was overcome by referring to national and international texts that recognize the intrinsic value of biological diversity. From the point of view of climate justice, it is a matter of taking into consideration one of the essential "partners" in executing the objective pursued[5] – namely, nature, even if it happens to be a symbolic partner. Environmental inequalities cover all environmental degradation and, therefore, all damage to ecological integrity.

Justice for future generations is no longer a debatable point. It is now commonly admitted that the right to sustainable development is a right belonging to future generations. Therefore, what is needed is to consider the preservation of economic, social, cultural and environmental rights as an ensemble for future generations. That means doing everything possible to conserve the possibility of choice for them, leaving future generations an environment at least equal in quality to that of present generations, and preserving equitable access for everyone to all the resources of a common heritage. This last point is developed in the book by Edith Brown Weiss specifying that "the members of the present generation have to refrain from degrading the available heritage and that, wherever some of them are too poor to exercise their right of access, others help them".[6]

Climate justice is an integral part of this cementing of solidarity between generations that accounts for the different capacities of different people. The members of a generation that cannot benefit from their "planetary heritage" (an expression also borrowed from Edith Brown Weiss) will not be able to transmit this heritage to future generations. Thus, vulnerability to climate change could contribute to the rupture of inter-generational links.

Behind this capacity for transmission hides the notion of irreversibility. Global warming puts us face to face with a "morally unacceptable danger" – in the sense used by the World Commission on the Ethics of Scientific Knowledge

---

5 D. Schlospberg, *Defining Environmental Justice. Theories, Movements and Nature*, Oxford University Press, U.K., 2007.

6 E. Brown Weiss, *Justice pour les générations futures* [*Justice for Future Generations*], United Nations University Press, 1989, UNESCO translation 1993, Editions Sang de la terre, Paris, 1993, p. 41.

and Technology (COMEST), of a danger to life that is serious, truly irreversible, inequitable for present as well as future generations, and imposed without any heed for the rights of those who suffer it.[7] The reality of climate change is no longer contested. Its consequences threaten the future of humanity. Climate justice involves confronting that reality. Constructing a project of justice for humanity in the future means looking into the consequences of our actions and admitting that our actions can have irreversible effects. Denying their irreversibility amounts to denying our responsibility with respect to future generations, whereas climate justice seeks above all to create a legal logic oriented towards the future.

II. Climate Justice at the Service of Future Generations: What Are the Prospects?

To bring about a climate justice "project" as envisaged by the 2016 French CESE opinion, it is necessary to activate the most innovative principles of environmental law possible; we must try to inject a new logic for the creation and articulation of public policies to preserve the rights of future generations effectively and enduringly.

A. Innovative Principles to Enable Us to Rise to the Climate Challenge

In the 2016 French CESE opinion, the fundamental principles of environmental law constitute a mainstay of climate justice, together with the principles of social justice and the major role played by research. The principle of prevention is, of course, a particularly appropriate way of preserving all the options for future generations. This is supplemented by the principle of precaution, which makes it possible to foresee potential risks and, thus, adopt a prudent approach to the development of projects that could have an impact on the environment. The essential principles of the 1998 Aarhus Convention – concerning access to information, public participation in the decision process and access to justice – are, moreover, essential in firmly establishing climate justice at a national and international level.

---

7 World Commission on the Ethics of Scientific Knowledge and Technology (COMEST), Report, *Les implications du changement climatique mondial* [*The Implications of Global Climate Change*], UNESCO, Paris, 2010, p. 31.

Two principles recently introduced in Law No. 2016-1087 of 8 August 2016 (for the restoration of biodiversity, nature and landscapes) also help underpin the implementation of climate justice for future generations.

Firstly, the principle of non-regression (according to which the protection of the environment cannot but be the object of improvement) goes hand in hand with the theory of constant progress applied in social law and, therefore, is also paramount in strengthening climate justice. Non-regression also reiterates basic human rights, of which the right to a healthy environment is an integral part – in that, non-regression of human rights is ensured by the guarantee of inviolability and irreversibility.[8] Guaranteeing constant improvement of the environment is, of course, a pledge to carry out our duty to protect the rights of future generations.

Next, the principle of ecological solidarity listed in the fundamental principles[9] under Title 1 of the law, opens up a number of possibilities even though it is defined in a restrictive manner, "6: The principle of ecological solidarity, which calls for the taking into consideration in all public decision-making having a significant impact on the environment of the areas affected, the interactions of ecosystems, living beings and natural or developed sites".

Thus, ecological solidarity is part of a dynamic approach (with "interactions"); instead of targeting specific localities, it targets ecosystems, natural or developed sites and, above all, living beings. This last aspect of the definition could be interpreted as referring to both present and future living beings.

The principle of ecological solidarity should inspire each of the following: knowledge, protection, enhancement, restoration, refurbishment, management, preservation of the ability to evolve, and the safeguarding of services ensuing from the various elements that constitute the common heritage of a nation, especially biodiversity. Elevated to the level of a principle, ecological solidarity could give rise to new texts that would define its scope more precisely. The jurisprudence could also seize on ecological solidarity to raise the thresholds of

---

8 M. Prieur, "De l'urgente nécessité de reconnaître le principe de 'non régression' en droit de l'environnement" [The Urgent Need to Recognize the Principle of "Non-regression" in Environmental Law], *in* Conference Proceedings of the French Society of Environmental Law (*SFDE*) of La Rochelle, 2010, A. Michelot (ed.), *Equité et environnement. Quel(s) modèle(s) de justice environnementale ?* [Equity and Environment: What Model(s) of Environmental Justice?], Larcier, Bruxelles, 2012, pp. 71–93.

9 It should be remembered here that French legislation uses the concepts of general principles and fundamental principles interchangeably in the different codes.

environmental responsibility where the protection of the interests of future generations is concerned.

Environmental law is evolving and enhancing our capacity to avoid environmental degradation that could have irreparable effects and prejudice the interests of future generations. Nevertheless, climate justice needs an operational dimension and, thus, a series of measures to ensure an ecological transition that is fair for everyone, including future generations.

B. Measures to Preserve the Interests of Future Generations: Anticipating Climate Risks

The 2016 French CESE opinion on climate justice currently constitutes the most advanced project of its sort at the national level. It is based on the pragmatic observation that France enjoys particularly favorable conditions for the implementation of a climate justice project befitting a developed country. The territories under French sovereignty constitute a broad geographic spread of diverse lands across several regions of the world thanks to the Overseas Territories. Consequently, France's natural heritage comprises varied land and sea ecosystems that are exposed to a broad diversity of climate risks. France is, therefore, particularly well placed to understand the issues of climate justice in all its forms. Moreover, rigorous social policies have been developed, backed up by a firm commitment to an ecological transition to guide the economic choices that determine the future.

The aim is to create synergy between economic, social and environmental policies and thus create transversal measures capable of engendering a suitable climate justice project. A number of measures recommended by the CESE demonstrate the priority given to the rights of future generations.

One of these is the support given to research into the trajectories of vulnerability in the territories that are most exposed to climate risks, taking into account the social criteria of this exposure.[10] Vulnerability is defined in the Intergovernmental Panel on Climate Change (IPCC) report glossary as a "Propensity or predisposition to be adversely affected. Vulnerability encompasses a variety of concepts and elements including sensitivity or susceptibility to harm and lack of capacity to cope and adapt".[11] The trajectories of vulnerability are

10 J. Jouzel & A. Michelot, 2016, p. 36.

11 IPCC, Climate change 2014: Summary report. Contribution of Work Groups I, II and III to the fifth Assessment Report of the Intergovernmental Panel on Climate Change,

based on an understanding of past phenomena that gives us the ability to anticipate the occurrence of future phenomena. The aim is to increase our ability to anticipate and, thus, facilitate adaptation to climate change for future generations to fight the maladaptation that characterises the neediest populations and, potentially, future generations.

Another measure that illustrates the preoccupation with implementing measures to protect the rights of future generations is that which consists in reviewing the rules for evaluating investment projects. The CESE thus suggests that the "methodological framework of the ex ante evaluation needs to be modified to take greater account of the poorest and of future generations".[12] This involves "setting a discount rate that more effectively takes into account the well-being of future generations".

This preoccupation with a framework for public investment that supports the fight against climate change in the interest of present and future generations is also found, with the same spirit but in the appropriate forms, in a recommendation relating to international investment. International investment is, of course, a major factor in development – one which carries much weight in the implementation of environmental policies. Poorly managed, it can work against the aims of the battle with global warming. Accordingly, the CESE recommends that "France should integrate into its foreign investment agreement model obligations relating to the impact study evaluations that take into account the objectives of climate justice".[13]

Conclusion

Climate justice has made great strides in its definitions, objectives, as well as in achieving social and institutional recognition. It is largely founded on the rights of future generations and has fully integrated the defence of the rights of humanity in the future by seeking to increase awareness as well as the accountability of present generations. Climate justice promises a legal logic for the future that can help change substantive law applicable in different economic, social and environmental fields in the context of economic transition. If a major objective of climate justice is preservation of the right to a healthy environment for those

---

[Under the direction of the core writing team, R.K. Pachauri & L.A. Meyer], IPCC, Geneva, Switzerland, 2014, p. 144.

12 J. Jouzel & A. Michelot, 2016, p. 46.

13 *Ibid.*, p. 44.

who are most exposed and vulnerable to climate change, there is little doubt – in view of the climate changes expected – that future generations are the most concerned. Given the under-representation of future generations before the highest national and international authorities, the creation of a climate justice project able to influence all public policies would therefore seem all-the-more essential. The deliberations surrounding reform of the French CESE – which could become the "Assembly of the future", as parliament debates a draft constitutional law for a more representative, responsible and efficient democracy – illustrate this preoccupation.

PART 4. PROSPECTIVE LEGAL ACTIONS ON BEHALF OF FUTURE GENERATIONS?

In the fourth Part of this book, we explore convergent and prospective paths of legal actions on behalf of Future Generations.

Dr. Marie-Angèle Hermitte examines the need to refocus legal categories as a vehicle for better recognizing and protecting the co-evolving relationship between humans and nature. Hermitte summarizes failures associated with regulation of common resource exploitation, including initial as well as modern attempts to address climate change. Some limited progress has been made by courageous "climate-aware" judges who have begun to shake the balance of powers by applying three forms of legal animism that give concerned citizens a greater role, including indigenist, spiritual and scientific inspirations (essay #11 on "Each Object has its own Subject! The Legal Revolutions of the Human-Nature Relationship")

Matthias Petel studies the potential impact of recognizing the rights of nature on the judicial protection of ecosystems. He first retraces the genealogy of our relationship with nature in the Western world and the shift provoked by granting legal personhood to nature: from anthropocentric ethics to ecocentrism, from neoclassical to ecological economics, and from appropriation to subjectivization within our legal orders. Secondly, Petel attempts to determine the extent to which the rights of nature can facilitate access to justice for environmental issues. He answers the common objections raised by opponents of this proposal, and analyzes examples where this revolution has become a reality including the concrete effects of such recognition. Finally, Petel argues that upon entering the Anthropocene, contrasting humankind and nature no longer makes sense – as our survival depends on the protection of the biosphere. Rather, he claims that the current struggles pit vulnerable human communities against profit-driven logics of corporations and/or States, in a manner that is detrimental to social and environmental objectives. Therefore, he believes that the effectiveness of the rights of nature will depend on the political or cultural practices of the human communities fighting for their land's protection. In that sense, beyond the anthropocentrism vs. ecocentrism debate, human rights and nature rights complement each other in the pursuit of ecological justice, defined as respect for the ecological limits imposed by nature while ensuring the well-being and the fundamental rights of all human beings (essay #12 on "The Rights of Nature: A Legal Revolution for Ecological Justice").

Attorney Juan Ignacio Pereyra begins his essay by noting the serious transgenerational harm caused by certain technological advances. He praises the positive influence of international law on Argentina's adoption of constitutional provisions and national legislation that respect the rights of future generations. Pereyra then surveys judicial decisions interpreting this major step forward under Argentinian law, but concludes that further development is necessary in the form of regulations that provide specific objective standards to be developed by specialized bodies charged with safeguarding the indispensable rights of future generations (essay #13 on "The Recognition of Rights for Future Generations in Argentinian Lawsuits: Review and Prospects").

David M. Forman identifies links between Native Hawaiian cultural values and the intergenerational equity concepts introduced at the beginning of this book by Professors Delmas-Marty, Brown Weiss and Robinson. Forman then describes a missed opportunity to apply relevant provisions of the Hawai'i constitution in support of local government efforts to fill gaps in both federal and state regulation of pesticide use, in addition to other impacts associated with more than fifty years of open-air field tests in Hawai'i involving genetically engineered seed crops (essay #14 entitled "Marooned in the Doldrums While Ignoring Indigenous Ecological Knowledge: Attempting to Regulate Pesticide Use in Hawai'i").

Professor Michel Prieur describes an effort to build upon two international covenants – concerning Civil and Political Rights (ICCPR), as well as Economic, Social and Cultural Rights (ICESCR) – with a third covenant that reinforces rights relating to the environment, by closely linking them to human rights. This draft third covenant: sets forth justiciable rights and obligations exercised with equity, solidarity between generations, without discrimination and in the framework of environmentally sustainable development; mandates international cooperation; and, provides for effective implementation through specific monitoring measures as well as enforcement through existing procedures administered by the ICESCR under its Optional Protocol (essay #15 on "The Project of an International Covenant on the Human Right to the Environment").

Attorney Corinne Lepage & Professor Emilie Gaillard address the same dynamic renewal of contemporary legal humanism in their essay concerning efforts to draft a Universal Declaration on the Rights and Duties of Humankind. Perhaps even more daring than the third covenant on a human right to the environment, this initiative seeks to extend the rights of humanity to future generations (essay #16 on "Towards the Recognition of a Universal Declaration of the Rights and Duties of Humankind").

Marie-Angèle HERMITTE

11. Each Object Has its Own Subject! The Legal Revolutions of the Human-Nature Relationship

Aware of the widening gap between Global warning alerts and the legal apparatus meant to deal with them, jurists are looking for new principles such as the non-regression principle, and new norm hierarchies such as the inclusion of climate and biodiversity issues in national constitutions. Each step is important. In spite of a variety of principles, rules and international conventions, our Earth system is entangled in a downward spiral. Would we be better off if we were to redesign "objects of law" and "subjects of law"?[1] This would involve a drastic reconstruction of the legal ontology, which inspires all operations of law.[2] We don't know for sure, but maybe these two complementary tracks deserve to be followed simultaneously. In this paper, I intend to focus exclusively on the ontological perspective.[3] Indeed, constituents, lawmakers, judges and plaintiffs tend to redesign legal categories in order to grasp global issues (*see* Part I below). We will further examine in which circumstances some legal systems have come to posit that natural entities are subjects of law, in order to evidence how different objects call for different subjects (*see* Part II below).

---

1 This essay raised difficult translation questions because the French and English categories are not identical. Francophones use the words "nature juridique", "ontologie juridique", to refer to law in general, while the word "legal", in French, refers to legislative act; English most often does not make any difference between the two. I will use the most common English translation, "legal nature". On the other hand, I will make a *verbatim* translation for the concepts of "sujet de droit" and "objet de droit", designated as "subject of law" and "object of law". This allows me to highlight this first logical level, which is very abstract. At a second level, there are two sub-categories, natural persons and legal persons. Natural entities must constitute a third sub-category, independent of the first two.

2 Y. Thomas, *Les opérations du droit [*Legal Operations*]*, Le Seuil, 2011.

3 Given the limited length of this essay, please see some previous works which this paper is a follow up to: M.-A. Hermitte, *Le droit saisi au vif. Sciences, technologies et formes de vie* [*Law Transformed: Science, Technology and Life Forms*], Interviews with F. Chateauraynaud, éditions Petra, 2013; and M.-A. Hermitte, "Artificialisation de la nature et droit(s) du vivant" [Artificialization of Nature and Law for Living Species], *in* P. Descola, *Les natures en questions* [*The Natures in Question*], Odile Jacob, 2018.

I. Global Hazards and Refocus of Legal Categories

This conference has fully evidenced how slowly worldviews towards the environment have changed: there is no point in further discussing it. Nature, once viewed as a pool meant for exploitation has turned into something with which we, as humans co-evolve.[4] The current challenge is to develop the tools relevant to this new approach that values the relationship. Such tools are currently available, in France *via* the preamble of the Charter for the Environment; in Ecuador, *via* its Constitution; and in Colombia, *via* its Supreme Court. How do we qualify in law these new objects we want to protect, such as climate which until then had been viewed as meta-legal? Our first intuition is to think of them in terms of commons to humankind as a whole (*see* Section I.A. below). How are we re-articulating these new objects to acting subjects? Climate disputes, which are the main expression of this global identity, reveal a more complex situation than action taken on behalf of the sole "humankind" (*see* Section I.B. below).

A. Things for Humankind as a Whole[5]: Is There a Lack of Operative Categories for Common Goods and Common Evils?

In Roman law, both air and the sea were viewed as commons that no-one was allowed to privatize, since they needed to be accessible to all. In the twentieth century, the category of "Common Heritage of Humankind" was meant to express, in the same line of thought, this intuition that some objects of law essential to Humankind as a whole might exist at a given time and for future generations. This was an attempt to link new objects of law (extra-atmospheric space, celestial bodies or atmosphere) to these new subjects of law, namely humankind or future generations. Soon it turned out that the basic characteristics of the newly designed regime, conservation and equitable access as well as the more or less consensual notion of its non-appropriable and inalienable character (all imprescriptible) did not meet the expectations of mainstream liberal economics. Although these objects have all found a regime, still under discussion, it serves mainly for their exploitation.[6]

---

4 O. Barrière & others, *Coviability of Social and Ecological Systems: Reconnecting Mankind to the Biosphere in an Era of Global Change*, Springer, 2019, Vols. 1 & 2, *available online at* https://www.springer.com/gb/book/9783319784960.

5 Things *extra patrimonio*.

6 For a history of this change in the law of the sea, which had been the most sophisticated avatar of the Common Heritage of Mankind, *see* J.-P. Beurier, "L'autorité internationale des fonds marins, l'environnement et le juge" [The International Seabed Authority,

In 1992, global warming issues were merely a "common concern of humankind", as mentioned by the Rio Convention on Climate Change, taken up again in the Paris Agreement. It was not until 11 July 2018 that this concern turned into a "security risk", at a session of the United Nations Security Council. A plan was set out to create an information and warning body in charge of registering correlations between climate change, wars, terrorism and displaced population.[7] In spite of this growing awareness, the climate's legal nature is not addressed.

Let us note that a number of investigations focus on these "positive" objects, "global public goods"; less energy is dedicated to investigating "negative" objects – these "global public evils" – that form all the negative externalities of the production systems. However, some consider waste accumulation as a more serious source of concern than the increasing scarcity of non-renewable resources.[8]

The scientific evidence concerning these issues has been fully disseminated, well enough to trigger action in what is coined "our knowledge societies". However, most administrations are reluctant to take relevant actions that would involve a more frugal economic system.

---

the Environment and the Judge], *in* Collectif, *La représentation de la nature devant le juge : approche comparative et prospective* [*The Representation of Nature Before the Judge: Comparative and Prospective Approach*], VertigO, 2017.

7 In 2018, the Security Council noted that Iraq and Egypt were forced for the first time to reduce their arable surface area. L. Maertens, "The UN Security Council debates on climate change", *Revue internationale et stratégique*, 2018/1, No. 109, pp. 105–114.

8 *See* P. Hugon, *L'ECONOMIE ETHIQUE PUBLIQUE : Biens Publics Mondiaux et Patrimoines Communs* [*THE PUBLIC ETHICAL ECONOMY: Global Public Goods and Common Heritage*], UNESCO, Economie Ethique, No. 3, *available online at* https://unesdoc.unesco.org/ark:/48223/pf0000130599 (accessed 16 June 2019). Hugon often deals with "public ills", but more in the sense of being the opposite of commons, and relevant in the same conceptual sphere as an independent category that has its own regime. On the notion of "common risks" and the uncontrolled circulation of data, *cf.* J.-S. Bergé & D. Le Metayer, "Phénomènes de masse et droit des données" [Mass Phenomena and Data Rights], to be published in *Communication-Commerce-Electronique*, Lexis Nexis. I do not agree with many of the statements in P.-N. Giraud, *L'homme inutile* [*The Useless Man*], Paris, Odile Jacob, 2015, but the book does raise the question of an inventory of disparate types of waste, with which to address the question of economic model structures.

B. Climate Change Litigation and the "Schism of Reality": Climate-Aware People as Opposed to Government Denials[9]

The whistle has been blown long ago and many citizens around the world received the message; however, the obvious incapacity of climate skeptic and climate paralyzed[10] governments to react properly to the threat represents a "schism of reality".[11] Jurists have paid little attention to this notion, coined by political scientists. However, law provides a specific form of visibility for this notion, obvious in what have become known as climate change litigation: lawsuits triggered by some climate-aware individuals, often under age. These claimants submitted to the courts their State's climate policies, whose blindness could violate their fundamental rights, legal mode of reasoning based on this denial of reality: the difficulties they met (*see* subsection I.B.1. below) will not prevent the slight increase in the power of "young people" and of the future generations (*see* subsection I.B.2. below).

---

9 In this essay, I deal with the climate disputes solely in the context of what they reveal about the legal ontology I am trying to form – which is very reductive. Regarding doctrine, please refer to the long and elaborate bibliography by M. Hautereau-Boutonnet, "Les procès climatiques par la doctrine du procès climatique" [Climatic Processes by the Doctrine of the Climatic Process], *in* C. Cournil & L. Varison, *Les procès climatiques : du national à l'international* [*Climatic Processes: From the National to the International*], Pédone, 2018.

10 Focusing our attention on the climate skeptics, who are decreasingly credible, has become counterproductive. Inability to address the problem now comes from climate-paralyzed people (who give lip-service but in practice defend the conventional economic activity) and climate-indifferent people (who make up the majority of the world population that refuses to change its lifestyle).

11 G. Marshall, *Le syndrome de l'autruche – Pourquoi notre cerveau veut ignorer le changement climatique* [*The Ostrich Syndrome – Why our Brain Wants to Ignore Climate Change*], Actes Sud, 2017; S. Akyut & A. Dahan, *Gouverner le climat ?* [*Governing the Climate?*], Presses de Sciences Po, 2015; M.-A. Hermitte, "*Edouard Bonnefous et la biodiversité : 'Vox clamantis in deserto' ou illustration du schisme de réalité*" [Edouard Bonnefous and Biodiversity: "The voice of one crying in the wilderness" or Illustration of the Schism of Reality], C. Bréchignac, G. de Broglie & M. Delmas-Marty (eds.), *L'environnement et ses métamorphoses* [*The Environment and its Metamorphoses*], Hermann, 2015.

1. *Difficulty of Identifying the Relevant Objects of Law in Order to Curb Global Change*

The argumentation submitted to the Supreme Court of Pakistan by a seven-year-old petitioner highlighted precisely that Pakistan continues to invest in coal, despite the country's participation in the COP 21, the existence of a climate minister of a climate plan, and the availability of considerable renewable energy sources. At a global level, "enormous sums of money and resources were spent on further destabilizing climate systems".[12] The International Monetary Fund support to fossil fuel for year 2015 was up to 5,300 billion dollars, including both subsidies and corrections of the negative externalities related to fossil energy. Carrying on in this manner is simply incomprehensible. From a legal standpoint, the first task to undertake would be to correctly delineate the objects in question.

a. *The Climate Is Not a Subject of Law*

Let us exclude from the start the possibility that the climate could be a subject of law. The climate may happen to be personified by humans complaining about floods, heat waves or the storms; however, there is no way to identify specific needs that would serve as a base to define the right of the climate to be protected from change. One might even assume the climate is enjoying such blasts, so it is unclear which rights the climate could claim to fight for.

b. *Few Operative Objects of Law Pertaining to Climate Change Emerge*

Greenhouse gases (GHG) are definitely "tangible things" that form an indistinct mass trapped by the greenhouse effect. As a mass, is it a "common evil" to which no clear category is associated?[13] But should we consider them as "goods", things *in patrimonio*? Yes, indeed, assuming we agree with William Dross that they are involuntary and undesirable fruits of human activity. Dross proposes to put an end to the "free faculty of abandon" granted to property owners in

---

12 The petition cited was received and made public. *Ali v. Federal of Pakistan & Another*, Constitutio Petition/No. I of 2016, Supreme Court of Pakistan (Islamabad), *available online at* https://www.elaw.org/system/files/Pakistan%20Climate%20Case-FINAL.pdf. However, no judgment was ever given.

13 It is made up of different molecules, but converted into units of contribution to warming, is undifferentiated. For more on the interest that such masses could have generated, *cf.* J.-S. Bergé & D. Le Metayer, *Communication Commerce Electronique*, Dec. 2018, Issue 12, Study No. 20, *available online at* http://www.universitates.eu/jsberge/?p=23762.

favor of an "obligation to reallocate" the GHG emissions at the request of their "neighbor". This solution sounds interesting, yet it seems so unpractical on a day-to-day basis, that it undermines the idea.[14] The current situation entails considering GHG by default as freely abandoned things at the very moment of their production, which has the drawback of placing them in a category of objects for which no-one is responsible and leads to the current dead end. Dross criticizes the modern waste regime, which creates some exceptions for certain objects to the freedom of abandon principle, and imposes various obligations on the producer; thus, transforming waste into an object "of negative value" – not with regard to private interests, according to the most well-known model, but with regard to general interest[15]: producers are forced to limit waste production, recycle it, take into account its dangerousness, dump it in the appropriate landfill, and give it a negative economic value at the expense of its producer. However, waste law functions on a case-by-case basis, with all the delays and sluggishness that permits.

This is the solution favored by the Kyoto Protocol and the tools that implement it. The emissions ("released into the atmosphere of certain gases from certain sources"), gases and sources are defined as juridical facts because they are at the core of a network of obligations created by law in order to achieve emissions reduction in certain territories and for certain emitters, and to set a temperature reduction target. The technical device will be an emission permit implemented through the creation of accounting units characterized by their "contribution to global warming"; emission and absorption units, likely to join an existing legal category, "intangible movable property", traded on markets segmented according to their fungibility.[16]

The climate too is defined as a fact: a set of average weather conditions, locally observed over a 30 years period. Climate change is defined as a wider planetary

14 W. Dross, "De la revendication à la réattribution: la propriété peut-elle sauver le climat ?" [From Claim to Reallocation: Can Property Save the Climate?], *Recueil Dalloz*, 2017, p. 2,553. We could also think of the category, "*res nullius*" because GHG emissions could be involuntarily compared to these wild animals that prosper on appropriated land and tend to cause damage to the neighborhood.

15 D. Chilstein, "Les biens à valeur vénale négative" [Goods with Negative Market Value], *Revue trimestrielle droit civil*, 2006.

16 For an article with vast bibliography on this type of property, *see* F-G. Trébulle, "Les titres environnementaux" [Environmental Titles], *Revue Juridique de l'Environnement*, 2011/2, p. 203, *available online at* https://www.cairn.info/revue-revue-juridique-de-l-environnement-2011-2-page-203.htm.

process evolving over a much longer period of time. In legal terms, the climate cannot be reduced to a thing endowed with tangibility because it has no materiality nor localization. On the other hand, it is unclear how the climate can be established as an intangible thing, because if it fits with the basic idea of immaterial wealth, we do not see how to delineate a variety of complex processes, involving fuzzy or unexpected elements. The atmosphere, as a set of gaseous bodies precisely located around the globe, could be more easily classified as a tangible thing common to all humankind. To date, the doctrine struggles to establish these things as global public goods, whose progress is barely visible in positive law.[17]

Yet certain judicial rulings reveal that the "climate system" can be qualified in two different directions: an economic vision based on the climate as a natural resource or environmental asset; and an axiological approach that considers the climate as a value, object of a fundamental right, like freedom or life. These avenues are being explored by emerging subjects.

2. Emerging Subjects of Law: "Young People" and Future Generations

So far, no subjects of law have been stabilized. However, there are some emerging stakeholders, mostly young people and future generations.

a. The Paris Agreement and Non-Party Stakeholders: A Status in the Form of a Call for Help.[18]

The Paris Agreement, following the *Lima-Paris Action Plan,* dedicated an entire chapter to the notion of "non-party stakeholders" – in other words, any physical

---

17 B. Boidin, "Approche économique" [Economic Approach], *in Dictionnaire des biens communs*, M. Cornu, F. Orsi, J. Rochfeld (eds.), Quadrige, Presses Universitaires de France, 2017.

18 *See, e.g.,* J.-M. Arbour, "L'impossible défi canadien: lutter efficacement contre les changements climatiques, exporter davantage de pétrole, respecter les compétences constitutionnelles des provinces" [The Impossible Canadian Challenge: Efficiently Fight Climate Change, Export More Oil, Respect the Constitutional Authorities of the Provinces], *in Après l'accord de Paris, quels droits face au changement climatique?* [*After the Paris Agreement, What Rights for Climate Change?*], *Revue Juridique de l'Environnement*, Lavoisier, 2017, No. Special, pp. 73–103; *ibid.*, pp. 105–117 (I. Michallet, "De l'action locale au droit global: l'engagement climatique des villes" [From Local Action to Global Law: Cities Responding to Climate Change]); *ibid.*, pp. 119–133 (M.-P. Blin-Franchome, "Quel rôle pour l'entreprise après l'Accord de Paris?" [The Company's Role After the Paris Agreement?]); *ibid.*, pp. 135–139 (R. Bettin, "Les

or legal persons other than States. Although the role of NGOs has long been recognized in international public law, those who work spontaneously for the good of the climate are now being treated as indispensable partners who will be associated "in parallel" with the COP. These new partners are encouraged to join their efforts and coalesce: this obviously involves the civil society, but also financial institutions, corporations[19] and above all urban areas, which will be home to seven out of every ten inhabitants by 2050. In this regard, they should be the leading players at climate conventions. This shows how maladapted international public law is given its focus on State stakeholders. From this standpoint, the boom of "non-party stakeholders" sounds as a confession by the States' of their own insufficiency. However, that confession does not generate any specific international power, such as a generalized system of preferences between urban areas active in reducing atmospheric pollution.[20]

b. Humankind?

In legal technique, the solution could have been to recognize humankind as the subject of a right to a climate beneficial to the development of the human species, or of the living world in general, under an eco-centric perspective. But what legitimate representatives could have been found? Every person may stand before any court and plead in their own name wherever they are in the world, but in a much wider perspective than their own interest. Let us mention two cases that recently made headlines.

First, the Court of Appeal in Hamm, Germany, ruled that it would hear the case of Saúl Luciano Lliuya, a Peruvian farmer and high mountain guide, against Rheinisch-Westfälisches Elektrizitätswerk (RWE), the main energy emitter of

---

ONG: moteurs de l'avant, actrices de l'après" [NGOs: Drivers of the "Before", Actors of the "After"]).

19 Professor Hautereau-Boutonnet anticipated the possible development of a new branch of the *lex mercatoria*, specific to awareness of climate change. M. Hautereau-Boutonnet, "Is the climate *lex mercatoria* a representation of global law?", *Revista de direito international*, Direito Ambiental Global, UniCEUB, 2017, Vol. 14, No. 3, p. 31.

20 M.-P. Blin-Franchomme, "Quel rôle dans la lute le changement climatique pour l'entreprise?" [What Role for Companies in the Fight Against Climate Change?], *in* M. Hautereau-Boutonnet (ed.), *Quel droit pour sauver le climat?* [*What Right to Save the Climate?*], 2018, p. 9, *available online at* https://halshs.archives-ouvertes.fr/halshs-01684948/document (accessed 16 June 2019) (discussing the "climate social responsibility" dynamic that encourages companies to engage in the Non-State Actor Zone for Climate Action, or NAZCA, portal set up under the Paris Agreement).

Global Energy Services (GES) Europe. Each and every emission by RWE adds to the overall increase in temperature in some way. The farmer's legal theory sought to dilute the traditional concept of the causality link in the sense that, instead of being detrimental to the victim (as can often be the case), it would actually work in their favor because all emissions in some way add to different damages, whereever they take place. The Court ordered a group of experts to establish the causality link between the pollutant waste of RWE and the damages noted in Peru because of the melting glaciers in the Andes and all its local consequences.[21] RWE does not have a power plant in Peru and, of course, argued that an emitter is not responsible for phenomena that are a result of multiple causes; RWE instead asserted that recognizing such a cause of action could lead to an anarchic situation where everyone sues everyone because each and everybody suffers from and contributes to climate change.[22] Indeed, the consequences of recognizing such harm could have financial impacts that would be the most convincing way of engaging industries in a serious energy transformation – one that governments have not managed to impose upon them. These individual cases, which at least at first, may not go very far, thus take on evident collective value.

We may also consider the case of Ashgar Leghari, who petitioned the High Court of Lahore regarding the government's failure to act in the fight against climate change – arguing that the absence of action and delays jeopardized water supplies and food security.[23] The initial governmental action ordered by the court in 2015[24] appears to have been somewhat effective, because the court's 2018

---

21 The Peruvian farmer sought an award of damages so he could carry out the necessary work to reconstruct his village. *Cf.* M. Hautereau-Boutonnet & L. Canali, "Jalons pour une responsabilité civile climatique préventive" [Paving the Way for a Preventive Climate Change Tort Liability Regime], *Journal International de Bioéthique,* 2018, No. 3, *n° spécial La responsabilité climatique.*

22 D. Nerbollier, "Réchauffement climatique, un agriculteur péruvien contre le géant allemand de l'énergie" [Global Warming, a Peruvian Farmer against the German Energy Giant], *La Croix*, 14 Nov. 2017, *available online at* https://www.la-croix.com/Sciences-et-ethique/Environnement/Rechauffement-climatique-agriculteur-peruvien-contre-geant-allemand-lenergie-2017-11-14-1200891945.

23 Order Sheet, *Ashgar Leghari v. Federation of Pakistan*, W.P. No. 25501/2015, Lahore High Court Green Bench, 04 Sep. 2015, *available online at* https://elaw.org/system/files/pk.leghari.090415_0.pdf.

24 The court directed several government ministries to: nominate "a climate change focal person" to implement the Framework [of Climate Change Policy (2014–2030)], and to present a list of action points by 31 December 2015, in addition to creating a Climate Change Commission composed of representatives of key ministries, NGO's, and technical experts to monitor the government's progress. *Leghari v. Federation of Pakistan*,

final judgment acknowledges a number of improvements – although admittedly insufficient – in the government's implementation of action plans adopted pursuant to the earlier orders.[25] The successful petitioner referred to himself first and foremost as a farmer (therefore, an individual), then as a citizen of Pakistan – i.e., an individual member of a Nation – without taking a step further by identifying himself as a "world citizen" and representing humankind in the legal action.

c. *The "Youth Plaintiffs"*

Judges are also recognizing "youth" plaintiffs who petition the courts under the intervention of their parents, tutors or guardians – as well themselves. These youth stand before their national judges demanding respect for their rights to a sustainable climate: a sufficient quality of life and a reasonable life expectancy for themselves, their fellow countrymen and their descendants. Some "youth" also stand on behalf of all humankind.[26]

W.P. No. 25501/2015, *Lahore High Court Green Bench*, 04 Sep. 2018, *available online at* http://blogs2.law.columbia.edu/climate-change-litigation/wp-content/uploads/sites/16/non-us-case-documents/2015/20150512_Case-No.-CHR-NI-2016-0001_petition-1.pdf (Summary, with link to "Decision"). The court subsequently issued a supplemental decision on 14 September 2015, naming 21 individuals to the Commission and vesting it with various powers. *Leghari v. Federation of Pakistan*, W.P. No. 25501/2015, *Lahore High Court Green Bench*, 14 Sep. 2018, *available online at* http://blogs2.law.columbia.edu/climate-change-litigation/wp-content/uploads/sites/16/non-us-case-documents/2015/20150512_Case-No.-CHR-NI-2016-0001_petition-1.pdf (Summary, with link to "Decision").

25 According to the judgment issued by Judge Syed Mansoor Ali Shah, the government took 66% of priority measures for the implementation of policies concerning climate change. *Leghari v. Federation of Pakistan*, W.P. No. 25501/2015, *Lahore High Court Green Bench*, 25 Jan. 2018, *available online at* http://blogs2.law.columbia.edu/climate-change-litigation/wp-content/uploads/sites/16/non-us-case-documents/2015/20150512_Case-No.-CHR-NI-2016-0001_petition-1.pdf ("Judgment").

26 Since 2011, Emilie Gaillard has noted the acceptance of the concept by environmental law, its migration towards fundamental rights, and the premises for legal action. E. Gaillard, *Générations futures et droit privé. Vers un droit des générations futures* [*Future Generations and Private Law: Towards a Law for Future Generations*], Librairie Générale de Droit et de Jurisprudence, 2011, pp. 655–673.

(i) "Youth Plaintiffs": Future Generations Embedded in Present Generations

Strangely enough, while the "future generations" category might have been directly seized, "suspended" as it was in numerous texts without binding force, it was the "youth plaintiffs" category that emerged more directly: a group of *young* people aged between eight and nineteen ("youth plaintiffs"), Earth Guardians – an association of *young* environmental activists – and Dr. James Hansen, acting as guardian for *future generations*.[27] The main focus was on their determination and their precarious future.[28] However, the lawsuit also highlighted their incapacity to vote, since they were under age, arguing that the judge was their only recourse.[29] Some judges are moved by their youth. They recognize their interest in demonstrating a causal link between past and present decisions, their vulnerability and that of their descendants; these children who are the present generations, already impacted, represent the present generation, engrossed with future generations, facing a grim fate.

The Supreme Court of Colombia is the only court that emphasized the specific characteristics of the youth plaintiffs' standing: aged 7 to 25, their life expectancy is 78 years and their adulthood will take place from 2041 to 2070. During this period, the temperature will rise between 1.6°C and 2.14°C, and they will be affected by all the hazards involved.[30]

---

27 I have chosen to discuss Judge Ann Aiken's ruling because it is particularly well worded. *Juliana v. United States*, No. 6:15-cv-01517-TC, United States District Court for the District of Oregon, 10 Nov. 2016, slip opinion, *available online at* https://static1.squarespace.com/static/571d109b04426270152febe0/t/5824e85e6a49638292ddd1c9/1478813795912/Order+MTD.Aiken.pdf. The trial scheduled to start 29 October 2018 has been stayed pending an interlocutory appeal to the United States Court of Appeals for the Ninth Circuit. *See* E. Brown & others, essay #9 (this book) on "Securing the Legal Right to a Healthy Atmosphere and Stable Climate for the Benefit of All Present and Future Generations".

28 According to her father, a lawyer specialized in environmental law, the seven-year-old Rabab Ali is deeply concerned about climate change that is affecting her and millions of Pakistanis, and will affect future generations. Ali, who swore allegiance to the Earth on 23 April 2015 on "World Earth Day", has never seen the dew on the leaves; only fine particles. She has never heard the birds sing; only rickshaws.

29 *Juliana v. United States*, p. 16 (section I.D., entitled "Summary: This Case Does Not Raise a Nonjusticiable Political Question").

30 This ruling is generally studied in the light of the biological diversity and nature as a subject of law, but it is also relevant to deforestations. The plaintiffs focused on the commitments taken by Colombia in this respect during the Conference of the Parties (COP) 21, therefore in the framework of the climate mechanism.

Conversely, in the *Urgenda* case,[31] the claim was launched by a "platform" of activists bringing the action as Dutch citizens. They came from all segments of society involved in the ecological transition. They stood on behalf of present and future generations, all over the world. However, the Dutch State argued that the plaintiffs did not have standing to bring claims on behalf of the rest of the world. To justify its ruling in favor of the Urgenda Foundation, the court highlighted the characteristics of a climate system which is global by nature. From then on, all NGOs concerned about climate change have rightly argued that everything done in the small state of the Netherlands has a global reach, and everything that is done at the present time will impact future generations.[32] Therefore, there is no need to establish Urgenda's capacity to represent some specific generation or country, since the interests of some serve the interest of others.[33]

In Switzerland there is a "Climate Seniors Association". As if youth and seniors have distinguishable interests in the climate debate.[34]

(ii) Consensual Fundamental Rights

From one ruling to the next, the youth plaintiffs claim the same fundamental rights.[35] In *Juliana*, Judge Aiken mentions the youth plaintiffs' standing to challenge American climate change policy by asserting constitutional rights: the right to freedom, life and property, plus dignity, including access to water and consequently food security.[36] The Supreme Court of Colombia similarly recognized

---

31 *Urgenda Foundation v. Kingdom of the Netherlands,* Case No. C/09/456689/HA ZA 131396, The Hague District Court, 24 June 2015.

32 *Ibid.*, paragraphs 4.6 to 4.8.

33 *Ibid.*, paragraphs 4.79, 4.83 & 4.92.

34 Klima Seniorinnen, Aînées pour la protection climate [Elders for Climate Protection], *available online at* https://ainees-climat.ch.

35 C. Cournil, "Les droits fondamentaux au service de l'émergence d'un contentieux climatique, Des stratégies contentieuses des requérants à l'activisme des juges" [Fundamental Rights at the Service of the Emergence of a Climate Dispute, Applicants' Contentious Strategies to the Activism of Judges], *in* M. Torre-Schaub, C. Cournil, S. Lavorel & M. Moliner-Dubost (eds.), *Quel(s) droit(s) pour les changements climatiques?* [*What Right(s) for Climate Change?*], éditions Mare & Martin, 2017.

36 Several rulings enrich this basis of diverse principles attached to it: the principle of equity, which not only leads to the principle of common responsibilities, that are different for developing countries, but also to the obligation to take the needs of future generations into account in current policies (*Urgenda*, paragraphs 4.55 and 4.56); the principles of precaution and sustainable development that have an impact on fundamental individual rights (*Urgenda*, paragraph 4.63).

that it can judge the violation of fundamental rights to life, health, freedom and human dignity as determined by the environment and ecosystems: without a healthy environment, subjects of law and sensitive beings in general cannot survive (*see* Part II below).

(iii) *Public Trust* vs. the Obligation of Protection and Diligence

The youth plaintiffs' invocation of the right to life is based on specific legal tools. Thus, "Public trust" is an institution of English common law that can also be found in other countries from the U.S. to Pakistan.[37] In the *Juliana* case, Judge Aiken defined the public trust as encompassing powers so central to the exercise of sovereignty (like the police power), that the State cannot ever waive. Natural resources are a group of assets that the successive governments must preserve to meet the needs of the successive generations of citizens. The legislator cannot therefore bar the State from these rights, just as he cannot bar ports from navigable waters: the legislator is in a similar position as the trustees who are in charge of protecting the common property from damage in the interest of current and future beneficiaries. This imposes limits on the exercise of legislative powers. According to the judge, the American energy and climate policy shows that the State has abdicated that responsibility stemming from its position as a trustee, and this presumed renouncement must be challenged as a violation of substantive due process. The word "abdicate" is the key to these disputes, because it expresses in legal terms the denial of reality that makes governments climate-paralyzed.

In *Urgenda*, the Dutch judges based their ruling on a concept that is more familiar to continental laws: the State's obligation of due diligence in implementing its duties of protection, of both environment and people. It is thus obliged to design a climate plan in accordance with scientific data, to be further implemented and monitored. However, even though the Constitution, the

37 This capacity to contribute to developing environmental law was addressed long ago in an article by Joseph Sax, highly acclaimed to this day. J. Sax, *The Public Trust Doctrine in Natural Resource Law: Effective Judicial Intervention*, *Michigan Law Review*, 1969, Vol. 68, p. 417, *available online at* https://scholarship.law.berkeley.edu/cgi/viewcontent.cgi?article=2359&context=facpubs; E. Cornu-Thenard, "Eléments sur l'apport de la doctrine du public trust à la représentation de la nature devant le juge" [Elements on the Contribution of the Public Trust Doctrine to the Representation of Nature Before the Judge], *in* Collectif, *La représentation de la nature devant le juge, approches comparative et prospective* [The Representation of Nature Before the Judge, Comparative and Prospective Approaches], *VertigO*, 2017, p. 187.

European Convention on Human Rights and International Climate Change Law are not directly relevant to the case, their norms can serve as guidelines in order to assess whether the State has failed in its obligation to protect vis-a-vis *Urgenda* and more precisely to assess to what extent this limits its discretionary power.[38] The court concluded that there was indeed a breach of due diligence because emission reductions were not of a sufficient magnitude to curb the trajectory, causing "reduced future options".[39]

(iv) Separation of Powers, Right to Trial and Legitimacy of The Judge to Impose an "Order" on the State

The "right to trial" is currently at the heart of climate disputes and reveals, in the domain of law, the schism of reality. Indeed, citizens, as individuals or as groups, are not targeting any specific illegality, but their State's climate policy as a whole, poorly adjusted to scientific data. Consequently, they beg the judges to order governments to change their climate policies. This request is being made in relation to: the American climate policy in general in the *Juliana* case; the percentage and pace of emissions reduction chosen by the State in the *Urgenda* affair; as well as, the development and exploitation of a coal reserve in the petition by the young Rabab Ali. Both urgency and depth of focus feed a conflict between "climate-conscious" citizens and "reality-denying States".[40]

These claims address the separation of powers issue, because political choices are at least partly adjourned for further deliberation. In *Urgenda*, the court deviates from the topic by making the following statement: strictly speaking, there is no separation of powers, but rather a distribution of functions between executive and judicial power, because the Rule of Law demands that the action of political bodies could be assessed by an independent court, even though the court should not get involved in political decisions.[41] A judge, although not elected, has democratic legitimacy of another kind, in another respect, and the obligation to protect citizens from the State, albeit "restrained".[42] The way and the rate in which the objective of 2°C maximum warming is to be achieved,

38 *Urgenda*, paragraphs 4.36 to 4.52.
39 *Ibid.*, paragraph 4.75.
40 *Ibid.*, paragraph 4.65.
41 *Ibid.*, paragraph 4.95.
42 *Ibid.*, paragraphs 4.97 and 4.100.

is certainly within the discretionary power of the government, but this broad power is not unlimited.[43]

In the *Juliana* case, Judge Aiken recalled that although separation of powers is a defensive wall against tyranny, it should not bar any right to file a complaint when fundamental rights protected by the constitution are at stake. All youth plaintiffs brought evidence that they had been personally and tangibly hurt by phenomena such as algae proliferation, a flooded house, and asthma aggravated by forest fires. They were thus able to prove the causal link between the damages they suffered on the one hand and, on the other hand, the United States energy policy since 1751 and the considerable contribution this State makes to global emission levels. A judicial order to change this policy could partly repair their damage. They therefore have the right to "due process": the "genius" of the constitution, which enables it to adapt to new needs as Thomas Jefferson did, this time by taking future generations into account. Judge Aiken thus has "no doubt that the right to a climate system capable of sustaining human life is fundamental to a free and ordered society".[44] A stable climate is the foundation of society, "without which there would be neither civilization or progress",[45] especially for future generations. Without taking a stance on the ultimate result, the judge posits that there is a "cause of action". The Supreme Court of Colombia, on the other hand, fulfills its commitment by compelling the State to move towards a more eco-centric society by changing its "an anthropocentric and selfish model",[46] characterized by dramatic population growth, adoption of a consumerist system and over-exploitation of natural resources. In this regard, the presidency and other

---

43 *Ibid.*, paragraphs 4.53 and 4.54. The issues of pace and urgency are important in all these cases. The plaintiffs and the judges all insisted on the urgency of reducing emissions. Some also insisted on the urgency of *not* taking or implementing decisions that obstruct the reduction target. This is particularly dramatic in the case of the enormous coal deposit in Pakistan: according to the young petitioner Rabab Ali, it should not be mined at all. It is also evident in the Dutch case, where the court insisted on the need to speed up the transition to renewable energies. *Ibid.*, paragraph 4.65. Based on data provided by the IPCC, the judges argued that taking immediate action is more cost-effective than acting later. *Ibid.*, paragraphs 4.71 to 4.73.

44 *Juliana v. United States*, p. 1250.

45 *Ibid.*

46 *Future Generations v. Ministry of the Environment and others*, Supreme Court of Colombia, No. STC4360-2018, 5 Apr. 2018, translated by Dejusiticia (unofficial translation of excerpts), p.16, *available online at* http://blogs2.law.columbia.edu/climate-change-litigation/wp-content/uploads/sites/16/non-us-case-documents/2018/20180405_11001-22-03-000-2018-00319-00_decision-1.pdf

regional and municipal authorities were ordered to work with the plaintiffs, impacted communities and the concerned public, to formulate an action plan against deforestation and its effects on the climate. The court also ordered the presidency and all the local authorities to make an intergenerational pact against deforestation.[47]

These judges are calling for a revitalization of the "third power". They are encouraged by the need to shake the balance of powers by giving "concerned" citizens a greater role, demanding that scientific data, international law and the general principles of fundamental rights be respected. Christian Huglo[48] highlights the transformation of the judge's function by taking into consideration global and intergenerational issues that most States have abandoned, by incorporating new sanctions in their orders (or *imperium*, for Mathilde Hautereau-Boutonnet).[49] These would force the defective States to take more serious reduction and adaptation measures.[50] This is what the Dutch judges did: they ordered the State to

---

47 This obliges a fight against the interests of the powerful, who are involved in land grabbing, crops for illicit use, infrastructure, agro-business and illegal tree cutting – all profitable activities that aggravate climate change. The separation of powers issue is less relevant to Latin American jurisdictions, using very specific procedures. *Cf.* E.F. Fernandez, "Les controverses autour de l'intérêt à agir pour l'accès au juge constitutionnel: de la défense du droit à l'environnement (Costa Rica) à la défense des droits de la nature (Équateur)" [The Controversies Surrounding the Interest in Acting for Access to the Constitutional Judge: From the Defense of the Right to the Environment (Costa Rica) to the Defense of the Rights of Nature (Ecuador)], *VertigO – La revue électronique en sciences de l'environnement*, Special Issue No. 22, Sep. 2015.

48 *See* C. Huglo, essay #8 (this book) on "Global Warming and the National Courts: A Global Legal Revolution?"; *cf.* A.-S. Tabau & C. Cournil, "Nouvelles perspectives pour la justice climatique : Cour du District de La Haye, 24 juin 2015, Fondation Urgenda contre Pays-Bas" [New perspectives for Climate Justice: LaHaye District Court, 24 June 2015, Urgenda Foundation Against the Netherlands], *Revue Juridique de l'Environnement*, 2015/4, p. 200, *available online at* https://notreaffaireatous.org/. *See also* London School of Economics and Political Science, Grantham Research Institute on Climate Change and the Environment, http://www.lse.ac.uk/GranthamInstitute/, for an overview as well as rulings linked to all the climate disputes throughout the world.

49 M. Hautereau-Boutonnet, Climatic Processes by the Doctrine of the Climatic Process, 2018.

50 Pakistan is currently a low contributor, but its emissions are increasing; the opening of the mine will make a major contribution. The Netherlands is a small country and therefore a low contributor at a global level, but the emission level per inhabitant is high. In every contributing State, we must cease to reason in a segmented manner because the phenomenon is global.

change the reduction target from 17% to 25-40% by 2020, and this over a short period of time, as required by climate change science as well as the international policy that stems from it.[51]

The comments of these "climate-aware" judges are severe. Judge Aiken sees the Government's incapacity to admit that its action can be disputed in court as a profound "resistance to change".[52] She regrets that the federal courts have too often been "cautious" and filled with "deference" regarding old habits[53]: the world has suffered for this because the legal system has not protected humanity from the collapse of finite natural resources, caused by the uncontrolled pursuit of profit. This fresh look at the third power that must make these issues a "cause of action", completely overturns the argument of the separation of powers. Pakistani judge Syed Mansoor Ai Shah said nothing more[54]: environmental protection has become a central aspect of the fundamental rights system, and environmental justice that is localized to global climate justice must be developed. The renewal of fundamental rights must take place through the invention of "judicial toolkits" capable of compelling governments to respond to climate change.

However, although some progress has been achieved thanks to these courageous judges, the decision of the Supreme Court of Colombia is the only final ruling so far. It is a decision on the merits by the nation's highest court, based

---

51 "The courts impose themselves as a substitute for the political institutions, judged as failures by the victims of climate change. The judge has gradually become a decision-making figure and therefore concurrent to executive and legislative power, awakening existing tensions between law and politics". Author's translation of L. Canali, "Droit du process et climat" [Procedural Law and Climate], *in* M. Hautereau-Boutonnet, *Quel droit pour sauver le climat ? sous la direction de Mathilde Hautereau-Boutonnet* [What Right to Save the Climate?: Under the Direction of Mathilde Hautereau-Boutonnet], 2018, Université Lyon, p. 10, *available online at* https://halshs.archives-ouvertes.fr/halshs-01684948/document (accessed 16 June 2019).

52 *Juliana v. United States*, p. 1262.

53 In his ruling of 4 September 2015, the Pakistani judge cited the defense of the Minister of Climate Change, the main target of the farmer, Ashgar Leghari, who gave an account of the framework to other ministers so that each ministry may take part in reducing GHG emissions. He evoked the lack of support from other government bodies and concluded by saying that a period of awareness raising is still necessary. What environmental minister could not adhere to this proposal?

54 The Court of Lahore recognized that the State's failure to act violates its fundamental rights and ordered each ministry to nominate a head of action for climate change, responsible for putting the 2012 climate plan into practice. It also ordered the Government to create a commission responsible for the implementation of its commitments.

in part on specific laws about standing in Colombia. Its tangible effectiveness still remains to be proven.[55] Without being able to assess the effectiveness of the movement in favor of natural elements considered as legal subjects, the opening of the category is following different cultural pathways (*see* Part II below).

II. The Three Paths of Legal Animism

In 1972, Christopher Stone wanted to provide all natural entities – from forests to oceans – with the quality of legal subjects able to plead on their behalf in the courts.[56] Published in 1988, "*L'homme, la nature et le droit*"[57] proposed a legal approach "of all living things", based on the need to think of the "living system" as a totality that links the environment and biomedicine: it was proposed that categories of res and persona be redesigned so as to consider, "the common destiny of humankind and nature, subjects and objects of techno-sciences" and make biological diversity a legal subject. These solutions were both technical, and utopian.

Since then, they have been developed to and fro, based on: concerns about the planet's capacity to function; the change of outlook towards animals and vegetables by some life sciences and society in general; the expansion of indigenous cultures; and, the failures of governments.[58]

55 M. Hautereau-Boutonnet, "Les procès climatiques par la doctrine du procès climatique" [Climatic Processes by the Doctrine of the Climatic Process], 2018. The author has carried out precious research on the reality of climate disputes and the doctrine that determines a particular subject in all the environmental disputes; in her article on liability, she provides examples to show that the separation of powers is currently the essential cause of plaintiffs' failures.

56 C. Stone, *Should Trees Have Standing? Law, Morality, and the Environment,* Oxford University Press, 3rd edition, 2010.

57 B. Edelman & M-A. Hermitte (eds.), *L'homme, la nature et le droit* [Man, Nature and the Law], C. Bourgois, 1988, p. 238; *see also* M. Callon, "Éléments pour une sociologie de la traduction. La domestication des coquilles Saint-Jacques dans la Baie de Saint Brieuc" [Elements for a Sociology of Translation: The Domestication of Scallops in the Bay of Saint Brieuc], *L'Année sociologique,* 1986, No. 36.

58 A. Geslin, "États et sécurité environnementale, états de l'insécurité environnementale : de la recomposition normative des territoires à l'esquisse d'un droit de l'anthropocène" [States and Environmental Security, States of Environmental Security: From the Normative Recomposition of Territories to the Outline of an Anthropocene Right], *in* J. Tercinet (ed.), *États et sécurité internationale* [*States and International Security*], coll. Études stratégiques internationales, Bruylant, Brussels, 2012, pp. 87–104; B. Favre, *Umwelt et droit – Le droit de l'environnement au prisme de l'éthologie,* Mémoire à la

Indeed, one of the possible paths in law entailed changing the modalities of confrontation between human short-term interests and the ongoing interests of all living beings. To this end, non-humans, including the ecosystems, had to become subjects of law capable of expressing their needs in court: associations were no longer to merely defend their love for non-humans, but actually be their voice.[59] Although still widely criticized, the idea of integrating non-humans is included in many texts[60]: constitutional provisions, legislative enactments that oblige the States to organize territories of co-existence between humans and non-humans,[61] and in legal decisions that recognize animals or ecosystems "as if" they have rights. All these legal texts describe (at times expressly and others implicitly) non-human subjectivities. Along the same lines, the possibility of pure ecological damage under tort law is recognized in several legal orders. The

Faculté de droit de Lausanne, July 2016; T. Lefort-Martine, *Des droits pour la nature? : L'expérience équatorienne* [*Rights for Nature: The Ecuadorian Experience*], L'Harmattan, 2018. An unjustly forgotten thesis also makes these points. A. Zabalza, *La Terre & le Droit* [*The Earth & the Law*], Editions Bière, 2007.

59 This idea was at the heart of the minority opinion of Judge Douglas in the Sierra Club affair that inspired Christopher Stone. *See, e.g.*, Stone, 2010. The judge wrote: "The river as plaintiff speaks for the ecological unit of life. The sole question is, who has standing to be heard? Those people who have a meaningful relation to that body of water must be able to speak for the values which the river represents". *Sierra Club v. Morton*, United States Supreme Court, *United States Reports*, 1972, Vol. 405, p. 727, p. 743 (dissenting opinion by Justice Douglas). Anthropologists say it differently. *See, e.g.*, E. Kohn, *Comment pensent les forêts : Vers une anthropologie au-delà de l'humain* [*How Forests Think: Towards an Anthropology Beyond the Human*], Zones sensibles, 2017, p. 313, translated by G. Delaplace; *ibid.*, p. 136 (describing "parler-chien"); B. Morizot, *Les diplomates : Cohabiter avec les loups sur une autre carte du vivant* [*Diplomats: Cohabiting with Wolves on Another Map of Life*], Wildproject, 2017, p. 60, *available online at* https://www.wildproject.org/diplomates ("According to werewolf diplomats, it's a case of starting to include categories of animal lifestyles in our language"); *ibid.*, pp. 201 and 203 ("Stratégie de l'interprète" [Interpreter Strategy]).

60 Simone Goyard-Fabre went so far as to speak of "perfidious", "absurd" renaturation, and "cynical rerouting". S. Goyard-Fabre, "Sujet de droit et objet de droit, défense de l'humanisme" [Subject of Law and Object of Right, Defense of Humanism], *Cahiers de philosophie politique et juridique*, Presses Universitaires du France, 1992, No. 22, p. 7. For a recent critique, *see* G. Giudicelli-Delage & K. Martin-Chenut, "Humanisme et protection de la nature" [Humanism and Nature Protection], *in L'environnement et ses métamorphoses* [*The Environment and its Metamorphoses*], Le Monde – Hermann, 2015, p. 227.

61 The network, Natura 2000, accounts for nearly 13% of the metropolitan area in France, 40% in some municipalities and half in La Guyane.

French civil code declares compensable, "non trivial harm caused to the elements or the functions of ecosystems [...]"; therefore, free of all human interest.

My assumption is that these are not unrelated whims, but rather different forms of animism that craft the law by taking three different paths.[62]

A. Legal Animism with Some Indigenous Touch

Ecuador was the first country to launch this movement. Its 2008 Constitution linked the recognition of nature as a legal subject with indigenous communities. This bold step inspired Bolivia and Colombia, whose Supreme Courts linked classic fundamental human rights to the environment: without a healthy environment, subjects of law and living beings in general cannot survive. This also involves our children and future generations. All environmental shortages (of air, water, etc.) reduce our expectancy of a dignified life.[63] It specifies that fundamental rights involve recognition of "the other" – of otherness, these other people that inhabit the planet, encompassing also the other animal and plant species, the unborn, who should enjoy the same environmental conditions as ours, our relatives and neighbors as such (this is based on the solidarity principle).[64]

---

62 I define legal animism as the different ways the law has to animate the world. In other words, to cause effects to be produced based on the fact that every living entity has needs that extend to the psycho-chemical world it depends on. *See* M-A. Hermitte & F. Chateauraynaud (eds.), 2013, p. 94 and onwards.

63 This ruling of Colombia's Constitutional Court of 5 April 2018, followed a previous ruling on May 2017, regarding the pollution of the river *Atrato* by a mining exploitation. After having declared the river a legal subject, the Court ordered the Government to give it a legal representative: a guardian who, working with the inhabitants, would be in charge of taking the necessary action against the illegal mine that used toxic substances (mercury, etc.). In the 2018 judgment, it is worth noting the numerous tangible obligations ordered by the Court: action against illicit crops, illegal mines, irrational expansion of agricultural borders, the obligation to fill the void left by the FARC. *See* Environmental Law Alliance Worldwide, "STC4360-2018 de la Corte Suprema de Justicia, Sala de Casacion Civil, M.P. Luis Armando Tolosa Villabona (2018)", *available online at* https://www.elaw.org/CO_Amazon.

64 M.V. Berros, "Defending Rivers: Vilcabamba in the South of Ecuador", *in* A.L. Tabios Hillebrecht & M.V. Berros, *Can Nature have Rights? Legal and Political Insights*, Rachel Carson Center for Environment & Society, 2017, No. 6, pp. 37-44; M. V. Berros, "The Constitution of the Republic of Ecuador: Pachamama Has Rights", *Environment & Society Portal, Arcadia*, 2015, No. 11, *available online at* http://www.environmentandsociety.org/arcadia/constitution-republic-ecuador-pachamama-has-rights; M.V. Berros, "El estatuto jurídico de la naturaleza en debate (meulen en el

The Court stigmatizes the ineffectiveness of the measures adopted in the conventional legal ontology and infers from it the need to recognize nature as an authentic legal subject, in accordance with an ecocentric perspective. It also recognizes the need to protect life forms solely on the ground that they are living things and cultural representations, and therefore identifiable as individual legal subjects, all interconnected in the biosphere. This took on particular importance in the Colombian case because of its cultural and ethnic pluralism, and the knowledge of the indigenous communities, recognized as guardians of the environment. A new "bio-cultural rights" approach, based on the interdependence between nature and the human species has to be implemented. This compels us to take seriously the fact that nature and its environment require the full range of rights granted to legal subjects.

The New Zealand model of the *Whanganui River* is technically the most elaborate because it established the new governance in great detail.[65] Ending a conflict that dated back to the nineteenth century, an agreement endorsed by the Parliament in 2017 was reached between the Maoris and the Crown declaring the Whanganui River "an indivisible and living whole, incorporating all its physical and metaphysical elements", "as a legal entity".[66] The text of the agreement combines classical environmental interests in terms of degradation and pollution with political and cultural interests, pertaining to the capacity of the *Whanganui iwi*, the tribe affected most, to take its destiny into its own hands. The whole change involves a modification of the river governance based on the tribe's cosmological view that enables the river to speak: "I am the river and the river is me". They are the descendants of this "living whole", and are represented by *Te Pou Tupua*, the "human face" that allows the river to speak with its own voice. This being can no longer be the object of property rights, like an inanimate being. Considering that the voice of the river as well as its physical and

---

mundo del derecho)" [The Legal Status of Nature in Debate (Swirling Wind in the World of Law)], *Revista de Derecho Ambiental*, 2013, No. 36, pp. 133–151.

65 C.J. Iorns Magallanes, "Nature as an Ancestor: Two Examples of Legal Personality for Nature in New Zealand", Sep. 2015, *Vertigo – la revue électronique en sciences de l'environnement*, Special Issue No. 22, Sep. 2015, p. 4, *available online at* https://journals.openedition.org/vertigo/16199.

66 V. David, "La nouvelle vague des droits de la nature. La personnalité juridique reconnue aux fleuves Whanganui, Gange et Yamuna" [The New Wave of the Rights of Nature. Recognized Legal Personality at Whanganui, Ganges and Yamuna Rivers], *Revue juridique de l'environnement*, 2017, No. 3, p. 418.

spiritual manifestations were silenced by the Crown's legislation for 150 years, it now must be discussed *by the descendants of the river.*[67]

B. Legal Animism with Religious or Mystical Background

On 30 March 2017, two rulings of the High Court of Uttarakhand at Nainital, now overruled by the Supreme Court, declared that two rivers – the Ganga and the Yamuna – as well as glaciers and a number of other natural elements, were legal subjects. Their rulings were based on a combination of common law, Hindu religious tradition, and scientific data.[68]

The judges declared the Ganga and the Yamuna legal subjects as *parens patriae*, holders of all the "rights, duties and liabilities" of nature to preserve them.[69] This prerogative allows the sovereign to use its authority to serve defenseless subjects poorly protected by their neighbors, or to settle conflicts related to access to water. Some physical person has to be designated to act "*in loco parentis*": they will act as "the human face" that will protect the rivers and promote their health and wellbeing.[70] The ruling for the dispute over the Gangotri and Yamunotri glaciers is generally similar to those in cases for rivers, lakes, air, forests and prairies, etc. The Secretary of State was ordered to appoint representatives to ensure that industries, hotels, and Ashrams no longer dump waste into the rivers, thus damaging the health and well-being of the rivers.

---

67 M-A. Hermitte, "Souveraineté, peuples autochtones : le partage équitable des ressources et des connaissances" [Sovereignty, Indigenous Peoples: Equitable Sharing of Resources and Knowledge], *in* F. Bellivier & C. Noiville (eds.), *La bioéquité* [Bioequity], Autrement, 2009, p. 115. V. David focuses on the influence of the historical context on these rulings – the imposition of foreign laws that violate traditions: the moghole invasions, British colonization; V. David, 2017, p. 421; M. V. Berros & R. Colombo, "Miradas emergentes sobre el estatuto jurídico de los ríos, cuencas y glaciares" [Emerging Views on the Legal Status of Rivers, Basins and Glaciers], *Rivista quadrimestrale di diritto dell'ambiente*, 2017, pp. 31–72.

68 *Lalit Miglani v. State of Uttarakhand & others* (*Yamuna*), Writ Petition (PIL) No. 140 of 2015, High Court of Uttarakhand at Naintial, 30 Mar. 2017, *available online at* http://lobis.nic.in/ddir/uhc/RS/orders/31-03-2017/RS30032017WPPIL1402015.pdf; *Mohd. Salim Petitioner Versus State of Uttarakhand & others* (*Ganga*), Writ Petition (PIL) No.126 of 2014, High Court of Uttarakhand at Naintial, 20 Mar. 2017, *available online at* https://elaw.org/system/files/attachments/publicresource/in_Salim__riverpersonhood_2017.pdf?_ga=2.14546295.1338751871.1564992986-985906626.1564992986.

69 *Ganga*, pp. 11–12, point 19; *Yamuna*, p. 64, point 2.

70 *Ganga*, pp. 11–12, point 19; *Yamuna*, pp. 64–65, point 3.

In the *Ganga* case, the Honorable Rajiv Sharma and Alok Singh debated at length which circumstances might induce a jurisdiction to address the "juristic person" category, whenever it is necessary for "necessities in the human development".[71] Having recalled the precedent of granting the status of "juristic entity" to a Hindu divinity who could own and manage its own property,[72] the ruling linked the creation of new legal personhood to the needs of human development.[73] This reflection is the universal part of these rulings, which were unfortunately overruled by the Supreme Court of India on the ground that it would be unrealistic under constitutional law, would entail legal complications, and would trigger an unsustainable flow of disputes.

In this specific case, the High Court judges link the religious aspect (i.e., the attachment of Hindus to this sacred and venerated river that provides humans with health and well-being)[74] to global scientific data, evoking the push of "socio-political-scientific development" that justified this creation.[75] They condemn both the *Uttar Pradesh* and *Uttarakhand* States, and the Central State's inertia – "sign of non-governance"[76] – and order them to form the *Ganga Management Board* in charge of implementing the ban on mining exploitations, making decisions regarding irrigation, as well as energy and water supplies in both rural and urban areas, regulating navigation, and developing industries that respect environmental protection laws, as they were enshrined in the Indian Constitution. In these rulings, the judges note that the principles of environmental law are outdated. A commission for the rights of nature must thus be established, made up of citizens and "uncorrupted scientists" with no political bias. This commission will be in charge of implementing the right to existence for rivers and lakes, the right to be unpolluted, and the right to have their viability restored. The judges also mention the constitutional rights of Mother Earth, concluding solely that the category of legal person allows us to integrate mountains, glaciers and all-natural elements in the functioning of society.

---

71 *Ganga*, pp. 7–8, point 14.
72 *Ibid.*, pp. 6–7, point 13.
73 *Ibid.*, pp. 7–8, point 14; *cf. ibid.*, p. 10, point 16.
74 *Ibid.*, p. 11, point 17; *see also* V. David, 2017, pp. 413 & 420.
75 *Ganga*, p. 10, point 16.
76 *Ibid.*, p. 4, point 9.

C. Western Legal Systems: Science-Based Animism

So far, Western legal systems do not expressly acknowledge that natural elements may be legal subjects. However, the institution of an interconnected lattice of spaces organizing the division of territories between humans and non-humans should be justified. It is through justification (mostly based on science) of rules that curb human activities in the name of the vital needs of non-human beings, that European law sheds light on the implicit subjectivization of natural elements.[77]

For example, migratory birds enjoy a right that prevents a vast protected area in Bulgaria from being divided up, in order to preserve the area's "functional unity" and satisfy the birds' needs.[78] In Germany, the (river as well as sea) lamprey and salmon who migrate through the Elbe enjoy a protected migratory corridor several hundreds of kilometers long, intended to ensure their reproduction. Yet, Germany planned to develop a water supply point viewed as indispensable to cooling a coal power station in *Morburg* downstream of the protected area. Considering the interconnections between ecosystems and the possibility that the plant's operations might increase the river's temperature, the Court of Justice for the European Union decided to extend existing upstream restrictions to the downstream area.[79]

Along the same lines, the French Act of 2016 on the reconquest of biodiversity uses several devices to reinforce the objective of co-existence between humans

---

77 Generally, in Western laws, there is no doctrinal movement towards a legal personality of natural elements. I have tried to demonstrate that, if this affirmation is perfectly precise, with a few limited exceptions, the contents of rules and more importantly, the reasons behind legal rulings, show implicit but extremely widespread subjectivization. M-A. Hermitte, *La nature sujet de droits* [The Nature Subject of Rights], *available online at* https://www.cairn.info/revue-annales-2011-1-p-173.htm. Please refer to the above. I will take two of the most recent examples from it.

78 Accordingly, Bulgaria was condemned in a proceeding before the Court of Justice for the European Union based on the country's failure to fulfil its legal obligations as a member state. *European Commission v. Republic of Bulgaria,* No. C-141/14, Court of Justice of the European Union, 14 Jan. 2016, *available online at* http://curia.europa.eu/juris/document/document.jsf?text=&docid=173520&doclang=EN.

79 *Construction of the Morburg power station*, No. C-142/16, Court of Justice of the European Union, 26 Apr. 2017. An interesting attempt on the indivisibility of Pacha Mama evoked without success before an Ecuadorian judge with regard to the British Petroluem platform explosion in the Gulf of Mexico. M.V. Berros, "The Rights of Nature Recognition", *in* S. Kalantzakos, *Energy & Environmental Transformations in a Globalizing World*, Nomiki Bibliothiki, 2015.

and non-humans. A step towards biocentrism was made since the expression, "living beings" that also encompasses Human beings, replaces the former expression "animal and vegetable species", that used to exclude it. Humans and non-humans are thus both involved in land management: the creation of "hotspots for biodiversity", a "principle of ecological solidarity", of "ecological continuity", and recognition of the value of ecosystem and environmental services.[80]

The evolution of Western legal systems justifies the term, "scientifically-based legal animism".[81] We are no longer descendants of our rivers and our forests, and we no longer have pre-established human faces to speak legitimately on their behalf. However, nothing can prevent us from forming an inclusive relationship with living beings, based as much on scientific knowledge as on common knowledge and new awareness.

***

I share the theoretical equanimity of the Indian judges: we do have to create those subjects "needed" by modern societies; however, I also share this combination of anxiety, sadness and anger, that irrigates the doctrine, some texts (without mandatory legal value), and the most important court rulings. There is absolute urgency in all the domains pertaining to climate and biodiversity change. However, to this end, the current environmental law is insufficient. We do need a

---

80 C. Cans & O. Cizel, *Loi biodiversité ce qui change en pratique* [Biodiversity Law: What is Changing in Practice], Legislative, 2017, p. 68 (S. Mabile, "Principe de solidarité écologique" [The Principle of Ecological Solidarity]); *ibid.*, p. 364 (T. Dubreuil, "Les zones prioritaires pour la biodiversité" [Priority Areas for Biodiversity]); *ibid.*, p. 371 (T. Dubreuil, "Espaces de continuités écologiques" [Spaces of Ecological Continuity]); *see also* S. Vanuxem, "Les services écologiques ou le renouveau de la catégorie civiliste de fruits" [Ecological Services or the Renewal of the Civilian Fruit Category], *McGill Law Journal,* 2017, Vol. 62, No. 3, pp. 739–776; *ibid.*, p. 743 (distinguishing between "ecosystem services" – meaning benefits that one ecosystem can bring to other ecosystems, or human societies – and "environmental services", meaning benefits that humans bring to ecosystems).

81 This type of animism is obviously not included in the categories described by Philippe Descola, in reference to animism, analogism, totemism and naturalism. In fact, the author outlined pure categories while the hybrid western legal systems outlined at least three of them, from which he borrows traits that he redistributes in a new model that puts scientific foundations in the first place, aware that certain scientific approaches are more suitable than others (e.g., ethology v zootechny), and that anthropomorphism, if described, is a precious instrument for changing awareness. This point is developed in M.-A. Hermitte, "Artificialisation de la nature et droit(s) du vivant" [Artificialization of Nature and Law for Living Species], *in* P. Descola (ed.), *Les natures en questions* [*The Natures in Question*], Odile Jacob, 2018, p. 257.

revolution of powers that will make action mandatory, and a revolution of categories encompassing the law of liability as well as fundamental rights, the theory of property rights as well as the theory of persons. In its attempt to balance risks and benefits, along with a list of exceptions that would allow principles to be pragmatic,[82] the current government technique fails to restrain the unlimited spiral of technological desire. The new legal ontology, which partly gives way to animist paths, must enable us to re-establish friendly relations between humans and non-humans, reinvent shared ownership and non-appropriable things,[83] manage resources in such a way that they renew oneself, manage risks according to an ethic of relationship, as opposed to a cold calculation, and rely on non-humans to overcome obstacles. This is indeed a brand-new science of subjects and objects, likely to incorporate the various aspects of the living world.

82 *See* C. Noiville & T. Berger, "L'accès à l'information sur l'environnement, réflexions sur deux causes d'ineffectivité" [Access to Environmental Information, Reflections on Two Causes of Inefficiency], *in Sciences et droits de l'homme* (Collectif), éditions Mare & Martin, 2017, p. 173.

83 S. Vanuxem & C. Guibet-Lafaye (eds.), *Repenser la propriété, un essai de politique écologique* [Rethinking Property, an Environmental Policy Test], Presses Universitaires Aix-Marseilles, 2015, *Droit(s) de l'environnement* [*Law(s) of the Environment*], p. 194; M. Cornu, F. Orsi & J. Rochfeld (eds.), *Dictionnaire des biens communs* [*Common Goods Dictionary*], Quadrige, Presses Universitaires due France, 2017.

Matthias PETEL

12. The Rights of Nature: A Legal Revolution for Ecological Justice

Introduction

We are living in a world that is in transition. We are moving from the period of the Holocene to the Anthropocene. This changes everything.[1] A convergent and growing scientific literature claims that we are dangerously reaching a global tipping point,[2] which could lead us to face unprecedented, brutal, and irreversible modifications of our current living conditions. Anthropic activities are putting pressure on ecological balances to the point that we are on the verge of a genuine breakdown. Those facts are not quite new. The first warnings of a potential collapse caused by our growth-based system were present in the Club of Rome Report on the Limits to Growth.[3] More recently, the emergence of the concept of "planetary boundaries" developed by the Stockholm Resilience Center reminds us of the necessity to live within ecological limits if we want to avoid major catastrophes.[4]

The calls urging us to operate an ecological transformation are coming from the scientists, civil society, and international organizations. A certain consensus around the need to radically change our ways of life – as well as the economic system itself – begins to emerge. However, one must admit that this switch from a destructive consumerist model towards a harmonious socio-ecological world has yet to happen.

---

1 N. Klein, *This Changes Everything*, London, Penguin Books, 2014.

2 Contrary to what one might think, ecosystems do not respond to disturbances in a gradual and proportionate way. Scientific literature talks about "tipping points" involving subtle alterations that cause drastic, uncontrollable, and irreversible changes. When so called "ecological thresholds" are passed, sudden collapse can occur. A group of 22 scientists claim that Earth is close to a global tipping point. *See* A.D. Barnosky & others, "Approaching a state shift in Earth's biosphere", *Nature*, 2012, Vol. 486, pp. 52–58.

3 D.H. Meadows, D.L. Meadows, J. Randers & W.W; Behrens III, *The Limits to Growth: A Report for the Club of Rome's Project on the Predicament of Mankind,* Universe books, 1972.

4 W. Steffen & others, "Planetary Boundaries: Guiding human development on a changing planet", *Science*, 2015, Vol. 347, No. 6223.

In light of the ecological threats, all disciplines must be reinvented in order to facilitate the transition process. The law cannot remain indifferent to those metamorphoses. It must operate its own transition. Legal systems have thus far failed in preventing the degradation of the biosphere. According to all the relevant scientific indicators, the environment is in a worse state than it was at the adoption of the first environmental laws. This does not mean that those laws have fostered the destruction of our habitats, nor does it imply that environmental law has been not useful in slowing down the speed of the destruction. However, it is clear that the explosion of norms on environmental issues – from the Stockholm declaration in 1972 to the Paris Agreement in 2015 – has not allowed our societies to take the path of sustainability and resilience.

The conclusion is, thus, quite radical: "law has failed, the ecosystems have clearly lost the war".[5] To explain the paradoxical relationship between a growing number of environmental regulations and the increasing degradation of the nature, I argue that the underlying philosophical foundations of the legal and economic order are incompatible with a harmonious relationship between humankind and nature.[6] Beyond new laws, we need a shift in paradigm. The marginal adaptation of a flawed system will not offer relevant solutions.

If a deeper transformation is needed, at which legal concepts should we aim? I will defend the idea that recognition of the rights of nature is a powerful tool, not only to provoke a cultural change, but also to improve access to justice for the protection of ecosystems, the living beings of our planet, and future generations. I believe in the emergence of an ecological justice, protecting the interdependent future of both humanity and the biosphere. Rights of nature are the first step in that direction.

First, I will describe the traditional conception of nature and how it has facilitated the emergence of a destructive relationship with our own environment. I will analyze the ethical, economic and legal consequences of consecrating rights to nature. Secondly, I will answer the objections generally raised by opponents of this proposal and offer examples to demonstrate that this idea is becoming a reality. I then discuss the possible positive impact of recognizing the rights of nature on the judicial protection of ecosystems. Finally, I will argue that one

---

5 I. Lowe, "Wild Law Embodies Values for a Sustainable Future", *in* M. Maloney & P. Burdon (eds.), *Wild Law – In Practice*, Abingdon, Routledge, 2014, p. 4.

6 M. Petel, "La nature : d'un objet d'appropriation à un sujet de droit. Réflexions pour un nouveau modèle de société" [Nature: From an Object of Appropriation to a Subject of Law. Reflections for a New Model of Society], *Revue Interdisciplinaire d'Etudes Juridiques,* 2018, Vol. 80.

should not oppose human rights and nature rights. Instead of a dualistic opposition, we need to recognize their complementarity, as the present and future well-being of humankind depend on healthy ecosystems.

I. The Rights of Nature from a Philosophical, Economic and Legal Point of View.

The article published in 1972 by Christopher Stone, "Should trees have standing?",[7] was the first to defend the recognition of rights to nature itself. Instead of protecting nature indirectly through the prism of human interests, he argued in favor of protecting nature for its own intrinsic value. The context of this proposal was the decision accepting the implementation of a large-scale tourism project in the Mineral King Valley (California, United States). The Sierra Club, a nature conservation association, decided to sue the company to bring the project to a halt. However, no individual, nor the organization itself, had been directly and personally affected by this project. As a result, the Sierra Club did not possess the right to bring a lawsuit against the corporation. Therefore, American legal scholar Christopher Stone defended an idea before the U.S. Supreme Court that would give legal personhood to nature so one could represent it before the courts and claim nature's own rights. The idea was simple: although the Sierra Club and its members were not directly harmed by the decision, it was the valley itself that was endangered and must be protected. Stone's proposal was based on a simple but profoundly avant-garde idea: nature must cease to be a mere object devoid of legal existence and rights, sporadically protected in the interest of human individuals, and instead become a legal person that must be protected from injury by human activities.[8] Faced with the failure of lawsuits based on lack of standing or with decisions favoring economic interests, the idea is to "make nature talk" so that we are more sensitive to its interests.

I wish to consider seriously this proposal and to explore its potential consequences. What would be the impact of acknowledging all life forms have the right to exist, persist, maintain and regenerate their vital cycles?[9] I will examine this question from philosophical, economic and legal perspectives.

---

7 C. Stone, "Should trees have Standing? Toward legal rights for natural objects", *Southern California Law Review*, 1972, Vol. 45, pp. 450–501.

8 V. David, "La lente consécration de la nature, sujet de droit. Le monde est-il enfin Stone ?" [The Slow Consecration of Nature as a Subject of Law: Is the World Finally Stone?], *Revue juridique de l'environnement*, 2012/3, Vol. 37, p. 474.

9 Global Alliance for The Rights of Nature, "What is Right of Nature", *available online at* https://therightsofnature.org/frequently-asked-questions/.

A. An Ethical Revolution: From Human Superiority to Earth Jurisprudence

Our vision of the world is essentially dualistic, in the sense that humankind is considered as being completely separated from nature. According to Descartes' ontology, human beings are the only one to benefit from rationality, which makes them sovereign beings.[10] It is a binary conception that dissociates the human individual – holder of a logical mind (*res cogitans* or thinking substance) – from the rest of the world (*res extensa* or extended thing), perceived as a sum of inert objects.[11] This metaphysical position led to a famous quote from Descartes enjoining us, as human beings, to behave as "masters and possessors of nature".[12] The "humankind vs. nature" dichotomy has been further accentuated by the rise of modern science, which has defended a mechanistic conception of nature. Nature was analyzed not as a complex networks of living beings but as a machine that could be understood and divided by the power of human beings' intellect. Cartesian dualism and modern scientism credos go hand in hand, both objectifying nature. The world is nothing but an inanimate and fragmented machine. Instead of perceiving ecosystems in their multitude of relationships and interactions, the living are dissected, divided and mastered.

These conceptions (dualism and mechanism) have moved us away from the rest of the living world. Man is no longer part of nature: instead he masters it, modifies it, exploits it and supplants it. The supposed superiority conferred by science allows humanity to dream of an absolute hegemony where Man would be emancipated from the shackles represented by the laws of nature, slowing us down on the path towards progress. More recently, Luc Ferry reiterated this position of man as an antinatural being and for whom freedom is understood as the complete separation from nature.[13]

Those postures are the foundations of what is considered as our anthropocentric moral conceptions. Humans are the only ones who possess an inherent dignity and an intrinsic moral value. The human individual is the yardstick of

---

10 S. Gutwirth, "Trente ans de théorie du droit de l'environnement : concepts et opinions" [Thirty Years of Environmental Law Theory: Concepts and Opinions], *Environnement et société*, 2001, No. 26, p. 7.

11 F. Flipo, "Pour des droits de la nature" [For Rights of Nature], *Mouvements,* 2012/2, No. 70, p. 131.

12 R. Descartes, *Discours de la méthode* [*Discourse on Method*], Paris, Gallimard, 1966, p. 168.

13 L. Ferry, *Le Nouvel Ordre écologique. L'arbre, l'animal et l'homme* [*The New Ecological Order: The Tree, the Animal and the Man*], Paris, Grasset, 1992.

our values, actions and ethical models. In this context, nature can only have an instrumental value. It will be considered and protected only if it benefits the human kingdom. Nature is only a tool to fulfill our desires and needs. The natural world (defined as anything that is not human) is a means and not an end. As expressed by Bryan Norton, only humans are worthy of moral consideration, and the value of other objects is derived solely from their contribution to human well-being. The environment is therefore valued for its usefulness.[14]

However, the ecological crisis teaches us a fundamental lesson: dualism leads to a dead end.[15] The conviction of our separation and our superiority vis-à-vis nature causes the feeling of "hubris": an excessive self-pride based on the conviction that human ingenuity will solve environmental problems via technoscience, allowing us to fulfill our unlimited desires. This "humanism of domination" has shown its limits since our ideal of conquering nature has led us to threaten the safety of the planet and the survival of humanity.[16] In other terms, "the collapse of ecosystems and species, as well as the acceleration of climate change, are clear indications that a fundamental change in the relationship between humankind and the natural world is necessary".[17]

By contrast, the movement underlying the proposal of the rights of nature seeks to overcome the humanity-nature dichotomy. I will not go into the details of all the existing theories (deep ecology, land ethic, biocentrism, ecocentrism, sociocentrism, etc.). However, these different environmental ethics have a common denominator; namely, the revolutionary idea that the world does not exist only in the interest of humanity.[18] In other words, all these conceptions, grouped by Adrian Armstrong under the name of "intrinsic valuations",[19] recognize nature's own value without reference to its use by humans. Contrary to the instrumental value, which is often translated by a monetary valuation method

---

14 A. Armstrong, *Ethics and Justice for the Environment*, London, Routledge, 2012, p. 44.

15 F. Ost, *La nature hors la loi : L'écologie à l'épreuve du droit* [*Nature Out of the Law: Ecology Under the Law*], 2nd edition, Paris, La Découverte, 2003, p. 11.

16 *See* the foreword of M. Delmas-Marty, *in* L. Neyret (ed.), *Des écocrimes à l'écocide. Le droit pénal au secours de l'environnement* [*From Ecocrimes to Ecocide: Criminal Law Saving the Environment*], Bruylant, 2015.

17 M. Margil, "Press Release: Colombia constitutional Court Finds Atrato River Possesses Rights", 4 May 2017, Community Environmental Legal Defense Fund, *available online at* https://celdf.org/2017/05/press-release-colombia-constitutional-court-finds-atrato-river-possesses-rights/.

18 R. Nash, *The Rights of Nature: A History of Environmental Ethics*, Wisconsin, University of Wisconsin Press, 1989, p. 13.

19 A. Armstrong, 2012, pp. 47–48.

(and the environmental problems solved through a cost-benefit analysis), the intrinsic value recognizes that nature is no longer a mere resource but an end in itself.[20]

This is the idea underlying the "*Earth Jurisprudence*" movement created by Thomas Berry. It defends a new governance whose main task is to create a mutually beneficial system for humans and all living things of the Earth system. The earth community as a whole must share the "commons" of land, water, air and ecosystems in a healthy and sustainable way so that the well-being of all is respected.[21] The aim is to promote a new system whose objective is to enable a symbiotic relationship within the biosphere.[22] In addition, laws must be aligned with planetary boundaries and respect biophysical realities.[23] Following Aldo Leopold's lead, the idea is that we abuse the Earth because we consider it as a good that we own.[24] Instead, the movement conferring rights to nature claims that humankind is part of moral community in which we are no longer omnipotent conquerors but responsible citizens.[25]

B. An Economic Revolution: From Neoclassical Economics to Ecological Economics

Originally, nature was absent from the dominant economic models based on neoclassical assumptions. Nature was considered as infinite (hence the dogma of infinite economic growth) and freely available to serve the appetite of nation states and corporations during the industrial revolution. Nature was perceived as being capable of endlessly feeding the productive cycle and fostering economic development. In order to develop itself, the capitalist economy needed a commodification of the world tending to subject anything possible to private

20 F. Flipo, "Droits de la nature, mythe ou réalité ?" [Rights of Nature, Myth or Reality?], 12 July 2012, *available online at* http://mouvements.info/droits-de-la-nature-mythe-ou-realite-2/

21 T. Berry, *The Great Work: Our Way into the Future*, New York, Bell Tower Press, 1999, pp. 61–62.

22 T.L. Timmons, "Earth Jurisprudence and Lockean Theory: Rethinking the American Perception of Private Property", *Earth Jurisprudence & Environmental Justice Journal*, 2011, Vol.1, p. 105.

23 M. Maloney & P. Siemen, "Responding to the Great Work: The Role of Earth Jurisprudence and Wild Law in the 21st Century", *Earth Jurisprudence & Environmental Justice*, 2015, No. 6, p. 22.

24 A. Leopold, *A Sand County Almanac*, Ballantine Books New York, 1966, p. 238.

25 *Ibid.*, pp. 239–240.

appropriation, free use, and free disposition. Capitalism is based on a constant need for new areas of investment and consumption to maintain profits. In this context, nature was either used freely by corporations in the productive processes (and thus conservation of nature and mitigation of polluting impacts were simply irrelevant) or sold as a simple commodity. The capitalist economy pursued the ethical dualism described above with nature instrumentalized as a reservoir of resources at the disposal of humankind, either used to promote economic expansion, or valued for its economic contribution to allow the accumulation of capital. It is not so much a question of meeting human needs but of responding to the infinite and insatiable appetites of capital.[26] Those evolutions have resulted in the "virtual absorption of environmental concern by the desire to promote development".[27] Nature has been engulfed in the irresistible expansion of international trade, the booming of economic growth, and globalization. In Herman Daly's terms, the founding assumptions of neoclassical economics were developed in an empty world, with infinite space and abundant resources.[28]

Facing environmental threats, neoclassical economics has tried to adapt its models, leading to the development of environmental economics. In this perspective, proponents of "free market environmentalism" or "green capitalism" advocate an extension of ownership regimes and market mechanisms to the natural world. The origin of the ecological crisis stems from the lack of economic and financial value for nature, and the fact that ecosystem services are not taken into account in mainstream economic calculations.[29] In this thought pattern, what is free has no value (since value is considered purely from a monetary perspective) and will not be protected. Therefore, the solution is to give a price to the "ecosystem services" freely provided by nature in order to integrate nature

26 R. White, *Crimes Against Nature, Environmental criminology and ecological justice*, Devon, Willan Publishing, 2008, p. 163.

27 Author's translation of D. Shelton, "Réflexion introductive: environnement international et patrimoine commun de l'humanité" [Introductory Reflection: International Environment and the Common Heritage of Humanity], *in* M.-P. Camproux Duffrène & J. Sohnle (eds.), *Marché et environnement, le marché : menace ou remède ?* [*Market and Environment, the Market: Threat or Remedy?*], Bruxelles, Bruylant, 2014, p. 6.

28 H. Daly, "Economics for a Full World", *Great Transition Initiative: Towards a Transformative Vision and Praxis*, June 2015, *available online at* https://www.greattransition.org/publication/economics-for-a-full-world (accessed 16 June 2019).

29 G. Azam, C. Bonneuil & M. Combes, *La nature n'a pas de prix – Les méprises de l'économie verte* [*Nature is Priceless – The Misunderstandings of the Green Economy*], Paris, Les liens qui libèrent, 2012, p. 12.

into the market system, renaming the natural world's diversity as natural capital[30] and opening up new growth prospects, considered to be green. The objective is to allow a perfect substitution between all the types of capital (financial, social, human and natural), since they are reducible to the common denominator of financial value.[31] In this approach, the intrinsic value of nature is denied since it can be replaced by any other capital of equivalent economic value. It is one of the foundations of so-called "weak sustainability".[32] The assumption of weak sustainability is that technical progress will always allow humanity to substitute depleted natural resources with manufactured resources through technological input.[33] On this basis, the economic model promotes a supposedly infinite economic growth since nature will never stop providing us with resources and, where appropriate, technology will take over to keep the system afloat.[34]

More concretely, how are environmental issues integrated within mainstream economics models? The first step is to privatize the natural world. The method of valuing nature is indeed intimately linked to its prior privatization. It is necessary to have owners so that the economic value of natural elements becomes profitable.[35] Therefore, missing or incomplete property rights must be defined and collective goods completely privatized. Following Garret Hardin's hypothesis (according to which common resources lead inexorably to overexploitation since everyone seeks to maximize their performance to the detriment of the viability of the common resource), instead of degrading nature, private property has an ecological function and must even be considered as the "guardian of nature".[36]

---

30 C. Figuieres, H. Guyomard & G. Rotillon, "Sustainable Development: Between Moral Injunctions and Natural Constraints", *Sustainability*, 2010, No. 2, p. 3611.

31 J.-M. Harribey, "La nature, un capital ?" [Nature, a Capital?], *L'Âge de faire*, Feb. 2014, No. 83.

32 E. Gudynas, "Développement, droits de la Nature et Bien Vivre : l'expérience équatorienne" [Development, Rights of Nature and Living Well: The Ecuadorian Experience], *Mouvemen*ts, 2011/4, No. 68, p. 17.

33 J.-M. Harribey, "Marchandisation de la nature versus préservation du bien commun" [Commodification of Nature versus Preservation of the Common Good], *Revue francophone du développement durable*, Oct. 2013, No. 2, p. 69.

34 M. Barlow, "Building the Case for the Universal Declaration of the Rights of Mother Earth", *in Does Nature Have Rights? Transforming Grassroots to Protect People and the Planet, Right of Nature Report*, 2010, p. 7.

35 J.-M. Harribey, "La nature n'est pas à vendre" [Nature is Not For Sale], *Politis*, 28 June 2012, No. 1209.

36 J. De Malafosse, "La propriété gardienne de la nature" [The Guardian Property of Nature], Études offertes à J. Flour, *Répertoire du notariat Defrénois*, 1979, pp. 335–349.

The environment will be protected as soon as "every tree and every animal will have an owner, and therefore a defender".[37]

After privatization, nature can make its entry into the market. However, for exchange to occur, it is necessary to set a common value. The market will thus operate a complete homogenization of various elements, a standardization of multiple references by a simple monetary conversion: everything is converted into its financial value.[38] Rather than calling into question their *modus operandi*, the applications of market mechanisms to the biosphere appeals to the decision-makers and entrepreneurs because environmental issues are converted into a language they understand: money.[39] The ultimate aim is to incorporate nature into the productive process and allow its maintenance by private companies, as their production capacities will rely on the sustainable use of nature. The hope rests on the idea that the integration of nature as a factor of production will push companies to be reasonable in their use of resources. I must note significant progress, since this approach accepts the finitude of resources.

According to neoclassical assumptions, this double hegemony (privatization and commodification) applied to resources will lead to better conservation of nature. We must keep faith in the market's capacity to be an efficient environmental regulator: market prices must determine the price for destruction of nature, and resources will be exploited to an optimal degree assessed by the market.[40]

However, the danger is clear: the extension of a utilitarian vision applied to nature, which is perceived as a mere factor of production for infinite economic growth and absorbed in the capital cycle. In order to protect the environment without causing systemic upheaval, the proposed solutions do not push for systemic change, but seek to adapt the system and minimize its negative effects,

---

37 F.L. Smith, "Économie de marché et protection de l'environnement" [Market Economy and Environmental Protection], *in* M. Falque & G. Millière (eds.), *Écologie et liberté, une autre approche de l'environnement* [*Ecology and Freedom: Another Approach to the Environment*], Paris, Litec, 1992, p. 239.

38 J.C. Fritz, "Protection de l'environnement et marché: coexistence ou guerre des mondes" [Environmental Protection and Market: Coexistence or War of the Worlds?], *in* M.P. Camproux Duffrène & J. Sohnle, 2014, p. 21.

39 G. Barnaud, "Des fonctions écologiques au marché des services écosystémiques, une avancée conceptuelle ou une gageure" [From Ecological Functions to the Ecosystem Services Market, a Conceptual Advance or a Challenge], *in* M.P. Camproux Duffrène & J. Sohnle, 2014, p. 57.

40 S. Alexander, "Wild Law from below, Examining the anarchist challenge to Earth Jurisprudence", *in* M. Maloney & P. Burdon, 2014, p. 35.

without addressing the root of the problem. In contrast, the rights of nature seek to push us towards another path traced by ecological economics. This new school of thought does not try to adapt the neoclassical models in response to the ecological crisis; instead, its objective is to radically change the models. Two elements must be stressed.

Firstly, man-made capital cannot substitute for natural capital. The weak sustainability assumptions that nature can be replaced through technological innovations and capital accumulated to date, are ruled out by the philosophy underlying rights of nature. The incommensurability of nature's value is proclaimed, converging with the assumptions of the "strong sustainability" approach: certain functions performed by nature cannot be duplicated by humans, or by human made capital. Instead of encouraging the monetary homogenization of heterogeneous elements, one should recognize the "irreducibility of nature to capital".[41] Similarly, the application of cost-benefit analysis to environmental issues leads to ecological breakdown; that approach does not appreciate that ecological processes and functions are unique, fragile, and cannot be translated into a financial value. The conviction embodied in rights of nature is that the biosphere will not be saved through its commodification. Nature must remain outside of the market realm.

Secondly, ecological limits are non-negotiable. Nature was non-existent in neoclassical economic theorems; nature was then integrated in its models through monetary valuation, and must now be considered as the overarching constraint surrounding our economic organization. The economy should be recognized as a subsystem of the biosphere (the opposite of today's objective to make ecosystems a subsystem of the market economy). Economic activities should respect the regenerative capacity of ecosystems, as well as planetary boundaries (cycles and processes that maintain the stability of the planetary environment). Therefore, economic growth is necessarily limited.[42] The global economy is so large now, that society can no longer safely claim that it operates within a limitless system. Rights of nature will have the effect of acknowledging those uncontestable facts: "the biosphere is finite, nongrowing, closed (except for the constant input of solar energy), and constrained by the laws of thermodynamics. Any subsystem, such as the economy, must at some point cease to grow

41 J.-M. Harribey, "Sur la valeur de la nature, éviter du fétichisme" [On the Value of Nature, Avoid Fetishism], *Les Possibles*, Printemps 2014, No. 3, p. 3.

42 *See, e.g.*, T. Jackson, *Prosperity Without Growth: Foundations for the Economy of Tomorrow*, 2nd edition, London, Routledge, 2017.

and adapt itself to a dynamic equilibrium, something like a steady state".[43] The prevailing obsession with economic growth puts us on the path to ecological collapse, sacrificing the very sustenance of our well-being and survival. To reverse this ominous trajectory, we must transition toward a steady-state economy focused on qualitative development, as opposed to quantitative growth, and the interdependence of the human economy and the global ecosphere.[44]

C. A Legal Revolution: From Appropriation to Subjectivization

Considering the philosophical premises discussed above, legal personhood has logically been reserved to human beings who are the sole holders of these rights. Kelsen defined the humanist-centered approach that characterizes the law: mankind is the producer of legal norms and through them, determines the condition of legal personhood, which – unlike many legal objects – can only be the human itself.[45] In this thought pattern, nature is a property.

Locke has provided a strong foundation for legitimizing nature's appropriation. According to him, the land belongs to the person who deserves it, namely the one who exploits it. The labor theory of property (also called the labor theory of appropriation) holds that property originally comes about by the exertion of labor upon natural resource. Through labor, each individual subtracts a part of the available resources, which become his property.[46] This is rooted in a utilitarian position that denies the value of the thing by following a conception of the "capital residing in the added value".[47] The surplus value conferred by labor confers a property title. According to the Lockean philosophy, man exercises his natural freedom by his labor and through this process he gives resources a specification and an added value; he can then legitimately own them.[48] To prevent any abuses, Locke developed safeguards such as the concept of strict sufficiency (not exceeding the satisfaction of one's needs) and the respect for the needs of others

---

43 H. Daly, "Economics in a Full World", *Scientific American*, Sep. 2005, Vol. 293, No. 3, p. 101, *available online at* https://pages.wustl.edu/files/pages/imce/fazz/ad_5_2_daly.pdf (accessed 16 June 2019).

44 *Ibid.*

45 Quoted by S. Goyard-Fabre, "Sujet de droit et objet de droit: défense de l'humanisme" [Subject of Law and Object of Right: Defense of Humanism], *Cahiers de philosophie politique et juridique*, 1992, No. 22, p. 20.

46 A. Zabalza, *La Terre & le Droit* [*The Earth & the Law*], Editions Bière, 2007, p. 280.

47 Author's translation of F. Ost, 2003, p. 280.

48 *Ibid.*, p. 52.

(ensuring that the rest is sufficient for other members of the community).[49] These limits have been progressively set aside in order to allow the infinite accumulation made possible in particular by the monetary system.[50] The sovereign owner – the despotic dominion to borrow the expression of Blackstone[51] – is the natural legal embodiment of nature's master as described by Descartes.

The appropriation of nature is a logical consequence of the dualistic, mechanistic and anthropocentric dogmas outlined in this contribution. In the eighteenth century, property was conceived as an inviolable right[52] creating a sacred link between the owner and the good (in our case natural elements).[53] Property rights were thus considered as natural rights, in the sense that they were inherent by virtue of human nature and endowed by God. The discourse linking property and the divine world order has been replaced by a legal positivist perspective. Legal scholars differentiate between things that are goods (that is, appropriated or likely to be appropriated) and those that are not. Nature's appropriation is thus the result of a social construction consecrated through the law. Thus, even though it may seem counterintuitive, appropriation as a relationship to nature is not a universal model but comes from cultural conceptions and politico-legal choices hidden behind the pseudo-neutrality of the law.[54] This construction is not explicitly recognized, as the legalist approach is "characterized by the paradox of holding a discourse of truth about constructed objects and claiming to describe them in a depoliticized manner while they are full of politics and ideologies".[55] This relatively recent model is far from being universal,[56] but has become a dogma structuring and homogenizing the doctrinal discourses.[57] Under the

---

49 J. Locke, *Deuxième traité du gouvernement civil* [*Second Treaty of the Civil Government*], Paris, Librarie Philosophique J. Vrin, 1977, p. 91.

50 T.L. Timmons, 2011, p. 108.

51 W. Blackstone, *Commentaries on the Laws of England*, 1765–1769, Vol. 2, Ch.1, p. 2, *available online at* http://avalon.law.yale.edu/18th_century/blackstone_bk2ch1.asp.

52 Déclaration universelle des droits de l'homme et du citoyen de 1789 [Universal Declaration of the Rights of Man and the Citizen of 1789], art. 17.

53 J.P. Chazal, "La propriété : dogme ou instrument politique ? Ou comment la doctrine s'interdit de penser le réel" [Property: Dogma or Political Instrument? Or How the Doctrine Refrains from Thinking the Real], *Revue trimestrielle de droit civil,* 2014–12, No. 4, p. 766.

54 J.P. Chazal, 2014, pp. 794–795.

55 Author's translation of J.P. Chazal, 2014, p. 768.

56 A. Van Lang, *Droit de l'environnement* [*Environmental Law*], Paris, Presses Universitaires de France, 2002, p. 168.

57 J.P. Chazal, 2014, p. 768.

influence of legal positivists and mercantile activity, "property became detached from theological reflection and more readily associated with commercial value".[58]

The private property paradigm makes it possible for humans to "dispose of" nature, which becomes the essential modality of our relationship to the world. In the words of François Ost, the net of appropriation has captured nature "to corporeal and concrete things, we apply private property; to abstract elements, we adapt the mechanisms of intellectual property since things that cannot be controlled and cannot be appropriated, such as air and water, they will be the object of public property while tolerating the privative appropriation of their constitutive elements".[59] In conclusion, the right to private property allows us to enjoy an absolute and exclusive disposition of natural elements, including the right to destroy them.[60] Even if this "right to destroy" is constrained by legal safeguards in order to preserve the general interest, it remains a question of preserving human interests and not of respecting nature itself.[61] For some authors, including Michel Serres, the right to property is the cultural source of pollution in the sense that the exclusivity claimed by the individual on nature legitimizes destructive behavior.[62]

A body of environmental law has been developed to mitigate the destruction of our industrial system on the environment. However, this environmental law is itself the result of an approach according to which nature is a reservoir of resources available to humanity that has to be managed to foster our prosperity. The environmental standards we adopted were not intended to profoundly challenge our current relationship to nature, but rather to preserve natural resources in order to allow the continuation of economic exchanges and to maintain the objective of economic growth.[63] Contrary to the 1972 Club of Rome report mentioned in the introduction, the concept of sustainable development reflected in the 1987 Brundtland Report maintains its confidence in technoscientific

---

58 T. Jayatilaka, *Rights of Nature: The Right Approach to Environmental Standing in the EU?*, 2016–2017, LLM Paper, Ghent University, p. 25.

59 Author's translation of F. Ost, 2003, pp. 47–48

60 M. Rémond-Gouilloud, *Du droit de détruire – essai sur le droit de l'environnement* [*Right to Destroy – Environmental Law Test*], Paris, Presses Universitaires de France, 1989, p. 12

61 S. Gutwirth, 2001, p. 8.

62 M. Serres, *Le Contrat naturel* [*The Natural Contract*], Paris, François Bourin, 1990.

63 M. Stenmark, *Environmental Ethics and Policy-Making*, New York, Routledge, 2002, pp. 21–22.

solutions and in our ability to maintain consumerist lifestyles.[64] A "green cloak" has draped our economic order, leaving the financial interests present in global capitalism unchallenged and giving the system an ecological legitimacy.[65] More specifically, since the end of the 1970s, a neoliberal shift has inspired European environmental policies based on the idea that market values must be applied not only to economic life, but also to social, political and environmental issues.[66] This is the rise of market-based ecology or "free market environmentalism". According to this perspective, the environmental crisis is seen as a simple market failure. The dominant economic system must not be questioned in order to achieve sustainable development. Instead, nature must simply be better integrated within the existing mechanisms and models. In other words, a normative filter has been placed on environmental law based on the fetishism of growth and the market: the norms that are supposed to protect nature are accepted as long as they do not contradict the objectives of accumulation and growth, which lie at the heart of the ecological crisis.[67]

The current legal system is essentially anthropocentric and pro-growth. The law maintains the *status quo* most notably though private property law, investment law and international trade law. If an environmental law exists, it is a mere mitigation of the negative impacts of industrial production rather than a true paradigmatic shift. It has accompanied the industrial recklessness and our materialistic bulimia instead of developing an overarching framework limiting human activities so as to respect the regenerative capacity of ecosystems.

The rights of nature could be one massive step in another direction. The carrying capacity of ecosystems and the ecological limits should become the boundaries of our development in order to remain within a "safe operating space" for humanity.[68] Just as human rights limit the decisional power of our democracies to better respect human dignity, rights of nature should constrain our decisions to preserve Earth's systems and the biodiversity that rely on them. Such rights should be defined as unbreachable limits framing all political structures and

64 S. Coyle & K. Morrow, *The Philosophical Foundations of Environmental Law – Property, Rights and Nature,* Oxford, Hart Publishing, 2004, p. 203.

65 S. Kingston, *European Perspectives on Environmental Law and Governance*, New York, Routledge, 2013, p. 12.

66 N. Castree, "Neoliberalising Nature: The Logics of Deregulation and Reregulation", *Environment and Planning A*, 2008, No. 40, pp. 131–152.

67 S. Alexander, 2014, pp. 34–35.

68 J. Rockström & others, "A safe operating space for humanity", *Nature*, 24 Sep. 2009, Vol. 461.

placing the respect of ecosystems outside of the vagaries of the political game. Therefore, "recognizing that nature has legal rights and accepting these rights as part of our legal systems require not only the introduction of new laws observing these rights, but also a shift in paradigm for them to fit in a contemporaneous legal puzzle".[69]

II. Rights of Nature and Justice

It is clear that recognition of the rights of nature carries symbolic weight. The significance of such symbolism should not be overlooked. Indeed, the essential function of the law is to enact a reality that corresponds to the values defended by the norm and its authors. However, this process is not instantaneous. Individual and collective consciousness can be profoundly transformed by new norms conveying powerful symbolism. In the same vein, Thomas Berry argued that the law was not only intended to regulate human behavior but also played a subtler role: to defend a certain vision of the world and to shape our perceptions of it.[70] In this conception, the law is recognized as a lever for cultural change. A constitutional recognition of the rights of nature would certainly influence political discussions, public opinion, and the interpretations of judges, in addition to acting as a catalyst for new legislation.

However, could we expect more immediate impacts and direct results from recognizing the rights of nature? What could be the concrete impact of such recognition on environmental issues? Could it strengthen the judicial claims of social and environmental movements? I will first answer practical objections commonly raised by opponents of the idea. I will then provide a few significant examples from around the world recognizing rights of nature. Finally, I present some of our conclusions and tentative answers to the following question: can the rights of nature enable access to justice for the protection of ecosystems?

---

69 L.C. Pecharroman, "Rights of Nature: Rivers That Can Stand in Court", *Resources*, Molecular Diversity Preservation International publisher, 2018, Vol. 7, 13, doi:10.3390/resources7010013, p. 1, *in* J. Emel & A. Cantor, *New Water Regimes*, Molecular Diversity Preservation International, 2018, p. 23, *available online at* https://www.mdpi.com/books/pdfview/book/630.

70 P. Burdon, "The Rights of Nature: Reconsidered", *Australian Humanities Review*, Nov. 2010, Issue 49, p. 86.

A. Common Objections

I distinguish three types of objections. The first objection claims that rights are a human construction, which applies only to humans. Using the language of rights is not adequate for nature. Granting rights to nature is nonsense, an "absurdity"[71] since only the human individual is endowed with enough subjectivity to hold rights. Nature cannot speak out or plead, and therefore cannot claim rights. This objection rests on the idea that legal personality is an institution embedded in the human figure exclusively.

In response, two elements must be considered. Firstly, the objective is not to confer upon nature all the rights recognized to humans. An absurdity could indeed appear if that were the case. If some people think rights are not applicable to nature, it is partly because they fear that nature may claim all the rights developed within the framework of our legal orders. However, extending recognition of rights to an entity must be based on the entity concerned.[72] Certain rights will have to be adapted or will not be recognized to natural entities, because they are suitable only for human beings. Thomas Berry stated that the rights of nature must be looked at through a flexible and complementary understanding of rights: rights are specific to the role each entity plays in the ecosystem.[73] Similarly, Christopher Stone anticipated this reproach: "To say that the environment should have rights is not to say that it should have every right we can imagine, or even the same body of rights as human beings have".[74]

Secondly, it is necessary to adopt a more flexible conception of the legal personhood that allows attribution of this quality according to the needs/values of society. It is this same approach to legal personhood that made possible the development of the concept of legal person (or legal entity) recognized for companies or associations, as opposed to the personhood of natural persons. Yet, companies do not have any more capacity to express themselves than nature. Corporations, public institutions and other entities can stand in court in our legal systems, why not nature? A legal person is an abstract, fictitious notion and yet it does hold rights and obligations. It can take legal action and defend its interests through individuals. The legal person does not have the same attributes

---

71 L. Nouhalt, "Pachamama mia!" [My Mother Earth!], *Libération*, 23 Aug. 2010, *available online at* http://www.liberation.fr/terre/2010/08/23/attac-pachamama-mia_673655.

72 P. Burdon, 2010, p. 79.

73 T. Berry, *Evening Thoughts: Reflections on Earth as Sacred Community*, San Francisco, Sierra Club Books, 2006, p. 150.

74 C. Stone, 1972, p. 457.

as the natural person: its rights are adapted to its specificities and objectives. The conclusion is logical: legal personhood is a purely legal construct and it does not exclude in principle subjects that do not fit the figure of individual human beings.[75] Insofar as a legal person is not necessarily a human person, whether or not rights can be recognized in nature and other entities depends on our desire to extend the benefits of the consecration of legal personhood. It is a political decision.[76]

The second objection to recognizing rights of nature claims is that the elements composing nature (trees, rivers, mountains) cannot have rights because they cannot have obligations. Following this criticism, if nature cannot be a legal person, it would be more relevant to impose duties on human individuals towards nature in order to avoid upsetting the spirit of our current legal system.

It is true that if nature is granted rights, it will have no correlative obligations. For instance, a river cannot be forced to respect the rights of the inhabitants of a village through which it passes. Why not then talk about duties vis-à-vis nature instead of recognizing rights? Firstly, I reject the idea that there must be a link between legal personhood and the ability to bear duties: those are two different issues.[77] For instance, children have rights that can be enforced in court by their legal representatives, but children do not bear any responsibility.[78] Nature must be protected regardless of whether or not it has obligations. Moreover, corresponding duties would not have the same impact. The precise aim of rights of nature is to create a change of perspective through the consecration of nature's dignity/intrinsic value. Thus, human beings' duties towards nature maintain the *status quo* where the rights of nature are meant to be a paradigmatic shift. Besides, in practice, the rights of nature would have a much greater weight in balancing the interests of judges when a decision requires limits on certain human activities. The rights holder is granted the highest protection.

A third objection is that it is impossible to distinguish the interests of nature. Mark Sagoff quickly challenged Stone's thesis on the basis that it was impossible to express oneself in the place of objects that do not have the ability to

75 M.-A. Hermitte, "La nature, sujet de droit?" [Nature, Subject of Right?], *Annales, Histoire, Sciences Sociales*, 2011/1, 66th Year, p. 197.

76 D. Shelton, "Nature as a legal person", *VertigO – La revue électronique en sciences de l'environnement*, Special Issue No. 22, Sep. 2015, p. 5.

77 H. Leimbacher, "Gender and Nature in Comparative Legal Cultures", *in* D. Nelken (ed.), *Comparing Legal Cultures*, New York, Routledge, 2016, p. 146.

78 Pecharroman, 2018, p. 2.

communicate their will.[79] How could an entity have rights when it has no conscience, desires or goals, and therefore no interests?

If it is difficult to express the interest of a tree or a swamp individually; it is necessary to focus on an ecosystemic perspective instead. At this scale, it is possible to determine that the ecosystem has the right to balance, regeneration, non-destruction and the capacity of resilience. The species and plants that form an integral part of nature are also protected as essential to the ecosystem. It is possible to claim the river's interest in continuing to flow and thus allowing the life that depends on the river to flourish. This approach requires a precise understanding of the components of the ecosystem in question, and the dynamics of their relationships. The ecosystemic approach also answers the criticism that the concept of "right" is intrinsically individualistic and not adapted to nature. Recognition of such rights would impose a competition of interests between deeply connected elements.[80] However, the rights I defend are not focused on isolated elements disconnected from their ecosystem function. Each element is protected in relation to the role it plays in the local and global ecosystem. Following the "systemic paradigm" of ecology, I focus on the interdependence of the elements of the biosphere, humans included. A purely individualistic rights approach would create a situation in which competing rights would be ranked so that one entity's rights would prevail over the right of a different entity. Following this logic, rights of nature would fragment an integrated system. On the contrary, a relational rights approach allows for compromise in order to maintain the overall balance and resilience of the ecosystem.

Moreover, if nature cannot express itself, it is possible for others to express themselves in the name of nature. People who lack legal capacity in our legal system (children, people with disabilities) are represented, but still hold rights. If incapacitated persons cannot speak for themselves, they still have interests that deserve to be defended. As is the case for disabled persons and minors, nature is the weaker party and must be protected. Similarly, it is possible to appoint legal representatives for nature. The first possibility is to choose a "guardian", a specific "protector". For example, a community that has a symbiotic relationship with its territory might have great legitimacy. This would be particularly relevant in countries with strong indigenous communities. In the context of Western states where such relationships with nature are less common, the "guardian" or

79 M. Sagoff, "On Preserving the Natural Environment", *Yale Law Journal*, 1974, Vol. 84(2), pp. 221–222.

80 P. Burdon, 2010, p. 83.

"protector" may consist of local communities, groups spontaneously gathered around the defense of a biotope, environmental associations, or any individual.

B. From Utopia to Reality: Nature Has Legal Standing

To the extent that the groundbreaking 1972 proposal of giving legal personhood to nature was seen as "frightening or laughable",[81] an increasing number of legislative enactments and court rulings are recognizing rights of nature today. I will not go into the details of various legislative changes taking place around the world at every level,[82] but I will provide a few representative examples.

Historically, the first example of such recognition occurred in 2006 within the United States of America (USA). The local government of Tamaqua, Pennsylvania, gave nature rights in a sludge ordinance that banned corporations from dumping toxic waste. Similar provisions were then adopted at the local level in more than 180 American communities in the fight against polluting projects such as hydraulic fracturing ("fracking"). These legislative changes resulted from political struggles in communities that were fighting to protect their land and resources against private interests.[83]

The case of the Ecuadorian Constitution has been widely analyzed.[84] Article 71 explicitly recognizes Nature's "right to integral respect for its existence and for the maintenance and regeneration of its life cycles, structure, functions and evolutionary processes" as well as the right for "all persons, communities, peoples and nations can call upon public authorities to enforce the rights of nature". Anyone, alone or collectively, can stand before courts as nature's representative. As soon as the rights of nature are suspected to have been violated, anybody is entitled to engage the judicial process. The first ruling of this kind was delivered by an Ecuadorian court in Vilcabamba. The provincial government of Loja had authorized the construction of a road close to the Vilcabamba River. Upon launching the project, materials used in the process polluted the waters and negatively affected citizens. Those citizens decided to take the company to court by filing an action on behalf of the river. The judge decided that the rights of nature

---

81 C. Stone, 1972, p. 455.

82 *See, e.g.*, Pecharroman, 2018, pp. 4–6.

83 N. Greene, "Le cas des constitutions équatorienne et bolivienne" [The case of Ecuadorian and Bolivian Constitutions], *in Des droits pour nature* [*Rights for the Earth*], Utopia, 2016, pp. 72–73.

84 M. Tanasescu, "The Rights of Nature in Ecuador", *Environment, Political Representation, and the Challenge of Rights*, 2016, pp. 85–106.

had been violated; in particular, the river's rights to exist and be maintained, including regeneration of its vital cycles, structures and functions. This ruling "recognizes the rights of nature as a constitutional right to be observed and emphasizes that every citizen can defend such rights in court when violated".[85] Applying the precautionary principle, the court concluded that construction could start again on the condition that the company demonstrated there was no risk of environmental damage.[86] This decision is of considerable importance, since the Court held that the rights of nature took precedence over the rights of residents to benefit from the route.[87]

In New Zealand, a settlement was reached before the Waitangi Tribunal granting legal personhood to the Whanganui River as well as recognizing the indigenous community of Whanganui iwi (the local Maori tribe) as guardian responsible for protecting the health and well-being of the river, based on the community adage: "I am the river and the river is me". This agreement was the result of long-standing negotiations over ownership issues involving the tribe and the Crown (New-Zealand government). The actors designing the new framework and the institutional arrangement were the ones affected by the changes, which "gave the actors a feeling of ownership over the end result and allowed for local knowledge to be incorporated into the decision-process and framework".[88] The agreement recognizes the river as a living entity with rights and interests to defend; its designated "owner", the river bed itself. The river is no longer considered property. Every decision impacting the river must be negotiated by a council whose membership is equally divided between the government and the tribe's representatives. This agreement was ratified by Parliament on 15 March 2017 in the Te Awa Tupua Act. Interestingly, the Act's aim was to protect nature as well as to respect human rights and, more particularly following colonization, the right

85 Pecharroman, 2018, p. 7.

86 E. Daly, "The Ecuadorian Examplar: The First Ever Vindications of Constitutional Rights of Nature", *Review of European, Comparative & International Environmental Law*, 2012, Vol. 21, Issue 1, *available online at* https://onlinelibrary.wiley.com/doi/abs/10.1111/j.1467-9388.2012.00744.x ().

87 D. Shelton, 2015, p. 6.

88 J. Talbot-Jones, "Flowing from fiction to act: The challenges of implementing legal rights for rivers", 14 May 2018, *Global Water Forum, available online at* http://www.globalwaterforum.org/2018/05/14/flowing-from-fiction-to-fact-the-challenges-of-implementing-legal-rights-for-rivers/.

of the Maori natives who had lost their lands and natural treasures.[89] Henceforth, the river can be represented by the community, considered as a trustee entitled to lodge submissions on matters affecting the river whose interest transcends the general interest of the public according to the text of the Act.

C. What Impact on Access to Justice for Environmental Protection?

One of the biggest issues in environmental law is legal standing. Standing refers to the entitlement and ability of a party to justify its participation by demonstrating a sufficient connection to the case.[90] Rights of nature bypass the issue of standing. The rights of nature clearly facilitate access to a judge for both physical persons and associations. Individuals can become representatives of nature without having to justify a direct and personal interest; nature's interest alone is taken into consideration. Many ecological damage incidents do not directly affect humans, but only the environment in general. For instance, deforestation of primary forests does not necessarily affect human communities in the short-run, but this phenomenon is a major threat to biodiversity. In such situations, the rights of nature provide mechanisms for transcending the human perspective.

Does this imply that rights of nature are the only solution for ensuring protection of nature in the courts? I do not believe this to be the case. There are many developments in legal thought that could promote access to justice in environmental matters. Innovative mechanisms would lead to results comparable to those that could be obtained through rights of nature.

Several hypotheses can be explored. First, the environment could be recognized as an interest of humankind as a whole. This would lead to the consecration of an *actio popularis*, a universal right to initiate a lawsuit or prosecution involving environmental matters. The environment could become a universal general interest,[91] the logical corollary of new fundamental human right to a

---

89 C.J. Iorns Magallanes, "Nature as an Ancestor: Two Examples of Legal Personality for Nature in New Zealand", *VertigO – la revue électronique en sciences de l'environnement*, Special Issue No. 22, Sep. 2015, p. 4,

90 European Commission, *Communication from the Commission: Commission Notice on Access to Justice in Environmental Matters*, 28 Apr. 2017, *available online at* http://ec.europa.eu/environment/aarhus/pdf/notice_accesstojustice.pdf.

91 V. Jaworski, "Les représentations multiples de l'environnement devant le juge pénal : entre intérêts général, individuel et collectif" [Multiple Representations of the Environment Before the Criminal Judge: Between General, Individual and Collective Interests], *VertigO – La revue électronique en sciences de l'environnement ?*, Special Issue No. 22, Sep. 2015, p. 8.

healthy environment.[92] This *actio popularis* would lead to the exact same results contemplated under article 71 of the Ecuadorian Constitution.

In order to mitigate the individualistic bias of *actio popularis*, the "diffuse interest theory" should also be considered to allow a "socialization of interests".[93] Unlike the so-called collective interests that are carried by organized people around a stable legal bond such as an association, the diffuse interests concern individuals united by a common interest arising from factual circumstances.[94] This notion transcends the classical categories (public interest protected by the State, collective interests embodied by associations, and the individual interests of a person). Nor should it be reduced to a simple addition of individual interests. The personal interest of each individual might be limited, causing them to gather for the protection of a common goal – which resonates with the characterization of the environment as a common good that cannot be appropriated.

Finally, and this may be the most logical option, we should also consider opening up the courtroom to environmental organizations to the largest extent possible. Relying on the State as the guardian of the general interest tends to favor a pro-growth perspective and a productivist logic; instead, organizations should be allowed to defend the collective interest in protecting the environment, as is the case in many countries. Not necessarily to demonstrate the direct impact on humans, but activating the altruistic rationale of organizations to protect nature for its own sake.

These initiatives would maintain a largely mitigated anthropocentric perspective and would not have the same symbolic weight as rights of nature. However, they could achieve effects similar to recognizing the rights of nature – at least as far as legal standing and judicial access are concerned. This was the conclusion reached by Edgar Fernandez Fernandez when he compared the issue of standing in a system with indirect protection of the environment as in Costa Rica, with protection based on fundamental rights recognized to nature in the context of Ecuador. Despite the absence of rights of nature, the Costa Rican Constitutional Court recognizes that "any person has an interest to act […] to defend the right to the conservation of the country's natural resources" and "to protect the right

92 *Ibid.*, p. 10.

93 A. Aragao, "Les intérêts diffus, instruments pour la justice et la démocratie environnementale" [Diffuse Interests, Instruments for Justice and Environmental Democracy], *VertigO – La revue électronique en sciences de l'environnement*, Special Issue No. 22, Sep. 2015, p. 3.

94 *Ibid.*, p. 4.

to maintain the natural balance of the ecosystem".[95] An *actio popularis* is thus recognized in Costa Rica, which provides judicial access similar to Ecuador with regard to environmental issues. Therefore, although this represents a major ethical claim, the personification of nature is not an indispensable condition for facilitating judicial access because "this objective can also be achieved by recognizing an interest in acting as broadly as possible, to any person, individually or in community, to access the judge for the purpose of protecting the environment".[96]

As discussed above, several concepts could be developed to improve environmental justice without recognition of the rights of nature. However, this option could have very concrete effects and offers other advantages beyond the standing issue: it would give a higher value to nature. Its destruction could not be compensated only by money; compensations for nature itself would have to be recognized ("préjudice écologique pur" as it exists in France since the Erika case). It would make it harder to set nature aside when balancing competing rights. Property rights would be understood in the broader context of nature's resilience and integrity, etc. All those aspects should be further analyzed as the case law on the rights of nature continues to grow. In the meantime, I can already state that the rights of nature are not only a symbolic measure but also a source of effective change for ecological justice: understood as the respect of ecological limits imposed by nature, while ensuring the well-being and the fundamental rights of all human beings.

III. Nature's Rights vs. Human Rights? Beyond the Anthropocentrism and Ecocentrism Debate

True ecological justice will not depend on the answer given to the long-lasting debate between anthropocentrism and ecocentrism. Rather, it will come from the understanding that social justice and environmental justice are intertwined, just as human rights and nature rights complement each other. Three main points will allow us to support the view according to which human rights

95 *See* E.F. Fernandez, "Les controverses autour de l'intérêt à agir pour l'accès au juge constitutionnel : de la défense du droit à l'environnement (Costa Rica) à la défense des droits de la nature (Équateur)" [The Controversies Surrounding the Interest in Acting for Access to the Constitutional Judge: From the Defense of the Right to the Environment (Costa Rica) to the Defense of the Rights of Mature (Ecuador)], *VertigO - La revue électronique en sciences de l'environnement*, Special Issue No. 22, Sep. 2015, pp. 3–6 (quoting and analyzing relevant Costa Rican Constitutional Court case law).

96 *Ibid.*, p. 6.

advocates and nature's rights activists should align their interests. First, I will return to the examples of rights of nature's recognitions to show that their consecration and effectiveness depends on the political or cultural practices of the human communities fighting for their land's protection. Secondly, entering in the Anthropocene, opposing humankind and the planet no longer makes sense as our survival depends on the protection of the biosphere. Finally, the notion of ecocide will illustrate this combination of anthropocentric and ecocentric motivations as this legal concept protects human and nature's rights equally.

A. Behind the Rights of Nature? Resistance Movements of Human Communities

From the examples discussed above, it seems clear that recognizing rights of nature is the result of human communities defending their interests, cosmologies, rights, and traditions. In the USA, the provisions recognizing such rights are human-centric and intended to protect the resources that municipalities rely on against corporations' appetite for profit. If the Ecuadorian Constitution is ecocentric (as it clearly acknowledges the intrinsic value of nature), it also reflects the human values of indigenous populations and their cosmology. In New Zealand, too, the rights of nature represent recognition of the Maori's specific relationship to nature, and compensation for the human rights atrocities and other destructive consequences of colonization vis-à-vis indigenous minorities.[97] This is not to say that an apparently ecocentric legislation is ultimately just another anthropocentric tool, but that in the end human interests and nature's interests coincide. In the same vein, the Ganges and the Yamuna rivers in India were recognized as legal persons by the High Court of Uttarakhand. The court did not justify its ruling based on the intrinsic value of these rivers, but rather on the cosmology of Hindus and their religious beliefs. The rights recognized to nature are generally the reflection of cultural and collective rights that are also a powerful alternative to the dominant paradigm of private property.[98] As shown through these examples, the rights of nature are not opposed to human rights; on the contrary, rights of nature very often allow for their protection against financial interests. It is a battle between powerless communities or minorities against big corporations or a state's polluting policies, more often than a conflict between nature and humankind.

---

97 T. Jayatilaka, 2016–2017, p. 12.

98 C.J. Iorns Magallanes, "Maori cultural rights in Aoeteara New Zealand: protecting the cosmology that protects the environment", *Widener Law Review*, 2015, vol. 21, p. 327.

Therefore, the political and collective practices of human communities defending their respective territory are decisive as far as environmental justice and ecological integrity are concerned.[99] Regardless of the legal qualification of the resource, collective struggles and practices offer a genuine alternative to the profit-driven paradigm based on private property. This is also why we cannot expect rights of nature, as powerful as they might become, to be a magical solution that will destroy our capitalistic structures and allow the emergence of a harmonious system. The effectiveness of this new legal tool in helping to solve the ecological crisis will depend on the political context underlying its consecration.

Rights of nature could remain toothless if not supported by human communities willing to fight for their present and future well-being or if public authorities remain passive against the greed of private interests. Ecuador is a telling example of the limited impact rights of nature will have when not supported by true political will. Few cases have been judged on the basis of nature's rights in Ecuador; on the rare occasions where this has occurred, these decisions were not systematically enforced.[100] There is a gap between rhetoric and the reality.[101] This illustrates the difficulty of implementing such rights when the national economy relies on the exploitation of natural resources,[102] leading the country to maintain support for extractive industries to the detriment of ecosystems. In 2013, an Ecuadorian judge clearly stated that development, as a matter of public interest, will always prevail over the rights of nature despite clear evidence of their violation.[103] The pursuit of economic growth remains the main objective of public authorities in Ecuador.[104]

By contrast, recognizing the rights of nature could become a strong legal tool to strengthen the global contestation against environmental injustices, and could also be used "to advance a post-neoliberal development agenda rooted in

99 F. Ost, "Personnaliser la nature, pour elle-même, vraiment?" [Personifying Nature, for Itself, Really?], *in* P. Descola (ed.), *Les Natures en question* [*Natures in Question*], Odile Jacob, 2018.

100 E.F. Fernandez, 2015, p. 135

101 *See* L. Kotze & P. Villa Vicencio Calzadilla, "Somewhere between rhetoric and reality: environment constitutionalism and the rights of nature in Ecuador", *Transnational Environmental Law*, Nov. 2017, Vol. 6, Issue 3, pp. 1–33.

102 *See* C. Kaufmann & P. Martin, "Testing Ecuador's Rights of Nature: Why Some Lawsuits Succeed and Others Fail", Paper presented at the International Studies Association Annual Convention, Atlanta, 18 Mar. 2016.

103 *Ibid.*

104 K. Herold, *The Right of Nature: Indigenous Philosophies Reframing Law*, 6 Jan. 2017, Earth Law Center.

harmony with nature".[105] If the rights of nature may become a true alternative to the fatal trajectory of our capitalist system, it will only be possible with the support of social and environmental movements. For example, a recent study analyzing the granting of legal rights to rivers as a new paradigm for water governance concluded that the effectiveness of those rights was likely to depend on the participation of communities impacted in the process and their capacity to influence the decisions in the given framework.[106] In other words, I believe that those already fighting for the protection of the "commons" could be strengthened by the recognition of the rights of nature. The effectiveness of nature's rights in preserving the Earth for future generations (humans and non-humans alike) will depend on our commitment to make them a true limitation on our economic gigantism.

In conclusion, the rights of nature will not provide a miraculous recipe for harmony between humankind and nature. Remaining issues include the enforcement of judgments, the protection of activists fighting for those rights, the tradeoffs between economic growth and environmental protection, etc. Nevertheless, this could become a powerful legal concept in the hands of civil society. It could help make the political powers and the corporations accountable for their environmental crimes, especially before the courts. Such strategic litigation is becoming increasingly common in light of political inertia, especially in the fight against global warming.[107] The rights of nature could help those movements to achieve historical decisions. Many uncertainties remain, but this should not hinder us from supporting the potential legal revolution it represents for rethinking our current system, our definition of progress and success, our vision of prosperity, our societies' goals and our paradigms.

105 C.M. Kauffman & P. Martin, "Can Rights of Nature Make Development More Sustainable? Why Some Ecuadorian lawsuits Succeed and Others Fail", *World Development*, 2017, Vol. 92, pp. 130–142.

106 J. Talbot-Jones, 2018.

107 For a complete database of the climate change litigation cases, *see* Sabin Center for Climate Change Law, Climate Change Litigation Databases, *available online at* http://climatecasechart.com/.

B. The Anthropocene: A Common Destiny for Humankind and Nature

Rights of nature denounce both the ecological and the human impact of industrial societies.[108] When mobilized by individuals gathering around the protection of the ecosystems on which they rely, rights of nature are a tool for reconciling social justice and ecological integrity. The rights of nature framework seeks to combine human and nature's interests by claiming that they are intimately interdependent. Integration of future generations into our moral and political concerns shares a common objective with nature's rights: moving away from a system incompatible with the earth's life support systems. One could even say that human communities and ecosystems have a common enemy: short-term, profit-driven thinking, and reduction of the living to a monetary value. The exploitation of nature by man goes hand-in-hand with the exploitation of man by man: the rights of nature do not deny the importance of human rights, they extend their logic to the natural world.[109]

The Anthropocene is defined as the current epoch, in which humans and our societies have become a global geophysical force[110] with the power to radically and irreversibly modify the conditions of existence on Earth. Hence, it is no longer relevant to frame the debate as if a choice was to be made between saving humankind or saving the planet. Since we are capable of transforming the biosphere to such an extent that we might annihilate various forms of living including ours, it is now about protecting ourselves and the rest of the Earthly community against a certain development path. Since the "health and well-being of humankind depend on the health of the environment, these goals will often be so mutually supportive that one can avoid deciding".[111]

The ecological crisis is deeply rooted in the inequalities and the domination that results from the domination of humankind over nature, of the rich over the poor, of the North over the South and, in general, the powerful over the powerless. When ecosystems are pushed to collapse for the purpose of satisfying the

108 A. Boutaud, "Ecologie: les grandes controverses" [Ecology: The Big Controversies], *Millénaire,* 3 Feb. 2010, p. 4.

109 D.E. Fisher, "Jurisprudential challenges to the protection of the natural environment", *in* M. Maloney & P. Burdon, 2014, p. 96.

110 W. Steffen, P.J. Crutzen & J.R. McNeill, "The Anthropocene: Are Humans Now Overwhelming the Great Forces of Nature?", *Ambio*, 2007, Vol. 36, No. 8, pp. 614–621.

111 Pecharroman, 2018, p. 3.

elite's interests, neither human rights nor rights of nature can be respected. In other words, human rights cannot be protected in the long run without rights of nature, since the full enjoyment of many human rights depends on the health of ecosystems.[112] This is why the recognition of rights of nature is a necessary step in the direction that I call ecological justice.

My position is perfectly summarized in the "People's Agreement" of the World People's Conference on Climate Change and the Rights of Mother Earth: "Under capitalism, Mother Earth is converted into a source of raw materials, and human beings into consumers and a means of production, into people that are seen as valuable only for what they own, and not for what they are".

C. The Notion of Ecocide in the Name of Ecological Justice

In our view, ecocide is a vivid example of a concept that could very well reconcile the logics of human and nature's rights. It is a true ecological justice concept where humans and ecosystems are both protected from companies and/or states that are driven by the quest of profit to the detriment of social and environmental concerns.

How could this notion be defined? Broadly, ecocide is the destruction of our natural environment.[113] More specifically, Eradicating Ecocide, a citizen movement that advocates for the recognition of ecocide as a fifth international crime, proposes to define the concept as "the extensive damage to, destruction of or loss of ecosystem(s) of a given territory, whether by human agency or by other causes, to such an extent that peaceful enjoyment by the inhabitants of that territory has been or will be severely diminished".[114] Ecocide thus refers to a lasting, significant alteration of ecological balances that threatens ecosystems, non-human species, and humans' living conditions. The etymology of the term quite clearly shows why I consider ecocide as a concept at the crossroads of human rights and the rights of nature. The term comes from the ancient Greek "oikos": the "house" or the "home", and from the Latin "caedere": "to strike down, to demolish, to kill". Literally, it must be translated as "killing our house". We destroy what allows

112 J. Knox, Statement, "Annual Report: Biodiversity and Human Rights and Country Visit to Madagascar", Human Rights Council, 34th Session 8 Mar. 2017.

113 S. Metha & P. Merz, "Ecocide – A New Crime Against Peace?", *Environmental Law Review*, 2014, Vol. 17, p. 4.

114 *See* Eradicating Ecocide, Proposed Amendment to the Rome Statute, *available online at* https://eradicatingecocide.com/the-law/what-is-ecocide/.

our own conditions of existence. Ecocide is an attack on what Pope Francis calls our "common home".[115] If there are similarities with the definitions of the crime against humanity and war crimes which are focused on human dignity, ecocide is an autonomous crime that goes beyond anthropocentric motivations.

What is protected by the prohibition of ecocide? Is it nature for itself, with all its diversity, or human beings? In other words, is it the safety of the planet as such, or the safety of the planet as the condition of human life? No clear answer can be given, as ecocide does not protect a single value but a "network of values, themselves interdependent".[116] What is protected is planetary safety[117] or, more precisely, "the guarantee of the substantial integrity of the Earth".[118] Therefore, prohibition of ecocide provides double protection: of the environment for itself, and of affected populations.

Concretely, two components can be included in the planet's safety. The first component is the protection of nature for its intrinsic value. This covers the Earth's components, processes and life cycles.[119] The second component protects the environment because its preservation is a condition of the existence of human communities. The idea is to limit human activities that endanger and threaten our future. In this perspective, the safety of the planet refers to anthropocentric motivations considerably mitigated by collective apprehension of the following concept: "It is humanity, or at least a population in the collective sense and not the individual, which is targeted here".[120] In this sense, ecocide is a crime against the environment and against humanity; the crossroads of humanistic and eco-centric conceptions must be recognized so that no one can escape justice in the name of national sovereignty or through market-based instruments.

---

115 Encyclical Letter Laudato Si' of the Holy Father Francis *On Care for Our Common Home*, *available online at* http://w2.vatican.va/content/francesco/en/encyclicals/documents/papa-francesco_20150524_enciclica-laudato-si.html.

116 E. Fonza & others, "Vers une définition du crime international d'écocide" [Towards a Definition of the International Crime of Ecocide], *in* L. Neyret, 2015, p. 132.

117 H. Hellio, "De la valeur partagée de la sûreté de la planète à la répression internationale de l'écocide. Une nouvelle quête" [From the Shared Value of the Safety of the Planet to the International Repression of Ecocide: A New Quest], *in* L. Neyret, 2015, p. 110.

118 *Ibid.*, p. 111.

119 *Ibid.*, pp. 112–113

120 *Ibid.*

Conclusion

Western society's ethical, economic and legal foundations are based on obsolete paradigms incapable of solving the challenges we face in today's world. The mastery of nature and the emancipation of man through technology are presented as inevitable processes, a continuum tending towards prosperity and abundance. This concept is particularly striking in the economic sphere: the biosphere is subjected to the economic rationale (most notably through privatization and economic valuation mechanisms) rather than the other way around. As far as the legal world is concerned, I believe that the law's failure to push our societies towards sustainability can be explained, at least in part, by the fact that our legal orders have been built around the cartesian credo of human domination over nature, without deeply questioning that belief. The conquest culture deeply embodied in our growth-driven system has been only marginally revised by current legal norms. Quoting Serge Gutwirth: "From the scientific, philosophical, ethical, legal and economic points of view, the instrumentalist conception of nature is deeply rooted in Western culture. Respect for the right of property, the laws of the market and the epistemological principle of control and possession have a head start on ecological awareness".[121]

Despite the unprecedented development of environmental standards in recent decades, climate change, biodiversity loss and ecosystem degradation, depletion of fish stocks, ocean acidification, and desertification are all phenomena that have worsened in recent decades. On the basis of this observation, I believe in the potential that rights of nature will foster the emergence of new paradigms that can enable us to transform our models. Applying Albert Einstein's maxim "no problem can be solved without changing the level of consciousness that engendered it", we cannot hope that the models which contributed to the degradation of nature will bring relevant solutions. Hence, the need for rights of nature as the first step in a philosophical, economic and legal revolution that will redefine our prosperity within planetary limits. From neoclassical economics to ecological economics, from anthropocentric philosophy to environmental ethics, and from appropriation to legal personhood, nature must return to the center of our preoccupations.

I have tried to demonstrate that, beyond its powerful symbolism, rights of nature could have massive concrete effects on current struggles in the name of environmental justice. Legal standing would be opened for individuals as well as organizations to protect ecosystems, regardless of whether or not human

121 Author's translation of S. Gutwirth, 2001, p. 9.

interests are directly harmed. The judge would have to consider the fundamental rights of nature in his decisions, which could be particularly effective to limit polluting human activities.

Above all, a simple observation has become clear in our minds: since humanity and nature are interdependent, in the long-term, protecting one is protecting the other. Separating social issues from environmental issues would be absurd since the dominance of nature reflects the myriad of exploitations of man by man.[122] Social and environmental crises are intimately linked and responding to them separately is meaningless. As I have demonstrated, the rights of nature are a necessary condition for protecting the rights of present and future generations. Rights of nature are a tool for the protection of human communities against financial interests and polluting projects. Therefore, I agree with Catherine Larrère, who eloquently stated that: the choice is not between humankind or the nature, but between a uniform world, shaped solely by economic interests and a diverse world, making room for the plurality of our aspirations as well as the plurality of living beings.[123]

---

122 M. Bookchin, *Social Ecology and Communalism*, Oakland, AK Press, 2007, p. 13.
123 C. Larrère, "Questions d'éthique environnementale" [Enviromental Ethics Issues], *Les grands dossiers des sciences humaines*, 2006, No. 2, p. 87.

Juan Ignacio PEREYRA

13. The Recognition of Rights for Future Generations in Argentinian Lawsuits: Review and Prospects

Technological progress made by humankind in the twentieth century generated a hitherto unknown danger: the capacity to harm future generations.

This risk first became apparent at the beginning of the 1900s with the conflict of the First World War, and prompted the founding of the first supranational organizations. These included the League of Nations (1919/1946), in order to promote international co-operation and to achieve international peace and security,[1] and later, at the end of World War II, the United Nations – which recognized the duty to protect future generations as one of its main objectives in the Charter of San Francisco to save succeeding generations from the calamities of war.[2] It was thus a fundamental precursor to *Transgenerational Law*,[3] whose goal is to protect future generations from the serious damage that current generations can cause.

From the second half of the twentieth century onwards, it became clear that certain technological advances applied to civil and commercial life were causing

---

1 League of Nations, Covenant of the League of Nations, 28 April 1919, p. 1, *available online at* https://www.refworld.org/docid/3dd8b9854.html (accessed 13 June 2019).

2 United Nations, Charter of the United Nations, 24 October 1945, 1 UNTS XVI, p. 1, *available online at* https://www.refworld.org/docid/3ae6b3930.html (accessed 13 June 2019).

3 *See* E. Gaillard, "L'équité transgénérationnelle : perspectives de justice pour les générations futures ?" [Transgenerational Equity: Opportunities to Pursue Justice for Future Generations?], *in* A. Michelot (ed.), *Equité et Environnement. Quel(s) modèle(s) de justice environnementale ?* [Equity and Environment: What Model(s) of Environmental Justice?], Larcier, 2012, p. 52 (explaining that the use of "transgenerational equity" is preferable to "intergenerational equity". According to Émile Littré, the prefix "trans- added in the composition of certain words (allows to integrate) the idea of beyond, through". To the extent that human generations are not clearly distinct from each other, our hypothesis is that they participate in a community of terrestrial destinies here and now as well as beyond present time – which is better captured by the term "transgenerational". Use of this term instead of "intergenerational" accounts for the continuous succession of human generations).

serious transgenerational harm. Examples include: Thalomide (1957-1963); pesticides, as exposed by Rachel Carson in *Silent Spring* (1962); the Club of Rome report, *The Limits to Growth* (1972); polychlorinated biphenyl (PCB) pollution in Japan (1968) that left children malformed by Yushu disease; PCB pollution in Lake Michigan (1985); the Union Carbide chemical explosion in Bhopal that affected 500,000 people (India, 1984); the Chernobyl disaster (1986); pollution caused by Chevron in Ecuador (1972-1992); Monsanto's PCBs in Annistan, Alabama (USA), resulting in the health disaster reported in Marie-Monique Robin's documentary, *The World According to Monsanto* (2008); the oil spill from the British Petroleum (BP) drilling rig in the Gulf of Mexico (2010); and, the Fukushima nuclear disaster (2011).

Hobbes once said that Man is a wolf to man.[4] After analyzing the twentieth century, we can now say that, *current generations are a wolf to future generations*. This is a historical moment: humanity faces a distinctive phenomenon where certain social groups are capable of causing transgenerational harm.[5] This harm is defined as affecting commons that are essential for the life and development of present and future generations. The purpose of transgenerational law is to safeguard *transgenerational commons*. Transgenerational harm is clearly unjust and illegal, because its harmful consequences are transferred to others – in this case, future generations – who must not only suffer its consequences, but also bear the cost of reparation. This situation clearly breaches the overall principle of the law, alterum non laedere (do no harm to others) which is the second of the three iuris praecepta (general principles of Law established by Ulpiano, Ulpiano: Digesto 1, 1, 10, 1)[6] – which provides an indisputable basis for the legal regime of civil responsibility, as well as a juridical foundation for the duty to repair damage, *cuius est commodum eius est incommodum* (he who receives the benefit should also bear the disadvantage).[7]

4 T. Hobbes, *Leviathan* (reprinted from the edition of 1651), Clarendon Press, 1909.

5 E. Gaillard, "Pour la reconnaissance du dommage juridique transgénérationel" [For the Recognition of Transgenerational Legal Damage], *in* J.-P. Markus (ed.), *Quelles responsabilité juridique envers les générations futures ?* [What Legal Responsibility for Future Generations?], Dalloz, 2012, pp. 245–260.

6 *Diccionario Jurídico Español* [*Spanish Legal Dictionary*], Real Academia Española, https://dej.rae.es/lema/alterum-non-laedere [accessed 9 June 2019] (Alterum non laedere).

7 *Ibid.*, https://dej.rae.es/lema/cuius-commodum-eius-est-incommodum (Cuius est commodum eius est incommodum) (accessed 9 June 2019).

The Civil and Commercial Code of the Argentine Republic defines "abuse of the law" in article 14 as follows: "The law does not protect the abusive exercise of individual rights when it may affect the environment and collective rights in general".[8] In the case of harm that can affect future generations, this constitutes an *abuse of transgenerational rights*.

I. The Law Should Regulate "Transgenerational Externalities"

Since transgenerational harm is now a reality, the Law is obliged to develop adequate legal mechanisms to prevent and repair this harm. In order to do so, a profound analysis of the social dynamics that cause and permit harm is necessary in order to establish appropriate principles, institutions, bodies and procedures to prevent harm from being caused, or repair it in the event that it is generated. When damage is caused, future generations are in the most defenseless position possible due to the fact that they do not yet exist. Here follows a brief outline of legislation and case law relative to current transgenerational safeguards. These safeguards will be analyzed and innovations proposed to make the legal protection of future generations more effective.

II. International Transgenerational Law

International Law includes many legal documents that recognize the responsibilities of current generations towards future generations. Given the huge influence these pronouncements had on the formulation of Argentine Law, it is worth mentioning some of them:

- The San Francisco Charter of the United Nations (1945) begins as follows: "We the people of the United Nations, determined to save succeeding generations from the scourge of war […]".[9]
- The universal nature of Universal Declaration of Human Rights (1948) extends to both present and future generations.

---

8 Código Civil y Comercial de la Nación, 1st edition, Oct. 2014, Art. 14, *available online at* http://www.saij.gob.ar/docs-f/codigo/Codigo_Civil_y_Comercial_de_la_Nacion.pdf.

9 United Nations, Charter of the United Nations, 24 Oct. 1945, *United Nations Treaty Series*, Vol. 1, No. 16, p. 1, *available online at* https://www.refworld.org/docid/3ae6b3930.html (accessed 9 June 2019).

- The Stockholm Declaration on the Human Environment (1972) recognizes that, "to defend and improve the human environment for present and future generations has become an imperative goal for mankind".[10]
- The Convention for the Protection of World Cultural and Natural Heritage was adopted at the UNESCO General Conference on 16 November 1972 (Article 4).[11]
- The report, *Our Common Future*, referred to as the Brundtland Report (1987), incorporated the concept of sustainable development as meeting "the needs of the present without compromising the ability of future generations to meet their own needs".[12] This means that compromising the needs and interests of future generations incurs an abuse of rights in relation to the use of transgenerational commons, as we mentioned earlier.[13] The concept of sustainable development thus implicitly recognizes that future generations are legal subjects who must be protected from the abusive use of transgenerational commons, defined as transgenerational harm.
- The United Nations Framework Convention on Climate Change and the Convention on Biological Diversity approved in Rio de Janeiro on 5 June 1992.
- The Rio Declaration on Environment and Development approved by the United Nations Conference on Environment and Development in June 1992, was an important step forward as it recognized "the integral and interdependent nature of the Earth, our home […]"[14] and nature as commons. It thus gave nature a higher legal status and established the need for special legal safeguarding of the essential and life-giving purpose it fulfils. The Rio Declaration also established the principles of transgenerational equity and sustainability, thus laying the foundations for Transgenerational Law.

---

10 The United Nations Conference on the Human Environment (Stockholm), A/CONF.48/14/Rev.l, 5–16 June 1972, point 6 & principes 1 and 2.

11 UN Educational, Scientific and Cultural Organisation (UNESCO), Convention Concerning the Protection of the World Cultural and Natural Heritage, 16 Nov. 1972, *available online at* https://www.refworld.org/docid/4042287a4.html (accessed 13 June 2019).

12 G. Brundtland, *Report of the World Commission on Environment and Development: Our Common Future*, United Nations General Assembly document A/42/427, 1987, p. 24.

13 *See* E. Gaillard, *Générations futures et droit privé. Vers un droit des générations futures* [*Future Generations and Private Law: Towards a Law for Future Generations*], Librairie Générale de Droit et de Jurisprudence, 2011, pp. 434–435 (Nos. 524–525).

14 The United Nations Conference on Environment and Development, Rio de Janeiro (3–14 June 1992), The Rio Declaration on Environment And Development, A/CONF.151/26, 1992, Vol. 1, p. 1.

- The Vienna Declaration and Programme of Action approved by the World Conference on Human Rights on 25 June 1993, and the resolutions of the United Nations General Assembly on the protection of the global climate for present and future generations, approved since 1990.
- The Stockholm Convention on Persistent Organic Pollutants (1997) recognizes the dangers of Persistent Organic Pollutants (POPs)[15] for future generations and establishes a set of public and private obligations aimed at protecting future generations.
- The Declaration on the Responsibilities of the Present Generations Towards Future Generations approved by UNESCO on 12 November 1997 was the culmination of the new law, asserting the need to establish "new, equitable and global links of partnership and intragenerational solidarity, and for promoting inter-generational solidarity for the perpetuation of humankind"[16] so as to, "contribute towards the solution of current world problems through increased international co-operation, to create such conditions as will ensure that the needs and interests of future generations are not jeopardized by the burden of the past, and to hand on a better world to future generations".[17] "Bearing in mind that the fate of future generations depends to a great extent on decisions and actions taken today, and that present-day problems, including poverty, technological and material underdevelopment, unemployment, exclusion, discrimination and threats to the environment, must be solved in the interests of both present and future generations",[18] and "[c]onvinced that there is a moral obligation to formulate behavioral guidelines for the present generations within a broad, future-oriented perspective".[19] These are the foundations on which the Declaration recognized a plexus of obligations of the present generations to protect the interests of future generations. They must be transposed into national legal codes to ensure they are observed.

---

15 Persistent Organic Pollutants (POPs).

16 General Conference of the United Nations Educational, Scientific and Cultural Organization, Paris, France, Declaration on the Responsibilities of the Present Generations Towards Future Generations, 12 Nov. 1997, preamble, *available online at* http://portal.unesco.org/en/ev.php-URL_ID=13178&URL_DO=DO_TOPIC&URL_SECTION=201.html (accessed 14 June 2019).

17 *Ibid.*

18 *Ibid.*

19 *Ibid.*

III. Transgenerational Law in Argentina

The first legal recognition of the future generations in Argentine law can be found in the preamble of the National Constitution (1853) that states: "We, the representatives of the people of the Argentine Nation, gathered [...] in order to form a national union, guarantee justice, secure domestic peace, provide for the common defense, promote the general welfare and secure the blessings of liberty to ourselves, *to our posterity*".[20]

This transgenerational recognition was sufficient to establish the protection of future generations in one of the most important rulings regarding environmental matters, in the 10 May 1983 case of *Alberto E. Kattan & other vs. the National Government*,[21] which we will return to later (*see* Section III.C. below).

A. Constitutional Transgenerational Law

With the 1994 constitutional reforms of Argentina, future generations gained constitutional recognition as legal subjects. Article 41 incorporated the environmental paradigm, constitutionalizing Environmental Law and its principles – including the duty to protect future generations – in the following terms: "All inhabitants are entitled to the right to a healthy and balanced environment fit for human development in order that productive activities shall meet present needs without endangering those of future generations; and shall have the duty to preserve it".[22] The Argentine constitution thus recognizes the environment as a commons protected by law for all inhabitants, but also grants it transgenerational status by establishing a clear boundary as to the extent present generations may exercise their rights with respect to the commons without compromising the needs of future generations. Since 1994, future generations have thus had constitutional recognition as collective legal subjects in the Argentine legal system.

---

20 Author's translation of Constitución de la Nación Argentina [Argentine Constitution], Santa Fe, 22 de Agosto de 1994, Boletín Oficial [Official Bulletin], 23 Aug. 1994, *available online at* http://www.saij.gob.ar/nacional-constitucion-nacional-constitucion-nacion-argentina-lns0002665-1994-08-22/123456789-0abc-defg-g56-62000scanyel (accessed 14 June 2019) (emphasis added).

21 *Kattan, Alberto E. Y Otro C. Gobierno Nacional -Poder Ejecutivo* [*Alberto E. Kattan & other v. the National Government* (Executive Power)], Juzgado Nacional de 1a Instancia en lo Contencioso-administrativo Federal No. 2, Buenos Aires, 10 May 1983, La Ley 1983-D, 576, *available online at* http://center-hre.org/wp-content/uploads/2011/07/1983-05-10-kattan-.pdf (accessed 14 June 2019).

22 Author's translation of Argentine Constitution, article 41.

These constitutional laws bore fruit in environmental legislation at both national and provincial levels and became a point of reference for case law. Future Generations were also incorporated into the Buenos Aires provincial legislation through the provincial constitutional reform of 1994, which set out in article 28 that "the inhabitants of the province have the right to enjoy a healthy environment and the duty to preserve it and protect it, to their own benefit *and that of the generations to come*".[23] Also, the constitutional reform of the Autonomous City of Buenos Aires of 1996 stated in article 26 that: "The environment is common heritage. Everyone has the right to enjoy a healthy environment, as well as the duty to preserve and defend it for the benefit of present and future generations".[24]

The duty to protect future generations has also been incorporated into the provincial constitutional reforms of Córdoba (art. 68), Chubut (art. 109), Mendoza (art. 1), and Santiago de Estero (art. 35).

B. Transgenerational Legislation

Consequently, Argentina passed the Law on National Environmental Policy (Law 25,675).[25] In article 1, this law sets out sustainable management as an objective, clearly implying that present generations have a duty to refrain from affecting the environment in in a manner detrimental to its use and enjoyment by future generations.[26] The law then asserts under article 2(b), that national environmental policies must: "Promote the improvement of quality of life of present and future generations as a priority".[27] Article 4 further establishes the principles of environmental law and policy, affirming the Principle of Intergenerational Equity: "Those responsible for protecting the environment must ensure appropriate use and enjoyment of the environment by present and future generations".[28]

---

23 Author's translation of Constitución de la Provincia de Buenos Aires, article 28, *available online at* http://www.gob.gba.gov.ar/dijl/constitucion/cpppal.htm (accessed 14 June 2019) (emphasis added).

24 Author's translation of Constitución de la Ciudad de Buenos Aires, article 26, *available online at* https://www.buenosaires.gob.ar/areas/leg_tecnica/sin/normapop09.php?id=26766&qu=c (accessed 14 June 2019).

25 Información Legislativa, Politica Ambiental Nacional [National Environmental Policy], Ley 25.675, Ley General del Ambiente [General Law of the Environment], 27 Nov. 2002, *available online at* http://servicios.infoleg.gob.ar/infolegInternet/anexos/75000-79999/79980/norma.htm (accessed 14 June 2019).

26 *Ibid.*

27 *Ibid.* (author's translation).

28 *Ibid.* (author's translation).

In addition, article 4 establishes the Principle of Sustainability: "Economic and social development and use of natural resources must be carried out through appropriate environmental management in such a way that it does not compromise the opportunities of present and future generations".[29]

The Law on Environmental Protection in the Province of Buenos Aires No. 11,723,[30] in turn provides for environmental transgenerational protection in article 1: "according to article 28 of the Constitution of Buenos Aires, the purpose of this law is to protect, conserve, improve and restore the natural resources and environment in general in the Province of Buenos Aires. The aim of this [article] is to preserve life in its broadest sense, ensuring the conservation of the environmental quality and biological diversity for present and future generations".[31] These standards – among others – set out the public and private obligations aimed at preserving transgenerational commons, to prevent their diminishment through use or enjoyment to the detriment of future generations.

Thanks to the extraordinary praetorian endeavors of certain judges, case law doctrine based on these guidelines has been constructed with great lucidity and sensitivity, putting these decisions at the frontlines of transgenerational law. Their application is worthy of consideration and analysis.

C. Case Law in Argentina for Protecting Future Generations

We will begin our analysis with the memorable *Kattan* ruling, as an example of commitment, courage and innovation. The plaintiff requested annulment of two executive authorizations to fish/hunt 14 pink bottlenose dolphins in the Argentine Sea pending completion of studies about the environmental and wildlife impact such hunting could cause.[32] The court's exemplary ruling:

(1) Recognized Nature and natural resources as legal commons, with a higher status than other commons due to their importance in the development of human life[33];

---

29 *Ibid.* (author's translation).

30 Ley N° 11 .723, Ley Integral del Medio Ambiente y los Recursos Naturales [Comprehensive Law on the Environment and Natural Resources], Provincia de Buenos Aires, 9 Nov. 1995, *available online at* http://www.opds.gba.gov.ar/sites/default/files/Ley%20%2011723.pdf (accessed 14 June 2019).

31 *Ibid.*, article 1 (author's translation); *see also* Constitución de la Provincia de Buenos Aires [Constitution of the Province of Buenos Aires], 1994, article 28, *available online at* http://www.infoleg.gob.ar/?page_id=173 (accessed 14 June 2019).

32 *Ibid.*, p. 1, paragraph I (author's translation).

33 *Ibid.*, p. 5, paragraph XVIII (author's translation).

(2) Recognized the massive and transgenerational harm caused to "collective and essential commons", establishing the need for special protection[34];
(3) Recognized that the plaintiff, who in this case was an individual, had active, ample and sufficient legitimacy to initiate legal action for environmental safeguarding[35]; and
(4) Upheld anticipatory safeguarding so as to "avoid future harm" as a precautionary measure due to the lack of sufficient information on the how the capture of these 14 bottlenose dolphins could affect the species, and consequently the environment.[36]

Absent sufficient information to protect the species, the court annulled the permits based on the principle of iura novit curia (the court knows the law).[37]

Prior to the 1994 Constitutional reform, *Schroder v. Secretary of Natural Resources*[38] established special procedural protection (Environmental Amparo) to safeguard the rights of present and future generations, applying the *Principle of Sustainability* along with *Transgenerational Equity*:

> It is appropriate that the plaintiff – citizen of the Province of Buenos Aires – has the right to bring amparo proceedings requesting the annulment of a call for tender for the construction of a hazardous waste plant (Law 24,051) [...]. The National Constitution expressly established that all inhabitants are entitled to a healthy and balanced environment fit for human development in order that productive activities shall meet present needs without endangering those of future generations; and shall have the duty to preserve it (National Constitution, article 41), establishing special procedural protection for the new right set out herein through Amparo proceedings. According to article 43 of the National Constitution, when the action concerns the protection of rights relative to the environment, such proceedings may be brought by the damaged party.[39]

---

34 *Ibid.*, paragraphs IV & V (author's translation).
35 *Ibid.*, paragraph XVIII (author's translation).
36 *Ibid.*, paragraph XXI (author's translation).
37 *Ibid.*
38 *Schroder, Juan c. Estado Nacional -Secretaría de Recursos Naturales* [*Juan Schroder v. the National State* (*Secretary of Natural Resources*)], Camara Nacional Federal de Apelaciones en lo Contencioso Administrativo, Sala No. 3 (Buenos Aires), 8 Sep. 1994, *available online at* http://www.planetaius.com.ar/fallos/jurisprudencia-s/caso-Schroder-Juan-c-Estado-Nacional-Secretaria-de-Recursos-Naturales.htm (accessed 14 June 2019).
39 *Ibid.*, paragraphs III-IV (author's translation).

Almada v. Copetro S.A.,[40] established the *Principle of Prevention in favor of Future Generations*:

> Taking it to be proven that the defendant's facilities caused damage to the environment, and despite the absence of pathological signs in the plaintiffs who fundamentally argued for a definitive end to the aforesaid damage, the Chamber, making use of the preventive order to "prevent the feared harm becoming real, effective and irreparable harm" (page 2722) implemented the provision of article 42 [sic: 41] of the National Constitution that guarantees the right to a healthy and balanced environment fit not only for all inhabitants but also for future generations.[41]

The court further applied and interpreted the *Principle of Intergenerational Equity* as follows: "Inspired by the same formulation and in accordance with the national Magna Carta text, the text of our province also incorporated articles 28 and 20".[42] The court explained that the "first of these ensures that the inhabitants of the Province have [...] 'the right to enjoy a healthy environment [...] to their own benefit and that of the generations to come' ".[43] The second guarantees the right "to participate in defending the environment, and natural and cultural resources".[44] Moreover, this "offense not only compromises the health and well-being of those who currently suffer the consequences, but also of the future generations whose life prospects we must not in any way infringe".[45]

Y.P.F. Limited Liability Company, 80,866 Oikos Association Environmental Network v. the Government of the Province of Mendoza,[46] applied the *Principle of Sustainability*:

---

40 *Almada, Hugo Néstor c/ Copetro S.A. y otro s/ Daños y perjuicios* [*Hugo Nestor Almada v Copetra S.A (Damages)*], Ac. 60.094, Suprema Corte de Justicia. La Plata, Buenos Aires, 19 May 1998, *available online at* https://juba.scba.gov.ar/VerTextoCompleto.aspx?idFallo=111708 (accessed 14 June 2019).

41 *Ibid.*, paragraph I.f) (majority opinion by Judge Dr. Hitters, concerning the second question raised) (author's translation).

42 *Ibid.*, paragraph 5 (concurring opinion by Judge Dr. Pettigiani) (author's translation).

43 *Ibid.* (quoting article 28, paragraph 1 of the Buenos Aires constitution) (author's translation).

44 *Ibid.* (quoting article 20, paragraph 3 of the Buenos Aires constitution) (author's translation).

45 *Ibid.*, paragraph 7 (author's translation).

46 *Y.P.F. Sociedad Anónima en j° 80.866 Asociación Oikos Red Ambiental c/ Gob. de la Prov. de Mza. p/ Acc. de Amp. S/Inc. Cas.*, No 78.245, Sala Primera de la Excma. Suprema Corte de Justicia, 11 Mar. 2005, *available online at* http://www.revistarap.com.ar/Derecho/constitucional_e_internacional/accion_de_amparo/ypf_sociedad_anonima_en_j_176_80866_asoc.html (accessed 14 June 2019).

> When examining the substantial aspects of the dispute, the emphasis is placed on the essential basis of our abundant and prestigious doctrine dedicated to developing environmental law, in the sense that protection of the environment has a vision that is fundamentally humanistic: it serves to satisfy the needs of the current population without disregarding the repercussions on future generations, on the basis of rational and sustainable use of natural resources, thus ruling out the interest of caring for the environment in itself.[47]

The court's mandamus order in the *Sofia A. Bordenave*[48] case extended the Precautionary Principle to the protection of future generations, including a praetorian development on interpretation and application of the *Transgenerational Precautionary Principle*.[49] The court called upon the local government of Bariloche to observe a city ordinance requiring authorized stores to make a list of transgenic products available to their users/consumers, as well as a visible sign indicating the availability of this list.[50] The court explained that "from the second half of the twentieth century onwards, with the appearance of 'technological mega-dangers' and the so-called 'global risk' produced by the likes of atomic energy and the introduction of genetic engineering [...], prevention is no longer sufficient because we are now facing uncertainty: doubts based on the harm that could be caused".[51] The court added that, "the precautionary principle is part of the wide spectrum of environmental protection and includes protecting the interests of future generations (art. 41, National Constitution) in order to prevent harm to the ecosystem, essential for the survival of the human race".[52]

---

47 *Ibid.* paragraph I.5.b ("On the first question, vote of Dr. Alejandro Pérez Hualde") (author's translation).

48 *Bordenave, Sofia s/ Mandamus*, No. 18726/03-STJ, Superior Tribunal de Justicia de la Provincia de Río Negro, 17 Mar. 2005, *available online at* https://www.informea.org/sites/default/files/court-decisions/COU-143734E.pdf (accessed 14 June 2019).

49 *Ibid.*, p. 44 (vote of Judge Víctor H. Sodero Nievas, concerning "Responsabilidades" [responsibilities]) (author's translation) ; *ibid.* (citing Bergel, Salvador, Cátedra de UNESCO Bioethics., "Transgenic varieties and the precautionary principle", Communication, *in* Seminar International "Biotechnology and Society", 16 & 17 Nov. 1999, at the Faculty of Law, National University of Buenos Aires; cf. Isidoro H Goldenberg and Néstor A. Cafferatta, "The principle of caution", JA. 2002-IV-1442, Lexis N * 0003/009138).

50 *Ibid.*, p. 57 (second resolution) (author's translation).

51 *Ibid.*, p. 44 (author's translation).

52 *Ibid.*, pp. 49–50 (concerning preventive action and the principle of precaution) (author's translation).

The Matanza-Riachuelo River Basin Case[53] recognized the duty of all citizens, especially judges, to protect the environment as "transgenerational commons".[54] The court explained that:

> Protecting the environment requires that each citizen carries his or her duty to care for the rivers, flora and fauna diversity, neighboring land and the atmosphere. This duty corresponds to the right that these same citizens have to enjoy a healthy environment, for themselves and for future generations, because when someone harms the commons, they are harming themselves. The improvement or degradation of the environment benefits or harms the whole population because it is a resource that belongs to the social sphere and the transindividual. This is why judges must work exceptionally hard to apply these constitutional mandates.[55]

Two dissenting judges in *Asociación de Superficiarios de la Patagonia*[56] sought to apply the principles of *Sustainability* and *Intergenerational Equity*, arguing that the Argentine constitution requires that laws must be interpreted in a manner that does not endanger the needs of future generations.[57]

> With the indicated understanding, the reforming constituents in art. 41 of the Fundamental Law not only established the right to enjoy a healthy environment but, for the purposes of enforcing the law, it set out a directive aimed at ensuring an environment, "fit for human development in order that productive activities shall meet present needs without endangering those of future generations". This definition entails recognition of the collective interests with precise distinction of those which are strictly

---

53 *Mendoza, Beatriz Silvia y otros c/ Estado Nacional y otros s/ daños y perjuicios (daños derivados de la contaminación ambiental del Río Matanza - Riachuelo)*, No. M.1569. XL, Corte Suprema de Justicia de la Nacion (Capital Federal, Ciudad Autónoma De Buenos Aires), *Sistema Argentino Información Juridica*, 20 June 2006, *available online at* http://www.saij.gob.ar/corte-suprema-justicia-nacion-federal-ciudad-autonoma-buenos-aires-mendoza-beatriz-silvia-otros-estado-nacional-otros-danos-perjuicios-danos-derivados-contaminacion-ambiental-rio-matanza-riachuelo-fa06000248-2006-06-20/123456789-842-0006-0ots-eupmocsollaf (click on link to.pdf "Ver archivo adjunto" [*see* attached file]) (accessed 14 June 2019).

54 *Ibid.*, p. 16, point 18.

55 *Ibid.* (author's translation).

56 *Asociación de Superficiarios de la Patagonia c/ Y.P.F. S.A. y otros*, No. A. 1274. XXXIX, Corte Suprema de Justicia de la Nación, 29 Aug. 2006, *in* Corte Suprema de Justicia de la Nación: Secretaría de Jurisprudencia [Supreme Court of Justice of the Nation: Secretariat of Jurisprudence], "Derecho Ambiental" [Environmental Law], Nov. 2012, pp. 62–77, *available online at* https://sj.csjn.gov.ar/sj/suplementos.do?method=ver&data=sda (accessed 15 June 2019).

57 *Ibid.*, pp. 73–74, points 19 & 20 (dissenting opinion of Judges Juan Carlos Maqueda and Eugenio Raúl Zaffaroni) (author's translation).

individual. Consequently, the infra-constitutional laws dictated, or to be dictated, must be interpreted in such a way that they build appropriate means by which to make the proposals and purposes of the Fundamental Law applicable. If the constitutional mandate was not as such it would be reduced to a mere dogmatic declamation without any possibility of being put into practice. [...] This aspect must be taken into consideration, as the same law provides that these kinds of questions must be examined in the light of the principle of interjurisdictional equity, when those responsible for protecting the environment must ensure appropriate use and enjoyment of the environment by present and future generations".[58]

Salvador Yane v. Municipality of General Alvarado[59] likewise applied the principles of *Sustainability* and *Intergenerational Equity*, emphasizing the "duty" of the public to protect the environmental heritage for future generations.[60] "Internal public law entails protecting not only nature and landscapes but also quality of life, the framework of its architectural and urbanistic manifestations, and, in short, the environmental heritage with its biological, physical and cultural resources so they are passed on intact to future generations".[61]

Sociedad Anónima Garovaglio y Zorraquin c/Provincia de Buenos Aires (O.S.B.A.) s/ demanda contencioso administrativa [*Garovaglio y Zorraquin SA v. the Province of Buenos Aires (O.S.B.A.)*],[62] once again applied the principles of *Transgenerational Equity* and *Sustainability* under article 41 of the Argentine Constitution and article 28 of the Constitution of the Province of Buenos Aires:

---

58 *Ibid.*

59 *Yane, Salvador contra Municipalidad de General Alvarado. Materia a categorizar*, Case No. C.90.020, Suprema Corte de Justicia de la Provincia de Buenos Aires, 14 Nov. 2007, *available online at* www.scba.gov.ar/falloscompl/SCBA/2007/11-14/c90020.doc (accessed 15 June 2019).

60 *Ibid.* p. 5, point III (Judge Héctor Negri, citing articles 41 and 43 of the Argentine constitution, along with international agreements on human rights that have higher standing than laws under article 75 of the constitution, in addition to numerous regulations on environmental defense at the national, provincial, and municipal levels) (author's translation).

61 *Ibid.*, pp. 6–7, point III, paragraphs 6–7 (author's translation); *see also ibid.*, p. 9–10 (quoting article 28, Constitution of the Province of Buenos Aires, as a guiding principle to justify protecting the rights of future generations under article 1 of Law 11,723); *ibid.*, p. 15 (reiterating that Law 11,723 was adopted in accordance with this same constitutional provision).

62 *Sociedad Anónima Garovaglio y Zorraquin c/Provincia de Buenos Aires (O.S.B.A.)*, No. B 57.805, Suprema Corte de Justicia de la Provincia de Buenos Aires, 26 Sep. 2007, *available online at* http://www.scba.gov.ar/falloscompl/SCBA/2007/09-26/B57805.doc (accessed 15 June 2019).

> These provisions determine that all inhabitants are entitled to the right to a healthy and balanced environment. The duty to conserve and protect it (art. 28, Provincial Constitution) lies primarily with the public authorities (doctr. Case 1. 1982, "Y.P.F", ruling of 31 October 2001), although also with the general public, so that our natural surroundings are appropriately safeguarded, so as to guarantee development that is socially, economically and technologically sustainable; in other words, in harmony with the environment for current and future generations (art. 41, National Constitution and art. 28, Provincial Constitution).[63]

Salas, Dino y otros c/ Salta, Provincia de y Estado Nacional s/ amparo [*Dino Salas & others v Salta Province and National State* (*Amparo*)],[64] applied the "Precaution Principle" in favor of future generations and outlined the procedural characteristics of the "Transgenerational Precautionary Principle":

> It has been clearly demonstrated that authorizations for tree felling and clearing have been granted where the environmental impact of each authorization has been considered on an individual basis, *but no studies on the accumulative effects of all the authorizations have been carried out.* […] *These accumulative effects result in a clear situation of danger of serious harm* because they could substantially change the region's whole climate regime, affecting both present inhabitants *and future generations, and this potential harm would be irreversible and there is a lack of information regarding such damage* [in the environmental impact studies]. […] The precautionary principle obliges extended and anticipatory precaution by civil servants. Therefore, the law is not observed if authorizations are granted without knowing their effects, aiming to act once this harm manifests itself. On the contrary, administrators presented with two options based on risk, must act with precaution and obtain previously sufficient information to be able to take a decision based on an adequate balance of risks and benefits. […] The application of this principle entails harmonizing environmental protection and development through a process of reasonable deliberation. This is why the two elements must not be in opposition but rather complementary: protecting the environment does not mean stalling progress; on the contrary, it means making it long-lasting so that future generations may also benefit from it".[65]

The court also ordered an Evaluation of Accumulative Effects that takes into account the consequences on future generations; thus, establishing the *Transgenerational Environmental Impact Evaluation*:

---

63 *Ibid.*, p. 22, point V.2., paragraph 2 (author's translation).

64 *Salas, Dino y otros c/ Salta, Provincia de y Estado Nacional s/ amparo,* No. S.1144.XLIV, Corte Suprema de Justicia de la Nación, 26 Mar. 2009, *available online at* https://sjconsulta.csjn.gov.ar/sjconsulta/documentos/verDocumentoById.html?idDocumento=6641951 (accessed 8 January 2020).

65 *Ibid.*, pp. 1–3, point 2, paragraphs 2 & 5–7 (author's translation, emphasis added).

> The application of the precautionary principle in this case obliges us to suspend the authorizations for, and realization of, tree felling and clearing in the four departments in question until a study of the accumulative impacts of these processes has been carried out. […] The aforementioned study must be carried out by the Province of Salta in collaboration with the Nation's Secretary for the Environment and Sustainable Development who must ensure respect for the relative minimum requirements. […] Furthermore, there must be high participation of the communities inhabiting the affected zones in the study. […] This study must focus on analyzing the accumulative environmental impact of the aforementioned tree felling and clearing on climate, landscape and environment in general as well as the living conditions of the inhabitants. It must also propose a solution that combines protection of environmental commons with development based on the costs and benefits involved. In this sense, probability margins for the tendencies noted must be identified and the *benefits relative to the stakeholder parties and future generations must be assessed.*[66]

Longarini v. Ministry of Production[67] applied the principles of *Sustainability* and *Transgenerational Equity* in addition to recognizing that citizens (especially public authorities) have transgenerational duties to conserve and protect nature:

> All inhabitants have the right to a healthy and balanced environment, the responsibility of which lies primarily with the public authorities (doctr. Case 1. 1982, "Y.P.F", ruling of 31 October 2001), although also with the general public (art. 28, Provincial Constitution), so that our natural surroundings are appropriately safeguarded, so as to guarantee development that is socially, economically and technologically sustainable; in other words, in harmony with the environment for the current and future generations (art. 41, National Constitution and art. 28, Provincial Constitution)".[68]

Infringing this right not only compromises the health and well-being of those who are currently suffering the consequences, but also that of the future generations whose life prospects we must not infringe in any way.

Conclusions

Forty years have now passed since the Stockholm Declaration on the Human Environment. Thirty-one years since the Brundtland Report. Twenty-six years since the Declaration of Rio. Twenty-four years since the Constitutional reform

66 *Ibid.*, pp. 3–4, point 3, paragraphs 1–3 (author's translation, emphasis added).
67 *Longarini, Cristian Ezequiel y otros contra Ministerio de la Producción y otros. Amparo. Recurso extraordinario de inaplicabilidad de ley*, Case No. A.70.082, Suprema Corte de Justicia de la Provincia de Buenos Aires, 29 Mar. 2017, *available online at* https://juba.scba.gov.ar/VerTextoCompleto.aspx?idFallo=141823 (accessed 15 June 2019).
68 *Ibid.*, paragraph 2, Votación [Vote] V.2.b (Judge Daniel Soria) (author's translation).

of Argentina. And, twenty-one years since the Declaration on the Responsibilities of the Present Generations Towards Future Generations. As a result, we can draw the following conclusions:

First, future generations require international and national legal protection. The formulation of this became obligatory when the commitments were made in the 1992 Rio Convention.

Second, the recognition of future generations as legal subjects in Argentine law constituted a major step forward. It recognized their right to a healthy environment fit for human development and also established that the authorities and all citizens are obliged to preserve the environment so as not to compromise their needs.

Third, their current legal protection is insufficient because the duties and procedures aimed at ensuring their protection have not yet been regulated. The absence of specific objective standards that regulate their protection hinders the effective safeguarding of future generations. As in other historical moments, when it was necessary to generate a second or third generation of rights with specific principles and rules, today calls for a fourth generation in which the rights of future generations are engraved. This requires a system of standards, with its own principles and rules, for the effective protection of the human rights of people who have not yet been born, but in the future will be.

Fourth, it is of paramount importance that we continue to develop this in International Law, which has a major influence on national legislation. It would therefore be appropriate to set up international and national bodies to work towards the achievement of the full recognition and application of the Declaration on the Responsibilities of the Present Generations Towards Future Generations.

Fifth, in the framework of National Law, forming laws and specialized bodies to safeguard the rights of future generations is indispensable. For example, the formulation of a Law of Minimum Requirements for the Protection of Future Generations (art. 41, National Constitution) would be most valuable as it would regulate the basic concepts of the protection of future generations such as:

(a) *A legal definition of transgenerational commons and their protection regime.*

This would entail limits to property rights relative to the conservation of property according to its social, environmental (essential) and transgenerational function.[69]

---

69 *Cf.* L. Duguit, *Función social de la propiedad – Las transformaciones generales del derecho privado desde el Código de Napoleón* [*The Social Function of Property – General*

(b) *Defining transgenerational harm and establishing a liability regime, given the legal vacuum in this area.*

For example, take the case of harm derived from technological errors: when new technologies are developed and cause serious harm to health and the environment (as a result of risk assessment flaws). In such cases, the copyright owners or obtainers – *or patent holders* – must be held liable as parents of the beast: those who have invented and profit from the technology. This situation is being addressed by a new scientific discipline referred to as Technopathogenology.[70] It studies the consequences of non-evident technical errors in the development of new technology that is integrated into the market and environment and causes serious harm. It is therefore necessary to establish a liability regime for those who patent technological innovations that end up causing harm to people. Today there are companies or individuals who, in their haste to make a profit, develop and integrate new substances and molecules with unknown consequences. Yet when these harmful consequences are discovered, there are no legal instruments to make their inventors liable. Imagine the difference it would make if whoever patented or introduced new technology into the world, knew in advance that they would be liable for its harmful consequences. Today, those who suffer such harmful consequences are innocent victims – in many cases future generations – who have no connection with the development of or profits gained from such technology.

Transformations of Civil Law Since the Napoleonic Code], 2nd edition. Madrid: Francisco Beltrán, Librería española y extranjera, 1920, p. 170.

70 Miguel Eguiazu and Alberto Motta developed the concept of technopathogenology, which addresses hidden errors in technology that have negative impacts on human health and the preservation of living conditions. The negative consequences must be registered as early as possible and in a timely manner, not just in future years or by future generations. One of the many examples of this is the Thalomide scandal. Hidden errors are theoretically possible in all scientific disciplines and their technical implementation because it can often be difficult to discover them using methods that are currently in ordinary usage. There is no scientific discipline that is commonly used to prevent it. Above all, Eguiazu and Motta ask scientists to take responsibility for their research. *See, e.g.*, G.M. Eguiazu, *Tecnogenia, Tecnología, riesgos y vías de prevención [Technopathogenology, Technology, Risks and Prevention Paths]*, Universidad Nacional de Rosario Editora, 1997; G.M. Eguiazu, *Plaguicidas y Error Tecnogénico [Pesticides and Technopathogenological Errors]*, Publicaciones Universidad Nacional de Rosario, 1998, p. 30.

(c) *A regulatory systemization of the principles of Transgenerational Law is fundamental.*

Although some of these principles have already been incorporated, such as the Principle of Sustainability and the Principle of Transgenerational Equity, others require further clarification of their legislative recognition – for example, the Principles of Transgenerational Prevention and Precaution. Contrary to conventional preventative or precautionary principles, we need to incorporate transgenerational temporal criteria into risk assessments. An analysis of the "accumulative effects of other activity taking place in the surrounding area" and their repercussions over time is equally necessary, so that the consequences on future generations are taken into account.

(d) *This requires establishing objective mechanisms and criteria for transgenerational protection and inclusion of the following in the environmental impact assessments analyses: (1) the effects that an activity could have over a period of 30 consecutive years (the number 30 is merely by way of illustration); and (2) the accumulative and synergic effects with other activity taking place in the ecosystem where it is being developed over a transgenerational period of time.*

The incorporation of these variables would transform a conventional environmental impact assessment into a Transgenerational environmental impact assessment. Currently, in the face of certain activity that could cause transgenerational harm, the Transgenerational Environmental Impact Assessment (abbreviated as "EIATranG" in Spanish) is an indispensable prevention tool.

(e) *Furthermore, it is important to establish public bodies specialized in protecting collective and transgenerational rights.*

These could include courts, district attorney offices, attorney general's offices, public defenders, etc. – i.e., lawyers who defend on behalf of future generations.

Let us finish by saying that transgenerational law is a very new law; it belongs to the so-called "fourth generation" and requires much further development in order to become effective. To this end, we invite you all to participate in its development so that we may become the best ancestors possible.

David M. FORMAN[1]

14. Marooned in the Doldrums While Ignoring Indigenous Ecological Knowledge: Attempting to Regulate Pesticide Use in Hawai'i

Professor Mireille Delmas-Marty opens this book with her essay #1 on "Adapting Juridical Order in the Age of the Anthropocene", which warns we are facing the risk of miring ourselves in the doldrums[2] unless we adopt a new legal spirit and a new world governance heading – one that recognizes the interdependency of man and nature as well as our obligations to future generations. To steer clear of the doldrums, Professor Delmas-Marty urges us to adopt an approach that balances a multiplicity of regulatory "winds". Despite the temporary silence imposed as a result of colonization and modernism, the environmental knowledge cultivated by indigenous peoples across millenia provides a valuable database for addressing the seemingly intractable challenge posed by Delmas-Marty.[3] For example, a Native Hawaiian legend about The Wind Gourd of La'amaomao

1 Consistent with the theme of this international symposium, the Mission Statement for the Environmental Law Program (ELP) concludes by stating its goal to address the "challenges of promoting sustainable development that maintains the integrity of our diverse ecosystems and unique species for present and future generations" (emphasis added). The author thanks Miranda Steed '19, ELP Research Associate and 2017 Jarman Fellow, for her assistance with substantive content and French language translation of the author's 17 November 2017 presentation in Caen, France.

2 Delmas-Marty defined the "doldrums" as "the place in the middle of the oceans where the meeting of north and south is so violent that their encounter produces, at best, calms (i.e., neutralizes one another and paralyzes vessels) and, at worst, causes storms and shipwrecks"; M. Delmas-Marty, "10x10 (Global): Homage to Norman Dorser", *International Journal of Constitutional Law*, 2010, Vol. 8, pp. 445–52.

3 *See, e.g.*, D.M. Forman, "Applying Indigenous Knowledge for the Protection of Environmental Commons: Case Studies from Hawai'i for the Benefit of Island Earth", *University of Hawai'i Law Review*, 2019, Vol. 41, p. 300 (discussing the reciprocal obligation to mālama honua, or care for the earth; describing evolving international recognition of indigenous environmental knowledge and the principle of intergenerational equity as a tool for protecting the environment; and, providing three contemporary examples at the state and local level); *cf.* D.K. Sproat, "An Indigenous People's Right to Environmental Self-Determination: Native Hawaiians and the Struggle Against Climate Change Devastation", *Stanford Environmental Law Journal*,

describes all the winds of Hawaiʻi – which Native Hawaiians have identified and named based on their particular qualities, including: relationships with birds, ocean swells, geographic areas, and other natural aspects.[4] Wikini Sage[5] fittingly described the paradigm-shifting impact of The Mālama Honua Worldwide Voyage,[6] stating that indigenous knowledge not only demonstrates how to avoid the doldrums as an actual geographical phenomenon, but also in the figurative sense described by Delmas-Marty. Sage added that the traditional Native Hawaiian sailing canoes triggered deep genealogical memories while sailing across the Earth's oceans to join and grow the global movement toward a more sustainable world.

In her essay #2 on "Intergenerational Equity as Change of Paradigm", Professor Edith Brown Weiss likewise acknowledges notions of intergenerational solidarity and future needs that are deeply rooted in diverse cultural and religious

---

2016, Vol. 35, p. 197 (proposing an "an analytic framework for the development of remedial measures to redress the consequences of colonization, including climate change [...] to guide, and possibly compel, local decision-makers to proactively combat climate change" by "infusing international human rights norms into local laws and embracing restorative justice to realize the indigenous right to environmental self-determination").

4 S. Iaukea, "'A lot is riding on sun, surf, and souvenirs' – Tourist longing and conservation: landscaping agendas of the state", *Proceedings of the Indigenous Knowledges Conference Reconciling Academic Priorities with Indigenous Realities*, Dr. J. Kidman, Dr. J. Te Rito & Dr. W. Penetito (eds.), Nov. 2007, pp. 88–90, *available online at* http://www.maramatanga.co.nz/sites/default/files/TKC%202005.pdf.

5 Sage serves as President of the Economic, Social, and Cultural Committee of French Polynesia; unfortunately, his symposium presentation on "The Transformation of Polynesian Society with Nuclear Tests" was not converted into an essay for this book. *But see* E. Gaillard, essay #20 (this book) on "Legal Bases for Protecting Future Generations?" (referencing Sage's presentation).

6 "Mālama honua [...] means to 'care for our Earth'". Polynesian Voyaging Society, "The Mālama Honua Worldwide Voyage continues into 2018", *available online at* http://www.hokulea.com/worldwide-voyage/ (scroll down and click on "Read more about the Mālama Honua Worldwide Voyage"); *ibid.* (explaining that the traditonal Native Hawaiian sailing canoes named Hōkūle'a [Star of Gladness (Arctura)], and Hikianalia [Spica] visited "more than 150 ports, 23 countries and territories, and eight of UNESCO's Marine World Heritage sites" to "connect with more than 100,000 people [...] across the South Pacific, Tasman Sea, Indian Ocean, Atlantic Ocean, and the Caribbean Sea, including Samoa, Aotearoa [New Zealand], Australia, Indonesia, Mauritius, South Africa, Brazil, U.S. Virgin Islands, Cuba, the East Coast of the United States, Canada, Panama, and the Galapagos Islands").

traditions, specifically recognizing rights held in relationship to our ancestors which must also be protected for our descendants.[7] Professor Brown Weiss cites opinions by two judges from the International Court of Justice,[8] which provide a normative framework for evaluating legal challenges that involve the interests of future generations. In short, these opinions contend that intergenerational equity and the precautionary principle[9] must inform collective decision-making processes that focus on conservation and management principles instead of continuing to tip the scales in favor of industrial interests.

Like Wikini Sage, Professor Nick Robinson explicitly connected intergenerational equity with indigenous cultural values in his essay #3 on "Evolutionary Roots Nurturing Equity Across Generations". Citing the ancestral mandate of the Peacemaker for the Onondonga Nation of New York, Professor Robinson described how decisions made on behalf of the seven generations to come ensured peace by sustaining life rather than simply setting aside assets for the future. Native Hawaiians developed cultural values like those of the Onondonga Nation and other indigenous peoples around the world.[10] For example, under

---

7 *See also* E. Brown Weiss, *In Fairness to Future Generations: International Law, Common Patrimony, and Intergenerational Equity*, Tokyo/New York, United Nations University/ Transnational Publishers, 1989.

8 Judgment, *Whaling in the Antarctic (Australia v. Japan; New Zealand intervening)*, International Court of Justice, *International Court of Justice Reports*, 31 Mar. 2014, p. 226; *ibid.*, pp. 348, 351–353 & 362–367 (paragraphs 7, 10–12 & 41–47) (Separate Opinion of Judge Antônio Augusto Cançado Trindade); *Legality of the Threat or Use of Nuclear Weapons*, Advisory Opinion, 8 July 1996 International Court of Justice Reports, p. 226; *ibid.*, pp. 429 & 455–456 (Dissenting Opinion of Judge Christopher G. Weeramantry).

9 The "precautionary principle or approach" is reflected, among other documents, in Principle 15 of the 1992 Rio Declaration on Environment and Development, which was "intended to provide guidance in the development and application of international environmental law where there is scientific uncertainty" by requiring "caution and vigilance in decision-making in the face of such [scientific] uncertainty." *Whaling in the Antarctic*, 2014, pp. 371–372, paragraph 62; *see also ibid.* pp. 374–375, paragraphs 62, 66–67 & 69–71.

10 *See, e.g.*, M. Burkett, "Indigenous Environmental Knowledge and Climate Change Adaptation", *in* R.S. Abate & E.A. Kronk (eds.), *Climate Change and Indigenous Peoples: The Search for Legal Remedies*, Edward Elgar Publishing Limited, 2013, pp. 105–112 & 115–118 (citing the Iroquois' "Seventh Generation" planning principle, and Hawai'i's public trust doctrine, and explaining how the principle of intergenerational equity plays a foundational role in deploying indigenous ecological knowledge to improve environmental laws and policies); D.K. Sproat, An Indigenous People's Right to Environmental Self-Determination: Native Hawaiians and the Struggle Against Climate Change Devastation, *Stanford Environmental Law Journal*, 2016, Vol. 35,

the Native Hawaiian ʻAha Moku [District Council] system, recognized "experts in fisheries management, hydrology and water distribution, astronomy and navigation, architecture, farming, healing arts, etc." managed natural and cultural resources "not just for the people of that time, but for all successive generations".[11]

This essay briefly outlines a missed opportunity to apply the intergenerational equity/precautionary framework in the context of grass-roots efforts to regulate genetically engineered (GE) crops or genetically modified organisms (GMO) in Hawaiʻi.[12] Part I introduces the historical context for GE/GMO seed production

---

pp. 157, 197 (proposing an "analytical framework for the development of remedial measures to redress the consequences of colonization, including climate change . . . to guide, and possibly compel, local decision-makers to proactively combat climate change" by "infusing international human rights norms into local laws and embracing restorative justice to realize the indigenous right to environmental self-determination."); S.K. Serrano, "A Reparative Justice Approach to Assessing Ancestral Classifications Aimed at Colonization's Harms", *William & Mary Bill of Rights Journal*, 2018, Vol. 27, pp. 501, 523 ("For Indigenous inhabitants of the territories, in particular, the preservation of their deep connections to land (and where applicable, the return of land), the reclaiming of knowledge systems, language, and life ways, and the regeneration of self-government, are also central to their self-determination"); M. Akutagawa, "The ʻAha Moku Rules of Practice and Procedure: Weaving ʻŌiwi Governance and Expertise in Mālama ʻĀina" (draft on file with author); Final Rules of Practice and Procedure for the ʻAha Moku Advisory Committee [AMAC], State of Hawaiʻi Department of Land and Natural Resources, sections 1–1 to 4–1 (Oct. 2016), *available online at* http://www.ahamoku.org/wp-content/uploads/2016/12/FINAL.AMAC_.Admin_.Rules_.effective.102016.pdf (incorporating millenia-old Native Hawaiian natural resource management knowledge and practices into the duly promulgated administrative rules of an advisory body that consists of the leaders from community-based management organizations on each island, who help the State of Hawaiʻi's Department of Land and Natural Resources in carrying out its mandate to sustain "the State's marine, land, cultural, agricultural, and natural resources" and foster "protection and conservation of the State's natural resources").

11 AMAC Rules of Practice and Procedure, section 2–2(a); *see also id.*, section 2–2(e)(3)(iv) (requiring the AMAC to "[a]dopt measures and implement solutions that [...] establish abundance and sustainability for future generations").

12 "*Genetically engineered* and *genetically modified* are often used interchangeably when referring to varieties of crops developed by means other than conventional breeding. *Genetic modification* refers to the process used to modify the genome of an organism. *Genetic engineering* is one type of genetic modification process by which humans introduce or change DNA, RNA, or proteins in an organism to express a new trait or change the express of an existing trait". The National Academy of Sciences, Engineering and Medicine (NAS), "A Science-Based Look at Genetically Engineered Crops: FAQS on GE Crops", *available online at* https://nas-sites.org/ge-crops/2014/06/04/faq-on-ge-crops/

in Hawai'i. Next, Part II describes some of the actual and perceived regulatory gaps in federal as well as state laws that governing the industry. To finish setting the stage for an international audience, Part III briefly explains American concepts of preemption and home rule. Part IV then summarizes federal court decisions that invalidated local efforts to fill some of these regulatory gaps, by essentially ignoring state constitutional provisions that implicitly codify indigenous cultural values which are reflective of this intergenerational equity/precautionary framework.

I. "Hawai'i Appears to Be Ground Zero in the Debate Over Regulating GMOs"[13]

GE/GMO crops have been in Hawai'i for more than fifty years.[14] Beginning in the 1960s, Dr. James Brewbaker[15] lured seed companies away from the continental United States to take advantage of "mild winters and the availability of

(emphasis in original). Genetically engineered or genetically modified animals are beyond the scope of this essay. *See, e.g.*, Animal Health Protection Act, United States Code, 2013, Vol. 7, section 8305.

13 D.L. Callies, "GMO Regulation", *Zoning and Planning Reports NL*, Vol. 1, Nov. 2015, p. 38; *see also* P. Koberstein, "GMO companies are dousing Hawaiian island with toxic pesticides", *Grist*, 16 June 2014, *available online at* https://grist.org/business-technology/gmo-companies-are-dousing-hawaiian-island-with-toxic-pesticides/; A. McAvoy, "Hawaii emerges as battleground of debate over genetically engineered crops", *The Washington Post*, 19 Apr. 2014, *available online at* https://www.washingtonpost.com/national/health-science/hawaii-emerges-as-battleground-of-debate-over-genetically-engineered-crops/2014/04/19/ebd29b7a-c7d8-11e3-8b9a-8e0977a24aeb_story.html?noredirect=on&utm_term=.87757910ad16.

14 P. Brewbaker, Ph.D., "Fifty Years of Seed in the Fiftieth State: An Economic Report of the Hawaii Crop Improvement Association", Aug. 2016, p. 5, footnote 11 (citing J.L. Brewbaker and D.E. Hamill, "Winter corn seed production on the island of Molokai, Hawaii," Hawaii Agricultural Experiment Station Technical Progress Report 160, 1967, p. 21 (noting that "[t]he Hawaii Crop Improvement Association (HCIA) is a non-profit association [...] comprised of five member seed companies").

15 A few years prior to the economic report published by his son, the elder Dr. James Brewbaker endowed a million-dollar fellowship to support plant breeding research within the College of Tropical Agriculture and Human Resources at the state's flagship university. Press Release, C. Ernst, University of Hawai'i at Mānoa, "Plant breeder Brewbaker makes $1 million gift to support future work", 30 Nov. 2013, *available online at* http://www.hawaii.edu/news/article.php?aId=6164.

prime agricultural land as plantations began their long decline" in the Hawaiian Islands.[16]

In addition to its isolation and multiple annual growing cycles,[17] Hawaiʻi offered a favorable regulatory climate.[18] The single law regulating GMOs in Hawaiʻi was not adopted until 1988 (and has not been amended since); this law merely requires applicants for federal field testing permits to submit contemporaneous copies of their applications to the state Department of Health.[19] In this context,

> [h]erbicide resistance is the most frequently tested trait in [Hawaiʻi]. Data suggests that GMO producers in [Hawaiʻi] use an estimated eighteen tons of pesticides on their GM plots each year, with "stacked" pesticide formulations containing upwards of sixty active toxic ingredients. Applications of restricted use pesticides (RUPs), which are considered the most toxic to human health and require application by specially trained workers, are also far greater than the national average.[20]

---

16 P. Brewbaker, 2016, p. 19 (noting that the seed industry's initial growth involved more than 200 Midwestern seed companies – which later merged into five major entities – on the islands of Moloka'i, Maui and Kaua'i); *see also* J.L. Brewbaker, "Corn Production in the Tropics: The Hawaii Experience", College of Tropical Agriculture and Human Resources (CTAHR), 2003, pp. 3, 9, 67 & 68; *ibid.*, p. 67 (noting that "the first 5-acre winter nursery [... was] founded on Molokai in 1966").

17 P. Voosen, "King Corn Takes Root in Hawaii", *The New York Times*, 22 Aug. 2011, *available online at* https://archive.nytimes.com/www.nytimes.com/gwire/2011/08/22/22greenwire-king-corn-takes-root-in-hawaii-28466.html.

18 D.-R. Gibson, Comment, "Remembering the 'Big Five': Hawaiʻi's Constitutional Obligation to Regulate the Genetic Engineering Industry", *Asian-Pacific Law & Policy Journal*, 2014, Vol. 15, pp. 213 & 224–226 (noting the state's "history of being exploited by private commercial interests" as well as heavy reliance by the "plantation industry [...] on the use of pesticides to facilitate its industrial agricultural practices" for nearly two centuries), *available online at* http://blog.hawaii.edu/aplpj/files/2014/05/APLPJ_15.2_Gibson_FINAL.pdf; *Ibid.*, p. 230, footnote 129 (commenting that "[t]he presence of the 'Big Five' seed companies in Hawaiʻi [BASF, Dow AgroSciences, Monsanto, Dupont Pioneer, and Syngenta, *ibid.*, p. 217, footnote 23,] is eerily reminiscent of the 'Big Five' sugar companies that dominated Hawaiʻi during the 1800s and early 1900s"; observing, further, that the industry "is beginning to exercise increasing political influence, control over natural resources, and economic dominance").

19 *Ibid.*, p. 217, footnote 19 (citing section 321–11.6, Hawaiʻi Revised Statutes Annotated, Michie's, 2007 & Supplement 2017, which has not been amended since its enactment).

20 R. Barnett-Rose, "Judicially Modified Democracy: Court and State Preemption of Local GMO Regulation in Hawaii and Beyond", *Duke Environmental Law & Policy Forum*, 2015, Vol. 26, p. 71, 98 (citations omitted).

Agricultural biotechnology also received a major statewide boost with the election of Hawai'i Governor Benjamin Cayetano (1994-2002), who made support for the industry a significant part of his platform.[21] Bills to require further industry disclosures were (unsuccessfully) introduced in subsequent 2005 and 2012 Hawai'i legislative sessions, as well as a 2007 bill seeking to ban the testing of biopharmaceuticals.[22] As a result, during 2013 alone, over six times more test sites had been approved in Hawai'i (1,124) than in California (184),[23] despite California having nearly twenty-eight times more prime agricultural land than Hawai'i.[24] Following closure of Hawai'i's last sugar plantation at the end of 2016, GE/GMO seed is now the state's dominant agricultural crop.[25]

---

21 "Biotechs call Cayetano their governor of the year", *Pacific Business News*, 22 Oct. 2002 (2:20am), *available online at* https://www.bizjournals.com/pacific/stories/2002/10/21/daily22.html (referencing the enactment of "sweeping economic development and pro-technology legislation over the past several years" and "the governor's support of investment incentives for the Hawaiian biotechnology industry"); *see also* B. Dunford, "Cayetano: Anti-biotech vandalism should be punished", *The Garden Island,* 24 May 2000, *available online at* http://www.thegardenisland.com/2000/05/24/news/cayetanoanti-biotech-vandalism-should-bepunished/ ("The governor recently attended an international conference on biotechnology and champions the industry as a possible new source of economic growth for the islands").

22 *See Center for Food Safety v. Johanns* (*Johanns I*), No. Civ.03–00621 JMS/BMK, United States District Court for the District of Hawai'i, *Federal Supplement, Second Series*, West Publishing, 1 Sep. 2006, Vol. 415, p. 1165 (holding that issuance of federal permits for field testing of biopharmaceuticals without an environmental assessment or environmental impact assessment violated the National Environmental Policy Act).

23 Press Release, "Center for Food Safety, Victory! Maui Wins Community Protections From Chemical Companies: Ballot Initiative Requires Pesticide Companies to Suspend GE Crop Operations Pending Safety Review", 5 Nov. 2014, *available online at* https://www.centerforfoodsafety.org/press-releases/3585/victory-maui-wins-community-protections-from-chemical-companies (linking to federal government data compiled by APHIS).

24 *See* Farmland Information Center, California Statistics, *available online at* http://www.farmlandinfo.org/statistics/california (citing the 2012 National Resource Inventory for a total of 6,006,100 acres); *ibid.*, Hawaii Statistics, *available online at* http://www.farmlandinfo.org/statistics/hawaii (citing the same inventory for a total of 216,100 acres).

25 L. Imada, "HC&S closure will pull plug on power deal", *The Maui News*, 29 Nov. 2016, *available online at* http://www.mauinews.com/news/local-news/2016/11/hcs-closure-will-pull-plug-on-power-deal/ (reporting that in early January 2016, Hawaiian Commercial & Sugar Company's "parent company, Alexander & Baldwin [one of the original 'Big Five'], announced the closure of Hawaii's last sugar plantation at the end of

II. The Regulatory Context for GE/GMO Seed Production

More than half the European Union (including France) has voluntarily opted-out of a European Commission directive that authorizes GMO usage.[26] By comparison, the United States chose to promote industry development by issuing a 1986 policy statement called the Coordinated Framework for Regulation of Biotechnology.[27] The Coordinated Framework identifies three federal agencies with pre-existing regulatory responsibilities that can be applied to the GE/GMO industry: the Food and Drug and Administration (FDA); the Environmental Protection Agency (EPA); and, the Department of Agriculture (USDA).

The FDA is charged with protecting the food supply from "any poisonous or deleterious substance which may render it injurious to health" and must approve additives before they are used in food, under the Federal Food, Drug and Cosmetic Act.[28] However, the FDA determined – *without* any risk assessments

---

this year"); *see also* Hawai'i Dept. of Agric., Statewide Agricultural Land Use Baseline, 2015, pp. 48–49 & fig. 13, *available online at* http://hdoa.hawaii.gov/salub/ (click on "State AG Land Use Baseline Report 2015").

26 "15 member states opt out of GMO culture", EURACTIV, 1 Oct. 2015, *available online at* https://www.euractiv.com/section/science-policymaking/news/15-member-states-opt-out-of-gmo-culture/; Directive (EU) 2015/412, 11 Mar. 2015 (amending Directive 2001/18/EC and Regulation (EC) 1829/2003, which previously established a comprehensive legal framework for authorization of GMOs within the European Union). *See also* M. Kuntz, "The GMO Case in France: Politics, lawlessness and postmodernism", GM Crops & Food, 30 Oct. 2014, Vol. 5, Issue no. 3, *available online at* https://www.tandfonline.com/doi/full/10.4161/21645698.2014.945882 ("GMO cultivation in France is totally blocked (including field trials and GM research) for political reasons, with no foreseeable way to reverse this situation".).

27 Federal Register, 26 June 1986, Vol. 51, p. 23,302, *cited in* D. Farquhar and L. Meyer, "State Authority to Regulate Biotechnology Under the Federal Coordinated Framework", *Drake Journal of Agricultural Law*, 2007, Vol. 12, p. 439; *ibid.*, p. 440 & footnote 2; *see also* Environmental Protection Agency, "Modernizing the Regulatory System for Biotechnology Products: Final Version of the 2017 Update to the Coordinated Framework for the Regulation of Biotechnology", *available online at* https://www.epa.gov/sites/production/files/2017-01/documents/2017_coordinated_framework_update.pdf.

28 United States Code, 2013, Vol. 21, sections 301–399 f. *See, e.g., ibid.*, section 342(a)(1) (defining food as "adulterated" if it contains such poisonous or deleterious substances); *ibid.*, section 343(a) (regarding false or misleading labels); *ibid.*, section 348(a)(1) (regarding the safety of food additives); *ibid.*, section 348(c)(1) (regarding labeling for food additives); *ibid.*, section 393(b)(2) (requiring the FDA to "protect the public health by ensuring that [...] foods are safe, wholesome, sanitary and properly labeled").

or data to back up the agency's safety assumptions[29] – that foods created from GE/GMO crops would be "generally recognized as safe" by experts, because they are "substantially equivalent" to conventional crops.[30] As a result, use restrictions may not be imposed unless the authorities prove that a GE/GMO crop is unsafe.[31] The FDA relied on an analogous "same or substantially similar" assumption to determine that labels are not required for GE/GMO foods.[32] Further tipping the scales in favor of the GE/GMO industry, the FDA merely applies a *voluntary* consultation process (rather than requiring food additive manufacturers to submit data and information about plant-derived bioengineered foods); accordingly, manufacturers have little incentive to explore possible risks or determine up front that their GE/GMO products are actually safe.[33] In any event, FDA guidance encouraging manufacturers to consult with the agency early in their process to address safety issues has not been applied to plants engineered either to

---

29 M.R. Lee-Muramoto, "Reforming the 'Uncoordinated' Framework for Regulation of Biotechnology", *Drake Journal of Agricultural Law*, 2012, Vol. 17, p. 311; *Ibid.*, pp. 320–21, *cited in* Gibson, 2014, p. 234, footnote 158.

30 K. Aoki, "Food Forethought: Intergenerational Equity and Global Food Supply—Past, Present, and Future", *Wisconsin Law Review*, 2011, Issue no. 2, p. 399; *ibid.*, pp. 464–65. *See also* R. Bratspies, "Some Thoughts on the American Approach to Regulating Genetically Modified Organisms", *Kansas Journal of Law & Public Policy*, 2007, Vol. 16, p. 393; *Ibid.*, pp. 408–09.

31 Bratspies, 2007, pp. 406–07.

32 Statement of Policy: Foods Derived from New Plant Varieties, Federal Register, 29 May 1992, Vol., 57, p. 22,984; *ibid.*, p. 22,985 ("In most cases, the [GE/GMO] substances expected to become components of food [...] will be the same as or substantially similar to substances commonly found in food, such as proteins, fats and oils, and carbohydrates".); *ibid.*, p. 22,991 (concluding that whether food contains GE/GMO ingredients is not "material information" that must otherwise be disclosed pursuant to United States Code, Vol. 21, section 321(n)). *But see* Guidance for Industry: Voluntary Labeling Indicating Whether Foods Have or Have Not Been Derived from Genetically Engineered Plants, Food & Drug Administration, Nov. 2015, https://perma.cc/NRL5-CL3V, *cited in* R.K. Craig, "Labeling Genetically-Engineered Foods: An Update from One of the Front Lines of Federalism", *Environmental Law*, 2017, Vol. 47, p. 609; *ibid.*, p. 623, footnote 123.

33 R. Bratspies, "Myths of Voluntary Compliance: Lessons from the StarLink Corn Fiasco", *William & Mary Environmental Law & Policy Review*, 2003, Vol. 27, p. 593; *ibid.*, p. 595 (discussing the consequences of this voluntary consultation process where "[o]ne company, with one GM crop, managed to contaminate food for millions of households and brought an international commodities market to a standstill" after DNA fragments from StarLink corn were discovered in Taco Bell taco shells sold in grocery stores).

produce pesticides, or to be resistant to herbicide application (which describe an overwhelming majority of GMOs on the market). Although the agency "is tasked with both enforcing EPA tolerances for pesticides in food and removing food contaminated with unapproved pesticides or the unintended, unauthorized presence of unapproved transgenic material, it neither engages in any systemic compliance-monitoring of GM foods nor monitoring of the same for contamination".[34]

The EPA is authorized to set allowable tolerances for pesticide residue in food products, ensure safe pesticide use through pesticide labeling, and regulate plants that produce their own pesticide as "plant-incorporated protectants" or PIPs.[35] Although EPA prohibited residential use of chlorpyrifos in 2000, it did not ban industrial use and put "no regulatory mechanisms in place to review the cumulative environmental impacts of glyphosate before glyphosate resistant crops enter the U.S. marketplace".[36] Relying on the *absence* of evidence that Bacillus thuringiensis (Bt) genes or their proteins are toxic to humans, EPA exercised its discretion much like the FDA and granted many "exemptions from the requirement for a tolerance level" to GE/GMO crops that contain Bt.[37] As a

---

34 *Ibid.*, pp. 409–10. On 9 August 2018, a three-judge Ninth Circuit panel vacated a March 2017 EPA order (finally denying a petition to revoke the tolerances originally filed in 2007) that would have maintained tolerances for use of chlorpyrifos on food products; the Ninth Circuit instead ordered the agency to revoke all tolerances and cancel all registrations for chlorpyrifos within 60 days. *League of United Latin American Citizens v. Wheeler*, United States Court of Appeals for the Ninth Circuit, *Federal Reporter, Third Series*, West Publishing, 2018, Vol. 899, p. 814. That decision is pending *en banc* review by the Ninth Circuit. *Ibid.*, 2019, Vol. 914, p. 1189; D. Jenkins, "Groups argue over chlorpyrifos ban", *Capital Press*, 18 Oct. 2018, *available online at* http://www.capitalpress.com/Nation_World/20181018/groups-argue-over-chlorpyrifos-ban.

35 Gibson, 2014, p. 234, footnote 159 (citing United States Code, Vol. 21, section 346a(b)(1), the FIFRA, and Code of Federal Regulations, 2011, Vol. 40, Secs. 174.1 & 174.3); *see also ibid.*, Vol. 40, section 152.3 (defining PIP as "a pesticidal substance that is intended to be produced in a living plant, or in the produce thereof, and the genetic material necessary for production of such a pesticidal substance" as well as "any inert ingredient").

36 R.K. Stewart, "Weeds, Seeds & Deeds Redux: Natural and Legal Evolution in the U.S. Seed Wars", *Stanford Technology Law Review*, 2014, Vol. 18, p. 79; *ibid.*, p. 148 & n.384 (citing R.M. Bratspies, "Is Anyone Regulating? The Curious State of GMO Governance in the United States", *Vermont Law Review*, 2013, Vol. 37, p. 923; *ibid.*, p. 946).

37 Bratspies, 2007, p. 411 & footnote 86. *See also* M. Mendelsohn & others, "Are Bt crops safe?", Environmental Protection Agency, *available online at* https://www.epa.gov/regulation-biotechnology-under-tsca-and-fifra/are-bt-crops-safe ("the use of Bt corn

result, "superweeds will likely continue to multiply [... causing] increased use of herbicides[.]"[38] In addition, EPA does not require labeling of PIPs,[39] instead requiring registrants of pesticides to enter into "grower agreements" that merely make farmers comply with use restrictions that the registrants are tasked with enforcing through *private contractual* remedies[40] – i.e., agreements that are not enforceable by the government, or by its citizens.

For its part, the USDA evaluates "whether there is risk that a novel organism will pose a plant pest risk when introduced into the environment or interstate commerce" under the Plant Protection Act.[41] Through USDA's Animal and Plant Health Inspection Service (APHIS), the federal government regulates "organisms and products altered or produced through genetic engineering that are plant pests or are believed to be plant pests".[42] APHIS's Biotechnology Regulatory Services division considers petitions for *deregulation* of GE/GMO products unlikely to present a greater plant pest risk than an unmodified organism based upon field tests – i.e., a determination that the product is safe for commercial sale.[43] Accordingly, APHIS is authorized to permit the introduction of GE/GMO crops through *either* (i) a permitting process that requires an environmental impact statement (EIS) or environmental assessment (EA) to determine the potential risks associated with release of the crop, or (ii) a simple notification process where the permit applicant performs its own risk evaluation.[44] Nearly

---

and Bt cotton result in less risk to human health and the environment than chemical alternatives").

38 Stewart, 2014, p. 148, footnote 385.

39 Gibson, 2014, p. 243 & footnote 238 (citing Lee-Muramoto, 2012, p. 317).

40 M.R. Taylor & others, *Tending the Fields: State & Federal Roles in the Oversight of Genetically Modified Crops*, Dec. 2004, Pew Initiative on Food and Biotechnology, Resources for the Future, p. 52, *cited in* Gibson, 2014, p. 243 & footnote 239.

41 Plant Protection Act (PPA), United States Code, 2013, Vol. 7, sections 7701–7772; *ibid.*, section 7711(a), *cited in* Bratspies, 2007, p. 411 & footnote 87.

42 Code of Federal Regulations, 2018, Vol. 7, Part 340; *ibid.*, sections 340.1(a)(2), footnote 1 & 340.1, *cited in* Bratspies, 2007, p. 412 & footnotes 88–89.

43 Petition for Determination of Nonregulated Status, Code of Federal Regulations, 2018, Vol. 7, section 340.6(a). Following a sixty-day comment period after publication in the Federal Register, *ibid.*, section 340.6(d)(2), USDA has one hundred and eighty days to deny or approve the petition. *Ibid.*, section 340.6(d)(3). Once deregulated, there is no post-market monitoring of GE/GMO crops. Gibson, 2014, p. 239 (citing Lee-Muramoto, 2012, p. 319; Code of Federal Regulations, Vol. 7, section 340.6).

44 Code of Federal Regulations, Vol. 7, sections 340.3, 340.4; *see also* G.N. Mandel, "Gaps, Inexperience, Inconsistencies, and Overlaps: Crisis in the Regulation of Genetically

99% of APHIS permits for field trials are conducted without an EIS/EA,[45] and do not require the industry to evaluate whether the GE/GMO crop to be introduced is hazardous to human health or the environment.[46]

Like the FDA, USDA/APHIS starts with the assumption that GE/GMO products are "substantially equivalent" to their conventional counterparts,[47] a position that has been roundly criticized as "scientifically indefensible".[48] Moreover, "APHIS does not consider whether planting a GM crop modified to be resistant to a herbicide is likely to spread the trait of resistance more generally, nor does the agency consider the possible contamination that might result from pollen drift from GM plants to unmodified plants" – according to a government audit, such releases are "likely".[49] Meanwhile, APHIS is conducting less research and providing less information to states and the public about the nature and location of field trials involving GE/GMO crops, in deference to industry claims

Modified Plants and Animals", *William & Mary Law Review*, 2004, Vol., 45, p. 2167; *ibid.*, pp. 2231–2232, *cited in* Gibson, 2014, p. 235–36 & footnote 171.

45 Lee-Muramoto, 2012, p. 318, *cited in* Gibson, 2014, p. 236 & footnote 174. *But see Center for Food Safety v. Vilsack*, United States District Court for the Northern District of California, *Federal Supplement, Second Series*, West Publishing, 13 Aug. 2010, Vol. 734, p. 948, p. 955.

46 Code of Federal Regulations, 2018, Vol. 7, section 340.3(b), *cited in* Gibson, 2014, p. 236 & footnotes 177–179.

47 Bratspies, 2007, p. 412. Notwithstanding the regulatory assumption of "substantial equivalence," the legal standard for determining whether a patent may issue to protect the intellectual property represented by GE/GMO products is "new and useful". United States Code, 2013, Vol. 35, section 101; *see also Diamond v. Chakrabaty*, United States Supreme Court, *United States Reports*, United States Government Publishing Office, 16 June 1980, Vol. 447, p. 303 (analyzing the Patent Act of 1952, as derived from the original Patent Act of 1793, and authorizing the first patent for a genetically engineered, living organism that was "markedly different characteristics from any found in nature and […] the potential for significant utility").

48 U.S. Gen. Accounting Office (GAO), "Biotechnology: Managing the Risks of Field Testing Genetically Engineered Organisms", GAO/RCED-88-27, June 1988, p. 48, *cited in* Bratspies, 2007, p. 412 (quoting a report from the GAO's Resources, Community, and Economic Development Division).

49 Bratspies, 2007, p. 412. *See also* Gibson, 2014, p. 238 & footnote 192 (citing U.S. Government Accountability Office, *Report to the Committee on Agriculture, Nutrition, and Forestry, U.S. Senate, Genetically Engineered Crops, Agencies are Proposing Changes to Improve Oversight, but Could Take Additional Steps to Enhance Coordination and Monitoring*, 2008, p. 19, for the proposition that "the ease with which genetic material from crops can be spread makes future releases likely").

about the right to protect confidential business information from disclosure.[50] In addition, "the USDA does not inspect all field trial sites where GE crops are tested; instead it uses a risk-based approach to select sites for inspection" despite not even having "adequate resources to develop the methods necessary to determine whether regulated GE material has escaped the control of the GE developer" – this means that "escape is likely" and has, indeed, occurred in the past.[51]

Actual or perceived gaps are also present at the state level within the regulatory scheme for GE/GMO seed crops. Although the Hawai'i Department of Agriculture (HDOA) inspects imported GE/GMO seed crops for the presence of pests and viruses, it does not conduct any further investigation into the traits contained within the imported GE/GMO seeds.[52] Although the state has authority to review GE/GMO field test permit applications and suggest whether APHIS should grant the permit or impose additional conditions to protect local

---

50 Gibson, 2014, p. 237 (citing Mandel, 2004, p. 21; Lee-Muramoto, 2012, p. 318). *Center for Food Safety v. Johanns (Johanns II)*, No. 06-17319. United States Court of Appeals for the Ninth Circuit, *Federal Appendix*, West Publishing, 2 Feb. 2009, Vol. 310, p. 964, p. 965 (concluding that the lower court did not abuse its discretion by sealing certain industry documents "due to the risk of vandalism to the fields and the possibility that trade secrets would be stolen" even after the plaintiffs prevailed in their lawsuit challenging the issuance of permits for field trials of genetically modified plans in Hawai'i for failure to comply with the Endangered Species Act, Plant Protection Act, and the National Environmental Policy Act); *see generally*, *Johanns I*, pp. 1165–1196.

51 Gibson, 2014, pp. 237–239 & footnote 187 (citing a 2008 report by the U.S. Government Accountability Office). Other gaps in the regulatory regime may be demonstrated by the Trump Administration's decision to rescind "an Obama-era ban on the use of pesticides linked to declining bee populations and the cultivation of genetically modified crops in dozens of national wildlife refuges where farming is permitted". L. Zuckerman, "Trump administration lifts GMO crop ban for U.S. wildlife refuges", *Reuters*, 3 Aug. 2018, *available online at* https://www.reuters.com/article/usa-wildlife-pesticides/trump-administration-lifts-gmo-crop-ban-for-u-s-wildlife-refuges-idUSL1N1UU1X7 (citing a U.S. Fish and Wildlife Service memorandum that rolled back a policy that prohibited "biotech crops – such as soybeans and corn – engineered to resist insect pests and weed-controlling herbicides" along with "neonicotinoid pesticides, or neonics, [...] a class of insecticides tied by research to declining populations of wild bees and other pollinating insects around the world", in place of a case-base-case approach "to ensure adequate forage for migratory birds, including ducks and geese – favored and hunted by sportsmen" on 50-plus national wildlife refuges across the country).

52 Gibson, 2014, p. 240 & footnote 206 (citing an interview with then HDOA Chair Russell Kokubun, and an e-mail from Monsanto Hawaii's Community Affairs Manager, Alan Takemoto).

interests, the state's review is hampered when it does not have access to confidential business information.[53] Handcuffing state review in this manner, while APHIS insists upon "sound scientific data or a through risk assessment" in order to support a state's reliance on a "special need" for industry limitations, is doubly ironic in light of the USDA's decision not to require the GE/GMO industry to prove "substantial equivalence" with non-GE/GMO crops.[54] Thus, HDOA is essentially a "rubber stamp" for USDA/APHIS determinations about the safety of imported GE/GMO crops.[55]

Meanwhile, HDOA "suffered budget cuts that have stretched its pesticide oversight to the limit [… and there] are only six pesticide inspectors in the state, including one on [Kaua'i]" who "finished just seven of 72 investigations into possible violations on [Kaua'i] alone for 2011 and 2012"; moreover, "the state Department of Health has no program in place to regularly test for pesticide contamination in the soil, air, or water".[56] "In addition to minimal state regulation over GE crops as a whole, there [is] also a lack of state regulations regarding use or testing of PIPs, even though states have the authority to regulate the use of pesticides".[57] For example, Bt crop seeds "fall[] through the cracks because [they do] not fit neatly within either the federal or state regulatory scheme".[58] During

53 *Ibid.*, pp. 241–42 & footnotes 213–216, 222–227 (citing Taylor, 2004, pp. 46, 80, 113).

54 *See also* Code of Federal Regulations, 2018, Vol. 7, section 301.1(a)(2) (authorizing state restrictions when the USDA Secretary determines that there is a "special need […] based on sound scientific data or a thorough risk assessment"); *ibid.*, section 301.1(b).

55 Gibson, 2014, p. 232, footnote 227 (citing an interview with attorney Paul Atchitoff of the Earthjustice Mid-Pacific office in Honolulu, Hawai'i).

56 S. Cocke, "Frustrated By State's Inactivity, Kauai County Takes Pesticide Fight Into Its Own Hands", *Huffington Post*, 8 Oct. 2013, *available online at* http://www.huffingtonpost.com/2013/10/08/kauai-county-gmo-fight_n_4064787.html (reporting that the lone Kaua'i investigator was instead "responding to [time-sensitive] public records requests about pesticides [… which] kept her so bogged down she hasn't had time to concentrate on the job she was hired to do" – viz., pesticide inspection reviews that, by comparison, do not have any legally enforceable deadlines).

57 Gibson, 2014, pp. 244–245 & footnotes 247–249 (noting that the Hawai'i Pesticide Law is silent as to whether PIPs fall within HDOA's regulatory scope, that HDOA's "administrative rules [Hawai'i Administrative Rules, Title 4, Chapter 66, sections 1 to 67] are also silent as to PIPs" and that federal law only preempts state law on issues relating to the pesticide's label – which PIPs do not have). *See also* Craig, pp. 640–646 (regarding federal preemption as it applies to labeling requirements, in addition to state remedies for violations of federal law and gaps that suggest room for state regulation).

58 Gibson, 2014, pp. 245–246 & footnotes 250–252 (citing Hawai'i Administrative Rules, sections 11-55-01, -04(a), -34.02).

deliberations on a proposed county ordinance, the Branch Chief for the Hawai'i State Pesticide Branch offered damning testimony:

> We looked into stream sediments specifically for glyphosate, for Roundup, and *we found Roundup in all of the samples that we took*. All in all, we found 20 herbicides, 11 insecticides, 6 fungicides, 7 locations with glyphosate but [...] *there are no EPA benchmarks for* [...] *glyphosate*. So we found stuff but, frankly, we don't know what it means and [...] *we don't know how to compare that to any kind of health standards.*[59]

Finally, although the Hawai'i Department of Health requires a National Pollutant Discharge Elimination System permit for the discharge of biological pesticides including plant-incorporate pesticides (PIPs) into state waters, HDOA's rules and regulations do not even mention PIPs.[60]

III. The Principles of Preemption [Principe de Primauté] and Home Rule, as Distinguished from Preferential Municipal Acquisition [Droit de Préemption Urbain]

In the United States, the term "preemption" refers to laws passed by higher authorities that take precedence over laws passed by lower authorities. Federal preemption derives from the supremacy clause of the U.S. Constitution, which states that the "Constitution, and the Laws of the United States [...] made in Pursuance thereof [...] shall be the supreme Law of the Land; [...] any Thing in the Constitution or Laws of any state to the Contrary notwithstanding".[61] In short, the supremacy clause means that federal laws will often trump state or local laws on the same topic.

When Congress acts pursuant to one of its enumerated powers (e.g., regulating interstate commerce),[62] it may either expressly or impliedly preempt

59 Brief of Appellants, pp. *9–10, *Atay v. Robert Ito Farm, Inc.*, No. 15-15641, United States Court of Appeals for the Ninth Circuit, filed 30 Apr. 2015, *available online at* http://nomorefakenews.com/dir666/shaka-opening-brief-2015-4-30.pdf, *cited in* J. Rappoport, "Shocker: court documents assert Hawaii inspectors clueless about what Monsanto is spraying", *Activist Post*, 21 May 2015, *available online at* https://www.activistpost.com/2015/05/shocker-court-document-asserts-hawaii.html (quoting testimony by the Branch Chief, Pesticides Branch, Plant Industry Division, Hawai'i Department of Agriculture).

60 Gibson, 2014, p. 245, footnote 250.

61 U.S. Constitution, article VI, clause 2. *See, e.g.*, S.A. Gardbaum, "The Nature of Preemption", *Cornell Law Review*, 1994, Vol. 79, p. 767; *ibid.*, p. 769.

62 U.S. Constitution, article I, section 8, clause 3.

contrary state or local law on the subject. For example, "no political subdivision may regulate the movement in interstate commerce [...] to prevent the introduction or dissemination of a [...] plant pest, or noxious weed" that is subject to regulation by the Animal and Plant Health Inspection Service (APHIS), under the U.S. Department of Agriculture (USDA).[63] In addition,

> [n]o State or a political subdivision of a State may directly or indirectly establish under any authority or continue in effect as to any food or seed in interstate commerce any requirement relating to the labeling of whether a food (including food served in a restaurant or similar establishment) or seed is genetically engineered (which shall include such other similar terms as determined by the Secretary of Agriculture) or was developed or produced using genetic engineering, including any requirement for claims that a food or seed is or contains an ingredient that was developed or produced using genetic engineering.[64]

Also, states "shall not impose or continue in effect any requirements for labeling or packaging in addition to or different from those required under the Federal Insecticide, Fungicide and Rodenticide Act".[65]

---

63 *Compare* United States Code, Vol. 7, section 7756(b)(1), *with ibid.*, section 7756(b)(2) (providing exceptions for regulations that are consistent with and do not exceed federal regulations, or where a state demonstrates "special need" and the USDA Secretary agrees that additional prohibitions or restrictions are appropriate). Applicable USDA regulations require permits for the introduction of organisms and products altered or produced through genetic engineering, which are plant pests or when there is reason to believe the organisms or products are plant pests. *See generally*, Code of Federal Regulations, West Publishing (Westlaw current through 3 May 2018), Vol. 7, Part 340.

64 Public Law No. 114-216, United States Statutes at Large, U.S. Government Printing Office, Washington, D.C., 2016, Vol. 130, p. 834, *codified at* United States Code Annotated, West Publishing (Westlaw current through Public Law No. 115-140), Vol. 7, sections 1639–1639j (adopting both House Bill No. 1599, the National Bioengineered Food Disclosure Standard, and Senate Bill No. 764, the Safe and Accurate Food Labeling Act of 2015); *ibid.*, section 1639i (same). *See also ibid.*, section 1639b(3) ("no State or political subdivision of a State may directly or indirectly establish under any authority or continue in effect as to any food in interstate commerce any requirement relating to the labeling or disclosure of whether a food is bioengineered or was developed or produced using bioengineering for a food that is the subject of the national bioengineered food disclosure standard under this section that is not identical to the mandatory disclosure requirement under that standard").

65 Federal Insecticide, Fungicide and Rodenticide Act (FIFRA), United States Code, 2013, Vol. 7, sections 136–136y; *ibid.*, section 136v(b) (quoting the preemption language above, in a section entitled "Uniformity").

Powers that are neither delegated to the U.S. Congress nor prohibited to the states by the U.S. Constitution, are reserved to the states (or the people).[66] For example, Hawai'i and the other forty-nine states have traditionally exercised the so-called "police power" by regulating behavior and enforcing order within their territory for the betterment of the health, safety, morals, and general welfare of the state's inhabitants. Although most states have delegated some of their police power authority over land use control to local governments through a zoning enabling act, some (including Hawai'i, Oregon, and California) instead retain broad land use control authority.[67] Hawai'i is a so-called "Legislative Home Rule"[68] state because its constitution authorizes creation of political subdivisions (namely, county governments) with powers that are conferred under general law,[69] while at the same time expressly reserving the power to enact laws of state-wide concern.[70] The state's reserved powers include agricultural policies.[71] As a

66 U.S. Constitution, Amendment X.

67 D.R. Mandelker & others, *State and Local Government in a Federal System*, 2010, LexisNexis, 7th edition, p. 115; F. Bosselman & D. Callies, *The Quiet Revolution in Land Use Control*, Council on Environmental Quality, Washington, D.C., 1971, *cited in* Callies, 2015, footnotes 6–7 & accompanying text.

68 Callies, 2015.

69 Hawai'i Constitution, 1978, article VIII, section 1; *see also ibid.*, section 2 (giving the state's political subdivisions the power to frame and adopt charters for self-government within limits and procedures provided by law); Hawai'i Revised Statutes Annotated, Michie's, 2007 & Supplement 2017, Vol. 2, section 46–1.5(13) (delegating to counties "the power to enact ordinances deemed necessary to protect health, life, and property [...] on any subject or matter not inconsistent with, or tending to defeat, the intent of any state statute [...] disclos[ing] an express or implied intent that the statute shall be exclusive or uniform throughout the State").

70 *See, e.g.*, *Richardson v. City and County of Honolulu*, No. 16457, Hawai'i Supreme Court, *Pacific Reporter, Second Series*, West Publishing, 18 Feb. 1994, Vol. 868, p. 1193, p. 1209; *Marsland v. First Hawaiian Bank*, No. 12529, Hawai'i Supreme Court, *Pacific Reporter, Second Series*, West Publishing, 14 Nov. 1988, Vol. 764, p. 1228, p. 1232.

71 Hawai'i Constitution, 1978, article XI, section 3 ("The State shall conserve and protect agricultural lands, promote diversified agriculture, increase agricultural self-sufficiency and assure the availability of agriculturally suitable lands" and the "legislature shall provide standards and criteria to accomplish the foregoing"). The only express recognition of the counties' role with respect to agricultural policies is to promote the long-term viability of Important Agricultural Lands. *Id.* (providing that "important agricultural lands [...] shall not be reclassified by the State or rezoned by its political subdivisions without meeting the standards and criteria established by the legislature and approved by a two-thirds vote of the body responsible for the reclassification or rezoning action).

result, depending upon the circumstances, county ordinances in Hawai'i may be pre-empted by either federal or state law.

IV. Hawai'i Grassroots Efforts to Regulate the GE/GMO Seed Industry Invalidated by Federal Courts

Dramatic increases in GE/GMO seed company acreage/production[72] in Hawai'i contributed to community conflicts and led to state-wide protests by a broad cross-section of individuals including Native Hawaiians, environmentalists, doctors, and anti-GMO activists, along with many other residents and supporters.[73] These protests fueled efforts in three of four Hawai'i counties to adopt ordinances regulating the GE/GMO seed industry by expressly relying on state constitutional provisions that recognize public trust obligations for the benefit of current and future generations, along with the right to a clean

---

72 *See, e.g.*, P. Brewbaker, pp. 9–10, Figs. 3–5 (graphs illustrating Hawai'i seed industry: "out-shipments"; "cropped acreage"; and, "crop acreage shares"). *See also* Statewide Agricultural Land Use Baseline, pp. 23, 47–51, 55–57, 61, 67, 71, 77–78 & 98, *available online at* http://hdoa.hawaii.gov/salub/ (click on "View the Full Report Here: State AG Land Use Baseline Report 2015"); *ibid.* (scroll down and click on the first image marked "2015 Crop Summary by Acreage" listing a total of 23,729 acres – including: 13,299 acres on Kaua'i; 754 acres on Maui; 2,342 acres on Moloka'i; 7,333 acres on O'ahu; as well as 2,566 acres of primarily GE papaya on Hawai'i); *ibid.* (scroll down and click on the third through seventh images of 2015 crop summaries for Maui, Kaua'i, Moloka'i, Hawai'i, and O'ahu, respectively).

73 *See., e.g.*, C. Pala, "Pesticides in paradise: Hawaii's spike in birth defects puts focus on GM crops", *The Guardian*, 23 Aug. 2015, *available online at* https://www.theguardian.com/us-news/2015/aug/23/hawaii-birth-defects-pesticides-gmo (hereafter *Pesticides in Paradise*) (estimating 10,000 people marched through Waikīkī on the island of O'ahu); I. Altemus-Williams, "The struggle to reclaim paradise", *Waging Nonviolence*, 10 Apr. 2013, *available online at* https://wagingnonviolence.org/feature/the-struggle-to-reclaim-paradise/ (describing the first of the series of marches in Haleiwa on the north shore of O'ahu; a month-long series of actions against biotech chemical companies on Moloka'i in March/April 2013, culminating with "the last of a series of protests on the five Hawaiian islands that Monsanto and other biotech companies have turned into the world's ground zero for chemical testing and food engineering"; and, a 16 January 2013 march on the state capitol for a rally featuring India's Vandana Shiva); R. Daysog, "Anti-GMO rally attracts hundreds", *Hawaii News Now*, 2013, *available online at* http://www.hawaiinewsnow.com/story/24226906/anti-gmo-rally-attracts-hundreds (referencing earlier protests on the Big Island and Kaua'i); E. Summers, "A'ole GMO" [No GMO], *The Molokai Dispatch*, 31 Mar. 2013 (referencing "marches on Maui and Kauai [that] had more than 2,000 participants each").

and healthful environment. Temporary moratoria requiring the industry to conduct an Environmental Public Health Impact Statement analysis (EPHIS) were adopted by both Maui County[74] and Kaua'i County. Kaua'i County further required disclosure of GE/GMO crops and applications of restricted use pesticides, called for 500-foot pesticide-free buffer zones around public areas and bodies of water, in addition to prohibiting open-air testing of experimental pesticides and GM crops.[75] Hawai'i County imposed a permanent ban on new GE/GMO crops that prohibited open-air cultivation, propagation, development or testing (with exceptions for GE papaya where registered).[76]

Notwithstanding the regulatory gaps identified in Section II of this essay, concurrent November 18, 2016 decisions issued by the United States Court of Appeals for the Ninth Circuit (Ninth Circuit) invalidated all three county provisions based on federal and/or state preemption.[77] In *Atay v. County of*

---

74 Maui County Genetically Modified Organism Initiative (Nov. 2014), full text, *available online at* https://ballotpedia.org/Maui_County_Genetically_Modified_Organism_Moratorium_Initiative_(November_2014),_full_text, at section 1 (Summary Statement); *Id.*, section 3 (Rights and Authority, citing Hawai'i Revised Statues, section 46–1.5(13), as well as article XI, sections 1 and 9 of the Hawai'i Constitution, in addition to the precautionary principle as implicitly recognized in *Maine v. Taylor*, United States Supreme Court, *United States Reports*, United States Government Publishing Office, 23 June 1986, Vol. 477, p. 131).

75 C. D'Angelo, "Hooser introduces GMO bill", *The Garden Island*, 21 June 2013, *available online at* http://www.thegardenisland.com/2013/06/21/hawaii-news/hooser-introduces-gmo-bill/; M. Sergio, "GMO & Pesticide Experiments in Hawaii: The Poisoning of Paradise", *The Huffington Post*, 2 July 2013, *available online at* https://www.huffingtonpost.com/maggie-sergio/gmo-pesticide-experiments_b_3513496.html.

76 County of Hawai'i Ordinance 13–121 (effective Dec. 5, 2013); *see, e.g.*, Hawai'i County Code, sections 14–128, 14–130 & 14–133(a) and (b); "Hawaii's Big Island Bans Biotech Companies & GMO Crops", *The Huffington Post*, 19 Nov. 1993, *available online at* https://www.huffingtonpost.com/2013/11/19/big-island-bans-gmo_n_4305729.html (Bill 113 forbade biotech companies from operating on the Big Island and prohibited all new GMOs).

77 *Atay v. County of Maui*, Nos. 15-16466 & 15-16552, United States Court of Appeals for the Ninth Circuit, *Federal Reporter, Third Series*, West Publishing, 18 Nov. 2016, Vol. 842, p. 688, pp. 698–703 & 705–10; *Syngenta Seeds, Inc. v. County of Kauai* (*Syngenta Seeds I*), Nos. 14–16833 & 14–16848, United States Court of Appeals for the Ninth Circuit, *Federal Reporter, Third Series*, West Publishing, 18 Nov. 2016, Vol. 842, p. 669, pp. 676–81; *Hawai'i Papaya Industry Association v. County of Hawaii*, No. 14–17538, United States Court of Appeals for the Ninth Circuit, *Federal Appendix*, West Publishing, 18 Nov. 2016, Vol. 666, p. 631, pp. 633–34 (unpublished). *See also Syngenta Seeds, Inc. v. County of Kauai* (*Syngenta Seeds II*), Nos. 14-16833 & 14-16848, United States Court

Maui, the court held the Maui County ordinance expressly preempted where APHIS continues to exercise its regulatory authority under the federal Plant Protection Act.[78] Additionally, due to the central nature of the federal preemption question, the Ninth Circuit concluded that the lower court did not err in refusing to remand exclusively state law claims for declaratory relief back to the Hawai'i Supreme Court. The Ninth Circuit acknowledged the states' regulatory authority where APHIS has instead *deregulated* commercial plants, but nevertheless followed *Syngenta Seeds I* in holding that HRS chapter 149A (the Hawai'i Pesticides Law) "comprehensively regulates pesticides and creates a clear inference of legislative intent to preempt local regulations [sic] of pesticides[.]"[79] An unpublished opinion by the Ninth Circuit in *Syngenta Seeds II* likewise determined that the 'okina: Kaua'i ordinance's GMO crop notification provisions are impliedly preempted by state law.[80] And, a second unpublished decision by the Ninth Circuit similarly relied on *Atay v. County of Maui* and *Syngenta Seeds I* to overturn the GE/GMO ban in Hawai'i County.[81]

Interestingly, the Ninth Circuit stated that it was simply "not persuaded" that article XI, section 1 of the Hawai'i Constitution compelled the county to regulate pesticide use absent an express grant of such power by the state to the counties.[82] In a shockingly brief statement bereft of substantive analysis, the federal court

---

of Appeals for the Ninth Circuit, *Federal Appendix*, West Publishing, 18 Nov. 2016, Vol. 664, p. 669, pp. 671–73 (unpublished).

78 *Atay v. County of Maui*, 2016, pp. 701–703.

79 *Syngenta Seeds I*, 2016, p. 681; *see also ibid.*, pp. 676–81.

80 *Syngenta Seeds II*, 2016, pp. 672–73 (citing *Atay v. County of Maui*, 2016). About two months later, the Kaua'i County Council repealed Ordinance 960 from the county code. R. Bernardino, "Kauai Council removes invalid law regulation pesticides, GMOS", *Honolulu Star-Advertiser*, 25 Jan. 2017, *available online at* http://www.staradvertiser.com/2017/01/25/breaking-news/kauai-council-removes-invalid-law-regulating-pesticides-gmos/.

81 *Hawai'i Papaya Industry*, 2016, pp. 633–34.

82 *Ibid.*, pp. 675–76 (distinguishing *Robinson Township v. Pennsylvania*, Pennsylvania Supreme Court, *Atlantic Reporter, Third Series*, West Publishing, 19 Dec. 2013, Vol. 83, p. 901, p. 977, because Hawai'i's counties "lack inherent authority under the Hawaii Constitution [...] to conserve the public trust unless the State has delegated to them the authority to do so"); *id.* at 676 (observing that "the conservation clause may obligate counties to use their authority to conserve public-trust resources, but it does not permit counties to exercise power that the State has not granted them"); *see also Hawai'i Papaya Industry*, 2016, pp. 632, footnote 1 & 634, footnote 4 (citing *Syngenta Seeds I*, 2016).

instead called the Hawai'i constitutional provision "irrelevant" to the question presented.[83] Accordingly, the court declined to certify the fundamental and determinative question of state law preemption to the Hawai'i Supreme Court.[84] Ten years earlier, however, the state's highest court concluded that "as a political subdivision of the State of Hawai'i, the public trust duties imposed on the state [...] also apply to the County" based on the plain language of article XI, section 1, read in conjunction with article VIII, section 1.[85] Although a duly enacted state law required county governments to adopt relevant ordinances in cooperation

---

83 *Hawai'i Papaya Industry*, 2016, p. 676.

84 *Syngenta Seeds I*, 2016, p. 681 (concluding that "the district court did not abuse its discretion in denying Defendants' motion to certify" and "certification is unnecessary because the State's test for implied preemption is 'rather well-defined'"); *see also, e.g.*, Memorandum in Opposition to Plaintiffs' Motion for Partial Summary Judgment of Claims One, Three, Four, and Five of the First Amended Complaint Filed February 7, 2014, Filed April 14, 2014 and in Support of Defendant County of Kaua'i's Cross-Motion for Partial Summary Judgment of Claims One, Three, Four and Five of the First Amended Complaint Filed February 7, 2014, United States District Court for the District of Hawai'i, West Publishing (Westlaw), 2 June 2014, No. 14-00014 BMK (Kaua'i County MIO), p. 2758339 (Section IV.D., starting at page 51 of the trial memorandum). The county filed its memorandum approximately *three months* after the Hawai'i Supreme Court issued its opinion in *Kauai Springs, Inc. v. Planning Commission of Kaua'i*, No. SCWC-29440, Hawai'i Supreme Court, *Pacific Reporter, Third Series*, West Publishing, 28 Feb. 2014, Vol. 324, p. 951. *See, e.g.*, *ibid.*, p. 991–92 (Recktenwald, Chief Justice, concurring and dissenting) (observing that it "is *beyond dispute* that public trust doctrine imposes on the State *and its political subdivisions* a serious and significant duty to protect the natural water resources of the State") (emphases added).

85 *Kelly v. 1250 Oceanside Partners*, No. 26813, Hawai'i Supreme Court, *Pacific Reporter, Third Series*, West Publishing, 28 July 2006, Vol. 140, p. 985, pp. 1004–1005. In *Kelly*, the court held that both the county and the state had "an affirmative duty [...] under the public trust doctrine" to protect waters adjacent to a large-scale residential, recreational and agricultural project, although the plaintiffs failed to establish that either the county or the state breached their respective duties. *Ibid.*, p. 989. More specifically, the court rejected an argument that the act of vesting authority to manage state-owned public resources in a state agency through legislation, combined with the unexercised legislative power to transfer public lands to counties for public uses or purposes, left the county without any public trust obligations over those resources. *Ibid.*, p. 1003 & footnotes 21–22 (citing sections 171-3 & -11, Hawai'i Revised Statutes).

with appropriate state and federal agencies,[86] the Hawai'i Supreme Court nevertheless stressed that "the proponents of amendments to article XI intended to impose upon the State *and* its political subdivision an *affirmative duty* to preserve and protect the State's [natural] resources".[87] In other words, the public trust obligations that were elevated to constitutional status through article XI, section 1, are self-executing:

> For the benefit of present and *future generations*, the State and its political subdivisions shall conserve and protect Hawaii's natural beauty and all natural resources, including land, water, air, minerals and energy sources, and shall promote the development and utilization of these resources in a manner consistent with their conservation and in furtherance of the self-sufficiency of the State.
> *All public natural resources are held in trust by the State for the benefit of the people.*

The obligations inherent in this intergenerational equity/precautionary framework do not lie dormant awaiting enactment of state law provisions that grant the counties express legislative power to perform such fundamental duties.[88]

Conclusion

Provisions of the Hawai'i constitution reflect the intergenerational equity/precautionary framework introduced by Professors Delmas-Marty, Brown Weiss and Robinson in Part I of this book. However, the nation as a whole continues to languish in the doldrums as a result of the United States federal courts' flawed and dismissive treatment of these provisions.[89] Judicial decisions relying on federal and state preemption principles utterly failed to address numerous gaps in federal and state laws governing the GE/GMO seed industry. The veneer of regulatory protection provided by these laws and regulations is based on untested assumptions including "substantial equivalence" that do not provide adequate

86 *Ibid.*, pp. 1004–05 (citing sections 180C-2(a) and (b), Hawai'i Revised Statutes, which require the counties to adopt ordinances "for the purpose of controlling soil erosion and sediment" that meet specified standards at a minimum).

87 *Ibid.*, p. 1006 (emphasis in original).

88 *See, e.g.*, *Kauai Springs*, 2014, pp. 991–92; *Kelly*, 2006, pp. 989 & 1003–05.

89 The author delivered a presentation in October 2018 entitled "Critical Regulation: Re-Membering Indigenous Ecological Knowledge to Rebalance the Scales of Justice" at The Georgetown Law Center's Celebrating Commons Scholarship Conference; the presentation involved a more detailed analysis of these federal court decisions through the lens of critical legal theory.

assurance to skeptical members of the public who are concerned about whether health and safety concerns for present and future generations are being sacrificed in favor of industrial profit and other short-term economic interests.

A silver lining in the aftermath of this GE/GMO seed industry litigation was the successful effort to make Hawaiʻi the first state in the nation to enact a complete ban on chlorpyrifos.[90] Alongside the islands' commitment to the Paris Agreement, the establishment of 2045 target date for 100% renewable energy[91] and carbon neutrality,[92] Hawaiʻi's ongoing commitment to Mālama Honua [Care

90 Act 45 (2018) amends the Hawaiʻi Pesticides Law by creating a new Pesticide Reporting and Regulation Program that requires reports to the Hawaiʻi Department of Agriculture (HDOA) concerning restricted use pesticides (RUPs), and prohibits: use of RUPs within one hundred feet of a school during normal school hours (beginning January 1, 2019); use of pesticides containing chlorpyrifos as an active ingredient (beginning January 1, 2019; although DOA must grant a temporary permit upon request allowing use of such pesticides until December 31, 2022); and requires the HDOA to develop a pesticide drift monitoring study by July 1, 2019. *See also* C. Pala, "Hawaii bans use of harmful pesticide", *Ecologist*, 18 June 2018, https://theecologist.org/2018/jun/18/hawaii-bans-use-harmful-pesticide; C. Pala, "Hawaii Will Finally Force Companies to Say What Pesticides They're Spraying", *Live Science*, 15 June 2018, *available online at* https://www.livescience.com/62831-hawaii-bans-secret-spray-sites.html.

91 Act 33 (2017) expands strategies and mechanisms to reduce greenhouse gas emissions in the State of Hawaiʻi "through reduction of energy use, adoption of renewable energy, and control of air pollution among all agencies, departments, industries, and sectors, including transportation [...] and shall be closely aligned with the climate change principles and goals adopted in the Paris Agreement and Hawaii's share of obligations within the expectations apportioned to the United States in the Paris Agreement, regardless of federal action".

92 Act 15 (2018) further expands and makes permanent a new greenhouse gas sequestration task force whose charge includes identifying appropriate criteria to measure "improvements in soil health [...] and other key indicators of greenhouse gas benefits from beneficial agricultural [...] practices" in addition to encouraging "agricultural [...] practices and land use practices that would promote increased greenhouse gas sequestration, build healthy soils, and provide greenhouse gas benefits". Hawaiʻi State Legislature, 2018, Act 15, *available online at* https://www.capitol.hawaii.gov/session2018/bills/GM1115_.PDF (acknowledging that "Mayors from each county of the State have pledged to end the State's dependence on fossil fuels by eliminating fossil fuels from transportation by 2045" and that "as part of the United States Climate Alliance, [Hawaiʻi] joined leaders from every other country on earth and committed to upholding the objectives of the 2015 Paris Agreement").

for the Earth] is rooted in traditional cultural values that could help this archipelago in the middle of the Pacific Ocean demonstrate a new legal spirit and a new world governance heading that recognizes the interdependency of man and nature as well as our obligations to future generations.

Michel PRIEUR

15. Draft International Covenant on the Human Right to the Environment

Seventy years have passed since the Universal Declaration of Human Rights, and fifty-two since the United Nations adopted two International Covenants on Human Rights. The first of these Covenants enshrines Civil and Political Rights; the second, Economic, Social and Cultural Rights.[1] The time has thus come to codify at an international level the emergence of a third category of human rights: a Covenant for the environment.

To this end, a group of jurist co-authors[2] have developed a draft third covenant on international recognition of a human right to the environment. This work was initiated in response to an invitation by the President of the French Constitutional Council, Laurent Fabius, in the "Le Monde" newspaper (31 August 2016). His invitation related to the Paris Agreement approved at the United Nations Climate Change Conference in December 2015. At the time of the Paris Agreement, Fabius was the French Minister of Foreign Affairs and chaired the Paris Climate Change Conference in this capacity. Fabius called for the rapid ratification of the Agreement due to the climate emergency. People paid heed: to everyone's surprise, the number of ratifications necessary for the entry into force of the Paris agreement was reached in November 2016, on the eve of the Marrakech COP 22. But Fabius also launched another appeal. He called for, "a major step forward for humanity" through the preparation of a universal covenant for the environment: "a text within the current framework, in a mandatory treaty that reiterates the principles already recognized and agreed upon, and with particular recognition of each person's right to a healthy environment".

The International Center of Comparative Environmental Law [Centre International de Droit Comparé l'Environment (CIDCE)] welcomed this call to prepare a third covenant establishing a third pillar of human rights, and immediately set to work. The CIDCE is an international NGO. It was founded in 1982 in Limoges by Professor Michel Prieur. In 2015, it obtained official special

1 Adopted on 16 December 1966 and in force since 1976; the word "covenant" describes an international document that has the validity of a mandatory treaty.

2 M. Prieur, J. Bétaille, M-A. Cohendet, H. Delzangles, J. Makowiak & P. Steichen, *Droit de l'environnement* [*Environmental Law*], Dalloz, 8th edition, 2019.

consultative status with ECOSOC, the United Nations Economic and Social Council (*see* www.cidce.org).[3] In October 2016, the CIDCE's draft was the subject of an international consultation that brought together environmental and human rights jurists from every continent. In 2017, it was transmitted to the Human Rights Council in Geneva via a written statement.[4]

This text presents the grounds for a third Covenant, its precedents, sources of inspiration and legal foundations. It concludes with a brief analysis of the contents of the draft.

I. What Grounds Exist for an International Covenant on the Human Right to the Environment?

Since the conferences in Stockholm (1972) and in Rio (1992 and 2012), the human right to a healthy environment can be considered as a common concern for humanity and the subject of high international consensus.

There is an urgent need to put the environment at heart of the human rights issues. Today, a covenant on the right to the environment is all the more topical because women and men throughout the world are affected on a daily basis by: poverty; hunger; desertification; the degradation of the environment due to various forms of pollution; the risk of natural, industrial and nuclear disasters; and, climate change. The United Nations General Assembly highlighted these threats in several resolutions that address globalization and its impact on the full enjoyment of human rights (69/73), human rights and extreme poverty (69/183), and the strengthening of international cooperation in the area of human rights (70/153). The 2030 Agenda for Sustainable Development and its seventeen (17) sustainable development goals, adopted in 2015, are clearly based on human rights (resolution 69/315, paragraph 8).

According to John H. Knox, Special Rapporteur on human rights obligations relating to the enjoyment of a safe, clean, healthy and sustainable environment, "virtually all of the suggested methods of implementing human rights norms relating to the environment would also support achievement of the Sustainable Development Goals" (A/HRC/31/53, paragraph 11). Humanity is concerned about the risks human beings and nature are facing: the adverse effects of climate change; the acceleration of the loss of biodiversity; natural and

---

3 Professors Soukaina Bouraoui (Tunisia), Kaboğlu Ibrahim (Turkey), Paulo Affonso Leme Machado (Brazil), Mohamed Ali Mékouar (Morocco), and Mary Sancy (France) are vice presidents of the CIDCE.

4 Written statement A/HRC/34/NGO/60 of 15 February 2017.

technological disasters; as well as the degradation of soils, forests, oceans and coastal areas. These brutal or insidious upheavals all involve violations of fundamental rights in addition to constituting serious threats to both present and future generations.

It is now well recognized by competent international authorities and the regional human rights courts that harm to the environment is often accompanied by either direct or indirect violations of "classical" human rights. Disrespect of the environment may also be accompanied by a violation of the right to life, health, safe drinking water and sanitation, food, unpolluted air, respect for private and family life and the home, or freedom of opinion and expression. Indigenous and local communities are more often victims of these abuses because they have a very close and dependent relationship with nature. Exercising certain human rights can also involve destruction of the environment.

However, when harm to the environment does affect "classical" human rights, it is not always evident or acknowledged by all. The human rights covenants of 1966 are in fact a reflection of society in the second half of the twentieth century: they were formulated as early as 1948, in the Universal Declaration of Human Rights. At this time, environmental issues were not yet on the agenda. At mindset, scientific and legal levels, it is also currently necessary to formulate the human right to the environment using specific environmental vocabulary in a clear and direct manner. However, this is a very complex task: it involves addressing easily identifiable physical elements (air, water, soil), as well as apparently abstract and complex elements (biodiversity, landscape, ecological connectivity, climate, and genetically modified organisms); then, considering the interrelationship between these elements.

It could be said that the current wording of human rights treaties already allows for protection of the environment. But such interpretations are at times far-reaching or disputable; they also have limited scope and are without any judicial security. The time has therefore come to bring this right to the environment to the forefront by clearly articulating the close relationship between human rights and the environment, including nature. This effort to clarify the contents of the rights relating to the environment is proof of the progress made in the matter by international society. By codifying the right to the environment, we legally reaffirm what has already been reaffirmed politically by multiple declarations and resolutions, as well as legally, in international or regional conventions and in national constitutions.

II. The Sources of Inspiration of a Third Covenant

The idea of complementing the two Covenants of 1966 with a third Covenant is not new. For the past 40 years, a number of ideological or non-profit initiatives have worked for the recognition of a third wave of human rights relating to: the right to development, the right to peace, the right to self-determination and, more recently, the right to the environment and ownership in respect of mankind's common heritage. Until 2017, no State had officially undertaken a project of this kind.

Such initiatives include: the Universal Declaration of Human Rights; the Charter of Algiers (4 July 1976); the Declaration on the Rights of Humankind, adopted in Buenos Aires at the 10th Congress of the Argentine Association of International Law (11 November 1989); and, the Universal Declaration of the Collective Rights of Peoples adopted in Barcelona (27 May 1990) by the Conference of Stateless Nations of Europe.

Karl Vasak's proposal for a third category of human rights is of particular interest. He expounded it in an article in the UNESCO Courier entitled, "A 30-year struggle; the sustained efforts to give force of law to the Universal Declaration of Human Rights" (1977), and in his course at the Hague Academy of International Law (RCADI [Cours de l'Académie de Droit de la Haye], 1974-IV). According to Vasak, "because of the changing patterns of society in recent years, it has become imperative to formulate what the Director General of UNESCO has termed 'the third generation of human rights.'" But the first draft of a third covenant was the fruit of work realized at the Armand Hammer Conference. Hammer was a Doctor of Philosophy and conference organizer for the International Institute of Human Rights. A draft covenant on solidarity rights was drawn up during a symposium in Aix-en-Provence (21-23 August 1981), and published in French as part of a collection honoring Hector Gros Espiell [*Mélanges*].[5] According to article 13 of this draft: "Every person and all people collectively have a right to a healthy and ecologically balanced environment, conducive to their social, cultural, political and legal development as much as to their economic development". Article 19 is relative to the right to the respect of mankind's common heritage. In 1986, Tunisian Professor Abdelfattah Amor wrote a detailed article on "the human rights of the third generation" that included an ample section on the environment.[6]

---

5 H.G. Espiell, "Human Person and International Law", Bruylant, 1997, Vol. 2, p. 1673.

6 A. Amor, *Les droits de la troisième génération* [The Rights of the Third Generation], *Tunisian Journal of Law*, 1986, p. 13.

The environment as a direct subject of a new human right next emerged in several different initiatives. The most official of these is the proposal drafted by Madam Ksentini, Special Rapporteur for the United Nations Commission on Human Rights in Geneva. It is the first official document on the subject. The 1994 text is entitled "Draft Declaration of Human Rights and the Environment" and contains twenty-seven articles.[7] According to article 2: "All persons have the right to a secure, healthy and ecologically sound environment. This right and other human rights, including civil, cultural, economic, political and social rights, are universal, interdependent and indivisible". There was no follow up to this text.

The 2007 Paris Conference on Global Ecological Governance was chaired by the then French President, Jacques Chirac. The final declaration (or "Call of Paris"), made on 3 February, set out in paragraph four: "To promote ecological ethics, we call for the adoption of a universal declaration of environmental rights and obligations. This common charter will guarantee a new human right for present and future generations: the right to a healthy and preserved environment". The *Grenelle de l'environnement* [Grenelle Environment Round Table] instigated by the former French President, N. Sarkozy, was held September 2007. Professor M. Prieur, vice-president of the commission for "Ecological Governance and Democracy", proposed the formulation of a universal declaration of environmental rights and obligations that takes into account the achievements of international environmental law as jus cogens and the form of a conventional act, like the 1966 Covenants.

The most successful text is that of the International Union for Conservation of Nature (IUCN) and its World Commission on Environmental Law (WCEL). This is the initiative of Wolfgang Burhenne, Parvez Hassan and Nicholas Robinson, in particular. It is more of a program for a general convention on all environmental problems than a draft for a third international covenant. The first edition dates back to 1995; the fourth, 2010[8]; and the fifth, 2015. A version in French is currently being translated. It has been commented on in detail, article by article, and is primarily focused on obligations imposed on States by existing international declarations and conventions. In the fifth version, only article 15.1 evokes the right to the environment as follows: "Parties undertake to achieve progressively the full realization of the right of all persons to live in an ecologically sound environment adequate for their development, health, well-being and dignity". This

7 *Cf.* E/CN.4/Sub.2/1994/9, Annex I (1994).

8 Draft International Covenant on Environment and Development, Fourth Edition, Environmental Policy and Law Paper, no. 31, rev. 3.

right is immediately accompanied by an obligation in article 15.2: "Parties shall ensure that all physical and legal persons have a duty to protect and conserve the environment".

In 2016, a university initiative of Cardiff Law School and a South African university produced a declaration on human rights and climate change.[9] In Rio de Janeiro on 29 April 2016, the World Congress of Environmental Law was held by the IUCN's WCEL and chaired by Brazilian judge Antonio Benjamin. It adopted a statement stressing the close links between human rights and the environment. It asserted the right of all to enjoy nature as humankind's shared heritage and advocated non-regression of legal protection for the environment.

An initiative of the French President François Holland led to a draft Universal Declaration of the Rights and Duties of Humankind. This text was submitted to the French President by Corinne Lepage. In April 2016, President Holland submitted it to the Secretary General of the United Nations.[10] Four members of the CIDCE took an active part in its drafting. It had been preceded by a draft prepared by the experts of the CIDCE on 28 April 2015 (*available online at* www.cidce.org/publications/statements). It is intended that this text will receive political endorsement by the United Nations General Assembly, as did the Universal Declaration of Human Rights of 1948. Its content and drafting are an important source of inspiration for a future international Covenant and the current draft is largely inspired by it. However, the draft of the third Covenant is more conventional in that it focuses on establishing individual rights without addressing the complex judicial issue of legal representation of humankind. The latter issue has not yet been addressed in the Universal Declaration of Human Rights, which merely asserts the rights and obligations without presenting the procedural elements essential for ensuring that these rights are effective and justiciable.

In 2015, the *Club des juristes* [French legal think tank] coordinated by Yann Aguila, proposed formulating a Universal Environmental Charter as an extension of its reflections on the effectiveness of the right to the environment. In June 2017, it drafted a Global Pact for the Environment, formally establishing the commitments of the 1992 Rio Conference. President Macron presented this draft at the United Nations General Assembly in New York and at a launching summit on 19 September 2017. Given that it has the same goals as the CIDCE

9 Global Network for the Study of Human Rights and the Environment, Declaration on Human Rights and Climate Change, *available online at* http://gnhre.org/declaration-human-rights-climate-change.

10 C. Lepage & J.-L. Servan-Schreiber, *Déclaration Universelle des Droits de l'Humanité* [*Universal Declaration of the Rights and Duties of Humankind*], Chêne édition, 2016.

draft covenant, it may be possible, in the long term and for efficiency's sake, to merge the two drafts during future international negotiations. However, there is a difference in the formal content of the Global Pact proposed by France and the Third International Covenant proposed by the CIDCE in its capacity as an international NGO. The Third Covenant is a "human rights" convention in which all the conventional principles of environmental law become "rights to [...]", while the Global Pact is an "environmental law" convention that leaves the Rio principles as mere principles.

III. The Legal Foundations of the Third Covenant

The 1948 Universal Declaration of Human Rights had already recognized the right of all to a standard of living adequate for the health and well-being of themselves and their family (art. 25.1). Furthermore, the International Covenant on Economic, Social and Cultural Rights established the right of all to enjoy a better state of physical and mental health determined by the improvement of all aspects of the environment (arts. 12.1 and 12.2.b).[11]

This mandatory text only associates the environment to the right to health. Since then, international and national laws have supplemented and clarified the content of the rights relating to the environment – but have done so in a disorderly way. There has been international consensus since the declaration adopted by the United Nations Conference on the Environment in Stockholm in 1972 according to which man has a fundamental right "to adequate conditions of life, in an environment of a quality that permits a life of dignity and well-being, and he bears a solemn responsibility to protect and improve the environment for present and future generations" (Principle 1). This international recognition has been reiterated at the highest level at various United Nations conferences and summits on the environment and development: Rio (1992), Johannesburg (2002), Rio+20 (2012) and New York (2015) (adopting the 2030 Agenda for Sustainable Development).

Seven regional conventions on human rights have legally enshrined humankind's right to the environment: the African Charter on Human and Peoples Rights (1981); the American Convention on Human Rights in the Area of Economic, Social and Cultural Rights, or "Protocol of San Salvador" (1988); the Maputo Protocol on the Rights of Women in Africa (2003); the African

11 Note that the French version of the Covenant refers to "l'hygiène du milieu" [hygiene of surroundings] while the English and Spanish versions use the words *environmental hygiene* instead.

Convention on the Conservation of Nature and Natural Resources adopted in Maputo (2003); the Arab Charter on Human Rights (2004); the Interamerican Convention on protecting the human rights of older persons (2015); and the Escazú Convention for Latin America and the Caribbean (2018). A universal convention also recognized the right to the environment (art. 1 of the 1998 Aarhus Convention on access to Information, Public Participation in Decision-making and Access to Justice in Environmental Matters).

The Office of the High Commissioner for Human Rights, in accordance with resolution 16/11 of the Council of Human Rights presented a comprehensive report on the relationship between human rights and the environment in 2011.[12]

Since 1988 resolutions and reports of the Commission on Human Rights and the Human Rights Council have on several occasions addressed the human right to the environment.[13] In 2012, an independent expert was appointed to the Human Rights Council, marking a milestone in the reflection on the close relationship between the environment and human rights. Professor John H Knox, in 2015, also became the Special Rapporteur for mandatory issues on human rights and how to enjoy a safe, healthy, clean and sustainable environment.[14] One report in particular addresses the rights of children in relation to the environment.[15] In his last report of 24 January 2018, Professor Knox outlined the contents of a veritable future treaty, introducing 16 framework principles.

The regional jurisdictions on human rights have to varying degrees made the link between human rights and the environment, resulting in fairly well-developed case law, especially in Europe.[16]

---

12 Analytical study on the relationship between human rights and the environment, 16 Dec. 2011, A/HRC/19/34.

13 *Cf.* Commission on Human Rights: resolution 1988/26, Ksentini report 1994/14, 2005/60; the Human Rights Council: resolutions 16/11 of 2010, 19/10 of 2012, 25/21 of 2014; 28/11 of 2015 and 31/8 of 2016; on climate change and human rights: resolutions 7/23 of 2008, 10/4 of 2009, 18/12 of 2011, 26/27 of 2014, 29/15 of 2015, 32/33 of 2016, 34/20 of 2017, 37/L.19 in 2018.

14 *Cf.* the reports of John H. Knox A/HRC/22/43 of 2012; A/HRC/25/53 of 2013; A/HRC/25/53/Add.1 of the 2014 Mission in Costa Rica; A/HRC/28/61/Add.1 of the 2015 Mission in France; A/HRC/31/53 of 2015; A/HRC/31/52 of 2016; A/HRC/34/49 of 2017; A/HRC/37/59 of 2018.

15 A/HRC/37/58 of 24 January 2018.

16 *Cf.* the Chroniques of J.-P. Marguénaud and S. Nadaud in the French Environmental Legal Review. *See also* Council of Europe, *Manual on Human Rights and the Environment*, 2nd Edition, 2012, *available online at* https://www.echr.coe.int/LibraryDocs/DH_DEV_Manual_Environment_Eng.pdf (accessed 16 June 2019).

As progress has been made in international law, so have national laws made steps to enshrine the environment: more than 170 national constitutions have integrated the environment as a societal goal, making States responsible for the implementation of adapted public policies. More specifically, more than 100 national constitutions have also formally enshrined the right to the environment as a new fundamental right, with constitutional validity.[17]

All these international, regional and national sources enable us to propose the adoption of a new treaty on human rights to international public opinion and to the States; a treaty that enshrines the right to the environment by bringing together all the substantive and procedural rights arising therefrom and already recognized. This would transform the "principles of environmental law", set out in Rio (1992), into real individual and justiciable rights.

IV. Overview of the Content of the Third Covenant

The draft third Covenant (reproduced at the end of this essay), will be examined and completed by the Human Rights Council as well as the Economic and Social Council of the United Nations, considered for approval by the United Nations General Assembly, then submitted for adoption by the States. Raising awareness among Sates and NGOs is a prerequisite.

The intention is not to introduce new concepts into international law, but rather acknowledge achievements to date and prevent any regression of rights related to the environment. It aims to highlight that most of the rights related to the environment can be linked to the human right to the environment. These can give form to individual rights, according to the tradition of human rights, without actually neglecting the possibility of recognizing certain collective rights – just as classical human rights such as the right to strike or freedom of association are already recognized.

The third Covenant also demonstrates that environmental protection cannot be achieved merely through an indirect link with classical human rights. The full enjoyment of civil and political rights as well as economic, social and cultural rights has become impossible in the twenty-first century without recognition of the human right to the environment. It is therefore no longer possible to treat the environment as a marginal issue in society. Formal recognition would confirm all past commitments made by States on environmental matters; it would also

---

17 D.R. Boyd, *The Environmental Rights Revolution,* University of British Columbia Press, 2011; J.R. May & E. Daly, *Global Environmental Constitutionalism,* Cambridge University Press, 2015.

reify the current situation at a judicial level by introducing the environment as another genre of human rights. This is why the third Covenant draws from the first two Covenants of 1966. Although it is a more modern, and green version, it is based on control mechanisms of the earlier Covenants that have proved the test of time.

As stated in the Exposition of Motives and the Preamble, recognition of the human right to the environment at the international level will reinforce the obligations relating to peace, security, rule of law, democracy, political stability, and good governance. Furthermore, this recognition will contribute not only symbolically but more importantly legally: it will become a tool for strengthening the effectiveness of sustainable development, to the benefit of present and future generations. We can only win the fight against world poverty and hunger, desertification and the loss of biodiversity, and all types of pollution and climate change, if there is better environmental management and protection. In States governed by the rule of law, this requires that the right to the environment not only be juridically enshrined but also implemented in both international and national laws. This is why the draft third Covenant has an operational and procedural part that involves concrete implementation, contrary to all the previous drafts mentioned herein.

In the initial French version, the vocabulary used in the title of the new draft Covenant stands out from that of 1966. It no longer refers to "droits de l'homme" [human rights] but to "droits des êtres humains" [human being]. The text is preceded by a long Exposition of Motives that will eventually be deleted. It was kept for the dissemination and explanation stage of the draft. The Preamble establishes the rest of the text in practical and legal terms. It also has a more educational than legal function and could eventually be shortened or deleted.

The first part is the core of the Covenant. It is fundamentally sufficient in itself and affirms the right to the environment (art. 1). This right is immediately accompanied by obligations for both States and individuals. The point of this entire part is to establish from the outset individual rights and obligations (the term *every person* does in fact refer to both natural and legal persons; public and private) and State obligations. Although the Covenant may depend on the States for its ratification, it depends on individuals and people with effective and justiciable rights for its implementation. Human rights can be enforced by both States and individuals.

Most of the articles of this first part begin with, "the right to […]". This clearly denotes that they are justiciable and very different from mere principles. It also prevents the courts from arguing that the text can only be directly enforced between States. In order to reify the right to a healthy environment, the text presents a series of rights drawn from the general principles of environmental law as human rights: the right to a heightened level of protection and to non-retrogression; the right to precautionary measures; the right to prevention; the right to environmental assessment; the right to reparation of environmental damage; the right to education; freedom of opinion and expression; the right to information; the right to participation; the right to recourse; the right to water; the right to food; the rights of indigenous and local peoples; the rights of persons in disaster situations; as well as the rights of environmental refugees and internally displaced persons.

All these rights and obligations are exercised with equity, solidarity between generations, without discrimination and in the framework of development that guarantees the sustainable protection of the environment; in other words, environmentally sustainable development.

The second part concerns international cooperation, which is a mandatory element of the third Covenant. It requires respect for the principle of cooperation and urges the States to "progressively" ensure the full exercise of the rights set out in Part 1 by providing assistance, technology transfer, and cooperation – including on legal matters, when necessary. The obligation to notify the other States of disasters and to assist one another echoes back to Principle 18 of the 1992 Rio Declaration and is based on the International Law Commission's draft articles on the protection of persons in the event of disasters. With regard to the rules of interpretation of the Covenant (beyond the classical principles of the Vienna Convention on the Law of Treaties), the exercise of the rights recognized in the Covenant may not be interpreted as limiting the rights of nature or of any parts thereof when they are recognized by a State. It was not intended that the Covenant enshrine a law for nature, because this issue is not yet the subject of international consensus.[18] However, forward-looking States that have already given rights to nature and/or animals must not be penalized.

The third part is about the effective implementation of the Covenant through specific measures for monitoring how it is applied. This involves conventional measures of international law: the obligation to submit reports every four years and to present both interstate and individual communications. The means to demand that the Covenant is respected before a Compliance Committee, is an essential instrument that enables individuals and NGOs to take real legal action

---

18 *Cf.* the resolutions of the United Nations General Assembly on the reports relating to *Harmony with Nature:* 69/224 of 2014; 70/208 of 2015; 71/232 of 2016; and 72/223 of 2017.

of petition and complaint, obliging States to react and to make progress in effectively protecting the rights enshrined in the Covenant.

To avoid overloading the UN bureaucratic machine we choose the simplest procedure: the body responsible for monitoring and controlling compliance with the third Covenant is the existing enforcement body for the Covenant on Economic, Social and Cultural Rights. This Committee was established in 1985. Again, to avoid adding a new procedure, the Covenant shall use the existing one for the Optional Protocol for the International Covenant on Economic, Social and Cultural Rights, adopted 10 December 2008.

This third Covenant reinforces rights relating to the environment by closely linking them to human rights without increasing the burden on existing structures. In so doing, the CIDCE contributes to the implementation of resolution 53/144 of the United Nations General Assembly that invited civil society and experts to promote new ideas and principles in the subject area of human rights. Since the end of 2017, the international context has been particularly favorable thanks to several international instruments and bodies that gave renewed recognition to the right to the environment: the Advisory Opinion issued by the Inter-American Court of Human Rights in November 2017[19]; the judgment issued by the International Court of Justice on 2 February 2018, establishing the reparation of ecological harm as a general principle of international law; and, the Escazú Agreement on Access to Information, Public Participation and Justice in Environmental Matters in Latin America and the Caribbean (Costa Rica, 4 March 2018), which enshrined the principle of non-regression in a convention for the first time.

To conclude, future international negotiations appear to be on the table. Indeed, following the adoption of resolution 72/277 of the General Assembly of 10 May 2018 (A/72/L.51), "towards a global Covenant for the environment", a UN Secretary-General's Report addressing the shortcomings of International Environmental Law must be submitted by the end of 2018. A working group met at the beginning of 2019, but failed to agree on a new international instrument (*see* United Nations General Assembly, 30 August 2019, A/RES/73/333).

---

19 *Advisory Opinion* OC 23/17 (Requested by the Republic of Colombia), Inter-American Court of Human Rights, 15 Nov. 2017, *available online at* https://www.escr-net.org/sites/default/files/caselaw/iacthr_rt_to_a_healthy_env_judgment.pdf. The CIDCE filed an *amicus curiae* brief with the Court in 2017.

Will the new human right to the environment also permit recognition of nature's right to legally defend itself against human aggression? If so, the premonitions of Claude Lévi-Strauss will be confirmed. In 1983, Levi-Strauss wrote, "Environmental Law is a right of the environment over man and not a right of man over the environment".[20]

Draft of the International Covenant on the Human Right to the Environment[[21]]
Exposition of Motives

1. Human rights and fundamental rights being indivisible, the full realization of civil and political rights without the enjoyment of economic, social and cultural rights is impossible.[[22]]
2. The human right to the environment, which takes part of economic, social, and cultural rights, have come to complement and reinforce civil and political rights and economic, social, and cultural rights.
3. Sixty-nine years after the Universal Declaration of Human Rights and fifty-one years after the two international covenants for social, economic, and cultural rights, and for civil and political rights adopted and opened for signature, and for ratification and accession by the General Assembly of the United Nations in its Resolution 2200 A (XXXI) of 16 December 1966, the time has come to devote a third International Covenant to the human right to the environment.
4. A third International Covenant for the right to the environment is even more indispensable as globalization and poverty challenge human rights and require enhanced consideration of the environment. The General Assembly of the United Nations has specifically insisted on this evolution in its Resolution 69/173 of 18 December 2004 on Globalization and its impact on the full enjoyment of all human rights, 69/183 of 18 December 2014 on Human rights and extreme poverty and 70/153 of 17 December 2015 on the Enhancement of international cooperation in the field of human rights.

---

20 *Cf.* C. Lévi-Strauss, *Le regard éloigné* [*The View from Afar*], Plon, 1983, p. 371.

21 Centre International de Droit Comparé de l'Environnement (CIDCE), Draft of the International Convenant on the Human Right to the Environment, *available online at* https://cidce.org/wp-content/uploads/2016/08/Draft-of-the-International-Covenant-on-the-Human-Right-to-the-Environment_15.II_.2017_EN.pdf.

22 Tehran Proclamation of 1968 (UN doc A/CONF 32/41), paragraph 13; Vienna Declaration of 1993 (A/CONF.157.23), paragraph 5.

5. The economic, social, and cultural effects of environmental damage on human rights can sometimes have greater impact on vulnerable persons and communities. Autochthonous and local communities are most victimized by environmental damage because of their greater dependence on nature.[23]
6. Multiple threats to the environment, resulting from all forms of pollution, climate change, and loss of biodiversity, require an increased resilience of humanity. This resilience is based in particular on international human rights law and international humanitarian law which are now indivisible with the human right to the environment.
7. The human right to the environment has become in 45 years a quasi-customary obligation of international law, given its international and national recognition.
8. All of the international United Nations conferences on the environment and development have admitted by consensus the importance of the human right to a healthy and ecologically balanced environment permitting people to live with dignity and well-being; Stockholm Declaration of 1972, Rio Declaration of 1992, Johannesburg Declaration of 2002, the Rio Declaration of 2012.
9. Among the universal Goals of the 2030 Agenda for Sustainable Development adopted by the General Assembly of the United Nations in 2015 is the environmental dimension of sustainable development.[24] The Special Rappoteur for Human Rights and the Environment has emphasized the importance of new Sustainable Development Goals for human rights and the environment.[25]
10. The General Assembly of the United Nations has adopted resolutions in particular on the right to water in 2010 and 2015,[26] on the right to food in 2014,[27] on living in harmony with nature,[28] and on access to reliable and

23 Resolutions of the Human Rights Council A/HRC/Res/16/11 of 24 March 2011 and A/HRC/Res/28/11 of 26 March 2015; Report of John H. Knox, Special Rapporteur on Human Rights and the Environment, A/HRC/31/52 [section] 81 of February 1, 2016; Declaration of the United Nations on the Rights of Indigenous Peoples, 2007, RES 61/295, arts. 25, 28, 29; Special Rapporteur on the rights of indigenous peoples A/HRC/18/35, [section] 26.

24 Resolution 20/1 of 25 September 2015.

25 Report of John H. Knox, 28 December 2015, A/HRC/31/53, [section] 11.

26 Resolutions 64/292 of 28 July 2010 and 70/169 of 17 December 2015.

27 Resolution 69/177 of 18 December 2014.

28 Resolutions 64/196 of 21 December 2009, 65/164 of 2010, 66/204 of 2011, 67/214 of 2012, 68/216 of 2013, 69/224 of 19 December 2014 and 70/208 of 23 December 2015.

modern energy services.[29] It has also adopted in 1982 the World Charter for Nature.[30] Nature and the environment being indivisible, some jurisdictions recognize the rights of nature, giving it juridical personality. The right to the environment complements the rights of nature,[31] as was suggested in the Rio Declaration on the Environment and Development, Principle 1: human beings are "entitled to a healthy and productive life in harmony with nature."

11. Several international and regional conventions for the environment have created a judicially recognized a [sic] new human right to the environment,[32] as well as a convention with universal jurisdiction.[33]
12. Resolutions and reports of the Commission on Human Rights and later the Human Rights Council have on several occasions addressed the human right to the environment in its diverse aspects since 1988.[34]
13. The place of the human right to the environment at the heart of human rights was again reinforced with the nomination in 2012, by the Human Rights Council, of an independent expert, who became Special Rapporteur on the Issue of Human Rights Obligations Relating to the Enjoyment of a Safe, Clean, Healthy and Sustainable Environment.[35]

---

29 SDG 7-1 on sustainable development, Resolution of the General Assembly of the United Nation of 25 September 2015, A/70/1.

30 Resolution 37/7.

31 Articles 17 and 71 of the Constitution of Ecuador; in New Zealand, the River Whanganui (Ruruku Whakatupua, The Whanganui Iwi Deed of Settlement 2014), Te Urewera forest (section 11, Te Urewera Act 2014).

32 African Charter on Human and People's Rights of 1981; Additional Protocol to the American Convention on Human Rights in the Area of Economic, Social, and Cultural Rights (San Salvador Protocol) of 1988; Protocol to the African Charter on Human and Peoples' Rights on the Rights of Women in Africa (Maputo Protocol) of 2003; African Convention on the Conservation of Nature and Natural Resources (Maputo Convention) of 2003; Arab Charter on Human Rights of 2004.

33 Aarhus Convention of 1988 on Access to Information, Public Participation in Decision-Making and Access to Justice in Environmental Matters (Aarhus Convention).

34 Since 1988[,] the work of the Human Rights Commission (Resolution 1988/26) and the Ksentini Report of 1994/14 and 2005/60 (Ksentini Report); [s]ince 2010, Resolutions of the Human Rights Council on the environment 16/11 of 2010, 19/10 of 2012, 25/21 of 2014, 28/11 of 2015, 31/8 of 2016; [and,] on climate change 7/23 of 2008, 10/4 of 2009, 18/12 of 2011, 26/27 of 2014, 29/15 of 2015, 32/33 of 2016.

35 Reports of John H. Knox A/HRC/31/53 of 28 December 2015 and A/HRC/31/52 of 1 February 2016.

14. The International Court of Justice, in its advisory opinion of 8 July 1996 on the legality of the threat or use of nuclear weapons, found that "the environment is not an abstraction but represents the living space, the quality of life and the very health of human beings, including generations unborn."[36]
15. In parallel with these diverse forms of recognition of international human rights, more than 150 national constitutions have included the environment as a social obligation. Among them, more than 95 have recognized the human right to the environment as a new fundamental constitutional right.[37] In the absence of constitutional provisions, several constitutional courts or supreme courts have also recognized a right to the environment.
16. The recognition of the human right to a healthy environment at the international level will reinforce the obligations relating to peace, security, rule of law, political stability, and democracy and will reinforce the rights of humanity.[38] Moreover, the right to development in the context of the establishment of a new international economic order is indissoluble with protection for the environment.[39]
17. Several initiatives have been taken toward establishing a 3d international covenant on human rights. Among those that have had formal recognition,[40] the proposal of Mme. Ksentini, the Special Rapporteur for the United Nations on the human right to the environment deserves special attention. At the time of its publication in 1994, attention was only beginning to be paid to the

36 [*Legality of the Threat or Use of Nuclear Weapons*, International Court of Justice] Advisory opinion, I.C.J. Reports 1996, p.226[,] paragraph 29.

37 [D.]R. Boyd, The Environmental Rights Revolution, University of British Columbia Press, 2012; [J.]R. May and [E.] Daly, [*Global Environmental Constitutionalism*], Cambridge University Press, 2015.

38 Preamble of the Inter-American Democratic Charter, approved by the General Assembly of the Organization of American States on 11 September 2001; the African Charter on Democracy, Elections, and Governance of 2007 mandates the political and strategic protection for the environment within a framework of sustainable development for the benefit of present and future generations (Art. 42).

39 Resolutions of the United Nations General Assembly on the Right to Development 41/128 of 9 December 1986 and on the establishment of a new international economic order 3201 (S-VI) of 1 May 1974, 63/224 of 19 December 2008, 64/209 of 21 December 2009, 65/167 of 20 December 2010 et 67/217 of 21 December 2012.

40 *See* the earlier draft of the Third International Covenant on Solidarity Rights and the Hammer Projet, drafted in Aix-en-Provence in 1981 and published in Annex II of the Mélanges Hector Gros Espiell, "Personne humaine et droit international" [People and International Law], Bruylant 1997, vol. 2, p. 1673.

relationship between the environment and human rights. Twenty-three years later, the time has come to adopt a 3d International Covenant dedicated to the environment, recognized as a fundamental human right.[41]

18. Taking into account the invitation of the United Nations to promote new ideas and principles in the area of human rights to protect and make more effective environmental rights, and pursuant to United Nations General Assembly Resolution 53/144, the International Center for Comparative Environmental Law, as an organ of civil society, proposes the following International Covenant.[42]

Preamble

The State Parties to the present Covenant,

1. Considering that in accordance with the Charter of the United Nations, peoples are determined to promote social progress and better standards of life in larger freedom[43] and to promote universal respect for and observance of human rights and fundamental freedoms,[44]
2. Reaffirming that all human rights and fundamental freedoms, including the right to environment, are universal, indivisible and interdependent and that it is the responsibility of the States, individuals, and other public and private entities to protect and promote these rights,[45]
3. Convinced that peace, the rule of law, respect for human rights, sustainable development, the right to development, and environmental protection are indivisible,[46]

---

41 Ksentini Report, E/CN.4/Sub.2/1994/9, 26 July 1994, Annex 1.

42 Resolution 53/144 of 9 December 1998 ("Declaration on the Right and Responsibility of Individuals, Groups and Organs of Society to Promote and Protect Universally Recognized Human Rights and Fundamental Freedoms").

43 United Nations Charter, Preamble [section] 4.

44 United Nations Charter, Art. 55 and Universal Declaration of Human Rights, United Nations General Assembly, Universal Declaration of Human Rights (UDHR), 10 December 1948, 217 A (III), Preamble.

45 United Nations General Assembly Resolution 32/130 of 16 December 1977 and 41/117 of 4 December 1986.

46 Rio Declaration on Environment and Development (A/CONF.151/26, vol. I) and Agenda 21 (A/CONF.151/26, vol. II), adopted by the United Nations Conference on Environment and Development on 14 June 1992[] (Rio Declaration), Principle 25; on the right to development, Resolution AG NU 70/155 of 2015.

4. Recognizing that, in accordance with the Universal Declaration of Human Rights, everyone has the right to a standard of living adequate for his health and well-being and that of his family,[[47]]
5. Recalling that States must take measures to achieve the most efficient development and utilization of natural resources[[48]] and improve all aspects of the environment,[[49]] in accordance with the International Covenant on Economic, Social, and Cultural Rights,
6. Considering that the environment is understood in all its dimensions: earth, maritime, atmospheric and super-atmospheric, and that the right to a healthy environment applies to all public, private, and customary resources as well as to common goods,
7. Deeply troubled by the risks facing humanity and nature, in particular by the adverse effects of climate change, the accelerated loss of biodiversity, natural and technological disasters, degradation of lands and oceans, all of which give rise to violations of fundamental human rights and represent a vital threat to present and future generations,[[50]]
8. Finding that environmental damage, which necessarily affects all humanity, is often accompanied by direct or indirect violations of human rights, particularly the right to life, the right to health, the right to water, the right to food, the right to respect for private life, family and the home, and the right to freedom of opinion and expression,
9. Noting also, reciprocally, that some human rights abuses are accompanied by destruction of the environment,

47 UDHR, Art 25-1.

48 United Nations General Assembly, International Covenant on Economic, Social and Cultural Rights, 16 December 1966, United Nations, Treaty Series, vol. 993, p. 3[] ("ICESCR"), Art. 11-2-a.

49 Dans la version française du Pacte, l'article 12-2-b fait référence à « l'hygiène du milieu et [de] l'hygiène industrielle ». Dans les versions anglaises et espagnoles du Pacte, le terme « environnement » est employé en lieu et place de « hygiène du milieu ». [In the French version of the Covenant, Article 12-2-b refers to "environmental hygiene and industrial hygiene". In the English and Spanish versions of the Covenant, the term "environment" is used instead of "environmental hygiene".]

50 Draft Declaration of Humankind Rights, Preamble, para. 7, presented by F. Hollande, President of the French Republic to the Secretary General of the United Nations, 28 April 2016.

10. Considering that human rights are a form of resilience in the face of environmental degradation,[51]
11. Recalling the international consensus existing since the first principle of the Declaration adopted by the United Nations Conference on the Human Environment in Stockholm, of 16 June 1972, according to which each person has the fundamental right to freedom, equality and adequate conditions of life, in an environment of a quality that permits a life of dignity and well-being,
12. Finding that the human right to a quality environment is recognized by several international conventions, and by the constitutions of the majority of member states of the United Nations,
13. Considering that freedom of association recognized by article 22 of the International Covenant on Civil and Political Rights constitutes an important means of promoting and safeguarding respect for the rights included in the present Covenant;
14. Considering that it is nonetheless necessary to establish, in a universal convention, international rules for the human right to a healthy environment, binding on states, individuals, and other public and private entities, and enforceable by them,

The following articles are hereby agreed:

First part: The right to the environment and the rights and duties that pertain to its realization.

Article 1 – The right to a healthy environment

1. Everyone, including future generations, has the right to live in an ecologically balanced environment capable of assuring his or her health, security, and wellbeing.[52]
2. To that end, every person has the obligation to protect the environment and to contribute to its improvement.
3. The State Parties undertake to effectively implement the rights and duties in the present Covenant. They adopt all measures necessary to this end.

---

51 Conseil de l'Europe, EUROPA, Ethical principles on disaster risk reduction and people's resilience, Strasbourg, 2011.

52 Stockholm Declaration, Principle 1; Rio Declaration, Principle 1; Aarhus Convention, art. 1.

Article 2 – The right to a heightened level of protection and to non-retrogression.

1. Everyone has the right to a heightened level of protection of the environment and to non-retrogression in the levels already attained.
2. The State Parties adopt measures necessary to effectively combat threats to the environment.
3. These measures should be adapted to the state of the environment and ensure a heightened level of protection.[53]
4. These measures may not result, directly or indirectly, in the relation or transfer to other States of any activities and substances that cause severe environmental degradation or are found to be harmful to human health.[54]
5. These measures must contribute to enhanced protection for the environment and health. They must not lead to a reduction in the level of environmental protection already attained.[55]

Article 3 – Right to precautionary measures

1. Everyone has a right to proportional precautionary measures in case of risk of serious or irreversible damage and in the absence of scientific certainty regarding the effects of a legal act or activity on the environment.
2. To this end, everyone has a duty to take necessary precautionary measures.[56]

Article 4 – Right to prevention

1. Everyone has a right to have preventive measures taken.
2. To this end, every person has a duty to prevent damage he or she is likely to cause to the environment.

---

53 Rio Declaration, Principle 11.

54 Rio Declaration, Principle 14; Proposal of the IUCN Covenant 2015 ("IUCN Proposal"), Article 18.

55 Rio+ 20 Declaration, 2012, para. 20. Reports of John H. Knox A/HRC/25/53, 30 December 2013, para. 55; A/HRC/31/52, 1 February 2016, paras. 67, 68, 75; Resolutions IUCN 5.128 of the World Congress of [Jeju] in 2012 and 0.82 of the World Congress in Hawai'i in 2016; European Parliament resolution of 29 September 2011 on developing a common EU position ahead of the United Nations Conference on Sustainable Development (Rio+20), para. 97; IUCN Proposal, art. 10.

56 Principle 15 of Rio 1992; Article 6 of the 2015 IUCN Covenant; Article 5 of the 2005 French Charter on the Environment.

3. The costs of prevention, pollution reduction, and the fight against pollution, as well as the costs of repairing environmental damage, must be borne by the polluter[57].
4. Everyone, including States within the limits of their jurisdictions, must ensure that their activities and those activities under their control, do not cause damage to the environment of other States or of areas beyond the limits of national jurisdiction.[58]

Article 5 – Right to environmental assessment

1. Projects, plans or programs must undergo an assessment of their impact on the environment.
2. This evaluation must also include transboundary impacts. In this context, States must notify concerned States of their projects and hold consultations promptly and in good faith.[59]

Article 6 – Right to reparation of environmental damage

Everyone who is responsible for damage to the environment is obligated to restore to its original state. This obligation exists within and between States.[60]

Article 7 – The right to education

1. Everyone has the right to education and to lifelong environmental education.[61]
2. Environmental education emphasizes the acquisition of knowledge relating to balanced environmental uses and on different modes of management respectful of the natural environment.

Article 8 – Freedom of opinion and expression

1. Everyone has the right to have and to express his or her opinion and to communicate ideas and information about the environment.

---

57 Rio Declaration, Principle 16; on the internalization of costs of prevention and pollution controls well as the costs of environmental damage, recommendation of the OECD C (90) 177 (final) of 1991.

58 Stockholm Declaration 1972, Principle 21; Rio Declaration Principle 2.

59 Rio Declaration, Principle 17 and 19; Report of John H. Knox A/HRC/25/53, 30 December 2013, para. 30; Espoo Convention and the Kiev Protocol; International Court of Justice, Papeleras, 20 April 2010.

60 Art. 1386-19 of the French Civil Code.

61 ICESCR, Art. 13; IUCN Proposal 2015 Art. 54[.]

2. Environmental defenders must not be arbitrarily defamed, prosecuted, arrested, detained or exiled.[62]
3. States shall take all necessary measures to protect the exercise of fundamental rights by any individual or group working to promote environmental protection.[63]

Article 9 – Right to information

1. Everyone has the right, without having to prove an individual interest, to access to information on the environment, including information about hazardous materials and activities, and to obtain and disseminate it.
2. Such information must be disclosed in a way that is pertinent, comprehensible, and available at a reasonable cost.

Article 10 – Right to participation

1. Everyone has the right to participate effectively in decision-making in environmental matters, from the beginning of the process.
2. The right to participation in particular must apply to the planning, usage, and management for the protection of the environment.[64]
3. Results of public participation shall be taken into consideration.[65]

Article 11 – Right to Recourse

Everyone has the right to effective recourse before competent judicial or any impartial and independent administrative bodies in order to challenge acts or

---

62 UDHR, Article 9; United Nations General Assembly, Special Rapporteur on the situation of human rights defenders, *see* Environnement p. 16 (A/70/217, 30 July 2015); United Nations General Assembly Resolution A/RES/70/161, 17 December 2015 on human rights defenders and the Declaration on the right and responsibility of individuals, groups, and civil society organizations to promote and protect universally recognized fundamental human rights and freedoms.

63 Special Rapporteur on human rights defenders: environmental rights defenders, A/71/281 of 3 August 2016; Human Rights Council, Resolution 31/8 (A/HRC/RES/31/8) of 22 April 2016; Resolution 31/32 (A/HRC/31/32) of 20 April 2016 defenders of economic, social, and cultural rights; Special Rapporteur on human rights and the environment John H. Knox (A/HRC/28/61), 18 February 2015, p. 12; Inter-American Court of Human Rights, Kawas v. Honduras, 3 April 2009.

64 Protocol relating to the rights of women of the African Charter of Human and Peoples' Rights, Art. 18.

65 Aarhus Convention, Articles 6–8 and 8.

omissions of public or private persons who violate national or international environmental law.[66]

Article 12 – Right to water

Everyone has the right to safe drinking water and sanitation.[67]

Article 13 – Right to food

Everyone has the right to healthy and nutritious food in sufficient quantity.[68]

Article 14 – Rights of indigenous peoples

1. Indigenous, autochthonous, and local communities, as distinct populations, and because of their traditions and customs, have the right to protection of their environment, their lands, territories and resources,[69] taking into account their indigenous legal order.
2. They have access to natural resources essential to their subsistence and their culture and they have a right to share in the benefits associated with the exploitation of natural resources, including genetic resources, within their territories.
3. They have the right, in the case of forced displacement, to return to a place that permits their use of natural resources consistent with their life style.

Article 15 – Rights of persons in disaster situations

State parties undertake to ensure that all human rights provided under international law are guaranteed to those who are vulnerable to natural or industrial disasters. They have a right, in particular, to prior detailed information on the

---

66 United Nations General Assembly Resolution 60/147 of 16 December 2005 on "Basic Principles and Guidelines on the Right to a Remedy and Reparation for Victims of Gross Violations of International Human Rights Law and Serious Violations of International Humanitarian Law"; Rio Declaration, Principe 10; Aarhus Convention; IUCN Proposal, art. 15.

67 This right is exercised as an element of the right to adequate standard of living, as much as a human right necessary for the full enjoyment of life and of the exercise of all other rights. (United Nations General Assembly Resolutions 64/292 and 70/169). This right is inextricably related to the right to the highest attainable standard of physical and mental health, as well as to the right to life and human dignity. (United Nations General Assembly Resolution A/C.3/70/55 of 18 November 2015). The links of water and health are especially pronounced in the London Protocol of 1999 on water and health to the 1992 Convention on international water courses and lakes.

68 United Nations General Assembly, Resolutions 69/177 of 2014 and 70/154 of 2015.

69 Rio Declaration, Principle 22; IUCN Proposal, art 16; United Nations General Assembly Declaration on the rights of indigenous peoples 61/295 of 13 September 2007 A/RES/61/295.

present and future consequences of environmental accidents on their health and to the environment, and to information about previous losses as well as to an emergency alert system.[70]

Article 16 – Rights of environmental refugees and internally displaced persons

1. All civil, political, social, economic, cultural, and environmental rights are guaranteed to persons displaced whether voluntarily or by force, as a result of sudden or insidious changes to their environment.
2. Internally and internationally displaced persons have a right to special juridical status to ensure their right of "regular stay" and their fundamental rights.[71]

Article 17 – Fairness and solidarity

1. States Parties undertake to ensure that the rights and duties contained in the present Covenant shall be exercised with fairness and solidarity for the benefit of present and future generations.
2. They fulfill their obligations by taking into account their common but differentiated responsibilities.

Article 18 – Non-discrimination

States Parties undertake to guarantee that the rights contained in the present Covenant shall be exercised without discrimination whatsoever based on race, gender, age, language, religion, political or other opinion, national or social origin, property, birth or other status[72].

Article 19 – Sustainable protection

So that the rights contained in the present Covenant are protected for present and future generations, State Parties shall ensure that all public policies and all development processes integrate environmental sustainability.

---

70 Rio Declaration, Principle 18; International Law Commission Proposal for articles on the protection of persons in the event of disasters, 2016 ("ILC Proposal"), art. 9-2; IUCN Proposal, art 19; European Court of Human Rights, Tatar v Roumania, 27 January 2009, para. 122.

71 Proposal for the Convention of Limoges on the juridical status of environmentally displaced persons (www.cidce.org); Report of John H. Knox A/HRC/31/52, 1 February 2016, paras. 24 and 61.

72 ICESCR, Art. 2-2.

Second Part: International Cooperation

Article 20 – Cooperation

All States, international organizations, and all peoples shall cooperate in a spirit of global partnership to oversee, assess, conserve, protect and restore the health and integrity of the Earth's land and marine ecosystems, taking into account especially the needs of the most vulnerable populations, in particular in the least developed countries and small island developing States.[73]

Article 21 – Assistance

To assure the progressive realization of the rights recognized in the present Covenant, each State Party undertakes to take steps to the maximum of its available resources, by its own efforts and through assistance through technology transfer and international cooperation, particularly on the scientific, economic, legal, and technical matters.[74]

Article 22 – Disaster Notification

States Parties shall notify the other States of any risk of disaster that may affect the environment. They must assist one another and ensure respect for human rights in rescue and relief operations.[75]

Article 23 – Framework for limitations of rights

The States Parties to the present Covenant recognize that, in the enjoyment of those rights provided by the State in conformity with the present Covenant, the State may subject such rights only to such limitations as are determined by law only in so far as this may be compatible with the nature of these rights and solely for the purpose of promoting the general welfare in a democratic society.[76]

Article 24 – Interpretation of the Covenant

1. Nothing in the present Covenant may be interpreted as implying for any State, group or person any right to engage in any activity or to perform any act aimed at the destruction of any of the rights or freedoms recognized herein, or at their limitation to a greater extent than is provided for in the present Covenant.[77]

---

73 Paris Climate Agreement of 12 December 2015, Art 9 (9) and 11 (1); Rio Declaration Principles 5, 6, and 7.

74 ICESCR, Art 2-1.

75 Rio Declaration, Principle 18; International Law Commission Proposal, arts. 11, 12.

76 ICESCR, Art. 4; Protocol of San Salvador, Art. 5; European Convention of Human Rights, Art. 8.

77 ICESCR, Art. 5-1.

2. This Covenant may not be interpreted as limiting the rights of nature or of any parts thereof when they are recognized by a State.[78]

Part Three: Monitoring the Enforcement of the Covenant

Article 25 – Enforcement Body

The Committee on Economic, Social and Cultural Rights established by resolution 1985/17 of 28 May 1985 (hereinafter referred to as the "Committee") is responsible for monitoring and controlling compliance with obligations under the present Covenant.

Article 26 – Reports to the Committee

1. The States Parties to the present Covenant undertake to submit every four years reports on the measures they will have adopted and on the progress made to ensure respect for rights and duties contained in the present Covenant.[79]
2. Reports may describe the difficulties that states face in fulfillment of obligations under the present Covenant.
3. All reports are submitted to the Secretary General of the United Nations who shall transmit copies to the Economic and Social Council and the Committee.
4. The Secretary General of the United Nations may, after consultation with the Committee, transmit to the specialized agencies concerned copies of such parts of the reports as may fall within their field of competence.[80]
5. The Committee is responsible for reviewing these reports and making recommendations to the Economic and Social Council.
6. The States Parties may submit to the Economic and Social Council comments on any recommendation made under [section] 5 above or any mention of a recommendation contained in a Committee report.

Article 27 – Interstate Communications

Any State Party to the present Covenant may decide to any time that it recognizes the competence of the Committee to receive and consider communications in which a State Party claims that another State Party has not fulfilled its obligations under the present Covenant.

---

78 ICESCR, Art. 5-2; with particular regard to the rights of nature protected in Bolivia and Ecuador.

79 ICESCR, Art. 16.

80 International Covenant of Civil and Political Rights, Art. 40, [paragraph] 3.

Article 28 – Individual communications

1. Under the present Covenant, the Committee is responsible for receiving and considering communications from individuals, or groups of individuals, or on behalf of individuals, or groups of individuals, subject to the jurisdiction of a State party, who claim to be victims of a violation by that State Party of one of the rights or obligations relating to the environment set forth in the present Covenant.
2. A communication may only be submitted on behalf of individuals or groups of individuals with their consent, unless the author can justify acting on their behalf without such consent.

Article 29 – Procedure

The Optional Protocol to the International Covenant on Economic, Social and Cultural Rights adopted on 10 December 2008 by resolution A/RES/63/117 of the United Nations General Assembly[81] shall apply *mutatis mutandis* to the implementation of the present Covenant to receive and consider communications presented pursuant to Articles 27 and 28 of this Covenant.

Article 30 – Annual Report of the Committee

In its annual report, the Committee will include a summary of its activities under the present Covenant.[82]

Fourth Part: Final Provisions

Article 31 – Signature, Ratification, Accession

1. The present Covenant is open for signature by any State Member of the United Nations or member of any of its specialized agencies, and to any other State invited by the National Assembly of the United Nations to become a party to the present Covenant.
2. The present Covenant is subject to ratification and the instruments of ratification shall be deposited with the Secretary General of the United Nations.
3. The present Covenant shall be open for accession by any State referred to in paragraph 1 of this Article.
4. Accession shall be by deposit of an instrument of accession with the Secretary General of the United Nations.

---

81 Entered into force on 5 May 2013.

82 ICESCR, Optional Protocol, Art. 21.

5. The Secretary General of the United Nations shall inform all States which have signed this Covenant, which have ratified it, or which have acceded to the deposit of each instrument of ratification or accession.

Article 32 – Entry Into Force

1. The present Covenant shall enter into force three months after the date of deposit with the Secretary General of the United Nations of the thirty-fifth instrument of ratification or accession.
2. For each State ratifying the present Covenant or acceding to it after the deposit of the thirty-fifth instrument of ratification or accession, the present Covenant shall enter into force three months after the date of the deposit of its instrument of ratification or accession.

Article 33 – Reservations

No reservation to the provisions of the present Covenant shall be accepted.

Article 34 – Amendments

1. Any State Party to the present Covenant may propose an amendment and file it with the Secretary General of the United Nations. The Secretary General shall thereupon communicate any proposed amendments to States Parties to the present Covenant, asking them to indicate whether they favor convening a conference of States Parties to examine them and vote. If at least one third of the States are in favor of this conference, the Secretary General shall convene the conference under the auspices of the United Nations. Any amendment adopted by a majority of States present and voting at the conference shall be submitted for approval to the United Nations General Assembly.
2. Amendments come into force when approved by the United Nations General Assembly and accepted in accordance with their respective constitutional processes, by two thirds of States Parties to the present Covenant.
3. When amendments come into force, they are mandatory for States Parties which have accepted them, other States Parties still being bound by the provisions of the present Covenant and any earlier amendment which they have accepted.

Article 35 – Notification by the Secretary General

Irrespective of the notifications provided for in paragraph 5 of article 31, the Secretary General of the United Nations shall inform all States referred to in paragraph 1 of Article 31 of:

a) the signatures to the present Covenant and the instruments of ratification and accessions deposited under Article 31;
b) the date on which the present Covenant shall enter into force in accordance with Article 32 and the date for the entry into force of any amendments under article 34.

Article 36 – Official Languages

1. The present Covenant, of which the English, Arabic, Chinese, Spanish, French, and Russian texts are equally authentic, shall be deposited with the United Nations archives.
2. The Secretary General of the United Nations shall transmit certified copies of the present Covenant to all States referred to in Article 31.[83]

Draft Covenant prepared by the Center for International Comparative Environmental Law (CIDCE), an INGO with special consultative status as a UN ECOSOC INGO, and a group led by Professor Michel Prieur and consisting of Julien Bétaille, Marie-Anne Cohendet, Hubert Delzangles, Jessica Makowiak and Pascale Steichen (co-authors of "Right to the Environment" (Dalloz [8th edition 2019]).

Thanks to the network of correspondents of the CIDCE (www.cidce.org), the draft covenant has benefited from commentary and amendments from 40 legal scholars from 22 different countries from North and South America, Africa, Asia, Europe, and the Pacific. They are all gratefully acknowledged here for their timely contributions.

Thanks for the English translation by Erin Daly, professor of law, Delaware law school, USA.

83 Except for minor adjustments, the final provisions of the fourth part are entirely borrowed from Arts. 26–31 of the ICESCR.

Corinne LEPAGE & Emilie GAILLARD

16. For the Recognition of the Rights & Duties of Humankind

"[France was able, 70 years ago, to convene a major conference about universal human rights. Now we must drive the world to adopt a Declaration for the Rights of Humankind to preserve the planet]."[1] It was with these words that President François Hollande addressed the people of France on 31 December 2014, at the Elysee Palace. Former French Minister of the Environment, Corinne Lepage was appointed head of a mission to coordinate the drafting of a text which outlines these ambitions. After several months of meetings and preparatory work, especially with the Ministry of Foreign Affairs, the text was submitted to the French President in September 2015. Although intended for presentation at COP 21 in Paris, this draft Declaration was not formally presented for tactical reasons, notably following the influence of Foreign Minister Laurent Fabius – in order to give the Paris Agreement the best chance of being signed. Nevertheless, given the Declaration's historical significance and its particular resonance in helping to face the great challenges of our time, Madam Corinne Lepage has continued her work since 2015: seeking to bring together as many actors as possible around this text – from civil society, public and private stakeholders, NGOs, universities as well as professional orders.

It is clear that the time has come to affirm such a Declaration: Humanity is facing several major and unprecedented dangers (climate change, irreversible pollution from pesticides, human beings' distortion of humanity and large-scale genetic manipulation of living systems). Admittedly, many texts have already been adopted and COP 21 would have functioned as a historic moment to present the Declaration. In any event, the fate of this text will be insured by focusing on the long-term goal of rallying the global community, involving nations but also private actors, businesses and multinationals.

---

1 Presidential wishes of 31 Dec. 2014, *Déclaration Universelle des Droits de l'Humanité – Rapport à l'attention de Monsieur le Président de la République* [*Universal Declaration of the Rights and Duties of Humankind – Report for the President of the Republic*], p. 5, *available online at* www.ladocumentationfrancaise.fr/var/storage/rapports-publics/154000687.pdf.

This Declaration gives impetus to a new era in the way of thinking and posturing human rights. The time has come to officially recognize the third generation of fundamental rights: after civil and political rights (1st generation), as well as economic and social rights (2nd generation), it is now time to establish solidarity rights (3rd generation). These rights include, among others, the protection of the right to peace, the environment, the world heritage and sustainable development.[2] It is also a necessary step to support the significant transformation of strengthening solidarity rights with Humankind (past, present and future) with its/their ecological habitat. The legal utopia we are discussing here aims to establish "the right to live in a world whose future is not compromised by the present".[3]

The text, of course, does not bring into question the Universal Declaration of Human Rights of 1948 (UDHR). It presents itself as a new stage of evolution that is both necessary and complementary. This ideal of legally recognizing humanity has become a necessity for civilization in this twenty-first century. The topics we must now deal with are collective in nature: we have gone beyond the scale of individuals. It is no longer a question of defending only the integrity and rights of people individually. Specifically, the Universal Declaration of the Rights and Duties of Humankind (Declaration Universelle des Droits de L'Humanite, or DDHu) introduces a contemporary legal framework for the sustainable preservation of fundamental rights, whether individual or collective. Another remarkable development is that the Declaration recognizes both the rights and the duties of Humankind, in order to create a new legal horizon that reaches beyond the present and beyond state borders.

This Declaration is a tool that aims to be approved as widely as possible, accepted by the largest possible number of people around the world.[4] Indeed,

---

2 E. Gaillard, *Générations futures et droit privé. Vers un droit des générations futures* [*Future Generations and Private Law: Towards a Law for Future Generations*], Librairie Générale de Droit et de Jurisprudence, 2011, pp. 234–262.

3 Author's translation of Letter from François Hollande, Le Président de La République, to Madame Corinne Lepage, 4 June 2015 (engaging Madame Lepage for the purpose of drafting a "Declaration universelle des droits de l'Homme" or DDHu [Universal Declaration of the Rights and Duties of Humankind]), *in* C. Lepage & Equipe de Redaction, "Déclaration Universelle des Droits de l'Humanité : Rapport à l'attention de Monsieur Le Président de La République" [Universal Declaration of the Rights and Duties of Humankind: A Report to Monsieur the President of the Republic], 25 Sep. 2015, *available online at* https://www.ladocumentationfrancaise.fr/rapports-publics/154000687/index.shtml (in French).

4 The growing number of signatories – categorized by local governments, legal entities, economic entities, and countries – can be followed online at a dedicated website.

the legal context is favorable for such a project. Various Declarations and other non-binding texts have already paved the way for recognizing the idea of Humanity. In binding legal texts, the concepts of "laws of humanity",[5] "Crimes against humanity"[6] or "the interest of all mankind",[7] "Intangible Heritage of Humanity",[8] "common interest of all mankind"[9] or "common concern of

---

See http://droitshumanite.fr/?lang=en; http://droitshumanite.fr/newsletter-may-2019/?lang=en ("the International Association of Francophone Mayors signed the Declaration on [3 June 2019] in Kigali. After the unanimous vote of UCLG's Executive Committee in April, this is a major step forward as the association has more than 300 members in 52 countries, representing more than 130 million inhabitants"). The DHR complements the Draft International Covenant on the Human Right to the Environment by Michel Prieur. Although both documents take into account humanity's relationship to nature, the DHR more directly takes into account everything that is precisely related to humanity including: peace, technological progress, economic issues and access to resources. *See* Universal Declaration of the Rights and Duties of Humankind, *available online at* http://droitshumanite.fr/the-declaration:?lang=en.

5 The Hague Convention (II) with Respect to the Laws and Customs of War on Land and its annex: Regulations concerning the Laws and Customs of War on Land, 29 July 1899, *available online at* http://www.opbw.org/int_inst/sec_docs/1899HC-TEXT.pdf; The Hague Convention (IV) Respecting the Laws and Customs of War on Land and Its Annex: Regulations Concerning the Laws and Customs of War on Land, 18 Oct. 1907, *available at* https://www.refworld.org/docid/4374cae64.html; International Committee of the Red Cross (ICRC), Geneva Convention Relative to the Protection of Civilian Persons in Time of War (Fourth Geneva Convention), 12 Aug. 1949, 75 UNTS 287, article 158, *available online at* https://www.refworld.org/docid/3ae6b36d2.html.

6 United Nations, Charter of the International Military Tribunal – Annex to the Agreement for the prosecution and punishment of the major war criminals of the European Axis ("London Agreement"), 8 Aug. 1945, *available online at* https://www.refworld.org/docid/3ae6b39614.html?fbclid=IwAR0fshGqbtQ_rIqYTBYzuOFVB8_Aj78Ca-ydTG2UNwNVMP9iYfdVKD5sZ3c; *ibid.*, article 6(c) ("murder, extermination, enslavement, deportation, and other inhumane acts committed against any civilian population, before or during the war, or persecutions on political, racial or religious grounds").

7 The Antarctic Treaty, *United Nations Treaty Series*, 1961, Vol. 420, p. 71, 72.

8 United Nations Educational, Scientific and Cultural Organisation (UNESCO), Convention for the Safeguarding of the Intangible Cultural Heritage, 3 Nov. 2003, article 31, *available online at* https://ich.unesco.org/en/convention

9 Treaty on Principles Governing the Activities of States in the Exploration and Use of Outer Space, including the Moon and other Selestial Bodies (Outer Space Treaty), *United Nations Treaty Series*, 1967, Vol. 610, p. 205 *available online at* http://www.unoosa.org/oosa/en/ourwork/spacelaw/treaties/introouterspacetreaty.html.

humankind"[10] are already consecrated. This momentum reinforces the future of humanity as a new legal concept under International law. A large number of non-legally binding texts (or soft law, such as Declarations) incorporate this legal concept through the adoption of concepts such as: the "Human family",[11] taking into account the intrinsic diversity of Humankind,[12] the emergence

---

10 UN General Assembly, United Nations Framework Convention on Climate Change, 20 Jan. 1994, A/RES/48/189, preamble, *available online at*: https://unfccc.int/resource/docs/convkp/conveng.pdf?fbclid=IwAR3thuPZCzIQEKBtdTtiQPkB2ken46q0hnUB2oG3io6czsSCnNQaGpAO7c8 (signed 9 May 1992); United Nations Convention on Biological Biodiversity, 29 Dec. 1993, preamble, https://www.cbd.int/doc/legal/cbd-en.pdf (signed 5 June 1992).

11 Universal Declaration on Human Rights (UDHR), 10 Dec. 1948, preamble, *available online at* https://www.un.org/en/universal-declaration-human-rights/?fbclid=IwAR1k3tBnGSwOfz2kJa8qBSHkQc6xGRTr0Otsn7KcaY7PCoaxJiwf6Ca74uw.

12 *Three categories* of soft law derived from various UNESCO declarations provide persuasive authority that help pave the way for taking into account the intrinsic diversity of humanity:

First, the notion that "culture" is part of the "common heritage" of mankind/humanity. UNESCO Declaration on Race and Racial Prejudice, 27 Nov. 1978, preamble, *available online at* http://www.unesco.org/education/pdf/RACE_E.PDF?fbclid=IwAR1Cvk2BVvdLvIgMF4FYN8z6a_1eprCj9sGoDTxAXEQjBBoEWbI18DYecfk ("cultures [...] in their plurality and as a result of their interpretation; constitute the common heritage of mankind"); *ibid.*, article 5(1) ("Culture" is "a common heritage of mankind"); *see also* UNESCO Universal Declaration on Cultural Diversity, 2 Nov. 2001, article 1, *available online at* http://portal.unesco.org/en/ev.php-URL_ID=13179&URL_DO=DO_TOPIC&URL_SECTION=201.html?fbclid=IwAR0xOD3tEwsZ7jYFPrYif5_EBPk1ueYukhy0FRp0HYp1YUAW3JunukWfv4Q ("Culture [...] is the common heritage of humanity").

Second, "the fundamental unity of all members of the human family, as well as the recognition of their inherent dignity and diversity" is, in a "symbolic sense, [...] the heritage of humanity". UNESCO Universal Declaration on the Human Genome and Human Rights, 11 Nov. 1997, article 1, *available online at* http://www.unesco.org/new/en/social-and-human-sciences/themes/bioethics/human-genome-and-human-rights.

Third, "the preservation of the human species in particular through scientific and technical progress and the protection of the genetic heritage". UNESCO International Declaration on Human Genetic Data, 16 Oct. 2003, article 26, *available online at at* http://portal.unesco.org/en/ev.php-URL_ID=17720&URL_DO=DO_TOPIC&URL_SECTION=201.html (requiring UNESCO to "foster progress of the life sciences and their applications through technologies, based on respect for human dignity and the exercise and observance of human rights and fundamental freedoms"); United Nations Declaration on the Cloning of Human Beings, 8 Mar. 2005, *available online* at https://digitallibrary.un.org/record/541409/files/A_C.6_59_L.27_Add.1-EN.pdf ("Member

of the rights of "future generations",[13] and recognizing the importance of protecting the environment for Humankind.[14] These collective interests in

States are called upon to prohibit all forms of human cloning inasmuch as they are incompatible with human dignity and the protection of human life"; "Member States are further called upon to adopt the measures necessary to prohibit the application of genetic engineering techniques that may be contrary to human dignity"); UNESCO Universal Declaration on Bioethics and Human Rights, 19 Oct. 2005, preamble ("cultural diversity [...] is the common heritage of humanity, but emphasizing that it may not be invoked at the expense of human rights and fundamental freedoms"), *available online at* http://portal.unesco.org/en/ev.php-URL_ID=31058&URL_DO=DO_TOPIC&URL_SECTION=201.html.

13 The Hague Declaration on the Environment, *International Legal Materials*, Cambridge University Press, Sep. 1989, Vol. 28, No. 5 ("consequent duty of nations vis-à-vis present and future generations"); UNESCO Declaration on the Responsibilities of the Present Generations Towards Future Generations, 12 Nov. 1997, article 5 ("ensure that future generations benefit from the richness of the Earth's ecosystems" and "are not exposed to pollution which may endanger their health or their existence"; "preserve for future generations natural resources necessary for sustaining human life and for its development"; "take into account possible consequences for future generations of major projects before these are carried out"), *available online at* http://portal.unesco.org/en/ev.php-URL_ID=13178&URL_DO=DO_TOPIC&URL_SECTION=201.html; *ibid.*, article 7 ("present generations have the responsibility to identify, protect and safeguard the tangible and intangible cultural heritage and to transit this common heritage to future generations"); *ibid.*, article 8 ("present generations may use the common heritage of mankind [...] provided that this does not entail compromising it irreversibly"); *cf.* UN General Assembly Resolution No. 39/11, Declaration on the Right of Peoples to Peace, 12 Nov. 1984 ("preservation of human civilization and the survival of mankind"), *available online at* https://www.ohchr.org/EN/ProfessionalInterest/Pages/RightOfPeoplesToPeace.aspx;
Declaration of Principles Governing the Sea-Bed and the Ocean Floor and the Subsoil Thereof, beyond the Limits of National Jurisdiction, UNGA Resolution No. 2749/XXV, 12 Dec. 1970, paragraph 1 ("common heritage of mankind"), *available online at* http://www.worldlii.org/int/other/UNGA/1970/118.pdf. *Accord* E. Gaillard, 2011, pp. 223-299 & 468-494. pp. 223–299 & 468–494.

14 Declaration of the United Nations Conference on the Human Environment (Stockholm Declaration), 16 June 1972, paragraph 6 ("defend and improve the human environment for present and future generations"), *available online at* https://www.refworld.org/docid/3b00f1c840.html; World Charter of Nature, UNGA Resolution A/RES/37/7, 28 Nov. 1982, paragraph 11(c), 21(c) & 23 ("environmental impact studies of development projects" that "shall be planned and carried out so as to minimize potential adverse effects"; "conservation of nature and [...] protection of the environment"; "opportunity

the defense of humanity are confirmed in texts supported by NGOs and civil society.[15]

While the Declaration is breaking new ground, it is also clearly part of a historical and legal legacy that confirms the time has come for nations to gather

---

to participate […] in the formulation of decisions of direct concern to their environment; and […] access to means of redress when their environment has suffered damage or degradation"), *available online at* https://www.refworld.org/docid/3b00f22a10.html; UNGA Resolution No. 35/7, Draft World Charter for Nature, 30 Oct. 1980, paragraph 2 ("recognition of the supreme importance of protecting natural systems, maintaining the balance and quality of nature and conserving natural resources; in the interests of present and future generations"), *available online at* https://www.un.org/documents/ga/res/35/a35r7e.pdf; UNGA Resolution A/HRC/16/11, Human Rights and the Environment, 24 Mar. 2011 ("the right to development must be fulfilled in order to meet the development and environmental needs of present and future generations equitably"), *available online at* https://www2.ohchr.org/english/bodies/hrcouncil/docs/16session/A.HRC.RES.16.11_en.pdf; Johannesburg Declaration on Sustainable Development, United Nations Doc. A/CONF.199/20, 4 Sep. 2002, paragraph 8 ("protection of the environment" is "fundamental to sustainable development"), *available online at* http://ec.europa.eu/environment/archives/wssd/documents/wssd_pol_declaration.pdf.

15 The Cousteau Society, A Bill of Rights for the Future Generations, 1979 (quoting Jacques-Yves Cousteau, "Why should we preserve a livable planet if not for our children and grandchildren?"; recognizing "the rights of future generations to exercise options with respect to the nurture and continuity of life"), *in* E. Brown Weiss, *Justice pour les générations futures* [Justice for Future Generations], Éditions Sang de la terre, 1993, UNESCO translation, p. 339; Proposal [for a] Universal Declaration of the Rights of Mother Earth (Cochabamba Declaration), World People's Conference on Climate Change and the Rights of Mother Earth, 22 Apr. 2010, articles 3(1), 3(2)(e), 3(2)(f) ("[e]very human being is responsible for respecting and living in harmony with Mother Earth": and further obligating humans to "establish and apply effective norms for the defence, protection and conservation of the rights of Mother Earth" as well as to "respect, protect, conserve and where necessary, restore the integrity, of the vital ecological cycles, processes and balances of Mother Earth"), *available online at* https://pwccc.wordpress.com/programa/; P. Calame, Proposal for a Universal Declaration of Human Responsibilities, Foundation Charles Léopold Mayer pour le Progrès de l'Homme, June 2012, preamble, paragraphs 1, 2, 6 (referring to "community of destiny"; "preservation of the integrity of the planet, and […] safekeeping the interests of future generations"; "preserve our only, fragile planet, by preventing major unbalances from bringing about ecological and social disasters that will affect all the peoples of the Earth"), *available online at* http://base.alliance-respons.net/docs/declaration_universelle_en.pdf.

along with civil society around a new legal Humanism. The rights of Humankind function to complement the human rights already recognized in international human rights law. They build a bridge between the recognition of peoples' rights and human rights already in force. In the end, the rights of Humankind could not have preceded those of man. These news rights of Humankind constitute a new generation of rights, which encompasses the rights of future generations.

The Declaration was also drafted in a spirit of respect for diverse legal cultures. It is now important to present the content for these rights of Humankind (*see* Part I below), and to describe a gathering worldwide momentum of nations that is currently underway (*see* Part II below).

I. Universal Declaration of the Rights and Duties of Humankind: Contents

The mission of Corinne Lepage and her team was to draft a Declaration that was simple and acceptable for the States of the world. The Declaration is endowed with a Preamble that is divided into twelve points, four principles (*see* Section I.A. below), six rights (*see* Section I.B. below), and six duties (*see* Section I.C. below).

A. A Preamble and Four Principles

1. The Preamble

For the sake of simplicity, the DDHu contains a relatively short preamble. It commences with the observation that "Humanity is in danger". This calls into question the rights of present generations and introduces the issue of vital threats to future generations. Point 2 emphasizes the need to recognize the principles, rights and responsibilities of humanity. As the preamble reminds us, this text is inscribed in a line of texts originating from international human rights law and from international protection of the environment.

What does "Humanity" entail? The answer may seem obvious but it is not! Many authors have tried this delicate task.[16] This Declaration uses a definition

16 "[Suppose the people of Europe, instead of defying one another, to jealousy, hate one another, have loved one another: suppose they had told themselves that even before being French, or English, or German, one is a man, and if nations are homelands, humanity is a family; and now, that sum of one hundred and twenty-eight billion, so madly and so vainly spent by mistrust, make her spend by trust! These hundred and twenty-eight billion given to hatred, give them harmony! These hundred and twenty-eight billion given to the war, give them to peace!]" V. Hugo, "Un jour viendra" [One Day Will Come], Discourse First World Peace Congress, 1849. "Agis de telle sorte que les

that is both vertical and horizontal. On the one hand, a vertical definition: Humankind includes past, present and future generations. There are duties associated with the cultural heritage bequeathed by past generations. This is not about conservatism that prevents moving forward. It is about instituting an imperative of respect vis-à-vis the heritage of Humanity. On the other hand, a horizontal definition enriches and embraces the diversity of actors. In today's world, Humankind comprises everyone: from supra-state organizations to citizens. It is clear that citizens today defend and act in the name of Humanity and of future generations. Humanity is thus a *continuum* that has expressed itself from the United Nations to individuals. Humanity also includes businesses, NGOs and, in particular, multinationals.

Two sets of interdependencies are recalled in the preamble: first, between the Earth and Humankind (referring to the famous "*Recognizing the integral and interdependent nature of the Earth, our home*" accepted by the Rio Declaration on the 1th of June 1994)[17]; second, between the environment and Rights of Humankind. These interdependencies form a virtuous circle: the rights of Humankind serve both current and future generations, as well as nature and life in general. The Declaration therefore aims to create sustainable interdependencies that bring about democracy, justice, environmental protection and peace for the present and future of all humanity.

---

effets de ton action soient compatibles avec la permanence d'une vie authentiquement humaine sur Terre" [Act so that the effects of your actions are compatible with the permanence of a genuine human life]. H. Jonas, *Le principe responsabilité. Une éthique pour la civilisation technologique* [The Imperative of Responsibility. In Search of an Ethics for the Technological Age], éditions du Cerf, 1990, p. 40. "L'humanité entière est confrontée à un ensemble entremêlé de crises qui, à elles toutes, constituent la Grande Crise d'une humanité qui n'arrive pas à accéder à l'Humanité" [The whole of humanity is confronted with a set of crises that, together, constitute the Great Depression of a humanity that can not get to Humanity]. E. Morin, *Le chemin de l'espérance* [*The Path of Hope*], S. Hessel & E. Morin (eds.), éditions Fayard, 2011, Chap. 1 *in* C. Lepage & Equipe de Redaction, "Déclaration Universelle des Droits de l'Humanité : Rapport à l'attention de Monsieur Le Président de La République" [Universal Declaration of the Rights and Duties of Humankind: A Report to Monsieur the President of the Republic], 25 Sep. 2015, p. 10.

17 The Rio Declaration on Environment and Development, United Nations Conference on Environment and Development, 14 June 1992, preamble ("Recognizing the integral and interdependent nature of the Earth, our home"), *available online at* www.unesco.org/education/pdf/RIO_E.pdf.

The Preamble launches a clear call for responsibility involving all actors – not only States, although their main duty is to protect the existence of Humankind and living beings.

Finally, the Preamble establishes freedom, justice and world peace ruled in the principle of the dignity of Humanity. The positive perspective of this principle is that we will be able to read all human rights through the new lens of transgenerational rights.[18]

2. *The Principles*

Following the proclamation are four principles. Article 1 states that "The principle of intragenerational and intergenerational responsibility, equity and solidarity demands that the human family and in particular its States shall endeavor, in a common and differentiated manner, to safeguard and preserve humanity and Earth". The principle of responsibility is essential. This text only makes sense because Humanity considers itself responsible not only for itself and its environment, not only for future generations, but more broadly for all other species as well. We are the only species with a conscience that allows us to ensure the longevity of other species. That is what makes it possible to divorce ourselves from extreme positions: ecocentric and anthropocentric design. The Declaration builds a bridge between these two approaches. This is the fundamental objective of the DDHu.

Article 2 proclaims the principle of dignity for Humankind and its members, which entails the satisfaction of basic needs as well as the protection of the intangible rights of Humankind. This principle is transitive, since it continuously applies to each generation as a means of guaranteeing respect over time.

Article 3 proclaims the imperative of civilization: the principle of continuity of human existence principle. This principle requires us to conduct activities that are careful and respectful of nature, recognizing the need for transgenerational protection. This principle also offers the opportunity to witness the emergence of a new legal concept: the right to anticipate and prevent disasters. It means thinking about catastrophes at the earliest stage, keeping in mind that tragedies can happen, and enabling a legal imperative of protection for the continuity of Humankind.[19]

---

18 E. Gaillard, 2011, pp. 455–494.

19 *See* J.-M. Collin's essay #5 (this book) on "Treaty on the Prohibition of Nuclear Weapons: A Move Towards New Legal Action to Protect Future Generations"; F. Lemarchand's essay #6 (this book) on "The Bomb as a New Definition of Present

Article 4 establishes a principle of temporal non-discrimination.[20] The law can protect future generations from the long-term effects of actions taken by present generations. Thus, measures or activities that restrict choices for future generations by depleting resources, or perpetuating their excessive reduction, should not take place.

B. Six Rights of Humankind, Six Duties Towards Humanity

In the interests of balance, the Declaration recognizes Six Rights of Humankind (*see* subsection I.B.1. below) and Six Duties towards Humanity (*see* subsection I.B.2. below).

1. Six Rights of Humankind

The first right of Humankind is to live in a healthy and sustainable environment. This right is shared by all living species. Article 5 reaches beyond the traditional gap between ecocentric and anthropocentric approaches. The right for people to live in a healthy environment only makes sense, and can only be in a sustainable way, if it respects the preservation of nature.

The second right of Humankind is the right to responsible, fair, inclusive and sustainable development. This right is clearly in keeping with history, and further aligns with the 2030 Sustainable Development Goals.

Humanity is also entitled to protection of the common heritage and its natural, cultural, material as well as its immaterial patrimony. The Declaration also calls for preservation of common resources, especially air, water and soil, along with universal access to vital resources. Article 8 insists that future generations are entitled to their inheritance. Under the legacy of the San Francisco Charter, which seeks to protect future generations from the scourge of war, Humankind has the right to sustainable peace and human security. This concept is particularly rich in legal potentialities; it holistically and systematically encompasses environmental, food, health, economic and political security. Finally, the imperative of protecting the future translates as: "Humankind has freedom of choice to determine its fate".

---

and Future Humanity: What we Owe to Günther Anders' Thoughts"; E. Gaillard's essay #20 (this book) on "Legal Bases for Protecting Future Generations?".

20 E. Gaillard, 2011, pp. 431–454.

In light of Humankind future and our attitude towards non-human lives, the Declaration recognizes six duties towards Humanity.

2. Six Duties Towards Humanity

According to Article 11, "The present generations have a duty to ensure respect for the rights of humankind as well as of all living species. The rights of mankind as a whole and human rights are indivisible and applicable to all future generations". This article incorporates both a long-term perspective, as well as the imperatives of transgenerational transmission and respect.

Each generation has the duty to transmit ecological resources and preserve ecological balance. Every generation has the duty to transmit the natural common heritage of humanity (Article 12). Acknowledging the essential question of climate justice, the Declaration breaks new ground by declaring a duty to do all that is possible to preserve the atmosphere and climate balance (Article 13). This latter mandate includes the responsibility to do everything possible to avoid forcing people to migrate as a result of environmental disaster, as well as the duty to rescue and protect people who nevertheless must move from place to place due to environmental catastrophe.

These duties are fundamental at a time when many migrants – often victims of slavery, abuse and other forms of trafficking – are drowning in the Mediterranean Sea, while Member States of the European Union demonstrate the greatest indifference.

There is also a duty specifically dedicated to the management of technical and scientific progress. All that can be done does not necessarily have to be done! We are living in a time of profound changes and acceleration linked to technological "progress". It is important to remember that these upheavals have never been the subject of democratic choice! Past experiences like the advent of a "Biotech Century"[21] and all the appropriation of life that this process has generated, were achieved without democratic debate. Today, more than ever, the questions of artificial intelligence and augmented Humankind require such a debate. How can we establish a healthy basis to conduct this kind of research? This fundamental question has long been a blind spot due to globalization and the race for competitiveness beyond the traditional legal framework. Certain multinational companies have enriched themselves using these legal loopholes. This responsibility allows us to verbalize the question: where do we place our priorities? Is our

21 J. Rifkin, *The Biotech Century: Harnessing the Gene and Remaking the World*, TarcherPerigee, 1999.

priority to have an augmented reality, or to deal with climate change? Knowing how to manage scientific and technical progress is an extremely important issue. To say that this must be done in the interest of preserving Humankind and other species is extremely important and helps prioritize present interests.

Considering that these issues relate to the sustainability of life on Earth, Article 15 proclaims the responsibility of states and of all actors (public and private) "to integrate the long-term perspective [...] and to promote sustainable human development".

Finally, in order to intensify protective laws, Article 16 proclaims the duty of States to ensure the effective implementation of the principles and responsibilities recognized in the DDHu.

Thus, the proposed Declaration is modest in scope (i.e., non-binding) in order to make the prospects for adoption more favorable. This Declaration could be a prelude to more potent commitments. It paves the way for further discussions and new, transgenerational forms of rights including the rights to: sustainable human health,[22] integrity of the human species,[23] and food, environmental as well as sanitary security.

UNIVERSAL DECLARATION OF THE RIGHTS & DUTIES OF HUMANKIND

PREAMBLE

1. **Whereas humanity and nature** are in danger and in particular the adverse effects of climate change, accelerated loss of biodiversity, degradation of land and ocean, are all violations of human rights and a vital threat to present and future generations.
2. **Whereas the extreme gravity of the situation**, which is a concern for all humanity, requires the recognition of new principles, rights and duties.
3. **Whereas commitment to the principles and rights** recognized in the Universal Declaration of Human Rights, including equality between women and men, as well as to the purposes and principles of the UN Charter, are reaffirmed.
4. **Whereas the peoples of Earth** endorse the 1972 Stockholm Declaration on the Human Environment, the 1982 New York World Charter for Nature, the Rio Declaration on Environment and Development of 1992 and the 2000 Millennium Declaration and 2012 The Future We Want resolutions of the General Assembly of the United Nations.

22 E. Gaillard, 2011, pp. 481, 485.

23 *Ibid.*, pp. 541–553.

5. **Whereas the aforementioned danger** is recognized by civil society, especially networks of people, organizations, institutions, and cities in the 2000 Earth Charter
6. **Whereas humanity,** which comprises all human individuals and organizations, includes past, present and future generations altogether, and that the very continuity of humanity rests on this intergenerational link.
7. **Whereas the Earth, home to humanity,** constitutes a whole marked by interdependence and reaffirming that the existence and the future of humanity are inseparable from its natural environment.
8. **Whereas the fundamental rights of human beings and the duty** to preserve nature are inherently interdependent and with the conviction that good conservation of the environment and improvement of its quality are of vital importance.
9. **Whereas present generations are especially responsible,** this being especially true of all States, which have primary responsibility in the matter, but also of people, intergovernmental organizations, companies and notably multinational corporations, non-governmental organizations, local authorities and individuals.
10. **Whereas this historical responsibility** confers duties vis-à-vis the whole of humanity, and that these obligations are to be implemented through just, democratic, ecological and peaceful means.
11. **Whereas recognition of the inherent dignity of humanity and all members of the human family** is the foundation of freedom, justice and peace in the world.
12. **Proclaims the principles, rights and duties** that follow and adopts the present statement:

THE PRINCIPLES

I

The principle of intragenerational and intergenerational responsibility, equity and solidarity demands that the human family and in particular its States shall endeavor, in a common and differentiated manner, to safeguard and preserve humanity and Earth.

II

The principle of humanity and dignity of its members involves the satisfaction of their basic needs and the protection of their intangible rights. Each generation shall ensure compliance with this principle over time.

III

The principle of continuity of human existence guarantees the protection and future of humankind and nature through human activities that shall be prudent and respectful of nature, particularly of life, both human and non-human, and making every effort to prevent all serious or irreversible transgenerational consequences.

IV

The principle of non-discrimination between generations shall preserve humanity, particularly future generations, and requires that no activities or measures undertaken by the present generations shall have the effect of causing depletion or perpetuating excessive reduction of resources nor restriction of choices for future generations.

THE RIGHTS OF HUMANKIND

V

Humankind, like all living species, has the right to live in a healthy and ecologically sustainable environment.

VI

Humankind has the right to responsible, equitable, inclusive and sustainable development.

VII

Humankind has the right to protection of its common, natural, cultural, tangible and intangible heritage.

VIII

Humankind has the right to the preservation of common goods, especially air, water and soil, and the right to universal and effective access to vital resources. Future generations are entitled to their transmission.

IX

Humankind has the right to peace, the peaceful settlement of disputes, and the right to human security in all dimensions, specifically environment, food, sanitation, economy and politics. This right is aimed in particular at preserving succeeding generations from the scourge of war.

X

Humankind has freedom of choice to determine its fate. This right is exercised by taking the long term into account, especially where rhythms inherent to humanity and nature are concerned, in collective choices.

THE DUTIES TOWARDS HUMANITY

XI

The present generations have a duty to ensure respect for the rights of humankind as well as of all living species. The rights of mankind as a whole and human rights are indivisible and applicable to all future generations.

XII

The present generations, who are guarantors of resources, ecological balance, and of the common, natural, cultural, tangible and intangible heritage have a duty to ensure that this legacy is preserved and that it be used cautiously, responsibly and equitably.

XIII

To ensure the sustainability of life on Earth, the present generations have a duty to make every effort to preserve both the atmosphere and climate balance and to prevent, as much as possible, the displacement of people resulting from impact on the environment, and to otherwise rescue and protect the affected people.

XIV

The present generations have a duty to guide scientific and technical progress towards the preservation and health of mankind and other species. To this end, they must, in particular, ensure that any access and use of biological and genetic resources altogether respects human dignity, traditional knowledge and the maintenance of biodiversity.

XV

All States and other public and private stakeholders and entities have the duty to integrate the long-term perspective in their policies and to promote sustainable human development. This development, as well as the principles, rights and duties set forth in this Declaration shall be advanced through awareness raising, education and implementation initiatives.

XVI

All States have the duty to ensure the effectiveness of the principles, rights and duties proclaimed by this declaration, including through the implementation of appropriate mechanisms.

PART 5. PROTECTING THE HUMAN CONDITION OF FUTURE GENERATIONS, A NEW LEGAL QUESTION?

In the fifth Part, the book raises new and particularly difficult philosophical and legal questions involving transhumanism, the advent of a new ideology with multiple faces that aims to "improve" the human being and create a new humanity.

Judge Christian Byk describes posthumanism as the mere continuation of questions about social perfectibility that have been confronted by philosophers throughout our history. He considers whether the law can play a role by organizing human life around the concept of improved human capacity instead of sociability and, thus, becoming a medium for paradigm-shifting technoscientific changes that alter human nature? Recognizing that the boundaries of the law are being rebuilt on new criteria such as the rights of future generations, Byk characterizes transhumanism as a political question. He concludes that the law can either serve as a place of resistance and resilience, or a vehicle that facilitates transhumanism through regulation that helps democratize technoscience – for example, through a hybrid governance system that combines the political, legal, ethical and expertise-based dimensions of these transformative developments (essay #17 on "Law and the Idea of Human Perfectibility").

Professor Louise Vandelac considers transhumanism through a less neutral and far more critical lens, describing efforts to "improve" Humankind as a form of anthropocide that goes alongside the ecocide represented by our intertwined climate, biodiversity, energy, resources, health and fertility crises. She suggests that fantasies about transhumanism sap the limited time, resources, and collective imagination that will be required to confront our existing environmental and human rights challenges with the necessary sense of solidarity and empathy (essay #18 on "The Posthumous Post-human, or Abolishing The Future of Generations: By What Right?").

Lecturer Amandine Cayol & Professor Emilie Gaillard further criticize transhumanist ideology as an echo of Nazi ideology. Cayol and Gaillard call for a new legal humanism, starting with global recognition of crimes against the human species drawing upon a French law providing that "the human body is inviolable" as a principle of human dignity for future generations that preserves the human species (essay #19 on "Transhumanism(s) & Law(s) First Tracks and Thoughts").

Christian BYK[1]

17. Law and the Idea of Human Perfectibility

"We have given you, O Adam, no visage proper to yourself, nor endowment properly your own, in order that whatever place, whatever form, whatever gifts you may, with premeditation, select, these same you may have and possess through your own judgement and decision. The nature of all other creatures is defined and restricted within laws which We have laid down; you, by contrast, impeded by no such restrictions, may, by your own free will, to whose custody We have assigned you, trace for yourself the lineaments of your own nature [...]. We have made you a creature neither of heaven nor of earth, neither mortal nor immortal, in order that you may, as the free and proud shaper of your own being, fashion yourself in the form you may prefer. It will be in your power to descend to the lower, brutish forms of life; you will be able, through your own decision, to rise again to the superior orders whose life is divine."[2]

Introduction

The question raised by posthumanism is only the continuation of the question of human perfectibility. For some Western philosophers, perfectibility is an integral part of human nature itself, and is what distinguishes human beings from other living species. But what sort of perfectibility is referred to? The sources demonstrate that we have so far taken it to be social perfectibility. However, the twentieth century, because of excesses in the focus on progress, as well as on political systems that were meant to be "scientific", has led to a certain

1 Secretary General, International Association of Law, Ethics and Science. The association is an international and multidisciplinary network dedicated to reflection on politics in the field of the ethics of sciences and techniques. It publishes a quarterly bilingual journal, the Journal international de bioéthique et d'éthique des sciences [International Journal of Bioethics and of the Ethics of Sciences], Eska Publishing Co., *available online at* http://eska-publishing.com/fr/.

2 G.P. della Mirandola, *Oration on the Dignity of Man*, Gateway Editions, Regnery Publishing, 1996, translation A.R. Gaponigri.

disillusionment. Conversely, a technoscientific revolution would give humanity a new assurance, enabling it to break away from History and rebuild its destiny with the notion of improvement. (*See* Part I below.)

What role does law play in this change of paradigm? To respond, we need to question law not only as a system of thought, but also as the system of standards through which we organize our social structure. Is law able to organize human life such that the idea of its perfectibility is based on the improvement not of sociability but of capacities? Is law capable of becoming the medium of new technoscientific changes that affect human nature? (*See* Part II below.)

I. Is Law Undergoing an Ideology and Identity Change?

The sociologist Karin Knorr-Cetina asserts that we are now entering a "culture of life" where identities and society are thought of in biological terms, perhaps breaking away from modern "society culture".[3] Law, which thus far had participated in a cultural and political construction of mankind's future (*see* Section I.A. below), becomes the instrument of the perfectibility of human existence (*see* Section I.B. below).

A. Law and the Construction of Social Perfectibility

Perfectibility is a philosophical and religious ideal which has always inspired humanity in its Earthly project, and which has pervaded law.

1. *The Ideal of Social Perfectibility*

The question of perfectibility is a heritage rooted in ancient philosophical sources that were transformed during the Enlightenment.

a. *Ancient Sources*

How can we distinguish between humans and other animals? Philosophy has suggested several criteria: the hand (Anaxagoras),[4] politics (Aristotle),[5] and

---

3 K. Knorr-Cetina, "*Au-delà des Lumières : l'essor d'une culture de la vie*" [Beyond the Enlightenment: the Rise of a Culture of Life], *in* A. Kahn, E. Agazzi, G. Hottois & C. Djerassi (eds.), *Biologie moderne et visions de l'Humanité* [*Modern biology and visions of Humanity*], De Boeck, 2004, p. 31.

4 "[M]an is the most intelligent of animals because he posseses hands". Aristotle, *Parts of Animals*, Harvard University Press, 1961, translated by A.L. Peck & F.H.A. Marshall, p. 373 (quoting Anaxagoras).

5 M. Dufour, "L'homme animal politique" [Man the Political Animal], *in Bulletin de L'association Guillaume Budé*, 1928, Vol. 18, No. 1, pp. 35–37.

language.[6] But it is reason that seems to have prevailed over the other criteria (living "under the guidance of reason", Spinoza).[7] However, the Greeks and Romans did not extend this consideration to slaves or barbarians. It was Christianity that recognised this essential characteristic as constituting the essence of all human beings.[8] However, the Christian distinction between "fallen humanity" and a "regenerated humanity" through the Church, only accorded the possibility of perfectibility through reason to the latter.[9]

It was the philosophy of the Enlightenment that, by dissociating the concept of human nature from original sin, human nature acquired a historical dimension – i.e., perfectibility.

b. The Enlightenment and the Emergence of Historical Perfectibility

Perfectibility, a power granted to man to act upon his own nature, is not only recognition of the concept of progress applied to civilised man, it is also, according to Rousseau, the discovery of mankind's paradoxical erring between a return to and a departure from nature.

---

6 E. Cassan, "La raison chez Descartes, puissance de bien juger" [Descartes' Reason, the Power to Judge Well], *Le Philosophoire*, 2007/1, No. 28, p. 252.

7 "There is no individual thing in nature, which is more useful to man, than a man who lives in obedience to reason". B. de Spinoza, *On the improvement of the Understanding/The Ethics/Correspondence*, Dover Books, 1955, translated by R.H.M Elwes, Proposition XXXV, Corollary I.

8 "There is neither Jew nor Gentile, neither slave nor free, nor is there male and female, for you are all one in Christ Jesus". Galatians 3:28, *New International Version Biblical Theology Study*.

9 Saint Augustin (354–430) describes the four steps of Christian life as follows: "(1) L'Humanité avant la chute (innocence) est capable de pécher et de ne pas pécher; (2) L'Humanité après la chute est incapable de ne pas pécher (Humanité déchue); (3) L'Humanité régénérée (par la nouvelle naissance) est capable de ne pas pécher; (4) L'Humanité glorifiée (dans le ciel) est incapable de pécher" [1. Humankind before the fall (innocence) is capable of sinning and not sinning; 2. Humankind after the fall is incapable of not sinning (fallen humanity); 3. Humankind regenerated (by the new birth) is capable of not sinning; 4. Humankind which is glorified (in heaven) is incapable of sinning]. *Le Manuel de St Augustin traduit en Français*, Paris, 1658, translated by C. de Sercy, Manual of St. Augustin (Enchiridion and Laurentius), ch. 118, *available online at* http://www.ewtn.com/library/PATRISTC/PNI3-5.HTM (accessed 27 June 2019).

Taken in its primary sense, the notion of perfectibility may be seen as a kind of "anthropological optimism of the Enlightenment"[10]: it represents the capacities mankind has deployed to rise above his original capabilities. But above all this optimism inverts the order of things because it once more puts "man at the centre of Creation, [...] he becomes the embodiment of a policy of conquest, (and) improvement is [...] secularised".[11]

Jean-Jacques Rousseau speaks of perfectibility as "the ability to improve oneself", an ability that only develops with time and the exercise of freedom in accordance with one's needs and passions; hence, the essential role of education in this passage from a natural to a social state. According to Rousseau, this passage does not make mankind freer or happier because he is corrupted by society.[12] Rousseau's thoughts would later be mocked by Voltaire,[13] but were essentially embraced by Immanuel Kant[14] – who replaced Rousseau's somewhat pessimistic vision with anthropological and historical optimism.

Culture is thus ambivalent: it can be a factor in emancipation just as it can warp. But does not law itself contain this duality? It frees those who are enslaved by the harsh realities of life and at the same time brings restrictions to individual interests with a view to safeguarding the common good.

2. *The Function of Law in the Face Social Perfectibility*

It is the legacy of Rousseau and of Kant that nourishes this vision of law as having two essential characteristics: a political dimension and universal scope.

---

10 F. Lotterie, "*Les Lumières contre le progrès? La naissance de l'idée de perfectibilité*" [*Enlightenment Against Progress? The Birth of the Idea of Perfectibility*], Dix-huitième Siècle [Eighteenth Century], 1998, Vol. 30, No. 1, p. 384.

11 *Ibid.*, pp. 385–86.

12 J.J. Rousseau, *Discours sur l'origine et les fondements des inégalités parmi les hommes* [*Discourse on the Origin and Foundations of Inegality Among Men*], Folio essais, Gallimard, Paris, 1989.

13 Letter of 30 August 1755 from Voltaire to Jean Jacques Rousseau, *in* Voltaire, *Œuvres complètes de Voltaire* [*Complete Works of Voltaire*] Vol. 38, Letter No. 3000, Garnier, pp. 446–450.

14 *See* his analysis of the pragmatic disposition of man "in the progress of civilisation through culture," I. Kant, *Anthropologie du point de vue pragmatique* [*Anthropology from a Pragmatic Point of View*], Garnier-Flammarion, 1993, p. 312.

a. *Organising Society in a Rational and Political Way*

Freedom, in the sense of reason in action, is the basis of the human condition. It is in the framework of the "social contract" that mankind renounces natural liberty in favour of civil and moral liberty.[15] Kant extends this idea by proclaiming that the duty of the State consists in guaranteeing liberty and that national laws need to be confronted with democratic principles. This is the Rule of Law.

b. *Promoting Universalism of Values and Rights*

The revolution of the Enlightenment consisted essentially in the proclamation of the universality of humanity: "Like truth, reason, and justice, human rights, the interest of property, and freedom and health are the same everywhere", according to Condorcet.[16] And for Rousseau, "When considering human nature, the true philosopher is neither an Indian, nor a Tartar, neither from Geneva nor from Paris, he is but a man".[17] As for Montesquieu, "I am necessarily a man, and only accidentally am I French".[18] The equality of all before the law – all citizens at least – is the consequence of this.

As formulated by Rousseau in 1755, [the notion of perfectibility aims at the improvement of human beings within, by and for society, at the heart of the modern democratic ideal [...] in favor of a fairer and more decent society].[19] Since then, several phenomena have undermined this idea: the failure of

---

15 Kant remembers Rousseau's project to replace nature by law in *The Social Contract*. *Cf.* S. Goyard-Fabre, *Kant et le problème du droit* [*Kant and the Problem of Law*], Librarie Philosophique J. Vrin, 1975.

16 N. de Condorcet, *Observations sur le XXIXe livre de l'Esprit des lois* [*Observations on the Twenty-Ninth Book of The Spirit of Laws*], *in* A.D. de Tracy, Complete Works, *Commentaire sur l'Esprit des lois de Montesquieu suivi d'Observations de Condorcet sur le vingt-neuvième livre de l'Esprit des lois* [*Commentary on the Spirit of the Laws of Montesquieu followed by Concordet's Observations on the Twenty-Ninth Book of the Sprirt of the Laws*], Librarie Philosophique J. Vrin, 2016, Vol. 7, Ch. 18.

17 *Lettre à M. Philopolis* [*Letter to M. Philopolis*], *in* J.J Rousseau, Complete Works, Vol. 1, Geneva, 1782, p. 183.

18 *Pensées* [*Montesquieu's Thoughts*], No. 1437, Folio, Gallimard, 2014.

19 Entretien avec Nicolas Le Dévédec, La perfectibilité humaine des Lumières au transhumanisme [Interview with Nicolas Le Dévédec, Human Perfectibility, from the Enlightenment to Transhumanism], *La Revue du projet*, No. 55, Mar. 2016, *available online at* http://projet.pcf.fr/85874 (accessed 16 June 2019) ("la notion de perfectibilité vise une amélioration de l'être humain dans, par et pour la société, au cœur de l'idéal démocratique moderne et des principaux combats sociaux et politiques en faveur d'une société plus juste et plus décente").

"liberating" ideologies, the persistence of destructive conflicts, the fragility of democracies and the rule of law, individualism, and the inability to master the negative effects of technoscience. In the face of its inability to change the world in the political sense,[20] technoscience has paved the way for a new conquest, that of life and the extension of life. It is, thus, that law is called upon to serve the perfectibility of life.

B. Law and the Construction of the Perfectibility of Life

The characteristics of this law derive from a new social philosophy.

1. *Towards a New Social Philosophy*

What we call "loss of meaning" or "quest for identity" is for philosophers "a complete reversal of the humanist ideal […], the idea now prevailing being the improvement no longer of society but of human beings and life itself".[21]

a. *The Predicted End of History: No Longer an Attempt to Change Society, but the Desire to Improve Life*

The failure of the ideologies that proferred social projects in order to fulfill the hopes of the Enlightenment is only too obvious. Thus, in response to the prospects offered by Karl Marx to "men of progress",[22] the "No" of the "totalitarian" ideologies of the twentieth century amounted to a dual sacrifice: that of the current generations, and that of the idea that our social life has meaning.

What, therefore, can remain of reason,[23] other than the disenchantment, even the nihilism, perhaps, that leads to the end of History[24] and, consequently, to

---

20 In 1845, Karl Marx rendered obsolete a certain practice of philosophy by writing, "jusqu'ici, les philosophes n'ont fait qu'interpréter le monde de différentes manières, ce qui importe, c'est de le transformer" [until now, philosophers have only interpreted the world in various ways; the point is to change it]. K. Marx, "Theses on Feuerbach", *in* K. Marx, M. Rubel & Gallimard, *Œuvres* [Works], Bibliothèque de la Pléiade coll., 1982, Vol. III (Philosophy), p. 1033. The failure of political commitment to protect an endangered future seems to have broken the prior revolutionary momentum.

21 *Ibid.*

22 N. Le Dévédec Interview, 2016.

23 K. Marx & others, 1982.

24 F. Fukuyama, *La fin de l'Histoire et le dernier des hommes* [*The End of History and the Last Man*], Flammarion, 1992.

the triumph of individual desire exacerbated by a globalised technoscientific society?[25]

b. The Triumph of "Desire" Over Reason

The philosophers of the Enlightenment defined an individual as a being for whom reason is the basis for action. However, a human being is more complex than this.

The unconscious, the emotions, our desires all play a role alongside intelligence in decision-making.[26] In addition, biology and genetics currently rival the social sciences in the attempt to understand what it is that makes us human. Modern man, while protected by his fundamental rights, feels an increasing liberation from the social constraints that once restricted freedom, proportional to the use to which he can put modern technology. Joyously caught up in the happy "whirlwind of life",[27] he seems to be living the Olympic motto "Citius, Altius, Fortius".[28]

In parallel with this quest for individual identity and happiness, social structures and the State are discovering their limits. Networks, which are more flexible, and new ways of working and doing business are emerging. The commitment to collective belonging is no longer aiming at a "new world" but at preserving the old world from new perils.

Thus, the rejection of a future founded on an "achievable" Utopia leaves us with the choice of either: living in the present with consumerist hedonism or, shutting ourselves in a past that is venerated as a lost paradise. Carried away by our lack of reason, law totters on its foundations and vacillates unsteadily, or splits itself in two, torn between two opposing directions.

---

25 J.-M. Besnier, "Le post-humanisme ou la fatigue d'être libre" [Posthumanism or the Fatigue of Freedom], *La pensée de midi*, 2010/1, No. 30, p.75.

26 For example, O. Houdé & L. Degos, "La psychologie cognitive et le rapport sience/politique pour mieux comprendre l'homme" [Cognitive Psychology and the Relationship Between Science and Politics as a Means of Understanding Man], Colloque Regard sur l'homme contemporain [A Look at Contemporary Man Conference], Institut de France, 7 June 2010; F. Clément & L. Kaufmann, *La sociologie cognitive* [*Cognitive Sociology*], Maison des Sciences de l'Homme, coll. "Cogniprisme", 2011, p. 371.

27 We cannot resist offering a little musical interlude at this half-way stage, with the theme tune from *Jules et Jim, available online at* https://www.youtube.com/watch?v=dcVcwwo8QFE.

28 "Faster, Higher, Stronger". We owe this motto to Dominican Father Henri Martin Didon, who coined it on 7 March 1891 at Arcueil, where he was prior, in his closing speech of the first championships of the *Ecole Albert-le-Grand* Athletics Association.

2. *Law's New Clothes*

"Grasp all, lose all". This is the lesson we may eventually learn from a legal system that has become imperialistic through its normative aims, while its function within society appears ambivalent, tending to "say less with more".

a. *Law Embraces All Forms of Life*

With law in the clutch of biology, perhaps indeed carried away by it, the two would seem to have become inseparable.[29] The rediscovery of the human body by the law[30] takes due account of the biological reality of the human being but also of the mastery by mankind of this reality as biology becomes the instrument of human ambitions for mankind's own future.[31] Not only is the failing body revitalised but predictive medicine is now taking shape. Beyond medicine, the beginnings of life (for instance the organisation of a family and parentage) are turned upside down, while there is also a desire to control the end of life.

"Customary" law, which is steeped in daily repetition over a long period, fades and gives way to a new legal system, one derived from a logic of the satisfaction of personal desires (which constitutes an interpretative approach of human rights) and from economic aspects – i.e., the dismembered body and its products are being subjected to a market economy, all be it a regulated one. Moreover, because of similarities between human biology and that of other forms of life, the boundaries of law are being rebuilt on new criteria – such as the rights of future generations, and protection of biodiversity as well as the biosphere. This is the law of the living.

b. *The Law of the Living: A Law of Principles and a Law of Techniques*

Every legal system is based on the values or choices of a society, even when these are not explicit because they seem so obvious, so "natural". This was the case for a long time with the requirement for a couple entering into marriage to be composed of a man and a woman.[32] The rise of the biological sciences and the

---

29 C. Puigelier & F. Gros, *Biologie et droit, les étapes du vivant* [*Biology and Law, the Stages of Life*], Bruylant, 2016.

30 C. Byk, "Les nouvelles frontières du corps" [The New Frontiers of the Body], *Revue générale de droit médical*, No. 63, Les Etudes Hospitalières, June 2017.

31 I. Arnoux, *Les droits de l'être humain sur son corps* [*The Rights of Humans over Their Bodies*], Presses Universitaires de Bordeaux, Pessac, 2003.

32 During the annulment procedure of the marriage of two people of the same sex (the "Bègles Marriage" case in 2007), the Court of Cassation explicitly judged that: "[According to French law, marriage is the union of a man and a woman; [...]

social transformations they cause led to a more explicit affirmation of the values or choices implied in law, either because (i) we wish them to be recognized,[33] or (ii) it seems necessary to set the law in stone after traditional understandings are violated by new social practices,[34] resulting in a proliferation of fundamental rights.[35]

But besides this "matrix law",[36] the law of life sciences appears like a technical law because its aim is essentially to "regulate" new technologies and not to question them, except for the "sacrifice" of certain utilizations, such as genetic tests for insurance or employment purposes. What is expected from the law is to ensure quality, safety, liability and compensation, with everything else coming under the heading of individual choice in a zone that no longer bows to the State.

How, in these conditions, can law find its way to preserving some degree of social linkage within society? Must it bring about the new human perfectibility or, adhering to its independence, venture along a path of resistance, at the risk that legal normativeness becomes the means towards a new social messianism?

II. The Place of Law in the Dynamic of Evolution

It is difficult for the jurist, more so than for the philosopher, to construct systems that are not based on concrete realities. All the same, even if a positivist, he still has the right to reflect on the world that is emerging based on what he encounters of the world that is disappearing and to respond to the following

---

this principle is not contradicted by any of the provisions of the European Convention on Human Rights or of the EU Charter of Fundamental Rights, which in France does not have binding force]" (*Cass. civ.1ère, 13 Mar. 2007*; *Grands arrêts* [*Major Judgments*], Dalloz, 2007, No. 32, p. 1697, note E. Agostini). Law No. 2013–404 of 17 May 2013 opening up marriage to persons of the same sex, put an end to this assumption of an obvious truth formally recognized at a time when it was no longer obvious!

33 The right to "marriage for all" in 2013 and, possibly, the right soon to medically assisted procreation for all!

34 For example, the prohibition of "surrogate motherhood".

35 B. Mathieu, "Droits fondamentaux et Science biomédicale : Les données d'une prise de conscience universelle" [Fundamental Rights and Biomedical Science: the Data on the Rise to Universal Consciousness], *Revue de l'Actualité Juridique Française*, 2000, *available online at* http://webcache.googleusercontent.com/search?q=cache:ezqq3UnPHukJ:www.rajf.org/spip.php%3Farticle24+&cd=3&hl=fr&ct=clnk&gl=fr.

36 In 1994, Professor Bertrand Mathieu first used the expression "matrix" principles with regard to the principles of unavailability, inviolability and anonymity inscribed in the laws of bioethics.

imperative: how can law continue to exist as a factor of fair social stability when it totters on its foundations and gets caught up in conflicting aims? (*See* Section II.A. below.) Should he be a legitimist with regard to a new social thought and help bring it about or, in order to defend a world that is disappearing, must he resist in order to maintain the values of the Old World – unless the notion of legal "resilience" has, as we ourselves think, a more positive meaning, that of a hybridization between technical practice and social values? (*See* Section II.B. below.)

A. Law and the Issue of "Human Enhancement"

Experience with the relationship between law and new technologies acquired over the last part of the twentieth century has brought to the fore a question about the development process of a legal rule.[37] This experience enables us to better understand what the role of law will be, and what expectations of law are likely to arise from the shift of the transhumanist philosophy from a bioethical to a biopolitical dimension.

1. *The New Social Position of Law: A Law Centred Upon Social Expectations*

Underlining the two tendencies that mold law – a manipulation for the benefit of the economy and State policies on the one hand, and a moralistic ambition on the part of "civil society" for fair laws on the other hand – Jürgen Habermas suggests that the challenge of this "paradoxical evolution" is to understand the social position of law as this in itself "constitutes an indicator of what law is, halfway between ethics and politics, unable to be reduced to either one or the other".[38]

A means of systemic regulation, the law also legitimizes social sub-systems (e.g., the market, the State) within a rationalized lived-in world. Far from being alien to it, its moral dimension is embedded in the very procedures of developing and enforcing norms. Thus, law in the contemporary world has the power "of colonisation of the lived-in world".

---

37 J. Hervois, *La production de la norme juridique en matière scientifique et technologique* [*The Production of Legal Standards for Science and Technology*], Thesis, University of La Rochelle, 2011, *available online at* https://tel.archives-ouvertes.fr/tel-00688129/document.

38 J. Habermas, "Law and Morality", *in The Tanner Lectures of Human Values*, Cambridge University Press, 1986, p 264.

Why would its relationship with the technoscientific subsystem of society be any different? In fact, the autonomy of law implies that it has the same ability to interrelate with the new realities of the world as these realities must reshape it. Nonetheless, this "refocusing" of law in response to transhumanism assumes that the latter has a political dimension.

2. *Trans/Posthumanism and "Human Enhancement": From the Bioethical Dimension to the Biopolitical Dimension*

Is considering the technoscientific society as a subsystem of the "lived-in world" not a way of acknowledging the political dimension of trans/posthumanism? The nature of the debate between the different tendencies in the trans/posthumanism movement seems to confirm this hypothesis.

a. *Why Is Trans/Posthumanism a Political Question?*

Gilbert Hottois maintains that one should neither avoid transhumanist ideas nor treat them with contempt but, on the contrary, take them seriously.[39] The first essential is to differentiate between the idea of transhumanism and that of posthumanism, as this enables us to gauge the change from an ethical to a political dimension in the matter of "human enhancement".

Transhumanism and Posthumanism

For Hottois, "what characterises transhumanism is the reference to ethics [...]. Its main aim is the enhancement of human beings, not their transformation [...] or, worse still, elimination. The transhumanist ethic is not in itself original: it derives from utilitarian ways of thinking and draws upon the legacy of the Enlightenment [...]. Transhumanism seeks to reconcile ethics, technoscience and Evolution".[40]

"In autonomous posthumanism, we often find a straightforward cross between technoscience and Evolution (because it is) inclined towards an experimentalism that does not worry about the preservation of the human species or its values". It is this approach that is problematic because it potentially paves the way for radical changes in the political organization of society.

39 G. Hottois, *Philosophie et idéologies trans/posthumanistes* [*Trans/Posthumanist Philosophy and Ideology*], Librarie Philosophique J. Vrin, 2017, p. 286.
40 *Ibid.*, p. 291.

Ethical and Political Dimensions

> Transhumanism has an undeniably philosophical and ethical dimension since it invites us to confront the unfathomable aspects of the human condition. Yet "most human beings allow themselves to be blinded and forget or deny this unfathomable side as much through entertainment as through work (and) embrace the fillers that society, culture, tradition, religion and ideologies offer them".[41]

However, transhumanism shifts from this ethical dimension to a biopolitical dimension by offering to replace outdated "symbolic transcendence" with alternatives offered by technoscience. This shift is not risk-free but "the dangers are not consubstantial to the techniques and anthropotechniques themselves; they are related to the moral, economic and political organisation of society (and) the law that will regulate the anthropotechniques".[42]

This is why it is important to know the currents of thought behind the "transhumanism politics", as each one is likely to orient law in a different way.

b. The Main "Political" Currents of Transhumanism

Analysis of the writings and social projects of transhumanists allows them to be classified into five different ideological currents of thought.

First, and oldest, is the *neoliberal and libertarian* current of thought[43] – which asserts that utilization of human enhancement techniques cannot be decided by the State since these involve philosophical and religious beliefs that belong to individual freedom of choice.

Second, *social transhumanism* addresses issues related to inequalities – embracing the belief that human enhancement could provide solutions to them even if, at a transitional level, certain inequalities might increase.

Third, *technoprogressive* thought "believes that the acceleration of change triggers as many serious risks as benefits but that we can maximise the benefits and minimise the risks through public policy".[44]

---

41 *Ibid.*

42 *Ibid.*, p. 297.

43 R. Nozick, *Anarchy, State and Utopia*, Presses Universitaires du France, 1988; R. Bailey, "For Enhancing People", *in The Transhumanist Reader*, John Wiley & Sons, 2013.

44 D. Wood, "Four political futures: which will you choose?", *Transpolitica*, 24 July 2015, *available online at* https://transpolitica.org/2015/07/24/four-political-futures-which-will-you-choose/.

Fourth, *technoskeptical* thought admits that there has been rapid technoscientific change since the end of the twentieth century, but considers that the consequences of this need must be put into perspective.

Conversely, fifth, the *technoconservative* current of thought argues that technology will inflict terrible damage on the planet and, consequently, considers it necessary to slow down this change.[45]

This overview demonstrates that the "traditional" political families are shuffled around by transhumanist ideas since the bioconservative camp is as full of religious traditionalists as it is of environmentalists, while the other side of the spectrum attracts as many neo-liberals as advocates of the welfare state. It is from the directly opposing influences of these diverse currents of thought that a seemingly bipolar vision of law emerges.

B. The Two Faces of Law

Depending on whether technologies favoring human enhancement have the support of the different movements or not, any new law will appear as either the introducer of posthumanism or a factor of resilience opposed to it.

---

45 "L'une des principales oppositions soulevée à l'égard de l'augmentation humaine par les bioconservateurs tient au risque qu'elle ferait porter aux droits fondamentaux de l'être humain" [One of the principle objections raised by bioconservatives to the idea of human augmentation is the risk that it poses to the fundamental rights of human beings], N. Le Dévédec & F. Guis, "L'humain augmenté, un enjeu social" [The Enhanced Human, a Social Issue], *Sociologies*, 19 Nov. 2013, para. 10, *available online at* http://sociologies.revues.org/4409 (author's translation). Describing transhumanism as "l'idée la plus dangereuse au monde" [the most dangerous idea in the world], political scientist Francis Fukuyama, like philosopher Leon Kass and other thinkers including George J. Annas, Lori B. Andrews and Rosario M. Isai, defend the idea that "l'être humain se définit par une nature, au sens biologique du terme, sur laquelle s'étaierait l'idée même de dignité humaine" [the human being is defined by nature, in the biological sense of the word, and from this derives the very concept of human dignity]. *Ibid.* (citing F. Fukuyama, "Transhumanism: The World'[s] Most Dangerous Idea", *Foreign Policy*, 2004, No. 144, pp. 42–43; L. Kass, *Life, Liberty, and the Defense of Dignity: The Challenge for Bioethics*, San Francisco, Encounter Books, 2002; G. Annas, L.B. Andrews & R.M. Isasi, "Protecting the Endangered Human: Toward an International Treaty Prohibiting Cloning and Inheritable Alterations", *American Journal of Law and Medicine*, 2002, No. 28, pp. 151–178.

1. *Law, The Introducer of "Posthumanism"*

An analysis of what the concept of human enhancement covers reveals the different ways in which positive law could be useful to it, as well as its limitations.[46]

a. The Enhancement of Abilities

The enhancement of abilities is the possibility of using the progress of medicine in both a medical and a non-medical context. Its objectives are concrete and relate to physical as well as cognitive abilities, to lifespan and to quality of ageing. It of course raises ethical questions, such as whether the prescription of a growth hormone to "undersized" children in order to help them reach a "normal size" is acceptable. It is worth noting that law tends to face this challenge by condoning medical uses that have a social purpose (e.g., abortion) and often only prohibits obvious abuse.

b. The Enhancement of Human Nature

"The enhancement of human nature elicits a discussion that is more abstract",[47] but also more controversial. Indeed, "the idea of altering human nature is often presented as a project that is incompatible with a religious vision of the world ('Playing God') or with a respectful conception of Nature".[48] It would threaten the anthropological nature of mankind and blur the distinction between the human species, other species, and artifacts endowed with artificial intelligence. Moreover, it would increase inequalities in terms of access to these technologies, effectively creating obsolete, non-enhanced humans.

No legislation to date has openly supported this particular current of thought. On the other hand, numerous laws at both national and international level have strictly prohibited human cloning, embryo research, eugenics, gender selection and endangerment of the human species.

c. Self Enhancement

Finally, self enhancement "is on a different level [...], of quest for identity".[49] This can be as much an individual quest for meaning as the reminder of a common,

---

46 S. Bateman & J. Gayon, "L'amélioration humaine : trois usages, trois enjeux" [The Improvement of Humans: Three Applications, Three Objectives], *Médecine/Sciences*, Vol. 28, No. 10, Oct. 2012, p. 887, *available online at* http://www.philosophie.ens.fr/IMG/Bateman%20Gayon%20M%C3%A9decine%20Sciences.pdf.

47 *Ibid.*

48 *Ibid.*

49 *Ibid.*

Promethean quest. In the latter case, it would be "the continuity of the 'American dream'" since, "according to Tocqueville, Americans, in contrast to Europeans, do not look to their ancestors to guide their choices, but to their own judgment and public opinion".[50] But we could also see it as consistent with a European vision, one permeated by a culture of progress and liberation.

Whatever the specifics, the principle of freedom and its corollaries – in other words, the principles of equality and non-discrimination – open up the possibilities for such an approach. But can we then follow that path without asking the following question: what do we do when individual choices come into conflict with social acceptability? We may think that restoring the eyesight of a blind person or getting a physically disabled person to walk will be welcomed, while being fully aware of the discrimination transgender people suffer in our society. Is there not an additional risk of drifting from self enhancement into moral enhancement of oneself and of others? Might we make a violent person less violent or reintegrate into the community someone who promotes an "asocial ideology"?

It is true that new boundaries for the body[51] have led to changes in the scope of individual freedoms, both in family law and in health law. Nevertheless, the law remains a constraining factor even when rid of certain former concepts, because the profusion of standards and legal subsystems compounds its complexity and autonomy.[52] With its consent or without it, law is a place of resistance – even of resilience[53] – against change.

2. *Law as a Factor of Resilience*

What exactly does law resist? The transition to a transhumanist society (as the last protector of humanist values), or the advent of a society free of law (because, deep down, it no longer believes in the idea of human perfection), or the advent of a world without social class, inequality and injustice? In the one case its

---

50 C. Eliott, *Better than Well: American Medicine Meets the American Dream*, W.W. Norton & Company, New York, 2004.

51 H. Hurpy, "L'identité et le corps" [Identity and the Body], *La Revue des droits de l'homme*, 2015. Issue No. 8, *available online at* http://journals.openedition.org/revdh/1601; C. Byk, 2017, pp. 33–89.

52 C. Byk, "Droit et complexité: l'exemple du bio-droit" [Law and Complexity: the Example of Biolaw], *Revue de la Recherche Juridique – Droit prospectif*, 2016–4, Presses Universitaires Aix-Marseilles, p. 1537.

53 J. Dacheux, "Résistance et résilience" [Resistance and Resilience], *available online at* http://jeanpierredacheux.blogspot.fr/2010/08/resilience-et-resistance.html.

resistance is of an ideological type, while in the other it stems from an attitude of suspicion towards all ideologies, with law being of necessity the guarantor of social balance.

a. Resilience as the Rejection of Transhumanism

Bioconservatism "is an ideology that advocates total opposition to the idea of enhancement because of the uncontrollable risks involved […]. Instead of exerting ourselves to implement simple and common-sense solutions, we fall for the technoscientific lure […]. We may gain abundant electronic and chemical gratification, but we lose our souls in the process [… and] also our lives, if certain of the risks capable of affecting our existence become reality".[54] The radical nature of this view and the designation of a clear objective give this ideology appeal, as it positions itself as the last defense of humanist values and invites us to become the heroes, if need be the martyrs, of this ultimate battle before the changeover to an entirely different world.

Directing law towards this path would however be a serious error. In the first place, this position *denies the irreversibility of certain changes*. Bioconservatism wants not only the rate of technological change to be slowed down or even, in some cases, halted, but also to invert the relationship between ideology and science. In other words, ideology should dictate to science what it should and should not do. Bioconservatism leads to only one possible solution: stopping everything, or even turning backwards.

In the second place, the diversity of values and interests underlying the bioconservative ideology makes it such a nebulous affair that it cannot put forward a coherent political project. While traditionalist Catholics and feminists may agree to oppose the medicalization of the beginning of life, it is far from certain that this alliance could successfully develop a social project surrounding "new parenthood". Bioconservatism therefore appears to embody powerful resilience through its language but seems somewhat inefficient and even dangerous in its application. From a pragmatic point of view, resilience can offer no more than a means of regulating transhumanism.

54 D. Wood, 2015.

b. *Resilience as Regulation of Transhumanism: Technology and Democracy, the Realization of Fundamental Rights and the Search for a New Organisation of Democracy*

We concentrate here on two aspects: respect for social values, and the search for a new organization of democracy.

(1) Respect for Social Values

Regulating resilience – in the sense that it expresses neither systematic approval nor systematic opposition to all the utilizations of new technologies – does not translate as ideological relativism but, rather, as a policy that is rooted in social values and that applies them via a dynamic of action. If Jean Le Bon had not lost the battle of Poitiers in 1356, I would readily adopt the words of the future Philip the Bold to represent the role of law in action: "Father, beware on your right! Father, beware on your left!" Wherever they come from, we need to see the blows coming in order to win the battle of the future – a battle that is neither short term (deprived of vision), nor long term (with a scope so unfathomable that we can make no dent in it even though we cannot ignore it either), but medium term; that is, of a period of 20 to 50 years. We, therefore, need to civilize transhumanism in the light of the search for new organisations for the democritization of technoscience.

(2) A New Organization of Democracy[55]

How can we imagine that population aging and the rise of neurodegenerative diseases will not have an influence on the nature and functioning of the

55 N. Le Dévédec, "La démocratie à l'épreuve du posthumain: médicalisation de la société, dépolitisation de la perfectibilité" [Democracy Facing the Test of Posthumanism: Medicalisation of Society and Depolitisation of Perfectibility], 2009, *in* A. Sniadecki, *Dossier critique du transhumanisme* [*Critical dossier on transhumanism*], 2016, p. 56, *available online at* https://archive.org/stream/DossierCritiqueDuTranshumanisme/Dossier_Transhumanisme#page/n13/mode/2up. *See also* B. Laurent, "Des assemblages incertains aux technologies de démocratie : deux modalités de l'expérience démocratique" [From Uncertain Assemblies to Technologies of Democracy: Two Modes of Democratic Experience], *Quaderni*, Autumn 2012, Issue No. 79 (Produire la démocratie), p. 81; P. Vercauteren, "Gouvernance et démocratie : quel ordre?" [Governance and democracy: what order?], *in Fédéralisme, Régionalisme*, 2007, Vol. 7, No. 2 – Société civile, globalisation, gouvernance; L. Cardinal & C. Andrew, *La démocratie à l'épreuve de la gouvernance* [*Democracy Facing the Test of Governance*], University of Ottawa Press, 2000, Ottawa.

democratic system while already in many countries the younger age groups have lost all interest in voting?[56] How can we believe in the expression of political choices by a sovereign people when algorithms can predict collective and individual behaviour?[57] What type of role and social legitimacy are left to more rigid institutional organisations such as States and international organizations, by the networks[58] developed through communication technologies?[59]

As always, there are more questions than answers because the validity of answers can only be confirmed by experience. In this regard, the social phenomenon constituted by bioethics or risk management on an international scale offers an interesting field of study.

However, good governance is by no means the same thing as democracy of governance, and the large step from the one to the other is what keeps us grounded within Humanity. If good governance is undoubtedly capable of applying new technologies efficiently (optimizing costs and social objectives), it is democracy that can be expected to maintain and nurture the social relationships that experience the transformative nature of these technologies.

---

56 A. Parant, "Les enjeux du vieillissement de la population" [The Isssues of an Aging Population], *Revue française d'administration publique*, 2005/1, no. 113, p. 208.

57 Office of the Privacy Commissioner of Canada, "The Age of Predictive Analysis: From Patterns to Predictions", Report, Aug. 2012, *available online at* https://www.priv.gc.ca/media/1755/pa_201208_f.pdf.

58 In other words, the "giants" of the Web: Google, Apple, Facebook, Amazon, Microsoft.

59 P. Ségur & S. Piéré-Frey (eds.), *L'Internet et la démocratie numérique : Études* [*The Internet and Digital Democracy: Collected Studies*], Presses Universitaires de Perpignan, 2016. Although neither national nor international public institutions stay passive. Thus, for example, the Danish Minister for Foreign Affairs announced on 26 January 2017 the creation of the post of "Digital Ambassador" to Silicon Valley, to represent his country's interests among the Web giants. And on the subject of the protection of individual rights, the European Court of Human Rights ruled that, when it came to employees using their company's Internet for private emails, "an employer's instructions cannot reduce private social life in the workplace to zero" without striking a "proper balance" beween respect for the private life of staff and the rights of the employer to take measures to ensure smooth running of the company, which implies, in this particular context, the obligation to giver prior notification to staff that the Inernet was "monitored". *Barbulescu v. Romania*, No. 61496/08, European Court of Human Rights, Grand Chamber, 5 Sep. 2017.

Conclusion

Law is undeniably undergoing a change in its relationship with the idea of perfectibility: it is aware of the turning of a page in history,[60] yet is unsure which path to take.

However, if setting out all the arguments is necessary in order to reduce unjustified fears as well as disproportionate hopes, do we still have time to demystify the idea of human enhancement? What should we say to people who believe that "when the collapse of the species appears as a conceivable possibility, the situation of emergency will not be compatible with our lengthy and complex deliberative processes? In a state of panic, will the Western world not infringe its values of freedom and justice [...]"?[61]

Maybe we should "speak the truth" and prepare ourselves for a hybrid governance that combines political, legal, ethical and expertise-based dimensions? A humanism that recognises only History and not Evolution would give rise to an in-part obsolete vision of mankind while, "contributing to an updated image of mankind and its place in the universe [...], transhumanism [...] is [...] a humanism that is able to extend, diversify and improve indefinitely".[62]

---

60 "[Having given himself whole to the becoming world, God has no more to give: it is our turn now to give to him]". H. Jonas, *Le concept de Dieu après Auschwitz* [*The Concept of God After Auschwitz*], Payot et Rivages, 1994.

61 M. Rocard, D. Bourg & F. Augagneur, "Le genre humain, menacé" [The Human Race Threatened], *Le Monde*, 3 Apr. 2011.

62 G. Hottois, 2017, p. 302.

Louise VANDELAC

18. The Posthumous Post-Human, or Abolishing the Future of Generations: By What Right?

"Everything swallows me up".

R. Ducharme,

[The Swallower Swallowed],

Hamilton, 1967, p. 1,

Translation of L'Avalée des avalés by B. Bray.[1]

If Emilie Gaillard suggested that we should close this conference by launching open debates on transhumanism, she obviously had a feeling that the rights of future generations are about to collide, to be carried away – in fact, to get "swallowed" by our "sortie en douce de l'espèce humaine" [smooth and ongoing escape out of human kind], with transhumanism as one of its most troubling features.

She presumably also knows that we are running out of time. It took us 70 years to recover from the horrors of the Nazi extermination camps, the atomic bombings on Hiroshima and Nagasaki and the 60 to 70 million deaths of the Second World War. But we have only just begun to grasp the extent of the insidious war on the living world, attacking the very conditions of the regeneration of living environments, to the point of constituting, henceforth, a risk to ourselves. How then, likewise, are we to gauge the transhumanist wave that is crashing down on all humans – which, while intending to "improve" humankind, is about to undermine its foundations and thus risk its destruction? In a nutshell, how can we still, before it is too late, avoid being swept away by the great maelstrom of the intertwined climate and biodiversity crises emerging from the Anthropocene, as

1 This title and these first words of the novel by the Quebec writer Réjean Ducharme, capture all the burden of anxiety of this imperceptible slipping outside of ourselves. Would he have already grasped that much, in 1967?

well as from a transhumanist tsunami aiming to boot us out of humanity? How can we avoid the perils of ecocide as well as anthropocide? Can we hope for our laws to slow down the pace, divert the trajectory or even criminalize them?[2]

We therefore understand the unspeakable urgency to grasp the meaning of these tangled mutations of the living, to recognize their effects of fascination – as indeed they stun our thought itself – leaving us without words and without a voice. That is why it is important to understand the issues that play out, and that play with us, and to identify some keys to understanding. Hence also the importance of exploring what lies hidden there; in particular, this planned and soulless way to jettison entire populations into the hell of sub-humanity, which some transhumanists contrive to make their stepping stone. We are thus called upon from all sides – and so is the law.

In 1991, legal scholar Catherine Labrusse-Riou posed the following question:

> Does our law enable us to take care of future generations and apply the "Responsibility Principle", introduced by the philosopher Hans Jonas as an imperative, when in fact the law rather is taken up by the other aspect of science, that which, in the short term, aims for technical conquest, appropriation, production and exploitation of the living, including the human race, and which therefore meets concerns of ideology and economy?[3]

What is on the horizon?

In 2016, twenty-five years later, Jacques Testart, a watchful critic of the impact of technoscience on reproduction and on the future of the world, states that

---

2 L. Vandelac, "Sortir en douce de l'humanité. Pour une écologie politique du vivant" [The Smooth and Ongoing Escape out of Human Kind: for a Political Ecology of the Living], *Le Devoir*, 7 Oct., 2000, reprinted under "Nous risquons de sortir en douce de l'espèce humaine" [We Risk Slipping Out of Human Kind], *le Courrier international, Spécial Nouveau millénaire*, l'Homme-Dieu, Enquête sur la fabrique du surhumain. No. 529–530, 21 Dec.-5 Jan. 2000, p. 50; Revised and expanded version: L. Vandelac, "Menace sur l'espèce humaine […] ou démocratiser le génie génétique" [Threaten the Human Species … or Democratize Genetic Engineering], *Futuribles*. Paris, 2001, pp. 5–26.

3 C. Labrusse-Riou, "L'enjeu des qualifications: la survie juridique de la personne" [The Stake of Qualifications: the Legal Survival of the Person], *in Droits, La revue française de théorie juridique*, 1991, p. 20 ("Notre droit sait-il prendre en charge les générations futures et mettre en œuvre 'le principe Responsabilité' que le philosophe Hans Jonas nous présente comme impératif, alors que le droit est plutôt saisi par l'autre aspect de la science, celui qui, à court terme, vise la conquête technique, l'appropriation, la production et l'exploitation du vivant, humain compris, et qui rencontre alors l'idéologie et l'économie ?"), translated by Marie Noonan.

"[transhumanism advances as much through moral desertion as through desires for power]" and its "[advances are insidious because there are no clear stages for us to realize that we should worry]".[4]

Of course, the main themes of transhumanism were already charted starting in the nineteenth century, but without our noticing that its advances (in gestation since the end of the 1950s) have gradually been unfolding and unfurling over the last decades. The themes of transhumanism subtly insinuate themselves into our heads and our lives – especially into the lives of our children, who are glued to their so-called "smart" tablets and phones – interspersed with video games, widgets and friendly robots, "emoticons", substitutes of artificial intelligence (AI) and artificial emotions,[5] along with strange ego-portraits, sometimes seemingly taking the place of politics for certain heads of state. How many hours a day do we spend with the Web giants and with digital disruption, which shape our understanding of the world? And what will tomorrow bring?

The control and power of seduction exercised by the big data universe and augmented reality are so strong that they already know almost everything about our profiles and preferences, which they sometimes divert to their own benefit – shall we also, ourselves, share our medical details with them? As our thousands of daily clicks and tweets, weaving the digital web, feed off its infinite knowledge and the same time feed it with information, they thus consolidate unconceivable powers[6] and generate huge fortunes.[7] Indeed, the internet giants can both dictate their own law and multiply tax evasions – all while gleefully, with the apostles of AI, drawing on public funds, where the promises of the new Eldorado called artificial intelligence literally turn heads.[8] Masking powerful military, industrial

---

4 J. Testart & A. Rousseaux, *Au péril de L'Humain, les promesses suicidaires des transhumanistes* [*At the Risk of the Human, the Suicidal Promises of the Transhumanists*], Collections. Sciences ouvertes, Seuil, Paris, 2018, p. 9 ("le transhumanisme avance autant grâce à la désertion morale qu'aux désirs de puissance"; "avancées sont insidieuses car il n'existe pas d'étapes claires où il faudrait s'inquiéter"), translated by M. Noonan.

5 P. Aronson & J. Duportail, *The Quantify Hearth*, AEON, July 2018, *available online at* https://aeon.co/essays/can-emotion-regulating-tech-translate-across-cultures.

6 For example, the Cambridge Analytica Facebook scandal that siphoned the data of 87 million people.

7 According to *Forbes* Magazine, Jeff Bezos, the founder of *Amazon*, 54, has made US$120 billion between February 2017 and 2018. *See* J.-F. Nadeau, *Le Devoir*, 12 Mar. 2018, p. A3.

8 In Quebec, public money flows freely with hopes of ensuring the symbolic and financial success of AI: huge financial assistance, tax incentives and breaks, research grants of

and political stakes, people are entertained and distracted by self-driving cars, or the "intelligent" home, urgent marketing and growth priorities with poorly estimated impacts – as if AI were an inevitable but highly desirable fatality. Admittedly, like most socio-technical innovations, AI is not unequivocal; its innumerable applications already modify our everyday life so profoundly that it has become hard to do without it – which should not, however, prevent us from being aware of them.

Thus, somewhere out of the transhumanist nebula, billion-dollar markets open up, encompassing all kinds of experiments. These experiments range from banal computer applications to augmented reality (*via* deep learning, robots, artificial organs and avatars), on to human-machine hybridization. Credulous (and without really knowing it or wanting it), we move along on the discoursing clouds of life extension until "the death of death". We traverse from an ultra-performing body to horizons of cloning and cyborg, towards the singular Singularity: this historic moment when, around 2050, according to Ray Kurzweil, project manager at Google since 2012, human intelligence will be overtaken by the growth of technologies.[9]

As pointed out in a recent article published by *Foreign Affairs*, there is concern that AI has started overtaking human intelligence and is beginning to escape human control; Elon Musk emphasized the potentially disastrous consequences, particularly with respect to automatic weapons.[10] According to the same article, others fear that the industrial revolution of AI might replace humans by machines in all or most areas (ranging from transport to the army to health care). We shudder at the thought of a digital authoritarianism. AI could reshape our societies and redesign global geopolitics by providing States with sophisticated monitoring and automatic learning tools that facilitate the free flow of information for economically productive activities, while maintaining high levels of social

---

$94 million – in 2016 for IVADO 2018 [Institute for Data Valorization], digital action plan of 1.186 billion among others to strengthen the position in artificial intelligence, not to mention the purchase of products by the public administrations. J. Gélinas & M. Moore, "L'intelligence artificielle, l'industrie de la promesse" [Artificial Intelligence, the Industry of Promises], *Le Devoir, Idées*, 16 July 2018.

9 J.-G. Ganascia, "*Le mythe de la Singularité, Faut-il craindre l'intelligence artificielle ?*" [The Singularity Myth, Should we Fear Artificial Intelligence?], Seuil, Paris, 2017, p. 107.

10 In 2017, an open letter from *Tesla* CEO Elon Musk (along with about a hundred other robotics and AI researchers), called on the UN to banish such "weapons of terror" before they get out of control.

control at a reasonable cost.[11] Is this a dream or a nightmare? Programmed idleness, under the omnipresence of surveillance cameras and our mirror profiles drawn up by the keys of our keyboards – under the illusion that everything obeys our every word and move – in this brave new world where handmaids already wander around. How could we not be cynical, or not worry about it? But most people seem to prefer to wait and see, heedlessly thinking "It'll only be for the day after tomorrow. And after all they only want to improve us".

The path to Singularity (the antechamber of post-humanism) mobilizes, both literally and figuratively, unprecedented technical, economic and political means – the proliferation of patents, the privatization of common goods, the monopolization of scarce resources, the siphoning of public funds, and the accelerated erosion of the conditions of regeneration of the planet's creatures. It is a double movement of appropriation and loss of living conditions, deepening already abysmal socio-economic differences. And yet, the internet giants are praised, and their privileges multiplied. All while we silently witness the growing take-over of the world by artificial intelligence, holding the economy by invisible hand – already guiding more than 800 current geoengineering operations on climate, and experiments without safety nets (nor turning back from the synthetic biology of the species), accelerated since the advent of CRISPR-Cas9.[12]

In the meantime, as if caught on a hamster wheel, we turn in an obscene version of circular economy where (with the complacency of the States) producers of toxic molecules – directly linked to the epidemics of chronic diseases, cancers, accelerated loss of fertility,[13] and Autism-like

11 N. Wright, "How Artificial Intelligence Will Reshape the Global Order: The Coming Competition Between Digital Authoritarianism and Liberal Democracy", *Foreign Affairs*, 10 July 2018, *available online at* https://www.foreignaffairs.com/articles/world/2018-07-10/how-artificial-intelligence-will-reshape-global-order?cid=nlc-fa_fatoday-20180710.

12 The list of applications and the associated risks cannot be reproduced here, but let it be noted that, at the economic level, the use of CRISPR-Cas9 allows agrochemical giants, such as Dow/Dupont, Bayer/Monsanto and Syngenta, which already control 50% of the seed market, to multiply the patents on the technical processes, the seeds, the plants, the animals, livestock farming, even the yields, thus widening ever more their monopoly. Tech Biotech, 28/06/2018.

13 There has been a yearly decline of 1-3% per in spermatogenesis in European and North-American countries, where sufficient data exists to demonstrate this. Should this tendency persist, these statistics announce a reproductive breakdown by the end of the century. *See* S. Swann, "Sperm counts, testicular cancers, and the environment", *British Medical Journal*, 2017, 10 Oct. 2017 (359:j4517), *available online at* https://doi.org/10.1136/bmj.j4517.

disorders[14] – also provide miracle medicines and participate in the development of a personalized, sophisticated and expensive medicine. This circular economy grows to the boundless rhythm of people's needs and desires, from scalpel and implant driven body shaping[15] to the dismantling and marketing of procreation.[16] What a strange way ahead, where under the influences of fascination and stunned thought, the discourse of the apostles of transhumanism become commonplace; all the while imposing their tawdry tailor-made solutions on us.

I. Transhumanism Invades Our Sleepwalking Existence

Flashback: 7 August 2017, 6:00 a.m., Montreal. Coffee, newspaper, an ordinary morning; interrupted by the following secondary headline: "Mark Zuckerberg, fondateur et grand patron de Facebook, l'affirme : il ne sera pas candidat à la Maison-Blanche en 2020. Sauf qu'il ne cesse de quadriller les États-Unis et de recruter des stratèges démocrates" [Mark Zuckerberg, founder and CEO of

14 In Quebec, cases of children with Autism Spectrum Disorders (ASD) increased by 850% between 2001–2002 and 2014–2015 according to the *Ministère de la santé et des services sociaux* [Ministry of Health and Social Services] (MSSS, 2017). In Montérégie, the main agricultural region, the prevalence of children with ASD in schools was 1 child out of 46 in 2015–2016, compared to 1 out of 70 children in the province of Quebec. *See* M. Noiseux, "Fréquentation préscolaire chez les enfants de 0 à 4 ans de la MRC du Haut-Richelieu" [Pre-school attendance for children aged 0 to 4 in the Haut-Richelieu RCM], Portfolio thématique, Longueuil : Centre intégré de santé et services sociaux de la Montérégie-Centre, Direction de santé publique, Secteur Planification, évaluation et surveillance, 2017, *available online at* http://extranet.santemonteregie.qc.ca/userfiles/file/sante-publique/surveillance-etat-sante/Portrait-sante-anglophone-adulte.pptx

15 L. Vandelac, "De l'impensé du corps à sa mise en joue […] Chirurgies esthétiques ou l'effritement des limites" [From the Body Unthinkable to its Updating: Plastic Surgery and the Disappearance of Boundaries], *in Le lien social*, no. 59, Corps et Politiques, A. Quéniart & R. Hurtubise (éds.), 2008, pp. 125–137.

16 L. Vandelac, "Sexes et technologies de la reproduction 'Mères porteuses' ou la maternité déportée par la langue" [The Sexes and the Technologies of Procreation: "Surrogate Mothers" or the Appropriation of Motherhood through Language'], pp.168–197, reprinted in *Revue Illusio*, Numéro 8/9 Corps, Médecine, Santé, 439, p. 2012; L. Vandelac (ed.), "Clonage ou la traversée du miroir" [Cloning or Crossing the Mirror], *Le bord de l'eau* [The Edge of the Water], France, 2003, pp. 141–157, *in* I. Lasvergnas (ed.), *Éthique contemporaine et rationalité instrumentale* [Contemporary Ethics and Instrumental Rationality], Cahier de sociologie de l'UQAM, Éd. Liber, *available online at* https://www.erudit.org/en/journals/crs/2003-crs1517600/1002334ar.pdf.

Facebook, says he won't be running for the White House in 2020. However, he keeps criss-crossing the United States to recruit Democratic strategists].[17] After having to endure Trump's lies and tantrums, must we now also deal with the transhumanist fads of Facebook's naive founder (and fifth richest person in the world), who has stated that "l'un des principaux problèmes de Facebook est son 'idéalisme' parce qu'il n'a longtemps vu que les bons côtés de la connexion entre les personnes" [one of Facebook's biggest problems is its "idealism", because it has long seen only the good sides of connecting people]?[18]

Another flashback: 17 July 2016, in Montreal again, this time riveted to my computer. I watched the first *Novus Summit* chaired by Peter Diamandis, co-founder of the Singularity University. The summit was broadcast live from the United Nations (UN) headquarters in New York (UN Web TV). Legal scholar Emilie Gaillard brought the transmission to my attention while she was sitting in the audience at the UN amphitheater. Four months earlier, Gaillard had given a presentation to the UN about the draft *Universal Declaration of the Rights and Duties of Humankind* (which she had worked on under the direction of Corine Lepage)[19] – containing ideas directly opposed to the concepts expressed during the Novus Summit. Bearing that context in mind, Gaillard and I were both stunned into silence.

Was this a simple, symbolic poker bluff by Diamandis and Ray Kurzweil (who happens to be the co-president of a dozen companies with evocative names like: *Human Longevity Inc.*, which promotes gene and cell therapy; and *Planetary Resources*, which is involved in commercial developments of asteroid prospecting spacecraft)? For sure, this fabulous publicity stunt suggested that entry to the UN provided certain benefits to Kurzweil and Diamandis as co-founders of the Singularity University (which is financed by Nokia, Cisco, Genentech and

17 D. Hadni, "Zuckerberg se prépare-t-il à succéder à Trump ?" [Is Zuckerberg Preparing to Succeed Trump?], *Le Devoir*, 5 Aug. 2017, *available online at* https://www.liberation.fr/planete/2017/08/05/zuckerberg-se-prepare-t-il-a-succeder-a-trump_1588343. Among the consultants hired by its Chan Zuckerberg Initiative Foundation, with the noble goal to "advance human potential" were: former campaign directors and advisers of Bush and Obama, the former photographer of the White House and top dog in the Clinton polls.

18 "Facebook aurait besoin de 'quelques années' pour régler ses problèmes" [Facebook Would Need "a few years" to Solve its Problems], *Le Devoir*, 3 Apr. 2018, p. A2, *available online at* https://www.ledevoir.com/societe/science/524303/facebook-aura-besoin-de-quelques-annees-pour-resoudre-ses-problemes-zuckerberg.

19 Déclaration Universelle des Droits de l'Humanité [Universal Declaration of Human Rights], *available online at* http://droitshumanite.fr/.

Autodesk, among others). Unless, of course, they relied on the influence of the omnipresent "Technological Singularity" promoted at great expense by the "Web Giants" (Google, Amazon, Facebook, Apple and Microsoft) – also known by the acronym GAFAM, but sometimes including Twitter, Yahoo and PayPal, as well as NATU – if not the 4 major "digital disruption" companies, namely Netflix, Airbnb, Tesla and Uber[20]; connections that undoubtedly open doors at the highest levels.

A. A Tradition of Symbolic Manipulation, to Get out of the Symbolic

In 1999, strange predecessors indeed held the *First International Congress on Eternal Life* in the Jesuit-owned amphitheatre of the Gesù in Montreal. "Forget about death! Can there be better news?", shouted a happy and smiling Rael at an enraptured audience of 700 people.[21] As part of the only camera crew working with documentary filmmakers from Japan to "immortalize" the event (in *Clone inc.*),[22] we had the opportunity to listen to the ravings of Randolph Wicker, *Clone Right United Front* (U.S.). Wicker projected his own picture as a child on a giant screen and condemned as "true monsters" those who would refuse this child the right to be reborn without someone else's genes. Eugenics resurfaced (with all of its disturbing repression), but this time relying on a stranger's genes?

Among Rael's guests at this "fathom yourself" evening was Richard Seed, an auspicious-named scientist, who, due to claiming to have worked on human cloning, had been invited to lead a lecture at the Royal Society of London. It is no wonder then that, on Christmas in 2002, these hoax masters announced to the whole world: "She is born, the scientific child"? The birth of Eve, the first allegedly cloned baby! This fabulous sham presenting a "[parentless birth, allowing humans, freed from genealogy, to become a scientific experiment, replicable at will]",[23] immediately landed in the headlines, looped continuously all over the media – until, at last, the trickery dawned on some.

20 Ganascia, 2017.

21 Rael, guru of the Raelian Sect. *See* "2015 Secrets d'actualité" [2015 News Secrets] survey, *available online at* https://www.youtube.com/watch?v=0LkfRuusFAk.

22 *Clonage ou l'art de se faire doubler* [Cloning or the Art of Doubling], Documentaire de K. Parent et L. Vandelac, Office National du film du Canada, Studio Sciences et sociétés, 2000, 52 minutes. *See also Clone Inc*, Documentary by K. Parent & L. Vandelac (National Firm Board of Inter-American), Society and Science Studio, 2006.

23 M. Vacquin, "Fascination pour le Transhumanisme" [Fascination for Transhumanism], *La science entre archaïsme et démesure* [*Science between Archaism and Excess*], Actes du colloque Critique de la Raison Transhumaniste, Collège des Bernardins, 2017, Paris,

Despite the issues that are so dear to transhumanists, such as "the death of death" and cloning, one thing should not be misunderstood: Rael and his followers have never been included in the new "Pantheon of the Eternal 2.0". The technoprophet-like rhetoric of the engineers of Singularity – perfect examples of pragmatics,[24] imposing a new reality through a single word – differs, indeed, from that of the Raelians. Their rhetoric also differs from that of super-rich American evangelist Christians and tele-evangelists (who enjoy a strong influence at the highest levels of American politics due to their millions of "faithful" and their fortune), as revealed by Trump's election promises to those circles during the last U.S. Supreme Court appointment.

Despite their high-tech polish, the transhumanists 2.0 benefit nonetheless from this fertile evangelist soil of "deep America", which is so often underestimated by Europeans. Transhumanists adopt similar codes of psychological intimidation in which celebrity, wealth and high-profile political access hone people's feelings of inferiority; thus, enhancing the superiority of the transhumanists and their ilk. Transhumanists draw their power from the same anthropological melting-pot that is activated by fear of dying, of illness and of old age – fears that are at the origin of so many arrangements with Eternity and Afterlife, which were formerly the privileged territory of religions, but are now appropriated to fit the transhumanists' own stock-in-trade; although with no God, and no temple.[25] Nor do transhumanist movements flirt with the neo-conservatives or the Ayn Rand ultra-right, who were also key ingredients of Trump's election.[26] These young and wealthy technoscience and engineering entrepreneurs draw on the magic – preferring to dazzle and seduce the child in us (and, indeed, our own children: their future audience) – using futuristic registers punctuated

---

éditions du Cerf ("naissance sans parents, permettant à l'homme, débarrassé de la généalogie, de devenir une expérience scientifique, répliquable à merci" [Birth without parents allows humans freed from genealogy to become unlimited replicable scientific experiments?]).

24 C. Perelman & L. Olbrechts-Tyteca, *Traité de l'argumentation, la nouvelle rhétorique* [The New Rhetoric: a Treatise on Argumentation], Bruxelles, Éd. de l'Université de Bruxelles, 1958; new edition, 2009.

25 T. Metzinger, "Silicon Valley is selling an ancient dream of immortality", *Financial Times*, 18 Aug. 2017, *available online at* https://www.ft.com/content/7a89c998-828d-11e7-94e2-c5b903247afd.

26 N. Morgan, *Haine froide, A quoi pense la droite américaine* ? [Cold Hatred: What Does the American Right Think?] Paris, Le Seuil, 2012.

with managerial efficiency, and mingled with political ambitions to better recruit young engineers and other brilliant students for their exponential university.

In his analysis of speeches by seven of the main transhumanistic leaders,[27] Mehdi Ourabah points out that these leaders make their openness to change a criterion of competency as the self-appointed avant-garde of society.[28] Ourabah further explains the transhumanists' hope that their promising concepts will seduce investors to help bring their innovations on the market quickly – to have them be disseminated, trivialized and assimilated by the general public before ethical or legal questions can even be raised – thus preventing their development from being held back.[29] This is a classic recipe for limiting any scientific evaluation and supervision, which facilitates quick returns on investment (something that has now become a standard, as we have seen in the North American marketing of GMOs and nanotechnologies).

B. Transhumanism: Premises and Silent Gestation

Although sometimes laboring under the impression that we are among the first to see these issues unfold over the news, others already had a foretaste of their density and consequences through various prisms in the immediate post-war period. The context then was deeply marked by cybernetics, which tended to absorb everything within its categories including nature – assimilated to the ecosystem concept, which (even if it is very rich and promising in scientific terms) nevertheless remains terribly simplistic; especially if we now have to pay the price for it.

---

27 Ray Kurzweil and Peter Diamandis (Singularity University co-founders), with Craig Venter, scientist at Human Longevity Inc and Aubrey de Gray of the Matthuselah Foundation and Rejuvenation Research. Elon Musk, founder of Open AI, develops research in artificial intelligence and collaborates with Peter Thiel, close to Open AI to finance young talents via his Thiel Foundation. Finally, Max More, cryogenics specialist and his wife Natasha-Vita More, another custom-designed name, try to reassure the public by emphasizing the flourishing nature of these technologies and their compatibility with religion, especially with influential Mormons.

28 M. Ourabah, "*Les discours prometteurs des leaders du transhumanisme, Réponse aux peurs pour apparaître comme des sauveurs de l'humanité, ou stratégie managériale dans un environnement concurrentiel en construction*" [The Promising Speeches of Leaders of Transhumanism: Response to Fears of Appearing as Saviors of Humanity, or Management Strategy in a Competitive Environment Under Construction?], Mémoire de maîtrise, Dép. de sociologie, Univ. de Caen Normandie. 2017.

29 *Ibid.*, pp. 22–24.

In the midst of these tumultuous changes, the naturalist Julian Huxley (brother of Aldous Huxley) invented the term "transhumanism" in 1957.[30] Monette Vacquin writes:

> "[the human species can, if it wishes, transcend itself, not only sporadically, but as a whole and forever]",[31] then adds that "[Europe has barely emerged from the abyss. We enter what Georges Steiner will call the post-Nazi condition. And the end of the great stories, their pulverization, the religious discourses considered obsolete, the discredited ideologies, depriving us of an inexhaustible source of metaphors on the mystery that man is to himself. Everything happens as if the desire for belief were seeking shelter somewhere. Science becomes the only supposedly unfalsifiable discourse, with its operational evidence, its visibility, its proofs]".[32]

One year earlier in Germany, Günther Anders argued in his 1956 publication *L'Obsolescence de l'homme*, that "[the task of current science no longer consists … in discovering the secret and therefore hidden essence of the world or things, or the laws they obey, but in discovering the possible use they conceal. The metaphysical hypothesis (itself usually kept secret) of current research is therefore that there is nothing that is not exploitable]".[33]

---

30 J. Huxley, "Transhumanism", *in* J. Huxley, *New Bottles for New Wine*, Chatto & Windus, London, 1957, pp. 13–17.

31 M. Vacquin, 2017 ("l'espèce humaine peut, si elle le souhaite, se transcender elle-même, pas seulement de manière sporadique, mais dans son ensemble et pour toujours").

32 *Ibid.* ("L'Europe sort à peine du gouffre. On aborde ce que Georges Steiner nommera la condition post nazie. Et la fin des grands récits, leur pulvérisation, les discours religieux tenus pour obsolètes, les idéologies discréditées, nous privant d'une source inépuisables de métaphores sur le mystère que l'homme est à lui-même. Tout se passe comme si le désir de croyance cherchait à se loger quelque part. La science devient le seul discours supposé infalsifiable, avec son évidence opératoire, sa visibilité, ses preuves").

33 R.-P. Droit, *L'Obsolescence de l'homme. Tome II. Sur la destruction de la vie à l'époque de la troisième révolution industrielle, de Günther Anders : les exagérations prophétiques de "Monsieur autrement"* [The Obsolence of Man. Vol. II. On the Destruction of Life in the Epoch of the Third Industrial Revolution, by Günther Anders: the Prophetic Exaggerations of "Mr. Other"], *Le Monde des livres*, 9 June 2011, *available online at* https://www.lemonde.fr/livres/article/2011/06/09/l-obsolescence-de-l-homme-tome-ii-sur-la-destruction-de-la-vie-a-l-epoque-de-la-troisieme-revolution-industrielle-de-gunther-anders_1533798_3260.html ("La tâche de la science actuelle ne consiste […] plus à découvrir l'essence secrète et donc cachée du monde ou des choses, ou encore les lois auxquelles elles obéissent, mais à découvrir le possible usage qu'ils dissimulent. L'hypothèse métaphysique (elle-même habituellement tenue secrète) des recherches actuelles est donc qu'il n'y a rien qui ne soit exploitable").

A keen awareness has emerged of science becoming increasingly dominated by technoscience and ideology – where everything (ourselves included) can be reified, instrumentalized and exploited for the sake of projects which we do not even know exist. For Anders, "[Humanity is outdated. Expiration date: 1945, with the combined discovery of Auschwitz and the Hiroshima and Nagasaki bombs. Future, history, values, hope and the very idea of what we used to call 'man', in a jumble have become obsolete]",[34] says Roger Pol Droit, in *Le Monde*, emphasizing Anders' comments about "[the derealization of the world, the dehumanization of everyday life, the general commodification. The biggest surprise for the reader is finally to see how, on many points, Anders saw right, was right before all others]".[35]

Around the same time in Cambridge, Italian economist Piero Sraffa (a friend of Antonio Gramsci and Maynard Keynes) completed his major work, which was to be considered the foundation of the Neo-Ricardian Economic School. It took Sraffa four decades to write this little book published in 1960, *Production of Commodities by Means of Commodities* – a title that appears to have been portentous, especially seen through the rear-view mirror of transhumanism. On the fault line between the two great politico-economic systems of the Cold War, it appeared as if human beings were dissolving into the self-referential and implacable universe of the commodity-by-means-of-commodities production cycle – already reflecting Anders' *The Obsolescence of Man*, and Julian Huxley's transhumanist perspectives.

Similarly, a fourth figure (this time a biologist in the United States) analyzed the effects of the war on the living that was initiated by the chemical industry in the wake of its conversion of chemical weapons from the 1939-1945 war. Rachel Carson launched the contemporary environmental movement with her publication of *Silent Spring* in 1962, observing that these products – DDT, pesticides and other biocides – were dispersed in large quantities that impact everything and everyone in harmful ways: birds, children, and the author herself.

---

34 *Ibid.* ("L'humanité est périmée. Date de péremption : 1945, quand se conjuguent la découverte d'Auschwitz et les bombes d'Hiroshima et de Nagasaki. Sont alors devenus désuets, pêle-mêle : l'avenir, l'histoire, les valeurs, l'espérance et l'idée même de ce qu'on appelait, auparavant, 'homme' ").

35 *Ibid.* ("la déréalisation du monde, la déshumanisation du quotidien, la marchandisation générale. Le principal étonnement du lecteur, c'est finalement de constater combien, sur quantité de points, Anders a vu juste avant tout le monde").

C. A Singular Convergence

We could have added hundreds of others to these few figures, who broke with traditional thought patterns and echoed each other without even knowing about each other.[36] But the influence of these bright consciences is out of all proportion to the fulgurating power of technoscientific developments that emerged over the preceding decades, in addition to the scale of socio-cultural changes brought about by these developments. The transformative changes that resulted from the advances of nanotechnologies and their convergence with biotechnologies, information sciences and cognitive sciences (collectively referred to by the acronym NBIC), is fodder for the rise of artificial intelligence and transhumanist perspectives.

Based on their elementary components (atoms, DNA, bits and synapses) working on a nanometric scale, the first convergence of disciplines led to a second convergence towards the end of the century; the intersections and entanglements of the NBICs multiplied generations of innovations, thus striving to establish themselves as true techno-economic drivers. The 400-page report entitled *Converging Knowledges for Improving Human Performance*, published in 2002 by the National Science Foundation and the U.S. Department of Commerce, enabled NBICs to develop in a particularly favorable environment: with unparalleled public and private funding programs, as well as privileged relationships to the highest levels of national as well as international institutions of knowledge and power.

One of the main proponents of NBICs – Mihail Roco, senior advisor for nanotechnology at the U.S. *National Science Foundation*, with admitted transhumanist inclinations) – maintains that NBIC developments are now paving the way to a third level of convergence, with a rather transparent objective: *Convergence of Knowledge, Technologies and Society* (CKTS) "is the next stage in convergence; it expands emerging technologies at their interfaces and frontiers, and *intimately introduces them into the human-scale*, Earth-scale, and societal-scale platforms".[37] Can there be a more far-reaching and terrifying project than one

---

36 Including, for example, the visionary Mary Schelley, who was analyzed with finesse by Monette Vacquin. M. Vacquin, "Frankenstein aujourd'hui : égarements et délires de la science moderne" [Frankenstein Today : Delusions and Ravings of Modern Science], Paris, éditions Belin, 2016.

37 M.C. Roco, W.S. Bainbridge, B. Tonn, & G. Whitesides (eds.), *Convergence of Knowledge, Technology, and Society: Beyond Convergence of Nano-Bio-Info-Cognitive Technologies*, World Technology Evaluation Center Inc., July 2013, p. 2, *available online at* http://www.wtec.org/NBIC2-Report/ (accessed 16 June 2019).

that subordinates knowledge and societies in such a way, transforming everything, including us, into a platform dedicated to experimentation and innovation? And by what right?

II. From Humanism to Antihumanism, from Transhumanism to Posthumanism, and Straight to the Posthumous Post-Human

The jurist Catherine Labrusse-Riou points out the following:

> [We knew what humanism is; we unlearned it with anti-humanism; transhumanism – and its flight towards posthumanism – accredits the idea of modifying the human race to propagate a new species, arising from fusion and hybridization of humans and machines, from convergence of technologies (in particular NBICs), and this in order to escape the "*Promethean shame*" (G. Anders, 1956-2002)[38] of owing one's existence to chance or to undergo an incidental evolution after having created machines more powerful than humans].[39]

If we describe this dark horizon as posthumous post-human, it is because this manufactured, "augmented" and "improved" human is presented as the negation in acts of Otherness. It is the antithesis of humanism, a disembodied and soulless human who is seeking to put an end to body, diseases and finitude. It is also a depraved attack upon reproduction, birth and generations. This dreadful androcentrist project to eviscerate le "féminin maternel" and thus to cancel women, announces a new, massive eugenics based (given the nature of cloning) on the elimination of ancestors; hence its posthumous character.

---

38 G. Anders, *L'obsolescence de l'homme, sur l'âme à l'époque de la deuxième révolution industrielle* [The Obsolescence of Man: On the Soul at the Time of the Second Industrial Revolution], Encyclopédie des nuisances, Ivrea, Paris, 2002 (originally published in 1956).

39 C. Labrusse-Riou, "Transhumanisme. Entre progrès et nihilisme, l'humanité ne cesse de mettre en question sa condition" [Transhumanism: Between Progress and Nihilism, Humanity is Constantly Questioning its Condition], *Revue Lamy Droit Civil*, June 2016, No. 138 I ("On savait ce qu'est l'humanisme; on le désapprit avec l'antihumanisme; le transhumanisme – et sa poursuite vers le posthumanisme – accrédite l'idée de modifier l'espèce humaine pour engendrer une nouvelle espèce, résultat de la fusion et de l'hybridation de l'homme et des machines, de la convergence des technologies (en particulier les NBIC : nanotechnologies, biotechnologies, informatique, sciences cognitives), et cela afin d'échapper à la 'honte prométhéenne' (Anders G. 1956–2002) de devoir son existence au hasard ou de subir une évolution non dirigée après avoir créé des machines plus puissantes que l'homme").

In 1989, the jurist and philosopher Bernard Edelman asked:

> [Is not man about to be modified? Will the "biologization" of life not destroy, step by step, the representation we have of ourselves, of our "social being"? Will it not habituate us to the idea that we are "cellular beings", kinds of repositories of organs and therefore, that we can, *in parte qua*, that is to say part by part, be sold and supplied with a price tag? In short, would man have succeeded, at the end of an irresistible evolution of the commercial society, in this astonishing result of producing himself as a commodity?][40]

Considering this thesis on these methods of appropriation and unprecedented technical transformation of being (from frozen embryos to warm corpses), how it is possible not to be frightened by our entry into the "embryo-economy of the living". Our transition to this strange "embryo-economy of the living" undercuts begetting relationships – "the ethics of the word given to the child", that sensitive framework of filiation and the fundamental psychic reference points which allow children to be born to themselves?

We were then still far from imagining the attraction exercised; especially the power of the means implemented to act out *this delirious and megalomaniac utopia.*[41] An utopia that aimed to: disqualify the bond and the limit; to "unravel" the founding categories; as well as to de-differentiate and untie genders and generations – in other words, as Dany-Robert Dufour reminds us, the abscissae and ordinates that weave the fabric of our societies.[42] Although scarcely mentioned, it entails the jettisoning of those humans made inferior by the post-human; thus, accelerating the suicidal prospects of ecocide and anthropocide.

Hidden behind the "Human Enhancement" – which suggests both an increased, improved, implicitly manufactured, but also enhanced human (signing the agreement of his or her submission to the excessiveness of this

---

40 B. Edelman, "Le Droit et le Vivant" [The Right and the Living], *La Recherche*, 1989, No. 212 ("L'homme n'est-il pas en passe de se modifier, la 'biologisation' de la vie ne va-t-elle pas détruire, de proche en proche, la représentation que nous avons de nous-mêmes, de notre 'être social'? Ne va-t-elle pas nous accoutumer à l'idée que nous sommes des 'hommes cellulaires', des sortes de réceptacles d'organes et partant, que nous pouvons, in parte qua, c'est-à-dire partie par partie, être vendus et monnayés ? En deux mots, l'homme serait-il parvenu, au terme d'une évolution irrésistible de la société marchande, à ce résultat stupéfiant de se produire lui-même comme marchandise?").

41 M. Vacquin, 2017 (using the expression "cette utopie délirante et mégalomaniaque").

42 D.-R. Dufour, *L'art de réduire les têtes. Sur la nouvelle servitude de l'homme libéré à l'ère du capitalisme total* [The Art of Reducting the Teas: South the New Servitude of the Liberated Man to the Era of Total Capitalism], Éditions Denoël, Paris, 2003; D-R. Dufour, *The Art of Shrinking Heads: The New Servitude of the Liberated in the Era of Total Capitalism*, Polity Press, Cambridge, UK/Malden, Massachusetts, 2008.

"tailor-made" market) – there is certainly a will to overcome deficiencies. However, there is also the insatiable dissatisfaction of not being able to personally embody the dreamed-of whole, to the point of wanting to melt into aluminium and silicone then "complete" oneself with prostheses, computer chips and electronic circuits. In short, to "incarnate" oneself into a cyborg – if this word still has meaning. Therefore, we are not in the context of a New Human as tragically experienced during the twentieth century and its bleak memories associated with Stalinism, Nazism, and Maoism. Instead, the post-human is part of a singular, solitary, androcentric and self-referential universe. In this isolated universe, the obsession to produce oneself as a clone (i.e., a half-flesh, half-iron, half-silicone being with an extended lifetime that matches his fantasies of longevity, power and competitiveness), turns humans into hyper-individualists with terrifying destructive power.

As an over-the-top clone copy of the *homo oeconomicus* that self-duplicates *ad infinitum*, this "post-human" bases himself on and even exacerbates (while claiming the opposite[43]) the combined degradations of climate, biodiversity, and climatic events – with dreadful effects on the reproduction of living beings along with regeneration of the world; thus, literally leading to our demise! As a perfect embodiment of neoliberalism à la Hayek, transhumanism reduces both our lives and the planet to algorithms that serve a world entirely immersed in its economy. An economy for the benefit of a few billionaires with teenage dreams. This post-human is literally caught up in an allegedly endless growth rate, thus putting an end to our own growth.

Multiplying promises of eternal life through the abolition of death, this post-human fuels the "exponentials" – a key word for the Singularity University, whose status as a new figure of infinite growth is boosted by the omnipotence of the "Technological Fix" and its innovations; supposedly solving everything, including us. Is this hypothesis too violent? In his essay *Où atterrir*? [Where to Land?], Bruno Latour gives the word globalization an increasingly pejorative meaning, postulating that deregulation creates a vertiginous explosion of inequalities and climate change – where climate refers here to the very general sense of human relations to their material living conditions – as symptoms of the same historical situation. According to Latour, everything is happening as if part of the ruling classes (with their privileges and ecological footprints) have come

43 An excellent illustration is provided in P-H. Gouyon, "5 minutes pour changer votre vision de la Biodiversité" [5 minutes to Change Your Vision of Biodiversity], *Le Monde*, 13 July 2014, *available online at* http://mobile.lemonde.fr/sciences/video/2014/07/13/les-ogm-et-la-panne-de-la-biodiversite-agricole_4456266_1650684.html.

to the conclusion that there will no longer be enough room on earth for the rest of the world's inhabitants. Latour then adds that it is useless to pretend history will continue to lead towards a common horizon, where all men could prosper equally. Since 1980, the ruling classes no longer claim to rule the world; instead, they seek to protect themselves from it. Current U.S. President Donald Trump is an "eloquent" symbol of such escapism.

Latour further believes that we cannot understand anything about the political positions of the last 50 years (inequality, deregulation, populism, etc.) if we do not give a central place to the question of climate change and its denial – for which the United States offers an astonishing laboratory. This perspective effectively leads to the elimination of human beings. Is this deliberate decimation? In other words, indifference towards the erosion of vital conditions for the vast majority of the people on the planet in favor of profits for the few as they indecently grab the world's resources; thus, accelerating disintegration of the climate and Earth's biodiversity? Focusing on the multiplication of walls and on strategies of repression at the borders (including imprisonment, slavery and the tragedies of the Mediterranean), we can see that the fascist discourse on "vermin" has been replaced by that of post-humans. Revamped and hyper-connected post-humans who are essentially "the others" as "sub-humans"? In a world where conflicts, extreme climate events, and endemic poverty have already led to some 70 million displaced persons per year, the perspectives of the new eugenism should concern us a lot more than the pursuit of a sordid ideal based on the fusion of human and machine.

Hidden behind the fantasies of narcissistic self-reproduction, the blind spot of this new eugenics lies in the delirious claim to replace the conditions for regeneration of the world's creatures with an entirely artificialized and patented production regime that is controlled by a few. The fact that in just a few years, three giants of agrochemistry have succeeded in taking control of 60% of the world's seeds and three-quarters of the R&D in this domain, should no doubt alert us.

Behind daydreams like "killing death", finitude itself is called into question. From an anthropological point of view, Gilles Bibeau reminds us that death is the one thing that defines the human condition in its entirety. Death is not a regrettable imperfection of the human condition; we belong to the human species because we are mortal, because we are aware of it.[44] Indeed, finitude itself is

44 J.-C. Guillebaud, "Techno-prophètes ou savants fous ?" [Techno-Prophets or Mad Scientists?], *Le corps obsolète ? L'idéologie transhumaniste en question [The Obsolete Body?: The Transhumanist Ideology in Question]*, Revue Relations, Montréal, 2017, Vol. 792, p. 19, *available online at* http://cjf.qc.ca/revue-relations/publication/article/

the one thing that calls for the need of generations. From a philosophical perspective, Bibeau adds that the notion of humanity only becomes conceivable on the horizon of finitude, fragility, and the quest for meaning in addition to the concern that arises from our deep incompleteness.[45]

Let us add Guillebaud's subsequent contention that "[the logic of the dream of the death of death is that of the death of procreation]", and also of the death of the constantly renewed flows of generations[46]; whereas, "the *perpetual recommencement*" – defined by the structural constitutive requirement of humanity, whose price to pay is the "perpetual completion"[47] – already worried the Greeks, as Hans Jonas reminds us in "*Le principe responsabilité*" [The Responsibility Principle].[48] Behind these very singular projects of the Singularity, there is already a "post-human" obsessed with clone reproduction, whose androcentrist and self-referential universe erodes the conditions of reproduction, in addition to the conditions for regeneration of the planet, creatures as well as societies, and even that of thought itself.

As a true negation of Otherness, the post-human project agrees further with the abolition of human begetting, of the "*féminin maternel*" (i.e., the very *erasure* of women), as if seeking to conclude the height of oppression and exploitation of women by making women disappear altogether. Would post-humanism thus carry forward the great disappearance of the 122 million "missing" women? With 50 and 35 million women missing, respectively, China and India assume 76% of this "global women's deficit" based on figures compiled by the World Bank in 2013. In other words, this femicide represents twice as many victims as World War II and as all the genocides of the twentieth century in less than

corps-obsolete-lideologie-transhumaniste-question/ (subscription required) ("imperfection regrettable de la condition humaine, nous appartenons à l'espèce humaine parce que nous sommes mortels, que nous en sommes conscients").

45 G. Bibeau, "Choisir la vie" [Choosing Life], *Le corps obsolète ? L'idéologie transhumaniste en question*, 2017, Vol. 792, p. 19 ("dans une perspective philosophique, la notion d'humanité ne devient pensable que sur l'horizon de la finitude, de la fragilité, de la quête du sens et de l'inquiétude surgissant de notre profonde incomplétude").

46 Guillebaud, 2017 ("la logique du rêve d'élimination de la mort est celle de l'élimination de la procréation").

47 *Ibid.*

48 H. Jonas, *Das Prinzip Verantwortung: Versuch enier Ehtik für die technologische Zivilisation* [The Principle of Responsibility: Attempting an Ethic for Technological Civilization], Insel Verlag Frankfurt am Main, 1979; H. Jonas, *The Imperative of Responsibility: In Search of an Ethics for the Technological Age*, University of Chicago Press, 1984.

50 years![49] Lest we see the acceleration of damage to the reproductive tract, biological differentiation, and to fertility in humans (as already witnessed in fish and mammals), due to the effects of toxic cocktail induced endocrine disruption.

And what will be left of the body? Will it become nothing more than a transitional body, body-pedestal, hybridized with nanotechnologies, biotechnologies and AI applications to create a cyborg? A hyper-individualized body, bent, fed with "smart drugs", "cognitive amplifiers", or brain stimulators, boosting the new forms of exploitation and alienation of individuals to better meet the growing imperatives of performance, productivity and "hyper work"?[50] Would it be a "human capital" body (à la Gary Becker, 1992 Nobel Prize winner in economics) – i.e., an overinvested body that grows with personal investments (e.g., diplomas, diets, physical training, health care, etc.), to "put in the bank" for generationally deferred projects or post-mortem use (sperm, ova, embryos)?[51]

In other words, fascinated by artificial mirages, the calamitous post-human project (and its over-the-top ideal of a smooth body made of iron and silicone, subjecting the living being as a whole to operative devices of dismantling and patchwork, of circuiting and marketing), leads to a magnification of the endangerment faced by the world and humans. All while directing human gazes to promised feats, which are hardly adequate to camouflage the fate reserved for a few billion souls who will be sent back to the ranks of infra-humans. This strange and paradoxical "post-human" project combines ecocide and anthropocide (and is, therefore, doubly suicidal), even though this word has itself become obsolete in the Newspeak of the Eternal 2.0 (*see* Section I.A. above).

III. By What Right? And, Indeed, by What Rights?

At a time when being and living become entangled objects of appropriation and modification without precedent, can the law leave these questions unanswered without running the risk of cheating us? Behind the dazzling media sensationalism (which, for the most part, instantly fawns over and legitimizes such

---

49 L. Vandelac, "Et si l'avenir s'échappait [...] Savoir lire le monde et savoir être lu par lui" [And if the Future Escaped: Knowing How to Read the World and Who to be Read by Him], Dossier central, *Revue Liberté Art et Politique*, 2017, No. 315, pp. 23–27, *available online at* http://revueliberte.ca/content/et-si-lavenir-sechappait.

50 N. Le Dévédec, "Corps augmentés, êtres exploités" [Increased Bodies, Exploited Beings], *Revue Relations*, 2017, Vol. 792, p. 19.

51 C. Lafontaine, "La biocitoyenneté à l'ère du néolibéralisme" [Biocitizenship in the Age of Neoliberalism], *Revue Relations*, 2017, Vol. 792, p. 19.

developments), looms another kind of relationship to beings and to the world; a relationship where nature and human nature would have no other future than that which changes their own nature. Well beyond the science fiction horizon that too often obscures the stakes of power involved, however, this ideological remodeling draws up new economic and political relations under which our identity is the very object. How can we not worry about these deadly prospects, which aim to create a new techno-living segment that breaks with the human chain, blinded to the hidden stakes of the times. What kind of strange fate does our future hold?

In 1992, Tibon-Cornillot wondered whether we are not submitting ourselves (body and soul) to a particular conception of scientific rationality through an astonishing looped effect of Western rationality? A conception

> [that, through these radical transformations of the livings determined by their logic, no longer claims a status of universal truth, but of "unavoidable reality", whose stake would be the dilution, or even the dissolution, through the imaginary at work in biology, of the symbolic, traditional and classical structures that still exist and are still at work in Western societies]?[52]

These projects combining both mechanization and transfiguration, make us move from the symbolic to pure materiality. How then can we forget that this outburst constitutes a loss of meaning that erodes not only our representations of beings and of the world, but the structures of our thoughts at an even deeper level. How can we fail to see the unraveling – at the deepest cultural and anthropological levels, the sense of the *link* and the *limit* – of such essential elements that are inseparable from the vital, psychic, social, and intergenerational balance, without which nothing is conceivable? As the jurist François Ost points out:

> [Hence, the link: what connects and binds …, the lines (lineage), the strings, the knots, the ties, the connections, the affinities. The wedding ring. The couple (coupling) and filiation. The roots. The link, or what allows time and place: a rooting, a place in a transmission. The link, or "tied part", i.e. the opposite of the "whole part": in other words, the very possibility of otherness and sharing. […] One can only establish links between what is, by itself, distinct and virtually detachable. The identity procured by the link is thus the condition for emancipation, itself a condition for the obligation freely assumed].[53]

---

52 M. Tibon-Cornillot, *Les corps transfigurés. Mécanisation du vivant et imaginaire de la biologie* [*The Transfigured Bodies: Mechanization of the Living and Imaginary Body*], Paris, Seuil, 1992.

53 J.-F. Ost, *La nature hors la loi : l'écologie à l'épreuve du droit* [Nature Outside the Law: Ecology is Right], Paris, éditions La Découverte, 1995, p. 9 ("Soit le lien : ce qui relie et oblige […], les lignes [lignées], les cordes, les noeuds, les attaches, les liaisons, les affinités. L'alliance. Le couple accouplement) et la filiation. Les racines. Le lien, ou

To paraphrase Ost, the divergence and the limit as constitutive parts of identity, therefore, are the elements that enable the link. It is a principle of enclosure that is also the principle of transgression, ensuring demarcation but also allowing passage. The limit "[is a place of exchange as much as a sign of difference]".[54] However, the transhumanist project aims to implode the meanings of both the link and the limit. At least for the moment, according to the jurist Catherine Labrusse Riou, contemporary law hardly manages to stop this:

> [Transhumanism is part of the dominant tendencies of contemporary law (with variations, of course): as an expression of a liberal ideology, the various transhumanist movements benefit from individual freedoms relating to the body (transsexualism, assisted procreation, self-determination, etc.), promote free access to all means likely to develop physical, intellectual and reproductive capacities, and borderless freedom for scientific research and for the market. In short, they promote a society of individuals unbridled by social and moral constraints].[55]

Even in the event of failure, whether by default or malice – hypotheses that are rarely raised by transhumanist optimists – Labrusse-Riou asks if we will be able to use the responsibility laws? She continues by asking further, "[could the erosion of the man/machine distinction risk paralyzing the mechanism of imputation which serves as foundation of the law]" if the legal categories are adapted to realities previously not considered?

The questions raised at the end of the 1980s when setting up the commercial and institutional factory of human livings – some of whom are deemed to be born, and others suspended in liquid nitrogen to become nothing but laboratory material[56] – have ricocheted back to us. At that time,

---

ce qui permet d'avoir temps et lieu: un enracinement, une place dans une transmission. Le lien, ou 'la partie liée', c'est-à-dire le contraire de la 'part entière': autrement dit, la possibilité même de l'altérité et du partage. […] On ne relie que ce qui, de soi, est distinct et virtuellement détachable. L'identité que procure le lien est donc condition de l'affranchissement, qui lui-même est condition de l'obligation librement assumée".).

54 *Ibid.*, p. 9.

55 C. Labrusse-Riou, 2016 ("Le transhumanisme, s'inscrit dans les tendances dominantes du droit contemporain (avec des variantes, certes): expression d'une idéologie libérale, les divers mouvements transhumanistes profitent des libertés individuelles corporelles (transsexualisme, procréations assistées, autodétermination, etc.), promeuvent le libre accès à tous des moyens de nature à développer les capacités physiques, intellectuelles, reproductives, la liberté sans frontières de la recherche scientifique, du marché, en bref une société d'individus que la contrainte sociale ou morale ne doit pas brider".).

56 L. Vandelac, "Technologies de reproduction : l'irresponsabilité des pouvoirs publics et la nôtre" [Reproductive Technologies : the Irresponsibility of the Public Authorities and

Labrusse-Riou wrote: "[Shouldn't the law be concerned by these ongoing changes to confront them with certain fundamental principles, and elaborate or preserve concepts and categories without which judgment is no longer possible, without which social ties have no meaning, nor symbolic or ethical reference]"?[57]

In other words, can the law contribute any reflection on these changes rather than just silently nodding and consenting to the techno-scientific stranglehold? Can the law provide resistance to the symbolic erosion and loss of meaning? Perhaps by contributing toward preservation of the humanity of begetting, the very condition of humans and the polysemy of their intergenerational links? Can the law escape the domination of utilitarian principles in order to protect public standards and respect towards human beings from commercial privatization? Can it contribute to preserving humanity, dignity and otherness – that of children, women and men, when they come into the world as well as when they leave it? For example, can the law help avoid the risk of seeing those we "produced" deport us out of our very selves – or at least out of humanity as we have conceived of to date?[58] In short, Catherine Labrusse-Riou asks, "[can the law be a body of judgment and not simply an alignment with the facts nor a simple method of recording social or scientific demands, which are mostly economically induced]"?[59]

Beyond the expression of a remarkable indignation, "By what right?", the urgency of these issues certainly calls for plural and entwined readings of the various branches of the law. It also requires a courageous immersion in the very foundations of the Law – i.e., the history, epistemology and philosophy of the Law. We thus write:

> [How would a law look like if it were amnesic of its humanist conceptions, proved unable of thinking globally about beings and society, other than through the prism of

---

Ours], *Sociologie et sociétés*, 1996, Vol. 28, No. 2, Dép. de sociologie, Un. de Montréal, pp. 109–122.

57 C. Labrusse-Riou, 1991, p. 20 ("Le droit ne doit-il pas se pencher sur ces mutations à l'œuvre pour y opposer certains principes régulateurs et élaborer ou préserver des concepts et des catégories sans lesquels le jugement n'est plus possible, sans lesquels les liens sociaux n'ont ni sens, ni référence symbolique ou éthique ?") translated by Marie Noonan..

58 L. Vandelac, 1996, pp. 59–75, *available online at* https://www.erudit.org/en/journals/socsoc/1996-v28-n2-socsoc81/001819ar.pdf.

59 C. Labrusse-Riou, 1991, p. 20 , *op. cit.*

technology? What kind of law would it be if it could do nothing else but speculate on the marketing modalities of the being and its body? What kind of law would it be if it was reduced to the status of an executor in charge of performing the fragmentation of intergenerational principles and running out of integrating principles? Would such a ław not look like a pale copy of law?][60]

Can we then not rethink the law, if it fails to address such technical and "managerial" notions? A law that pays heed to matters of life, to the submission to hazards of power relations and to the domination of utilitarian principles – is such a law incompatible with fundamental principles? How about a law that realizes and takes into account the excessiveness and outrageous character of these ideological and technoscientific abuses, which are mainly focused on the disembodiment of reproduction: this triple "made into flesh", "made into sense", "made into links" of new born children? Indeed, this lies at the very heart of social relations between genders, at the intersection of the "personal" and the "social", at the crossroads between socio-economic, political and symbolic stakes – which have nothing to do with androcentrist (perhaps misogynous) conceptions that diminish engendering to a discourse of nature; even going so far as reducing motherhood to an animal instinct. Yet, it is on this very ideological basis that an unsettling discourse has been developing – in terms of technical externalization of childbirth, hereafter dismantled and marketed (institutionally or commercially) then assimilated as part of a "women's liberation".[61] Some have even claimed this cleavage that borders on the absurd[62] would allow them to escape a so-called state of nature, instead raising them to the highest levels of culture.

It is therefore the contours, the functions, the structures, the anthropological foundations at their deepest level, as well as the foundations of the law that are affected, just as are the boundaries and relations between various fields of the Law: health, environment, patents, contracts, bio-rights, or the emerging rights of humanity, those of future generations, of their rights protecting them against the ecocide, or even against the anthropocide? Is it really any wonder that so

---

60 L. Vandelac, "La famille reconstituée par la biologie : des flous du droit au droit floué ?" [The Family Reconstituted by Biology: Fuzzy Right to the Right Fuzzed?], 1999, *in* C. Masse (éd.), *Revue juridique Thémis,* vol. 33, no. 2, pp. 372–401.

61 C. Labrusse-Riou, "Les implications juridiques de la génétique" [The Legal Implications of Genetics], *Revue du droit public et de la science politique en France et à l'étranger,* 1989, No. 1369, p. 36.

62 *See generally* L. Vandelac, 1999.

many brilliant jurists are now getting interested in these crucial issues for the future of the world, eager to renew these perspectives?

What are the tools available to work on such a construction site? What are the tools that need developing? Labrusse-Riou proposes the following:

> [Since it is a question of changing species, wouldn't the law which claims to institute the protection of its integrity be itself the tool allowing us to react? … What could be induced by the notion of human species, which entered the vocabulary of French bioethics law in 1994 and has hitherto been little exploited ([…] [French Civil Code], art. 16-4). … Let us stop thinking merely at the level of individuals, but more broadly at the level of species, and let us start real casuistic work for a renewal of legal thought!][63]

Are the rights of future generations,[64] as the issue at stake in this conference, along with the Declaration of Human Rights, not precisely parts of such a profound renewal of the legal landscape?

IV. What Will the Horizon Lines of Post-Humanism Be Now?

They clearly pursue the vanishing lines of a landscape sketched out more than a century ago by such extravagant writings as Renan's:

> [It is up to science to continue the work to where nature left it off. … I have been told that you even possess a bias to make the immortality of individuals conceivable …. Reason, I say, will one day take over the stewardship of this great work, and, after organizing humanity, will organize God …. This higher world which we dream of for the realization of pure reason would have no women.][65]

---

63 C. Labrusse-Riou, 2016 ("Puisqu'il s'agit de changer d'espèce le droit qui prétend instituer la protection de son intégrité ne serait-il pas l'outil permettant de réagir ? […] Que pourrait-on induire de la notion d'espèce humaine entrée dans le vocabulaire du droit de la bioéthique français en 1994 et jusqu'ici bien peu exploitée (C. civ., art. 16-4) […]. Ne raisonnons plus seulement au niveau des individus mais carrément à celui de l'espèce et engageons un vrai travail casuistique de renouvellement de la pensée juridique").

64 *See* the brilliant thesis of Emilie Gaillard on the Rights of Future Generations. E. Gaillard, *Générations futures et droit privé. Vers un droit des générations futures* [*Future Generations and Private Law: Towards a Law for Future Generations*], Librairie Générale de Droit et de Jurisprudence, 2011, pp. 655–673.

65 M. Vacquin, 2017 ("C'est à la science de prendre l'œuvre au point où la nature l'a laissée […]. On m'a dit que vous possédiez même un biais pour rendre concevable l'immortalité des individus […] La raison, dis-je, prendra un jour l'intendance de ce grand travail, et, après avoir organisé l'humanité, organisera Dieu […] et […]. Ce monde supérieur que nous rêvons pour la réalisation de la raison pure n'aurait pas de femmes").

Will these horizon lines fade (as suggested by Jacques Testart) into the growing and entangled crises of the climate, biodiversity, energy, resources, major events, health and fertility – which literally threaten the body of the planet, the human body, the social body, as well as the body of thought[66]– thus, helping slow down and even paralyze these pretentions of silicon-men? Or, to the contrary, will we witness an increase in fantasies about supermen with exponential powers whose monopolizing and extravagant waste of resources saps what little time, energy, money and collective intelligence humanity has left – resources that are indispensable to the ecological shift that is as urgent as it is inevitable? What then will become of thought, solidarity and empathy, which represent the very meaning (and cement of our relations) to the world, in addition to the follow-up measures that must be implemented?

Before this strange movement of diluting beings and the world dissolves everything (including us) to the point of literally carrying us away – body and soul – to the world of *The Swallower Swallowed,* let us end with a joke. The great Quebec storyteller, Fred Pellerin, created pride and hope by turning his village one neighbor at a time, into a country that thinks as follows about the world: "We do not convince much", he says, "Where is Facebook? Where does this tank go?"[67] And, turning solidarity and happiness into a fabulous antidote, Perellin adds: "It would be a lot of people standing up together. From the world that sings and dances, it's hard to break".[68]

66 L. Vandelac, 2017.

67 J. Blanchette, "Il est où, le pays, il est où ?" [Where is the Country, Where is it?], *Le Devoir*, 13 July 2018, *available online at* https://www.ledevoir.com/opinion/chroniques/532325/il-est-ou-le-pays-il-est-ou?fbclid=IwAR0_jefg-nAk54h4U1ocPJJQDatT4EKRrjajoEhkQktkzImE5vjCXUopmXE ("On converge pas sur grand chose. C'est où Facebook ? Ça mène où, ce char-là ?").

68 *Ibid.* ("Ça ferait pas mal de monde qui se lève deboutte, ensemble [...]. Du monde qui chante pis qui danse, c'est dur à breaker!")

Amandine CAYOL & Emilie GAILLARD

19. Transhumanism(s) & Law(s): First Tracks and Thoughts[1]

According to Hannah Arendt:

> It could be that we, who are earth-bound creatures and have begun to act as though we were dwellers of the universe, will be unable to understand, that is, to think and speak about the things we are nevertheless able to do [...]. If it should turn out to be true that knowledge (in the sense of know-how) have parted company for good, then we would indeed become the helpless slaves not so much of our machines as of our know-how, thoughtless creatures at the mercy of every gadget which is technically possible, no matter how murderous it is.[2]

The historical link, established in the twentieth century, between knowledge and power, between science and technology, makes us wonder, today more than ever, whether everything that is technically possible should be achieved, particularly when it comes to research involving a radical transformation of human beings.

The High-Level Political Forum on Sustainable Development held July 2016 in New York was an opportunity to attend a "special event" at the margins of the conference on Sustainable Development Goals (SDGs). Organized on Sunday, 17 July 2016, during the United Nations General Assembly, the *Novus Summit* brought together, under the sponsorship of the United Nations Department of Economic and Social Affairs (UN-DESA) service – an assembly of people considered as instigators of transhumanism such as Peter Diamandis (co-founder of the Singularity University), and Maye Musk (Mother of Elon Musk).[3] Here are a few quotes giving an overview of thoughts shared during the summit:

---

1 The authors would like to warmly thank Gabriel Dorthe, author of a thesis entitled *Malédiction des objets absents : explorations épistémiques, politiques et écologiques du mouvement transhumaniste par un chercheur embarqué* [*Curse of Absent Objects: Epistemic, Political and Environmental Explorations of the Transhumanist Movement by an Embedded Researcher*], defended on 23 Jan. 2019, for his kind corrections. He is one of the leading members of the research team on "Law(s), Right(s) & Transhumanism" led by Amandine Cayol and Emilie Gaillard, with the support of the GIP Law & Justice (French Ministry of Justice Research Program).

2 H. Arendt, *La condition de l'homme moderne* [*The Human Condition*], Paris Calman-Levy, 1983, pp. 9–10.

3 Elon Musk is the entrepreneur at the head of SpaceX, Tesla and Solar City, which aim to change the world and humanity. Ranked as the 80th richest personality in the world

> "For the first time in the history of humanity, we have the power to consciously change the human race."
> "We are the most inventive and creative animals [...] there is nothing that technology can't solve!"
> "Of course people will be surprised [...] it's only natural, this is what is taught at the Singularity University: we're at the eve of an exponential evolution, and that's why people will necessarily be having trouble understanding it! It is the rebirth of biotechnology."

In the context of bathing in technology and a massive convergence toward "Nano-Bio-Info-Cogno" (NBIC),[4] the *Novus Summit* was an opportunity to bring all sciences together through the transhumanist ideology. Education is a major goal for transhumanists: teaching children about biotechnology and computer programming must become priorities for the world of tomorrow, an "ideal" world in which children will acquire socialization through computers. From this point onwards, it is important to get the whole planet connected. Without this "right to connection", the transhumanist project cannot be set up. According to transhumanists, it would be advisable to use "positive" psychology to take human improvement projects further: increasing digital presence for everyone around the world, ensuring a new empathy and a better social link through the digital monitoring of everyone's psychology. The "Mood Mapping" already available on Facebook is a pertinent example of it: each individual's psychology can be determined through tag clouds. Thus, an individual predominantly using the word "why?" should present a rather depressive personality. "Can you imagine what could be done if the governments could know the mood of their population?" One of the inventors of Google, presents the next stage of evolution: "You always have your phone in your hand, but it will soon be directly implanted in your forearm or in your brain". "What does 'coming to the world' mean – when it becomes possible to control a robot from a distance and see through its eyes?", Peter Diamandis asks.

---

and the 21st most powerful personality in the world in 2016, according to Forbes Magazine.

4 Convergence of NBICs refers to the acceleration and interrelation of advances in nanotechnology (N), biotechnology (B), computer technology (I) and cognitive science (C). For work carried out within the Risk, Quality and Sustainable Environment Division of Maison de la Recherche en Sciences Humaines (MRSH), *see* "La convergence Nano-Bio-Info-Cogno: myth, reality or potentiality?" [Nano-Bio-Info-Cogno Convergence: Myth, Reality or Potential?], F. Lemarchand (organizer), 28–29 May 2013, MRSH Caen, *available online at* http://www.unicaen.fr/recherche/mrsh/risques/1298.

The Singularity University aims to "educate, inspire and empower leaders to apply exponential technologies to meet the great challenges of humanity [by exploiting] emerging technologies such as artificial intelligence, robotics and digital biology".[5] As a result, it appears that the relationship to others and to the world would potentially be profoundly disrupted. A new humanism would be on the move, in which algorithms and Big Data would play a decisive role. Artificial intelligence would be the future of the human condition, man being both controlled and predicted. The semantics used (particular, unconditional) arouse the feeling that no doubt is possible on the feasibility or desirability of the project. A new ideal of human perfectibility[6] is being promoted, with billions of dollars of investment coming from GAFAM (Google Apple Facebook Amazon Microsoft), Web giants alongside BATX (for Baidu, Alibaba, Tencent and Xiaomi), and NATU (Netflix, Airbnb, Tesla, Uber).

Not a week goes by without news indicating that we are entering a period of accelerating announcements, projects and even achievements. We can mention: Elon Musk and the Neuralink project to improve human cognitive performance,[7] the correction of defective genes by the CRISPR-Cas9 chisel,[8] the

---

5 Singularity University, About SU, *available online at* https://su.org/about/.

6 N. Le Dévédec, *La société de l'amélioration : le renversement de la perfectibilité humaine, de l'Humanisme des Lumières à l'Humain augmenté* [*The Society of Improvement: the Overthrow of Human Perfectibility, from Enlightenment Humanism to the Human Augmented*], Thèse Sciences Politiques et Sociologie, cotutelle J. Beaudoine & C. Lafontaine, Universities of Rennes 1 and Montréal, 2013; C. Byk, "Le droit et l'idée de perfectibilité humaine" [The Right and the Idea of Human Perfectibility], International symposium organized with the support of the GIP Droit et Justice, *Agir en justice au nom des générations futures* [*Taking Legal Action on Behalf of Future Generations*], Caen, 2017.

7 Jean-Pierre Henry described the project as follows: "What Elon Musk's new project, Neuralink, proposes is the coupling of our brain with a computer, an achievement that would allow instant exchanges with all human brains through the global Internet network. This coupling would also relieve our memory and expand our knowledge by allowing direct access to Google-type databases without the need for a hardware intermediary. More translation, more dictionary and even our memories would be stored in the universal database". J.-P. Henry, "Le projet Neuralink, rêve ou réalité ?" [The Neuralink Project: Dream or Reality?], *Futuribles*, 26 Sep. 2017, *available online at* https://www.futuribles.com/en/article/le-projet-neuralink-reve-ou-realite/.

8 AFMTéléthon, CRISPR/CAS9, *available online at* https://www.afm-telethon.fr/glossaire/crisprcas9-90754. CRISPR stands for Clustered Regularly Interspaced Short Palindromic Repeats, and Cas9 is one of the enzymes produced by the CRISPR system that binds to DNA; CRISPR-Cas9 is a genome editing tool that enables geneticists

development of artificial intelligence, the acquisition of Saudi Arabian nationality by a humanoid robot,[9] the fact that a man claims to be a cyborg,[10] the quest for the death of death,[11] the development of a test to determine the sex of an unborn child only eight weeks after conception with the risks of abortion that this entails.[12]

The research prospects are staggering, in the military, medical and societal fields.[13] First, in the military field, autonomous weapons or "killer robots" could soon replace human soldiers. This has already been the case for three years in the demilitarized zone separating North Korea and South Korea. A robot designed by Samsung is capable of detecting movement over four kilometers and shooting intruders without any human intervention. Second, in the medical field, the use of artificial intelligence would make it possible to improve diagnosis, particularly

---

and medical researchers to edit parts of the genome by removing, adding or altering sections of the DNA sequence.

9 B. Condomina, "L'Arabie saoudite accorde la citoyenneté à un robot" [Saudia Arabia Grants Citizenship to a Robot], *Radio France Internationale Les Voix Du Monde*, 28 Oct. 2017, *available online at* http://www.rfi.fr/moyen-orient/20171028-arabie-saoudite-intelligence-artificielle-robot-sophia-nationalite-citoyenne.

10 "Un Britannique se Revendique Premier 'Cyborg', du Monde, Mi-Homme Mi-Robot" [A Brittannian Claims the World's First "Cyborg", Mid-Man's Mid-Robot], *Gènéthique*, 15 Feb. 2018, *available online at* http://www.genethique.org/fr/un-britannique-se-revendique-premier-cyborg-du-monde-mi-homme-mi-robot-69190.html (source: Daily Mail, 14 Feb. 2018).

11 L. Alexandre, M.D., *La Mort de la Mort : Comment la technomédicine va bouleverser l'humanité* [*The Death of Death: How Technomedicine Will Revolutionize Humanity*], JC Lattès, 2011.

12 "Garçon ou fille ? un nouveau test fiable dès 8 semaines pourrait provoquer une vague d'avortements sélectifs" [Boy or Girl? A New, Reliable Test After 8 Weeks Could Cause a Wave of Selective Abortion], *Gènéthique*, 25 Apr. 2018, *available online at* http://www.genethique.org/fr/garcon-ou-fille-un-nouveau-test-fiable-des-8-semaines-pourrait-provoquer-une-vague-davortements. (source: S. Matthews & G. Martin, *Daily Mail*, 24 Apr. 2018).

13 According to Jean-Gabriel Ganascia, it is a question of engaging in a reflection on "[the future of mankind at a time of convergence between molecular genetic technologies, neural implants, bionics, nanorobotics, artificial intelligence, data masses and deep learning]". J.-G. Ganascia, "Des humanités numériques à la Singularité technologique. Que reste-t-il de l'Humanisme ?" [From the Digital Humanities to the Technological Singularity. What is left of Humanism?], *Archives de Philosophie du Droit*, 2017, Vol. 59, p. 193.

with regard to melanomas.[14] In addition, the boundary between repair and improvement of the human body is becoming increasingly blurred.[15] The "artificial" creation of human beings, devoid of any genealogical link, becomes possible; the modification and selection of embryos even before birth, a reality. An "emancipation" of the human condition is said to be in progress thanks, in particular, to research on totipotent cells, genetic modifications, or even the 3D printing of organs.[16] Illness and death are no longer perceived as fatalities. People could tear themselves away from nature by programming and totally controlling life. Third and finally, at the societal level, human relations are undergoing profound changes. It is now possible, through the use of algorithms, to know people's state of mind and personality better than "real" friends. The profound difference in nature between human beings and machines is likely to gradually diminish. For example, some advertisements already resort to the eroticization of the bionic woman, announcing the advent of a new humanity.

Transhumanist ideology, sprawling in its ramifications and applications, is experiencing multiple currents.[17] While transhumanists all advocate the

---

14 An artificial intelligence system detects melanomas in a more efficient way (95%) than by dermatologists (86.6%). "Un nouvel outil pour aider au dépistage des mélanomes" [New Tool to Help Detect Melanomas], *Gènéthique*, 29 May 2018, *available online at* http://www.genethique.org/fr/un-nouvel-outil-pour-aider-au-depistage-des-melanomes-69790.html (source: S. Johnson, Daily Mail Australia, 29 May 2018). Medical diagnostic software is more effective (81% of correct answers) than medical students (72%). "Polémique: le logiciel britanique qui diagnostiquerait mieux que les médecins eux-mêmes ?" [Polemic: The British Software that Diagnosed Better than Doctors Themselves?], *Gènéthique*, 29 May 2018, *available online at* http://www.genethique.org/fr/polemique-le-logiciel-britanique-qui-diagnostiquerait-mieux-que-les-medecins-eux-memes-70012.html (source: P. Thomeret, *Le Quotidien du Médecin*, 29 June 2018)).

15 *See* "Les interventions non thérapeutiques sur le corps humain" [Non-therapeutic Interventions on the Human Body], *Droit de la famille,* June 2018.

16 The objective of this 3D printing would be to use patient cells to recreate damaged tissue, or even, in the long term, a complete organ. V.B. Tosseri, "LabSkin Creations, l'impression 3D dans le peau" [LabSkin Creations, the 3D Print in the Skin], *La Croix*, 07 Apr. 2017, *available online at* https://www.la-croix.com/Economie/Entreprises/LabSkin-Creations-limpression-3D-dans-peau-2017-04-07-1200837823.

17 G. Dorthe, *Malédiction des objets absents : explorations épistémiques, politiques et écologiques du mouvement transhumaniste par un chercheur intégré* [*Curse of Absent Objects: Epistemic, Political and Ecological Explorations of the Transhumanist Movement by an Embedded Researcher*], Doctoral thesis, University of Lausanne and University Paris I Panthéon-Sorbonne, 2018.

improvement of the human being through new technologies, there are still significant differences between techno-progressors, immortalists, libertarians and singularists in particular. The various currents are trying to get closer in order to gain in power – for example, as revealed by the European TransVision 2017 conference, which was held from 9 to 11 November 2017 in Brussels. A structuring of the movement is being implemented. This search for unity also requires the adoption of unifying texts: the World Association of Transhumanists adopted a Transhumanistic Declaration on 1 December 2002.[18] Point 1 clearly states that:

> The future of humanity will be radically transformed by technology. We consider the possibility that human beings may undergo changes, such as rejuvenation, increased intelligence through biological or artificial means, the ability to modulate their own psychological state, the abolition of suffering and the exploration of the universe.

Even now, potential critics are described as "bio-conservatives", driven by a "negative psychology". Their desire is to preserve the random nature of human life and to respect the finiteness of its existence.

However, it is important "not to ignore the realities as they are and to be able to organize them in a legal system that is capable of evolving".[19] It is therefore important to question the foundation of our legal rules in order to be able to adapt them to a profoundly changing society. The transhumanist project involving systemic improvement and metamorphosis of both the human condition and our civilization, undermines the anthropological categories on which the fundamental notions of law are based.

> The ultimate objective of the Transhumanists is to achieve the advent of posthumanism. From humans who simply need to have parts of their bodies repaired by means of robotic technologies, with the objective to give him back the capacities he has lost, we now move on to a trend of improving human beings with capacities that go beyond the ones they should normally have, and hence surpassing human nature.[20]

---

18 Transhumanisme et Intelligence Artificielle, "Le déclaration Transhumaniste" [Transhumanistic Declaration], translated by R. Gauthier, 2013, *available online at* https://iatranshumanisme.com/transhumanisme/la-declaration-transhumaniste/ (accessed 27 June 2019). This Declaration has been amended and other texts have marked the development of this ideology since then.

19 *See* C. Byk, "Le droit et l'idée de perfectibilité humaine" [Law and the Idea of Human Perfectibility], *Revue de la Recherche Juridique - Droit prospectif*, 2017, Issue 4, p. 1399.

20 N. Nevejans, *Traité de droit et d'éthique de la robotique civile* [Treaty of Law and Ethics of Civil Robotics], LEH Edition, 2017, p. 1138.

Whereas the humanism as defined in the Enlightenment period, as inherited from the Renaissance, was based on the idea of the perfectibility of human being through society (culture, education, the arts), transhumanism is based on the biotechnological improvement of individuals against society.[21]

Therefore, what kind of legal humanism could stand up against transhumanism, which is defined – in the rhetoric – as a new kind of humanism? According to the transhumanist ideology, nature has created "imperfect" human beings while technology will enhance the process to create a new "augmented" Humankind. However, this type of humanism will remain selective (targeting the small solvent part of humanity), with evolution (biological and technical) *ultimately* taking over the process to eliminate techno-resisters. It is now particularly necessary to conduct research within the depths of ethics and law(s). It is important to identify, for the sake of standardization, the discrepancies and desynchronization points between the state of positive law and the research carried out by transhumanists. There is no doubt that it will be necessary to mobilize a new legal imagination at a time when the pace of announcements and challenges to legal science from this ideology is accelerating exponentially. It is also necessary to identify the irreducible legal values that lay down the measures to protect the human condition, namely the ontology of Humanity.

A plurality of issues can be distinguished that are at once philosophical, ethical and legal, such as:

How does it feel to live in this world without belonging to the chain of Human generations, as is the case with the cloning process, for instance? How does it feel to begin a life when your birth was preceded by a eugenic selection or manipulation on a still unborn child? How can the law react, anticipate, and how can the legislation be adapted to such changes? How does it feel to live in a world framed by global connections and a possible humanization of robots that can be remotely controlled?

How does it feel to live in a world that is in quest of immortality? What are the potential hazards that can be identified for the sake of a project that pushes the limits of life? What kind of cross-referenced analyses involving psychiatry and philosophy would shed light on such a quest to achieve immortality?[22]

---

21 *See* Byk, 2017.

22 Nathalie Nevejans already proposes a beginning of reflection in this sense: "As an almighty Homo Faber, man feels a deep narcissistic wound of being so little – sick, fragile, mortal, limited – when he knows he is so great. Finally, transforming oneself to the means of biotechnological interventions means bringing one's body into conformity with what one feels. This is no news, even for law. The struggle of today's transhumanists is similar to that of the transsexuals of the past, who wanted to match

In fact, what is indeed at stake here are the fundamental anthropological categories, which themselves serve as the basis for the framework of legal norms. It therefore becomes particularly urgent to question the role of law in the context of the globalization of the transhumanist project. What are the consequences for the human condition and for future generations? What answers can law (including human rights) provide to address new vulnerabilities or even unprecedented violations of the human condition? What mode of governance could be implemented in order to avoid the risks of participating in a global and totalitarian project? Finally, what impulses can be identified to open a new stage of reflection?

I. The Advent of a New Humanity, a Source of New Vulnerabilities

The other objective of the transhumanist project is to claim the emergence of a new humanity, which would be "increased", improved, selected and created.

Human enhancement, already pursued before birth, would run the risk of dividing humanity into sub-categories disregarding the principle of human dignity that acknowledges the equal value of all people, thereby undermining *ipso facto* the principle of non-discrimination.

Moreover, it is very confusing for French lawyers to witness eugenic claims in a context of globalization that allows such research to be carried out where they are qualified as crimes against humanity under French law.[23] A society based on selection of human beings according to ideological criteria reminds us of the dark hours of our history. The transhumanist project strongly echoes the Nazi ideology, which was based on the selection of "good generations". However, if we

their appearance and marital status with their perceived sexual identity. The philosopher Günther Anders created the concept of 'Promethean shame' to describe the feeling that humans feel not only because of the obsolete nature of their origin, but also because of the imperfection of the machines, which are irreproachable because they are calculated in the smallest details. From now on, human beings feel a deep sense of inferiority in the face of machines, so that they nourish themselves to become a product [...]. Transhumanists feel a deep Promethean shame at the imperfection of their being, destined to age, pain and death, so that augmentative technologies appear to them as the only ways of salvation, their only remedy for their unbearable finiteness". N. Nevejans, 2017, p. 1140.

23 According to article 214-1 of the French Criminal Code, crimes against the human species are punishable by a fine of 7,500,000 euros and 30 years' imprisonment.

take a closer look, we may wonder if some of our current trends including fetus selection do not already raise the risk of eugenics.[24]

With human beings becoming "produced", there is a risk of infringing the genealogical principle: sometimes loosely bound to the genetic linkage sequence (three-person, assisted reproductive technology), sometimes unrelated to it (reproductive human cloning), future generations would have difficulty attempting to trace back their origins.

Finally, since it seems to be unthinkable for humanity as a whole, could it be that the quest for immortality results in a new type of vulnerability which law had not considered possible so far: that of some people facing death? Can discrimination before death be tolerable as a social project? Should the imbalance in human conditions and temporal existence be entrenched or disregarded by law?

Wouldn't the law conduct a Copernican revolution by introducing posthuman rights such as the right to be augmented? Imposing legal limits on such a project seems only possible by enacting new criminal provisions, such as global recognition of crimes against the human species.[25] For Louise Vandelac, transhumanism is nothing more or less than "anthropocide".[26] We are switching from protection of the human condition – as an individual right – to new forms of protection for Humankind and future generations.

II. At the Crossroads Between Humanity, Men and Robots

The human condition has been questioned against a background of accelerating the robotization of humans and the humanization of robots. Humans and robots have started getting closer to one another. This is a real civilizational challenge

---

24 In France, 1,552 of the 1,956 fetuses diagnosed with Down's syndrome in 2014, were eliminated before birth following a medical termination of pregnancy (IMG). "Trisomie 21: de l'IMG à l'IVG" [Chromosome 21: From Medical Termination of Pregnancy to Abortion], *Gènéthique*, 04 May 2018, *available online at* http://www.genethique.org/fr/trisomie-21-de-limg-livg-69654.html.

25 *See* E. Gaillard, "What future for the interpretative application of the bio-law? From the precautionary principle to the bio-right of anticipation", V Franco-Latin American Forum on Bioethics, Bioethics, the Judge and Human Rights, University of Panama, 11 Apr. 2017; D. Roets, "Réprimer pénalement les interventions biotechniques à nalité" [Penalizing biotechnical interventions for transhumanist purposes?], *in* X. Labbée (ed.), *L'homme augmenté face au droit* [*The Enhanced Man Facing the Law*], Presses Universitaires du Septentrion, 2015, p. 143.

26 *See* Louise Vandelac's essay #18 (this book) on "The Posthumous Post-human, or Abolishing the Future of Generations: By What Right?".

that historically captures the role and functions of law. The blurring of the very notion of humanity keeps losing transparency, so much that transhumanists have started undermining the fundamental legal categories. This is how the distinction between things and people is increasingly losing its meaning.

First, human robotization questions the very essence of what a human being is. How far can we develop technology before we start losing our humanity? Is there a minimum percentage of "human material" until we cannot be considered as people anymore and therefore as natural beings (a category currently covering only human beings born alive and able to live from birth to death)? Should a human being reacting under the control of his brain implant be legally considered responsible for his actions?[27] Is there a solution against hacking?

The humanization of robots, for its part (and according to some people) considers the right to recognition as a person before the law, especially in order to establish robots' legal liability.[28] However, this would lead to a complete loss of responsibility for the creators of these new technologies. The creation of the atomic bomb introduced this question earlier in our history. A similar study should be carried out with regard to transhumanism. These questions are already being tackled, particularly in the event of accidents involving autonomous cars.

The temptation to assimilate robots with humans also leads us to consider granting them rights. For example, could robots be considered as the creators of an intellectual work,[29] or even benefit from human rights rethought as "posthuman rights"?

A study of legal anthropology appears essential to identify the foundations of the legal concepts of things and persons, and to address the issues raised by both the robotization of humans and the humanization of robots.

---

27 "Ce n'est pas ma faute, mon implant cérébral m'a incité à le faire" [This is not my Scythe, my Brain Implant Made me do it], *Généthique*, 04 Apr. 2018, *available online at* http://www.genethique.org/fr/ce-nest-pas-ma-faute-mon-implant-cerebral-ma-incite-le-faire-69474.html (sources: L.Y. Cabrera & J. Carter-Johnson, *The Conversation*, 03 Apr. 2018).

28 A letter was sent by 156 AI experts to the European Commission on 12 April 2018 to alert it to the risks presented by the granting of legal personality to robots. "Statut juridique des robots : des experts alertent la commission Européenne" [Status of Legal Framework for Robots: Experts Alert the European Commission], *Généthique*, 18 Apr. 2018, *available online at* http://www.genethique.org/fr/statut-juridique-des-robots-des-experts-alertent-la-commission-europeenne-69586.html (citing sources "Marianne, Alexandra Saviana (13/10/2018); Editions Francis Lefèbvre, Audrey Tabuteau (18/04/2018)").

29 *Contra* C. Alleaume & A. Pigeon-Bormans, "Droit(s) d'auteur des robots: 'Nous cherchons à comprendre'" [Right(s) of robots: "We seek to understand"], *Légipresse*, Nov. 2017, pp. 523–524.

III. Transhumanism, a Global and Totalizing Project?

There is a kind of imperceptible shift towards a "soft" totalitarianism where nothing can be classified as secret, intimate or private: everything is traced, everything is recorded. Not to mention Edward Snowden's denunciation of the U.S. monitoring programme, we are faced with a new form of global and general control. Everyone voluntarily reveals elements of their private lives on Facebook, and loses the ownership of the photos and videos uploaded on those sites. This is why, insidiously, some multinationals happen to hold information that should, in principle, remain private. This is particularly dangerous considering the dramatic increase in data hacking.[30]

Combined with facial recognition, other cascading slides are already at work. In China, the population is constantly subject to facial recognition and controls of various kinds:

> If you travel around this country, then you should know that a camera will (most likely) filming you in real time, no matter where you are and you will be recognizable through artificial intelligence. If you dare crossing a road outside the pedestrian crossing area in front of a camera, then you should expect receiving a fine and if you do not pay it, you could be banned from the transport networks or airports.[31]

Mood control is also still used in China, whether in schools to assess students' attention,[32] or in companies to check employees' full working capacity.[33]

---

30 Agence France-Presse, "Sécurité : les principaux vols des données personnelles" [Security: Key Your Personal Data], *Le Point*, 15 May 2018, *available online at* https://www.lepoint.fr/high-tech-internet/securite-les-principaux-vols-de-donnees-personnelles-15-05-2018-2218483_47.php.

31 "La reconnaissance faciale en Chine : un outil de surveillance redoutable" [Facial recognition in China: a Formidable Surveillance Tool], *Généthique*, 13 Apr. 2018, *available online at* http://www.genethique.org/fr/la-reconnaissance-faciale-en-chine-un-outil-de-surveillance-redoutable-69535.html (source: É. Lefaix, Siècle Digital, 13 Apr. 2018).

32 Cameras recording high school students' attention: relying on facial expressions to determine their emotional state ("neutral, happy, sad, disappointed, angry, scared and surprised"), their score depends on their level of concentration. "Chine: des caméras intelligentes surveillent la concentration des lycéens" [China: Smart Cameras Monitor High-School Student Concentration], *Généthique*, 18 May 2018, *available online at* http://www.genethique.org/fr/chine-des-cameras-intelligentes-surveillent-la-concentration-des-lyceens-69741.html (source: N. Mackako, *20 minutes*, 17 May 2018).

33 Employees filmed during their work through the use of helmets with sensors that analyze their brain waves to adapt their work rhythm in the event of emotional changes such as stress, anger or fatigue. "Des capteurs cérébraux utilisés en chine pour détecter les émotions des employés" [Brain Sensors Used in China to Detect Emotions of

These first applications of facial recognition technology, coupled with an authoritarian regime raise questions about the future of democracy in a hyper-connected society.

IV. The "Unthoughts" of Transhumanism

Some of the hazardous aspects of the transhumanist project are rarely identified. First, it is a question of probing the ecological viability and environmental and health consequences of a project that aims at technologically modifying human beings. Based on the global connection (of the planet and humans to each other), transhumanism is an important source of various types of pollution: "the information and communication technology sector thus produces 50% more greenhouse gases than air transport".[34] The question about the finiteness of primary resources to bring about a Posthuman and the connected society that comes along with it, is thus particularly significant. Many voices are already denouncing the "hidden side of digital technology" and the obvious ecological limits of such a project.[35]

It is also important to consider issues relating to responsibility towards future generations. The increasing NBIC convergence raises questions about ethical and legal responsibilities that have not previously been entertained with respect to future generations. Can we predetermine the existence of someone on ideological criteria? Wouldn't a principle of non-determination be necessary to counter the tendency towards pre-determination of human existence, because "in the fate of each human being, in his safeguarded or lost dignity, the idea of humanity as a whole is at stake"?[36] On the scale of humanity, can the project of post-human beings progress be counterbalanced by the right of future generations to decide whether they want to be augmented and live in a consubstantially discriminatory society?

Employees], *Généthique*, 18 May 2018, *available online at* http://www.genethique.org/fr/des-capteurs-cerebraux-utilises-en-chine-pour-detecter-les-emotions-des-employes-69642.html (source: C. Levenson, *Slate*, 01 May 2018).

34 H. Védrine, preface by G. Pitron, *La guerre des métaux rares* [*The War of Rare Metals*], Les Liens qui Libèrent, 2018, p. 10.

35 M. Dobre, F. Flipo & M. Michot, *La face cachée du numérique : l'impact environnemental des nouvelles technologies* [The Hidden Face of Digital Technology: the Environmental Impact of New Technologies], éd. L'échappée, 2013.

36 R. Badinter, Colloquium of the Institut des droits de l'homme du Barreau de Paris, Preface.

Finally, it is important to rethink people's relationship to their own bodies. A new opposition has appeared: a possible "right to be enhanced" (claimed by transhumanists) versus that of "not being enhanced" (claimed by bioconservatives). Traditionally considered as "the person's *substatrum*",[37] the body is treated "as the person, as long as it is at his/her disposal (*i.e.*, from birth to death). The body then becomes a person by nature".[38] However, the possibility of separating elements of the human body (first blood, then gametes and organs) has led to the recognition of the real nature of these elements after their "detachment".[39] The nature of the whole body must be further questioned. The notion of legal person is in fact only an intellectual creation from which the body can be distinguished: it "refers only to a slew of obligations, responsibility and subjective rights, in other words, a set of norms".[40] The body is therefore a legal thing, and even an appropriated thing – in other words, property. Contrary to what is usually stated, the right of ownership is not a property right. According to Frédéric Zenati,[41] it is indeed possible to redefine the right of ownership as a relationship that binds its holder to all of his property in an exclusive manner, whether that relationship is of a patrimonial or extra-patrimonial nature. Characterized by the power to exclude others from the use we make of the thing we own, the right of ownership could then become "private goods" of the person, such as the human body[42] or the attributes of personality. Positive law has already moved in this direction, even if the classification of property is not officially retained: as

37 J. Carbonnier, *Droit et passion du droit sous la Ve République* [*Law and Passion of the Law under the Fifth Republic*], Flammarion, 1996, p. 159.

38 X. Labbée, "Corps humain" [Human Body], *in* D. Alland & S. Rials (eds.), *Dictionnaire de la Culture juridique* [Dictionary of Legal Culture], Quadrige/Lamy-Presses Universitaires de France, 2003.

39 "Separated from the person, the body (organ, product, tissue or corpse) becomes a piece of furniture by nature". X. Labbée, 2003.

40 H. Kelsen, *Théorie pure du droit* [*Pure Theory of Law*], translated by H. Thevenaz, La Baconnière, 1953, p. 113.

41 F. Zenati, *Essai sur la nature juridique de la propriété : contribution à l'étude du droit subjectif* [*Essay on the Legal Nature of Property: Contribution to the Study of Subjective Law*], Thèse dactylographiée, Lyon, 1981.

42 F. Zenati-Castaing & T. Revet, *Manuel de droit des personnes* [Manual of the Law of Persons], Presses Universitaires de France, 2006; T. Revet, "Le corps humain est-il une chose appropriée?" [Is the Human Body an Appropriated Thing?], *Revue trimestrielle de droit civil*, 2017, p. 587 (text of an intervention at the conference "The human body seized by the law: between freedom and property", organized in Caen on 14 October 2016 by A. Catherine & A. Cayol).

stated in article 16-1 of the French Civil Code, "everyone has the right of respect for their own body" and "the human body is inviolable", which, in principle, prevents anyone from violating a person's physical integrity without his/her consent.[43] We could find here a legal basis to refuse any "improvement" of the body against our will. However, this prohibition only applies to France as a whole. A solution must be sought at the international level.

Acknowledging the existence of a property right over the body is often viewed as eventually problematic in that the power of self-determination would therefore necessarily be unlimited, opening the door to all imaginable abuses. This is not the case in France. In 1804, Article 544 of the Civil Code specified that the owner's prerogatives may be limited in order to take into consideration the general interest. The owner cannot be conceived as isolated from his property. Without going so far as to question the very existence of subjective rights,[44] as Léon Duguit did, it is possible to consider that they "[cannot be totally removed from the search of the general interest]".[45] The advent of the "third generation"[46] of fundamental rights shows the transition from an individualistic philosophy to a new legal "humanism": "the person is no longer seen as the bearer of individual interests, but as a being whose fundamental attributes he holds as a member of

43 Exceptions apply "in case of medical necessity for the person" or even "exceptionally in the interest of others" under article 16-3 of the French Civil Code.

44 L. Duguit, *Les transformations générales du droit privé depuis le code Napoléon* [General Transformations of Private Law Since the Napoleonic Code], Librairie Félix Alcan, 2nd edition, 1920, reprinted 1999, p. 21 ("La propriété n'est pas une droit; elle est une fonction sociale" [Property is No Right, it is a Social Function]).

45 J. Ghestin (ed.), *Traité de droit civil. General Introduction* [Civil Law Treaty. General Introduction], 4th edition, Librairie générale de droit et de jurisprudence, 1994, No. 198, p. 148; E. Gounot, *Le principe d'autonomie de la volonté en droit privé* [*The Principle of Autonomy of the Will in Private Law*], A. Rousseau (ed.), 1912, p. 339 ("Tout droit est un pouvoir, soit; mais un pouvoir au service de fins objectivement juste, un pouvoir correspondant à une fonction").

46 The so-called "first generation" included civil and political rights based on individual freedom and proclaimed by the 1789 Declaration of the Rights of Man and the Citizen; the "second generation" included economic and social rights from the Preamble of the 1946 Constitution. These "rights-credits" imply a positive intervention by the State; and, the third generation includes "solidarity rights" such as the right to the environment. K. Vasak, "Pour une troisième génération des droits de l'homme" [For the Third Generation of Human Rights], *in* C. Swinarski, *Études et essais sur le droit international humanitaire et les principes de la Croix rouge* [*Studies and Essays on International Humanitarian Law and the Principles of the Red Cross*], Martinus Nijhoff Publishers, 1984, p. 843.

Humankind [that] must be preserved".[47] These "new" fundamental rights, "solidarity rights",[48] bear a collective dimension and impose correlative duties on their holders.[49]

Can the principle of human dignity provide a bulwark to protect against the desires of transhumanists to transform the human condition? Traditionally, the principle of human dignity is conceived in an individualistic way, as "the eminent value of the individual in view of the unique, irreplaceable nature of his personal accomplishment".[50] Now, dignity also includes the means of preserving the human species.[51] In other words, should we be able to limit the powers of individuals over their own body when the acts they envisage are likely to harm their very humanity?[52] Moreover, in view of the many legal actions taken in the name of, and on behalf of future generations, it is becoming increasingly clear that a principle of dignity for future generations is emerging. This development opens up new legal perspectives, paving the way to limitations on transhumanist ideology.

---

47 V. Monteillet, *La contractualisation du droit de l'environnement* [The Contractualization of Environmental Law], Dalloz, 2017, No. 577, p. 458.

48 *Ibid.*, No. 574, p. 455.

49 "As generations of human rights succeed one another, the share of right seems to gradually yield to the share of obligation". F. Ost, "Réflexions sur les enjeux éthiques de la crise écologique?" [Enlarging the Political Community: Through Rights or Through Responsibilities?], *in* Th. Berns (ed.), *Le droit saisi par le collectif* [*The Right Seized by the Collective*], Bruylant, 2004, p. 245.

50 G. Lebreton, "Les ambiguités du droit français à l'égard de la dignité de la personne humaine" [The Ambiguities of French Law with regard to the Dignity of the Human Person], *in* P. Gélard & P. Fraisseix, *Mélanges Patrice Gélard; droit constitutionnel* [*Essays in Honor of Gélard Patrice: Constitutional Law*], Montchrestien, 2000, p. 55.

51 B. Edelman, "La dignité de la personne humaine, un concept nouveau" [The Dignity of the Human Person: a New Concept], Dalloz Collection, 1997, p. 185; M. Fabre-Magnan, "Dignité humaine" [Human Dignity], *in Dictionnaire des droits de l'homme* [*Dictionary of Human Rights*], Presses Universitaires de France, 2008, p. 285.

52 *See, e.g.*, the famous decision of the "dwarf throwing" case decided on 27 Oct. 1995. *Commune of Morsang-sur-Orge*, Conseil d'Etat [State Council], *La semaine juridique*, 1996, Vol. 2, Issue No. 22630, note F. Hamon.

PART 6. THE IMPERATIVE TO LOOK FORWARD

In this sixth and final Part, Professor Emilie Gaillard emphasises that the very protection of the future of the future is a new ethical and legal challenge. Incorporating symposium contributions that we were unable to integrate in this book, Gaillard provides an overview of multiple challenges raised by the complexity of transgenerational damage. The multiple faces of transgenerational damage – dual, systemic, transtemporal and transpatial – endanger the human condition as much as the integrity of all living beings, including all resources supporting life. The resulting influences on the cycle of life and its future present major challenges to scientific thought. Accordingly, it is important to extend all legal concepts, notions, principles and logic to the transgenerational field. Toward that end, an epistemological break in the law is necessary; several legal bases can be asserted in an effort to protect the rights of future generations. This essay identifies many direct and indirect paths that are possible from both theoretical and practical points of views (essay #20 on "Legal Bases for Protecting Future Generations?").

David Forman then introduces the man who opened all of these paths, Philippine environmental attorney Antonio A. Oposa, Jr., offering him a platform to conclude this book as he closed the symposium itself: by urging all of us – lawyers, scientists, and citizens all over the world – to actively participate in making a difference for future generations (essay #21 on "Making a Difference for Future Generations").

Emilie GAILLARD[1]

20. Legal Bases for Protecting Future Generations

The issue of legal protection for future generations is a matter of importance for our civilization, as it puts our future at risk. Reports regarding humanity, animal species and the equilibrium of our planet could not be clearer: we are facing a tipping point; key decisions must be taken to protect our civilization and other living species. Scientists warn of a sixth mass extinction of species due to actions carried out by man.[2] Biodiversity is declining before our very eyes while nothing seems to be done. From its very beginnings and throughout time, the building blocks of life are under sustained threat across generations. The earth, water and oceans are polluted, full of nitrate residue, pesticides, lingering organic pollutants, heavy metals, and radionuclides spread by winds and currents. Tiny micro-plastics can be found scattered throughout the planet, even in the depths of our oceans. These plastics act as sponges which absorb endocrine disruptors, creeping into our food chain and causing lasting harm. We breathe in polluted air, containing fine particles that can often be as harmful to our health as asbestos. Climate and geophysical cycles are disrupted, intensifying extreme weather events and disturbing natural life cycles. The most recent reports from the IPCC and the IPBES[3] are extremely worrying, forecasting a collapse in the foundations of life and biodiversity in the short to medium term. Reports on environmental health are equally alarming. Babies are born with more than 200 residual chemical products within their genes, which presents a grave risk to gene expression. All living beings are contaminated by residual

---

1 See collection of articles available online at http://unicaen.academia.edu/EGAILLARD.

2 G. Ceballos, P.R. Ehrlich, A.D. Barnosky, A. García, R.M. Pringle & T.M. Palmer, "Accelerated modern human–induced species losses: Entering the sixth mass extinction", *Science Advances*, 19 June 2015, Vol. 1, No. 5, *available online at* https://advances.sciencemag.org/content/1/5/e1400253.

3 The Intergovernmental Science-Policy Platform on Biodiversity and Ecosystem Services (IPBES), *Global assessment report on biodiversity and ecosystem services*, E.S. Brondizio, J. Settele, S. Díaz & H. T. Ngo (eds.), approved by the IPBES Plenary at its 7th session, Paris, May 2019, *available online at* https://www.ipbes.net/global-assessment-biodiversity-ecosystem-services.

chemical products, causing rates of cancer, autism, intellectual disabilities and congenital disorders to soar among species all over the world.

Given this catastrophic historical context – "catastrophic" in the philosophical sense of the word[4] – it is surprising, perhaps even criminal, that there remain those who question the very existence of global warming and invent stories to hide the damaging effects of substances such as pesticides. It is certainly difficult to face such a reality. The psychological reflex of preservation leads us to take refuge in denial, believing the reassuring words and casting aside those who warn us about the urgency required to protect our future. The philosopher Jean-Pierre Dupuy identified the phenomenon as follows: "We know, but we do not believe what we know".[5] We know that future generations are in danger, but many people simply do not want to believe it. Such short-sightedness when looking to the future is no longer possible when civilization is at stake.

We owe thanks to philosopher Hans Jonas for his brilliant work, laying the foundations for an ethics of the future, which take into account the technological age and the protection of future generations.[6] This ethical framework is rooted in the philosophical and concrete acknowledgement of a new and unprecedented influence that humanity has on the future. In his work *The Imperative of Responsibility: In Search of an Ethics for the Technological Age*, Jonas (1903-1993)

---

4 An accident must be distinguished from the concept of catastrophe, which requires a paradigm shift: "Le temps des catastrophes c'est cette temporalité en quelque sorte inversée. La catastrophe comme évènement surgissant du néant, ne devient possible qu'en se 'possibilisant' […] C'est bien là la source de notre problème. S'il faut prévenir la catastrophe, on besoin de croire en sa possibilité avant qu'elle ne se produise. Si inversement, on réussit à la prévenir, sa non-réalisation la maintient dans le domaine de l'impossible, et les efforts de prévention en apparaissent rétrospectivement inutiles" [Catastrophes are characterized by this temporality that is in some sense inverted. As an event bursting forth out of nothing, the catastrophe becomes possible only by "making itself possible" and that is precisely the source of our problem. For if one is to prevent a catastrophe, one needs to believe in its possibility before it occurs. If, on the other hand, one succeeds in preventing it, its non-realization keeps it it in the realm of the impossible, and as a result, the prevention efforts will appear useless in retrospect]. Author's translation of J.-P. Dupuy, *Pour un catastrophisme éclairé. Quand l'impossible devient certain* [*For an Enlightened Catastrophism: When the Impossible Becomes Certain*], Seuil 2002, p. 13.

5 *Ibid.*, p. 142.

6 H. Jonas, *The Imperative of Responsibility: In Search of an Ethics for the Technological Age*, University of Chicago Press, 1985; H. Jonas, *For an ethic for the Future*, Rivages, 1997, translated by S. Cornille & P. Ivernel.

opened the ethical field of responsibility towards future generations and the nature of tomorrow's world. This has become necessary because of the unprecedented power that man has acquired over future generations, over intrinsic human nature, and over the essential conditions for life on Earth. According to Jonas, the technological era requires new ethical rules, given that responsibility for the future had never before been contemplated. He talks of a complete "ethical void" in this regard.[7] Indeed, the future used to be outside of our moral and ethical boundaries, since it seemed better and more obvious to "let the distant future take care of itself".[8] The philosopher further recognizes the "altered nature of human action"[9]: Man has become an object of technology, putting *homo faber* above *homo sapiens*.[10] Jonas believes that mankind has no right to commit suicide,[11] and that Humankind's existence must not be put in danger.[12] He then goes on to outline moral imperatives. These include: "act in a way that is compatible with lasting, authentic human life"[13] and "act in a way that is not destructive for possible future life".[14] Jonassian thought is infinitely inspiring and valuable when considering ethics for the future.[15] The philosopher offers several fundamental

7 H. Jonas, *Le principe responsabilité. Une éthique pour la civilisation technologique* [The Imperative of Responsibility: In Search of an Ethics for the Technological Age], Flammarion, 2000, p. 60, translated by J. Greisch.

8 *Ibid.*, p. 79. It is important to qualify this approach, which remains essentially western. This transgenerational approach that consists in living together in harmony with nature is present in the norms and beliefs of many indigenous populations.

9 H. Jonas, 2000, pp. 21-62.

10 *Ibid.*, pp. 35 & 50 (Titles). Compare Hannah Arendt's famous warning: "[But it could be that we, who are earth-bound creatures and have begun to act as though we were dwellers of the universe, will forever be unable to understand, that is, to think and speak about the things which nevertheless we are able to do. [...] If it should turn out to be true that knowledge (in the modern sense of know-how) and thought have parted company for good, then we would indeed become the helpless slaves, not so much of our machines as of our know-how, thoughtless creatures at the mercy of every gadget which is technically possible, no matter how murderous it is]". H. Arendt, *La condition de l'homme moderne* [*The Human Condition*], Paris Calmann-Lévy, 1983, pp. 9-10.

11 H. Jonas, 2000, p. 84.

12 *Ibid.* ("Never must the existence or the essence of man as a whole be put at stake in the hazards of action").

13 H. Jonas, 2000, p. 40.

14 *Ibid.*

15 E. Gaillard, "L'équité transgénérationnelle: perspectives de justice pour les générations futures" [Transgenerational Equity: Opportunities to Pursue Justice for Future Generations?], *in* A. Michelot (ed.), *Equité et environnement : Quel(s) modèle(s) de justice environnementale ?*, editions Larcier, 2012, p. 51.

principles for the construction of a new utopia focusing on the future. It must be stressed that *The Imperative of Responsibility* encompasses both the future of humanity and that of nature; Jonas perfectly expresses their interdependence.

The influence that Humankind holds over the future of humanity – as well as the biosphere – is now so widely acknowledged that geologists have begun to use the term "Anthropocene"[16] referring to our entry into a new geological age, during which human activity has had a significant and global impact on the earth's ecosystem.

Authors from various disciplines agree that man has acquired the power to upset geophysical balances and great chemical cycles (nitrogen, ozone, phosphorus, ocean acidification, etc.). Several stratigraphic indicators have been put forward, including the presence of plastics and radionuclides across the planet and across time. Although the term anthropocene is not yet in official use by the international community of geologists, it is increasingly employed by authors to describe the current era. In 2009, this was the context under which the Stockholm Resilience Centre developed the theory of planetary boundaries,[17] recognizing that the continued existence of our civilization would be at risk beyond certain limits.

This theory is in line with Donella Meadows & others' 1972 report entitled *The Limits to Growth,* which already warned of the need to limit the "growth" process.[18] In addition to entering new philosophical and geological eras, we have also entered into a new legal era,[19] each of which are characterized by a pressing need for civilization to create and commit to a paradigm of the finite, including:

---

16 A. Sinaï, *Penser la décroissance. Politiques de l'Anthropocène* [*Envisioning Degrowth: Politics of Anthropocene*], Presses de Sciences Po, 2013; R. Beau & C. Larrère, *Penser l'Anthropocène* [*Conceptualizing Anthropocene*], Presses de Sciences Po, March 2018.

17 Study led by an international team of 26 researchers, under the direction of Johan Röckström, "Planetary Boundaries: Exploring the Safe Operating Space for Humanity", *Ecology and Society*, 2009, Vol. 14, No. 2, Art. 32, *available online at* http://www.ecologyandsociety.org/vol14/iss2/art32/.

18 D.H. Meadows, D.L. Meadows, J. Randers & W.W. Behrens, *The Limits to Growth: A Report for THE CLUB OF ROME'S Project on the Predicament of Mankind*, Universe books, 1972, *available online at* http://www.donellameadows.org/wp-content/userfiles/Limits-to-Growth-digital-scan-version.pdf.

19 The same disruption is desired by some economists. According to Kenneth E. Boulding, "[Anyone who believes that exponential growth can can go on forever in a finite world is either a madman or an economist]"! M.-A. Monique Robin, *Sacrée Croissance*, La Découverte, Arte Editions, 2019, p. 53.

- ethical limits with regards the unlimited effects of mankind's action on the safety of the future;
- economic limits for a capitalist system based on exponential, unlimited growth in a world with limited resources;
- legal limits to regulate technology and, more generally, all actions carried out by a part of humanity which places human and non-human life under its influence, across space and time.

Professor Alexandre Kiss set the tone by insisting that, for legal experts, including future generations within the law would constitute a "Copernican revolution".[20] In other words, the legal universe would no longer revolve around man solely in relation to his contemporaries. The revolution should look beyond this and create law to encompass many more areas. There would be an increase in the scope of legal fields to incorporate the protection of nature, its life cycles, and its regeneration. Also, future generations would be protected by law for the first time. The question remains, however: can and should law be used to protect future generations?

It has long been understood that the future must take care of itself. Traditionally, law that addressed the future was considered dangerous and illegitimate. The idea of transgenerational law was rejected for the first time during the Enlightenment, when it was declared that the law could not force obligations on future generations.[21] But today, the planet, Humankind and all living beings are at a crossroads. In this context, we must consider how law can be used and

---

20 "According to Alexander Kiss, this fundamental change in our conception of international environmental law can be compared to the Copernican revolution which proclaimed that the center of the universe was not the earth but the sun: states are less and less the center of international relations, the focus becoming more and more mankind and its individual representatives, both living now and in the future. We are increasingly recognizing that environmental issues have interests that are common to all humankind. International environmental norms tend to restrict the actions of states for the interests of the community of humankind as a whole". E. Agius, "Obligations of Justice Towards Future Generations: a Revolution in Social and Legal Thought", *in* E. Agius & S. Busuttil (eds.), *Future Generations & International Law*, Earthscan Publications, Ltd., 1997, p. 7.

21 This was clearly expressed in article 28 of the 1793 *Déclaration des droits de l'homme et du citoyen* [Declaration on the Rights of the Citizen], which never came into effect, and which explained that "a people always has the right to review, to reform, and to alter its constitution. One generation cannot subject future generations to its law". P. Türk, *Théorie générale du droit constitutionnel* [*General Theory of Constitutional Law*], Gualino, 2nd edition, 2009, p. 56 (referencing article 28 of the *Déclaration des droits* of 1793, in addition to quoting title 7, article 1 of the French Constitution of

which legal measures can ensure protection of the future. We must also contemplate how to protect future generations, and whether this is actually possible.

According to Professor Mireille Delmas-Marty, we share a "community of destinies".[22] We are without a doubt at a civilizational crossroads. Law concerning future generations is designed to express this community of destinies in legal terms and establish respect for the future. This new type of law is based upon two main, interrelated approaches. The first approach concerns environmental law – i.e., the inclusion of the concept of future generations in the definition of sustainable development, which helps to ensure that civilization is aware of the limits of our natural resources. The second concerns law and bioethics, and protecting the human condition of humanity in the future. These considerations regarding transhumanism open up new areas of legal protection that must be shaped and strengthened.

In order to extend our legal imagination and renew the law by widening its range to include the transgenerational field, it is useful to carry out a realistic and complete assessment concerning the extent of harm done. This awareness makes it possible to highlight the urgent ethical and legal necessity to protect the future human condition, as well as species integrity, through new spatiotemporal perspectives. As a result, new fundamental legal principles for a law of future generations can be put forward. Within this new legal matrix, law can branch off in varied and multiple directions.

The first section below considers multiple challenges raised by the complexity of transgenerational harm. The second section outlines the legal bases for transgenerational law that focuses on establishing respect for the future.

I. The Multiple Challenges Raised by the Complexity of Transgenerational Harm

During this international symposium we heard a great deal about the unprecedented scale of transgenerational harm.[23] This is without doubt a new reality that

---

4 September 1791: "The National Assembly declares that the nation has the imprescriptible right to change its constitution").

22 M. Delmas-Marty, "Sociétés de la peur et/ou Communauté de destins ?" [Societies of Fear and/or Community of Destiny?], 31 Mar. 2009 (public lecture: *Liberté et sûreté dans un monde dangereux* [*Freedom and Safety in a Dangerous World*], Chaire Etudes juridiques comparatives et internationalisation du droit, Collège de France).

23 Several contributions could not be included in this book; however, they all contribute to characterizing the multiples faces of transgenerational damage. For example, Winiki Sage spoke about the theme of "How nuclear tests transformed Polynesian

is both systemic and full of complexities (*see* Section I.A. below). Science is being posed new questions, and there is a call for an epistemological review of the role, direction, and mission of the sciences. This new reality is made more complex in that it requires a series of paradigm changes, not only within the area of legal science (*see* Section I.B. below).

A. Transgenerational Harm: A Complex and Systemic Reality

According to Gérard Cornu's *Vocabulaire juridique*, harm is "[an attack on a person's body, property or moral rights, which confers to the victim a right to compensation when this is a result of nonfulfillment of a contract, an offense or an action deemed unlawful by law or the courts]".[24] Even if there were laws establishing responsibility towards future generations, it is hard to believe that compensation could be sought from previous generations. Traditionally, the concept of damage has been understood as delimited in time – the time of man who is actually alive and in a relation of reciprocity with his contemporaries. In this classic conception, damage is experienced in flesh, property or in spirit.[25] Yet, the complex and systemic reality of transgenerational harm questions both the integrity of the human condition as well as its own integrity in interrelation with all living beings.

Transgenerational harm first and foremost endangers the human condition. There is a high risk of deviation when attempting to define this term, because such efforts can lead to the exclusion of Humankind. There seems to be a current consensus regarding eugenic research. Research that will likely lead to selection

---

society", Nadezha Kutepova appealed "For the transgenerational recognition of human rights: new legal cases related to the Mayak nuclear facility", and Gilles Eric Séralini focused on: "The transgenerational effects of pesticides and pollutants: how and why?" This essay includes some key elements from these rich oral presentations, which are *available online at* https://mrsh.hypotheses.org/250.

24 Author's translation of G. Cornu (ed.), *Vocabulaire juridique* [*Legal Vocabulary*], Presses Universitaires de France, 2017 ("une atteinte subie par une personne dans son corps, dans son patrimoine ou dans ses droits extrapatrimoniaux, qui ouvre à la victime un droit à réparation lorsqu'il résulte soit de l'inéxécution d'un contrat, soit d'un délit ou quasi-délit, soit d'un fait dont la loi ou les tribunaux imposent à une personne la charge").

25 E. Gaillard, "Pour la reconnaissance juridique du dommage transgénérationnel" [For the Recognition of Transgenerational Harm], *in* J-P. Markus (ed.), *Quelle responsabilité juridique envers les générations futures ?* [*Legal Responsibility Towards Future Generations*], éditions Dalloz, collection Thèmes et commentaire, 2012, p. 246.

of "good generations" should not be carried out. Some provisions exist in French law addressing this issue, recognizing the fact that such action could harm the integrity of the human species.[26] In the era of globalization, national laws or constitutional provisions related to fundamental civilization prohibitions neither serve as a deterrent, nor are they likely to be efficient. The Oviedo Convention for the Protection of Human Rights and Dignity of the Human Being – concerning the application of biology and medicine[27] – paved the way for an international law prohibiting all discrimination based on genetic inheritance. The convention also covers human genome sequencing. Nevertheless, we are now witnessing increases in both research as well as challenges to legal science. For instance, creation of the first genetically modified babies in China.[28] Put into perspective with the rise of Transhumanism, this genetic manipulation suggests the possibility of an uncontrolled and uncontrollable rise in actions that may compromise the future human condition. In this context, likely new discriminatory practices can be expected. Whether as a result of human cloning or genetic improvement, transgenerational harm to the human condition affects both the individual human being (the object of modification, cloning), and humanity itself (human species integrity, under French law). In other words, harm caused to the future human condition concerns both genetically modified or cloned children and the human family, thus placing duality at the core of the concept of transgenerational harm.

Transgenerational harm further endangers the human condition by polluting the environment, including flora and fauna as well as other natural resources – such as water and air – that we humans ingest for sustenance. Contamination of the food chain and of natural elements with residual pesticides, plastics or radionuclides are particularly alarming. Professor Gilles Eric Séralini,

26 Article 16-4 *Code civil* "Nul ne peut porter atteinte à l'intégrité de l'espèce humaine" [None can prejudice the integrity of humankind]; the French criminal code integrated a new subtitle, next to the crimes against humanity, there are now crimes against the human species written in the articles 214-1 *Code pénal* (collective eugenics), and 214-2 *Code pénal* (reproductive human cloning).

27 The *Convention for the Protection of Human Rights and Dignity of the Human Being with regard to the Application of Biology and Medicine*, presented to the states for signature in Oviedo on 4 April 1997, became applicable on 1 December 1999, *available online at* http://conventions.coe.int/Treaty/FR/Treaties/Html/164.htm.

28 The first use of the CRISPR method to create genetically modified babies, named Lulu & Nana, took place in China. M. Marchione, "Chinese researcher claims first gene-edited babies", *Associated Press*, 26 Nov. 2018.

molecular biologist at the University of Caen, has identified artificial products attached to fetal genes after analyzing cells from the placenta and the umbilical cord. These "xenobiotics" disrupt the normal expression of genes[29]and they are directly linked to petrochemicals. The scale of the impact of petrochemical multinationals in this regard is surprising. In fact, among the ten most significant pollutants, representing 60% of products in quantity, just 8 multinational firms were responsible.[30] The concept of endocrine disruptors, developed by

---

29 Professor Séralini provided some edifying figures: "plus de 400 produits artificiels sont collés par génome de cellules humaines, produits qui ont été essentiellement commercialisés depuis la seconde guerre mondiale, qui n'existaient pas auparavant sur les gènes humains. Ils habillent le génome et ont des effets que l'on appelle épigénétiques (cela signifie au-dessus du génome, qui couvre le génome et qui se transmet de manière héréditaire mais de manière plus fluide que le génome qui est le disque dur tandis que ces produits sont des clefs USB que l'on apporte et qu'on enlève à chaque génération, mais dont certains éléments peuvent se copier sur le génome) ou transgénérationnels" [more than 400 artificial products are attached to each human cell genome, products that were essentially commercialized since the Second World War, and which did not exist before in human genes. They coat the genome and have what we call transgenerational or epigenetic effects. This means above the genome, which covers the genome; and which is hereditary but in a more fluid manner than the genome which is the hard drive while these products are USB keys that we bring and take from each generation, but whose elements can be copied on the genome). Author's translation of G.E. Séralini, "The transgenerational effects of pesticides and pollutants: How and Why?", International Symposium Taking Legal Actions on Behalf of Future Generations, Caen, 18 Nov. 2017, Caen, *available online at* https://mrsh.hypotheses.org/250.

30 Professor Séralini specified further: "Quand on a pris les 10 premiers polluants les plus importants des 400, qui représentaient environ 60% des produits en quantité, ils appartenaient à 8 grandes multinationales : consortium de prétrochimie qui sont ceux qui dirigent l'agroalimentaire, les semences, le OGM, les pesticides, les médicaments, les nanoparticules et les plastifiants puisque tout provient du pétrole. On a donc focalisé les responsables d'une génération à huit réseaux financiers. Il se trouve que trois des principaux polluants parmi les 10 proviennent de la société Monsanto. C'est une société qui a commercialisé aussi, en tous cas la société mère Union Farben qui a travaillé beaucoup avec Hitler pour les gaz de concentration, le gaz sarin qui reste le plus toxique au monde, qui a été utilisé dans les années 30 comme pesticides. Ces personnes sont responsables de la commercialisation d'autant que ce sont les seules à faire les tests qui sont approuvés par les agences internationales qui permettent l'approbation des pesticides et OGM. Il y a un lien de 100% entre les OGM agricoles cultivés et l'utilisation de pesticides" [When we took the 10 main pollutants among the 400, which represented about 60% of products in quantity, they belonged to 8 large multinational firms : a petrochemicals consortium of the ones leading the food-processing industry, seeding,

biologist Théo Colborn, refers to synthetic hormones that mimic, block or disrupt the expression of hormones – which are chemical messengers necessary for all life: human and non-human, animal and plant. Endocrine disruptors represent grave, systemic and complex dangers for the future of the future. The interdependencies between living beings and bioaccumulated or dispersed pollution represent vectors of transgenerational harm across species and spaces. Russian lawyer Nadezha Kutepova highlighted the transgenerational reality of genetic and environmental harm linked to environmental pollution in the region of Mayak.[31] Although unknown for a long time, Mayak is a military site where the first nuclear disaster occurred – an explosion caused the release of many radionuclides into the environment.[32] This caused harm not only to the first hand victims, but also to future generations that will be born with birth defects as well as damaged genomes, and who will pass on to their children physiological ailments such as leukemia, which affects children even from a very young age. These people are victims of genetic, epigenetic and environmental transgenerational harm. Ingesting contaminated food is particularly dangerous because the adverse effects of internal radiation are ongoing.

Transgenerational harm also encompasses damage to life cycles through environmental pollution. Moreover, the loss of biodiversity speeds up transgenerational threats to food safety and, beyond that, environmental safety.

GMO, pesticides, medicines, nanoparticles and plasticizers; all coming from oil. So, we focused on eight financial networks as those responsible for an entire generation. Three of the main pollutants among the 10 happen to come from the Monsanto company. Their parent company Union Farben worked a lot with Hitler on concentration gas, and commercialized sarin gas which remains the most toxic gas in the world, and which was used in the 1930s as a pesticide. These people are responsible for this commercialization, even more so because they are the only ones to have made the tests that are approved by international agencies that allow for the pesticides and GMOs to be approved. There is a 100% link between the cultivated agricultural GMO and the use of pesticides]. *Ibid.*

31 In 1999, Russian sociologist and lawyer Nadezha Kutepova founded the NGO Planet of Hope, whose main objective is to inform the people living in the area of Mayak on the health effects linked to ionizing rays along with their rights as Russian citizens.

32 Mayak was a secret military complex where Kutepova's parents worked, and the first nuclear disaster occurred. Based on her personal experiences, Kutepova regularly denounces the terrible level of contamination in local rivers and lands. As a lawyer, she filed a claim on behalf of the six-year old girl who (along with her grandmother, a liquidator at Mayak) died of cancer – allegedly resulting from transgenerational genetic harm caused by radioactivity at the site.

Bees are now considered an endangered species, whose disappearance would condemn all living beings to dreadful food production losses at a global scale. Some have offered technological solutions such as "pollination drones"; however, it makes greater sense to focus on protection and the urgent development of measures to protect and preserve our biodiversity. Global environmental issues that go beyond a certain scale, for instance with climatic changes, are hard for Humankind to grasp. Indeed, our cognitive faculties are overwhelmed by this new reality including challenges presented by transgenerational harm to Humankind and all living beings along with the elements that support life itself.

Lastly, transgenerational harm can also be cultural, as explained by Mr. Winiki Sage, ex-president of the Economic, Social and Cultural Council of French Polynesia. Nuclear testing profoundly transformed Polynesian society, which took a "civilizational leap" from the age of harvesting to the nuclear age.[33] The cultural destruction was accompanied by a violation of the integrity of oceans, which are considered to be sacred Marae by peoples in Pacific Island nations. According to Sage, "[the Marae is a temple that should be preserved for future generations]".[34] The pollution linked to nuclear tests is now officially acknowledged by French authorities as a serious transgenerational violation. The

33 "Les polynésiens sont passés de l'âge de la cueillette, de la pêche, de l'agriculture à l'âge du nucléaire. Ils ont travaillé sur les sites nucléaires et eu la possibilité de gagner 100 fois plus. Cela a généré une déstructuration de l'économie. Avant 1960 il y avait un équilibre entre production et consommation. Le lien avec la Terre a par la suite été perdu et la société polynésienne s'est tournée vers une économie très dépendante des transferts de l'Etat et des importations. Le déséquilibre entre les classes sociales est très important. Il y a également eu une explosion démographique entre de 1960 à 2000 et une mutation des rapports des polynésiens avec les rapports ancestraux" [The Polynesian society went from the age of harvesting, fishing and agriculture to the nuclear age. They worked on nuclear sites where they were paid 100 times more than what they usually earned. This led to a reorganization of the economy. Before 1960, there was a balance between producing and consuming. Then a disconnection from the relationship to nature and culture to turn to an economy that depends more on state transfers and imports. There is a significant imbalance between social classes. There was also a demographic boom between 1960 and 2000, and a change in the relationship of the Polynesians with their ancestors]. W. Sage, "La transformation de la société polynésienne avec les essais nucléaires" [How nuclear tests transformed Polynesian society], Symposium Taking legal action on behalf of future generations, 17 November 2019, Caen, *available online at* https://mrsh.hypotheses.org/250.

34 *Ibid.* (author's translation).

resulting damage to oceanic food chains that provide the main food source for people in the Pacific, is invisible and hard to control.

Transgenerational harm thus comes in many forms: dual, systemic, transtemporal and transpatial. These impacts endanger the human condition, in addition to all living beings and all of the resources that support life. The cycles of life and their futures are now in humankind's hands. This raises many major challenges to scientific thought.

B. Transgenerational Harm: Significant Challenges Presented to the Sciences and Scientific Thought

The sciences (and scientific thought in general) seem poorly suited and perhaps even outdated, when it comes to addressing the complexity and multi-level interdependencies of transgenerational harm. It is important to understand the dual nature of this damage, and to invest in new areas of thought that encompass the transpatial, transtemporal and trans-species dimensions involved.

Endocrine disruptors provide a textbook case illustrating the crossroads of internal and environmental violations with respect to the human condition. Several cascading paradigm shifts are required to fully develop and implement public health, environmental and transgenerational policies. The initial challenges involved with understanding transgenerational harm are not necessarily legal. According to Professor Gilles Eric Séralini, "we have reached the limits of science"[35]; more specifically, the limits of epidemiological sciences, when it comes to comprehending endocrine disruptors and transgenerational harm. Indeed, epidemiological sciences are based on the paradigm of Paracelsus inherited from the sixteenth century, which claims that "the dose makes the poison". Expressed at a time when no chemical products existed, this paradigm is inadequate for considering the toxicity of such products – even less so for endocrine disruptors.

This symposium addressed multiple forms of transgenerational harm linked to the large-scale use of pesticides. Now, more than ever, we need new science that is systemic, complex and future oriented. Science that is, therefore, able to comprehend systemic damage, the phenomena of bioaccumulation, and the cocktail effect. Yet, our epidemiological sciences divide the analysis in ways that fail to take into account the synergystic processes of various pollutants.

35 G.E. Séralini, "The transgenerational effects of pesticides and pollutants: How and Why?", International Symposium Taking Legal Actions on Behalf of Future Generations, 18 Nov. 2017, Caen, *available online at* https://mrsh.hypotheses.org/250.

Epidemiological science must also be adjusted to consider the transgenerational nature of harm. Particular attention must be paid to concepts including the "window effect", "deferred effects" and "transgenerational effects" across and beyond present generations. This will require multiple paradigm shifts, introducing new theories like low doses[36] – according to which the harmful effects of some substances can be identified even (or, perhaps, even more so) at low doses – which would constitute a complete break in epistemology. Another paradigm shift would increase complexity at the forefront of sciences, integrating consideration of phenomena involving the complex synergies between substances currently studied in isolation. A final paradigm shift would involve the application of transgenerational logics, designed to carry out a more realistic analysis of harmful effects. According to Professor Séralini, "[we must create environmental medicine, just as we must create a right to lasting human health]".[37]

The case of nuclear power successfully illustrates the need for a series of paradigm shifts, particularly in the field of legal science. The presentations delivered by Alyn Ware,[38] Jean-Marie Collin[39] and Winiki Sage,[40] highlighted the interdependence of our destinies as we face the threat of nuclear weapons. It is no longer reasonable to think in terms of nation-states supervising the safety of humankind, a people or a part of the population. Andreas Nidecker warned about the risk of nuclear starvation that would result from a nuclear confrontation between India and Pakistan.[41] The recent September 2017 aerial dispersion of ruthenium 106 in Europe evidenced a major nuclear accident, demonstrating

---

36 On the theory of low doses, A. Cicollela, "Ce n'est pas la dose qui fait le poison" [It is not the Dose that Makes the Poison], *Le Point,* 30 June 2011, *available online at* https://www.lepoint.fr/societe/andre-cicolella-ce-n-est-pas-la-dose-qui-fait-le-poison-30-06-2011-1350177_23.php.

37 G.E. Séralini, 2017 presentation, *available online at* http://www.unicaen.fr/recherche/mrsh/forge/5133.

38 A. Ware, essay #4 (this book) on "Nuclear Weapons and Law for the Future: The Application of Principles Protecting Future Generations in International Tribunals".

39 J.-M. Collin, essay #5 (this book) on "Treaty on the Prohibition of Nuclear Weapons: A Move Towards New Legal Action to Protect Future Generations?".

40 W. Sage, 2017 presentation, *available online at* http://www.unicaen.fr/recherche/mrsh/forge/5043?fbclid=IwAR0EPTULN4R66-WincYeTHHA-0f12h7dQhPGy_bXKwSwjv8fgSY6LS9MKBc.

41 *See* IPPNW, *Nuclear Famine: Two Billion People at Risk—Global Impacts of Limited Nuclear War on Agriculture, Food Supplies, and Human Nutrition*, 2nd edition, *available online at* https://www.ippnw.org/pdf/nuclear-famine-two-billion-at-risk-2013.pdf.

the relative impossibility of protecting populations on a continental scale from the radioactive pollution generated in another state, no matter how remote.[42]

The interdependence of destinies is a key issue. All sciences, including legal sciences, must integrate the interdependence paradigm beyond national borders. International law has yet to reach the stage of maturity needed for an evolution toward authentic transpatial law. International law is currently based upon the paradigm of the nation-state and the opposition between war and peace. Therefore, huge changes must be undertaken in order to integrate transpatial issues.[43] The epistemological break is also temporal, because the damage itself is transtemporal/transgenerational. The fact is that we already represent a future generation whose fundamental rights have not been respected. Pollution of the ocean with plastics, residual antibiotics and persistent organic pollutants has resulted in large-scale contamination of water, soil and living beings. In addition to pollution of the oceans caused by chemical weapons used by both Nazi and Allied forces during the Second World War.[44]

This new transgenerational era must also address the cultural dimension of our human condition. Our existence only has meaning when linked to past generations and the cultural heritage of our ancestors. This cultural dimension is at risk due to both the disappearance of island states and the destruction of societies through integration of new technologies. The rise of a transhumanist society fuels doubts regarding our existence as free human beings. The rise of mass manipulation in the digital era likewise raises serious questions about whether free will can be maintained – and, thus, democratic choices – keeping in mind our responsibilities toward future generations.[45]

In our opinion, this new reality of systemic, complex and transgenerational threats calls for a law that can respond to these challenges. What

---

42 Institut national de recherche et de Sécurité pour la prévention des maladies professionnelles et des accidents du travail, "Détection de ruthénium 106 dans l'est et le sud-est de l'Europe" [Detection of Ruthenium 106 in Eastern and South-eastern Europe], *available online at* https://www.irsn.fr/fr/actualites_presse/actualites/pages/20171004_detection-ruthenium-106-en-europe.aspx#.XP4koS3pN0v.

43 *See* M. Delmas-Marty, essay #1 (this book) on "Adapting Juridical Order in the Age of Anthropocene".

44 *See* N. Koutsikas, E. Nadler & B. Cohen, *Armes chimiques sous la mer* [Chemical Weapons Under the Sea], *Arte* (France 2013) (documentary film, 88 minutes).

45 D. Coulon, *Propagande, la manipulation de masse dans le monde contemporain* [*Propaganda, Mass Manipulation in the Contemporary World*], Belin, 2019.

potential legal measures can be considered for extending the law to encompass the transgenerational field?

II. Legal Measures to Establish Transgenerational Law

We believe it is important to extend all legal concepts, notions, principles and logic to the transgenerational field. To do so, an epistemological break in the law is necessary. Until recently, the very heart of constitutional imagination included one founding premise: it would be illegitimate and dangerous for any generation to subject future generations to its laws.[46] Professor Alexandre Kiss set the tone by insisting that, for legal experts, including legal protection for future generations would operate a Copernican revolution. However, this transformation is already taking place, and multiple legal measures can now be deployed. Some of these levers address the general theory of law (*see* Section II.A. below), while others highlight legal technique and the concrete extension of rights or transgenerational legal action (*see* Section II.B. below).

A. Legal Measures Related to General Theory for Future Generations

Only a selection of the relevant legal measures will be described here. Theoretical questioning surrounds issues such as the definition of future generations; the matter of their legal representation; and in countries such as France, theoretical questions on certain legal topics.[47] However, it is clear that the reality of transgenerational harm demonstrates an abuse of power with respect to future generations. This represents an entirely new situation in which Humankind, through this abuse of power, endangers both the future of Humankind and the human condition of future generations. It has become necessary to question the legitimacy of different fields of law themselves, which are contained within a strict temporal matrix and therefore unable to address the challenges currently posed to civilization. Life on earth itself is at risk, and the law cannot ignore

---

46 Article 28 of the *Déclaration des droits de l'homme et du citoyen* [Declaration of the Rights of Man and the Citizen] (1793), which never came into effect (as distinguished from the 1789 version), explains that "a people has always the right to review, to reform, and to alter its constitution. One generation cannot subject to its law the future generations". P. Türk, *Théorie générale du droit constitutionnel*, Gualino, 2nd édition, 2009, p. 56.

47 *See* E. Gaillard, *Générations futures et droit privé. Vers un droit des générations futures* [*Future Generations and Private Law: Towards a Law for Future Generations*], Librairie Générale de Droit et de Jurisprudence, 2011, pp. 349-381.

this fact. Legitimate fields of the law must therefore be extended to integrate transtemporal and transpatial dimensions, including also the complexity of this reality. There are two founding legal principles of this new type of law.[48] The first, the principle of temporal non-discrimination, which would pave the way for a legal relationship with future generations. The second is the principle of dignity for future generations, which would allow for adjustment of the law's temporal range in order to ensure legal protection of future generations.

The principle of temporal non-discrimination conveys the idea of temporal priority; that the legitimacy of certain rights or values does not necessarily require actual existence. In other words, certain rights and values must be respected as of now and include the rights of non-human entities and future generations. The principle of temporal non-discrimination reveals a new strain between social values beyond the present. The absence of human existence no longer means the absence of rights.[49] The lack of human interests is no longer synonymous with the absence of legal protection. Instead, the rights of nature can be acknowledged, and offenses such as ecocide, crimes against the environment, or crimes against future generations can be established as actual criminal offenses. Creating links to future generations is systemic, complex and transtemporal, thus the principle of temporal non-discrimination must address these multiple theoretical challenges; allowing for extension of the law through systemic and complex thought, while integrating a new transgenerational temporal perspective. We believe the principle of temporal non-discrimination is already at work. All legal actions taken on behalf of future generations confirm the rise of this new principle, which affirms that the absence of human existence is no longer necessarily synonymous with absence of law, nor of legal protection. Therefore, while law for future generations is indeed at an early stage, it is also already successful and certainly bold.

Moreover, this principle of temporal non-discrimination is a founding principle that must be regarded in a dynamical, asymmetric and systemic manner. The principle does not apply equally to future generations of families in the narrow sense; or the protection of other flesh and blood beings of humanistic values. With regards to future generations of families, it seems *lex lata* that the protection of the future child already mirrors this principle of temporal non-discrimination. *Lex ferenda*, the principle of temporal non-discrimination will

48 For an exhaustive study, *see* E. Gaillard, 2011, pp. 429-495.

49 *See* C. Lepage & E. Gaillard, essay #16 (this book) on "For the Recognition of Humanity Rights & Duties".

allow for recognition of a human being's legal standing before birth or even before biological existence.[50] Respect for human existence would take precedence over biological reality once the interests of future generations are involved. It is important to recall that the principle of temporal non-discrimination only makes sense when future generations are endangered.

With regards future generations within human families, the principle of temporal non-discrimination takes on an essential dimension; that of the legal imperative to protect Humankind and the human condition. The challenges are related to civilization: what future should we preserve for our children and successive generations? The principle of temporal non-discrimination heralds the rise of irrevocable fundamental rights, of which no violation will be tolerated. To take one example, all living beings on Earth are part of the genealogical paradigm of generational succession.[51] Reproductive cloning would introduce a historical, irreversible break that would sever the transgenerational link in this chain of life. The principle of temporal non-discrimination also overcomes theoretical and practical difficulties relative to generational overlap. The principle makes it possible for the law to be applied dynamically by extending the matrix of liability before birth (i.e., the "window-effect" that describes a window of vulnerability during fetal development). Legal causalities can also be extended to invest in the long term, which would pave the way for consideration of delayed effects (e.g., endocrine disruptors). The principle of temporal non-discrimination makes it possible to realize that transgenerational harm is caused, consolidated and expressed through time. All conditions for implementation of the law, including responsibility and statutes of limitations, must then be revisited through the lens of the principle of temporal non-discrimination.

We believe that the principle of temporal non-discrimination must be applied in various, differing ways according to the state of scientific knowledge. It should not be applied in a uniform or linear manner and much less according to a logic of binary causality. Principles of prevention and, above all, precaution regarding transgenerational harm allow for legal protection to be reinforced in preparation for future generations. The principle of precaution is particularly necessary in our time as it anticipates severe and irreversible risks to both the environment and human health. It allows for protection of the future, by providing a

50 *See* E. Gaillard, 2011, pp. 437-440.

51 *Ibid.*, pp. 148-149, 152-153, 174, 330, 472, 474, 647-648, 668, 677, 699 (discussing "Principe généalogique de l'espèce humaine" [Genealogical Principle of Human Species]).

counterbalance to reliance on an otherwise harmful "wait-and-see" policy. The principle of precaution can be found in many legal systems,[52] especially in French law.[53]

By comparison, application of the principle of temporal non-discrimination is reinforced when transgenerational harm is certain. Implementation of best practices is no longer sufficient; efforts must instead be taken to prevent any health, environmental or cultural catastrophe because of the transgenerational effects involved. The question then becomes whether criminal law – national or international – can integrate this paradigm requiring protection of future generations. In other words, where the future is endangered either consciously or intentionally, criminal charges should be filed against any party who fails to fulfil fundamental obligations of environmental, health and/or cultural due diligence. As such, crimes against future generations,[54] and even ecocide[55] could one day exist. A new public order could be created based on the imperative to ensure a lasting and healthy existence for future generations.[56] There is one noteworthy pitfall: the fact that transgenerational harm will take place in the distant future and so is seen as uncertain.[57] However, if current knowledge can

---

52 E. Gaillard, "Fasc. 2415 : Le principe de précaution : Systèmes juridiques internationaux et européens" [The Precautionary Principle: International and European Legal Systems], Lexisnexis, 2015.

53 E. Gaillard, "Fasc. 2412 : Le principe de précaution : Droit interne" [The Precautionary Principle: French Law], Lexisnexis 2014.

54 E. Gaillard, "Crimes against Future Generations", *e-Pública*, Vol. 2, No. 2, 2015, p. 40, *available online at* http://www.scielo.mec.pt/pdf/epub/v2n2/v2n2a04.pdf.

55 F.J. Broswimmer, *Ecocide: a short history of the mass extinction of species*, Pluto Press, 2002; P. Higgins, *Eradicating Ecocide laws and governance to prevent the destruction of our planet*, Shepheard-Walwyn, 2010; L. Neyret (ed.), *Des écocrimes à l'écocide: le droit pénal au secours de l'environnement* [From Ecocrimes to Ecocide: Criminal Law Saving the Environment], Bruylant, 2015.

56 Interpol, "INTERPOL makes public appeal to help track environmental fugitives", 4 June 2019, *available online at* https://www.interpol.int/en/News-and-Events/News/2019/INTERPOL-makes-public-appeal-to-help-track-environmental-fugitives?fbclid=IwAR1EcWFmB4oqi49OMGB0llwAvqZMc9h6t2BTIqptWmA_HOqgWliK8UclLM4.

57 In France, final radioactive waste (non-nuclear but very dangerous, composed of asbestos, arsenic or even mercury for instance) are buried in an old salt quarry named StocaMine. A fire broke out in 2004 leading to its temporary closure. The prefect authorized its reopening in 2017. Yet, the quarries are collapsing in places and are located under the largest phreatic table in Alsace. The risks are high. Some expert assessments talk of a contamination which would remain just at the bottom

demonstrate that future generations will suffer harm, then this is proof enough of transgenerational harm. Thus, applying the principle of temporal non-discrimination allows for an extension of the scope of law to address this issue. In the same logic, more and more voices are pleading for the recognition of the principle of *In dubio pro Natura.*

A second founding principle of the law of future generations deserves to be noted: that of dignity of future generations. According to Robert Andorno: "law can [...] guarantee humane living conditions for future generations".[58] There is no doubt that the principle of human dignity can be extended to include future generations. This is already happening in legal actions. It is important to test the theoretical and conceptual potential of such a principle. The notion of dignity shows a certain receptiveness to the notion of future generations, both with regards to time and concept. It allows for a conceptual shift, to ensure the link and integrate the duality between the dignity of man and that of humanity. The principle of dignity of future generations articulates the following new humanist imperative: man, in his individuality, and humanity as a whole, is from now on responsible for future generations, for their own and others. Whether that be real people that may not exist yet or a humanist value including respect for life and natural elements.

In this way, the principle of dignity for future generations is a promising solution to stem current freedoms and to respect the interests of future generations. Read and applied in the light of the principle of temporal non-discrimination, the principle of human dignity changes profoundly. On the one hand, the notion of dignity would become transitive: each generation must ensure that the dignity of those that follow is preserved, whether or not they already exist.[59] The passing on of transgenerational responsibilities is something that is feasible. On

---

of the phreatic zone, suppressing any future risk of contamination. This case raises the question of the responsibility towards future generations who risk having their water contaminated.

58 R. Andorno, "le droit peut[-il] garantir des conditions humaines de vie aux générations futures ?" [Can the Law Guarantee Human Conditions of Life for Future Generations?], F. Chabas (ed.), *La distinction juridique entre les personnes et les choses: à l'épreuve des procréations artificielles* [*The Legal Distinction between Persons and Objects: Competing with Artifical Procreation*], Université Paris XII, Librairie Générale de Droit et de Jurisprudence, 1996, paragraphs 20-25.

59 *See* E. Brown-Weiss, "The Planetary Trust: Conservation and Intergenerational Equity", *Ecology Law Quaterly*, 1984, Vol. 11, p. 495.

the other hand, the notion of dignity of future generations could also pave the way for the consideration of non-human life and the integrity of ecosystems.

Applied and executed in the field of law, the principle of human dignity must include that of future generations. It opens the way for a transgenerational extension of human rights and marks the rise of humanity's rights and duties.[60] The notion of dignity of future generations is present in many constitutions, for instance that of Japan, which contains two articles that insist on the transgenerational understanding of human rights.[61] Legal actions examined here concerning the climate, the fight to stop deforestation, and the defense of nature, confirm the normative densification of this principle of dignity of future generations in interrelation with life in comparative law. From these changes, from pure general theory, come many legal and judicial measures that can now be used and strengthened in order to serve future generations. This corresponds to the immediate consequence of the paradigm shift that is the rise of future generation law.

B. The Legal Measures of Legal and Judicial Practices That Serve Future Generations

The legal paradigm imperceptibly guides the way law is thought about, created and applied. It plays the role of a conceptual matrix for legal experts by establishing boundaries to what seems legally advisable or even conceivable to them. Once the paradigm is established, i.e. dominant, it is generally not expressed, nor stated. Underpinned by the fact that it is obvious, its normative force seems invincible. When a new paradigm is emerging, there is a necessary reorganization of present normative forces. Whether or not the new paradigm replaces the former, a new expansion of dynamic and of normative creations is put into motion. The traditional concepts, notions and principles are renewed, and other, new ones become conceivable. New logics progress in turn, allowing

60 *See* C. Lepage & E. Gaillard essay # 16 (this book) on "For the Recognition of the Rights and Duties of Humanity".

61 This Constitution mentions equally the fundamental rights of current and future generations. Thus, article 11 of the Japanese Constitution states that "the people shall not be prevented from enjoying any fundamental human rights. These fundamental human rights guaranteed to the people by this Constitution shall be conferred upon the people of this and future generations as eternal and inviolable rights". Article 97 explains that "the fundamental human rights guaranteed to the people of Japan by this Constitution are fruits of the age-old struggle of man to be free; they have survived the many exacting tests for durability and are conferred upon this and future generations in trust, to be held for all time inviolable".

new solutions to be designed and implemented by all legal players. The normative force of the legal paradigm resembles a dynamic of creation, of orientation that brings law from the confines of legal imagination to its daily application.[62] Being aware of this dynamic of transformation, it is now possible to put into perspective the rise of new hybrid, complex fundamental rights that are open to the legal protection of future generations. More specifically, legal logic changes a great deal once the change of paradigm has occurred.

This can be illustrated by insisting on multiple processes of transformation or even of metamorphosis of fundamental rights that are currently at work (at the level of national as well as international rights). Although it is not entirely supported, human rights can traditionally be presented in three time periods. The rise of the first generation of human rights dates back to the eighteenth century. They appeared in a time of revolution, political and ideological disruptions particularly marked by the philosophy of the Enlightenment. Rights and freedoms were asserted and demanded in the first declarations of human rights in Corsica, England, in the USA and also France. The famous *Declaration of the Rights of Man and of the Citizen* in 1789 announced the existence of "droits de l'homme abstraits" (abstract human rights) or "droits-résistances" (resistant rights): individual and political liberties were asserted.

The second generation of human rights in France came after the Second World War. It consisted of collective and social rights, conceived by the *Conseil National de la Résistance* (National Council of the Resistance) which gathered together members of the Resistance of all political orientations during the occupation. These second-generation rights involved an active role played by the state in order to guarantee them. This is why they are called "droits de l'homme concrets" (concrete human rights) or even "droits-créances" (claim rights). Shaped by the historical context in which they were declared, they are marked by socialist ideology. These first two generations of human rights were movements that rose from the ground up.[63] They were also declared as part of the paradigm of the nation-state. Concurrently, an unprecedented transformation process began in another range of rules. It was new in that it operated at an international and regional scale and was a complete revolution in itself. In 1948, just three years after its creation, the United Nations Organization adopted the *Universal Declaration of Human Rights*. By transposing

62 E. Gaillard, "La force normative du paradigme juridique" [The Normative Force of the Legal Paradigm], *in* C. Thibierge (ed.), *La force normative. Naissance d'un concept* [The Normative Force: Birth of a Concept], Bruylant, 2009, p. 171.

63 M. Delmas-Marty, *Pour un droit commun* [For a Global Common Law], Seuil, 1994, p. 8.

the concept of human rights onto a supra-national scale, a new era began in the way of both imagining and expressing human rights. This text was the cornerstone of a new legal world that led to the creation of common law for human rights.[64] In the same year, the *American Declaration on Human Rights* was adopted at the Ninth International Conference of American States.[65] This declaration initiated another process of enrichment and further independence while still remaining in line with the intellectual legacy of the UDHR of 1948. In 1950, the *European Convention on Human Rights* was the first convention to be adopted by the Council of Europe.[66] These last two stages marked the beginning of a process of regionalization of human rights. At an international level, it was only in 1966 that binding international treaties were adopted.[67] Once these multiple processes had begun, a new step in the evolution began concerning the essence and the nature of fundamental rights. At the end of the 1970s, Professor Karel Vasak identified a third generation of human rights. Rights that were considered in solidarity through space and time.

New legal and judicial measures could from then on be applied. The integration of the paradigm of future generation law has ushered in a new era of progress in fundamental human rights. For instance, the rights of the first two generations could fall within the transgenerational field. Freedom of movement also includes the freedom of future generations to move within an environment that does not endanger their lives, such is already the case around the nuclear power plants of Chernobyl and Fukushima. Freedom of thought determines that future generations should be able to enjoy free will without being manipulated nor having cerebral implants likely to

---

64 According to one of the fathers of the Universal Declaration, this text elevates the concept of human rights to the level of universal society: "Grâce à elle [la DUDH], la société universelle prend sous sa protection l'ensemble des droits et des libertés proclamés jusqu'ici uniquement dans des Constitutions ou Déclarations issus du pouvoir constituant ou législatif de telles ou telles Nations agissant séparément" [Thanks to it [the UDHR], the universal society assumes the protection of all rights and freedoms currently declared only in Constitutions or Declarations created by the constituent or legislative power of nations acting individually]. R. Cassin, "La Déclaration Universelle des Droits de l'Homme" [The Universal Declration of Human Rights], *Recueil des cours l'Academie de Droit International de la Haye* [Collected courses of the Hague Academy of International Law], 1951, Vol. 2, p. 281; M. Delmas-Marty, 1994.

65 *American Declaration on Human Rights, available online at* https://www.cidh.oas.org/Basicos/English/Basic2.American%20Declaration.htm.

66 *European Convention on Human Rights, available online at* https://www.echr.coe.int/Documents/Convention_ENG.pdf.

67 *See* International Covenant on Civil and Political Rights; International Covenant on Economic, Social and Cultural Rights.

control them. The right to life of course includes the right to live in a healthy environment. The right to good health, often understood as the right to benefit from the social security system, could in turn be extended to the transgenerational field, and be understood as the right to live without residual pesticides or chemical products in the blood. A right to lasting human health could link different generations of fundamental rights and connect them to the rights of Nature.

A process of human rights transformation has been set in motion. Emerging solidarity rights and third generation rights now include humanity and future generations but they also move away from human interest.[68] The right to a healthy environment must include the protection of living beings and their livelihoods as a whole. Fundamental rights are complex and interdependent and are new requirements to protect civilization.[69] Lastly it is important to mention the work of Professor Helmons, who stresses the rise of a fourth generation of human rights, "ceux qui doivent protéger la dignité humaine de certains abus de la science" [those that must protect human dignity from some of the abuses of science].[70] We find this idea very interesting, and it is already implicit in many declarations adopted under the aegis of UNESCO. The time seems to have come to strengthen the rights of the fourth generation.

There exist many other noteworthy initiatives: legal action for the protection of common interests that exists in Portugal or Brazil, the possible action for the protection of common interest. The mobilization of the Public Trust mechanism or even that of the rights of Nature, are other examples of the influence and the plurality of expression of future generation law.

We are entering a new legal era that requires legal experts to mobilize around a new humanism that integrates the protection of the future of the future.[71] By revisiting law through the paradigm of the protection of future generations, a new universe is opening up to legal experts that is both immense and fascinating, as it strives for the common good of humanity.

---

68 *See* C. Lepage & E. Gaillard, essay #16 (this book) on "For the Recognition of the Rights and Duties of Humankind" (discussing Mission Lepage, *Déclaration Universelle des droits et devoirs de l'Humanité*).

69 *Ibid.*

70 S.M. Helmons, "La quatrième génération des droits de l'homme" [The Fourth Generation of Human Rights], *in Les droits de l'homme au seuil du troisième millénaire*: Mélanges en hommage à Pierre Lambert [*Human Rights on the Threshold of the Third Millennium*: Essays in honor of Pierre Lambert], éditions Bruylant, 2000, p. 549.

71 That is precisely the aim of the *Chaire Normandie pour la Paix* [Normandy Chair for Peace], created by the Normandy Region, CNRS and the University of Caen, administered by the MRSH (June 2019-June 2023).

David M. FORMAN[1] & Antonio A. OPOSA, Jr.[2]

21. Making a Difference for Future Generations

Introduction

It is my privilege to introduce our next speaker, Attorney Tony Oposa.[3] As someone with roots in the Philippines, it seems appropriate for me to use my mother's native language, and simply call him Kuya [Elder brother] Tony.

We almost lost Tony many years before the *Minors Oposa v. Factoran* case.[4] In a fire that burned his ancestral home in Cebu during his third year of law school, Tony suffered third degree burns on over seventy percent of his body. Tony's best friend died in that fire while spending the Christmas holidays with him. Given

1 David is the second son of a member of the first Peace Corps mission to the Philippines, Michael L. Forman (Ph.D. Cornell University), Emeritus Professor of Linguistics, University of Hawai'i at Mānoa (UHM), and Sheila M. Forman (nee da Silva; B.A. Maryknoll College, Quezon City, Early Childhood/Psychology; Ph.D. UHM, Child Psychology). David's parents met and married after his father convinced the Peace Corps to abandon its initial policy providing that knowledge of local languages was not necessary to fulfill the organization's mission in the Philippines, because most Filipinos also spoke English; the elder Forman extended his two-year commitment by one additional year to design and manage a language training program for Peace Corps volunteers and staff throughout the Philippines.

2 Tony is one of Asia's leading voices in the global arena of Environmental Law. He holds a business degree from the De La Salle University and a law degree from the University of the Philippines, in addition to an LLM degree from Harvard Law School.

3 A. Oposa Jr., University of Hawai'i Center for Philippine Studies, *available online at* http://www.hawaii.edu/cps/Oposa-biosketch.pdf. In spring 2015, Oposa served as the Dan & Maggie Inouye Distinguished Chair in Democractic Ideals, University of Hawai'i at Mānoa.

4 *Minors Oposa v. Factoran*, General Register No. 101083, Supreme Court of the Philippines, *International Law Materials*, 30 July 1993, Vol. 33, p. 173, *available online at* http://www.lawphil.net/judjuris/juri1993/jul1993/gr_101083_1993.html. *See also* M. Socorro, Z. Manguiat & V. Yu III, "Maximizing the Value of Oposa v. Factoran", *Georgetown International Environmental Law Revew*, 2003, Vol. 15, p. 487; E. Newburger, "Visionary of the Visayan Sea: For the sake of the planet, a lawyer wins the right to sue on behalf of future generations", *Harvard Law Bulletin*, Summer 2008, *available online at* https://today.law.harvard.edu/feature/visionary-of-the-visayan-sea/.

hardly any chance of survival himself, Tony finally woke up after more than a month in a state of coma; after a year of recuperation, he was back in law school.

That accident was transformative in another way: Tony abandoned his happy-go-lucky ways and started to live a life with purpose. In the late 1980s, with a young family, he began hands-on enforcement action against illegal logging in the Philippines. Working as an ordinary citizen with the then Secretary of the Department of Environment and Natural Resources, Tony organized law enforcement personnel, prosecutors, and citizens to "break the neck" of commercial illegal loggers. After three years of intensive hand-to-hand combat, the Secretary was replaced. This taught Tony a lesson about working with fickle and unreliable government. In his frustration, Tony decided to go on an extended holiday at Harvard Law School, where he pursued a Master of Laws. Tony was eventually chosen class commencement speaker. In the 2017 bicentennial anniversary of that prestigious institution, Tony was recognized as one of its most influential alumni (the only non-American and LLM graduate so chosen) who "changed the world by reason, question and action".[5]

I first learned about Kuya Tony when the Supreme Court of the Philippines issued the decision that bears the names of his children. I have since come to know Tony as a humble man who calls himself a "Certified Beach Bum," and says things like "there is no limit to what you can accomplish, if you are prepared to let others take the credit". Tony's humility is matched by his commitment to our environment. He has quite literally put his life on the line to protect marine resources in the Philippines.

Instead of capitalizing on his LLM degree, and United Nations Global Roll of Honor award, Tony gave up his entire law practice and decided to become the "lawyer of the fish, who do not pay attorney's fees". This time, he focused his efforts on the sea and organized a citizen-led enforcement campaign without any external funding.[6] They targeted criminal syndicates that produced explosives

---

5 Harvard Law School, HLS|200: Antonio Oposa Jr. LLM '97, 25 Apr. 2018, *available online at* https://www.youtube.com/watch?v=-sFxDE4en6o. Even more impressive is the fact that Tony received the 2009 Ramon Magsaysay Award, which is often considered to be Asia's equivalent of the Nobel Prize. *See* Ramon Magsaysay Award Foundation, Antonio A. Oposa, Jr., *available online at* http://rmaward.asia/awardees/oposa-antonio-jr/.

6 E. Newburger, 2008 ("Oposa started the Visayan Sea Squadron—with [Elpidio "Jojo"] de la Victoria and a host of others […]. They launched community-run sea patrols, led raids on producers of explosives and on commercial fishermen. One raid—aboard a Navy gunboat—ended in the arrest and jailing of three of a nearby city's most powerful

used for blast fishing, as well as rich commercial fishing boat operators who were illegally fishing in protected sea waters. This effort made such a dent that the syndicates offered a bounty of one million pesos to kill Tony and his buddy Jojo de la Victoria – the leaders of the Visayan Sea Squadron.[7] Although that threat was in fact carried out against Tony's friend,[8] our speaker somehow manages to inject humor into this tragic account. Tony jokes that the only reason he was not killed was because the killers could not find him: "Not even my wife could find me".

Professor Nick Robinson[9] and others sent money so Tony could hire bodyguards for himself and his family. Instead, Tony used that money as a seed fund – multiplied five times by an infusion of his own funds – to construct a School of the SEA (Sea and Earth Advocates).[10] Typhoon Yolanda [international name: Haiyan] destroyed the original site,[11] but Tony invites all of you to

---

commercial fishing boat operators, after Oposa and his team served outstanding warrants that the local police were not executing".).

7 Visayan Sea Squadron, 6 Aug. 2006, *available online at* http://vssq.blogspot.com/; J. Uy, "Dynamite fishing in Cebu decreases", *The Philippine Star*, 10 Aug. 2005, *available online at* https://www.philstar.com/cebu-news/2005/08/10/290850/dynamite-fishing-cebu-decreases.

8 E. Newburger, 2008 ("Elpidio de la Victoria, head of the local Bantay Dagat (or sea patrol) […] was shot and killed outside his home" two days after he and Oposa participated in an April 2006 enforcement action).

9 Nicholas A. Robinson is University Professor on the Environment and Gilbert and Sarah Kerlin Distinguished Professor of Environmental Law Emeritus, and Co-Director, Global Center for Environmental Legal Studies, with the Elisabeth Haub School of Law at Pace University. Nicholas A. Robinson, Pace | Elisabeth Haub School of Law, *available online at* https://law.pace.edu/faculty/nicholas-robinson ("He has served as legal advisor and chairman of the Commission on Environmental Law of the International Union for the Conservation of Nature and Natural Resources, engaged in drafting treaties and counseling different countries on the preparation of their environmental laws. He founded Pace's environmental law programs, edited the proceedings of the 1992 United Nations Earth Summit in Rio de Janeiro, Brazil, and is the author of several books and numerous articles".).

10 E. Newburger, 2008 ("when his friend Nicholas Robinson, co-director of Pace Law School's Center for Environmental Legal Studies, gave Oposa $5,000 to use for his security, Oposa had other ideas: It became seed money to build a structure that could better house the activism and education efforts on Bantayan Island: School of the SEA (Sea and Earth Advocates)".

11 A. Oposa Jr, "Victims or victors of the climate crisis?", *Rappler*, 26 Nov. 2013, *available online at* https://www.rappler.com/thought-leaders/civil-society/44532-victims-or-victors-of-the-climate-crisis.

Bantayan Island to see this symbol of Filipino resilience now known as Sea and Earth Advocates of Culture, Arts and Music for the Planet (SEA CAMP).[12]

I should also mention that Tony is a master storyteller. In the interest of time, and at Tony's request, I edited his audio message for this symposium, but his book *Shooting Stars and Dancing Fish* includes a more complete version of his presentation.[13] In any event, you should know that Tony offered to share with you the electronic version of his book.[14] One of the goals he seeks to implement in that book is a global citizens' movement and call to action voiced by previous speakers.[15]

We held an Intergenerational Climate Justice moot court at the sixth World Conservation Congress in Honolulu (Sep. 2016).[16] When health concerns prevented Tony from making the trip to Hawai'i, we renamed our ongoing project the Tony Oposa Intergenerational Moot Court in his honor. We were fortunate to have the participation of Emilie Gaillard and one of her students at that first moot. The following year, Emilie traveled with two more students to Tony's hometown in Cebu for the second the Tony Oposa Intergenerational Moot Court focusing on nuclear technology and disarmament.[17]

12 A video of the April 2018 re-launching of SEA CAMP is *available online at* https://drive.google.com/file/d/1gvpILtmA_W3QB6CpGSds1hzMxk_VDjJI/view?ts=5b6f94dd.

13 A. Oposa Jr., *Shooting Stars and Dancing Fish: A Walk to the World We Want*, 2017, Ramon Aboitiz Foundation.

14 *Ibid.*, *available online at* https://www.amazon.com/Shooting-Stars-Dancing-Fish-World/dp/9719599677.

15 *Ibid.*, pp. 213–33.

16 Initially named International Climate Justice before the International Court of Justice (or ICJ4ICJ), the inaugural Tony Oposa Intergenerational Moot Court was conceived as a unique, collaborative mock argument assuming that the United Nations General Assembly adopted a resolution requesting the International Court of Justice to issue an Advisory Opinion on the question "What is the responsibility under international law of States to address the global climate crisis for the benefit of present and future generations of humankind?" Environmental Law Program, University of Hawai'i at Mānoa, William S. Richardson School of Law, *available online at* http://blog.hawaii.edu/elp (click on the "IUCN" tab, then click on "1st Tony Oposa Intergenerational Moot Court – 2016"). The first moot took place in conjunction with the sixth IUCN World Conservation Congress held September 2016, in Honolulu, Hawai'i.

17 *Ibid.* (click on "2nd Tony Oposa Intergenerational Moot Court – 2017") (addressing nuclear weapons and nuclear technology disarmament). The second moot took place in conjunction with the IUCN Academy of Environmental Law annual colloquium held May 2017, in Cebu, Philippines.

Another moot court will take place in your lovely city of Caen, France (June 2018).[18]

Finally, before starting Tony's message, I have a warning for you: soon after a slide about the School of the SEA, Tony is requesting – well, actually, insisting – that you all stand and read aloud along with him. Anyone who has attended one of Tony's talks knows that he is very serious about this. He has actually stopped and started over when the audience does not speak with sufficient passion and volume.

I now give you the incomparable, Tony Oposa.

Plenary Presentation

Good day to you, bonjour, and hello from the Philippines. Thank you, Emilie, for this opportunity to have a chat with you and with your students. I apologize I could not be there.

Instead of giving a lecture, may I tell you a story? Once upon a time, in a faraway land, there was a group of islands so rich and so beautiful it was called de Perlas del Mar de Oriente – Pearl of the Orient Seas. The land was rich, but the sea was even richer, teaming with plants and animals. All kinds of plants. Everyone was happy. Money, they hardly had any; their only currency, their only money, was friends and family.

This country was known to be one of the seventeen *mega diversity* countries in the world, that hold almost all of the biological life on earth. It is reasonable to think of the Perlas as the Galapagos Islands multiplied tenfold. The Philippine Islands are that rich. People from foreign lands came and saw this group of islands in the 1900s; they saw how green it was. Everything was green but, then, they were of the mindset that the tree is money. All they could see about (and understand about) the tree, is that if you cut it down and turn it into lumber you can turn it into money. So, exercising what we call the economics of extraction and consumption, you recklessly extract from the land and you mindlessly

18 The fourth moot took place under the auspices of Normandy for Peace and the World Peace Forum held June 2018, in Caen, France. *Ibid.* (click on "4th Tony Oposa Intergenerational Moot Court – 2018") (addressing geoengineering and the rights of indigenous peoples). A third moot took place in conjunction with the Conference of Judges and Prosecutors on Water Justice at the eighth World Water Forum held March 2018, in Brasilia, Brazil. *Ibid.* (click on "3rd Tony Oposa Intergenerational Moot Court – 2018"). A fifth moot took place in August 2019 as a plenary session during the IUCN Academy of International Law annual colloquium held in Kuala Lumpur, Malaysia. Additional intergenerational moot court events are scheduled to take place during the second World Environmental Law Congress in 2020 (Rio de Janeiro, Brazil), and the seventh IUCN World Conservation Congress in 2021 (Marseilles, France).

consume and throw away. We call this EXCON economics. Using this kind of economic thinking, this is what happened barely 88 years later.

So, my friends, what can you do about this? There was great debate during 1988-1989 in the Philippine Senate about whether to selectively or totally ban legal logging, etc. And there was debate in the news and the TV and in the radio. I could not join that debate because I was a very young lawyer. Who is going to believe me? But looking at the issue, I saw that there was something wrong in this whole exercise.

You see, this is what happened: there was less than one million hectares left of virgin forest in the Philippines. Only 800,000 hectares left of virgin forest. Yet, government, because of previous administrations looking at trees as timber and wood and money, gave logging concessions to an area covering four million hectares. That means the government granted logging concessions to five times more than what was available. And we were cutting them down. We were cutting down our forest at the rate of more than 120,000 hectares per year.

I don't like numbers, but I just want you to understand how the numbers work. There were only 800,000 hectares left, and we were wiping them out at the rate of 100,000+ hectares per year. So, it does not take rocket science to understand that in less than eight years, there will be no forest left in the Philippines.

So here I was watching all of this – and I was a very young lawyer, slightly older than some of you there. I had a young family; my eldest was a three-year-old son. Deep in my heart I knew I had to do something about it. If I, for example, went to the media, who will listen to me? I was a nobody – I am still a nobody. But even assuming they would listen to me, they would give me maybe ten seconds of TV time, and that's it. It would all be forgotten again.

I sat back and said: "You know what, I am a lawyer". But, more important than a lawyer, I am, really, only a storyteller. I can tell this story, that there are only 800,000 hectares left of virgin forest, and we are cutting them down at a rate of more than a hundred thousand per year and will be wiping it out in less than 8 years. I can tell this story in a court of law, but the question was, who was going to be the plaintiff, the petitioner?

I figured out – this was 1990 – figured out that the proper petitioner, what we call in legal procedure the real parties in interest, those who stand to suffer irreparable injury and irreversible damage, is not me and my generation. It is my children. My eldest child was three years old; when he would grow to be ten years old, there would be nothing left of the forest in the Philippines. So, he, his brother, his sister, their cousins and their friends – their generation – would be the proper party in interest. So, I named them acting on behalf of their own generation and on behalf of generations of children that are not yet born.

You see, we lawyers are nothing more than storytellers. Words are our paintbrushes. Law is our medium. The courtroom is the canvas of our art. I consulted more senior lawyers – because I was a very young lawyer and I did not know what I was doing – everyone said I couldn't do it. Because everyone said I couldn't do it, I went ahead and did it anyway. So I filed the case in the trial court, hoping that I would at least get the chance to tell the story in court and present the facts backed up by evidence. Win or lose, one way or another, there would be a resolution.

However, the trial court had a different mind. The court said that there is no cause of action; there is failure to state a cause of action. In other words, the plaintiffs do not have a right of action, they cannot sue. So, I scratched my head – as I always do whenever I lose, or I win: I scratch my head, I smile, and then I ask myself – will I let this go? I lost in the trial court, will I let this go? After all, I was a very young lawyer, I was raising a very small family, a very young family – I did not even have a proper income. But then I am hard-headed, I wanted to continue telling the story. I wanted at least to tell the story.

So, I filed a petition directly to the Supreme Court. If I were smarter, I would have known that you cannot go directly to the Supreme Court. You have to first go to the court of appeals. But Mr. Mark Twain, the famous writer from America, said that there is a formula for success. The formula for success is confidence and ignorance. In my case, I was confident of my ignorance and I was ignorant of my confidence. That my friends, is a perfect formula for disaster, so we went on. I supported myself. I do not have any funding, even until now.

But, fortunately, the Supreme Court saw it my way. There was a question as to whether the children had the right because their right is not even stated in the bill of rights of the constitution. This provision on the environment is stated only in the section on state policy and principles. But the Supreme Court resolved this:

> If they [rights to the environment] are now explicitly mentioned in the fundamental charter, it is because of the well-founded fear of its framers that unless the rights to a balanced and healthful ecology and to health are mandated state policies by the Constitution itself, […] the day would not be too far when all else would be lost not only for the present generation, but also for those to come – generations which stand to inherit nothing but a parched earth incapable of sustaining life.[19]

19 *Minors Oposa v. Factoran*, General Register No. 101083, Supreme Court of the Philippines, *International Law Materials*, 30 July 1993, Vol. 33, p. 173, *available online at* http://www.lawphil.net/judjuris/juri1993/jul1993/gr_101083_1993.html

My friends, that was twenty-seven years ago; the decision was twenty-four years ago. The statement is prophetic because we now see the climate changing very negatively and very rapidly.

It took one generation, my friends, for this message to be heard. It was only in 2012 that the government totally banned logging in the Philippines; however, to the credit of then Secretary Fulgencio Factoran – who was the named respondent of the case (it was not against him in person, it was against the policy of the department) – he used the case to tell all the logging concessions to stop logging in the remaining virgin forests of the Philippines. This was in 1991, while the case was pending. He was so smart, he canceled all the logging concessions: from now on no more logging in the virgin forests and you can only log outside in the secondary growth forests. So, with his action, he was able to save the 800,000 hectares of virgin forests still remaining in the Philippines today, and it is now part of the national park system. That was the practical effect of the case. It spurred action.

Now, as rich as our land is – we are ten times richer than the Galapagos islands – our sea is even richer: a news article about a study by an American, Dr. Kent Carpenter, says the Philippines has the richest marine biodiversity on earth.[20] We are the "center of the center" of marine biodiversity on earth.[21] Yet, what have we done in Manila Bay? We have thrown all our garbage and all our sewage into Manila Bay. Again, this is 1999. I had given up my law practice in 1998, because I decided to make the fish and the trees my clients. I said, maybe I can tell another story.

So, in January of 1999, I initiated another case against eleven government agencies: Bureau of Fisheries; Department of Public Works; Department of Health; Department of Education; Coast Guard; local government; etc. I sued all of them – not in the sense that I was angry at them, but I was going to tickle them to enforce the law that says we must clean up the polluted bodies of water including Manila Bay. This case was started in the trial court; it went to the court of appeals and, finally, after ten years, it was in the Supreme Court. The Supreme Court decided that the government should clean up Manila Bay. These

---

20 M. Santos, "Chicago lecture cites threats to rich Verde Island marine life", *Philippine Inquirer*, 26 Oct. 2016 (citing a lecture by Old Dominion University professor of biological sciences, Kent Carpenter, Ph.D., entitled "Heart of Marine Biodiversity: Saving the Verde Island Passage").

21 K.E Carpenter & V.G. Springer, "*The center of the center of marine shore fish biodiversity: the Philippine Islands*", 21 Sep. 2009, Food and Agriculture Organization of the United Nations.

government agencies are mandated by the Supreme Court to report every three months about the progress of the case.

I will just tell you a little story, a short aside. When I was fighting this case, for about eight years, I had no funding, I had no money, I gave up my revenue generating practice and I was feeling burned out. I called up a friend, a more senior friend, who I looked at as Mother Earth herself, and I asked her, "What am I doing? I'm supposed to be a graduate of law, and this and that, but here I am defending the fish who do not even pay attorney's fees; and I am tired, I want to give up almost, I mean I was thinking of giving up". And then, tita [aunt] Odette Alcantara – who is now in some other star; she has left this world[22] – said to me, "Never mind Tony, don't worry, don't be concerned; because, a lawyer who defends the earth has god for a client". My friends, I leave that thought with you.

Later on, I also did real enforcement work: catching dynamite fishermen, because we have lots of crazy people, a lot of crazy people going dynamite fishing – and David Forman, there, is an honorary member of the legendary Visayan Sea Squadron, because he is the only foreigner that has joined a real enforcement operation, and I commend him for that. Because of that battle, fighting and fighting (we were not running after the small fisherman doing blast fishing, we were running after the syndicates), the criminal syndicates got mad at me and my buddy, my friend who was working with me. They were going to assassinate me, but they assassinated him[23]; I was supposed to be next, but they could not find me, not even my wife could find me.

So, my friends just to abbreviate, I will share with you some three lessons.

Number one, anything that is worth doing cannot be done in one lifetime. I started this case, for example, in 1990; and it was one generation after in 2012 that all logging was banned in the Philippines. I am lucky I am still around, I could see it. Manila Bay, I do not know. It took me ten years to get a piece of paper to say that government must clean it up. Is it clean now? I do not know, they are trying, but there is still a long way to go. But maybe in the next three

---

22 D. Laguyo, "In Memoriam: Ms. Odette Alcantara, Eco-crusader", University of the Philippines Manila, 23 Oct. 2009, *available online at* https://www.upm.edu.ph/node/708 (eulogizing Lourdes Benito-Alcantara, "a well-known ecological artist and environmentalist who networked people across many walks of life" coordinated the Earth Day Network in the Philippines, and lobbied for passage of the Clean Air Act and the Ecological Solid Waste Management Act).

23 "Cebu City Bantay Dagat chief slain", *The Philippine Star*, Apr. 16, 2006 ("De La Victoria earlier told reporters that he received information that there was a One Million reward for the person who could assassinate him and Oposa").

generations we will be able to swim in Manila Bay. But, my friends, even if anything that is worth doing cannot be done in this lifetime, in this lifetime we can only plant seeds. We must plant seeds, seeds of hope. I shared with you the story of these two cases, there are many more in my book – I sent an electronic copy to Emilie and David, they can share it all with you; you can share it with your Facebook friends and whoever.[24] The Hard copy is available on Amazon.[25]

Number two is the practical function of a legal action. I wanted to tell a story. I used the courtroom as the canvas of the art of telling the story, but there were practical effects in the children's case; many years later, it banned logging and the remaining virgin forests have been protected. In the case of Manila Bay, at least it has shaken up the system, and people in government now are doing something and are reporting to the government, to the Supreme Court on what they are doing now to clean up Manila Bay.

So, let me just put this in a short word, S-T-A-R; in French it is étoile, in Spanish it is estrella. A legal action is like a star; what is star? First, S: it tells a story. You are there to tell a STORY. Second, T: you put the issue on the TABLE for discussion in a manner that is orderly, logical, and backed up by evidence. Third, A: it sparks ACTION. Note what happened with Secretary Factoran; he was very good. He took it positively, he turned it around and was able to save the remaining 800,000 hectares of virgin forest. Fourth, R: it is RESOLUTION. One way or another, sooner or later, win or lose, there will be a resolution as to the story and issue that you presented on the table for discussion.

My friends, number three – and, again, I say this because I want you all to remember it – a lawyer who defends the earth has a greater power (you may call him god, or a great spirt) for a client. My friends, many, many years ago, we put up the School of the SEA. SEA stands for Sea and Earth Advocates. After Yolanda/Haiyan, the most powerful typhoon that hit landfall, we were not only destroyed, the whole place was erased. But, as a symbol of Philippine resilience, we are going to rebuild it and we will have a grand reopening of the School of the SEA on 20-22 April 2018. In front of that the school is a marine sanctuary teeming with fish. I am telling you that my friends, because I am inviting Emilie Gaillard, David Forman, and all of you to come and join us. If you cannot afford a ticket, buy a magic carpet!

---

24 Oposa, 2017, *available online at* https://digitalcommons.pace.edu/environmental/13/ (electronic version).

25 *Ibid.*

Because I have been inspired, we will also have a festival for the arts. My friends, remember. To protect the earth, you must use not the mind, but the heart and how? Because when you change the mind, it can change tomorrow, but when you change the heart it is forever. But how? Contained in the word earth and the word heart is one word, A-R-T. Art is the language of the soul, as music is the language of the heart.

My friends, inspired by your dear professor Emilie, we will draft the outline of the decision we want on how we can use the law. A draft decision of the International Court of Justice, just as an exercise. We will draft the decision on how the law can serve as a guide to the responsible behavior of supposedly the wisest animals on earth. And who are the wisest animals on earth? Homo sapiens. Why do we call them wise? Aren't they the only animals that dirty the water they drink? Aren't they the animals? Are they not the only animals that dirty, poison the air that they breathe? I leave that question to you.

Inspired by our discussions with Emilie and Nick and David, we went to the Netherlands in September 2018, where I served as a Scholar-and-Artist-in-Residence at Erasmus University. We painted, wrote a screenplay, performed theater arts, and engaged in other legal mischief.

My friends, in closing, I just want to leave you a little line. It is said that, if you want to be heard, tell a story. If you want to touch the heart, sing a song. If you want to start a revolution – even a peaceful revolution of the heart and of the mind – ask a question. My friends, I, we, only have one question: do you – young people, and your children, and the children that are yet unborn – do you deserve the kind of earth that we are leaving behind? If not, what is it that our generation must do?

My dear friends, from my inner most heart of hearts – I cannot be with you there, but I am there spiritually with you – I want to thank Emilie Gaillard, my dear brother David Forman (who is, by the way, half Filipino; that is why he is a very handsome gentleman), and our guru, the godfather, Nick Robinson of Pace Law School.

And, my friends, the biggest thank you belongs to all of you. You may think we have done a few things – we have done this and we have done that – yes, but we have generally failed. The world is not better because of what we have done. We have just prevented it from becoming much worse. But, my friends, if you think we are good, no. Maybe we've done a few things. But you my friends, my young friends, you must be ten times better. Why? Because you, my friends, the challenges that you will face in your generation and the generations thereafter will be ten or more times more difficult and more challenging.

My friends, they say humans are most active when they are standing up, they are most creative when they are lying down. The compromise is to sit down. You have been sitting down since the opening of this session, so may I ask everyone to please stand up.

Okay, please stand up. Read to this boy a certain poem that I wrote. Do not read it to Emilie, to David, to your teachers; do not even read to yourself. Read it to this boy, because this boy – when he grows up – he will hold us to account for what we do or what we have failed to do during our time. So, begin, begin together, begin to read aloud, and read not with your mouth, not with your tongue, not with your throat, but read with your heart:

Ten, fifty, a hundred years from now
and many generations here after
let it be said
that during our watch
while gifted with intelligence and insight
with privilege and position
with the wealth of wisdom
and with the freedom and power of the human will
let it be said
that in our time
and during our watch
we did our share
and maybe, just maybe
we will make a little difference.

– Antonio A. Oposa, Jr.

My friends, it is said that it is easy to make money, it is easy to make a name, but it is more meaningful – at the end of the day, when the sun sets it is more meaningful – to make a little difference. That my friends, I have no doubt, as David and as Emilie and as Nick have done, you will make not only a difference, but you will make the big difference. Thank you and bonjour!

List of Figures

Mireille DELMAS-MARTY
Adapting Juridical Order in the Age of the Anthropocene
Fig. 1: *Wind Rose, Identifying Opposing Winds.* 32
Fig. 2: *Wind Cycle, Dancing with the Winds.* 33

Martin WALTER & Andreas NIDECKER
Effects of Ionizing Radiation – Evidence of Genetic Effects: Greater Risks for Transgenerational Damage
Fig. 1: *The clonal theory.* Source: Adapted from E.G. Wright, "Radiation-induced Genomic Instability and Bystander Effects: implications for radiation leukaemogenesis", International Scientific Conference on Childhood Leukaemia, Sep. 2004, London (powerpoint presentation), *available online at* http://cwl2004.powerwatch.org.uk/programme/speakers/day2-wright-pres.pdf. 114
Fig. 2: *Genomic Instability.* Source: Adapted from E.G. Wright, 2004 114
Fig. 3: *Histological slide of bone tumor (white mass) in the lower part of a femur.* Source: Institute of Pathology, University of Basel. 115
Fig. 4: *Normal fruit fly on the left. Phenotypical aberration on the right (lack of wings).* Source: https://bugscope.beckman.illinois.edu/pdfs/insects/mutant.pdf. 119
Fig. 5: *Genetic effects in barn swallows.* Sources: T.A. Mousseau (c) 2006 (left and middle pictures); T.A. Mousseau (c) 2005 (right picture). 119
Fig. 6: *Examples of microsatellite germline mutations in three offspring (columns 3, 4 and 5) from barn swallows (father and mother, columns 1 and 2).* Source: Adapted from H. Ellegren & others, 1997. 120
Fig. 7: *Zizeeria maha, pale grass butterfly.* Source: https://en.wikipedia.org/wiki/Pseudozizeeria_maha. 121
Fig. 8: *Study concept relating to the blue grass pale butterfly after the Fukushima disaster.* Source: A. Hiyama & others, 2012. 122
Fig. 9: *Morphological damage in F1 and F2 butterfly generations.* Source: A. Hiyama & others, 2012. 123
Fig. 10: *Cow from a farm in the Fukushima prefecture with white spots on fur, indicating the possibility of radiation induced albinism.* Source: T.A. Mousseau & A.P. Møller, 2014. 125

Fig. 11: *Contamination of the Mogilev Region*. Source: United Nations Scientific Committee on the Effects of Atomic Radiation (UNSCEAR), Maps of radionuclide deposition, Fig. VI, *available online at* http://www.unscear.org/unscear/en/chernobylmaps.html 127
Fig. 12: *Examples of human minisatellite germline mutation.* Source: Y.E. Dubrova & others, 1996. 128

List of Tables

Martin WALTER & Andreas NIDECKER
Effects of Ionizing Radiation – Evidence of Genetic Effects: Greater Risks for Transgenerational Damage

Tab. 1: *Abnormality rate of Zizeeria maha*. Source: A. Hiyama & others, 2012. 124

Tab. 2: *Increased relative risk (RR) for children of fathers working at the Sellafield nuclear plant and receiving a total pre-conceptional ionizing radiation dose of 100 mSv or more*. Source: Adapted from M.J. Gardner & others, 1990. 126

Tab. 3: ^{137}*Cs surface contamination correlates with mutation rate.* Source: Adapted from Y.E. Dubrova & others, 1996. 129

Select Bibliography

I. Books

Agencia Argentina de Inversiones y Comerco Internacional, *Legal Environmental Handbook*, 2018, *available online at* http://www.inversionycomercio.org.ar/uploads/informes/1557920971-2018-07-06-Manual_de_normativa_ambiental_para_inversores_2018.pdf.pdf (accessed 16 June 2019).

E. Agius and S. Busuttil (eds.), *Future Generations & International Law*, Earthscan Publications, Ltd, London, 1997.

S. Akyut & A. Dahan, *Gouverner le climat ?* [*Governing the Climate?*], Presses de Sciences Po, 2015.

L. Alexandre, M.D., *La Mort de la Mort: Comment la technomédicine va bouleverser l'humanité* [*The Death of Death: How Technomedicine Will Revolutionize Humanity*], JC Lattès, 2011.

G. Anders,

- *L'homme sans monde. Écrits sur l'art de la littérature* [*Man without World: Writings on the Art of Literature*], Fario, 2015.
- *L'Obsolescence de l'homme: Sur l'âme à l'époque de la deuxième révolution industrielle* [*The Obsolescence of Man: On the Soul at the Time of the Second Industrial Revolution*], Éditions de l'Encyclopédie des Nuisances-Ivréa, 2002, Translated from the original 1956 version published by Beck'sche Reihe.
- *De la Bombe et notre aveuglement face à l'apocalypse* [*The Bomb and our Blindness to the Apocalypse*], Titanic, 1995.
- *Hiroshima ist überall* [*Hiroshima is Everywhere*], Munich, C.H. Beck, 1963.

A. Armstrong, *Ethics and Justice for the Environment*, London, Routledge, 2012.

I. Arnoux, *Les droits de l'être humain sur son corps* [*The Rights of Humans over Their Bodies*], Presses Universitaires de Bordeaux, Pessac, 2003.

O. Barrière & others, *Coviability of Social and Ecological Systems: Reconnecting Mankind to the Biosphere in an Era of Global Change*, Vols. 1 and 2, Springer, 2019.

B. Barrillot, *L'Héritage de la bombe : Polynésie – Sahara 1960-2002* [*The Legacy of the Bomb: Polynesia – Sahara 1960-2002*], Centre de Documentation et de Recherche sur la Paix et les Conflits, 2002.

T. Berry,

- *Evening Thoughts: Reflections on Earth as Sacred Community*, San Francisco, Sierra Club Books, 2006.

- *The Great Work: Our Way into the Future*, New York, Bell Tower Press, 1999.

J.-M. Besnier, *L'Homme simplifié* [*Simplified Man*], Paris, Fayard, 2012.

M. Bookchin, *Social Ecology and Communalism*, Oakland, AK Press, 2007.

D.R. Boyd, *The Environmental Rights Revolution*, University of British Columbia Press, 2011.

C. Bréchignac, G. de Broglie & M. Delmas-Marty (eds.), *L'environnement et ses métamorphoses* [*The Environment and its Metamorphoses*], Hermann, 2015.

F. J. Broswimmer, *Ecocide: A Short History of the Mass Extinction of Species*, Pluto Press, 2002.

E. Brown Weiss,

- *In Fairness to Future Generations*, Tokyo/New York, United Nations University/Transnational Publishers, 1989.
- *Establishing Norms in a Kaleidoscopic World*, The Hague Academy of International Law, 2018.

G. Brundtland, *Report of the World Commission on Environment and Development: Our Common Future*, United Nations General Assembly Doc. A/42/427, 1987.

J.-M. Collin, P. Quilès & M. Drain, *L'Illusion nucléaire, La face cachée de la bombe atomique* [*Nuclear Illusion: The Hidden Side of the Atomic Bomb*], Éditions Charles Léopold Meyer, 2018.

Committee for the Compilation of Materials on Damage Caused by the Atomic Bombs in Hiroshima and Nagasaki, *Hiroshima and Nagasaki: The Physical, Medical, and Social Effects of the Atomic Bombings*, New York Basic Books, 1981, translated by E. Ishikaa & D.L. Swain.

Council of Europe, *Manual on Human Rights and the Environment*, 2nd Edition, 2012.

C. Cournil & L. Varison, *Les procès climatiques: du national à l'international* [*Climatic Lawsuits: From the National to the International*], Pédone, 2018.

S. Coyle & K. Morrow, *The Philosophical Foundations of Environmental Law – Property, Rights and Nature*, Oxford, Hart Publishing, 2004.

M. Delmas-Marty, *Aux quatre vents du monde, Petit guide de navigation sur l'océan de la mondialisation* [*Four Winds of the World: A Short Guide to Navigating the Ocean of Globalization*], Seuil, 2016.

P. Descola, *Beyond Nature and Culture*, The University of Chicago Press, translated by J. Loyd, 2013.

M. Dobre, F. Flipo & M. Michot, *La face cachée du numérique: l'impact environnemental des nouvelles technologies* [*The Hidden Face of Digital

Technology: the Environmental Impact of New Technologies], éd. L'échappée, 2013.

G. Dorthe, *Malédiction des objets absents: explorations épistémiques, politiques et écologiques du mouvement transhumaniste par un chercheur intégré* [*Curse of Absent Objects: Epistemic, Political and Ecological Explorations of the Transhumanist Movement by an Embedded Researcher*], Doctoral thesis, University of Lausanne and University Paris I Panthéon-Sorbonne, 2018.

J.-P. Dupuy,

- *Petite métaphysique des tsunamis* [*A Short Treatise on the Metaphysics of Tsunamis*], Seuil, 2005.
- *Pour un catastrophisme éclairé : Quand l'impossible est certain* [*For an Enlightened Catastrophism: When the Impossible Becomes Certain*], Points Essais, éditions Seuil, 2004.

B. Edelman & M.-A. Hermitte (eds.), *L'homme, la nature et le droit* [*Man, Nature and the Law*], C. Bourgois, 1988.

G.M. Eguiazu,

- *Plaguicidas y Error Tecnogénico* [*Pesticides and Technogenic Errors*], Publicaciones Universidad Nacional de Rosario, 1998.
- *Tecnogenia, Tecnología, riesgos y vías de prevención [Technopathogenology, Technology, Risks and Prevention Paths],* Universidad Nacional de Rosario Editora, 1997.

C. Eliott, *Better than Well: American Medicine Meets the American Dream*, W.W. Norton & Company, New York, 2004.

Environmental Protection Agency, Final Rule, "Carbon pollution emission guidelines for existing stationary sources: electric utility generating units", *Federal Register*, 23 Oct. 2015, Vol. 80.

European Committee on Radiation Risks, *2010 Recommendations of the European Committee on Radiation Risk. The Health Effects of Exposure to Low Doses of Ionizing Radiation*, C. Busby, R. Bertell, I. Schmitz-Feuerhake, M. Scott Cato & A. Yablokov (eds.), Green Audit, 2010.

European Economic and Social Committee, *Climate justice (own-initiative opinion)*, 19 Oct. 2017, C. Lohan (reporter).

F. Fukuyama, *La fin de l'Histoire et le dernier des hommes* [*The End of History and the Last Man*], Flammarion, 1992.

E. Gaillard, *Générations futures et droit privé. Vers un droit des générations futures* [*Future Generations and Private Law: Towards a Law for Future Generations*], Librairie Générale de Droit et de Jurisprudence, 2011.

J.-G. Ganascia,

- "Des humanités numériques à la Singularité technologique. Que reste-t-il de l'Humanisme ?" [From the Digital Humanities to the Technical Singularity: What is Left of Humanism?], *Archives de Philosophie du Droit*, 2017, Vol. 59, p. 193
- "*Le mythe de la Singularité : faut-il craindre l'intelligence artificielle ?*" [The Singularity Myth: Should we Fear Artificial Intelligence?], Seuil, Paris, 2017.

M. Glasius, *The International Criminal Court: A Global Civil Society Achievement*, Routledge, London, 2006.

J. Habermas, "Law and Morality", *in The Tanner Lectures of Human Values*, Cambridge University Press, 1986.

J. Hansen, *Storms of My Grandchildren: The Truth About the Coming Climate Catastrophe and Our Last Chance to Save Humanity*, Paperback, 2009.

M.-A. Hermitte, *Le droit saisi au vif. Sciences, technologies et formes de vie* [*Law Transformed: Science, Technology and Life Forms*], Interviews with F. Chateauraynaud, Éditions Petra, 2013.

P. Higgins, *Eradicating Ecocide laws and governance to prevent the destruction of our planet*, Shepheard-Walwyn, 2010.

G. Hottois, *Philosophie et idéologies trans/posthumanistes* [*Trans/Posthumanist Philosophy and Ideology*], Librairie Philosophique J. Vrin, 2017.

C. Huglo, *Le contentieux climatique : une révolution judiciaire mondiale* [*Climate Litigation: A Global Judicial Revolution*], Éditions Bruylant, 2018.

P. Hugon, *L'ECONOMIE ETHIQUE PUBLIQUE : Biens Publics Mondiaux et Patrimoines Communs* [*THE PUBLIC ETHICAL ECONOMY: Global Public Goods and Common Heritage*], UNESCO, Economie Ethique, No. 3.

T. Jackson, *Prosperity Without Growth: Foundations for the Economy of Tomorrow*, 2nd edition, London, Routledge, 2017.

V.N. James & J.S. William (eds.), *The Children of Atomic Bomb Survivors: A Genetic Study*, National Academies Press, 1991.

T. Jayatilaka, *Rights of Nature: The Right Approach to Environmental Standing in the EU?*, 2016-2017, LLM Paper, Ghent University.

H. Jonas, *The Imperative of Responsibility: In Search of an Ethics for the Technological Age*, University of Chicago Press, 1985.

J. Jouzel & A. Michelot, *La Justice climatique : enjeux et perspectives pour la France* [*Climate Justice: Challenges and Prospects for France*], Les Éditions des Journaux Officiels, Sep. 2016, CESE27/09/2016.

L. Kass, *Life, Liberty, and the Defense of Dignity: The Challenge for Bioethics*, San Francisco, Encounter Books, 2002.

S. Kingston, *European Perspectives on Environmental Law and Governance*, New York, Routledge, 2013, p. 12.

N. Klein, *This Changes Everything*, London, Penguin Books, 2014.

E. Kohn, *Comment pensent les forêts – Vers une anthropologie au-delà de l'humain* [*How Forests Think: Towards an Anthropology Beyond the Human*], Zones sensibles, 2017, p. 313, translated by G. Delaplace.

X. Labbée (ed.), *L'homme augmenté face au droit* [*The Enhanced Man Facing the Law*], Presses Universitaires du Septentrion, 2015.

N. Le Dévédec, *La société de l'amélioration : le renversement de la perfectibilité humaine, de l'Humanisme des Lumières à l'Humain augmenté* [*The Society of Improvement: the Overthrow of Human Perfectibility, from Enlightenment Humanism to the Human Augmented*], Thèse Sciences Politiques et Sociologie, cotutelle J. Beaudoine & C. Lafontaine, Universities of Rennes 1 and Montréal, 2013.

T. Lefort-Martine, *Des droits pour la nature – L'expérience équatorienne* [*Rights for Nature – The Ecuadorian Experience*], L'Harmattan, 2018.

A. Leopold, *A Sand County Almanac*, Ballantine Books New York, 1966.

C. Lepage & Equipe de Rédaction, "Declaration Universelle des Droits de L'Humanite : Rapport à l'attention de Monsieur Le Président de La République" [Universal Declaration of the Rights and Duties of Humankind: A Report to Monsieur the President of the Republic], 25 Sep. 2015.

C. Lepage & J.-L. Servan-Schreiber, *Déclaration Universelle des Droits de l'Humanité* [*Universal Declaration of the Rights and Duties of Humankind*], Chêne édition, 2016.

G. Levitt, N. Bellinger, J. Margolis & D. Quirke, *Public Trust Doctrine in Environmental Decision Making*, Mar. 2016, The Environmental & Natural Resources Law Center.

D.R. Mandelker & others, *State and Local Government in a Federal System*, 2010, LexisNexis, 7th edition.

G. Marshall, *Le syndrome de l'autruche – Pourquoi notre cerveau veut ignorer le changement climatique* [*The Ostrich Syndrome – Why our Brain Wants to Ignore Climate Change*], Actes Sud, 2017.

J.R. May & E. Daly, *Global Environmental Constitutionalism*, Cambridge University Press, 2015.

D.H. Meadows, Dennis L.Meadows, J. Randers, W. W. Behrens, *The Limits to Growth: A Report for the Club of Rome's Project on the Predicament of Mankind*, Universe books, 1972.

A. Michelot (ed.), *Equité et environnement. Quel(s) modèle(s) de justice environnementale ?* [*Equity and Environment: What Model(s) of Environmental Justice?*], Larcier, 2012.

S. Milgram, *Obedience to Authority: An Experimental View*, Harper Collins, 2004.

R. Nash, *The Rights of Nature: A History of Environmental Ethics*, University of Wisconsin Press, 1989.

N. Nevejans, *Traité de droit et d'éthique de la robotique civile* [*Treaty of Law and Ethics of Civil Robotics*], LEH Edition, 2017.

R. Nozick, *Anarchy, State and Utopia*, Presses Universitaires du France, 1988.

A. Oposa, Jr., *Shooting Stars and Dancing Fish: A Walk to the World We Want*, Ramon Aboitiz Foundation, 2017.

F. Ost, *La nature hors la loi : L'écologie à l'épreuve du droit* [*Nature Out of the Law: Ecology Under the Law*], 2nd edition, Paris, La Découverte, 2003.

M. Prieur, J. Bétaille, M.-A. Cohendet, H. Delzangles, J. Makowiak & P. Steichen, *Droit de l'environnement* [*Environmental Law*], Dalloz, 7th edition, 2016.

C. Puigelier & F. Gros, *Biologie et droit, les étapes du vivant* [*Biology and Law, the Stages of Life*], Bruylant, 2016.

M. Rémond-Gouilloud, *Du droit de détruire – essai sur le droit de l'environnement* [*Right to Destroy – Environmental Law Test*], Paris, Presses Universitaires de France, 1989.

J. Rifkin, *The Biotech Century: Harnessing the Gene and Remaking the World*, TarcherPerigee, 1999.

M.C. Roco, W.S. Bainbridge, B. Tonn, & G. Whitesides (eds.), *Convergence of Knowledge, Technology, and Society: Beyond Convergence of Nano-Bio-Info-Cognitive Technologies*, World Technology Evaluation Center Inc., July 2013.

P. Roqueplo, *Penser la technique : pour une démocratie concrète* [*Thinking Technique: For a Concrete Democracy*], Seuil, 1983.

D. Schlospberg, *Defining Environmental Justice: Theories, Movements and Nature*, Oxford University Press, U.K., 2007.

M. Serres, *Le Contrat naturel* [*The Natural Contract*], Paris, François Bourin, 1990.

A. Sinaï, *Penser la décroissance. Politiques de l'Anthropocène* [*Think Decay: Policies of the Anthropocene*], Presses de Sciences Po, 2013.

J.W. Singer, *Property Law: Rules, Policies, and Practices*, 2010.

M. Stenmark, *Environmental Ethics and Policy-Making*, New Yok, Routledge, 2002.

Stockholm International Peace Research Institute, Yearbook 2018, *Armaments, Disarmament and International Security*, 2018.

C. Stone, *Should Trees Have Standing? Law, Morality, and the Environment*, Oxford University Press, 3rd edition, 2010.

D. Sumner, T.E. Wheldon & W. Watson (eds.), *Radiation risks: an evaluation*, Tarragon Press, 1990.

J. Testart & A. Rousseaux, *Au péril de l'Humain, les promesses suicidaires des transhumanistes* [*At the Risk of the Human, the Suicidal Promises of the Transhumanists*], Collections. Sciences ouvertes, Seuil, Paris, 2018.

M. Tibon-Cornillot, *Les corps transfigurés. Mécanisation du vivant et imaginaire de la biologie* [*The Transfigured Bodies: Mechanization of the Living and Imaginary Body*], Paris, Seuil, 1992.

Y. Thomas, *Les opérations du droit* [*Legal Operations*], Le Seuil, 2011.

M. Torre-Schaub, C. Cournil, S. Lavorel & M. Moliner-Dubost (eds.), *Quel(s) droit(s) pour les changements climatiques ?* [*What right(s) for climate change?*], éditions Mare and Martin, 2017.

UNICEF United Kingdom, *Climate Change: Children's Challenge* (2013).

UN Secretary General, *Intergenerational Solidarity and the Needs of Future Generations: Report of the Secretary-General*, United Nations Doc. A/68/322, 15 Aug. 2013.

A. Van Lang, *Droit de l'environnement* [*Environmental Law*], Paris, Presses Universitaires de France, 2002.

H. Védrine, preface by G. Pitron, *La guerre des métaux rares* [*The War of Rare Metals*], Les Liens qui Libèrent, 2018.

R. White, *Crimes Against Nature, Environmental criminology and ecological justice*, Devon, Willan Publishing, 2008.

M.C. Wood, *Nature's Trust: Environmental Law for a New Ecological Age*, 2013.

World Commission on the Ethics of Scientific Knowledge and Technology (COMEST), Report, *Les implications du changement climatique mondial* [*The Implications of Global Climate Change*], UNESCO, Paris, 2010.

World Commission on the Ethics of Scientific Knowledge and Technology (COMEST), Report, *The Precautionary Principle*, United Nations Educational, Scientific and Cultural Organization, 2005.

A. Zabalza, *La Terre & le Droit* [*The Earth & the Law*], Editions Bière, 2007.

II. Articles

S. Alexander, "Wild Law from below, Examining the anarchist challenge to Earth Jurisprudence", *in* M. Maloney & P. Burdon, 2014, p. 35.

C. Alleaume & A. Pigeon-Bormans, "Droit(s) d'auteur des robots : 'Nous cherchons à comprendre' "[Right(s) of robots: "We seek to understand"], *Légipresse*, Nov. 2017, p. 523.

American Academy of Pediatrics Council on Environmental Health (AAP), "Policy Statement on Global Climate Change and Children's Health", *Pediatrics*, 1 Nov. 2018, Vol. 136, p. 992.

A. Amor, "Les droits de la troisième génération" [The Rights of the Third Generation], *Tunisian Journal of Law*, 1986, p. 13.

G. Annas, L.B. Andrews & R.M. Isasi, "Protecting the Endangered Human: Toward an International Treaty Prohibiting Cloning and Inheritable Alterations", *American Journal of Law and Medicine*, 2002, No. 28, p. 151.

G. Anders, "Les bombes et les racines de notre aveuglement face à l'apocalypse" [The Bombs and the Roots of Our Blindness to the Apocalypse], *in* G. Anders, *L'Obsolescence de l'homme : Sur l'âme à l'époque de la deuxième révolution industrielle* [*The Obsolescence of Man: On the Soul at the Time of the Second Industrial Revolution*], Éditions de l'Encyclopédie des Nuisances-Ivréa, 2002, Translated from the original 1956 version published by Beck'sche Reihe.

K. Aoki, "Food Forethought: Intergenerational Equity and Global Food Supply—Past, Present, and Future", *Wisconsin Law Review*, 2011, Issue no. 2, p. 399.

A. Aragao, "Les intérêts diffus, instruments pour la justice et la démocratie environnementale" [Diffuse Interests, Instruments for Justice and Environmental Democracy], *VertigO – La revue électronique en sciences de l'environnement*, Special Issue No. 22, Sep. 2015, p. 3.

J.-M. Arbour, "L'impossible défi canadien : lutter efficacement contre les changements climatiques, exporter davantage de pétrole, respecter les compétences constitutionnelles des provinces" [The Impossible Canadian Challenge: Efficiently Fight Climate Change, Export More Oil, Respect the Constitutional Authorities of the Provinces], *in Après l'accord de Paris, quels droits face au changement climatique ?* [*After the Paris Agreement, What Rights for Climate Change?*], *Revue Juridique de l'Environnement*, Lavoisier, 2017, No. Special, p. 73.

G. Azam, C. Bonneuil & M. Combes, *La nature n'a pas de prix – Les méprises de l'économie verte* [*Nature is Priceless: The Misunderstandings of the Green Economy*], Paris, Les liens qui libèrent, 2012, p. 12.

R. Bailey, "For Enhancing People", *in The Transhumanist Reader*, John Wiley & Sons, 2013.

G.S. Bandazhevskaya & others, "Relationship between Caesium (^{137}Cs) load, cardiovascular symptoms, and source of food in 'Chernobyl' children – preliminary observations after intake of oral apple pectin", *Swiss Medical Weekly*, 18 Dec. 2004, No. 134(49-50), p. 725.

M. Barlow, "Building the Case for the Universal Declaration of the Rights of Mother Earth", *in Does Nature Have Rights? Transforming Grassroots to Protect People and the Planet, Right of Nature Report*, 2010, p. 7.

G. Barnaud, "Des fonctions écologiques au marché des services écosystémiques, une avancée conceptuelle ou une gageure" [From Ecological Functions to the Ecosystem Services Market, a Conceptual Advance or a Challenge], *in* M.-P. Camproux Duffrène & J. Sohnle (eds.), *Marché et environnement, le marché : menace ou remède ?* [*Market and Environment, the Market: Threat or Remedy?*], Bruxelles, Bruylant, 2014, p. 57.

R. Barnett-Rose, "Judicially Modified Democracy: Court and State Preemption of Local GMO Regulation in Hawaii and Beyond", 26 *Duke Environmental Law & Policy Forum*, 2015, p. 71.

A.D. Barnosky & others, "Approaching a state shift in Earth's biosphere", *Nature*, 2012, Vol. 486, p. 52.

B. Barrillot, "Essais nucléaires français. L'héritage empoisonné" [French Nuclear Tests: The Poisoned Inheritance], Observatoire des Armements/Centre de Documentation et de Recherche sur la Paix et les Conflits Editions, 2012.

S. Bateman & J. Gayon, "L'amélioration humaine : trois usages, trois enjeux" [The Improvement of Humans: Three Applications, Three Objectives], *Médecine/Sciences*, Vol. 28, No. 10, Oct. 2012, p. 887.

M.V. Berros,

- "Defending Rivers: Vilcabamba in the South of Ecuador", *in* A.L. Tabios Hillebrecht & M.V. Berros, *Can Nature have Rights? Legal and Political Insights*, Rachel Carson Center for Environment & Society, 2017, No. 6, p. 37.
- "The Constitution of the Republic of Ecuador: Pachamama Has Rights", *Environment & Society Portal*, Arcadia, 2015, No. 11.
- "The Rights of Nature Recognition", *in* S. Kalantzakos, *Energy & Environmental Transformations in a Globalizing World*, Nomiki Bibliothiki, 2015.
- "El estatuto jurídico de la naturaleza en debate (meulen en el mundo del derecho)" [The Legal Status of Nature in Debate (Swirling Wind in the World of Law)], *Revista de Derecho Ambiental*, 2013, No. 36, p. 133.

M. V. Berros & R. Colombo, "Miradas emergentes sobre el estatuto jurídico de los ríos, cuencas y glaciares" [Emerging Views on the Legal Status of Rivers, Basins and Glaciers], *Rivista quadrimestrale di diritto dell'ambiente*, 2017, p. 31.

J.-M. Besnier, “Le post-humanisme ou la fatigue d’être libre” [Posthumanism or the Fatigue of Freedom], *La pensée de midi*, 2010/1, No. 30, p. 75.

R. Bettin, “Les ONG : moteurs de l’avant, actrices de l’après” [NGOs: Drivers of the “Before”, Actors of the “After”], *in Après l’accord de Paris, quels droits face au changement climatique ? [After the Paris Agreement, What Rights for Climate Change?]*, p. 135.

J.-P. Beurier, “L’autorité internationale des fonds marins, l’environnement et le juge” [The International Seabed Authority, the Environment and the Judge], *in* Collectif, *La représentation de la nature devant le juge : approche comparative et prospective [The Representation of Nature Before the Judge: Comparative and Prospective Approach]*, VertigO, 2017.

G. Bibeau, “Choisir la vie” [Choosing Life], *in* Dossier : Le corps obsolète ? L’idéologie transhumaniste en question, Relations, 2017, Vol. 792, p. 19.

M.C. Blumm & R.D. Guthrie, “Internationalization of the Public Trust Doctrine: Natural Law and Constitutional and Statutory Approaches to Fulfilling the Saxion Vision”, *University of California Davis Law Review*, 2012, Vol. 45, p. 741.

B. Boidin, “Approche économique” [Economic Approach], *in Dictionnaire des biens communs*, M. Cornu, F. Orsi, J. Rochfeld (eds.), Quadrige, Presses Universitaires de France, 2017.

A. Boutaud, “Ecologie : les grandes controverses” [Ecology: The Big Controversies], *Millénaire*, 3 Feb. 2010, p. 4.

R. Bratspies,

- “Myths of Voluntary Compliance: Lessons from the StarLink Corn Fiasco”, *William & Mary Environmental Law & Policy Review*, 2003, Vol. 27, p. 593.
- “Some Thoughts on the American Approach to Regulating Genetically Modified Organisms”, *Kansas Journal of Law & Public Policy*, 2007, Vol. 16, p. 393.

P. Brewbaker, Ph.D., “Fifty Years of Seed in the Fiftieth State: An Economic Report of the Hawaii Crop Improvement Association”, Aug. 2016.

E. Brown Weiss, “The Planetary Trust: Conservation and Intergenerational Equity”, *Ecology Law Quaterly*, 1984, vol. 11, p. 495.

M. Burkett, “Indigenous Environmental Knowledge and Climate Change Adaptation”, *in* R.S. Abate & E.A. Kronk (eds.), *Climate Change and Indigenous Peoples: The Search for Legal Remedies*, Edward Elgar Publishing Limited, 2013, p. 96.

J. Burroughs,

- “The International Criminal Court, Weapons of Mass Destruction, NGOs and Other Issues: A Report on the Negotiations and the Statute”, *Lawyers Committee on Nuclear Policy*, New York, Apr. 1999.

- "The French Interpretative Declaration Regarding Nuclear Weapons", Lawyers Committee on Nuclear Policy, New York, 3 July 2000.

C. Byk,

- "Le droit et l'idée de perfectibilité humaine" [Law and the Idea of Human Perfectibility], *Revue de la Recherche Juridique - Droit prospectif*, 2017, Issue 4, p. 1399.
- "Les nouvelles frontières du corps" [The New Frontiers of the Body], *Revue générale de droit médical*, No. 63, Les Etudes Hospitalières, June 2017.
- "Droit et complexité : l'exemple du bio-droit" [Law and Complexity: the example of Biolaw], *Revue de la Recherche Juridique – Droit prospectif*, 2016-4, Presses Universitaires Aix-Marseilles, p. 1537.

D.L. Callies, "GMO Regulation", *Zoning and Planning Reports NL*, Vol. 1, Nov. 2015.

M. Callon, "Éléments pour une sociologie de la traduction. La domestication des coquilles Saint-Jacques dans la Baie de Saint Brieuc" [Elements for a Sociology of Translation: The Domestication of Scallops in the Bay of Saint Brieuc], *L'Année sociologique*, 1986, No. 36.

L. Canali, "Droit du process et climat" [Procedural Law and Climate], *in* M. Hautereau-Boutonnet (ed.), *Quel droit pour sauver le climat ?* [What Right to Save the Climate?], 2018, Université Lyon, p. 10, *available online at* https://halshs.archives-ouvertes.fr/halshs-01684948/document.

E. Cardis & others, "Cancer consequences of the Chernobyl accident: 20 years on", *Journal of Radiological protection*, 26 June 2006, Vol. 26, No. 2, p. 127.

D. Chilstein, "Les biens à valeur vénale négative" [Goods with Negative Market Value], *Revue trimestrielle droit civil*, 2006.

J.-M. Collin,

- "La convention d'interdiction des armes nucléaires : de la négociation au premier draft" [Nuclear Weapons Convention: From Negotiation to First Draft], Group for Research and Information on Peace and Security Analysis Note, 12 June 2017.
- "L'Assemblée générale de l'ONU ouvre la porte à un traité d'interdiction des armes nucléaires" [UN General Assembly Opens the Door to a Nuclear Weapons Ban Treaty], Group for Research and Information on Peace and Security (GRIP) – *Annuaire français de relations internationales* (AFRI), Vol. XVIII, 9 Dec. 2016.
- "Groupe de travail de l'ONU sur le désarmement nucléaire : bilan de ses sessions de travail de janvier à mai 2016" [UN Working Group on Nuclear Disarmament: Review of its Working Sessions from January to May 2016], *Note: Multipol*, 21 July 2016.

- "Dimension humanitaire du désarmement nucléaire et danger du nucléaire militaire en France" [The Humanitarian Dimension of Nuclear Disarmament and the Danger of Nuclear Energy in France], Group for Research and Information on Peace and Security Analysis Note, 16 Sep. 2015.
- "3rd conference on the humanitarian impact of nuclear weapons, a new cycle of action", Group for Research and Information on Peace and Security Analysis Note, 2015.
- "Nayarit conference on the humanitarian impact of nuclear weapons: A point of no-return!", Group for Research and Information on Peace and Security Analysis Note, 2014.
- "L'impact humanitaire des armes nucléaires: un nouveau forum du désarmement ?" [The Humanitarian Impact of Nuclear Weapons: A New Forum for Disarmament?], Group for Research and Information on Peace and Security Analysis Note, 2013.

E. Cornu-Thenard, "Eléments sur l'apport de la doctrine du public trust à la représentation de la nature devant le juge" [Elements on the Contribution of the Public Trust Doctrine to the Representation of Nature Before the Judge], *in* Collectif, *La représentation de la nature devant le juge, approches comparative et prospective* [*The Representation of Nature Before the Judge, Comparative and Prospective Approaches*], VertigO, 2017, p. 187.

R.H.J. Cox, "The Liability of European States for Climate Change", *Utrecht Journal of International and European Law*, 2014, Vol. 30(78), p. 125.

C. Cournil, "Les droits fondamentaux au service de l'émergence d'un contentieux climatique. Des stratégies contentieuses des requérants à l'activisme des juges" [Fundamental Rights at the Service of the Emergence of a Climate Dispute, Applicants' Contentious Strategies to the Activism of Judges], *in* M. Torre-Schaub, C. Cournil, S. Lavorel & M. Moliner-Dubost (eds.), *Quel(s) droit(s) pour les changements climatiques ?* [*What Right(s) for Climate Change?*], Mare & Martin, 2017.

R.K. Craig, "Labeling Genetically-Engineered Foods: An Update from One of the Front Lines of Federalism", *Environmental Law*, 2017, Vol. 47, p. 609.

J. Currie & L. Deschênes, "Children and Climate Change: Introducing the Issue", *The Future of Children*, Vol. 26, No 1, Children and Climate Change, p. 3.

H. Daly,

- "Economics for a Full World", *Great Transition Initiative: Towards a Transformative Vision and Praxis*, June 2015.
- "Economics in a Full World", *Scientific American*, Sep. 2005, Vol. 293, No. 3.

E. Daly, "The Ecuadorian Examplar: the First Ever Vindications of Constitutional Rights of Nature", *Review of European, Comparative & International Environmental Law*, 2012, Vol. 21, Issue 1.

D. Dana & S. Koniak, "Bargaining in the Shadow of Democracy", *University of Pennsylvania Law Review*, 1999, Vol. 148, p. 473.

V. David,

- "La nouvelle vague des droits de la nature. La personnalité juridique reconnue aux fleuves Whanganui, Gange et Yamuna" [The New Wave of the Rights of Nature. Recognized Legal Personality at Whanganui, Ganges and Yamuna Rivers], *Revue juridique de l'environnement*, 2017, No. 3, p. 418.
- "La lente consécration de la nature, sujet de droit. Le monde est-il enfin Stone ?" [The Slow Consecration of Nature as a Subject of Law: Is the World Finally Stone?], *Revue juridique de l'environnement*, 2012/3, Vol. 37, p. 474.

M. Delmas-Marty,

- "*Etudes juridiques comparatives et internationalisation du droit 'Cours : vers une communauté de valeurs ? – Les droits fondamentaux'*" [Comparative legal studies and the internationalization of law, "Lecture: Moving Towards a Community of Values? – Fundamental Rights"], *available online at* goo.gl/obJZhc.
- "10x10 (Global): Homage to Norman Dorser", *International Journal of Constitutional Law*, 2010, Vol. 8, p. 445.

A.G. Dimmen, "Gendered Impacts: The Humanitarian Impacts of Nuclear Weapons from a Gender Perspective", *International Law and Policy Institute – United Nations Institute for Disarmament Research Vienna Conference Series*, Paper No. 5 of 6, Dec. 2014.

W. Dross, "De la revendication à la réattribution: la propriété peut-elle sauver le climat ?" [From Claim to Reallocation: Can Property Save the Climate?], *Recueil Dalloz*, 2017, p. 2,553.

Y.E. Dubrova, V.N. Nesterov, N.G. Krouchinsky, V.A. Ostapenko, R. Neumann, D.L. Neil & A.J. Jeffreys, "Human minisatellite mutation rate after the Chernobyl accident", *Nature*, 25 Apr. 1996, Vol. 380, Issue 6576, p. 683.

M. Dutu, "Climate change and human rights: emergence of a new fundamental right to proper climate", *in* A. Michelot (ed.), *Justice climatique : enjeux et perspectives* [*Climate Justice: Issues and Perspectives*], Bruylant, 2016, p. 311.

H. Ellegren, G. Lindgren, C.R. Primmer, & A.P. Møller, "Fitness loss and germline mutations in barn swallows breeding in Chernobyl", *Nature*, 9 Oct. 1997, Vol. 389, No. 6651, p. 593.

D. Estrin, "Limiting dangerous climate change: the critical role of citizen suits and domestic courts, despite the Paris agreement", *Centre for International Governance Innovation*, No. 101, May 2016, p. 19.

J. Eule, "Temporal Limits on the Legislative Mandate: Entrenchment and Retroactivity", *American Bar Foundation Research Journal*, Spring-Summer 1987, Vol. 12, No 2/3, p. 379.

D. Farquhar & L. Meyer, "State Authority to Regulate Biotechnology Under the Federal Coordinated Framework", *Drake Journal of Agricultural Law*, 2007, Vol. 12, p. 439.

P. Fedirko, V. Sakovich & N. Garkava, "Vascular Pathology of an eye and the threat of developing age-related macular degeneration after radiation exposed", *Eureka: Health Science*, Nov. 2017, No. 6, p. 3.

E.F. Fernandez, "Les controverses autour de l'intérêt à agir pour l'accès au juge constitutionnel : de la défense du droit à l'environnement (Costa Rica) à la défense des droits de la nature (Équateur)" [The Controversies Surrounding the Interest in Acting for Access to the Constitutional Judge: From the Defense of the Right to the Environment (Costa Rica) to the Defense of the Rights of Nature (Ecuador)], *VertigO – La revue électronique en sciences de l'environnement*, Special Issue No. 22, Sep. 2015.

L. Ferry, *Le Nouvel Ordre écologique. L'arbre, l'animal et l'homme* [*The New Ecological Order: The Tree, the Animal and the Man*], Paris, Grasset, 1992.

C. Figuières, H. Guyomard & G. Rotillon, "Sustainable Development: Between Moral Injunctions and Natural Constraints", *Sustainability*, 2010, No. 2, p. 3611.

D.E. Fisher, "Jurisprudential challenges to the protection of the natural environment", *in* M. Maloney & P. Burdon (eds.), *Wild Law – In Practice*, Routledge, 2014.

F. Flipo, "Pour des droits de la nature" [For Rights of Nature], *Mouvements*, 2012/2, No. 70, p. 131.

E. Fonza & others, "Vers une définition du crime international d'écocide" [Towards a Definition of the International Crime of Ecocide], *in* L. Neyret (ed.), *Des écocrimes à l'écocide : le droit pénal au secours de l'environnement* [*From Ecocrimes to Ecocide: Criminal Law Saving the Environment*], Bruylant, 2015, p. 132.

D.M. Forman, "Applying Indigenous Knowledge for the Protection of Environmental Commons: Case Studies from Hawai'i for the Benefit of Island Earth", *University of Hawai'i Law Review*, 2019, Vol. 41 (forthcoming 2019).

E. Fox-Decent, "From Fiduciary States to Joint Trusteeship of the Atmosphere: The Right to a Healthy Environment Through a Fiduciary Prism", *in* K. Coghill & others (eds.), *Fiduciary Duty and the Atmospheric Trust*, 2012, p. 263.

M.-P. Blin-Franchehomme,

- "Quel rôle dans la lute le changement climatique pour l'enterprise ?" [What Role for Companies in the Fight Against Climate Change?], *in* M. Hautereau-Boutonnet (ed.), *Quel droit pour sauver le climat ? [What Right to Save the Climate?*], 2018, p. 9.
- "Quel rôle pour l'entreprise après l'Accord de Paris ?" [The Company's Role After the Paris Agreement?]; *in Après l'accord de Paris, quels droits face au changement climatique ? [After the Paris Agreement, What Rights for Climate Change?*], *Revue Juridique de l'Environnement*, Lavoisier, 2017, No. Special, p. 135.

J.C. Fritz, "Protection de l'environnement et marché : coexistence ou guerre des mondes ?" [Environmental Protection and Market: Coexistence or War of the Worlds?], *in* M.-P. Camproux Duffrène & J. Sohnle (eds.), *Marché et environnement, le marché : menace ou remède ? [Market and Environment, the Market: Threat or Remedy?*], Bruylant, 2014, p. 21.

E. Gaillard,

- "*Le Tribunal international Monsanto, un tribunal d'opinion atypique et audacieux*" [The International Monsanto Tribunal, an Atypical and Audacious Tribunal of Opinion], *Energie-Environnement-Infrastructures*, June 2017, No. 6, p. 62.
- *Amicus brief on Emerging law: Ecocide and the Rights of Future Generations*, People's International *Tribunal on Nuclear Weapons* and the Destruction of Human *Civilisation,* Centre for Peace and Conflict Studies, University of Sydney, *available online at* http://www.unfoldzero.org/wp-content/uploads/Emerging-law-.EGAILLARD.pdf (accessed on 14 June 2019).
- "Crimes againts Future Generations", *e-Pública*, Vol. 2, No. 2, 2015, p. 40.
- "Pour la reconnaissance du dommage juridique transgénérationel" [For the Recognition of Transgenerational Legal Damage], *in* J.-P. Markus (ed.), *Quelles responsabilité juridique envers les générations futures ?* [What Legal Responsibility for Future Generations?], Dalloz, 2012, p. 245.
- "L'équité transgénérationnelle: perspectives de justice pour les générations futures ?" [Transgenerational Equity: Opportunities to Pursue Justice for Future Generations?], *in* A. Michelot (ed.), *Equité et Environnement. Quel(s) modèle(s) de justice environnementale ? [Equity and Environment: What Model(s) of Environmental Justice?*], Larcier, 2012, p. 52.

S.A. Gardbaum, "The Nature of Preemption", *Cornell Law Review*, 1994, Vol. 79, p. 767.

M.J. Gardner, A.J. Hall, M.P. Snee, S. Downes, C.A. Powell & J.D. Terrell, "Methods and basic data of case-control study of leukaemia and lymphoma among young people near Sellafield nuclear plant in West Cumbria", *British Medical Journal*, 17 Feb. 1990, Issue No. 300, p. 429.

M.J. Gardner, M.P. Snee, A.J. Hall, C.A. Powell, S. Downes & J.D. Terrell, "Results of case-control study of leukaemia and lymphoma among young people near Sellafield nuclear plant in West Cumbria", *British Medical Journal*, 17 Feb. 1990, Issue No. 300, p. 423.

A. Geslin, "États et sécurité environnementale, états de l'insécurité environnementale : de la recomposition normative des territoires à l'esquisse d'un droit de l'anthropocène" [States and Environmental Security, States of Enviromental Security: From the Normative Recomposition of Territories to the Outline of an Anthropocene Right], *in* J. Tercinet (ed.), *États et sécurité internationale* [*States and International Security*], coll. Études stratégiques internationales, Bruylant, Brussels, 2012, p. 87.

D.-R. Gibson, Comment, "Remembering the 'Big Five': Hawai'i's Constitutional Obligation to Regulate the Genetic Engineering Industry", *Asian-Pacific Law & Policy Journal*, 2014, Vol. 15, p. 213.

G. Giudicelli-Delage & K. Martin-Chenut, "Humanisme et protection de la nature" [Humanism and Nature Protection], *in L'environnement et ses métamorphoses* [*The Environment and its Metamorphoses*], Le Monde – Hermann, 2015, p. 227.

J.-C. Guillebaud, "Techno-prophètes ou savants fous ?" [Techno-Prophets or Mad Scientists?], *Le corps obsolète ? L'idéologie transhumaniste en question [The Obsolete Body?: The Transhumanist Ideology in Question]*, Revue Relations, Montréal, 2017, Vol. 792, p. 19.

S. Goyard-Fabre, "Sujet de droit et objet de droit, défense de l'humanisme" [Subject of Law and Object of Right, Defense of Humanism], *Cahiers de philosophie politique et juridique*, Presses Universitaires du France, 1992, No. 22, p. 7.

N. Greene, "Le cas des constitutions équatorienne et bolivienne" [The case of Ecuadorian and Bolivian Constitutions], *in Des droits pour la Terre* [*Rights for the Earth*], Utopia, 2016, p. 76.

D. Green-Schloesser, M.E. Robbin, A.M. Pfeiffer & others, "Radiation-induced brain injury: a review", *Frontiers in Oncology*, 19 July 2012.

E. Gudynas, "Développement, droits de la Nature et Bien Vivre : l'expérience équatorienne" [Development, Rights of Nature and Living Well: The Ecuadorian Experience], *Mouvements*, 2011/4, No. 68, p. 17.

S. Gutwirth, "Trente ans de théorie du droit de l'environnement : concepts et opinions" [Thirty Years of Environmental Law Theory: Concepts and Opinions], *Environnement et société*, 2001, No. 26, p. 7.

O. Handt, M. Krings, R.H. Ward & S. Pääbo, "The retrieval of ancient human DNA sequences", *The American Journal of Human Genetics*, 1996, Vol. 59, Issue 2, p. 368.

J. Hansen & al,

- "Ice Melt, Sea Level Rise and Superstorms; Evidence from Paleoclimate Data, Climate Modelling, and Modern Observations that 2°C Global Warming Could be Dangerous", *Atmospheric Chemistry and Physics*, 2016, Vol. 16, p. 3761.
- "Global Temperature in 2015", *Climate Science, Awareness and Solutions*, 2016.
- "*Assessing Dangerous Climate Change*", 2013, p. 15.

J. Hansen & others, "Assessing 'Dangerous Climate Change': Required Reduction of Carbon Emissions to Protect Young People, Future Generations and Nature", *Public Library of Science ONE*, 3 Dec. 2013, 8(12):e81648, p. 15.

J.-M. Harribey,

- "Sur la valeur de la nature, éviter du fétichisme" [On the Value of Nature, Avoid Fetishism], *Les Possibles*, Printemps 2014, No. 3, p. 3
- "La nature, un capital ?" [Nature, a Capital?], *L'Âge de faire*, Feb. 2014, No. 83.
- "Marchandisation de la nature versus préservation du bien commun" [Commodification of Nature versus Preservation of the Common Good], *Revue francophone du développement durable*, Oct. 2013, No. 2, p. 69.
- "La nature n'est pas à vendre" [Nature is Not For Sale], *Politis*, 28 June 2012, No. 1209.

M. Hautereau-Boutonnet, "Les procès climatiques par la doctrine du procès climatique" [Climatic Processes by the Doctrine of the Climatic Process], *in* C. Cournil & L. Varison, *Les procès climatiques : du national à l'international* [*Climatic Processes: From the National to the International*], Pédone, 2018.

M. Hautereau-Boutonnet & L. Canali, "Jalons pour une responsabilité civile climatique préventive" [Paving the Way for a Preventive Climate Change Tort Liability Regime], *Journal International de Bioéthique*, 2018, No. 3, n° *spécial La responsabilité climatique*], *available online at* https://hal.archives-ouvertes.fr/hal-01875905/document.

R. Heede, "Tracing anthropogenic carbon dioxide and methane emissions to fossil fuel and cement producers, 1854-2010", *Climatic Change*, 2014, Vol. 122, Issue 1-2, p. 229.

S.M. Helmons, "La quatrième génération des droits de l'homme" [The Fourth Generation of Human Rights], *in* Les droits de l'homme au seuil du troisième millénaire : Mélanges en hommage à Pierre Lambert, [*Human Rights on the Threshold of the Third Millennium*: Essays in honor of Pierre Lambert], éd. Bruylant, 2000, p. 549.

J.M. Hermann, "Artificial transmutation of the gene", *Science*, 1927, Vol. 66, p. 84.

M.-A. Hermitte,

- "Artificialisation de la nature et droit(s) du vivant" [Artificialization of Nature and Law for Living Species], *in* P. Descola, *Les natures en questions* [*The Natures in Question*], Odile Jacob, 2018, p. 257.
- "*Edouard Bonnefous et la biodiversité* : '*Vox clamantis in deserto*' *ou illustration du schisme de réalité* " [Edouard Bonnefous and Biodiversity: "The voice of one crying in the wilderness" or Illustration of the Schism of Reality], C. Bréchignac, G. de Broglie & M. Delmas-Marty (eds.), *L'environnement et ses métamorphoses* [*The Environment and its Metamorphoses*], Hermann, 2015.
- "La nature, sujet de droit ?" [Nature, Subject of Right?], *Annales, Histoire, Sciences Sociales*, 2011/1, 66th Year, p. 173.
- "Souveraineté, peuples autochtones : le partage équitable des ressources et des connaissances" [Sovereignty, Indigenous Peoples: Equitable Sharing of Resources and Knowledge], *in* F. Bellivier & C. Noiville (eds.), *La bioéquité* [Bioequity], Autrement, 2009, p. 115.

A. Hiyama, C. Nohara, S. Kinjo, W. Taira, S. Gima, A. Tanahara & J.M. Otaki, "The biological impacts of the Fukushima nuclear accident on the pale grass blue butterfly", *Scientific Reports*, 2012, Vol. 2, Article no. 570, doi: 10.1038/srep00570

C. Huglo & C. Constantin, "Comment apprécier la portée de la réforme du droit des études d'impact issue du décret du 29 décembre 2011 au regard du droit de l'Union européenne ?" [How to Assess the Scope of the Reform of the Law of Impact Studies Resulting from the Decree of 29 December 2011 with regard to European Law?], *in Environnement et Développement*, Apr. 2012, p. 9.

H. Hurpy, "L'identité et le corps" [Identity and the Body], *La Revue des droits de l'homme*, Issue No 8, *available online at* https://journals.openedition.org/revdh/1601.

J. Huxley, "Transhumanism", *in* J. Huxley, *New Bottles for New Wine*, Chatto & Windus, London, 1957.

S. Iaukea, " 'A lot is riding on sun, surf, and souvenirs' – Tourist longing and conservation: landscaping agendas of the state", *Proceedings of the Indigenous Knowledges Conference Reconciling Academic Priorities with Indigenous Realities*, Dr. J. Kidman, Dr. J. Te Rito & Dr. W. Penetito (eds.), Nov. 2007, p. 88.

International Commission on Radiological Protection, Publication 103, "The 2007 Recommendations of the International Commission on Radiological Protection", 2007, Vol. 37, p. 2.

International Committee of the Red Cross, "Atomic weapons and non-directed weapons", *International Review of the Red Cross*, Vol. III, No. 4, April 1950, p. 70.

C.J. Iorns Magallanes,

- "Nature as an Ancestor: Two Examples of Legal Personality for Nature in New Zealand", Sep. 2015, *VertigO – la revue électronique en sciences de l'environnement*, Special Issue No. 22, Sep. 2015, p. 4.
- "Maori cultural rights in Aoeteara New Zealand: protecting the cosmology that protects the environment", *Widener Law Review*, 2015, vol. 21, p. 327.

V. Jaworski, "Les représentations multiples de l'environnement devant le juge pénal: entre intérêts général, individuel et collectif" [Multiple Representations of the Environment Before the Criminal Judge: Between General, Individual and Collective Interests], *VertigO – la revue électronique en sciences de l'environnement ?*, Special Issue No. 22, Sep. 2015, p. 8

L. Jeffrey & others, "2.7°C is Not Enough—We Can Get Lower", *Climate Action Tracker Update*, 8 Dec. 2015.

P. Kaatsch, C. Spix, S. Schmiedel, R. Schulze-Rath & others, "Epidemiologische Studie zu Kinderkrebs in der Umgebung von Kernkraftwerken (KiKK-Studie)" [Epidemiological Study on Childhood Cancer in the Vicinity of Nuclear Power Plants (KiKK Study)], Vorhaben 3602S04334, Deutsches Kinderkrebsregister, Mainz, Herausgegeben vom Bundesamt für Strahlenschutz (BfS), Salzgitter, 2007.

C. Kaufmann & P. Martin,

- "Can Rights of Nature Make Development More Sustainable? Why Some Ecuadorian lawsuits Succeed and Others Fail", *World Development*, 2017, Vol. 92, p. 130.
- "Testing Ecuador's Rights of Nature: Why Some Lawsuits Succeed and Others Fail", Paper presented at the International Studies Association Annual Convention, Atlanta, 18 Mar. 2016.

M. J. Klarman, "Majoritarian Judicial Review: The Entrenchment Problem", *Georgetown Law Journal*, 1997, Vol. 85, p. 491.

K. Knorr-Cetina, "*Au-delà des Lumières : l'essor d'une culture de la vie*" [Beyond the Enlightenment: the Rise of a Culture of Life], *in* A. Kahn, E. Agazzi, G. Hottois & C. Djerassi (eds.), *Biologie moderne et visions de l'Humanité* [*Modern biology and visions of Humanity*], De Boeck, 2004, p. 31.

P. Koberstein, "GMO companies are dousing Hawaiian island with toxic pesticides", *Grist*, 16 June 2014.

A. Köerblein, "Kinderleukämie um Kernkraft-werke: Neue episdemiologische Studie aus Frankreich" [Childhood Leukemia around Nuclear Power Plants: New Epidemiological Study from France], *Strahlentelex mit ElektrosmogReport*, 2 Feb. 2012, Vol. 26, No. 602-603.

L. Kotze & P. Villa Vicencio Calzadilla, "Somewhere between rhetoric and reality: environment constitutionalism and the rights of nature in Ecuador", *Transnational Environmental Law*, Nov. 2017, Vol. 6, Issue 3, p. 1.

H.M. Kristensen & R.S. Norris, "Global nuclear weapons stockpiles, 1945–2013", *Bulletin of the Atomic Scientists*, Sep. 2013, p. 75.

M. Kuntz, "The GMO Case in France: Politics, lawlessness and postmodernism", GM Crops & Food, 30 Oct. 2014, Vol. 5, Issue no. 3, p. 163.

C. Labrusse-Riou, "Transhumanisme. Entre progrès et nihilisme, l'humanité ne cesse de mettre en question sa condition" [Transhumanism: Between Progress and Nihilism, Humanity is Constantly Questioning its Condition], *Revue Lamy Droit Civil*, June 2016, No. 138 I.

C. Lafontaine, "La biocitoyenneté à l'ère du néolibéralisme" [Biocitizenship in the Age of Neoliberalism], *Revue Relations*, 2017, Vol. 792, p. 19.

C. Larrère, "Questions d'éthique environnementale" [Enviromental Ethics Issues], *Les grands dossiers des sciences humaines*, 2006, No. 2, p. 87.

C. Le Bris, "*Le Tribunal Monsanto ou l'écocide face à la justice des peuples*" [The Monsanto Tribunal or the Ecocide Against the Justice of Peoples], *Droit de l'environnement*, Jan. 2017, No. 252, p. 2.

N. Le Dévédec,

- "Corps augmentés, êtres exploités" [Increased Bodies, Exploited Beings], *Revue Relations*, 2017, Vol. 792, p. 19.
- "La démocratie à l'épreuve du posthumain : médicalisation de la société, dépolitisation de la perfectibilité" [Democracy Facing the Test of Posthumanism: Medicalisation of Society and Depolitisation of Perfectibility], 2009, *in* A. Sniadecki, *Dossier critique du transhumanisme* [*Critical dossier on transhumanism*], 2016, p. 56.

N. Le Dévédec & F. Guis, "L'humain augmenté, un enjeu social" [The Augmented Human, a Social Issue], *Sociologies*, 19 Nov. 2013.

B. Laurent, "Des assemblages incertains aux technologies de démocratie : deux modalités de l'expérience démocratique" [From Uncertain Assemblies to Technologies of Democracy: Two Modes of Democratic Experience], *Quaderni*, Autumn 2012, Issue No. 79 (*Produire la démocratie*), p. 81.

M.R. Lee-Muramoto, "Reforming the 'Uncoordinated' Framework for Regulation of Biotechnology", *Drake Journal of Agricultural Law*, 2012, Vol. 17, p. 311.

H. Leimbacher, "Gender and Nature in Comparative Legal Cultures", *in* D. Nelken (ed.), *Comparing Legal Cultures*, New York, Routledge, 2016, p. 146.

K.N. Loganovsky, S.V. Volovik, K.G. Manton & others, "Whether ionising radiation is a risk factor for schizophrenia spectrum disorders?", *The World Journal of Biological Psychiatry*, 2005, Vol. 6, Issue 4, pp. 212-230.

I. Lowe, "Wild Law Embodies Values for a Sustainable Future", *in* M. Maloney & P. Burdon (eds.), *Wild Law – In Practice*, Abingdon, Routledge, 2014, p. 4.

M. Maloney & P. Siemen, "Responding to the Great Work: The Role of Earth Jurisprudence and Wild Law in the 21st Century", *Earth Jurisprudence & Environmental Justice*, 2015, No. 6, p. 22.

L. Mampaey, "The ENMOD convention and the Programme HAARP: challenges and scope", *Analysis Note, GRIP*, June 2008.

G.N. Mandel, "Gaps, Inexperience, Inconsistencies, and Overlaps: Crisis in the Regulation of Genetically Modified Plants and Animals", *William & Mary Law Review*, 2004, Vol., 45, p. 2167.

D. Markell & J.B. Ruhl, "An Empirical Assessment of Climate Change In The Courts: A New Jurisprudence Or Business As Usual?", *Florida Law Review*, 2012, Vol. 64, p. 15.

J.D. Mathews, A.V. Forsythe, Z. Brady, M.W. Butler & others, "Cancer risk in 680,000 people exposed to computed tomography scans in childhood or adolescence: data linkage study of 11 million Australians", *British Medical Journal*, 21 May 2013, Vol. 346, doi: 10.1136/bmj.f2360

S. Metha & P. Merz, "Ecocide – A New Crime Against Peace?", *Environmental Law Review*, 2014, Vol. 17, p. 4.

A.J. McMichael, "Globalization, Climate Change, and Human Health", *New England Journal of Medicine*, 2013, Vol. 368, p. 1335.

I. Michallet, "De l'action locale au droit global : l'engagement climatique des villes" [From Local Action to Global Law: Cities Responding to Climate Change]; *in Après l'accord de Paris, quels droits face au changement climatique ?* [*After the Paris Agreement, What Rights for Climate Change?*], *Revue Juridique de l'Environnement*, Lavoisier, 2017, No. Special, p. 119.

D.L. Miglioretti, E. Johnson, A. Williams, R.T. Greenlee & others, "The Use of Computed Tomography in Pediatrics and the Associated Radiation Exposure and Estimated Cancer Risk", *JAMA Pediatrics*, 10 June 2013, Vol. 167, No. 8, p. 700, doi:10.1001/jamapediatrics.2013.311.

O. Molodanof & J. Durney, “Hope is a Song in a Weary Throat: An Interview with Julia Olson”, *Hastings Environmental Law Journal*, 2018, Vol. 24, p. 213.

A.P. Møller, A. Bonisoli-Alquati & T.A. Mousseau, “High frequency of albinism and tumours in free-living birds around Chernobyl”, *Mutation Research*, 18 Sep. 2013, Vol. 757, Issue 1, p. 52, doi: 10.1093/jhered/esu040.

T.A. Mousseau & A.P. Møller, “Genetic and ecological studies of animals in Chernobyl and Fukushima”, *The Journal of Heredity*, 1 Sep. 2014, Vol. 105, Issue 5, p. 704.

L. Neyret, “La reconnaissance de la responsabilité climatique” [Recognition of Climate Responsibility], *Recueil Dalloz*, 2015, p. 2278.

C. Noiville & T. Berger, “L’accès à l’information sur l’environnement, réflexions sur deux causes d’ineffectivité” [Access to Environmental Information, Reflections on Two Causes of Inefficiency], *in Sciences et droits de l’homme* (Collectif), éditions Mare & Martin, 2017, p. 173.

F. Ost, “Personnaliser la nature, pour elle-même, vraiment ?” [Personifying Nature, for Itself, Really?], *in* P. Descola (ed.), *Les Natures en question* [*Natures in Question*], Odile Jacob, 2018.

F. Pacini & others, “Thyroid consequences of the Chernobyl nuclear accident”, *Acta Paediatra Supplementum*, Dec. 1999, Vol. 88, Issue s433, p. 23.

L. Parker, M.S. Pearce, H.O. Dickinson, M. Aitkin & A.W. Craft, “Stillbirths among offspring of male radiation workers at Sellafield nuclear reprocessing plant”, *The Lancet*, 23 Oct. 1999, Vol. 354, Issue 9188, pp. 1407-1414, doi: https://doi.org/10.1016/S0140-6736(99)04138-0.

M.S. Pearce, J.A. Salotti, M.P. Little, K. McHugh & others, “Radiation exposure from CT scans in childhood and subsequent risk of leukaemia and brain tumours: a retrospective cohort study”, *The Lancet*, 2012, Vol. 380, Issue 9840, p. 499, *available online at* https://europepmc.org/articles/pmc3418594.

L.C. Pecharroman, “Rights of Nature: Rivers That Can Stand in Court”, *Resources*, 2018, Vol. 7, 13 doi:10.3390/resources7010013, p. 1, *in* J. Emel & A. Cantor, *New Water Regimes*, Molecular Diversity Preservation International, 2018, p. 23.

F.P. Perera, “Children Are Likely to Suffer Most from Our Fossil Fuel Addiction”, *Environmental Health Perspectives*, Aug. 2008, Issue No. 116(8), p. 987.

M. Petel, “La nature : d’un objet d’appropriation à un sujet de droit. Réflexions pour un nouveau modèle de société” [Nature: From an Object of Appropriation to a Subject of Law—Reflections for a New Model of Society], *Revue Interdisciplinaire d’Etudes Juridiques*, 2018, Vol. 80.

D.A. Pierce & D.L. Preston, "Radiation-Related Cancer Risks at Low Doses among Atomic Bomb Survivors", *Radiation Research*, 2000, Vol. 154, No. 2, p. 178.

G. Poissonnier, "*Tribunal Monsanto : vers une définition de l'écocide ?*" [Monsanto Tribunal: Toward a Definition of Ecocide?], *Recueil Dalloz*, 2016, p. 2512.

M. Prieur, "De l'urgente nécessité de reconnaître le principe de 'non régression' en droit de l'environnement" [The Urgent Need to Recognize the Principle of "Non-regression" in Environmental Law], *in* Conference Proceedings of the French Society of Environmental Law (*SFDE*) of La Rochelle, 2010, A. Michelot (ed.), *Equité et environnement. Quel(s) modèle(s) de justice environnementale* [*Equity and Environment: What Model(s) of Environmental Justice?*], Larcier, Bruxelles, 2012, p. 71.

N.A. Robinson,

- "The Charter of the Forest: Evolving Human Rights in Nature," *in Magna Carta and the Rule of Law*, D. Magraw & others (eds.), American Bar Association, 2014, p. 311.
- "The Resilience Principle," *in IUCN Academy of Environmental Law eJournal*, 2014, Vol. 5, p. 19.
- "Evolved Norms: A Canon for the Anthropocene," *in* C. Voigt (ed.), *Rule of Law for Nature*, Cambridge University Press, 2013, p. 46.

J. Rockström & others, "A safe operating space for humanity", *Nature*, 24 Sep. 2009, Vol. 461.

J. Rogelj & others, "Paris Agreement climate proposals need a boost to keep warming well below 2°C", *Nature*, 30 June 2016, Vol. 534, p. 631.

P.H. Sand, "Sovereignty Bounded: Public Trusteeship for Common Pool Resources", *Global Environmental Politics*, 2004, Vol. 4, p. 47.

M. Sagoff, "On Preserving the Natural Environment", *Yale Law Journal*, 1974, Vol. 84(2), p. 205.

J.L. Sax, "The Public Trust Doctrine in Natural Resources Law: Effective Juridical Intervention", *Michigan Law Review*, 1970, Vol. 68, p. 471.

D. Saxe & K. Mikadze, "The Dutch Climate Case: Beginning of a New Era of Climate Litigation?", *Slaw: Canada's online legal magazine*, 21 Aug. 2015.

S.K. Serrano, "A Reparative Justice Approach to Assessing Ancestral Classifications Aimed at Colonization's Harms", *William & Mary Bill of Rights Journal*, 2018, Vol. 27, p. 501.

D. Shelton,

- "Nature as a legal person", *VertigO – la revue électronique en sciences de l'environnement*, Special Issue No. 22, Sep. 2015, p. 5.

- "Réflexion introductive : environnement international et patrimoine commun de l'humanité" [Introductory Reflection: International Environment and the Common Heritage of Humanity], *in* M.-P. Camproux Duffrène & J. Sohnle (eds.), *Marché et environnement, le marché: menace ou remède ?* [*Market and Environment, the Market: Threat or Remedy?*], Bruxelles, Bruylant, 2014, p. 6.

J.W. Singer, "Co-tenancy and Joint Ownership", *American Jurisprudence*, Second Edition, 2012, Vol. 20, section 1.

F.L. Smith, "Économie de marché et protection de l'environnement" [Market Economy and Environmental Protection], *in* M. Falque & G. Millière (eds.), *Écologie et liberté, une autre approche de l'environnement* [*Ecology and Freedom: Another Approach to the Environment*], Paris, Litec, 1992, p. 239.

L. Spielberg, P. Potter & A. Leys, "Chapter 58. Radiation Retinopathy", *in RETINA*, S.J. Ryan, R.S. Srini, D.R. Hinton, A.P. Schachat, C.P. Wilkinson & P. Wiedemann (eds.), 2013, p. 1083.

D.K. Sproat, "An Indigenous People's Right to Environmental Self-Determination: Native Hawaiians and the Struggle Against Climate Change Devastation", *Stanford Environmental Law Journal*, 2016, Vol. 35, p. 197.

W. Steffen, P.J. Crutzen & J.R. McNeill, "The Anthropocene: Are Humans Now Overwhelming the Great Forces of Nature?", *Ambio*, 2007, Vol. 36, No. 8, p. 614.

W. Steffen & others, "Planetary Boundaries: Guiding human development on a changing planet", *Science*, 2015, Vol. 347, No. 6223.

R.K. Stewart, "Weeds, Seeds & Deeds Redux: Natural and Legal Evolution in the U.S. Seed Wars", *Stanford Technology Law Review*, 2014, Vol. 18, p. 79.

S. Swann, "Sperm counts, testicular cancers, and the environment", *British Medical Journal*, 10 Oct. 2017.

A.-S. Tabau & C. Cournil, "Nouvelles perspectives pour la justice climatique : Cour du District de La Haye, 24 juin 2015, Fondation Urgenda contre Pays-Bas" [New perspectives for Climate Justice: LaHaye District Court, 24 June 2015, Urgenda Foundation Against the Netherlands], *Revue Juridique de l'Environnement*, 2015/4, p. 200.

D. Takacs, "The Public Trust Doctrine, Environmental Human Rights and the Future of Private Property", *New York University Environmental Law Journal*, 2008, Vol. 16, p. 711.

M. Tanasescu, "The Rights of Nature in Ecuador", *Environment, Political Representation, and the Challenge of Rights*, 2016, p. 85.

T.L. Timmons, "Earth Jurisprudence and Lockean Theory: Rethinking the American Perception of Private Property", *Earth Jurisprudence & Environmental Justice Journal*, 2011, Vol.1, p. 105.

F-G. Trébulle, "Les titres environnementaux" [Environmental Titles], *Revue Juridique de l'Environnement*, 2011/2, p. 203.

M. Turnipseed & others, "Reinvigorating the Public Trust Doctrine: Expert Opinion on the Potential of a Public Trust Mandate in U.S. and International Environmental Law", *Environment Magazine*, 2010, Vol. 52, No. 5, p. 12.

UNICEF, "A brighter tomorrow: Climate change, child rights and intergenerational justice", 2010.

United States Department of Justice, "U.S. v. Volkswagen, 16-CR-20394: Volkswagen Diesel Engine Matters, Case No. 2:16-cr-20394-SFC-APP (E.D. Mich.)", 18 Dec. 2018.

M.C. Urban, "Accelerating Extinction Risk from Climate Change", *Science*, 2015, Vol. 348, p. 571.

M. Vacquin, "Fascination pour le Transhumanisme" [Fascination for Transhumanism], *La science entre archaïsme et démesure* [Science between Archaism and Excess], Actes du colloque Critique de la Raison Transhumaniste, Collège des Bernardins, 2017, Paris, éditions du Cerf.

L. Vandelac,

- "De l'impensé du corps à sa mise en joue [...] Chirurgies esthétiques ou l'effritement des limites" [From the Body Unthinkable to its Updating: Plastic Surgery and the Disappearance of Boundaries], *in Le lien social*, no. 59, Corps et Politiques, A. Quéniart & R. Hurtubise (éds.), 2008, p. 125.
- "Menace sur l'espèce humaine [...] ou démocratiser le génie génétique" [Threaten the Human Species ... or Democratize Genetic Engineering], *Futuribles*. Paris, 2001, p. 5.
- "La famille reconstituée par la biologie : des flous du droit au droit floué ?" [The Family Reconstituted by Biology: Fuzzy Right to the Right Fuzzed?], 1999, *in* C. Masse (éd.), *Revue juridique Thémis*, vol. 33, no. 2, p. 372.
- "Technologies de reproduction : l'irresponsabilité des pouvoirs publics et la nôtre" [Reproductive Technologies: the Irresponsibility of the Public Authorities and Ours], *Sociologie et sociétés*, 1996, Vol. 28, No. 2, p. 59.

S. Vanuxem, "Les services écologiques ou le renouveau de la catégorie civiliste de fruits" [Ecological Services or the Renewal of the Civilian Fruit Category], *McGill Law Journal*, 2017, Vol. 62, No. 3, p. 739.

P. Vercauteren, "Gouvernance et démocratie : quel ordre ?" [Governance and Democracy: What Order?], *in Fédéralisme, Régionalisme*, 2007, Vol. 7, No. 2.

D. Vine, "Achieving the United States' Intended Nationally Determined Contribution", *Center for Climate and Energy Solutions*, Sep. 2016.

H.S. Weinberg, A.B. Korol, V.M. Kirzhner, A. Avivi, T. Fahima, E. Nevo, S. Shapiro, G. Rennert, O. Piatak, E.I. Stepanova & E. Skvarskaja, "Very high mutation rate in offspring of Chernobyl accident liquidators", *Proceedings of the Royal Society of London, Series B: Biological Sciences*, 22 May 2001, Vol. 268, Issue 1471, p. 1001.

M. Wilensky, "Climate Change In The Courts: An Assessment Of Non-U.S. Climate Litigation", *Duke Environmental Law & Policy Forum*, Fall 2015, Vol. 26, p. 131, note.

M.C. Wood & D. Galpern, "Atmospheric Recovery Litigation: Making the Fossil Fuel Industry Pay to Restore a Viable Climate System", *Environmental Law*, Spring 2015, Vol. 45, Issue 2, p. 259.

M.C. Wood & G. Levitt, "The Public Trust Doctrine in Environmental Decision Making", *in* L. Paddock & others (eds.), *Decision Making in Environmental Law*, Edward Elgar Publishing, 2016.

Z. Xu & others, "The Impact of Heat Waves on Children's Health: A Systematic Review", *International Journal of Biometeorology*, 2014, p. 239.

III. Newspaper Articles

2018

D. Jenkins, "Groups argue over chlorpyrifos ban", *Capital Press*, 18 Oct. 2018.

L. Zuckerman, "Trump administration lifts GMO crop ban for U.S. wildlife refuges", *Reuters*, 3 Aug. 2018.

L. Hurley, "Supreme Court rejects Trump bid to halt climate change case", *Reuters*, 31 July 2018.

J. Gélinas & M. Moore, "L'intelligence artificielle, l'industrie de la promesse" [Artificial Intelligence, the Industry of Promises], *Le Devoir*, *Idées*, 16 July 2018.

N. Wright, "How Artificial Intelligence Will Reshape the Global Order: The Coming Competition Between Digital Authoritarianism and Liberal Democracy", *Foreign Affairs*, 10 July 2018.

Agence France-Presse, "Sécurité : les principaux vols des données personnelles" [Security: Key Your Personal Data], *Le Point*, 15 May 2018.

"La reconnaissance faciale en Chine : un outil de surveillance redoutable" [Facial recognition in China: a Formidable Surveillance Tool], *Généthique*, 13 Apr. 2018.

"Chine : des caméras intelligentes surveillent la concentration des lycéens" [China: Smart Cameras Monitor High-School Student Concentration], *Généthique*, 18 May 2018.

"Un Britannique se Revendique Premier 'Cyborg' du Monde, Mi-Homme Mi-Robot" [A Brittannian Claims the World's First "Cyborg", Mid-Man's Mid-Robot], *Gènéthique*, 15 Feb. 2018.

J.-M. Collin, "Loi de programmation militaire : le Parlement atomisé ?" [Military Planning Act: The Atomic Parliament?], *La Tribune*, 8 Feb. 2018.

2017

D. Rushe & agencies, "Oliver Schmidt jailed for seven years for Volkswagen emissions scam", *The Guardian*, 6 Dec. 2017.

D. Nerbollier, "Réchauffement climatique, un agriculteur péruvien contre le géant allemand de l'énergie" [Global Warming, a Peruvian Farmer against the German Energy Giant], *La Croix*, 14 Nov. 2017.

B. Condomina, "L'Arabie saoudite accorde la citoyenneté à un robot" [Saudia Arabia Grants Citizenship to a Robot], *Radio France Internationale Les Voix Du Monde*, 28 Oct. 2017

D. Hadni, "Zuckerberg se prépare-t-il à succéder à Trump ?" [Is Zuckerberg Preparing to Succeed Trump?], *Le Devoir*, 5 Aug. 2017.

T. Khan, "How climate change battles are increasingly being fought and won in court", *The Guardian*, 8 Mar. 2017.

2016

L. Imada, "HC&S closure will pull plug on power deal", *The Maui News*, 29 Nov. 2016.

D. Shepardson, "Three U.S. states sue Volkswagen, say executives covered up diesel cheating", *Reuters*, 19 July 2016.

J.-M. Collin, "La bombe juridique des îles Marshall contre les puissances nucléaires" [The Marshall Islands' Legal Bomb Against the Nuclear Powers], *Le Monde Diplomatique*, June 2016.

2015

"15 member states opt out of GMO culture", EURACTIV, 1 Oct. 2015.

C. Pala, "Pesticides in paradise: Hawaii's spike in birth defects puts focus on GM crops", *The Guardian*, 23 Aug. 2015.

J. Rappoport, "Shocker: court documents assert Hawaii inspectors clueless about what Monsanto is spraying", *Activist Post*, 21 May 2015.

2014

P. Koberstein, "GMO companies are dousing Hawaiian island with toxic pesticides", *Grist*, 16 June 2014.

A. McAvoy, "Hawaii emerges as battleground of debate over genetically engineered crops", *The Washington Post*, 19 Apr. 2014.

2013

R. Daysog, "Anti-GMO rally attracts hundreds", *Hawaii News Now*, 2013.

A. Oposa Jr, "Victims or victors of the climate crisis?", *Rappler*, 26 Nov. 2013.

S. Cocke, "Frustrated By State's Inactivity, Kauai County Takes Pesticide Fight Into Its Own Hands", *Huffington Post*, 8 Oct. 2013.

M. Sergio, "GMO & Pesticide Experiments in Hawaii: The Poisoning of Paradise", *The Huffington Post*, 2 July 2013.

C. D'Angelo, "Hooser introduces GMO bill", *The Garden Island*, 21 June 2013.

I. Altemus-Williams, "The struggle to reclaim paradise", *Waging Nonviolence*, 10 Apr. 2013.

E. Summers, "A'ole GMO" [No GMO], *The Molokai Dispatch*, 31 Mar. 2013.

2011

P. Voosen, "King Corn Takes Root in Hawaii", *The New York Times*, 22 Aug. 2011.

R.-P. Droit, "L'Obsolescence de l'homme. Tome II. Sur la destruction de la vie à l'époque de la troisième révolution industrielle, de Günther Anders : les exagérations prophétiques de 'Monsieur autrement' " [The Obsolence of Man. Vol. II. On the Destruction of Life in the Epoch of the Third Industrial Revolution, by Günther Anders: the Prophetic Exaggerations of "Mr. Other"], *Le Monde des livres*, 9 June 2011.

M. Rocard, D. Bourg & F. Augagneur, "Le genre humain, menacé" [The Human Race Threatened], *Le Monde*, 3 Apr. 2011.

2010

L. Nouhalt, "Pachamama mia!" [My Mother Earth], *Libération*, 23 Aug. 2010.

2002

"Biotechs call Cayetano their governor of the year", *Pacific Business News*, 22 Oct. 2002.

2000

L. Vandelac, "Sortir en douce de l'humanité : Pour une écologie politique du vivant" [The Smooth and Ongoing Escape out of Human Kind: for a Political Ecology of the Living'], *Le Devoir*, 7 Oct. 2000.

1989

B. Edelman, "Le Droit et le Vivant" [The Right and the Living], *La Recherche*, 1989, No. 212.

Select Case Law

2020

Juliana v. United States, No. 18-3602, United States Court of Appeals for the Ninth Circuit, 17 Jan. 2020 (slip opinion).

2019

United States v. United States District Court for the District of Oregon, No. 17-1692, United States Court of Appeals for the Ninth Circuit, 4 June 2019.

Juliana v. United States, No. 18-36082, United States Court of Appeals for the Ninth Circuit, 7 Jan. 2019 (slip opinion).

2018

Juliana v. United States, No. 18-80176, United States Court of Appeals for the Ninth Circuit, 26 Dec. 2018 (slip opinion).

In re United States, No. 18-73014, United States Court of Appeals for the Ninth Circuit, 26 Dec. 2018 (slip opinion).

Juliana v. United States, No. 6:15-cv-01517-AA, United States District Court for the District of Oregon, 21 Nov. 2018 (slip opinion).

In re United States, No. 18-73014, United States Court of Appeals for the Ninth Circuit, 8 Nov. 2018 (slip opinion).

In re United States, No. 18A410, United States Supreme Court, *Supreme Court Reporter*, United States Government Publishing Office, 2 Nov. 2018, Vol. 139, p. 452 (memorandum opinion).

In re United States, No. 18A410, United States Supreme Court, *Supreme Court Reporter*, United States Government Publishing Office, 19 Oct. 2018, Vol. 139, p. 16.

Future Generations v. Ministry of the Environment & others, STC4360-2018, Radicación No. 11001-22-03-000-2018-00319-01, Corte Suprema de Justicia de Colombia, 5 Apr. 2018.

United States v. District Court of Oregon, No. 17-71692, United States Court of Appeals for the Ninth Circuit, 7 Mar. 2018.

Order, *Maritime Delimitation in the Caribbean Sea and the Pacific Ocean (Costa Rica v. Nicaragua)*, International Court of Justice Reports, 2 Feb. 2018.

Föreningen Greenpeace Norden & Natur og Ungdom v. The Government of Norway through the Ministry of Petroleum and Energy, No. 16-166674TVI-OTIR/06, Oslo District Court, 4 Jan. 2018.

2017

Friends of the Irish Environment CLG v. Fingal County Council & others, Case No. 344 JR, High Court of Ireland, *High Court of Ireland Decisions* 695, 21 Nov. 2017.

Advisory Opinion OC 23/17 (Requested by the Republic of Colombia), Inter-American Court of Human Rights, 15 Nov. 2017.

Foster v. Washington Department of Ecology, No. 75374-6-I, Court of Appeals, State of Washington, 5 Sep. 2017 (unpublished opinion),

Order, *North Dakota v. Environmental Protection Agency*, Case No. 15-1381, United States Court of Appeals for the District of Columbia Circuit, 10 Aug. 2017.

Common Cause v. Union of India & others, Case No. SC WP 2014, Supreme Court of India, 2 Aug. 2017.

J. Waweru Karuma v. Republic of Kenya, Case No. 166 OF 2016, High Court of Kenya (Kiambu), Criminal Appeal, 15 June 2017.

Order, *North Dakota v. Environmental Protection Agency*, Case No. 15-1381, United States Court of Appeals for the District of Columbia Circuit, 28 Apr. 2017.

Construction of the Morburg power station, No. C-142/16, Court of Justice of the European Union, 26 April 2017.

Longarini, Cristian Ezequiel y otros contra Ministerio de la Producción y otros. Amparo. Recurso extraordinario de inaplicabilidad de ley, Case No. A.70.082, Suprema Corte de Justicia de la Provincia de Buenos Aires, 29 Mar. 2017.

Earthlife Africa Johannesburg v. Minister of Environmental Affairs & others, Case. No 65662/16, High Court of South Africa (Pretoria), 8 Mar. 2017.

United States of America v. Volkswagen AG, Case No 2:16-cv-10006-LJM-MJH, United States District Court for the Northern District of California, 4 Jan. 2017,

2016

Lliuya v. RWE AG, File No. 2 O 285/15, Regional Court Essen, 15 Dec. 2016.

Atay v. County of Maui, Nos. 15-16466 & 15-16552, United States Court of Appeals for the Ninth Circuit, *Federal Reporter, Third Series*, West Publishing, 18 Nov. 2016, Vol. 842, p. 688.

Syngenta Seeds, Inc. v. County of Kauai (*Syngenta Seeds I*), Nos. 14-16833 & 14-16848, United States Court of Appeals for the Ninth Circuit, *Federal Reporter, Third Series*, West Publishing, 18 Nov. 2016, Vol. 842, p. 669.

Hawai'i Papaya Industry Association v. County of Hawaii, No. 14-17538, United States Court of Appeals for the Ninth Circuit, *Federal Appendix*, West Publishing, 18 Nov. 2016, Vol. 666, p. 631 (unpublished).

Syngenta Seeds, Inc. v. County of Kauai (*Syngenta Seeds II*), Nos. 14-16833 & 14-16848, United States Court of Appeals for the Ninth Circuit, *Federal Appendix*, West Publishing, 18 Nov. 2016, Vol. 664, p. 669 (unpublished).

Juliana v. United States, No. 6:15-cv-01517-TC, United States District Court for the District of Oregon, *Federal Supplement, Third Series*, 10 Nov. 2016.

Obligations concerning Negotiations relating to Cessation of the Nuclear Arms Race and to Nuclear Disarmament (*Marshall Islands v. India*), International Court of Justice, *International Court of Justice Reports*, 5 Oct. 2016.

Obligations concerning Negotiations relating to Cessation of the Nuclear Arms Race and to Nuclear Disarmament (*Marshall Islands v. Pakistan*), International Court of Justice, *International Court of Justice Reports*, 5 Oct. 2016.

Obligations concerning Negotiations relating to Cessation of the Nuclear Arms Race and to Nuclear Disarmament (*Marshall Islands v. United Kingdom*), International Court of Justice, *International Court of Justice Reports*, 5 Oct. 2016.

In re Court on its own Motion v. State of Himachal Pradesh & others, National Green Tribunal (India), 9 May 2016, Application No. 237 (T_{HC}) of 2013

Constitutional Petition, *Rabab Ali v. Federation of Pakistan & Another*, Supreme Court of Pakistan, 1 Apr. 2016 (decision pending).

European Commission v. Republic of Bulgaria, No. C-141/14, Court of Justice of European Union, 14 Jan. 2016.

2015

Zoe and Stella Foster v. Washington Department of Ecology, No. 14-2-252951 SEA, Superior Court, State of Washington (King County), 19 Nov. 2015.

North Dakota v. Environmental Protection Agency, Case Nos. 15-1381, United States Court of Appeals for the District of Columbia Circuit, 23 Oct. 2015.

Ashgar Leghari v. Federation of Pakistan, Case W.P. No. 25501/2015, High Court of Lahore, 14 Sep. 2015.

Obergefell v. Hodges, United States Supreme Court, No. 14-556, *Supreme Court Reporter*, West Publishing, 26 June 2015.

Urgenda Foundation v. Kingdom of the Netherlands, Case No. C/09/456689/HA ZA 131396, The Hague District Court, 24 June 2015.

In re Greenpeace Southeast Asia, Case No. CHR-NI-2016-001, Philippine Commission on Human Rights, 12 May 2015.

2014

Kanuk v. Alaska Department of Natural Resources, No. S-14776, Supreme Court of Alaska, *Pacific Reporter, Third Series*, 12 Sep. 2014.

AD (Tuvalu), [2014] NZIPT 501370-371, New Zealand: Immigration and Protection Tribunal, 4 June 2014.

Goa Foundation v. Union of India & others, Case No. 435 OF 2012, National Green Tribunal (India), 21 Apr. 2014.

Whaling in the Antarctic (Australia v. Japan: New Zealand intervening), International Court of Justice, *International Court of Justice Reports*, 31 Mar. 2014.

Kauai Springs, Inc. v. Planning Commission of Kaua'i, Hawai'i Supreme Court, No. SCWC–29440, *Pacific Reporter, Third Series*, West Publishing, 28 Feb. 2014, Vol. 324, p. 951.

2013

Iberdrola S.A. & others, European Court of Justice (Fifth Chamber), Case No. C-566/11, 17 Oct. 2013.

Native Village of Kivalina v. ExxonMobil Corporation, United States Supreme Court, *United States Reports*, United States Government Publishing Office, 20 May 2013.

In re Court on its own Motion v. State of Himachal Pradesh & others, Application No. 237 (T_{HC}) of 2013, National Green Tribunal (India), 9 May 2016.

Agrargenossenschaft Neuzelle eG v. Landrat des Landkreises Oder-Spree, Case No. C-545/11, Court of Justice of the European Communities (Fourth Chamber), 14 Mar. 2013.

2012

Native Village of Kivalina v. ExxonMobil Corporation, No. 09-17490, United States Court of Appeals for the Ninth Circuit, *Federal Supplement, Third Series*, West Publishing, 21 Sep. 2012.

Turp v. Minister of Justice and Attorney General of Canada, Docket No T-110-12, Federal Court of Canada, *Federal Court Reports*, 17 July 2012.

2011

American Electric Power Company v. Connecticut, United States Supreme Court, *United States Reports*, United States Government Publishing Office, 20 June 2011.

2010

Comer v. Murphy Oil USA, Inc., United States Court of Appeals for the Fifth Circuit, *Federal Reporter, Third Series*, West Publishing, 28 May 2010.

2009

Ministerio Publico Federal v. H Carlos Schneider S/A Comercio e Industria e Outro [*Brazil v. H Carlos Schneider Inc.*], Superior Tribunal de Justiça – RECURSO ESPECIAL No. 650.728- SC (2d Panel), Relator: Ministro [Justice] António Herman Benjamin, 2 Dec. 2009.

Commission of the European Communities v. Italian Republic, Case No. C-540/07, European Court of Justice, 19 Nov. 2009.

Friends of the Earth v. Canada (Governor in Council), Docket No. A-572-08, Federal Court of Appeal, *Federal Court of Appeal Decisions*, 15 Oct. 2009.

New Zealand Recreational Fishing Council v. Sanford Limited & others, Case No. SC40/2008 NZSC 54, New Zealand Supreme Court, 28 May 2009.

Salas, Dino y otros c/ Salta, Provincia de y Estado Nacional s/ amparo, No. S. 1144. XLIV, Corte Suprema de Justicia de la Nación, 26 Mar. 2009.

Center for Food Safety v. Johanns (Johanns II), No. 06-17319. United States Court of Appeals for the Ninth Circuit, *Federal Appendix*, West Publishing, 2 Feb. 2009, Vol. 310, p. 964.

2008

Friends of the Earth v. Canada (Governor in Council), Docket Nos. T-2013-07, T-78-08 & T-1683-07, Federal Court of Canada (CanLII), *Federal Court Reports*, 18 June/20 Oct. 2008.

2007

Yane, Salvador contra Municipalidad de General Alvarado. Materia a categorizar, Case No. C.90.020, Suprema Corte de Justicia de la Provincia de Buenos Aires, 14 Nov. 2007.

Ministerio Publico do Estado de Sao Paulo v. Companhia Acucareira Sao Geraldo [*Sao Paulo State v. Sao Geraldo Sugar Co.*], Superior Tribunal de Justiça – RECURSO ESPECIAL, No. 948.921/SP (2d Panel), Relator: Ministro [Justice] António Herman Benjamin, 23 Oct. 2007.

Sociedad Anónima Garovaglio y Zorraquin c/Provincia de Buenos Aires (O.S.B.A.), No. B 57.805, Suprema Corte de Justicia de la Provincia de Buenos Aires, 26 Sep. 2007.

People of the State of California v. General Motors Corporation, No: C-06-05755 MJJ, United States District Court for the Northern District of California, *Westlaw*, Westlaw Publishing, 17 Sep. 2007, p. 2726871.

Comer v. Murphy Oil USA, Inc., United States District Court for the Southern District of Mississippi, Civ. No. 1:05-CV-436-LG-RHW, *Westlaw*, Westlaw Publishing, 30 Aug. 2007, p. 6942285.

Massachusetts v. Environmental Protection Agency, United States Supreme Court, *United States Reports*, United States Government Publishing Office, 2 Apr. 2007, Vol. 549, p. 497.

2006

Asociación de Superficiarios de la Patagonia c/ Y.P.F. S.A. y otros, No. A. 1274. XXXIX, Corte Suprema de Justicia de la Nación, 29 Aug. 2006.

Kelly v. 1250 Oceanside Partners, No. 26813, Hawai'i Supreme Court, *Pacific Reporter, Third Series*, West Publishing, 28 July 2006, Vol. 140, p. 985.

Mendoza, Beatriz Silvia y otros c/ Estado Nacional y otros s/ daños y perjuicios (daños derivados de la contaminación ambiental del Río Matanza - Riachuelo), No. M.1569.XL, Corte Suprema de Justicia de la Nacion (Capital Federal, Ciudad Autónoma De Buenos Aires), *Sistema Argentino Información Juridica*, 20 June 2006.

Center for Food Safety v. Johanns (Johanns I), No. Civ.03–00621 JMS/BMK. United States District Court for the District of Hawai'i, *Federal Supplement, Second Series*, West Publishing, 1 Sep. 2006, Vol. 415, p. 1165.

2005

Gbemre v. Shell Petroleum Development Company of Nigeria Ltd. & others, Suit No. FHC/B/CS/53/05, Federal High Court of Nigeria (Benin), 14 Nov. 2005.

Bordenave, Sofia s/ Mandamus, No. 18726/03-STJ, Superior Tribunal de Justicia de la Provincia de Río Negro, 17 Mar. 2005.

Y.P.F. Sociedad Anónima en j° 80.866 Asociación Oikos Red Ambiental c/ Gob. de la Prov. de Mza. p/ Acc. de Amp. S/Inc. Cas., No 78.245, Sala Primera de la Excma. Suprema Corte de Justicia, 11 Mar. 2005.

2004

BGP Properties Pty Limited v. Lake Macquarie City Council, Case No. NSWLEC 399, Land and Environment Court of New South Wales, 12 Aug. 2004.

2001

Social and Economic Rights Action Center (SERAC) and Center for Economic and Social Rights (CESR)/Nigeria, Decision 155/96, African Commission on Human and People's Rights, 13-27 Oct. 2001.

1998

Almada, Hugo Néstor c/ Copetro S.A. y otro s/ Daños y perjuicios [*Hugo Nestor Almada v Copetra S.A (Damages)*], Ac. 60.094, Suprema Corte de Justicia. La Plata, Buenos Aires, 19 May 1998.

1996

Northcompass Inc. v. Hornsby Shire Council, Case No. NSWLEC 213, Land and Environment Court of New South Wales, 26 Aug. 1996.

Advisory Opinion, *Legality of the Threat or Use of Nuclear Weapons*, International Court of Justice, *International Court of Justice Reports*, 8 July 1996.

1994

Schroder, Juan c. Estado Nacional -Secretaría de Recursos Naturales [*Juan Schroder v. the National State* (*Secretary of Natural Resources*)], Camara Nacional Federal de Apelaciones en lo Contencioso Administrativo, Sala No. 3 (Buenos Aires), 8 Sep. 1994.

Richardson v. City and County of Honolulu, No. 16457, Hawai'i Supreme Court, *Pacific Reporter, Second Series*, West Publishing, 18 Feb. 1994, Vol. 868, p. 1193, p. 1209.

1993

Minors Oposa v. Factoran, General Register No. 101083, Supreme Court of the Philippines, *Supreme Court Reports, Annotated*, 30 July 1993, Vol. 224, p. 792.

1992

Arizona Center for Law v. Hassell, Arizona Court of Appeals, Docket No1CA-CV89-134, *Pacific Reporter, Second Series*, West Publishing, 6 Oct. 1992, Vol. 837, p. 158.

1988

Marsland v. First Hawaiian Bank, No. 12529, Hawai'i Supreme Court, *Pacific Reporter, Second Series*, West Publishing, 14 Nov. 1988, Vol. 764, p. 1228.

1984

Chevron U.S.A., Inc. v. Natural Resources Defense Council, Inc., No. 82-1005, United States Supreme Court, *United States Reports*, United States Government Publishing Office, 25 June 1984, Vol. 467, p. 837.

1983

Kattan, Alberto E. Y Otro C. Gobierno Nacional -Poder Ejecutivo [*Alberto E. Kattan & other v. the National Government* (Executive Power)], Juzgado Nacional de 1a Instancia en lo Contencioso-administrativo Federal No. 2, Buenos Aires, 10 May 1983, La Ley 1983-D, 576.

1973

Judgment (9 May 1973), *Nuclear Tests (New Zealand v. France)*, International Court of Justice, *International Court of Justice Reports*, 1974.

Judgment (20 December 1974), *Nuclear Tests (Australia v. France)*, International Court of Justice, *International Court of Justice Reports*, 1974.

1955

Brown v. Board of Education, United States Supreme Court, *United States Reports*, United States Government Publishing Office, 31 May 1955, Vol. 349, p. 294.

1954

Brown v. Board of Education, United States Supreme Court, *United States Reports*, United States Government Publishing Office, 17 May 1954, Vol. 347, p. 483.

1932

Donoghue (or McAlister) v. Stevenson, Case No. AC562, House of Lords, *The All England Law Reports*, 26 May 1932.

1927

The Case of the S.S. Lotus (*France v Turkey*), Permanent Court of Arbitration, 7 Sep. 1927.

1920

Missouri v. Holland, No. 609, United States Supreme Court, *United States Reports*, United States Government Publishing Office, 19 Apr.1920, Vol. 252, pp. 416, 435.

1896

Geer v. Connecticut, No. 87, United States Supreme Court, *United States Reports*, United States Government Publishing Office, 2 March 1896, Vol. 161, p. 519.

1892

Illinois Central Railroad Co. v. Illinois, Nos. 419, 608 & 809, United States Supreme Court, *United States Reports*, United States Government Publishing Office, 5 Dec. 1892, Vol. 146, p. 387.

1879

Newton v. Commissioners of Mahoning County, United States Supreme Court, *United States Reports*, United States Government Publishing Office, 1 Oct. 1879, Vol. 100, p. 548.

Stone v. Mississippi, United States Supreme Court, *United States Reports*, United States Government Publishing Office, 1 Oct. 1879, Vol. 101, p. 814.

1803

Marbury v. Madison, United States Supreme Court, *United States Reports* (Cranch, Vol. 1), 24 Feb. 1803, Vol. 5, p. 137.

Notes on Editors

Emilie GAILLARD is lecturer at Sc Po Rennes, and co-head of the Network on Risks, Quality and Sustainable Environment at MRSH, CNRS/University of Caen Normandy. She teaches Bioethics, International Environmental and Human Rights Law at SciencesPo Rennes. In 2008, she defended a thesis entitled *Générations futures et droit privé. Vers un droit des générations futures* [*Future Generations and Private Law: Towards a Law for Future Generations*], Librairie Générale de Droit et de Jurisprudence (LGDJ), 2011. The book was awarded by the French Academy of Political and Moral Sciences (Charles Dupin's Prize, 2010). Her works highlight the emergence of a new temporal paradigm that renews the legal framework, and also initiates new legal logic. She strives for a revitalized legal humanism that respects humankind through time and space, in interdependency with the living species and by supporting conditions for life. She writes primarily about: Philosophy of Law; Legal Theory; International Human Rights Law ("Pour une approche systémique, complexe et prospective des droits de l'homme" [For a Systemic, Complex and Prospective Approach to Human Rights], *in Enjeux environnementaux globaux et droits de l'homme*, Bruylant, 2012); International Environmental & Criminal Law ("Crimes Against Future Generations", *The Law of the Future and the Future of the Law*, e-Publica, No. 2, July 2015); Constitutional Environmental Law; Biolaw & Bioethics. She is a member of the Mission Lepage, which wrote the *Universal Declaration of the Rights and Duties of Humankind* for the President of the French Republic (2015). She is also a member of the organizing committee for the International Monsanto Tribunal. In addition, she heads a two-year collective research project on the topic "Transhumanism(s) & Law(s)", Research Mission Law and Justice, French Ministry of Justice. She is the general coordinator of the Normandy Chair for Peace on Law and Future Generations led by Tony Oposa (Sept. 2019–Sept. 2023) and Prof. Robinson (Chair Emeritus). She is member of the WELC (IUCN).

David M. FORMAN is Director of the Environmental Law Program, William S. Richardson School of Law, University of Hawai'i at Mānoa, and a Faculty Specialist with the Ka Huli Ao Center for Excellence in Native Hawaiian Law. He has taught or co-taught courses including Administrative Law, Appellate Advocacy, Climate Justice for Future Generations Food Security, IUCN Motions Workshop Lawyering Fundamentals Pacific Islands Environmental Legislative Drafting, Philippine Environmental Law, and other legal writing classes. Among other publications, he co-authored a chapter on "Traditional and Customary

Native Hawaiian Rights" in *Native Hawaiian Law: A Treatise* (M. MacKenzie, D.K. Sproat and S.K. Serrano, eds., Kamehameha Publishing, 2015). He is a member of the World Commission on Environmental Law and served on the Host Committee/Program Committee for the International Union for the Conservation of Nature (IUCN) 6th World Conservation Congress, held September 2016 in Honolulu, Hawai'i. Forman convened and co-organized a unique, collaborative moot court that debuted during the 2016 Congress. *See* http://blog.hawaii.edu/elp/international/tony-oposa-integenerational-moot-court/. Subsequent iterations of this innovative "proof of concept" took place in: Cebu, Philippines (2017), as part of the IUCN Academy of Environmental Law's 15th annual colloquium; Brasilia, Brazil (2018), as a special event during the Conference of Judges and Prosecutors on Water Justice at the 8th World Water Forum; Caen, France (2018), as a side event in connection with the inaugural World Peace Forum; and Kuala Lumpur, Malaysia (2019), as part of the IUCN Academy of Environmental Law's 17th annual colloquium. He is the organizer of the sixth intergenerational moot court, which will be held in conjunction with the 2nd World Environmental Law Congress in Rio de Janeiro, Brazil (rescheduled for September 2020), and is also assisting with organizing efforts for the seventh intergenerational moot court, which will be held in conjunction with the IUCN World Conservation Congress in Marseilles, France (rescheduled for January 2021). He was nominated by the Hawai'i State Judicial Selection Commission for vacancies on the Hawai'i Supreme Court (2012), in addition to the Hawai'i Intermediate Court of Appeals (2017, 2018). He is also a member of the Normandy Chair for Peace on Law and Future Generations (Attorney Antonio A. Oposa, Jr., and Professor Nicholas A. Robinson), leading an initiative concerning Indigenous Peoples.

Notes on Contributors

Elisabeth BROWN is a former Global Program Manager for Our Children's Trust, the U.S. based NGO that established and now leads the youth-led and science-based global legal campaign to secure the binding legal right to a healthy atmosphere and stable climate. At Our Children's Trust, Elizabeth supported a global network of attorneys and youth in bringing legal actions against governments seeking science-based climate recovery planning. Elizabeth was part of the legal team litigating *Juliana v. United States*, the landmark case against the United States government, brought by 21 youth under the U.S. Constitution and the Public Trust Doctrine. Elizabeth holds a Juris Doctor degree with concentrations in public interest environmental law and international law from the University of Oregon School of Law and a Master of Arts degree in International Public Policy from Central European University.

Edith BROWN WEISS is Francis Cabell Brown Professor of International Law at Georgetown Law School. In September 2002, she was appointed to the World Bank Inspection Panel and from 2003-2007 served full-time as the Chairperson, an appointment at the level of World Bank Vice President. Previously, she was President of the American Society of International Law, Associate General Counsel for the U.S. Environmental Protection Agency, where she established the Division of International Law, and U.S. Special Legal Advisor to the North American Commission on the Environment. She is a member of UNEP's International Advisory Council on Environmental Justice. She is an editorial board member of many international journals. Her book *In Fairness to Future Generations* (1989) has been translated into Japanese, French, Spanish and Chinese. She delivered the General Course on Public International Law at The Hague Academy of International Law in 2017. She has been a director, trustee, or advisor to national and international organizations.

Christian BYK is a Judge at the Court of Appeals, Paris, and chairs the UNESCO Intergovernmental Bioethics Committee. He was advisor to the Secretary General of the Council of Europe responsible for drafting the European Convention on Biomedicine (1991-1993), and participated in the elaboration of the Universal Declaration on Bioethics and Human Rights (2005). He is the author of 10 books and more than 200 articles as well as the general editor of the *International Journal of Bioethics and Ethics of Science* and the *Law, Health and Society* review.

As a member of the International Council on Monuments and Sites, he has an interest in gardening history.

Amandine CAYOL is a lecturer in Private Law at the University of Caen Normandie. Her fields of expertise are Tort Law, Contract Law and Property Law. She defended her thesis entitled *Le contrat d'ouvrage* in 2009 (published at Bibliothèque de l'Institut de recherche juridique de la Sorbonne, 2013). The book received the 2010 Dupin Ainé Prize from the Chancellery of the Universities of Paris. Her thesis led to a renewed analysis of work contracts under the angle of Tort Law: as owner of a workforce, the contractor is also the original owner of the work produced by his workforce. Cayol is now particularly interested in the legal status of the human body. She organized a 2016 symposium in Caen on this topic and currently participates in a research group about transhumanism. She also has specific expertise in the matter of compensation for bodily injury. In addition, she heads a two-year collective research project on the topic "Transhumanism(s) & Law(s)", Research Mission Law and Justice, French Ministry of Justice.

Jean-Marie COLLIN is an expert working on international disarmament and national security issues in France. His area of expertise covers arms control, nuclear deterrence, non-proliferation, disarmament, and the nuclear humanitarian initiative process. He is Associate Researcher in the Group for Research and Information on Peace and Security (GRIP), as well as expert and spokesman for ICAN (International Campaign to Abolish Nuclear Weapons) France, which received the Nobel Peace Prize in 2017. He is the author of numerous articles about the French nuclear arsenal, and the Ban Treaty. His last book was published in May 2018, *L'illusion nucléaire : La face cachée de la bombe atomique* [*Nuclear Illusion: The Hidden Side of the Atomic Bomb*] (with co-authors P. Quilès & M. Drain). His expertise has allowed him to be heard by numerous Parliaments (Belgium, Costa-Rica, Czech Republic, Monaco, etc.), the French National Assembly, Senate Defence and Foreign Affairs Committees, the Centre des Hautes Etudes Militaires, as well as numerous universities and Think Tanks, in addition to participating in humanitarian conferences (Oslo, Nayarit, Vienne) and in UN negotiation processes for the Treaty on the Prohibition of Nuclear Weapons.

John DAVIDSON has served as a Professor and Instructor in the University of Oregon Department of Political Science since 2003, where he teaches courses on U.S. Constitutional Law, Intergenerational Justice, and related subjects. His primary research involves the intersection between constitutional law and intergenerational justice (including the ethical and legal rights and responsibilities that exist between earlier and later generations within a political society). John has regularly published and presented at conferences on the subject. His published work in that area includes "Tomorrow's Standing Today: How the Equitable Jurisdiction Clause of Article III, Section 2 Confers Standing Upon Future Generations", *Columbia Journal of Environmental Law*, 2003, Vol. 28, p. 185. John received his Juris Doctor degree from the University of Oregon School of Law. John is a retired member of the Oregon State Bar, and is an *amicus curiae* in *Juliana v. United States*.

Mireille DELMAS-MARTY teaches Law in several universities (located in France, Europe and many others countries, including the U.S. and Canada, China, Japan, Iran, Brazil, Mexico, and Africa). Mireille Delmas-Marty was elected at the Collège de France (Chair 2003-2011, "Etudes juridiques comparatives et internationalisation du droit"), and as a member of the Institut de France in 2007. First specialized in Criminal Law, she worked also on Human Rights Law, Comparative Law, European Law, International Law and Globalization of Law. For example, *Towards a truly common law: Europe as a laboratory for legal pluralism*, Cambridge University Press, 2002; *Ordering Pluralism: A Conceptual Framework for Understanding the Transnational Legal World* (trans. N. Norberg), Oxford, Hart Publishing, CERDIN, coll. French Studies in International Law, 2009; and, "International Law as the Articulation of Universalism and Pluralism", *in Conversations on Justice from National, International, and Global Perspectives*, J.-M. Coicaud & L.E. Sieger (ed.), Cambridge University Press, 2018. Starting from a practical observation of different legal orders, she elaborated a new theory ("Ordering pluralism") considering the dynamic processes towards a common legal order that would progressively incorporate the diversity of legal orders throughout the World. She has published more than twenty books; the last of them being a series of 4 volumes (*Les forces imaginantes du droit* [The Imaginary Forces of Law], Seuil, 2004-2012; *Aux quatre vents du monde. Petit guide de navigation sur l'océan de la mondialisation* [*Four Winds of the World: A Short Guide to Navigating the Ocean of Globalization*], Seuil, 2016; and, *Une boussole des possibles. Gouvernance mondiale et humanismes juridiques* [*A Possible Compass: Global Governance and Legal Humanisms*], Éditions du Collège de France, collection "Leçons de clôture" [Closing Lessons], 2020).

Christian HUGLO (Doctor in Law) has dedicated his career as an attorney and teacher of environmental law in all sectors of public life as well as the economy, both nationally and internationally. He specializes in litigation, including international pollution and environmental affairs – e.g., the Amoco Cadiz case and the Chicago case (1978-1992), the Erika case (1999-2012), as well as international pollution cases of the Mediterranean, the Rhine, the Bay of Seine, and the Moselle. He participated in the drafting of the *Universal Declaration of the Rights and Duties of Humankind* submitted to the United Nations with attorney, and former French Minister of Environment, Corinne Lepage. His recent book, *Le contentieux climatique: une révolution judiciaire mondiale* [Climate Litigation: A Global Judicial Revolution], published by Bruylant Editions in April 2018, provides an in-depth study of climate justice litigation.

Marie-Angèle HERMITTE is Emeritus Director of Research at CNRS (Centre National de la Recherche Scientifique), and Director of Studies at EHESS (École des Hautes Etudes en Sciences Sociales). Her area of expertise covers the emerging status of nature, biodiversity, indigenous peoples and communities of inhabitants, health and environmental safety, the human body, medically assisted reproduction, as well as transhumanism. Her last article was published in October 2018, "Artificialisation de la nature et droit(s) du vivant" [Artificialization of Nature and Law for Living Species], *in* P. Descola (dir.), *Les natures en question* [*The Natures in Question*], Collège de France, Odile Jacob, 2018, and her last book, *L'emprise des droits intellectuels sur le monde vivant*, Editions Quae, 2016.

Frédérick LEMARCHAND is Professor of Sociology at the University of Caen Normandy, Head of the Center for Research on Risks and Vulnerabilities (CERREV – Caen) and co-Head of the Network on Risks, Quality and Sustainable Environment (MRSH, CNRS/University of Caen Normandy). His research specializes on technological risks and nuclear disasters (co-author of *Les silences de Tchernobyl: L'avenir contaminé* [The Silences of Chernobyl: Contaminated Future], Autrement, 2004). He is coordinating important research programs on the topic of ecological transitions, particularly in the field of energy and hydrogen. He is also director of a Master degree in Governance des Risques et de l'Environnement [Risk and Environment Governance] (GREEN) at the University of Caen Normandy. He is lecturer at the University of Québec (Montréal) and member of the editorial board of the e-reviews *VertigO* and *Ecologie & politique* [Ecology & Politics]. He co-directs a working group on human transformation at the Association Internationale des Sociologues de Langue Française [International Association of French-Speaking Sociologists] (AISLF).

Corinne LEPAGE, French politician, trained as a lawyer before setting up a practice specialised in public and environmental law, where she made her name defending victims of the Amoco Cadiz oil spill in 1978. She went to defend victims of the Erika disaster in 1999. In 1995, she became Environment minister in the French government. She has often acted as an expert at the European level and was named on a UNEP list in 2006 of the ten most important women for the environment in Europe. She teaches at the Institute of Political Studies in Paris, where she heads the sustainable development section. Since 2015, she has lead the project to develop a Universal Declaration on Rights and Duties of Humankind. She is the author of a number of books including La Politique de précaution, with François Guéry (2000), Vivre autrement (2009), La vérité sur le nucléaire (2011), La vérité sur les OGM (2012), L'état Nucléaire (2014), Les femmes au secours de la République, de l'Europe…, de la planète (2015).

Agnès MICHELOT is Senior Lecturer in Public Law, Faculty of Law at the University of La Rochelle, supervising doctoral theses (Habilitation à Diriger des Recherches) and specializing in International Environmental Law (IEL). Her research includes IEL and comparative environmental law, climate justice and environmental justice, biodiversity law, natural risks in coastal areas, and ecological refugees. Formerly, Senior Special Fellow Expert for the Training Program on Environmental Law at the United Nations Institute for Training and Research (Geneva), and Consultant for UNESCO's Man and the Biosphere Programme. Currently, President of the Société Française pour le Droit de l'Environnement [French Society for Environmental Law] (SFDE), and member of the Environmental Section of the French Economic Social and Environmental Council (ESEC). She is co-rapporteur with Jean Jouzel of the ESEC opinion on *Climate Justice: Challenges and Prospects for France*. She is a participant in the interdisciplinary research project STORISK – Small Islands addressing climate change: towards storylines of risk and adaptation (2016-2020) related to French Polynesian islands.

Andreas NIDECKER, M.D., is Professor Emeritus of Radiology at the University of Basel, Switzerland, and a specialist in musculo-skeletal radiology. He was a member of the Bonetumor study group of the "Deutsches Krebsforschungs Zentrum" [German Cancer-Research Center] (DKFZ), Heidelberg. He is also Past President and board member of Physicians for Social Responsibility/International Physicians for the Prevention of Nuclear War (PSR/IPPNW), Switzerland, as well as Member of the organizing Committees of the IPPNW World Congress in Basel (2010) and of "U and health" meetings in Mali (2012), Tanzania (2013), and South Africa (2015). Furthermore, he is one of the organizers of the symposium "Human Rights, Future Generations and Crimes in the Nuclear Age" which took place in Basel from 14-17 September 2017. He is interested in radiation effects, in particular the topic of ionizing low-level radiation. Additionally, he is co-initiator and board member of "sun21", a think tank dedicated to use of renewable energies, resource utilization and sufficiency.

Danny NOONAN is a former Global Program Coordinator at Our Children's Trust, where he supported staff attorneys with coordinating global litigation and related legal actions. Danny was also part of the legal team behind *Juliana v. United States*. Prior to joining Our Children's Trust, he worked for the Australian law firm Maurice Blackburn. Danny is admitted as a lawyer in the Australian state of New South Wales, and has professional experience in the class action, "native title" (indigenous land rights) and public interest environmental law sectors. He has presented on the topic of climate change litigation at various academic and industry conferences. Danny graduated from the University of Sydney with a Bachelor's degree in International Studies 2013, and with a J.D. in 2017. He now lives in Eugene, Oregon.

Antonio A. OPOSA, Jr., is internationally known based on his work in *Minors Oposa v. Factoran* (1993), which adopted the principle of intergenerational responsibility concerning the remaining old-growth forests in the Philippines. He was selected as commencement speaker for his 1997 Master of Laws class at Harvard; he was also named to the UNEP Global 500 Roll of Honor that year. Oposa waged a ten-year legal battle to secure an order from the Supreme Court of the Philippines in 2008, requiring the government to clean up Manila Bay. In 2008, he became the only Asian to receive the Washington D.C.-based Center for International Environmental Law Award. In 2009, Oposa received Asia's highest recognition for public service: the Ramon Magsaysay Award (citing "his path-breaking crusade to engage Filipinos in acts of enlightened citizenship using the power of the Law to nurture the environment, for themselves, their children, and for generations yet unborn"). He leads the Normandy for Peace Chair on Law and Future Generations (Sept. 2019–Sept. 2023), co-created by Region Normandy, CNRS, University of Caen Normandy and hosted by the MRSH.

Richard L. OTTINGER served in the United States Air Force from 1955-57, retiring as a captain. He was also a founding member of the Peace Corps, and its director of programs for the West Coast of South America from 1961-1964. First elected to Congress in 1965, he served eight terms in the U.S. House of Representatives (1965-1971 & 1975-1985). He authored a substantial body of energy and environmental laws, including co-sponsorship of the 1977 Clean Air Act Amendments. In addition, he played a pioneering role in educating Members of Congress and the public about the advantages of energy efficiency and renewal energy, as Chair of the House Energy Conservation and Power Subcommittee of the Energy and Commerce Committee. After retiring from Congress in 1984, Ottinger began inspiring new generations of environmental lawyers at Pace Law

School, including his service as Dean from 1994-99. As co-director of the Pace Global Center for Environmental Legal Studies, he founded the Pace Energy & Climate Center, which raises more than $1 million dollars per year, advocating for promotion of clean energy resources. As Dean Emeritus, he continues to advise students and involve them in national and international environmental and energy efficiency initiatives as well as renewable energy research and presentations.

Juan Ignacio PEREYRA was born in Buenos Aires, Argentina in 1978. In 2005, he graduated as a lawyer at the University of La Plata. In 2012, he completed his postgraduate studies in Environmental Law at the University of Buenos Aires and specialized in Law for Future Generations. He is an active member of several NGOs dedicated to the protection of the environment: the Red Nacional de Municipios y Comunidades que fomentan la agroecología [National Network of Municipalities and Communities that Promote Agroecology] (RENAMA), the Red de Abogados de Pueblos Fumigados [Network of Lawyers of the Fumigated Peoples of Argentina] (RAPF), Foro Ambiental de Rojas [Environmental Forum de Rojas] and Justice Pesticides (France). He participated in the International Monsanto Tribunal (The Hague, October 2016), offering evidence from Argentina about the violation of human rights caused by this corporation. He also participated as a contributing author in the *Dictionnaire Juridique des Transitions Écologiques* [Legal Dictionary of Ecological Transitions], Fondation Varennes, 2018. He currently works as a attorney in various fields, especially in environmental lawsuits.

Matthias PETEL is a Researcher at the Université Catholique de Louvain in Belgium as well as the Coordinator of the Human Rights Law Clinic Rosa Parks, which provides legal assistance to NGOs with their environmental and social struggles. Petel's main field of research concerns Human Rights and their potential to foster ecological transition, rights of nature, as well as climate litigation. He is currently pursuing a Ph.D. under the guidance of Professor Olivier de Schutter, Special Rapporteur on extreme poverty and human rights.

Michel PRIEUR is a highly active emeritus professor of environmental law involved in promoting the Principle of Non-Regression in Environmental Law. He created the Société Française pour le Droit de l'Environnement [French Society for Environmental Law] (SFDE) and the *Revue Juridique de l'environnement* [*Environmental Law Review*] in the 1970's. He published books entitled: *Droit de l'environnement* [*Environmental Law*], Dalloz, 2019; *La non régression en droit de l'environnement* [*The Non-Regression Principle*], Bruylant, 2012; and, *Droit de l'environnement et développement durable* [*Environmental*

Law as Sustainable Law], Bruylant, 2014. He is President of the Centre International de Droit Comparé de l'Environnement [International Center for Comparative Environmental Law] (CIDCE), an international NGO with special consultative status at the UN and UNEA, which is also accredited to the Organisation Internationale de la Francophonie [International Organization of Francophonie] (OIF). Professor Prieur is currently working on: Human Rights and the Environment; a draft International Covenant on the Human Right to the Environment; the Legal Status of Environmental Displaced Persons; and, Legal Indicators to measure the Effectiveness of Environmental Law Implementation (*see* www.cidce.org).

Nicholas A. ROBINSON is an Environmental Law Professor with the Elisabeth Haub School of Law at Pace University. Since the 1972 Stockholm Conference on the Human Environment, Professor Robinson has been a leader in the environmental legal programs of the International Union for the Conservation of Nature (IUCN). He edited the United Nations' travaux preparatoires for the 1992 Rio Earth Summit, served on the drafting team for the UN World Charter for Nature, and was both IUCN's Legal Advisor and Chair of its World Commission on Environmental Law. He led formation of the IUCN Academy of Environmental Law. He has specialized in the law of environmental impact assessment since 1969, and founded the environmental legal education programs at Pace University in New York. He is Chair Emeritus of the Normandy for Peace Chair on Law and Future Generations (Sept. 2019–Sept. 2022).

Louise VANDELAC, Ph.D. is a full Professor in the Sociology Department and Institute of Environmental Sciences at the University of Québec (Montréal). She is also co-editor in chief of VertigO, the first francophone scientific journal in Environmental Sciences. Her interdisciplinary and intersectoral research at the crossroads of health, environment and public policies, explores the links between ecocide and anthropocide. She is involved with many research groups, among them: Centre d'études des interactions entre la santé et l'environnement [Center for the Study of Biological Interactions in Human Health] (CINBIOSE), a World Health Organization/Pan-American Health Organization collaborating center; and the Pôle Risques, Qualité et Environnement Durable [Risks, Quality and Sustainable Environment Center], MRSH, CNRS/University of Caen Normandy. She also directs the Collectif de recherche écosanté sur les pesticides, les politiques et les alternatives [Research Group on Eco-health Approach of Pesticides, Policies and Alternatives] (CREPPA). She was chair of the Human, Social and Natural Sciences Sectoral Commission of the Canadian Commission for UNESCO until the end of 2017. She is on the board of the international scientific council of the Réseau National des Maisons des Sciences de l'Homme [The French National Network of Houses of Human Sciences] (RnMSH) (23 universities and CNRS).

Martin WALTER, M.D., obtained his medical degree from the University of Basel in 1976, after writing a dissertation on coagulation factor XIII. He then trained as a specialist in internal medicine, receiving clinical training in internal medicine at the University Hospital of Basel in Switzerland. He also worked as a senior physician at Bruderholz Hospital from 1978 to 1981. Dr. Walter had a private practice in internal medicine from 1981 to 2013. He was a founding member of the Swiss affiliate of Physicians for Social Responsibility and International Physicians for the Prevention of Nuclear War Switzerland (PSR/IPPNW), serving as its president from 1988 to 1990. He remains active today as a member of the board of PSR/IPPNW, Switzerland. Dr. Walter also served as a board member of Greenpeace Switzerland from 1996 to 2002. His main interests are radioprotection and radiation biology, resulting in several visits to the Chernobyl and Fukushima nuclear disaster regions.

Alyn WARE is a nuclear policy expert from New Zealand. He is Director of the Basel Peace Office, Consultant for the International Association of Lawyers Against Nuclear Arms (IALANA) and Coordinator for Parliamentarians for Nuclear Non-proliferation and Disarmament (PNND). Mr. Ware was a leader in the New Zealand nuclear weapons prohibition movement, the 1996 International Court of Justice case against nuclear weapons, and the Model Nuclear Weapons Convention circulated by the UN Secretary-General to guide nuclear disarmament negotiations. Mr. Ware has won a number of awards including: the Right Livelihood Award, Sweden (2009); UN International Year for Peace Award, New Zealand (1986), and World Peace Award, Canada (2014). He was also nominated for the Nobel Peace Prize in 2015.

Index

A

Advisory Opinion on the *Legality of the Threat or Use of Nuclear Weapons* 50, 66–67, 69, 72–73, 77, 81.

African Charter on Human and Peoples' Rights 136–137, 291, 299–300, 306.

Albinism 119, 125, 130.

Anthropocene 29–43, 50–60, 110, 133, 211, 237, 261, 353, 400.

Artificial Intelligence 30, 111, 325, 346, 354–358, 365, 380–381, 389–390.

Atomic Bomb

See also Nuclear Bomb

B

Best Climate Science 153–154.

Bioaccumulation 404–406.

Biological diversity 45–46, 175, 195, 202, 246, 250.

Brundtland Report 53, 223, 246.

C

Cancer 67, 115–116, 125, 357, 398.

See also Leukemia

Catastrophe 98, 108–111, 127–130, 157–158, 211, 324–325, 397, 404–407, 413.

See also Disasters

Civil society 74, 89, 100, 144, 171, 191–192, 211, 236, 296, 301, 305, 315, 320, 326, 342.

Charter of the United Nations 69–71, 96, 243–246, 301.

Chernobyl 119, 124–130, 243, 418.

Clean Air Act 141, 146, 429.

Clean Power Plan 139, 143.

Climate

- change 48, 51, 133–134, 143–145, 154–158, 163, 167, 171–180, 188–194, 196–197, 200, 246, 285, 368–369.
- litigation 135–151, 153–170, 188–202.

Cloning 106, 318–319, 345–346, 356, 358, 360–361, 366, 385, 387, 404, 413

Common but Differentiated Responsibilities 35, 39, 162, 308.

Common Heritage of Mankind 27, 31, 37, 186, 217, 288, 317–319, 325, 328–329.

Conference on Disarmament, 87–90, 94–95.

Conference on the Humanitarian Consequences of Nuclear Weapons 74, 86–91, 94, 97, 100, 101.

Congenital Disorders 398, 405–406.

Constitution 5, 29, 49, 51, 59–60, 85, 135, 140, 145–147, 154, 161, 164–167, 169–170, 185–186, 196–197, 199, 203–204, 207, 215, 229–230, 232, 234, 248–258, 265–266, 275, 277–282, 287, 293, 299, 300, 303, 312, 392, 402, 411, 416, 427.

Constitutional Duty to Protect the Environment for Future Generations 49, 248–249, 251, 254–255, 281–282.

Constitutional Right to a Climate System Capable of Sustaining Human Life 154, 165, 199.

Court of Justice of the European Union 139, 148, 208.
Cosmology 205, 234.
Crimes against Future Generations 76, 414.
Crime against Human Species 332, 387.
Crimes against Humanity 30, 35, 39, 75, 150, 239, 317, 386, 404.

D

Declaration on Cultural Diversity 37, 318.
Declaration on the Responsibilities of the Present Generations towards Future Generations 62, 162, 173, 247, 258, 319.
Democracy 37, 180, 289, 294, 300, 322, 349–350, 390.
Dignity
- Human 27, 35–37, 41, 132, 168, 172–174, 196–197, 214, 224, 239, 289, 291, 298, 307, 319, 329, 345, 390, 393, 404, 419.
- of Humanity 323, 327, 374.
- of Future Generations 291, 332, 412, 415–416.
- of Nature 227, 303.

Disasters 15, 52, 61, 109, 156, 286–287, 295, 302, 307, 320, 323.
See also Catastrophes
Domestic margin of appreciation 35, 39.
Due diligence 149, 165, 197–198.
Due process 52, 197, 199.
Duty of care 147, 149, 254.
Duty of vigilance 40.

E

Ecocide 33, 36, 40, 75–76, 151, 234, 238–239, 331, 354, 367, 371, 375, 412, 414.
Ecological
- Civilization 60.
- Damage 31, 107, 151, 203, 212, 296.
- Integrity 132, 172, 174–175, 235, 237, 298, 325, 329, 390.
- Solidarity 177, 209, 287.
- Transition 178, 196.

Encyclical Letter *On Care for Our Common Home* 50, 162, 239.
Endocrine Disruptors 108, 405–406, 408, 413.
Environmental health 16, 58, 60, 97, 101, 107, 136–137, 153–154, 161, 174, 177, 179, 197, 204, 232, 248–249, 251–252, 254, 256–258, 279, 285, 286, 289, 292, 298, 300, 302, 304, 308, 326, 390, 397, 406, 408, 414.
Environmental Impact Assessment 55, 134, 136, 260, 267, 271.
Epidemiological Studies 115–116, 126, 130, 408–409.
Equity
See also Intergenerational Equity
See also Transgenerational Equity
Extreme Weather Events 51,155–156.
European Economic and Social Committee 132, 171.

F

Fairness 28, 51, 56–57, 59–60, 170, 308.
Fetus 387.
Forest
- Charter 54.
- Deforestation 49, 59, 169–170, 195, 200, 231, 416.
- Fire 156, 199.
- Restoration 54, 59, 135, 153, 177.
- Rights 202, 206.

- Tropical/Virgin 7, 58, 231, 426, 428, 430.
Fossil Fuels 153, 164–165, 283.
French Polynesia 75, 104, 107, 262, 402, 407.
Fukushima 62, 115, 120–125, 130, 244, 418.
Fundamental rights 31, 46–47, 60, 77, 81, 134, 136–137, 140, 153, 160, 165, 167, 169–170, 173, 182, 188, 191, 196–197, 199–201, 204, 210, 231–233, 241, 291, 293, 297, 300–303, 306, 308, 316, 327, 339, 341, 345, 349, 392–393, 410, 413, 416–419.
See also Rights/Human Rights

G

Genetically Modified
- Babies 404.
- Organism 264–265, 269, 271–273, 287.
Globalization 29–31, 33–34, 36, 39, 217, 286, 297, 325, 368, 386, 404.
Global Guardians for Future Generations 45.
Global Public Goods 31, 187, 191.
Global Trust 27, 43, 131, 139, 161.
Glyphosate 150, 270, 275.
Greenhouse Gas 39–40, 52, 135, 139–140, 142–143, 146, 148, 155–156, 189–190, 201, 283, 390.
Günther Anders 62, 103–111, 324, 363–363, 366, 386.

H

Hans Jonas 62, 105, 108, 111, 322, 351, 354, 370, 398–400.
Heede Report 149
Hibakushas 86, 98.
Hiroshima 6, 85, 98, 103–105, 107, 116, 118, 128, 353, 364.
Human nature 52, 56, 215, 222, 333–335, 337, 346, 372, 384, 399, 408.
Humanitarian
- Initiative 85, 87–88.
- Law 61, 66, 68–71, 74, 76, 79, 94, 100, 298.
- Pledge 89.
Humankind 29, 61, 181, 191–192, 202, 212–217, 234, 236–237, 241, 243, 247, 291, 331, 353, 404, 408– 409.
- Common Concern 231.
- Common Heritage 186.
- Concept of 161–162.
- Declaration on the Rights of (Argentina) 288.
- Representation of 194, 290, 387.
- Threat to 61–62, 74.
- Universal Declaration of the Rights & Duties (of) 30, 38, 182, 290, 302, 315–329, 359.

I

Indigenous 41, 51, 54–55, 204–206, 228, 230, 234–235, 261–284, 289, 295, 298, 307, 399, 425.
Interdependancies 30, 32, 35–38, 40, 205, 212, 221, 228, 237, 239, 241, 284, 289, 301, 322, 327, 400 , 406, 409–410, 419.
Intergenerational
- Equity 27, 43–50, 165–166, 170, 182, 243, 261, 264–265, 282, .
- Justice 156.
- Law 76, 162–163, 249.
- Moot Court 424–425.
- Obligations 46–47, 160.
- Pact for the Life of the Colombian Amazon 49.
- Principles 163, 166, 169, 249, 252, 254–255.

- Rights 46–47, 165.
- Solidarity 262.
International Committee of the Red Cross 69, 85–86, 95, 317.
International Court of Justice 49, 55, 61, 63–66, 68–69, 73, 75–76, 81, 99, 101, 133, 150–151, 263, 296, 300, 305, 424, 431.
International Criminal Court 61, 63, 77–78, 80–81, 150.
International Humanitarian Law 61, 66, 68–71, 76, 79, 88, 94, 100–101, 298, 307.
International Monsanto Tribunal 40, 101, 150–151.
International Security 64, 76, 84, 87, 90, 101, 172.
Islamic Declaration on Global Climate Change 162–163.
Ionizing Radiation 62, 65, 67, 76, 86, 96, 98, 113–130, 406.

J
Jean-Pierre Dupuy 15, 105, 109, 398.
Jellyfish Babies 68, 86.
Juliana case 131, 141, 145, 148, 154, 158, 163–170, 195–201.

K
Kant 29–30, 36, 105, 336–337.
Klimaatzaak case 145.

L
Laudato Si'
See also Encyclical Letter On Care for Our Common Home
Legal Animism 41, 181, 202–210.
Legal Pluralism 37.
Leghari case 135, 140, 193–194, 201.
Leukemia 62, 113, 166, 125–126, 406.
Lotus case 72, 474.

M
Marshall Islands 67–68, 73–74, 81, 86, 95–96, 101.
Martens Clause 68–69.
Meadows' Report 211, 400, 441.
Mondialité 31, 36.
Mother Earth 30, 35, 207, 218, 226, 238, 320, 429.
Mutations 62, 65, 118–120, 127, 130, 354.

N
Nagasaki 6, 85, 98, 104, 116, 118, 128, 353, 364.
Nature
- Rights (of) 181–182, 200, 203, 207, 211–241, 295, 299, 310, 412, 419.
- Rights of Nature Tribunal 40.
NGO's 30, 41, 78, 140, 172, 192–193, 196, 285, 291, 293, 295, 313, 315, 320, 322.
Non-discrimination principle 308, 324, 328, 347–386, 412–415.
Non Proliferation Treaty 61, 83, 85, 87–91, 95.
Nuclear
- Age 61–62, 85, 104, 108.
- Accident 117, 409.
- Arsenal 83–84, 87, 97.
- Bombs 85–86, 89, 98, 101, 103–105, 108, 116, 118, 353, 364.
- Catastrophe 99, 110, 121, 124, 128–130, 244, 286, 403, 406.
- Disarmament 61–62, 64, 66, 73–74, 81, 85, 87–97, 99–101, 109, 111, 424.
- Deterrence Doctrine 70, 75, 84, 87, 97, 100–101.

- Liquidators 129–130.
- Power plant 115–116, 125–126, 130, 418.
- Tests 64–67, 86, 90, 97, 107, 262, 402, 407.
- Test-Ban Treaty 90, 95, 97.
- Wastes 44–46, 110, 414, .
- Weapon free-zone 97.
- Weapons 5–6, 49, 61–81, 84–85, 87–101, 105, 300, 323, 409.

O

Oceans 34, 44, 51, 58–59, 161, 202, 261–262, 287, 302, 397, 410.
Ombudsperson for Future Generations 45, 47–48.
Onondaga 54–56, 58.
Oposa case 14, 48, 161, 165–166, 421, 427.
Our Children's Trust 15, 131, 140, 153–170.
Oviedo Convention for the Protection of Human Rights and Dignity of the Human Being 404.

P

Paradigm Shift 43–50, 58, 105, 114, 163, 212, 224–225, 227, 236, 240, 262, 331, 398, 403, 408–410, 414, 416, 418–419.
Paris Climate Agreement 6, 35, 38–39, 141, 156–157, 168, 171, 187, 191–192, 212, 283, 285, 309, 315.
People's International Tribunal On Nuclear Weapons and the Destruction of Human Civilization, 61, 63, 74–77, 81.
See also International Monsanto Tribunal

Planetary
- Boundaries 211, 216, 220, 400.
- Solidarity 27, 36, 38–39, 41, 43.
Plastic Waste 51, 58, 397, 400, 404, 406, 410.
Precautionary Principle 13, 72, 130, 148, 230, 253, 256–257, 260, 263, 279, 387, 414.
Prevention Principle 151, 252, 260, 305, 413.
Principle of Dignity of Future Generations 332, 393, 412, 415–416.
Principles of Intergenerational Equity:
- Principle of Comparable Option 44.
- Principle of Comparable Quality 44.
- Principle of Comparable Access 44.
Principle of Temporal Non-Discrimination 324, 412–415.
Posthuman/Posthumanism 111, 331, 333, 343, 345–346, 366, 384, 387–388, 390.
Psychological capacities 41, 109, 111, 346, 361, 381, 398, 407.
Public Trust Doctrine 131, 139–140, 145–146, 158–161, 165–167, 170, 197, 263.

R

Radionuclides 76, 113, 397, 400, 404, 406.
Resilience 28, 43, 56, 58–60, 212, 228, 233, 298, 331, 342, 345, 347–349, 424, 430.
Resilience Principle 55.
Right
- to a healthy environment
- *See also Environmental Health*

– to life 150, 154, 156, 163, 169, 173–174, 191, 194, 197, 287, 302, 419.
Rights
– *See also Intergenerational Rights*
– *See also Transgenerational Rights*

S
Sabin Center for Climate Change Law 134, 148, 236.
Soils 44, 46, 55, 283, 287.
Solidarity Rights 288, 316, 418–419.
Supreme Court
– of Alaska 148.
– of Bolivia 204.
– of Colombia 49, 169, 195–196, 199, 201, 204.
– of Hawaiʻi 277, 280–282.
– of India 48, 207.
– of New Zealand 49.
– of Pakistan 146, 189.
– of the Philippines 7, 48, 161, 165–166, 421–422, 427–430.
– of South Africa 136.
– of the United States 142, 145–146, 159, 165, 167–168, 203, 213, 279.
Sustainable
– Development 31, 44, 48, 53, 175, 196, 223–224, 246, 257, 294–295, 298, 301, 316, 324, 328–329, 379, 402.
– Development Goals (SDGs) 35, 38, 52, 59–60, 299, 324, 379.
– Peace 29, 31, 58.

T
Third International Covenant on the Human Right to a Healthy Environment 30, 182–183, 285–313, 317, 418.
Tony Oposa Moot Courts 424–425.
Transnational corporations (Responsibilities) 40, 192, 213, 226, 234–236, 327.
Transgenerational
– Damage 15, 31, 107, 113–130, 182, 244–246, 251, 259, 395, 402–408, 411, 413–415.
– Impacts 67, 69, 74, 107, 328, 409.
– Rights 326, 416.
– Threats 61–62, 410.
Transhumanism 41, 108, 331–351, 353–377, 379–393, 402, 404.
See also Posthuman
Treaty on the Prohibition of Nuclear Weapons 61–62, 80, 83–101.

U
Uttarakhand (High Court of) 206–207, 234.
United Nations Framework Convention on Climate Change (UNFCCC) 6, 134, 156–157, 162, 172–173, 246, 318.
Universal Declaration on Human Rights (UDHR) 35, 37–38, 301–302, 306, 316, 318, 326, 418.
Universal Declaration of the Rights of Man and the Citizen of 1789, 30, 222, 392, 417.
Universal Declaration on the Rights and Duties of Humankind [Déclaration Universelle des Droits et Devoirs de l'Humanité] (DDHu) 30, 38, 182–183, 290, 315–329, 323, 419.
Universal Declaration of the Rights of Mother Earth 30, 320.
Urgenda Case 39, 135, 146–147, 149, 196–198, 200.

W
Water
- Resources 55, 60, 155–156, 216, 223, 229, 274, 281, 287, 324, 397, 404, 410, 423.
- Right to 196, 295, 298, 302, 307, 328.
World Health Organization 99, 117.
Wind Rose 32–33.

X
Xenobiotic 110, 405.

Y
Youth 15, 43, 49–50, 140, 154, 163–169, 195–199.

Board of Advisers – Normandy Chair For Peace Collection

www.ingramcontent.com/pod-product-compliance
Ingram Content Group UK Ltd.
Pitfield, Milton Keynes, MK11 3LW, UK
UKHW021828100926
8556IPUK00004B/228

9 782807 61528